Systemic Development:
Local Solutions in a Global Environment

Systemic Development:
Local Solutions in a Global Environment

Edited by
James Sheffield

Cover Image: The Pohutukawa tree (*Metrosideros Excelsa*) with its crimson flower symbolizes New Zealander's ties with the land.

Systemic Development: Local Solutions in a Global Environment
Edited by: James Sheffield

Library of Congress Control Number: 2009922909

ISBN13: 978-0-9817032-7-5

Printed in the United States of America

CONTENTS

Theme 2:
Creativity in Systemic Problem-Solving

Theme 3:
Conceptual Modelling

Theme 4:
Information Systems

Theme 5:
Managing Systemic Development

Theme 6:
Organizational Systems

Theme 7:
Regional and Environmental Systems

Theme 8:
Social Systems

41. Increasing Cycle Commuting, *Stephen McKernon*

Theme 9:
System Dynamics

42. Local Solutions to Global Problems: An Integrated System Dynamics Model for Analyzing Policy Options for Tobacco Control in New Zealand, *Robert Cavana & Martin Tobias*

43. The Harnessing of Systems Methodologies to Enhance Understanding of the Systemic Structure of Industry Based Dilemmas, *John Davies, Bronwyn Howell & Victoria Mabin*

44. Pandemic Influenza Mitigation Strategies and their Economic Impacts, *Mary Ewers & Lori Dauelsberg*

Theme 10:
Systems Theory / Systems Thinking

Appendix A: **Miscellaneous Abstracts**

Editorial

James Sheffield
Department of Information Systems and Operations Management,
University of Auckland Business School, NZ

Following the success of previous conferences it was a pleasure to announce the 13th Annual ANZSYS conference. The conference was held in the city of Auckland, New Zealand from 2-5 December 2007, and was co-chaired by Kay Fielden, Unitec and James Sheffield, University of Auckland.

Currently the globally-connected world creates complexity for local decision makers. Environmental, social, organizational, and informational problems are pluralistic and messy. Systems approaches are required to reduce conflict and confusion. A key challenge is to apply holistic systems concepts to improve the lives of those served by systems of all kinds. This challenge motivated the theme for 2007's ANZSYS conference—'Systemic development: local solutions in a global environment'.

The conference provided a lively yet respectful forum for discussion and debate on systems perspectives and their applications. Papers were grouped according to their relationships with the following topics:

- A globally-connected virtual world;
- Applications of creativity to systemic problem-solving;
- Conceptual modelling;
- Critical systems;
- Information systems;
- Managing systemic development;
- Organizational systems;
- Regional and environmental systems;
- Social systems;
- System dynamics;
- Systems theory/systems thinking.

In each topic area some key papers were selected for presentation in plenary sessions. These plenary papers are marked with an asterisk. A feature of this conference was the high quality of the reviewing process. In total the 66 participants provided more than 200 double-blind reviews. Most submissions received three reviews and 63 papers were accepted. All of these adopted a systems perspective and met reviewer's consensus on quality requirements.

It is hoped that this volume will stimulate the reader to produce more robust local solutions in a complex global environment.

James Sheffield
University of Auckland Business School, NZ

About the Editor

Dr James Sheffield is Senior Lecturer, Department of Information Systems and Operations Management at the University of Auckland Business School. He graduated with a PhD from the University of Arizona in 1990. His doctoral work in group support systems led to the creation of a Decision Support Centre at the University of Auckland. He has designed, implemented and evaluated more than 100 action research initiatives. Most of these initiatives centre on complex inter-organisational situations involving considerable confusion and conflict. Major action research initiatives include the development of economic strategy, science policy, and comprehensive regional planning. He has over 100 publications, including articles in journals such as: *Decision Support Systems; Group Decision and Negotiation; International Journal of Applied Systemic Studies; International Journal of Business Information Systems; International Journal of Knowledge Management; Journal of Arts Management, Law and Society; Journal of Knowledge Management; Journal of MIS; People and Performance;* and *Systems Research and Behavioural Science.* Current interests include: Analytical frameworks for intervention design; ethical inquiry; group support systems; knowledge management; and research methods.

James may be contacted at:

University of Auckland Business School
Owen G Glenn Building
12 Grafton Road
Private Bag 92019
Auckland
New Zealand

Theme 1:
A Globally-Connected Virtual World

1. Welcome to the Culture Economy: An Evolving Cardinal Disruptive Innovation

Eli Berniker
Pacific Lutheran University, USA

Lilac Berniker

The emerging cultural economy driven by converging developments including the economics of plenty, increasing cultural consumption, and many-to-many networking constitutes a cardinal disruptive innovation that is likely to reshape all aspects of human society and create a better world. Societies experiencing plenty shift consumption towards cultural goods. Young adults today opt for participative interaction experiences and away from material consumption. Many-to-many technology is turning the millennial generation into cultural producers. Capitalist market society has experienced many disruptive technologies. The printing press, a cardinal disruptive technology, established the one-to-many broadcast society with impacts on religion, the nation-state, economics, and every aspect of society. The many-to-many Internet, coupled with the above shifts, represents a new cardinal disruptive innovation. This paper will explore the implications of these developments with respect to our ecological, economic, and social future.

Welcome to the Culture Economy: An Evolving Cardinal Disruptive Innovation

The thesis of this paper is that there is a convergence between three concurrent developments, a shift from the economics of scarcity to an economics of plenty, a shift towards cultural consumption away from material consumption, and the disruptive innovation of the many-to-many Internet that signals the emergence of a new societal paradigm and economic system.

Checkland (1988) identifies a system as a "framework" of understanding or a *weltanschauung* that makes a *"human activity system"* meaningful. A new system implies emergent properties that cannot be reduced to the elements of the old system. In particular, Checkland would require that the four characteristics of a new human activity system involve hierarchy, emerging properties, communications, and control all in forms that are in opposition to the existing global economic system. We suggest that what we label the *Cultural Economy* represents a new system, recognizing as, Checkland reminds us that our present *weltanschauung* will necessarily be inadequate for the task of its description.

A Cultural Economy does not imply the atrophy of the material economy. Rather, it suggests that the most rapidly growing element in the production of value will be the production and consumption of cultural artifacts and, as a result, the material economy will be relegated to maintenance. That shift would greatly benefit society and global sustainability.

Our thesis will be developed on the basis of the theory of disruptive innovation (Christensen, 1997) that is a model for change within capitalist market society and, as such, may be understood as an example of systems theory. However, we will postulate a concept of a "cardinal disruptive innovation" to signal disruptions that herald a new system.

Plenty and Enough

We live in an economy awash in plenty that we must experience as scarcity to sustain economic activity. The old adage "waste not, want not" has been inverted. We must waste extravagantly so that others will find employment and not starve. "Too much" must be perceived as "not enough" so that people can subsist.

Economic development operates under the same calculus. Subsistence economies are destroyed by globalization so that their citizens can participate in the world economy and become dependent on the growing waste of overdeveloped economies. "Scarcity" has become an economic addiction that can only be maintained if ever-increasing populations cannot securely sustain themselves.

In this age of enormous CEO salaries, Jeff Wales' declaration of "Enough" (Poe, 2006) is an anomaly if not subversive. Enough is a moving boundary floating between scarcity and plenty denoting sufficiency. The domain of economics is restricted to scarcity. We do not understand the economics of plenty. Yet, plenty has a long history

Marshall Sahlins (1972) called aboriginal tribes lining in the Australian bush the "original affluent society." They, along with similar "stone age" hunting and gathering tribes around the world, enjoyed material plenty, suffered no poverty, ate well, and worked an average of 15 to 20 hours a week. Sahlins noted that the "hunter is an uneconomic man" whose wants are scarce and means plentiful, did not accumulate material goods and were not motivated by scarcity.

Sahlin's insights have been confirmed by subsequent anthropological studies collected in a remarkable book, *Limited Wants, Unlimited Means* (Gowdy, 1998). Hunting and gathering peoples the world over organize their economic activity on the basis of sharing and exchange without markets in remarkably stable, egalitarian, and peaceful societies. They held land in common, and maintained a strong ethic of sharing and against accumulation suggesting that for much of human history, humanity enjoyed relative plenty.

In the late 1960s, one author, designing self-service systems for kibbutz dining halls, discovered a paradox. While most food was free choice, some menu items were portioned to control consumption. When made free choice, consumption immediately dropped. Portion control creates a perception of scarcity leading to increased consumption. Free choice implies plenty and consumption falls. The effect was immediate and replicated over many kibbutzim.

The paradox is: *Measures to limit consumption increase consumption while measures that free consumption reduce consumption.*

We might summarize our understanding basic human consumption behaviors with the following proposition: *Beyond basic physiological necessities, the experiences of "plenty" and "scarcity" are socially constructed.*

Demand is generated by the perception of scarcity. Thus, the economics of scarcity is a factor in increasing the very demand that is studied as an independent variable. Princen (2005) argues for a concept of "sufficiency" in opposition to "efficiency" as the key organizing principle for future society.

A reviewer raised questions that require making explicit and justifying two propositions.

Scarcity leads to distrust, necessitating power and controls which, in turn leads to societal transaction costs and reduced efficiency for society as a whole.

Plenty leads to trust leading to reduced transaction costs and, therefore, greater efficiency for society as a whole.

Leacock (1998), discussing the radical equality between men and women in hunting and gathering societies, points out that "*the direct relation between production and consumption was intimately connected with the dispersal of authority.* Unless some form of control over resources enables persons with authority to withhold them from others, authority is not authority as we know it." If anyone can gather their own sustenance any day in a matter of a few hours, no one can exert power over others and the conditions for trust are enabled. Moreover, the administration of power and control do not consume a large part of society's productive effort.

That reviewer questions that plenty begets efficiency and raises the non-trivial question: If efficiency means the optimal use of resources, optimal for whom?

Our economic system only counts as value that which is exchanged in markets. Thus the work of wives and mothers is excluded. A self-sustaining community that does not engage in trade is also excluded. At a recent mine accident, many millions were futilely expended to rescue the miners. Those expenditures add to the GNP. The lost lives of the miners are not a cost. Checkland (1988) postulates that every system has an owner defined as a person or persons with the capacity to modify or destroy the system. As Goldratt (1992) has pointed out, a system all of whose elements are working at peak efficiency cannot be optimally efficient. Taken together, if we consider the global economic system as belonging to humanity, as a whole, what is optimal for subsystems owners cannot be optimal for society as a whole.

Buckminster Fuller (1981) makes that point explicit when he estimates that maybe 30% of our employees are engaged in adding value while the rest are "checkers of checkers" necessary because of economic distrust. Consider prisons, courts, lawyers, and police. While they may be necessary, what value do they contribute to society? They are all part of the transaction costs in a society driven by scarcity. An economics of plenty can afford trust, reduce transaction costs, and, thereby, can be very competitive with the economics of scarcity. Fuller's estimate is remarkably similar to Marshall Sahlins' (1972) data. Humanity could enjoy plenty if we all created value about 15 to 20 hours a week.

The Cultural Economy

Jeff Wales said "Enough" and goes on to found Wikipedia (Poe, 2006).

Welcome to the Cultural Economy. Cultural economics appears to be governed by the following proposition:

Societies experiencing plenty invest time and resources into cultural production.

Cultural goods are products of human imagination such as art, literature, music, games, sports, theater, film, blogs, chat-rooms, and, more generally, knowledge.

Societies experiencing scarcity have great difficulty supporting cultural activity: On the other hand, Sahlin's hunters and gatherers had plenty of time to invest in social and cultural activities although little inclination to invest in artifacts (Sahlins, 1972).

Consider the famous Lascaux Cave paintings 17,000 years ago in Paleolithic times, one among 120 caves in Europe with Stone Age animal images; Many are works of great art. Archeologists discovered a 30,000 year old flute (Flutes, 2007). All of our history tells us that such works can only emerge from well-developed and practiced artistic endeavors. People, we believe lived in subsistence societies experienced sufficient plenty to invest resources into great art.

Thousands of years later, Europe found itself in the middle ages, plagued by disease, poverty, and harsh living conditions. Cultural production dropped significantly from the preceding era, only to be re-born through the Renaissance years later. The Renaissance marked the resurgence of economic strength in the region, and was accompanied by scholarly and artistic pursuits that consumed the excess resources of time and money. In times of perceived plenty, societies re-allocate efforts towards enrichment and away from needs.

A lifestyle revolution is occurring among young people in developed societies the world over. It is not an ideological revolution. Nor is it expressed as opposition to the economic order. They are opting out of the economics of scarcity and directing their time, energy, and resources into culture production and consumption.

Today's youth are the first generation, in the developed world, to experience plenty. They take for granted the basic necessities of life. Their grandparents suffered through The Great Depression and World War II. Their parents grew up in the shadow of those experiences. We were determined to protect our children from those experiences. The result is a secure sense of plenty and a shift towards cultural consumption and production.

In 1999, a student built the game called Counterstrike that in a few months had millions of players. 1.7 million people *played* 2.4 billion minutes a month compared to the Friends show that generated 2.9 billion viewer minutes per month. Today, MMORPG's, Massively Multiplayer Online Role Playing Games draw millions of players (Keighley, 2000). NASA's 85,000 click-workers voluntarily classify Martian craters creating knowledge for the fun of it (Benklar, 2002). MySpace and YouTube have become the default hangout locations for youth worldwide. YouTube and MySpace are now rated as the fourth and sixth most popular English websites (Alexa, 2007).

Most telling is the attitude towards the automobile. A surprising number of students, with other priorities, at a local high school of the arts did not drive. Given Internet surfing begins at age two, children will have surfed the web for 14 years before they are allowed to drive. A cultural shift away from automobiles, even a weak trend, may have profound disruptive effects on business.

What is happening here? There has been a massive shift among the young, and the not so young, away from the material and service economy towards the Cultural Economy. 2.4 billion minutes participating in Counterstrike was time not spent listening to advertising, shopping, or driving.

Three phenomena enable this change in behavior. First, as discussed above, the young are not experiencing scarcity. They do not apply economic metrics to their generosity. Disseminating their creative works freely runs counter to a fundamental value of prior generations: what is it worth, and can you sell it? Secondly, technology has enabled a zero-marginal-cost system by which this sharing can occur. Finally, cultural goods and knowledge are non-rival goods (Benklar, 2002). They are experienced not consumed.

As with every generation, the desire for freedom is overriding. However, for this generation, it means the freedom to surf the web, download what they like, blend and fuse cultural products from anywhere without limit. For this generation, status will be achieved on the web via cultural artifacts.

Cultural Shifts as Disruptive Innovations

Levitt, memorably formulated a theory of jobs-to-be-done with the phrase "*people are not buying a quarter inch drill, they are buying a quarter-inch hole*" (Christensen, 1997). The theory states that individuals do not make purchases; rather, they hire products to get certain jobs done. These jobs are remarkably consistent through time, though the products being hired are always changing.

The job being done by these cultural collaborative products is similar to that met by movies and television, hanging out at the mall, or, in prior generations, at the soda fountain. It can be cast as "be entertained while interacting with my peers," and indeed, is the same job that drives adults to cocktail parties. The distinction is this younger generation's selection of very different products to get their jobs done.

These new products constitute a disruptive innovation (Christensen, 1997). Disruptive innovations enter the market at a lower level of performance on the traditional trajectory, but provide some increased benefit on another performance attribute. Individuals whose needs are overshot by an incumbent product begin to consume a poorer alternative and are satisfied. Brushed off by incumbents, the alternative inevitably climbs up the trajectory of performance to become a viable competitor. The cell phone is an excellent example.

While few of the cultural products being consumed by the young are of the same quality or "caliber" as their commercial equivalents, these products vastly compensate in their accessibility. Technology has enabled culture to be produced by a much less trained individual, using common means in the comfort of their own basement. This phenomenon of democratizing a capability and delivering it to a larger population is a classic pattern by which disruption occurs.

A particularly disruptive aspect of the new cultural consumption is that production and consumption are the same activity and, while they involve rich exchanges and much time, none of these activities involve prices and markets.

At no cost, or nearly no cost, anyone with an Internet connection can easily consume or produce these products. These are interactions and exchanges between people without transactions. Essentially, they are not part of the traditional economy. Parents view the young as being lazy without understanding that the alternative is not work but shopping.

At this particular juncture – the interaction of price and product – the cultural economy we have been discussing interacts with the theory of disruption. In order for these products to be free, the producers must not only be able to produce them at no cost, but *they must also be willing to part with them for zero profit.* The former is the result of technological advancement. The latter is the psychological cultural shift we are experiencing.

Furthermore, the peculiar nature of these goods is that they are non-rival goods.

If another million players participate in Counterstrike games, the game is likely to become more enjoyable to all of its players. If more people chat on MySpace, the experience becomes richer for all users. And in the absence of scarcity of these experiences, there are no limits to the population that can participate. The strong network effect, combined with the inextinguishable supply creates the fundamental distinction from material goods. Material goods and services are consumed while cultural goods are experienced.

Historically, both the economics of plenty and the shift of societal resources into cultural activity and artifacts have occurred before. They are not sufficient conditions for a new *weltanschauung* or system of meaning. To assert the conditions for a new system, we must postulate the concept of a *cardinal disruptive innovation.*

Cardinal Disruptive Innovation

Over the history of human evolution, there have been cardinal disruptive innovations that changed every aspect of human work and society. The control of fire, evolution of language, discovery of metals, agriculture, the alphabet and invention of movable type and printing press come to mind as such innovations. The many-to-many Internet appears to be the next cardinal disruptive innovation.

The printing press changed religion, law, languages, economics, education, and science and lead to the modern nation-state. The printing press powered the Reformation. Luther's doctrine that all should read the Bible were unimaginable without a printed Bible. The Gutenberg Bible was the world's first mass produced product.

The printed book necessitated the standardization of modern languages with dictionaries, grammar, and punctuation so that meanings could be more clearly defined. Mass production emerged as the dominant mode of production. The printing press was the archetypical broadcast technology, the movement of products, information, culture and information in a "one to many" mode. The New York Times, Proctor and Gamble, Toyota, Dreamworks textbooks in colleges, the US Government, radio and television are all examples of broadcast technologies. And the many-to-many Internet threatens all of them.

That threat becomes evident when we examine Wales' Wikipedia. Wikipedia undermines the authority of academe by democratizing the generation and organization of knowledge, an attack on the very basis of academe. Blogs threaten the journalism. You Tube and My Space already constitute alternative forms of entertainment. Between TiVo and the Internet, many are able to bypass advertising disrupting the reach of advertising so central to commerce. The point is not that higher education, journalism, religion, entertainment, or advertising will disappear. Their traditional roles and power are not sustainable. Their new forms will have to evolve within a many-to-many society.

The threat of the Internet on the nation state is subtler. Consider millions of World of Warcraft players spread across the world's continents or aficionados of rock music varieties as widely distributed. These people are evolving shared cultures, in multiple communities, that transcend national boundaries. They may have more in common with one another than with their parents, teachers, and national leaders. That suggests that "People who play World of Warcraft together may never make war with one another." The ability to make war has always been a central aspect of the nation state. If the Internet erodes the ability of nations to rally their people to war, how long can we expect that form of governance to survive?

The many-to-many Internet has the capacity to change all of human society, as have cardinal disruptive technologies before it.

A New *Weltanschauung*– Identities

Checkland (1988) identifies a system as a "framework" of understanding or a *weltanschauung* that makes a *"human activity system"* meaningful. In addition, a new global economic system would have to exhibit hierarchy, emergent properties at each level, communication, and control in ways that are opposed to the system it replaces. To support our thesis, it is necessary to demonstrate the differences in Checkland's four elements.

In market society where everyone is treated as if they were equal and their identity is encoded in numbers, the burden of creating an identity falls on the individual. And since that identity can only be confirmed by others, all but a very few are nobodies. In this Hobbesian society, only the market confers identity.

The many-to-many Internet is a networked hierarchy constituted by the millions of postings by its participants. The most significant emergent property of that network is the capacity for individuals to create and identities and have them confirmed by others. As one wit put it, "I post, therefore, I am." For this generation, status and identity will be achieved on the web via cultural artifacts. And, given that those identities emerge in networked communities that transcend national boundaries, they threaten the primary basis for the nation state and the marketing basis of over-consumption.

The movement of information is communication. The one-to-many broadcast economy is being supplanted by the Internet with a consequent shift in power. Control, required to maintain systems stability, has shifted from power centers to participants. Linux, Wikipedia, and the emerging overlapping communities enabled by the Internet are all controlled by participants; self-regulation achieved without the bureaucracies characteristic of traditional economic organizations. All four dimensions of Checkland's (1988) systems model are constituted by elements in radical opposition to the current global economic system. Central to the new *weltanschauung* is the emerging capacity of individuals to create and project their own identities.

Accepting Checkland's (1988) admonition that our conceptual systems may not capture an emerging meaning system, we can venture some projections.

Economics of Plenty

- Exchanges will continue in a networked society. With talent and knowledge as primary assets in a cultural economy, the role of capital is likely to diminish;
- The leading edge of economic activity and development will be in cultural consumption and production;
- The shift from material towards cultural consumption will dramatically reduce pressure on ecological systems;
- An economics of plenty will reduce the demands for material goods;
- People will work less;
- Trust, and plenty, will reduce the enormous transaction costs of our present distribution systems;
- Trust will allow for very efficient organized economic activity.

Cultural Consumption/Production

- There will be increases in cultural and knowledge production beyond what we can imagine as sustainable today;
- Individuals will become more proactive, independent, and interactive resulting in a strengthening of individual responsibility as a social norm;

- Identities and status will be tied to our roles in the global cultural economy rather than be homogenized in the national material economy;
- Social norms will emerge that regulate networked relations.

Networked Society

- Most of the institutions of society will undergo major changes in purpose, structure, and functioning;
- Nation states will recede as boundaries become meaningless;
- New elites and power structures will emerge;
- The world will be more democratic and egalitarian.

Coda

This imagined future rests upon four pillars: The displacement of the economics of scarcity with an economics of plenty, the shift in consumption towards cultural and experiential goods and away from material goods, and the many-to-many nature of the Internet have been discussed above. The fourth leg is the impending ecological crisis of global warming, pollution, and the extinction of species that cannot be ignored any longer.

We cannot expect an easy path forward. The cultural economy represents a massive disruptive innovation and all of the evidence about such innovations suggests difficult adjustments across society. Powerful elites will not yield their power readily. We can expect future elites will emerge along with different systems of power. That appears to be the human condition. Nevertheless, we can expect a better world with more open societies based upon a stronger foundation of democratic institutions and sustainable economics.

References

Alexa.Com July 10,2007 http://www.alexa.com/

Checkland, Peter (1981) *Systems Thinking, Systems Practice* Wiley: Chichester ISBN 0-471-27911-0.

Benklar, Yochai (2002) "Coase's Penguin or Linux and The Nature of the Firm" Yale Law Journal vol 112 ISSN 0044-0094.

Christensen, Clayton M. (1997). *The Innovators Dilemma* Boston: Harvard Business School Press, ISBN 0-06-052199-6.

Fuller, R. Buckminster (1981). Critical Path. New York: St. Martin's Press, ISBN 031217488.

Goldratt, Eliahu and Cox, Jeffrey (1992). *The Goal* North River Press; 2nd ISBN-10: 0566086654.

Gowdy, John (ed) (1998). *Limited Wants, Unlimited Means* Washington DC: Island Press ISBN 1-55963-555.

Keighley, Geoff (2000). "Game development a la Mod" Business 2.0 October 1, 2000 ISSN 1938-7326l.

Leacock, Eleanor (1988) "Women's Status in Egalitarian Society: Implications for Social Evolution" in Gowdy, John (ed) *Limited Wants, Unlimited Means* Washington DC: Island Press ISBN 1-55963-555 pp139-16

Sahlins, Marshall (1972). "The Original Affluent Society" extracted from his book

Stone Age Economics ISBN 0202010996 http://www.primitivism.com/original-affluent.htm

Princen, Thomas (2005) *The Logic of Sufficiency* MIT Press, Cambridge,MA 2005 as cited by Hayden, Anders (2007) in *Ecological Economics* Vol 63, 4 ISSN 0921-8009. pp 828-829.

Poe, Marshall (2006) "The Hive" The Atlantic Monthly vol 298 Number 2 ISSN 1072-7825 pp 29-30,

Flutes (2007) Wikipedia http://en.wikipedia.org/wiki/Flutes

2. The Social World's Parts and Whole: Globalization and the Future of Some Non-Western Cultures in the Civilization and World-System Theories Perspectives

Dmitri M. Bondarenko
Institute for African Studies, Russian Academy of Sciences, RUS

While there are a diverse range of approaches to contemporary social and cultural theory, two particular approaches, civilization and world system, would seem to be at opposite poles of the conceptual spectrum. However if these are not seen as in opposition, we will be more likely to understand the current processes in the world and in its parts. In particular, the association between globalization and Westernization may be misleading: The global civilization can form only as a federation of local civilizations by absorbing their features at the universal level. Indeed, the correlation between the individual and the society will become crucial for both the global civilization and local civilizations. Neither a completely Western nor any non-Western influences will be able to dominate the emerging synthesis of a global civilization. So, the global civilization cannot form as purely Western or purely non-Western.

Globalization: The world system and civilization theories perspectives

While there are a diverse range of approaches to contemporary social and cultural theory, two particular approaches would seem to be at opposite poles of the conceptual spectrum: one seeing emerging social structures in terms of civilizations, the other in terms of global world systems. This may look like the former rejects the possibility of the global community emergence by emphasizing the insurmountable differences in the local civilizations' cultural backgrounds, while the latter insists on the global economic processes' ability to integrate the world into a global civilization by the cultural differences' transcending and elimination. However, I will try to demonstrate that it is wrong to set these two views in opposition to each other, and that if we do not do so, we will have a better chance to understand the nature of the processes that are nowadays taking place both in the world as a whole (as a system of societies and relations between them) and in its different parts (culture areas and relations within them).

"World-economies" and "world-empires" are among the key notions of the world-system conception as introduced by its "founding father", Immanuel Wallerstein. Remarkably, according to him, "world-economies" and "world-empires" must be considered precisely as alternatives, and not as two stages of social evolution. The examples of the ancient Greek poleis, and especially of the precolonial Maya and Yoruba polities, are significant in this respect. The heterarchic Greek poleis system was never transformed into an empire. The Maya and Yoruba interpolity networks consisted of the non-democratic societies. However they were never integrated as empires too, though in all the three cases particular polities dominated during some historical periods.

Nonetheless, I do not find it productive to describe the alternative to a world-empire as a world-economy, as this tends to downplay some other vital dimensions of such systems; the cultural dimension first and foremost. For example, in the European Union (a typical world-economy in Wallerstein's terms), the economic links no doubt play a significant part, but the links of other types – political, cultural and so on – are no less important. Besides, the EU can be treated as an element of wider world-economies (for instance, the European economy in general and, even wider, the Western industrial and high-tech economy), as well as of the global – "trans-", or "supra-national", economy. On the other hand, not all the parts of the EU communication networks are currently completely integrated economically (e.g., as testified by the refusal of some of the EU member countries to join the euro zone, and the debates on the future of the euro in some others). This shows that world-economies are not the only possible type of politically decentralized intersocietal networks. Rather, in this case we are dealing with a politically decentralized civilization.

For most of the last few millennia of human history, decentralized civilizations constituted the most effective alternative to world-empires. Besides the Classical Greek inter-poleis system, there is the example of the intersocietal communication network of Medieval Europe. Furthermore, politically decentralized networks of societies, close to each other socio-culturally, and tightly connected economically and politically, appeared effective alternatives to a separate society's development long before the formation of the first empires. For example, the networks of Sumerian cities prior to the rise of Akkad and of Egyptian nomes before the country's integration are readily recalled. Wallerstein suggests that in the age of complex societies, exclusively world-economies and world-empires could be treated as units of social evolution in general. Yet, I believe that both politically centralized and decentralized civilizations should be treated as such units. At this point, the significance of the cultural dimension of such systems should be stressed once again. Of course, the exchange of what Wallerstein calls "bulk goods" is important. But exchange of information is also always important, especially in our time.

Thus, not only is it essential to take into account the general character and type of particular cultures for an understanding of particular societies and the whole world's pathways of transformation, as well I believe that it is not correct to reduce the globalization process to primarily its economic aspect (the current transition from the "international" to "transnational" market economy) and the political aspect derived from it (consolidation of the multiparty democracy all over the world), though such a reduction is evident in many publications. Moreover, taking the cultural aspect of globalization into account also allows a more sensible approach to the prospects of globalization in the economic and political spheres. I also believe that this aspect of the problematic might be well examined within the civilization approach framework. Furthermore, as has been pointed out above, I will try my best to show that there is no real contradiction between the two respective approaches, i.e., world-system (generally globalistic) and civilization (generally particularistic in most of the contemporary versions).

Originally, in the mid-18th century, the Enlightenment thinkers developed the idea of civilization as the highest progressive stage of the essentially unilineal evolutionary process. It did not possess any substantially spatial connotations: though the stage of civilization was considered to be achieved by that time in Europe and its settler colonies only, it was regarded basically possible for other peoples of the world to rise up to this level, too. That time the study of civilization took into account predominantly the spiritual dimension of human life; the formation of civilization was regarded as the result of the human nature's "improvement", the increase in morality, the development of civil feelings, and, eventually, of "progress". Out of this the formation of the socio-political and economic institutions of the civil society, attributed by those thinkers to "civilized" nations, was derived by them.

Later on, the approach was becoming more and more diversified. Febvre (1991: 280–281) wrote that in the second half of the 19th century there happened the "... divergence of the notion of the civilization into two;.. [the supporters of] one of them finally arrived at the conclusion that any group of human beings, notwithstanding the means of its influence, material and intellectual, on the surrounding world, possesses a civilization of its own; the other (now old) is the conception of the higher civilization, which white nations of Western Europe and North America possess and spread..." So, the spatial approach to this notion, i.e., the idea of "civilizations", consolidated and this viewpoint did not suppose a direct link between the notion of civilization and a certain stage of development (though the foundations of such an approach also date back to the 18th century, ascending to Vico, Voltaire, and Herder).

But in this context the stress on the spiritual essence of the phenomenon of civilization has become even stronger. It is evident in the works of the first "local civilizations" theories creators (Rückert, Buckle, Danilevsky, Spengler and others). They demarcated a local civilization's boundaries on the basis of religion, mental characteristics, "the cultural-historical type", etc. of the population of a given large region. This tradition found its further development in the works by Toynbee and many other theorists.

During the 20th century a new trend within the civilization approach appeared. Its essence is manifested precisely in the attempts to combine the global aspect with the local one, i.e., to reveal the connection between changes of cultural types and human spirituality at the universal scale on the one hand, and local civilizations on the other. Jaspers and Eisenstadt are those who represent this tradition in the most prominent way. My approach basically stems from this tradition.

Globalization as a long-term historical process

At least from the Neolithic revolution era on, cultural distinctions between different areas tended to increase and to dominate the globalizing tendencies till the period of the Great Geographic Discoveries of the Early Modern Time. The results achieved on the pathway to globalization in the times of Hellenism, the invasions of the Eurasian steppe nomads and so on were most often temporal, reversible, and did not touch many parts of the world at all. From the era of the Great Geographic Discoveries the most important period in the history of all the local civilizations began. Now the inter-civilization interactions of various kinds involved practically the whole universe. The impact of those interactions on absolutely all their participants has increased many times. The immanent smoothing effect of the newly-born capitalism has also significantly contributed to the respective processes. As a result, the changing of the civilizational map has been quickened due to the absorption of some civilizations by others. Since then, new civilizations have appeared only as a synthesis of different older civilizations, and not many such syntheses have appeared; the formation of the Latin American civilization being the most significant event of that sort.

Thus, the process of globalization can be seen as not a completely recent and purely economic phenomenon, but as stemming from the formation of global civilization due to the long-lasting and multidirectional inter-civilization interaction. From a definite standpoint, a global civilization is not emerging nowadays, but rather the whole human history is that of gradual and up to the Modern Time slow process of the global civilization's revealing as the common background for particular civilizations' existence. It would be a mistake to present the humankind as a simple sum of separate cultures or even separate local civilizations for any historical period. World history demonstrates vividly that the globalization process can be effective only if it takes the shape of mutual adaptation and synthesizing of various civilizations' backgrounds, and this imperative has become more and more categorical in the course of time.

The explication of the global civilization in no way means the disappearance of particular civilizations but rather presupposes the formation of a kind of "federation". In this federation some common basic principles obtained in the course of globalization will be combined with, not only visual (ethno-cultural), but also to some extent with essential (precisely civilizational) diversity of the federation's members. Furthermore, the local civilizations' existence is a pledge of socio-cultural variability of the humankind. This variability between local civilizations is necessary and just as vital as the internal variability within any particular civilization (the fact, broadly recognized by the civilization approach theorists starting with Danilevsky and Gizaut). This is even more so if one speaks about the macro-civilizational units that is about the East and the West. To put it mildly, it is not obvious at all that the division between East and West will become irrelevant in the visible future. What might tend to happen is that at least some of the culture traits that separate different civilizations will be supplemented (gradually and often painfully for people) by new traits, original for another civilization but becoming common for them all. In the meantime, the East and the West are not geographical but socio-cultural, macro-civilizational phenomena; their borders having changed more than once, the present-day borderline being drawn only by the end of the 17th century (e.g., Konrad, 1966: 452). It looks like there are no good reasons to rule out at the outset that this borderline will move east- or westwards again in the future.

However, there is an important restriction for the process of the global civilization's revealing. Some features of this or that civilization may contradict sharply that imposed by global forces. So, we are coming here to the problem of the limits for globalization. It seems unreasonable and even misleading and counterproductive to attempt to solve this problem from the universalistic viewpoint. As every civilization is distinguished by a unique set of traits and features, a unique complex of cultural characteristics, each civilization has its own globalization limits.

Globalization and the prospects of non-Western civilizations: Tropical Africa, Russia, the Muslim world

The leading role of the Western civilization in the process of globalization is determined not just historically, but culturally (civilizationally) as well. This is not just by chance. Many non-Western peoples (the Arabs, Chinese, Polynesians, etc.) were experienced in navigation, even more peoples implemented into life expansionistic projects, and economically the East was generally leaving the West behind till the 18th century (see, e.g., Wallerstein, 1974; Kennedy, 1989). Nevertheless, it was only the Europeans who accomplished the Great Geographical Discoveries, introduced the colonial system and redrew the civilizational map of the world. The point is that the European civilization is practically the only one among those still existing today in which socio-cultural dynamism has been characteristic throughout its whole history. Dynamism was tightly connected with deeply rooted rationality of thinking, individualism, and other features the enumeration of which is a common place in many studies of the "European phenomenon". Dynamism this or that way revealed itself even in the most traditionalized period of the European history that is in the Middle Ages (Gurevich, 1999: 43–131). Europe realized the advantages of such a transformational mode when all its direct or indirect partners in the game for the role of the locomotive of globalization had already exhausted their civilizationally determined potential of dynamism. It was just this that eventually permitted the West to impose its rules and terms of globalization, to declare its civilizational values "global" and "universal"; thus, in fact, to identify globalization with Westernization.

If we now compare, or even better contrast, the present-day East Asia and Tropical Africa, we will see how crucially and dramatically the socio-cultural (i.e., civilizational) possibilities to adapt to the Western rules and values differ from one civilization to another. We should stress that what we mean is not the adaptive potential as such, but just the possibilities for adaptation to the civilizational features of the Western civilization that common people, politicians and academics associate with a global civilization. There is a paradox. On the one hand, this association is correct: volens nolens one should agree that the global civilization is now revealing itself first of all due to the attempts of the West and hence in accordance with its civilizational code and model. On the other hand, the respective association is basically wrong: the global civilization cannot but absorb in a non-contradictory manner the features of various civilizations. Another aspect of the problem of the local civilizations' adaptation to globalization is that of their contribution to its still emerging complex of features; globalization remains a history's "work in progress". The potential for peoples and states to adapt and contribute to the global civilization is crucial for their future prospects: for their equal or non-equal position in the reshaping system of international economic and political relations.

For example, the civilization of Tropical Africa, as its fortunes from the 15th century on demonstrate, seems to be adaptable to the features of the Western civilization to a rather limited degree. What can globalization mean for Africa? In my opinion, globalization may be the last chance for her to move from the periphery of contemporary world at least a little bit, to integrate into it on a more deserved basis than before. Unfortunately, this chance is not that great. Nevertheless, at least, the very existence of this opportunity is determined on the one hand by the transference of the centre of gravity of the world economic processes from the national and international level (as it was during not only the colonial but also neocolonial period) to the transnational, universal level and on the other hand, by the global civilization's inability to reveal itself without synthesizing of different local civilizations' backgrounds. So, I believe that it would be unwise to attempt to shut off from the universal integration processes as from new manifestations of harmfulness of the West but rather the policy of reasonable economic and information openness, of gradual but steady inclusion into these processes could be most profitable for the African countries. However, one should not expect that the inclusion of Africa into the new, global, system of economic relations must automatically result in the general acceptance of such fundamental Western values as the liberal (market) economy and democratic political regime at the national level. If we look at globalization as the process of cultural interaction, we will have to recognize that it is senseless and politically dangerous to expect their true (not formal) world-wide consolidation, at least in their purely Western shape.

The contribution of some other non-Western civilizations, such as the Russian and Muslim civilizations, to the global civilization cannot but turn out significant. This is not just because of the vast territories and big population, but it is likely that these civilizations, especially the latter one, are able to play the role of main "stabilizers" of the globalization process on the whole. Furthermore, these are able to be "correctors" of the Western values at the global civilization's consolidation, because these have a good chance to occupy merited positions in it. While not being part of the West, it is precisely because the Russian and Muslim civilizations are the closest to the West, that this is possible. The closeness arises partly because of the common cultural and undoubtedly common religious roots related to the monotheistic Abrahamatic religions – Christianity and Islam. Note that while in reality the modern Western civilization has lost religiosity in the proper sense to a considerable degree, it is still implicitly based, culturally and ethically, on the values of Christianity that made a significant contribution to its formation. It is quite evident that Russia is closer to the West in this respect than the Muslim world, owing to the greater similarity of the predominant religious doctrines (different versions of still one Christianity) on the one hand, and a vaster positive experience of inter-civilizational dialogue with the West. However, the Muslim world, notwithstanding its evident present-day contradictions in the relations with the West, does not oppose; rather the West and the Muslim world supplement each other. In the specifically medieval way this was realized in Europe as long ago as in the 12th century when the Papacy frightened by the Tartars who ravaged the Christian and Muslim countries equally, advocated that Muslims should not longer be regarded as pagans but as heretics.

Besides, also importantly, the economic and intellectual potential of the societies of these two civilizations allows them to adapt to the demands of the supra-national economy and to make use of the modern high technologies. In this respect, the societies of the Russian and the Muslim civilizations may become "well-equipped" for the postindustrial age, hence, increasing the likelihood that they will play important active parts in the global world. The ability of their social and political systems to adapt to the postindustrial era looks much more problematic as the prospects of transformations in these spheres always depends more crucially on the civilizational – socio-cultural – characteristics. The present state of the socio-political systems in the Muslim world, and the problems Russia is still currently experiencing, are in many cases really disappointing or even discouraging in the context under discussion. Nevertheless, the civilizational backgrounds of the respective societies encourage the hope of the transformation of their socio-political systems (although not rapid at all) in the direction the globalization within the post-industrialization of the world presupposes.

Thus, in the future, the Russian and Muslim civilizations can occupy highly merited positions in the global civilization. Having preserved their most significant socio-cultural traits (at least because they do not contradict the general backgrounds of globalization as cultural process) they will "share" some of them – those which will form parts of the global civilization's cultural code – with other local civilizations on the one hand, and will acquire from them some new features, on the other. Today it would still be too speculative to talk about it in more definite terms but it is likely that in the socio-cultural realm, the correlation between the individual and the society will become the key issue both in the global civilization and in the local civilizations. Precisely in this one can find the basic difference between contemporary civilizations of "the West and the rest". It is evident that neither a completely Western nor any completely non-Western solution is appropriate for the global civilization. Probably every local civilization will elaborate a specific version of the new correlation between the individual and the society but there is no doubt that, in absolutely all of them, this correlation will have to become more balanced, that is some will have to acquire more elements of collectivism while others – of individualism.

Conclusion

So, to this or that degree, there will inevitably be changes in the codes of all civilizations, including not only non-Western but Western as well. Though the West is still the main locomotive of the globalization process, some other civilizations, the East Asian civilization first of all, have already demonstrated their ability not only to adapt, but also to contribute, considerably and productively, to the global civilization's set of features. The "third way" synthesis is to be based on adaptation to natural environment by means of high technologies at a high level of production. This is possible only in the postindustrial world when the role of human conscious activities will become even greater than it is today, being supplemented by qualitative increase in the sense of social responsibility. This means that it is necessary for the appearance of new principles and forms of human existence in the natural and social milieu, accompanied by, and to a great extent determined by changes in human mentality.

The methods of studying globalization, that see the complete opposition of the world-system and civilization approaches, often claimed by the supporters of each approach, is no more than a perception. On the contrary, they are mutually complementary, as the present contribution is to demonstrate.

References

Febvre, L. (1991). Boi za istoriju [Struggles for History]. Moscow: Nauka, ISBN 5-02-009042-5.

Gurevich, A. (1999). Izbrannye trudy [Selected Works]. Vol. 2. Moscow; St. Petersburg: Universitetskaja kniga, ISBN 5-7914-0034-9.

Kennedy, F. (1989). The Rise and Fall of the Great Powers. Economic Change and Military Conflict from 1500 to 2000. New York: Oxford University Press, ISBN 0-679-72019-7.

Konrad, N. I. (1966). Zapad i Vostok [The East and the West]. Moscow: Nauka, no ISBN given.

Wallerstein, I. (1974). The Modern World-System: Capitalist Agriculture and the Origins of the European World-Economy in the Sixteenth Century. New York: Academic Press, ISBN 0127859209.

3. A Systems Approach to Global Sustainability

Sean Devine
Victoria Management School, Victoria University of Wellington, NZ

There is no overarching framework for economists, environmentalists and social scientists to address the key issues facing human kind. The global warming debate indicates that each discipline's insights have little credibility outside a core of true believers. Unless an acceptable framework can be found, self interest and power dynamics will determine how we face our future. This paper uses a generalization (Devine, 2005) of the Viable Systems Model (see Beer, 1981) to inquire into the high variety socio-economic system and its underpinning global ecosystem. The key issue is not how to quantify the system, but what questions to ask so that the underlying structural relationships can emerge. System coherence, stability, resourcing and survival against change, become the organizing framework to generate the necessary insights and a common language to help resolve the conflicts that exist between an economics and ecological world views.

Introduction

Human society has not yet developed adequate sense-making and decision tools to address critical issues such as global warming or the growing wealth gap between rich and poor nations. Indeed effective ways to decrease global poverty may well exacerbate the globe's environmental problem. As E.O. Wilson, using Rees and Wakernargel's concept of the ecological footprint (Rees & Wakernargel, 1996) points out that the ecological foot print of a first world human is 4-5 hectares; i.e., the productive land needed to keep them (us) in the style to which we are accustomed. If all humans are to have a similar lifestyle two more planet earths will be needed.

Traditional environmental, social or economic sense-making frameworks provide separate insights into these problems, but not in ways that provides clear directions for decision makers.

For example, environmental economists absorb environmental issues into a traditional economics framework by putting a price on environmental resources to signal value to the market. One example, the Stern Review on the Economics of Climate Change (Stern, 2006) expresses the environmental impacts of global warming as the cost of taking insurance type actions to avoid a more serious loss to the next generation. On the other hand, ecological economics look at the interface between ecological and economic systems at the large scale, but says little about how to manage an economy. Within an ecological economics framework, Costanza, *et al.* (1997) argue that the economic value of our global ecosystem is conservatively estimated as between US 16-54 $ trillion per year, clearly an important limit on global economic development. Those with a predominantly environmental perspective certainly highlight problems, but often come with an ideological perspective that ignores the complexity of an economy involving 6.6 billion people.

We urgently need an overarching conceptual framework to bring together different sense-making perspectives to, find ways to minimize the mismanagement of our environment while increasing global well being and protecting inter-generational security. This paper argues that the ecological generalization of the Viable Systems Model (VSM) of Stafford Beer (1984) provides a suitable overarching framework to ask the kinds of questions that need to be asked in order to make some sense of the global situation- how to understand it rather than how to quantify it. The VSM forces one to take a holistic view of the system and provides tools to make some sort of sense of the system without being locked in to particular approaches.

In what follows to avoid ambiguity, the world 'bio-environment' will be used to refer to the human life support environmental system while 'system environment' or 'external environment' will refer to the environment of the VSM model.

The Viable Systems Model

The VSM developed by Stafford Beer (1984) integrated emerging understandings of open systems (von Bertalanffy, 1950, 1995) with the cybernetic concepts of information and regulation through feedback (Ashby, 1964). While this is appropriate for well structured systems such as a firm, the approach is limited as it relies on a neuro-cybernetic metaphor (Ackoff & Gharajedaghi, 1966). However the author has shown (Devine, 2005) that the VSM can provide insights into high variety human systems if it is framed within an ecological, rather than a neuron cybernetic perspective. In what follows the traditional VSM approach will be outlined, then the paper will show how the ecological metaphor, that sees a human system as a highly interdependent ecology, can provide insights into the function of high variety systems.

Figure 1 is a schematic diagram of one layer of the traditional VSM (e.g., Flood & Jackson, 1991: chap. 6).

- The system's purpose is achieved through the operational component, S1 that contains the nested semi-autonomous subsystems. These themselves are viable systems;
- The S2, S3 and S3* components manage the S1 subsystems in real time, coordinating, controlling, monitoring behavior and allocating resources;
- S4 and S5 components, like the human brain, model the future (S4), set directions and manage the system as a whole (S5).

For an open system to be viable it must have the capacity to adapt to a changing environment (von Bertalanffy, 1950, 1968). As Ashby's law of req-

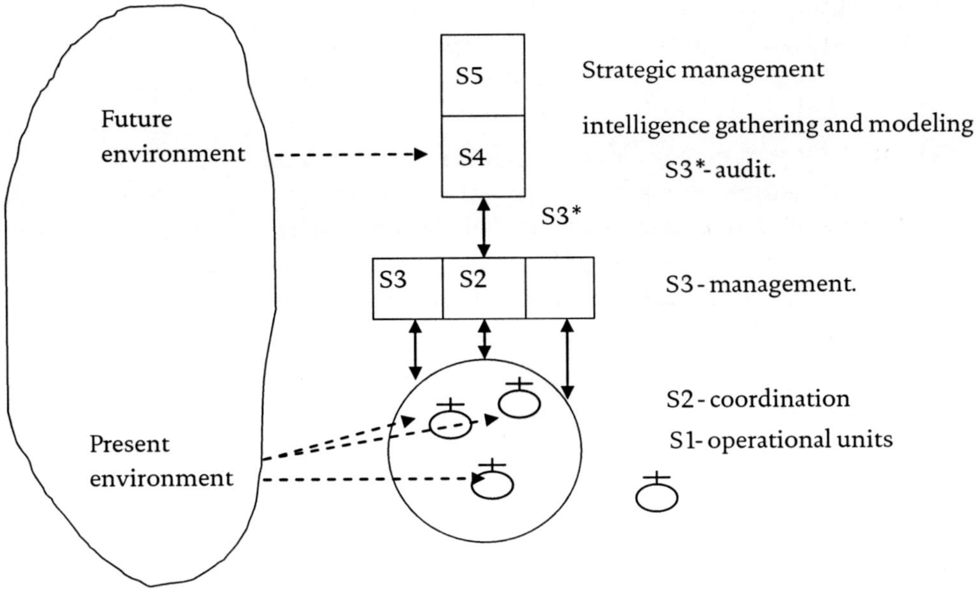

Figure *1 A schematic diagram of the VSM.*

uisite variety implies, the system must generate sufficient internal variety to match the variety embodied in the threats and opportunities of its external environment (Ashby, 1964) if the system is to maintain itself in a stable (homeostatic) regime.

General features of the VSM within an ecological metaphor

The traditional VSM can be adapted to inquire into complex human system provided it is framed within an ecological metaphor. The following shows how this metaphor provides insights into complex system behavior.

- Learning in human high variety systems is no longer mechanistic but is emergent. This system learning is the equivalent of Beer's (1984) non cognitive algedonic learning. Variety encapsulated in the behaviors of the organizational components of the socio-economic system (e.g., people, firms, NGOs, families etc) can be considered as behavioral routines. These behavioral instructions are typically observed in cultural, legal and cognitive forms and are analogous to computer software. On the other hand, the variety embodied in the organizational structures that express the routines are analogous to computer hardware. System learning takes place when changes in the external environment select the most appropriate behavioral routines and organizational structures. The selection processes can take place at the S1 subsystem level (e.g. in an economy, firms with effective behavioral routines survive) or in the real time management structures (economies with effective legal systems are more viable). For example, where cooperation enhances the system's effectiveness, cooperating behaviors will become more prominent in the organizational landscape and the system will appear to have learned cooperative behaviors;

- Where there is insufficient variety for the system to adapt, 'system failure' can be avoided by high-level S5 strategic interventions. E.g. in an economy, where market-oriented routines give rise to disruptive monopolies, legislation can enhance viability;
- The high level management or control embodied in the S4 and S5 levels of the socio-economic viable system may take place through government, powerful business, aristocratic rulers and military or religious leaders. However in general, survival is enhanced if 'double loop learning' is possible, e.g., when democratic or quasi-democratic processes align the high level purpose of the system with its operational parts;
- Because of the high variety implicit in socio-economic systems, and the autonomous nature of the subsystems in liberal democracies, high-level strategic management (S4, S5) is constrained. Government's role is limited to providing effective real time management and encouraging a variety-creating environment as Government usually has insufficient information to pick economic winners;
- A key point is that, at a given level of viability, there is a trade-off between maintaining sufficient embedded variety for adaptation to occur and consciously adapting through high-level strategic interventions (Devine, 2005; Espejo, 1989). The trade off in the form of indifference contours is illustrated in Figure 2. In general, if variety exists deep within the system there is little need for centralised management. However, if there is insufficient variety for the system to adapt internally any residual variety not matched must be matched through central management if the system to remain viable.

The Viable System as the global life support system

While all life is interconnected, in the absence of accurate information and effective models, a traditional economic approach to human development fails to adequately deal with long-term bio-sustainability issues. As the VSM provides a framework to visualize each system in terms of a hierarchy of subsystems nested within subsystems, the overarching life support human system is seen to contain both the biosystem and the global socio-economic system. This overarching system will be termed the bio/economic system. Nested within this is the global socio-economic system which in turns nests the national economic systems each with its organizations and communities. For simplicity this paper looks at three levels of nesting. The first level is a national economic system, with some recognition of social drivers. Next is the global economic system and finally the global bio/economic system.

A national economy

A VSM analysis of a national economy highlights some of the key features. The S1 component includes the providers of goods and services and consumers. The providers of goods and services can be considered as wealth generators and include the unwaged producers outside the traditional economy.

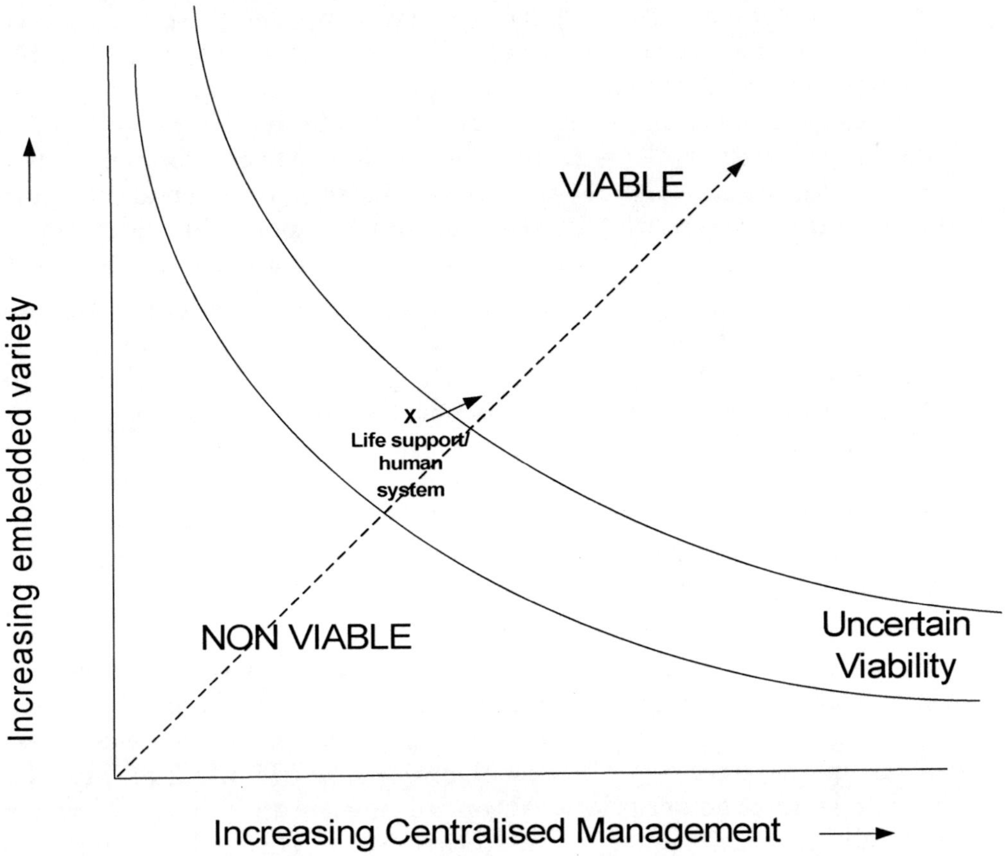

Figure 2 *The trade off between variety and centralised management*

The VSM within an ecological metaphor highlights the following:

1. Algedonic learning, the emergent learning taking place through the selection of behavioral routines, has been outlined in the previous section. This learning is limited to the here and now. For example competitive free- mark routines may be effective in a time of stability but may threaten viability in a time of uncertainty- as is the case over environmental issues. In this case cooperative routines may be necessary to maintain viability;
2. Internal variety must match external variety. This can take place within the system. For example if oil prices rise, producers within the system might develop alternative sources of energy and consumers might look at energy conservation. Alternatively if there is insufficient variety or capability to absorb the change, the high level S4 and S5 parts of the system may be called to take action; for example by imposing rationing, or funding new sources of energy;
3. The external environment of the socio-economic in the VSM includes the biosystems that support the national economy and the trading environment of other national economies. At this level, the conflict faced by a national economy emerges. One national economy might be environmentally re-

sponsible, but it may trade with nations that are not and these can undercut the local economy because of lower labour costs and, worse, exploit the bio-environment at the expense of the next generation. The national response to this can only be at the S4 and S5 level as the ability of local producers to counter the variety challenge from the external system environment may be limited. From a national point of view, imposing environmental conditions on trade may be necessary. Yet these will tend to be politically unacceptable, particularly if the voting population has not come to grips with the issues;

4. In a socio-economic system, centralised management is weak. Governments in liberal democracies cannot command. Governments maintain system coherence through the S3 and S3* parts of the system through the infrastructure and regulatory controls, developing appropriate legal systems and influencing the cultural norms of society. As the trade off between variety and control indicates, for high variety systems there may be insufficient information for Governments to be able to make effective decisions. Where Government cannot manage, the only option is to encourage variety generation within the system;
5. Furthermore, while the Governments operate at the S5 level and exert official control, there are other parts of the system that also have levels of control. These include the opinion leaders, the media, unions and religious leaders. These other influences may undermine the strategic thrust of Government. For example the front page of a recent Dominion Post (7 July, 2007) attacked the rising winter power prices. Yet, price rises are an indicator of system vulnerability. Viability may require price rises to encourage conservation and investment in alternative energy sources. Self interest of the S1 units may threaten viability by rejecting unpleasant indicators;
6. Government needs to access strategic information at the S4 level from its ministries in order to provide effective action to ameliorate bio-environmental and other variety threats. Alternative strategic information may come from NGOs, unions and opinion leaders.

The Global Economic system

If we move up one level of recursion to consider the global economic system as the viable system, the bio-environment becomes part of the external environment of the global economy. The S1 components are taken to be the national economies, coupled with local environmental resources, (figure 1). These national economies interact through trade, at cultural and at religious levels, as well as at the level of governments. These interactions may not always be benign. Power relationships exist between Governments, through the way business controls resources, and through cultural/religious systems. At this level, the national economies can be seen to operate in the light of self interest. At the global economic level, both the S4 strategic capability and the S5 management structures are weak as is discussed below

There is no one source of reliable strategic information to feed into the high level system decision making process. This strategic information may come from organizations such as the UN, or be provided at the pan-government level such as the Intergovernmental Panel on Climate Change report on global warming (IPCC 2001), and the Stern Review on climate change (2006). At this level the IPPC and the Stern reports, become indicators of system malfunction. The Stern report in particular has been influential because Stern was able to articulate the issues in a way that made sense to the economic community, even though some environmentalists rubbish it.

Think tanks, NGOs and academics etc. also provide formal and informal strategic information. One example is the Club of Rome's *Limits to Growth* (Meadows, *et al.*, 1974) and more recently the *Limits to Growth: The 30-Year Update* (Meadows, *et al.*, 2004). The difficulty is that these different sources may be contradictory allowing decision makers to choose information that best suits their predisposition. For example Lomborg in his book The *Skeptical Environmentalist: Measuring the Real State of the World* argues that many of the claims of ideological Green organizations exaggerate global problems; poverty is actually falling, potable water supplies are increasing. Lomborg wins on points on some issues. On the other hand, ideological Greens are perceived to be crying; "wolf, wolf" over every environmental issues, and so doing lose credibility. Looking at the situation from a systems perspective clarifies where the informational problems lie. The Greens are primarily future oriented and, raising critical issues, even though their 'here and now' data may be suspect. On the other hand the Lomborg approach is not future oriented. It fails to look beyond the present. There is no recognition of the bio-environment as an interconnected system and the big picture, concerned with the bio-environment's ability to continually support humanity's demands, is obscured. Sir John Houghton, co-Chair of the IPPC, offers a robust critique (Houghton, 2006) of Lomborg's book. Only when the bio-environment becomes part of the total system, will we be forced to face the limitations of the planet's limited bio- environmental resource.

At this level, the ecological economists, such as the previously mentioned Costanza (1997) provide an important input into the decision making process as they attempt to quantify the global ecosystem's limits.

The second issue is the weakness of the S5 control system. The UN, the G8 or Kyoto agreements are manifested as an action of the S5 system. However none of these have the ability to manage the system as a whole. Multinational corporations and religious organizations may at times exercise global control. Global management at best is through negotiation with the sub systems; the national economies. Because of this, figure 2 would suggest that, in order to adapt to external threats, as much variety as possible needs to be embedded within the system. Where this variety is embedded in communities and nations, learning and system adaptation can take place. The variety can be manifested in terms of alternative energy options, recycling, energy conservation protocols and behavior drivers such as tradeable carbon credits. From a VSM point of view no variety options should be ruled out. For example, despite immense criticism from his green compatriots, James Lovelock, who as the first global system thinker developed the Gaia concept, sees nuclear power as the only way forward in the short term (Lovelock, 2006). Within 30 years, New Zealand too may well need to allow nuclear powered merchant ships in its waters if it wishes to continue to trade.

Cultural alignment is going to be key to much of our future progress. The recent *Live Earth* concerts, supported by ex Vice President Al Gore, indicate that global cultural forces can be turned to good. In this respect, the potential cultural drivers may not be embodied in traditional structures. Diffuse or virtual networks supported through, for example, the internet, and cell phone texting can touch millions of people in a short time. Those nations able to create internal variety should be able to better survive bio-environmental threats of the future

The global bio/economic system

However if we move up a scale and recognise that the global socio-economic system as a subsystem of the all-embracing life-support/human system, some points emerge. The bio subsystem does not manage itself. It is sustained through having sufficient diversity to adapt to environment shocks such as drought or fire. However, ecological selection processes operate over time frames that are long relative to the scale and pace of human impacts. Humankind must therefore become the *de facto* S5 managers of the bio/economic system; otherwise its capability to sustain us is at risk. Unfortunately, the weak management structures of the global economic system are even less able to manage the whole bio/economic system. At this level, the finiteness of resources becomes a critical management issue, despite inadequate information or management structures to deal with the viability threats. Referring to figure 2, the trade-off between variety and control suggest that this global system is in the uncertain region of the viability curve. In the uncertain environment viability can only be improved by shifting the system to the higher variety region of Figure 2. In the absence of any real understandings, the default strategy is to ensure the ecological variety (its bio diversity) of the environment is sustained. In this context, the viability of the earthworm or the bee is infinitely more important than the preservation of the giant pander. At the economic level, sufficient management structures and incentives are required to ensure diversity in methods of food production and energy provision.

System coherence is essential, particular as S4 and S5 governance of the bio/economic system has limited ability to directly control human behavior. The evolution of better adapted cultural practices needs to be encouraged by debate, information dissemination and even ideology. Another interesting response has been from the secular humanist E O Wilson who recently published *The Creation: An Appeal to Save Life on Earth.* Here Wilson tries to reach the conservative Christians of the US. As the publisher's blurb says; "Wilson, a leading secular humanist, draws upon his own rich background as a boy in Alabama who took the waters, and seeks not to condemn this new generation of Christians but to address them on their own terms".

When this is done, what were previously indicators of mismatch between the socio-economic system and its bio-environment are replaced by whole system indicators and feedback mechanisms.

Conclusion

This particular systems approach needs credibility if it is to inform discussion on global issues. The first step is to repackage critical environmental and economic insights within the VSM framework from a New Zealand perspective, in order to identify the issues or trade-offs that need to be faced. Inevitably, any trade-offs will involve an understanding the purpose of the overall system's and its subsystems. For example, the economic system tends to identify purpose in terms of material well being, while the social system tends to define purpose in terms of relational well being and coherence. Not only can the social system be seen as a separate sub system, it also can be seen as a driver to align overall system behavior as part of the "here and now" management. While the VSM identifies the need for aligning the system, and can suggest S5 system interventions, such as implementing a carbon tax, or providing information about climate change, the VSM by itself does not provide the tools for aligning social behaviors. A better understanding of what motivates human communities will be needed if progress is to be made.

This paper offers no solutions to global human impact issues. What it does claim is that these issues are unlikely to be adequately dealt with using the fragmented approaches based on traditional silos of knowledge. Where progress is being made it is because the actions make sense from a whole systems point of view.

References

Ackoff, R. and Gharajedaghi, J. (1966). "Reflections on Systems and their Models," *Systems Research,* ISSN 1099-1735, 13: 13-23.

Ashby, W. R. (1964). *Introduction to Cybernetics,* London: University Paperbacks, ISBN 0416683002.

Beer, S. (1979). *The Heart Of Enterprise,* Chichester: Wiley, ISBN 0471275999.

Beer, S. (1981). *Brain of the Firm, 2nd ed.,* Chichester: Wiley, ISBN 0471276871.

Beer, S. (1984). "The Viable System Model: Its Provenance, Development, Methodology and Pathology," *Journal of the Operational Research Society,* ISSN 0160-5682, 35: 7-25.

Costanza, R., D'Arge, R., de Groot, R., Farber, S., Grasso, M., Hannon, B., Limburg, K., Naeem, S., O'Neill, R. V., Paruelo, J., Raskin, R. G., Sutton, P. and van den Belt, M. (1997). "The value of the world's ecosystem services and natural capital," *Nature,* ISSN 0028-0836, 387: 253-260.

Devine, S. D. (2005). "The Viable Systems Model applied to a National System of Innovation to inform policy development," *Systemic Practice and Action Research,* ISSN: 1094-429X 18: 491-517.

Espejo, R. (1989). "The VSM Revisited," in R. Espejo and R. Harnden (eds.), *The Viable Systems Model-Interpretations and Applications of the VSM,* Chichester: Wiley, ISBN 0471922889, pp. 77-100.

Flood, R. L. and Jackson, M. C. (1991). *Creative Problem Solving,* Chichester: Wiley, ISBN 0471930520.

Houghton, J. (2006). "Review of the skeptical Environmentalist by B Lomborg", http://www.jri.org.uk/index.php?option=com_content&task=view&id=23&Itemid=56

IPCC (2001). "Third Assessment Report - Climate Change 2001", http://www.ipcc.ch/pub/online.htm.

Lomborg, B. (2001). *The Skeptical Environmentalist: Measuring the Real State of the World,* Cambridge: University Press ISBN 0-521-01068-3.

Lovelock, J. (2006) *The Revenge of Gaia: Why the Earth Is Fighting Back — and How We Can Still Save Humanity,* Perseus. ISBN: 978-0-393-06217-5.

Meadows, D. H. Meadows, D L Randers, J and Behrens III. (1972),.*The Limits to Growth,* New York: Universe Books, ISBN 0-87663-165-0.

Meadows, M., Randers, J. Meadows D. (2004). *Limits to Growth: The 30-Year Update,* Chelsea Green Publishing Company, ISBN: 9781931498586.

Wakernargel, M. and Rees, W. (1996). *Our Ecological Footprint: Reducing Human Impact on the Earth,* Gabriola Island, BC: New Society Publishers, ISBN 0-86571-312-X.

Stern, N. (2006). *The Economics of Climate Change: The Stern Review,* Cambridge: University Press, ISBN-13: 9780521700801, www.hm-treasury.gov.uk/independent_reviews/stern_review_economics_climatechange/ stern_review_report.cfm

Ulrich, W. (1983). *Critical Heuristics of Social Planning,* Berne: P. Haupt, ISBN 325803219X.

von Bertalanffy, L. (1950). "The theory of open systems in physics and biology," *Science,* ISSN 0036-8075, 111: 23-29.

von Bertalanffy, L. (1995). *General System Theory. Foundations, Development, Applications,* New York: Braziller, ISBN 0807604534.

Wilson, E. O. (1998). *Consilience: The unity of Knowledge,* Abacus: London: ISBN 0 349 11112X.

Wilson, E. O. (2006). *The Creation: An Appeal to Save Life on Earth,* ISBN: 978-0-393-06217-5.

4. Normative Self-Regulation in the Emergence of Global Network Institutions: The Case of Wikipedia

Chris Goldspink
Centre for Research in Social Simulation, University of Surrey, ENG

Acknowledgements

The work on which this paper is based has been supported in part by EMIL, "Emergence In the Loop: simulating the two way dynamics of norm innovation", a three-year EU funded project (Sixth Framework Programme - Information Society and Technologies - Citizens and Governance in the Knowledge Based Society) involving six Partners: Institute of Cognitive Science and Technology, National Research Council, Italy; University of Bayreuth, Dept. of Philosophy, Germany; University of Surrey, Centre for Research on Social Simulation, Guildford, United Kingdom; Universität Koblenz – Landau, Germany; Manchester Metropolitan University, Centre for Policy Modelling, Manchester, United Kingdom; and, AITIA International Informatics Inc. Budapest, Hungary. I thank the partners for their contributions to the research.

This paper presents the findings of a case study into the self-regulative mechanisms of the Wikipedia. It examines the means by which a volunteer community of heterogeneous actors self-organize and self-regulate to give rise to and maintain a global network institution. Theoretically, the study is concerned with the reciprocal interplay between macro and micro phenomena. More specifically it examines how macro level 'normative' structure emerges from the micro interaction of agents and fold-back to influence agent behavior as revealed through the only coordination mechanism available to them - that of linguistic utterance. A detailed analysis of illocutionary speech acts is undertaken on Wikipedia articles labelled as controversial. This analysis is used to identify the self-organizational and self-regulatory mechanisms at work. Practically, the findings have relevance to the study of computer mediated communication and the interplay between technology, social artefacts and individual agency, particularly in the context of 'open source' global networks. The findings are relevant, therefore, to understanding network organizations (Miles & Snow, 1978; Miles *et al.*, 1997), network governance (Jones *et al.*, 1997) and the so called 'Bazaar Governance' of open source (Bonaccorsi & Rossi, August, 2003; Christley *et al.*, 2004; Lattemann & Stieglitz, 2005; Raymond, 2001). This paper forms a part of a three year EU research project titled 'emergence in the Loop' (EMIL).

Introduction

The World Wide Web has made possible new production processes that are global in scale. A new production model has resulted built around an 'architecture of participation' (O'Reilly, 2004). By exploiting the very low transaction costs of web media, the possibility exists to attract a small contribution from a very large and diverse group of contributors to develop information intensive products and services.

This is the general model which is argued to have made 'open source' possible. The Open Source movement is attracting attention as it represents a form of self-organization of social and productive activity quite different to both command and control and market based governance systems (Demil & Lecocq, 2003; Raymond, 2001). Open Source arguably lacks or has reduced reliance on the more common social ordering mechanisms, relying instead on self-organization across distributed networks (Muffatto & Faldani, 2003). The evidence makes clear that the mechanisms upon which open source relies were not preconceived but rather have been discovered through practice. Theory is struggling to catch up with and to explain the phenomena (see Rossi, 2004 for an overview). Understanding it is important if we are to appreciate how small local contributions can be effectively brought to bear on large scale global problems. How can the loosely orchestrated contribution of hundreds or even thousands of actors self-organise in order to generate a solution to some target issue or problem?

Interestingly, many Open Source projects have their rational beginnings in more traditional organizational and governance models. The Wikipedia is a good example of this. It began as an experimental side project to Nupedia (Sanger, 2005). Nupedia was intended to be a free encyclopaedia, but one assembled by conventionally constituted panel of 'experts' who would produce articles or peer review those contributed by others. It was anticipated that articles submitted on the new and experimental Wiki technology would feed into the Nupedia review process. The intrinsic openness of Wikipedia attracted increasing numbers of contributors and it quickly developed a life of its own, functioning independently to Nupedia and eventually overtaking it. It is, therefore, a genuinely novel emergent global institution and provides a useful case study through which to explore the wider Open Source phenomena as well as the self-organizing and self-regulatory mechanisms which underpin it. What are these mechanisms and how can we both study and model them? What theory and methods appear useful for understanding them?

The case study detailed here represents an initial attempt to answer such questions, focusing in particular on the micro mechanisms. It is part of a wider EU funded project tilted 'Emergence in the Loop: Simulating the two way dynamics of norm innovation' (EMIL). EMIL aims to advance our understanding of emergent social self-organization: Contributing both to conceptualization and furnishing methods for its study. Within EMIL, the target problem is cast as involving two intertwining processes – that of *emergence*; and the reverse process of *immergence*. Emergence is a concept widely used within systems, complex systems and multi-agent modelling communities (Gilbert, 1995; Holland,

1998; Schroder, 1998) to describe the process whereby (macro) pattern emerges from but is irreducible to a set of local (micro) interactions. Its widespread use is not, however, uncontroversial (Castelfranchi, 1998; Gilbert & Conte, 1995; Sawyer, 2001). The term immergence was coined by Castelfranchi (1998) to refer to the reciprocal process whereby (macro) pattern feeds back and influences (constrains, changes) the actions of (micro) agents Within EMIL, this interrelationship is to be examined by focusing on the emergence and immergence of social 'norms'. In other words it brings together a complex systems perspective and a sociological one.

Gibbs (1981) argues that *'Sociologists use few technical terms more than norms and the notion of norms looms large in their attempt to answer a perennial question: How is social order possible?'*. Not surprisingly then the concept has been incorporated into a wide range of alternative and often competing bodies of theory.

The normative literature can be largely divided into two fundamentally distinct groups. In the social philosophical tradition (Lewis, 1969) norms are seen as a particular class of emergent social behavior which spontaneously arise in a population. From this perspective, a 'norm' is a pattern identified by an observer ex-post. The defining characteristic of the pattern is the apparently prescriptive/proscriptive character – people behave 'as if' they were following a rule. By contrast, the view offered by the philosophy of law sees norms as a *source* of social order. This standpoint assumes the prior existence of (powerful) social institutions and posits them as the source of rules, which, when followed, lead to social patterns.

Therborn argues (2002: 868) people follow norms for different reasons. The extremes run from habit or routine to rational knowledge of consequences for the world. Between these lie:

- Identification with the norm or values – linking sense of self (identity) to the norm source (person, organization or doctrine) often leading to in-group-out-group;
- Deep internalization – self-respect – done independently to what others are doing.

Bicchieri (2006: 59) provides a rare hint at the cognitive process involved stating:

"To 'activate' a norm means that the subjects involved recognise that the norm applies: They infer from some situational cues what the appropriate behavior is, what they should expect others to do and what they are expected to do themselves, and act upon those cues."

This suggests a complex process of self-classification (how am 'I' situated with respect to this group and what is the nature of the situation in which 'I' find myself, does a norm pertain to 'me' in this situation and under what conditions and to what extent am I obliged to comply?).

The specific mechanisms by which norms reflect or reveal emergence/ immergence, therefore, remain ill defined. To begin to identify which (if any) of these loosely defined mechanisms might be supported by evidence and to aid in the development of a theory of norms helpful for understanding the more general emergence/immergence mechanism, we selected the Wikipedia as a preliminary case study.

Analysis of Wikipedia activity

We began with the observation that the volunteers that have participated in creating the Wikipedia have emerged a set of permissions, obligations, rules and norms which appear to bring it into being and maintain it as an institution. These have been documented as guidelines and etiquettes as well as embedded in technical artefacts such as style bots. However, from a governance perspective there are relatively few means within Wikipedia by which formal control can be exercised using these rules and the community relies instead on the use of informal or 'soft' control. These mechanisms need to be effective in the face of perturbation from 'vandals' (task saboteurs), 'trolls' (social saboteurs), as well as turnover of contributors in the context of a task which can require the accommodation of emotionally charged and value based issues.

At its beginning in 2001 the only rule in Wikipedia was 'there are no rules' (Sanger, 2005). The aim was to live with 'good natured anarchy' until the community itself could identify and posit a suitable rule-set – to grow the rule-set based on experience of what was needed and what might work. Many rules emerged as the community struggled to deal with its exponential growth (Viegas *et al.*, 2007). The need for, the nature of, and mechanisms for enforcement of these rules has, however, been a very controversial aspect of Wikipedia's development (Sanger, 2005, 2007). The founding Editor Larry Sanger has argued that in the early stages 'force of personality' and 'shaming' was the only means used to control contributors and that no formal exclusion occurred for six months, despite there being difficult characters from the beginning. Sanger notes that this took place within the context of a rapidly developing wider wiki culture which was opposed to rules of any kind.

As Wikipedia evolved, items were added to the 'What Wikipedia is not' page. These essentially clarified the aim of producing a credible encyclopaedia and marked out the distinguishing qualities of the genre. This clarification of goal – identifying what Wikipedia was intended to be by comparing it with what it was not – was initially the primary means for steering contributions. Founder Jimmy Wales then added the 'Neutral Point of View' (NPOV) rule which emphasised the need for contributions to be free of bias. The combination of clear purpose and the principle of neutrality provided a reference point against which all contributions could be easily judged.

Wikipedia can, therefore, assist us better to understand:

- The role and contribution of norms and rules to self-organization processes in volunteer on-line communities;

- The range and type of rules and norms used to self-regulate open global volunteer communities where there is little to no hierarchy and limited capacity for formal sanction;
- How these norms and rules are invoked, maintained and modified through communicative and administrative acts and the effectiveness of such acts;
- The relationship between goal, technical artefacts and social structures and the exercise of individual agency in self-regulation in volunteer online communities.

In Wikipedia there are two classes of activity: editing activity; and conversation about editing activity. This study is not concerned with the editing activity but with the self-organising and self-regulating phenomena which make it possible. Insight into this can be gained by examining the Discussion pages which accompany many of the articles rather than the articles themselves. The activity on the Discussion pages comprises a series of 'utterances' or speech acts between contributors about editing activity and the quality of product. On the face of it then, these pages should provide a fertile source of data to support analysis of how social norms operate. Discussion pages associated with articles identified as controversial were chosen as they represent an area of activity where the quality of relationships can be expected to be more critical to goal attainment and where social norms could be expected to play an important role in regulating behavior. We expected to see attempts by editors to influence the behavior of one another through the only means available to them – communicative acts. We anticipated that these may exhibit some regularity which would allow us to examine both the range and type of events that led to the explicit invocation of rules and norms and which revealed emergent influence patterns which were themselves normative. We wanted also to examine what conventions prevailed and how these compared and interacted with the goal of the community and its policies. A convention is defined here as a behavioural regularity widely observed by members of the community. Policies include explicit codes of conduct as well as guidelines (etiquettes) and principles.

Methodology

For the study we randomly selected a sample of thirty five discussion pages associated with controversial articles. At the time of the study (May/June 2007) there were 583 such articles. The preliminary analysis reported here is based on a sub-sample of nine of these articles.

Coding

As the computer mediated nature of Wikipedia communication means that no behavioural cues (other than linguistic) are possible. Wikipedia can be viewed as an institution founded on networks of commitments established, maintained and modified, exclusively in and through computer mediated linguistic exchange. It was anticipated that the process may involve quite subtle use of linguistic cues.

There exist a wide variety of coding schemes for natural speech. We considered a range of these before choosing to use the Verbal Response Mode (VRM) taxonomy (Stiles, 1992). VRM has been developed over many years and used in a wide range of communication contexts. Stiles defines it as *'a conceptually based, general purpose system for coding speech acts. The taxonomic categories are mutually exclusive and they are exhaustive in the sense that every conceivable utterance can be classified.'* (Stiles, 1992: 15). The classification schema has attributes very attractive where there is a need (as here) to capture many of the subtleties of natural language use that derive from and rely on the intrinsic flexibility and ambiguity of natural language yet map them to a more formal or axiomatic system needed for computer simulation.

VRM uses three structural (rather than functional) principles to classify utterances. These are a concern with whether the speaker frames an utterance on the basis of:

- His/her own or the others source of experience;
- Presumptions the speaker makes about the others experience (feeling, perceiving or intending), and;
- Whether the speaker presents the experience from his/her own viewpoint or a viewpoint shared or held in common with another.

Using the above principles all utterances can be assigned a unique code. This code is classificatory and does not require a judgement to be made about degree. However a gauge of illocutionary 'force' is available through the resulting modes. The modes are defined by the points of intersection of the three dimensional matrix resulting from application of the three principles.

Mode	Descriptors
Disclosure	Informative, unassuming, directive
Edification	Informative, unassuming, acquiescent
Advisement	Informative, presumptuous, directive
Confirmation	Informative, presumptuous, acquiescent
Question	Attentive, unassuming, directive
Acknowledgement	Attentive, unassuming, acquiescent
Interpretation	Attentive, presumptuous, directive
Reflection	Attentive, presumptuous, acquiescent

Table 1 *Descriptors associated with Verbal Response Modes (Source: Stiles, 1992: 63)*

The discussion pages were coded using VRM categories applied to both the literal and pragmatic intent. Additional codes were applied to identify: valence, subject of communication, explicit invocation or norms or rules and the associated deontic, whether the receiver/s accepted the illocutionary force of the utterance, and the registration status of the person making the utterance.

Initial Findings

Analysis revealed that utterances which involved a specific invocation of a norm or rule were rare (only 3.2%). Of these, 44% were generated in response to the form or presentation of an article, 28% in response to an editor's behavior, 22% in response to an edit action and 6% an article fact. Sixty three percent of all invocations involved specific Wikipedia rules or guidelines rather than general norms. All Wikipedia rules were invoked by registered users while 33% of general norms were invoked by unregistered users.

Sixty five percent of all utterances were phrased in a neutral or objective manner a further 22% were negative and 14% positive. The most common negative form was 'dismissive' (55% of all negative utterances), while the most common positive utterance was 'encouraging' (39% of all positive utterances). This suggests a convention of using neutral language. The observation that utterances were predominantly phrased in neutral terms should not be interpreted as saying anything about their factual basis. Some quite exotic ideas were expressed in neutral terms.

Twenty one percent of all positively phrased utterances were explicitly validated (accepted) and a further 56% went unquestioned. Only 3% of positive utterances were rejected and 20% ignored. It is surprising then that there was such a low usage of positive style, particularly as many of the Wikipedia etiquette guidelines encourage it. By comparison only 8% of negatively phrased utterances were accepted and 24% unquestioned with 27% explicitly rejected and a further 41% ignored. Negative behavior was clearly punished. The majority (52%) of neutrally phrased utterances went unquestioned, 21% were ignored, 11% rejected and 16% accepted.

Within VRM an utterance is coded twice, once to capture the form and once for the intent. In table two above, the rows relate to the grammatical form of the utterance (its strict literal meaning) while the columns relate to the pragmatic intent of the utterance. A typical utterance may take one form but reflect an alternative intent – for example, the utterance 'could you close the door?' has the form of a *question* but the intent of *advisement* – the speaker intends and listener to close the door. The relation of form to intent is expressed, "in service of" (Stiles, 1992) , in this case question in service of advisement (QA).

Edification in service of Edification (EE) is the most frequent form of utterance – 33% of all utterances were of this mode. The Edification mode is defined as deriving from the speaker's frame of reference, making no presumption about the listener and using a neutral (objective) frame of reference shared by both speaker and listener. This mode is informative, unassuming and acquiescent. As a strategy for influencing others it reflects attempts to convince by neutral objective argument.

The second most common mode is that of Disclosure in service of Disclosure (DD). Disclosure is defined as being from the speakers experience, making no presumption, but being framed using the speakers frame of reference. This is summarized as informative, unassuming but directive. Unlike EE mode, DD mode represents an attempt by the speaker to impose or have the listener accept the speakers frame. Eleven percent of all utterances adopted this form.

Pragmatic Intent									
Form	Edific.	Confirm	Qn	Ackmnt	Interpn	Disclo-sure	Reflec-tion	Adviset	Total
Edification	336	3	3	1	15	17	2	53	430
Confirmation	0	4	0	0	0	0	0	2	6
Question	4	0	55	0	1	2	1	18	81
Acknowledgment	2	2	0	49	0	0	0	0	53
Interpretation	1	0	0	0	30	0	0	4	35
Disclosure	101	2	4	3	7	106	0	53	276
Reflection	0	0	1	0	0	0	10	0	11
Advisement	0	0	0	0	0	0	0	84	84
Total	444	11	63	53	53	125	13	214	976

Table 2 *Verbal Response Mode Form by Intent – number of utterances coded*

The third most common mode is Disclosure in service of Edification (DE). The DE mode represents an utterance which is from the speaker's frame of reference but as if it is neutral or from a shared frame. Ten percent of all utterances used this mode. This is a somewhat neutral mode where the speaker offers clearly labelled personal knowledge as information.

The forth most common mode is Advisement in service of Advisement (AA). AA mode represents speech from the speaker's experience, which makes presumptions about the listener and adopts the speaker's frame of reference. It can be summarized as informative, presumptuous and directive. It commonly takes the form of 'you should….' Approximately 9% of utterances were in this mode. A further 11% of utterances have the directive pragmatic intent of advisement masked by using a less presumptuous form – that of Edification or Disclosure.

Fifty two percent of all questions were ignored as were 42% of all interpretations.

It was apparent from both the coding and the qualitative data that a great many utterances went unchallenged (47%) or were ignored (25%).

Discussion

What is significant about the utterance strategies is that they typically involve an exchange of assertions delivered with a neutral – i.e., non-emotive style. There are very few explicit praises, or put downs and few niceties like explicit acknowledgements of one another. Seldom do contributors refer to one another by name – the exchanges are rather impersonal. This does not tally with what one would expect if the Wikipedia etiquette (http://en.wikipedia.org/wiki/Wikipedia:Etiquette) had been institutionalized. If we assume that the etiquette captures the community's ideal, the emerged conventions do not conform to that 'ideal'. Similarly we see low levels of questioning or of reflection (i.e., feeding back the words of the speaker to check understanding or to come to better understand the others intentions). This is arguably inconsistent with the task needs – the need to reach consensus on controversial topics. The frequency with which utterances were ignored also suggested low engagement by participants in the discussion. Why might this be?

The absence of any expression of intimacy or acknowledgement of emotions and/or similarity of attitude (homophilly) among many contributors suggests that Wikipedia lacks many of the qualities of verbal exchange that would identify it as strong community. It is more consistent with being a place to share coordination of a task.

This could suggest that the goal is the primary orientating point. However, the lack of quality of discourse needed to achieve consensus is more indicative of a brief encounter between different and established milieu's which struggle to find common understanding rather than of a community committed to a common goal (Becker & Mark, 1997). This might suggest that the shared goal may be subordinate to more personal goals by a considerable proportion of contributors. Or it may be that the technology and environment simply will support no more than this. This environment includes the existence of saboteurs who can use the opportunity afforded by the open and anonymous platform to use identity deception i.e. to mimic the language and style of an 'expert' or to present as a genuine editor while trying to pursue personal or political agenda hostile to the aims or interests of the Wikipedia. The discussions about controversial articles provide particularly fertile ground for such sabotage. This could have an overall influence on the type of conventions which arise. Editors may, for example, display reserve and suspicion, withholding trust and taking conventional signals of authority and identity (Donath, 1998) as unreliable. The first principle in the Wikipedia etiquette is 'assume good faith'. To do so would, however, leave the process more vulnerable to 'troll' activity. This is more suggestive of the convention having arisen as a social artefact based on what works rather than concern with 'unrealistic' explicit codes of conduct.

Utterance strategies between registered and unregistered editors did not vary greatly, although unregistered editors were more likely to use disclosure intent and more likely to ask questions (possibly associated with the increased likelihood that they are relatively new to Wikipedia). There was no significant difference between registered and unregistered editors either on the tendency to use neutral compared to positive or negative utterances.

There was considerable evidence of mind reading (theory of mind) – i.e., editors appeared to form judgements about the intent of others on relatively little information. There was, however, little evidence of the use of utterance strategies to better understand or check these theories of mind. The latter would include the use of questioning, reflection, interpretation and confirmation VRM modes. Editors appeared quick to judge and to then follow response scripts consistent with those judgements (e.g., ignoring or accepting utterances of others) on the basis of those judgements. Consistent with this, there were few instances of renegotiated patterns of communication style. Positions and styles stayed relatively constant over the period of the interaction. Only occasionally would an editor modify his/her style significantly if challenged. Of the rule invocations 26% were accepted, a similar proportion were rejected or ignored and the remainder went unquestioned (but generally had no affect on behavior). This is consistent with norms viewed as being triggered by a limited range of cues which allow individuals to locate themselves and select identities appropriate to a context and which then remain essentially stable.

Conclusions and future work

In this study we set out to begin to identify mechanisms which underpin the emergence of systemic self-organization in a volunteer on-line global institution and methods by which they may be identified. The findings have challenged some of our assumptions and expectations, in particular:

- The more detailed and specific behavioral etiquette seems to have little influence on the overall character and style of interaction.
- The overall quality of interaction of editors falls short of the range and quality of communicative style characteristic of a community and consistent with what one would expect given the nature of the task.

Most regulation is achieved without the need for frequent explicit invocation of rules or norms. Rather, behavior seems to accord to a convention which editors quickly recognise and conform to and which minimally accommodates what needs to be done to satisfy the task in a context of somewhat heterogeneous personal goals.

There was a lack of evidence of active negotiation of expectations and standards and convergence of behavior towards a norm. Within the discussion pages there appeared to be an accommodation of a set of conventions and little obvious norm innovation, evolution, adaptation or extension. This suggests that on first encounter with Wikipedia editors read a set of cues as to what constitutes appropriate or acceptable behavior and then accommodate it.

The paper provides an example of how micro-influence processes may operate through the illocutionary force of speech acts and a method for studying how these relate to emergent self-organization in computer mediated institutions.

The research to date has raised a number of questions which require further investigation. We now propose to conduct this analysis for both archival discussion pages (from a period before the rules of Wikipedia became established and of current Featured articles. Our expectation is that in the former we may see more active use of norm invocation as a) editors will be more likely new to the wiki environment and b) there are few situation specific rules to draw on leaving only recourse to wider social norms as a means of checking inappropriate behavior of new users. Features sites reflect sites of high quality and this presumably may be based on effective social coordination of a diverse range of talents. It may be that greater community spirit will be evidenced on these pages.

References

Becker, B. & Mark, G. 1997. Constructing Social Systems through Computer Mediated Communication. Sankt Augustin, Germany: German National Research Center for Information Technology.

Bicchieri, C. 2006. The Grammar of Society. Cambridge: Cambridge University Press. ISBN 0521574900

Bonaccorsi, A. & Rossi, C. August, 2003. Altruistic individuals, selfish firms? The structure of motivation in Open Source software, Sant'Anna School of Advanced Studies, Institute for Informatics and Telematics.

Castelfranchi, C. 1998. Simulating with Cognitive Agents: The Importance of Cognitive Emergence. In J. S. Sichman & R. Conte & N. Gilbert (Eds.), Lecture Notes in Artificial Intelligence. Berlin: Springer Verlag ISBN 3-540-65476-3.

Christley, S., Xu, J., Gao, Y., & Madey, G. 2004. Public Goods Theory of the Open Source Development Community. Paper presented at the Agent2004 conference, Chicago, IL.

Demil, B. & Lecocq, X. 2003. Neither market or hierarchy or network: The emerging bazaar governance, Université Lille/Institut d'Administration des Entreprises.

Donath, J. S. 1998. Identity and deception in the virtual community. In P. Kollock & M. Smith (Eds.), Communities in Cyberspace. London: Routledge ISBN 0415191408.

Gibbs, J. P. 1981. Norms, Deviance and social control: Conceptual matters. New York: Elsevier. ISBN 0444015515

Gilbert, N. 1995. Emergence in Social Simulation. In N. Gilbert & R. Conte (Eds.), Artificial Societies. London: UCL Press ISBN 1-85728-305-8.

Gilbert, N. & Conte, R. 1995. Artificial Societies. London: UCL Press. ISBN 1-85728-305-8

Holland, J. H. 1998. Emergence: from chaos to order. Ma.: Addison Wesley. ISBN 0-201-14943-5

Jones, C., Hesterly, W. S., & Borgatti, S. P. 1997. A General Theory of Network Governance: Exchange Conditions and Social Mechanisms. Academy of Management Review 22(4), ISSN: 0363-7425: 911-945.

Lattemann, C. & Stieglitz, S. 2005. Framework for Governance in Open Source Communities. Paper presented at the 38th Annual Hawaii International Conference on System Sciences (HICSS'05) - Track 7 Hawaii.

Miles, R. E. & Snow, C. C. 1978. Organizational strategy, structure and process. New York: McGraw-Hill. ISBN 0804748403

Miles, R. E., Snow, C. C., Mathews, J. A., Miles, G., & Coleman, H. J. 1997. Organizing in the Knowledge Age: Anticipating the Cellular Form. Academy of Management Executive, 11(4), ISSN: 0896-3789: 7-24.

Muffatto, M. & Faldani, M. 2003. Open Source as a Complex Adaptive System. Emergence: Complexity and Organization, 5(3), ISSN 1521-3250: 83-100.

O'Reilly, T.; Open Source Paradigm Shift, http://tim.oreilly.com/articles/paradigmshift_0504.html

Raymond, E. S. 2001. Cathedral and the Bazaar: Musings on Linux and Open Source by an Accidental Revolutionary (Revised ed.): O'Reilly Media. ISBN 0596001088

Rossi, M. A. 2004. Decoding the "Free/Open Source (F/OSS) Puzzle" - a Survey of Theoretical and Empirical Contributions, University of Sienna, Sienna, Italy.

Sanger, L.; The Early History of Nupedia and Wikipedia: A Memoir, file:///C:/data/surrey/Case%20Studies/wikipedia/early%20history%20of%20nupedia%20and%20wikipedia.htm

Sanger, L.; How to Think about Strong Collaboration among Professionals, http://www.citizendium.org/collab_prof.html

Sawyer, K. R. 2001. Emergence in Sociology: Contemporary Philosophy of Mind and Some Implications for Sociology Theory. American Journal of Sociology, 107(3), ISSN: 0002-9602: 551-585.

Schroder, J. 1998. Emergence: Non-Deducibility or Downwards Causation? The Philosophical Quarterly, 48(193), ISSN 0031-8094: 434-452.

Stiles, W. B. 1992. Describing Talk: A Taxonomy of Verbal Response Modes: Sage. ISBN 0803944659

Therborn, G. 2002. Back to Norms! On the Scope and Dynamics of Norms and Normative Action. Current Sociology, 50(6), ISSN 0011-3921: 17.

Viegas, F., Wattenberg, M., Kriss, J., & van Ham, F. 2007. Talk Before you Type: Coordination in Wikipedia, 40th Hawaii International Conference on System Science. Hawaii.

5. Globalization and the Transformation of National Sovereignty

Leonid E. Grinin
Volgograd Center for Social Research, Russia

The process of globalization undoubtedly contributes to the changes and reduction of nomenclature and scope of state sovereign powers. At the same time this is a bilateral process: On the one hand, we see the growth of strength of those factors that actually undermine the countries' sovereignty, on the other – most states voluntarily limit the scope of their sovereignty including the right to use the capital punishment, to establish the nomenclature and size of taxation, the size of monetary emission and borrowings etc. We believe that among the range of factors influencing the process of change of national sovereignty, the factor of voluntary reduction of the scope of sovereign powers to obtain some additional prestige and benefits appears to be of the utmost importance. At the same time the limiting of sovereignty inevitably leads to great changes in the policy patterns of states as well as ones of common people.

The problem setting

Can the 21st century be already called the age of globalization? Will it really be of this kind? It is quite probable. But what will happen in the future with nation-state' sovereign rights? And will such states remain as before the leading players at the political scene, or will they give this place to some new political units?

At the end of the 20th and the beginning of the 21st century political science (especially in connection with the problems of globalization and new world order) start raising a considerable number of issues of national sovereignty change, "diffusion", "disappearing" etc. (e.g,. Giddens, 1990; Gilpin, 2001; Held & McGrew, 2003b; Ilyin, 1993). Nevertheless, in comparison with an avalanche of works on globalization, the number of publications dedicated to the transformation of sovereignty in modern world is incomparably smaller, and above all, in a sizeable part of those publication the problem itself is not studied thoroughly and profoundly enough, as they do not take into account to a sufficient degree the complexity of the present-day world political processes, whereas some of their important aspects are virtually not studied at all. Meanwhile in our view, the processes of change of sovereignty appear to be among the most important for the present.

In the present paper we try to demonstrate that on the whole globalization contributes to the change and reduction of nomenclature and scope of state sovereign powers and besides it is a bilateral process: on the one hand, we observe the strengthening of such factors that actually undermine nation-state sovereignty, on the other – most states voluntarily limit the scope of their sovereignty. And since the tendency to change and reduce the sovereign prerogatives (of course with considerable fluctuations) most likely will strengthen, it will inevitably and fundamentally influence all spheres of life including the change of ideology and public psychology. However, the last point is evidently underestimated by analysts. We think that to give an appropriate estimation of those changes within the global system one needs some new approaches to the problems of national sovereignty and the role of nation-states in the process of globalization. In the present paper we suggest and partially develop some of such approaches.

Introduction on Sovereignty and Globalization

In political science the sovereignty is usually defined as the most essential attribute of a state in the form of its complete self-sufficiency, i.e., its supremacy in the domestic policy and independence in the foreign one (e.g., Jerry and Jerry, 1999: 311; Held, 2003: 162-163). This notion became widespread in the 19th century. But already at the beginning of the Modern Age it got quite a definite interpretation in the works by Niccolo Machiavelli, Jean Bodin, Thomas Hobbes and others (see, e.g., Held, 2003: 162-163). In the system of international affairs which appeared after Peace Treaties of Westphalia of 1648 after the Thirty Years' War the principles of state sovereignty gradually obtained the all-European appreciation. However, it is important to note that this "normative trajectory" of international law was fully described only by the end of the 18th – early 19th century. At present in the UN Charter and in some other international agreements there are regulations on sovereign equality of states and nations' right to self-determination which together with the increasing degree of external security of most countries, in our view has sufficiently contributed to the consolidation of the idea of national sovereignty in international affairs in the second half of the 20th century. Indeed as we will see further, the tendency of recognizing the sovereign rights has been combined with the tendency of their voluntarily constraint by the sovereigns themselves. However the notion of sovereignty is one of the most difficult and ambiguous (see, e.g., Stankiewicz, 1969: 291) and its content has constantly changed and continues to change in connection with changes of international affairs and characteristics of the states themselves (see, e.g., Grinin, 2007; Grinin & Korotayev, 2006) and also depending on who was the supreme sovereign (see, e.g., Yan, 1996). Besides, the absolute (in theory) sovereignty of states as well of nations is always strongly and even fatally limited by different factors. Sovereignty can be considered in different aspects and variants. In other words the notion of sovereignty is not univocal and indisputable but provokes numerous debates and thus demands a considerable elaboration.

Globalization is an exceptionally many-sided process. Practically all spheres of life experience its impact (see, e.g., Giddens, 1990). It is the result of a very difficult allegation of political, social, economic, civilizational and many other processes in the modern world. But among these numerous factors one should especially mark out the huge changes in modern productive forces, media, world trade and specialization. Technology and trade entangle the world with new network connections and make national boundaries transparent. Together with other factors this harshly complicates the conditions external for a society. As a result globalization strongly reduces and changes the scope of national sovereignty, undermines the position of a state as the major actor of international affairs (see Grinin, 1999; 2005; 2007). Thus the changes in production forces in this or that way lead to the changes of all other spheres of life including the political one.

Of course, globalization is far from always giving a positive effect and this is constantly emphasized by its critics. In particular they point to the disparity in benefiting from globalization and the increasing gap in life rate of different countries though the last point is quite an ambiguous conclusion. That is why it is rather natural that the reduction of national sovereignty has not only positive side but also brings many negative consequences, e.g., weakening of such features as patriotism. And also the openness of boundaries is good in some way and wrong in another, e.g. in the field of terrorism and drugs spreading.

Globalization and reduction of Sovereignty

As we said above, sovereignty is usually defined as a state supremacy in the domestic policy and independence in the foreign one. Undoubtedly, in reality the state sovereignty has always been limited by different factors. But it is important to mention that today the idea of states' complete freedom of action even in mere theory looks false. The matter is that the scope of internal sovereignty has greatly narrowed de jure due to the international agreements including the issues of human rights and actually to a greater degree – in connection with already prevalent traditions.

As it has been already said there are comparatively not many works dedicated to the transformation of the position and role of a state in modern world. At that in most cases, as Michael Mann fairly observes, there is going on a one-sided debate on the issue whether the state system becomes stronger or weaker, meanwhile the process appears to be quite complicated and ambiguous; in some way these positions are weakening but in some way they become stronger (Mann, 1997; see also Giddens, 1990). Thus Susanne Strange insists that under the influence of powerful economic processes the state power is declining and at the same time she notes with surprise that the state has started to regulate the issues which people solved themselves before, in particular how to build their own house, how to maintain family relations, so that in her point of view 'less and less of daily life is immune from the activities and decisions of government bureaucracies' (Strange, 2003: 128). She calls it a paradox though these are quite natural things as the processes never go unilinearly and only in a single direction. The general trajectory is always a complicated balance of alternate changes, at the same time the system's weakening usually combines with strengthening of some its aspects although it occurs at the expense of the components conversion and changes in hierarchy levels.

Sometimes one may get an impression that scholars study the problem of state fortune in globalizing world only from the angle that great world economic powers – supranational and to a large degree anonymous – influence the transformation of national sovereignty, changing it on the whole as if in spite of or even contrary to the will of the states themselves (see, e.g., Clark, 1999; Held, 2003; Keohane, 1995; Slaughter, 2000; Strange, 2003). The list of threatens to the state sovereignty often includes: global financial flows, multinational corporations, global media empires, Internet etc. (see, e.g., Held & McGrew, 2003: 124). The globalists maintain that state authority is greatly weakened by these processes which lead to the boundaries transparency. At the same time another aspect of the problem is almost unnoticed (or it is not attached a sufficient importance) which we consider exactly an exceptionally important one: sovereignty to a large (probably, prevalent) degree is reduced *voluntary by national states themselves.*

It appears that it is not completely comprehended that since the afterwar time there is going on the most important process as a result of which many countries deliberately start to limit themselves in seemingly most sovereign things. We marked out and analyzed these aspects of globalization in a number of our works (see Grinin, 1999, 2005, 2007).

The basic trends of voluntarily reducing of the scope of sovereign prerogatives

To agree with the above-said it is enough to cast a brief glance at the spheres where sovereignty has reduced. The right to impose duties and taxation and define their rate; to forbid and reward import and export of goods (capitals) and some types of activity; to issue currency; to borrow; to set the rules of keeping the imprisoned and usage of their labour; to use the capital punishment; to proclaim these or those politic liberties or restrict them; to define fundamental rules of elections (and to hold them proper) and electoral qualification and also a great number of other important things have stopped to be defined only by the wishes of a state itself. Not so long ago the Europeans refused the sanctum sanctorum – their own national currencies that had been gained for centuries for the sake of a common currency (euro). Finally, what has always been regarded the main thing in sovereignty – the right of war and peace – is under international control. World wars and totalitarianism showed that absolute sovereignty including also the right to unleash wars and repressions is dangerous. Hence it is possible to make an important though on the whole obvious conclusion: the domestic affairs of a state where nobody intervenes and which are regulated only by national law and traditions, are getting narrow and international law or law of a definite community (of collective participation) is expanding (Grinin, 1999, 2005, 2007).

Of course, the processes of internationalization have started not today but have been already going on for centuries increasing all the time. But the prevalence and power of these processes yesterday and today are incomparable. First, they have involved the whole world. Second, the economic alliances were uncommon before and now they have become the most typical form of associations. And some of the economic organizations (such as WTrO, IMF) encompass the majority of countries of the world. The scale and aims of political associations have also changed. Third, enormously grew the intensity and consistency of country leaders` contacts. And the problems they solve have changed greatly. Fourth, only a few countries are able today to carry out an isolationist policy and avoid any associations (for more detail see: Grinin, 2005: 16-17).

To emphasize the above said it is worth mentioning though it may sound strange that the maximal sovereignty is gained by the countries ideologically (China, Iran, Saudi Arabia) and economically closed such as North Korea, Cuba; or exactly because of their "sovereign rights" (in particular to create nuclear weapon) there happen sharp conflicts. But on the whole even these countries` sovereignty starts to diminish. As for sufficiently open and developed countries, in our point of view the tendency to delegate their powers to the international, regional and world organizations and associations is absolutely obvious. The only exception are the USA which at times permit themselves to act regardless of many countries opinion, openly putting their national interests above the world and allied ones. But it seems to us that just in this confrontation of the USA and other countries which express a certain collective opinion, probably roots the main intrigue of the change of the world in the future and also the transformation of sovereignty content (see Grinin, 1999: 28–29, 2005: 9, 25–26).

Transformation of Sovereignty and the Systems of international relations

Thus there is completely no doubt that today in comparison with the past the sovereignty of completely free and independent countries has become much smaller. And what is extremely important, many countries quite often give away a part of their sovereign powers voluntarily indeed. We think that such altruism can be seriously explained only by the fact that such restriction becomes profitable as instead the countries gain quite real advantages. It is quite natural that such an "exchange" has become possible in principle only as a result of the powerful influence of the described (and many unmentioned) processes. As an important cause of sovereignty reduction in our view it must be noted a kind of world public opinion: the wider is the circle of countries voluntarily limiting their sovereignty the more undeveloped seem those states which do not make such restrictions.

Actually the notion of sovereignty itself undergoes very significant changes. In political science there is realized to a certain degree that the doctrine of national sovereignty has become old-fashioned and there is required a complex re-thinking and re-evaluation of the notion of sovereignty in connection with the emergence of world political community as well as in connection with the specifying of the limits of particular sovereignties, principles of their combination with each other and construction of their hierarchy and also in connection with the actions of other different subjects such as multinational corporation and non-state organizations as well as multinational structures and arrangements (see, e.g., Utkin, 2000: 41-41). However it seems that most researchers still underestimate the gravity of changes of sovereignty and the necessity to re-think this notion itself in the context of modern processes.

Well, of course, a state still principally remains (and will endure for quite a long time) the superior unit of political life. However, today there have appeared new powerful factors which in the long run will lead the state to stop being the limit of expressed and will give this place to large supranational formations. And in our opinion this tendency will increase. On the other hand, we would like without fail add that this is not a one-sided and univocal but a many-sided process: sovereignty will reduce in the main but in some way it will become stronger and even grow. That is why it is dangerous to hurry too much to bury national state, for a long time it will remain the leading player in international affairs. Besides, as some scholars fairly point out, the abrupt reduction of sovereignty and traditional functions of a state may cause chaos (Utkin, 2000: 41-42).

Though sovereignty is getting narrow but this principle itself will long remain one of the most important in the international affairs. That is why its open disrespect will continue to provoke condemnation. When old ideas are still alive and the new ones have not become firmly established the collisions may obtain a form of opposition of principles which hides their historical significance. In that case it is difficult to understand who is right, who is wrong. For instance, if basing on the right of the strong to openly trample on the sovereignty principle even in the respect of a dictatorial regime the sympathy may appear on the per se reactionary side. The war in Iraq in 2003 proves this. That is why it appears that in the legal and moral aspects really irreproachable arguments are desirable which would base on the world organizations decisions (UNO in the first place). That is why to support the actions against the regimes-disturbers the sanctions of exactly this kind are important.

So since the post-war time (since 1945) the tendency is more clearly revealed that countries gradually delegate a part of their sovereignty to the world international organizations. Even a larger part of sovereignty passes to regional associations and courts of arbitration. And the integration of states in suprastate economic associations is becoming more and more important part of globalization. Such supranational units and formations are present on almost all continents and in some cases a transformation of economic alliances into political ones is outlined. Of course, the process of creating really formed, systematically and profoundly integrated suprastate formations can not be quick. Neither will it be smooth since all its members can not ignore their own interests and in this or that way will oppose them to each other. Besides within the countries themselves different political powers interpret national aims quite in a different way. In other words the adjustment of the supra- and intrastate interests is a difficult problem, and different confrontations are inevitable here. Besides, common aims also may be interpreted in a different way. In this sense a very significant example is that of the USA which were able to bring together into a tight knot their purely national narrow political problems (such as the coming elections or the necessity to increase the president popularity) with world interests.

Globalization though it has started far from today on the whole is a new, unknown, most complicated and in many ways unpredictable process. At that still it is not worth exaggerating that anyway great role of economy in the transformation of the state, as, e.g., Turaev (2001: ch. 2) does it. The economy comes forward as the leading factor in this sense only in the long run. We think for a radical change of sovereignty there are also required some serious changes in other spheres of life just as for the formation of bourgeois society the changes in economy were insufficient and also there was needed a political revolution (see in detail Grinin, 1999, 2005, 2007). That is why in our opinion, for a long time the most important problem will be that of combining national and supra-national, group and world interests. After all only an institutionalized solution of this huge problem will establish a more or less stable world order. But this will not be the order which is spoken about with confidence in the USA but let us hope it will be a system of a more balanced account of interests of different regions and countries. However, the way to such an order is unclear, complicated and discrepant. Naturally, it will take some time during which there must occur a profound turn in the elites and people's outlook as a result of which the national problems will start to be considered primarily through the prism of common interests and only next in the context of common (regional and world) tasks and problems.

References

Clark, I. (1999). *Globalization and International Relations Theory*, ISBN 0198782098.

Giddens, A. (1990). *The Consequences of Modernity*, ISBN 0804717621.

Gilpin, R. (2001). *Global Political Economy: Understanding the International Economic Order*, ISBN 069108677X.

Grinin, L. E. (2007). *Gosudarstvo i istoricheskiy protsess. Politicheskiy srez istoricheskogo protsessa.* [State and Historical Process. The Political Cut of Historical Process], ISBN 978-5-484-01007-3.

Grinin, L. E. (2005). "Globalizatsiya i natsionaljnyj suverenitet" ["Globalization and National Sovereignty"], *Istoria i sovremennostj*, ISSN 1811-7481, 1: 6-31

Grinin, L.E. (1999). "Sovremennye proizvoditiljnye sily i problemy natsionaljnogo suvereniteta" ["Modern Productive Forces and Problems of National Sovereignty"], *Philosophiya i obschestvo,* ISSN 1681-4339, 4: 5-44.

Grinin, L. E. and Korotayev, A. V. (2006). "Political Development of the World System: A Formal Quantitative Analysis," in Turchin, P., Grinin, L. E., de Munck, V. and Korotayev, A. V. (eds.), *History & Mathematics: Historical Dynamics and Development of Complex Societies*, ISBN 978-5-484-01002-8, pp. 63-114.

Held, D. (2003). "The Changing Structure of International Law: Sovereignty Transformed?", in Held, D. and McGrew, A. (eds.), *The Global Transformation Reader: An Introduction to the Globalization Debate*, ISBN 0745631355, pp. 162-176.

Held, D. and McGrew, A. (2003). "Political Power and Civil Society: A Reconfiguration?", in Held, D., and McGrew, A. (eds.), *The Global Transformation Reader: An Introduction to the Globalization Debate*, ISBN 0745631355, pp. 121–125.

Held, D. and McGrew, A. (eds.). (2003a). *The Global Transformation Reader: An Introduction to the Globalization Debate*, ISBN 0745631355.

Ilyin, M. V. (1993). "Sobiranie i razdelenie suvereniteta" ["Collecting and Dividing Sovereignty"], *Politicheskie issledovanija*, ISSN 0321-2017, 5: 144-147.

Jerry, D., and Jerry, G. (1999). *Bolshoy tolkovyj sotsialogicheskiy slovarj* [Big Explanatory Sociological Dictionary]. 2 vols. Vol. 2, ISBN 5783804277.

Keohane, R. O. (1995) "Hobbes Dilemma and Institutional Change in World Politic: Sovereignty in International Society," in Holm, H.-H., and Sørensen, G. (eds.),

Whose World Order? Uneven Globalization and the End of the Cold War, ISBN 0813321875, pp. 165-186.

Mann, M. (1997). "Has Globalisation Ended the Rise and Rise of the Nation-State?", *Review of International Political Economy*, ISSN 0969-2290, 4(3) (Autumn): 472-496.

Slaughter, A. M. (2000). "Governing the Global Economy through Government Networks," in Byers, M. (ed.), *The Role of Law in International Politics: essays in International Relations and International* Laws, ISBN 0198268874, pp. 177-205.

Stankiewicz, W. J. (1969). "The Validity of Sovereignty," in Stankiewicz, W. J. (ed.), *In Defense of Sovereignty*. London, Toronto: Oxford University Press, no ISBN given, pp. 291–298.

Strange, S. (2003). "The Declining Authority of States," in Held, D., and McGrew, A. (eds.), *The Global Transformation Reader: An Introduction to the Globalization Debate*, ISBN 0745631355, pp. 127–134.

Turaev, V. A. (2001). *Globaljnye problyemy sovremennosti* [Global Problems of Modernity], ISBN 5940101178.

Utkin, A. I. (2000). "Vectory globaljnykh peremen: analiz i otsenki osnovnykh faktorov mirovogo politicheskogo razvitiya" [Vectors of Global Changes: Analysis and Evaluation of the Main Factors of World Political Development], *Politicheskie issledovanija*, ISSN 0321-2017, 1: 38–54.

Yan, E. (1996). "Demokratia i natsionalism; edinstvo ili protivorechie?" [Democarcy and Nationalism: Unity or Opposition?], *Politicheskie issledovanija*, ISSN 0321-2017, 1: 114–123.

6. Groupware and Socialware: Overview and Perspectives

Ivan Tomek, Rick Giles, Hai Zhang and **Li Di**
Jodrey School of Computer Science, Acadia University, CAN

Social and work communities are complex systems due to the nature and number of their components, the complexity, variety, and dynamics of their internal processes, and the range of tools that they employ. As more and more communities are geographically dispersed, tools are required to minimize the effect of their physical separation. The purpose of this paper is to illustrate software supporting these environments and show that socialware and groupware share essential features. This conclusion is then used to contemplate directions for their future joint evolution as a class of related software applications.

Introduction

Work and social environments are complicated open systems with many sophisticated components. They use a variety of tools and processes to respond to external stimuli and affect them in return. As the size, variety, and sophistication of work teams and social groups evolve and as individuals become increasingly geographically dispersed, these environments require new means of support. Fortunately, this is becoming possible thanks to powerful and affordable information technology.

Computer support of teamwork (groupware) and social interaction (socialware) has a long history. From initial single-function single-machine programs, groupware evolved into applications integrating many functions and running on many interconnected machines. Support for social interaction has a shorter history and is less researched. Beginning in the 1980s groupware and socialware started to overlap somewhat and although substantial differences remain, there are many similarities. The purpose of this paper is to support this claim and propose directions for future work taking advantage of the commonalities.

The rest of this paper is organized as follows: Section 2 provides a brief characterization of work environments. Section 3 offers a groupware classification and describes representative examples of the main categories. Section 4 deals with socialware and describes recent socialware products. Section 5 summarizes our position and suggests directions for future work.

A brief characterization of traditional work environments

To characterize work environments, let's examine the components of a typical conventional work situation.

Conventional work environments

A work environment consists of people, tools, work processes, and physical space. Members of a traditional work team share the same physical location and work in offices providing a degree of privacy that helps to maximize productivity and ensure a measure of personal comfort. Private work spaces are complemented by shared spaces such as meeting rooms and libraries. Work space is equipped with furniture such as whiteboards, and tools including personal computers running programs such as planning and scheduling applications.

Company employees typically form work teams dedicated to specific projects or tasks and individual members play multiple roles. Besides sharing a common task, groups also share documents, tools, and work places. They are formed mainly around projects and for limited durations.

Work teams use more or less formal processes to accomplish their tasks. Their nature depends on the discipline - teams of engineers, teams of architects, and teams of programmers use different work procedures. Work processes also evolve over time and even teams with similar tasks and within the same company may use different approaches.

A major part of work is communication within and across teams and with customers and suppliers. Some of it is formal but informal communication is very important too. The latter occurs beyond the 'strongly tied' part of the organization, and network theory shows (Grannoveter, 1973) that this kind of communication can bring new perspectives leading to fresh ideas.

Because work environments are open systems, they continuously evolve and the ability to change and adopt new tools is among the critical enablers of an organization's success.

Work environments at the time of global economy and Internet

As society and economy become global, organizations are increasingly geographically dispersed. Communication and information exchange become more difficult because face-to-face meetings often become impossible and significant savings in time and money can be achieved by eliminating excessive travel through alternatives to collocated work. Fortunately, technology evolves as fast as the demands, easing the problem somewhat. In dealing with geographical dislocation, groupware (Andriessen, 2002) is now one of the most important facilities.

Groupware classification

Before describing examples of groupware products, we will propose a classification that will help to see the range of available groupware and place our examples in perspective. By prevailing technology, we can initially classify groupware as Graphical User Interface (GUI)-based, or using surround technology or virtual reality. GUI-based products use windows with standard GUI controls and are best suited for tasks where text-based information is the major component of work as in software development. Products based on surround technology use cameras, large screens, and similar technology to create the feeling of physical collocation and are best suited for meetings. Products using virtual reality typically use computer-generated characters moving in a virtual 3D space. They are most appropriate where the dimensionality of physical space is particularly important, for example in architectural applications.

Surveying all three categories would require too much space and we will thus focus on GUI-based groupware. To understand it better, we will subdivide it further on the basis of the underlying metaphor – the characteristic used by the developers as the driving design principle, a restricted view of the essence of the targeted type of collaboration. In the following, we will adopt classification based on three metaphors: document-centric, meeting-based, and virtual-space based.

Supporters of the document-centric metaphor maintain that work revolves around project documents, such as specifications and blueprints. To proponents of the meeting-based metaphor, group- and individual meetings are the essence of work. And builders of virtual-space-based environments believe that software emulating spatial characteristics of work approximates the ideal collocated environment best. To illustrate these principles, we will now give examples of environments from each of the three categories.

Groupware examples

The purpose of the following examples is to illustrate typical groupware products and demonstrate that they share many common features in spite of the different metaphors that they use.

Foldera

Foldera is a *document-centric* application. Its centerpiece is a folder, a collection of documents. In addition to the folder tool, Foldera offers many other facilities to provide complete support for geographically dispersed teams, but all activity is initiated from an Activity Folder and kept within its context. As an example, a change to a document stored in the folder generates a notice that is communicated to all members registered in the project. Foldera is accessed via a Web browser, which provides accessibility from any place where Internet is available and eliminates the need to install or update client software because all software is on the central server. Foldera components include the following:

- *Activity Folder* - created for a project or task along with its users and their access rights. To provide a feeling for Foldera, Figure 1 shows Activity Folder's user interface.
- *E-mail* is Foldera-specific (non-interoperable with other e-mail systems) and works within the context of the folder from which the mail is sent.

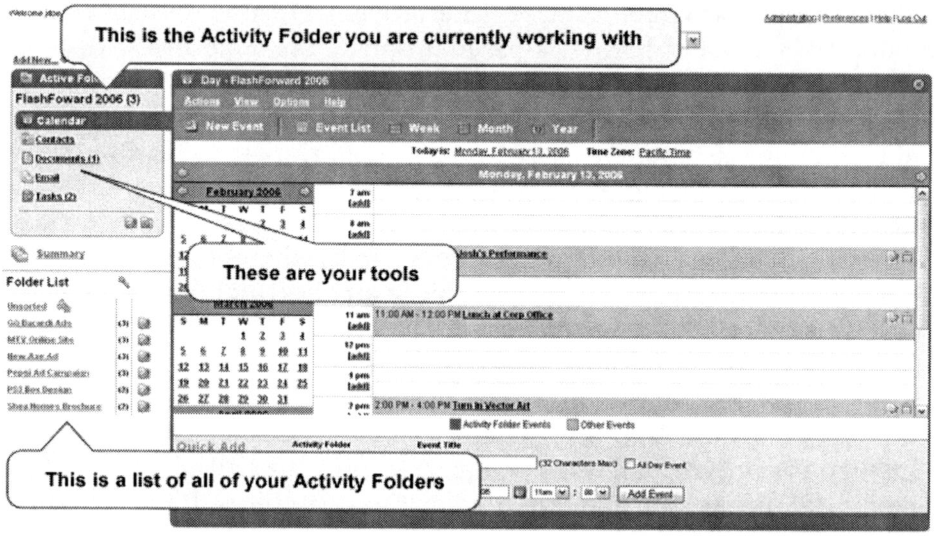

Figure 1 *Foldera's Activity Folder*

- *Document Manager* provides access to folder documents and document information. Access is controlled by user authorization and can use private, public, or custom setting. Documents are created and accessed by client-resident applications and document annotations facilitate document-centered discussions.
- *Task Manager* allows creation of project-related tasks, their assignment to project members, and progress monitoring. Access is private, public, or custom, and task changes are reported via notifications.
- *Calendar* is used to define events and can be programmed to send notifications when a new event is created or an existing event changed. Reminders and recurring events can also be programmed.
- *Contact Manager* maintains a list of contacts which can be imported from e-mail applications.
- *Comments* is a tool that mediates discussions around a document, task, or event. It is used, for example, to assist in shared document editing.
- *Instant Messenger* allows use of several popular chat products, such as MSN Messenger and Google Talk within the context of an Application Folder.
- *Administration tool* is used to create new Activity Folders, their users, and groups. It enables limited product customization.
- *Sharing Manager* allows users to control access to tasks, events, contacts, and documents.

Foldera is a black-box application and its implementation resides on a central site; users do not have any programming access to it and all updates and bug corrections must be performed by the Foldera team.

Marratech

Marratech (2007a, b) is a commercial product using the *meeting metaphor*. Its users typically run a client continuously and use it to contact other users to arrange virtual private or team meetings in a virtual office equipped with several built-in tools. These tools include an interactive whiteboard, video- and audio-conferencing, and instant messaging. Marratech also allows application sharing, and lets meeting participants control an application running on another user's machine. Meetings including voice, video, and whiteboard support can be recorded and played back. All functionality is available via a simple single window (Figure 2). Although users can access documents while together in a virtual room, Marratech does not allow virtual objects residing in a persistent virtual space.

Marratech is highly scalable because its clients perform much of the processing and offload the server. The client's operation is adaptive in that it automatically adjusts to the current state of the network. Marratech is a black-box product that does not allow customization, adaptation, or extension by users.

CVW, FCVW, FVE

CVW (Collaborative Virtual Workspace) is open source groupware developed by MITRE Inc. (CVW, 2007; Maybury, 2001). It uses the *virtual space metaphor* that emulates those aspects of the physical world that are most important for collaboration through the concept of a virtual building.

When users log in, they are placed in their home offices. Starting here, they can move around the virtual building, communicate with other users, and view room contents such as documents created within CVW or imported from client machines. Other virtual objects include whiteboards, chat recorders, and other facilities programmed with the built-in LambdaMOO programming language (LambdaMOO, 2007). Depending on their access rights, users can examine objects, modify them, and move them from room to room. Imported documents can be viewed using the application software that created them. Communication tools include chat, popup messaging, e-mail, video- and audio-conferencing, and acoustic phone. CVW also supports user groups to control access to rooms and documents, to simplify simultaneous communication with multiple users, etc. Using LambdaMOO, authorized users can program new types of objects and functionality or modify definitions of existing objects at runtime.
Figure 3 shows CVW's desktop user interfaces. Essential functionality is provided in the main window, less commonly needed tasks can be performed from specialized windows, and rarely used functionality is accessible via a command line in the main window.

CVW and its descendents, such as FCVW (Tomek, 2006) and FVE (Tomek, 2007) are the only products in this section that are user-programmable.

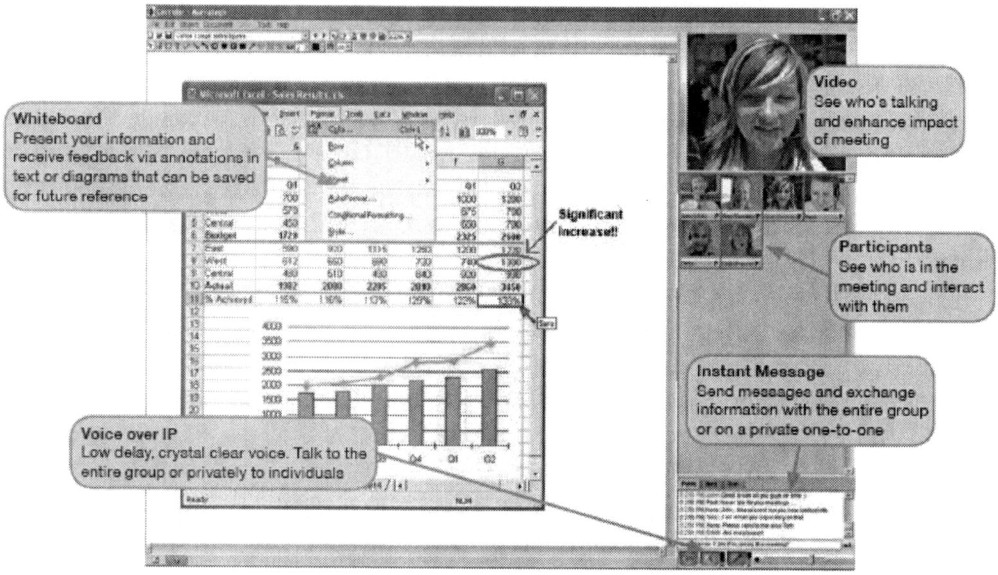

Figure 2 *Marratech user interface*

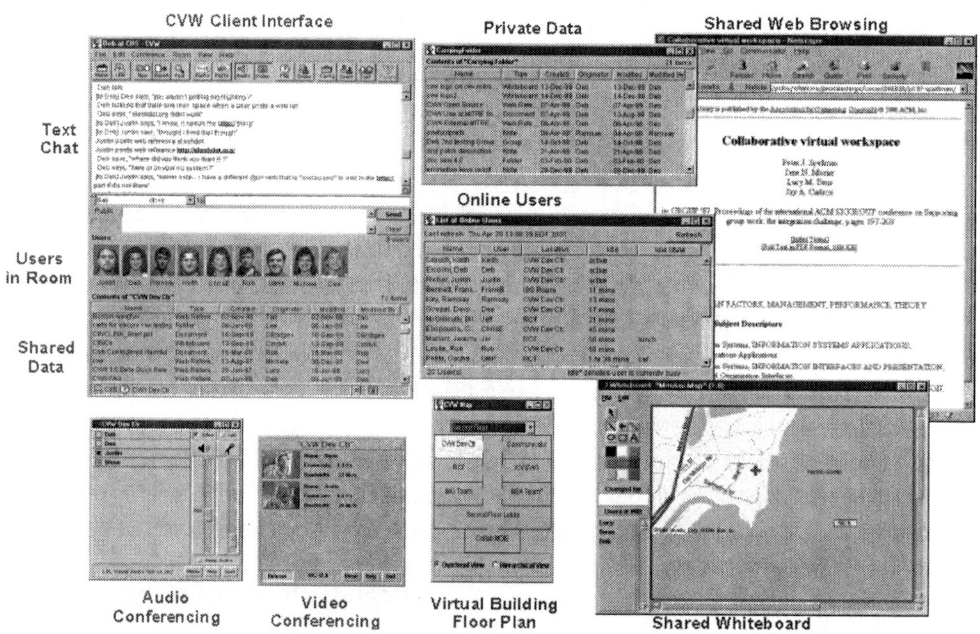

Figure 3 *CVW user interfaces. The main window is in upper left corner*

Conclusion: Groupware

Although different groupware applications use different work metaphors, they all share numerous common features or would greatly benefit from them. They all use client-server architecture and require secure and efficient network interfaces, must be scalable to accommodate varying numbers of users, persistent, reliable, and provide a shared core of user functions. These functions include, for example, ways to establish each user's personal identity, various forms of synchronous and asynchronous communication, ability to import, export, and share documents created by external application, support for groups, and the ability to define individual- and group-based authorizations for resource access.

Socialware with examples

Socialware is software for social interaction and support of on-line communities (Preece, 2000). Its history partially overlaps with groupware and its origin arguably dates to late 1970s MUDs and MOOs (Hayes, 2001) - text-based multi-player networked versions of the fantasy game Dungeons and Dragons. MUDs and MOOs introduced the concept of a virtual universe and today's related environments not only depend on the same principle but even use the original MOO server. Within a short time of their creation, MUD and MOO communities realized that the concept of a virtual universe has uses beyond gaming and started using it to support social interaction, as groupware (Churchill, 1999), and in education (Holmevik, 1999). Several MUD and MOO communities exist even today and their most extensive use is clustered around the enCore Consortium (enCore, 2007). We will not discuss this type of environments further because they are quite similar to CVW.

Most other socialware applications are either various forms of enhanced chat or software centered on information sharing. All are limited-purpose products lacking the wide range of features available in sophisticated groupware discussed above. To illustrate the current state of the functionally richer socialware applications, the following describes two products that explicitly claim to support social groups constructed around specific shared interests or concerns.

Ning

Ning is a client-server application that lets its users create social networks by combining a variety of features available from the Ning Web site (Ning, 2007). A quick scan of the many communities created with Ning shows social networks set up by groups as diverse as film-makers, bicycle riders, music group fans, soccer enthusiasts, and thousands of others.

Ning uses a Web browser client to access social networks hosted on the company's server. It offers free service to regular users, and enhanced service to paying business users. Started in October 2004, it claims to host tens of thousands of social networks. The company encourages users to discuss advantages and shortcomings of the platform and suggest new features, but selection and implementation is left to the development team. In other words, Ning is basically a black-box application. A limited form of client-side control is achieved with the help of the "View Source" tool, which allows users to see the source code behind any running site, and the 'Create' page that allows limited customization via one of several templates or a Cascading Style Sheet (CSS).

Ning members can access most existing Ning networks but some allow only invited members. Users can create their personal profile pages, a 'chatter-wall' is available for asynchronous chat, and uploaded photos and videos can be organized into albums, commented upon, and rated. Other features include photo and video sharing, a discussion forum, and blog posts. A part of Ning's Creator window is shown in Figure 4. Advertisements on the side of the page pay for the otherwise free services.

I-Neighbors

Project I-Neighbors (I-Neighbor, 2007a, b) is a free online service started as an MIT research project. It grew out of the widely shared suspicion that Internet increases virtual communication at the expense of interactions within real-world communities (Barney, 2004). I-Neighbors attempts to show that Internet can have a positive effect even on such communities and strengthen real-world neighborhoods by providing Web-based support for community-related needs.

The I-Neighbors web site allows anybody to become a member, create a personal profile, and select a 'home' neighborhood. Neighborhoods are organized by postal codes and users are free to become members of any neighborhood besides their home. They can also easily create a new neighborhood.

Once logged into a neighborhood (Figure 5) users can access, create, and update community-related data, and use several neighborhood services. These include polls, event schedules, reviews of local establishments, links to lists of elected officials, lists of registered neighbors and their personal information, neighborhood-based e-mail, uploading and sharing of documents, and directories of neighbors, photos, documents, reviews, and polls. One can also view adjacent neighborhoods and access US and Canadian neighborhoods by their postal code.

I-Neighbors runs on a central server and modifications are up to its developers and owners. The fact that some of the administrative processes are rather awkward and highly centralized shows that centralization is not necessarily the best approach. For example, to delete a document one must contact the central site, even if the party is the user who uploaded the document. Similarly, inappropriate photos and e-mail may only be deleted by the central authority.

The I-Neighbors service has been used to conduct substantial sociological research on the effect of socialware on physical neighborhoods (Faber, 2006). The findings indicate that the application helps to increase the sense of community belonging and involvement, and the ability of users to react to important issues and emergencies. The e-mail list of subscribed neighbors and elected officials was found to be the most appreciated service. On the negative side, the social ties created through I-Neighbors were characterized as weak compared to relationships established through face-to-face contact. It was found that interest in the service was greatly influenced by the type of community, and the age, technical sophistication, and other personal characteristics of its inhabitants.

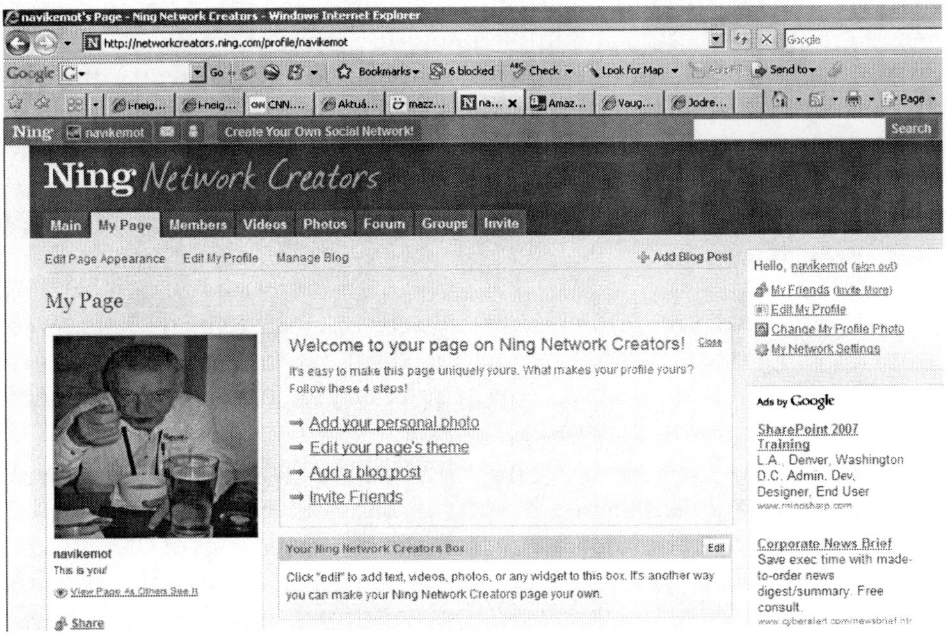

Figure 4 *Part of Ning's Creator page*

Figure 5 *Part of I-Neighbors page*

Conclusion: Socialware

Our brief survey of socialware suggests feature needs similar to those of advanced groupware. We conclude that it is therefore logical to approach socialware and groupware design and implementation from one perspective and develop a software framework that implements shared functionality and allows relatively easy extension and customization for more specific needs.

Closing notes

Our groupware and socialware characterization and examples lead us to the following conclusions:

1. Work- and social environments are complex open systems with many components and a variety of continuously evolving types of activities. Increasing globalization and new technologies require and enable IT-based support for these systems - groupware and socialware.
2. Groupware and socialware are not only tools that support complex open systems; they are complex open systems themselves. They are affected by factors outside their boundaries such as the characteristics of their users and teams, work processes, and technology, and their features affect their users and the productivity and quality of their work and their lives.
3. The history of groupware and socialware provides many examples of possible approaches but more research of both human and technical aspects is needed before such systems are accepted by their users as widely as they deserve.
4. Although work teams and social groups have different goals, groupware and socialware share many requirements: They must provide global connectivity, personalized support for individual users and user groups, synchronous and asynchronous communication among individuals and within groups, sharing of documents produced by applications outside the environment itself, awareness of activities taking place in the virtual space, and the ability to create private individual and group spaces for work, meetings, and documents. Efficiency, security, scalability, persistence, and support for new technologies are essential.
5. User needs differ among different communities and keep changing as technologies, processes, and goals evolve. Implementation of individual features changes as well, as better solutions and new technologies become available. As a consequence, design must allow existing feature implementations to be replaced by new ones and new features to be added without disrupting the operation of the environment. This requires modular architecture in which functional modules can be replaced at runtime, operation and interfaces customized, and new features programmatically added without interrupting operation. Because technological and social evolution is fast, the slow and selective response of centralized development teams is unacceptable. Users themselves should thus be able to intervene via module replacement or ad-

dition, as well as by using built-in programmability with minimal recourse the developers of the product.

6. Because groupware and socialware applications are complex and their development expensive and time-consuming, it is important to minimize duplication of effort in their development. The best way to do this is to create a software framework providing common functionality and facilities for customization, expansion, and modification to support adaptation. The bottom level of this software framework should support requirements shared by all social and work applications. The middle layer should define components for particular types of groupware or socialware communities, and specialized components should be defined in the top layer.
7. Groupware and socialware should be easy to learn and use. While user interfaces play a significant role in user satisfaction, the fundamental determining factor is the metaphor underlying the design. We believe that the most powerful and natural metaphor is that of a user-programmable virtual universe and that this metaphor is the best overarching conceptual principle for both socialware and groupware.
8. Successful examples of open software show that even large and high-quality systems can be developed as open source projects. We believe that a groupware and socialware framework along the lines proposed above could also be advantageously developed as an open source product. A suitable type of license would allow space for open extension, improvement and continued growth, offer room for rapid development of commercial products of professional quality, and provide an incentive for the development of a test bed for research.

References

Andriessen J.H. (2002): *Working with Groupware.* ISBN 185233603X.

Barney D. (2004): *Community in the Digital Age: Philosophy and Practice.* ISBN 0742529592.

Churchill E.F. and S. Bly S. (1999):*Virtual Environments at Work: Ongoing use of MUDs in the Workplace.* International Joint Conference on Work Activities Coordination and Collaboration.

Faber, J. (2006): *I-Neighbors.org: A Study of Technology and Community.* American Sociological Association, Montreal, Quebec, Canada, 2006.

Foldera (2007). http://www.foldera.com/index.htm

CVW (2007). http://cvw.sourceforge.net/

Granovetter, M. (1973). *The Strength of Weak Ties.* American Journal of Sociology, 78, (May), ISSN 0002-9602.

Hayes C., Holmevik J. (2001) *High Wired: On the Design, Use, and Theory of Educational MOOs.* ISBN 0472088386.

Holmevik J. N., Haynes C. (1999). *MOOniversity. A Student's Guide to Online Learning Environments.* ISBN 0205271146.

I-Neighbors (2007a). *New MIT web site encourages neighborliness* (2004). http://web.mit.edu/newsoffice/2004/ineighbors.html

I-Neighbors (2007b). http://www.i-neighbors.org/

LambdaMOO (2007). *LambdaMOO programmer's manual.* ftp://ftp.research.att.

com/dist/eostrom/MOO/html/ProgrammersManual_toc.html

Marratech, (2007a). *The Arrival of the Virtual Office – whitepaper* (2005). http://www.marratech.com/blog/archives/2005/08/the_arrival_of.html

Marratech (2007b): *See how the most complete collaboration and conferencing environment on the Internet creates the true 'virtual office'.* http://www.marratech.com/support.html

MIT News Office (2007). *New MIT web site encourages neighborliness, I-Neighbors.* http://web.mit.edu/newsoffice/2004/ineighbors.html

Maybury M. (2001). *Collaborative virtual environments for analysis and decision support*, Communications of the ACM, ISSN 0001-0782, December 2001.

Ning: *Create Your Own Social Network for Anything* (2007). http://www.ning.com/

Preece J. (2000). *Online Communities: Designing Usability and Supporting Sociability*, ISBN 0471805998.

Tomek I., et al. (2006). *FCVW: A Federated Collaborative Virtual Workspace*, IADIS International Conference on Applied Computing, San Sebastian, Spain, February 26,-28, 2006.

Tomek I., et al. (2007). *FVE – work in progress*, poster, GROUP 2007.

THEME 2:
CREATIVITY IN SYSTEMIC PROBLEM-SOLVING

7. Creativity, Ethics and Transformation: Key Factors in a Transdisciplinary Application of Systems Methodology to Resolving Wicked Problems in Sustainability

Jane Palmer, Tanzi Smith, Juliet Willetts and **Cynthia Mitchell**
Institute for Sustainable Futures, University of Technology, AUS

Sustainability is a wicked problem that requires a transdisciplinary approach. The defining characteristics of transdisciplinarity include collaborative, creative, higher order thinking which transcends discipline boundaries, the explicit contribution of an ethical or moral perspective to problem resolution, and the generation of new knowledge and new resolutions not available in multidisciplinary and interdisciplinary environments. These characteristics align well with theories on transformative learning and Wilber's theories on consciousness evolution. However we need ways to translate this thinking into practice. Soft systems methodology could provide this practical element, but does not necessarily emphasise transformative learning, or moral perspectives aligned with sustainability i.e. valuing of ecologically restorative, socially just, economically profitable resolutions. This paper explores how integration of a transformative learning process with soft systems methodology might provide a useful transdisciplinary approach to sustainability.

Introduction

Sustainability problems may well be described as wicked problems. Rittel and Webber (1973: 161-167) have identified certain characteristics of wicked problems. These include:

- There is no definitive formulation of a wicked problem;
- We stop work on a wicked problem not because *a* or *the* solution has been found, but because we finally say "That's good enough" or "I like this solution";
- Solutions to wicked problems are not true-or-false, but good-or-bad;
- "The choice of explanation [of the problem] determines the nature of the problem's resolution";
- The planner [problem-solver] has no right to be wrong. "Planners are liable for the consequences of the actions they generate; the effects can matter a great deal to those people that are touched by those actions".

According to Conklin, problem wickedness is not necessarily about a higher degree of complexity, "it is about a fundamentally different kind of challenge…one that makes solution secondary and problem understanding central" (Conklin, *et al.*, 2007: 2). Wickedness helps to explain "why no level of linear thinking…would ever present a workable solution to some problems" (Conklin, *et al.*, 2007: 3). As such, wicked problems call for a qualitatively different approach from conventional problem solving. In this paper, we adopt the term 'problem resolution' in place of 'problem solution' to reflect this difference.

Various authors have posited the need for a transdisciplinary approach to sustainability (Max-Neef, 2005, Meppem and Gill, 1998, Wickson, *et al.*, 2006). Rather than providing a particular process for addressing a problem, transdisciplinarity:

- Calls in a general way for collaborative, creative, higher order thinking which transcends discipline boundaries (Ramadier, 2004);
- Requires coordination between various levels of knowledge ranging from the empirical to values oriented level (Max-Neef, 2005);
- Allows for new knowledge and new resolutions not available in multidisciplinary and interdisciplinary environments (Thompson Klein, 2004, Wickson, *et al.*, 2006);
- Involves a combination of different types of knowledge (Després, *et al.*, 2004: 477) such that "the whole is more than the sum of its parts" (Ramadier, 2004: 432);
- "[I]s a way of self-transformation oriented towards the knowledge of the self, the unity of knowledge, and the creation of a new art of living" (Nicolescu, 1998: 2);
- Explicitly necessitates the contribution of an ethical or moral perspective to problem resolution (Max-Neef, 2005).

As we shall see, the last two points are particularly significant to this paper.

If a wicked problem is the *subject* of our problem-resolving process then transdisciplinarity offers a *framework* for guiding the application of the *tools* to resolve the problem. Soft systems methodology (SSM), described as an 'inquiring system' (Checkland, 1999: 285), is a *tool* which draws on systems thinking to help us address wicked problems by including multiple stakeholders and moving beyond up front claims about who is right or wrong.

Beginning with Max-Neef's point above, a moral perspective is required at the *framework* level to resolve Rittel and Webber's (1973) ethical dilemma: the moral vacuum which arises in the absence of "a theory that can locate societal goodness, [or] one that might dispel wickedness". This results in an inability to conclude, in the problem-solving process, "which group is right and which should have its ends served" (Rittel & Webber, 1973: 169).

Nicolescu's point above (Nicolescu, 1998) suggests that self-transformation is a key feature of transdisciplinarity. It was the authors' own experience of deep personal change when working on wicked problems which led us beyond

Checkland's descriptions of learning in SSM to explore Taylor and others' work on transformative learning and Wilber's theories on consciousness evolution. We found that key moral and creative elements are fundamental to these learning processes. In this paper we seek to explain how the application of SSM to wicked problems could reflect the concepts of transformative learning and consciousness evolution and more closely meet the requirements of a distinctively transdisciplinary approach to problem solving. In so doing, it may at least in part resolve Rittel and Webber's ethical dilemma. Most importantly, this learning would also contribute to problem resolutions that align with sustainability that is, they are ecologically, socially, and economically preferable.

Soft Systems Methodology

The resonance between SSM and wicked problems is clear. The driver of SSM since its earliest days has been that 'analysis is not enough' (Checkland, 1999: A5) i.e. that the whole purpose of the process is to enable accommodations to be reached by the group of people concerned that would allow action to be taken in a situation that they perceive to be unsatisfactory, as Figure 1 shows.

One area of resonance is between the wicked problem idea of stopping work when we reach a point 'that's good enough' and SSM's intent to uncover 'culturally feasible and systemically desirable' actions.

A second area of resonance lies with the numerous ways of conceptualizing a wicked problem. SSM is a structured process for creating logically coherent models as the basis for a process of finding out about the situation at hand. It carries an expectation that many such models exist (see Figure 1), each with a different 'desired change' (the term 'transformation' is also used, but to avoid confusion in this paper we reserve the latter term for personal transformation through learning) and *weltanschauung* (worldview) at its heart, and a different set of criteria that define its efficacy, efficiency, and effectiveness.

Having demonstrated the resonance between SSM and wicked problems, we move now to explain a little of the process of SSM. Checkland (1999) notes that Vickers' social constructivist writing on appreciative systems most completely mapped his and his colleagues' experiences in applying SSM. We argue that through the judgement processes in Vickers' appreciative systems that underlie the application of SSM (Checkland, 1999), some shift (transformation) must happen for at least some of the individuals involved, but that the ethical and moral direction of that shift is implicitly beyond the concern of the methodology as it is currently applied.

The application of SSM incorporates criteria of cultural feasibility and systemic desirability, and requires an analysis of roles, norms, values, and commodities of power. Using Vickers' appreciative system, SSM recognizes that our perceptions of reality are based on norms and values, and that these:

"lead to readinesses to notice only certain features of our situations; they determine what 'facts' are relevant; the facts noticed are evaluated against the norms, a process which both leads to our taking regulatory action and modifies the norms

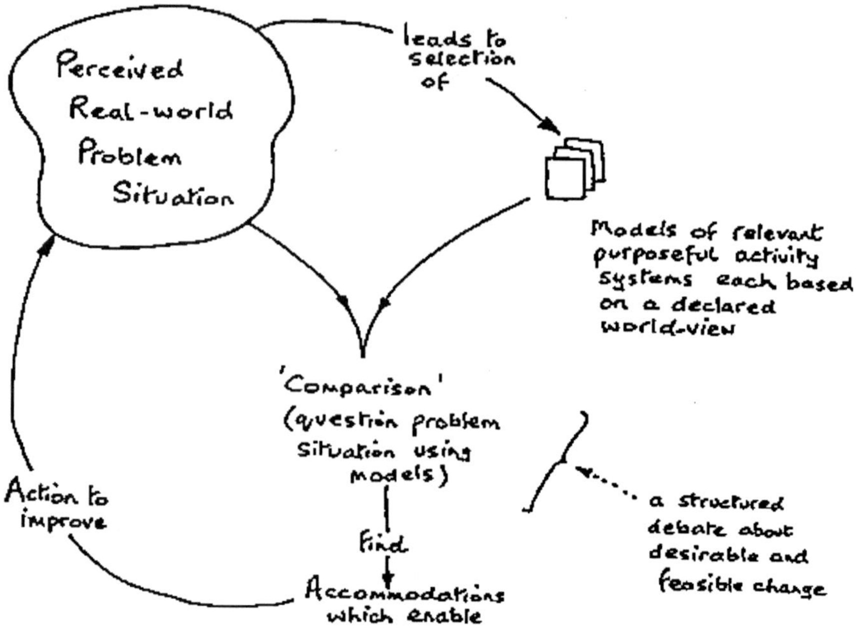

Figure 1 *The inquiring/learning cycle of SSM (Checkland, 1999: A9)*

or standards, so that future experiences will be evaluated differently" (Vickers, 1970 cited in Checkland, 1985: 762).

Value and reality judgements are at the core of the 'comparison' activity in Figure 1 which depicts the process of making models and comparing them with the perceptions about the real world problem situation. Since the point of this comparison process is to arrive at a set of accommodations, i.e. some set of actions that are sufficiently acceptable, or in SSM terms, culturally and politically feasible and systemically desirable, we argue that some transformations (changes in worldview or moral framework) are necessary on the part of at least some of the individuals involved in the application of an SSM learning system of inquiry.

In his earlier work focused on information systems, Checkland raised the possibility that SSM activities could take place within a moral vacuum (Checkland, 1988: 240). While the learning which takes place within an individual during Checkland's SSM process includes understanding various social and political perspectives, it does not include a way of developing criteria (an over-arching moral framework) for *weighing up* these perspectives and resolving a course of action.

SSM is silent on the issue of the nature and direction of the 'accommodations'. An accommodation that is culturally feasible and systemically desirable in an ego-centric worldview may be neither in a socio-centric or world-centric view (these Wilberian terms are explored later in the paper). An overarching moral framework, as Rittel and Webber (1973) suggest, would appear necessary to guide the way these accommodations occur and, for example, who is involved. This is in part the basis of Flood and Jackson's critique of SSM, and their adaptation of Habermasian 'emancipation' to give an over-arching and explicit moral and political purpose to the application of systems methodologies in the form of Critical Systems Thinking (Midgley, 1996).

The calls for transdisciplinary approaches to sustainability problems provide little guidance on the practicality of what do. SSM may be one way of filling that gap, in that it provides a tool for improving a perceived problematic situation. However for SSM activities to be undertaken within a moral framework which calls for sustainability, they would need to be structured with the intention of developing in participants a more world-centric view, i.e. one which seeks solutions which are socially just, ecologically restorative, and economically profitable (see Abeysuriya, *et al.*, 2007 for further discussion). In the following sections, we explore transformative learning and integral theory's evolution of consciousness as a means of doing that.

Transformative Learning

The descriptions Taylor provides below of transformative learning make clear how the adoption of this kind of learning by SSM would promote the distinctively creative discipline-transcending problem solving approach sought by transdisciplinarity, and also diminish the prospect of the moral vacuum in which Rittel and Webber potentially located our ways of approaching wicked problems.

Jack Mezirow describes perspective transformation, in which a person's 'meaning perspectives' are transformed, usually as a result of confronting a 'disorienting dilemma' (Taylor, 1998: 7). This results in a shift to a more inclusive and discriminating world view (Taylor, 1998: 11). A perspective transformation is "more (a) inclusive, (b) differentiating, (c) permeable [open to other points of view], (d) critically reflective, and (e) integrative of experience" (Jack Mezirow quoted in Taylor, 1998: 7).

Robert Boyd sees transformative learning as a process of individuation: "a fundamental change in one's personality involving conjointly the resolution of a personal dilemma and the expansion of consciousness resulting in greater personal integration". He proposes that "the purpose of such a transformation is to free the individual from his or her unconscious content and reified cultural norms and patterns that constrain the potential for self-actualization" (Robert Boyd quoted in Taylor, 1998: 13). Whereas Mezirow's perspective transformation is a cognitive one where the ego is 'the central psychic player', Boyd's concerns the role of the whole person in society. In contrast to Mezirow's focus on autonomy, Boyd claims that through transformative learning "the individual develops a greater interdependent relationship with and compassion for society" (Taylor, 1998: 14). In Wilber's terms, "the individual's cognitive and perceptual capacities apparently become so pluralistic and universal that they begin to reach beyond any narrowly personal or individual perspectives or concerns" (Ken Wilber quoted in Taylor, 1998: 14). Wilber (1995, 2000) extends this sense of interdependence and compassion to include both nature and society (see below).

Paulo Freire is more concerned with social change "via the unveiling or demythologizing of reality by the oppressed through the awakening of their critical consciousness" and thus the "fostering [of] an emancipatory transformative process" (Taylor, 1998: 16). Freire puts the concept of praxis at the centre of his approach, so that "action happens in concert with reflection; it is a process of continually looking over our shoulders at how our actions are affecting the world" (Taylor, 1998: 18).

In these types of transformative learning, the individual achieves not just a *changed* perspective but a *broader, deeper* perspective, a critical questioning of assumptions and a deeper compassion and commitment to the social good.

In the following section we consider Wilber's theory of the evolution of consciousness as another process of transformational learning.

The evolution of consciousness

Like many theories of transdisciplinarity (Max-Neef, 2005, Nicolescu, 1998, Ramadier, 2004), Ken Wilber's integral theory on the evolution of consciousness is also based on the view that there are wider and deeper perspectives from which new and creative ideas and understandings emerge. This process of evolution, or learning about the cosmos, also expands our moral focus to include and care about more and more of the world.

Wilber adapts the work of Piaget on the evolution of a child from a state of 'egocentrism' or 'narcissism' where the child "is unable to differentiate himself from the rest of the world, through to decentering of the self by increased interior awareness" (Wilber, 1995, 2000: 264-265); the individual becomes more autonomous and 'socio-centric', and, eventually, if the process of interior evolution continues, 'world-centric'.

Wilber proposes that, in ascending to a higher and wider identity, we also "expand the circle of our own compassion for more and more beings" (Wilber, 1995, 2000: 349). Our evolution as rational beings in the Age of Reason enabled us to question and to dream of other possibilities (Wilber, 1995, 2000: 179), and developed in us a concern for all citizens to be *legally, morally* and *politically* free subjects (Wilber, 1995, 2000: 251). However he maintains that self-transcendence eventually goes beyond the rational to the transrational (Wilber, 1995, 2000: 330). Inclusiveness, freedom from cultural constraints, compassion, and critical consciousness are all qualities of Wilber's transrational being. "[Beyond the problem-solving] stage are the *truly creative* scientists and thinkers who define important problems and ask important questions" (Wilber, 1995, 2000: 266) (authors' highlights).

"*In* transformation [self-transcendence]...a whole new world *of available stimuli becomes accessible ... these 'new worlds' are not physically located someplace else; they exist simply as a* deeper perception...*of the available stimuli in* this world" (Wilber, 1995, 2000: 67).

This higher level of consciousness is available to "any individual, at any time, who chooses to continue his or her own evolution within and beyond" (Wilber, 1995, 2000: 323). Change occurs when individuals achieve this higher level of consciousness and their new worldviews "feed back into the ongoing mainstream of social institutions". "The revolution as always will come from the within and be embedded in the without" (Wilber, 1995, 2000: 202).

Wilber's conclusion for the future of the world and for resolving wicked problems such as those of sustainability is that:
".... the real problem is *not* exterior. The real problem is *interior*. The real problem is how to get people to *internally transform* from egocentric to socio-centric to world-centric consciousness, which is the *only* stance that *can* grasp the global dimensions of the problem in the first place" (Wilber, 1995, 2000: 541).

Wilber's 'whole new worlds' and deeper *perception* connect closely to the writing of other transdisciplinary theorists and suggest a creative potential in individuals to make hitherto unperceived connections (Conklin, *et al.*, 2007: 9,10), resolve apparent paradoxes through perceiving different levels of reality (Nicolescu, 1998: 2) and 'rise above' existing kinds of knowledge to set problems in a wider context (Ramadier, 2004: 434). The individual with a world-centric consciousness also increases his/her circle of compassion and it is this which provides the moral framework for all of his/her action.

This view of learning, like that described by Taylor, is one which provides a moral and creative framework for approaching the resolution of problems in a transdisciplinary way. If problem solving tools such as SSM were applied with a view to enabling participants to engage in this kind of learning, we propose that we would be able to address Rittel and Webber's moral vacuum, and the problem of transcending disciplines to achieve creative and transdisciplinary solutions. The following example aims to demonstrate what this kind of learning might look like.

The Institute for Sustainable Futures in December 2006 conducted a Deliberative Forum (Citizens' Jury) to explore community values relating to the urban water supply system in the Yarra Valley, Victoria, Australia. (Note that while this process was facilitated along the principles of inclusiveness, and open discussion among multiple perspectives, it does not represent a full application of the SSM developed by Checkland and others). In the case of the practitioners involved (researchers from the Institute), a wide perspective, inclusive worldview and commitment to social change were something they 'brought to the table' as part of their framework for working. They aimed to engage participants in a learning process through presentations by experts and discussion of alternative ideas on how we can best supply water whilst maintaining social and environmental values.

The report on the Forum contains the following comments:

"The majority of participants indicated that their views about water supply and the rivers has changed....Some indicated that they were now going to be much more personally responsible for their actions and choices and wanted to share their learning" (Institute for Sustainable Futures, 2007: 9)

Quotes from participants include:

- "Enabling people to think through these things is empowering";
- "The three days [have taken] me out of my comfort zone...involving me in issues that I have not given as much thought as I should have been";
- "I will leave the forum a different person... I will be seriously considering new technologies" (Institute for Sustainable Futures, 2007: 11-12).

Through the experience of this forum, change in individuals appears to have occurred at both the perspective (cognitive and caring) level (Mezirow and Wilber) and at the level of agency and social responsibility (Boyd, Freire).

Conclusions

This paper seeks to link the moral imperative associated with sustainability to the need for a transdisciplinary approach, which to make a difference, requires traction in practice, and transformation of at least some actors. We proffer Soft Systems Methodology as a process that sits well with complex or 'wicked' problems like sustainability, and could provide the necessary traction.

For individuals working within a transdisciplinary framework, two issues emerge:

- Engaging a creativity which transcends discipline boundaries;
- Developing a moral framework within which conflicting realities (including values, norms and worldviews) can be considered and assessed.

Although SSM can likely assist with the former, it is largely silent on the latter, so further guidance is necessary. We propose transformative learning as a possible source of that guidance. In particular, both issues are important elements in the kind of transformative learning discussed by Taylor and the kind of consciousness evolution discussed by Wilber. Both writers describe ways in which individuals can 'learn' a wider, 'world-centric' perspective, with an associated expanded circle of compassion and sense of social justice, and a creative ability to see further and make more connections between the various levels of reality in the world.

The distinguishing feature of a truly transdisciplinary approach to complex problems in the future may well involve a transformative learning process that embodies the systemic principles of SSM and seeks explicit answers to the following questions:

- Who learns?
- Who decides who learns?
- What is the nature of the learning?
- What happens as a result of the learning?
- What ought the balance be between problem resolution and learning?
- What would it take for the learning process to provide a sufficiently creative, morally justifiable resolution?

We suggest that further research and practice on the role of transformative learning in SSM problem-solving processes would be an important contribution to the resolution of wicked problems in sustainability.

References

Abeysuriya, K., Mitchell, C. and White, S. (2007). 'Can Corporate Social Responsibility resolve the sanitation question in developing Asian countries?' *Ecological Economics*, ISSN 0921-8009, 62 (1): 174-183.

Checkland, P. (1985). 'From optimising to learning: A development of system thinking for the 1990's', *Journal of Operational Research Society*, ISSN 0160-5682, 36 (9): 757-767.

Checkland, P. (1988). 'Information Systems and Systems Thinking: Time to Unite?' *International Journal of Information Management*, ISSN 0268-4012, 8: 240.

Checkland, P. (1999). *Systems Thinking, Systems Practice*, ISBN 0471986062.

Conklin, J., Basadur, M. and VanPatter, G. (2007). *"Rethinking Wicked Problems" - Conversation between Jeff Conklin, Min Basadur and GK Van Patter*, NextD Journal, NextDesign Leadership Institute, viewed 28 August 2007 <www.nextd.org/02/10/1/index.html>.

Després, C., Brais, N. and Avellan, S. (2004). 'Collaborative planning for retrofitting suburbs: transdisciplinarity and intersubjectivity in action', *Futures*, ISSN 0016-3287, 36: 471-486.

Institute for Sustainable Futures. (2007). *Yarra River Values Forum Participants' Report*, A Citizens Forum held in Ivanhoe, Melbourne 1-3 December 2006, University of Technology Sydney.

Max-Neef, M. A. (2005). 'Foundations of transdisciplinarity', *Ecological Economics*, ISSN 0921-8009, 53: 5-16.

Meppem, T. and Gill, R. (1998). 'Planning for Sustainability as a learning concept', *Ecological Economics*, ISSN 0921-8009, 26: 121-137.

Midgley, G. (1996). 'What is this thing called CST?' in R. L. Flood and N. R. A. Romm (eds), *Critical Systems Thinking: Current Research and Practice*, ISBN 0306454513, pp. 11-24.

Nicolescu, B. (1998). 'The Transdisciplinary Evolution of the University – Condition for Sustainable Development', *Rencontres Transdisciplinaires: Bulletin Interactif du Centre International de Recherches et Etudes* ISSN 1777-8549, vol. No 12, viewed 26 August 2007, < http://nicol.club.fr/ciret/bulletin/b12/b12c8.htm>.

Ramadier, T. (2004). 'Transdisciplinarity and its challenges: the case of urban studies', *Futures*, ISSN 0016-3287, 36 (4): 423-439.

Rittel, H. W. J. and Webber, M. M. (1973). 'Dilemma in a General Theory of Planning', *Policy Sciences*, ISSN 0032-2687, 2: 155-169.

Taylor, E. W. (1998). *The Theory and Practice of Transformative Learning: A Critical Review*, in ERIC Clearinghouse on Adult Career and Vocational Education (ed.), Information Series No 374, vol. 2006, no 27 September, Center on Education and Training for Employment, Columbus, Ohio, viewed 27 September, 2006 <http://www.cete.org/acve/mp_taylor_01.asp>.

Thompson Klein, J. (2004). 'Prospects for transdisciplinarity', *Futures*, ISSN 0016-3287, 36: 515-526.

Vickers, G. (1970). *Freedom in a Rocking Boat*, ISBN 0465025447.

Wickson, F., Carew, A. and Russell, A. (2006). 'Transdisciplinary research: characteristics, quandaries and qualities', *Futures*, ISSN 0016-3287, 38: 1046-1059.

Wilber, K. (1995, 2000). *Sex, Ecology and Spirituality: The Spirit of Evolution*, ISBN 1-57061-744-4.

8. The Modern Generalist Universal Conceptual Model

Vincent Vesterby

The modern generalist conceptual model, and the techniques used to create it, are to qualitative analysis what math is to quantitative analysis. Factors intrinsic to the nature of reality are used as tools to explore, analyze, understand, and describe reality. These factor tools occur in two basic forms, the first being general patterns of organization that occur in space and in structure—patterns that establish the nature of the situations in which they occur. Second are the factors of connections in time—factors of origins, transformations, consequences, and interactions. One of these factors, development, is universal in that it is the pattern of organization within which all other patterns occur. Understanding development provides a universal conceptual model in which all factors of the nature of reality can be placed in correct relation to one another. This conceptual model powerfully enhances the accuracy of judgment by making explicit intrinsic deep structure.

Introduction

In 1998 Edward O. Wilson said, "A united system of knowledge is the surest means of identifying the still unexplored domains of reality. It provides a clear map of what is known, and it frames the most productive questions for future inquiry" (1999: 326).

In 1988 the evolutionary biologist Ernst Mayr said, "Twenty-nine years ago the physicist C. P. Snow vividly described the unbridgeable gap between the physical sciences and the humanities. If biologists, physicists, and philosophers working together can construct a broad-based, unified science that incorporates both the living and the nonliving world, we will have a better base from which to build bridges to the humanities, and some hope of reducing this unfortunate rift in our culture" (1988: 21).

Other researchers have been hoping for the methods of deep structure analysis that are being used to create the universal conceptual model.

In 2002 the mathematician Ian Stewart said "[W]e can hope to see the beginnings of a qualitative, contextual theory of dynamic pattern formation" (2002: 39).

Rodney Brooks, Director of the MIT Artificial Intelligence Laboratory, is clear about his need for a more general, deeper mode of understanding.

"The question then is whether there [is] something else, besides computation, in all life processes? We need [a] conceptual framework such as computation that

doesn't involve any new physics or chemistry, a framework that gives us a different way of thinking about the stuff that's there" (Brooks, 2007b).

and,

"*Maybe there's something beyond computation in the sense that we don't understand and we can't describe what's going on inside living systems using computation only... There's some other tool—some organizational principle—that we need to understand in order to really describe what's going on*" (Brooks, 2007a).

What Brooks is missing, and what Stewart hopes to see are techniques and understanding that answer the why questions. Not just what, not just how, but why do patterns form, why does computation work the way it does, and why do life processes behave as they do, sustaining progressive change over billions of years? The modern generalist techniques and the resulting universal conceptual model provide answers to Why?

There is one further situation that gives urgency to the need for a universal conceptual model. The serious problems we face in the world today, such as overpopulation, environmental degradation, resource depletion, the HIV epidemic, and social, educational, medical, economic, and political inequality, have a spread of sources and consequences that range from our geological and climatic context through all the levels of biological organization, from the cellular level through the levels of organism, society, and ecosystems. To solve these problems requires a breadth and depth of conceptual understanding that incorporates this entire range.

The universal conceptual model presented here incorporates all the sciences and humanities, and integrates them into a single sweep of understanding. It does so by way of their natural interrelations, their natural interconnections, by way of the manner in which chemistry emerges from physics, biology emerges from chemistry, psychology from biology, society from biology and psychology, and culture from psychology and society. Emergence is a form of progressive change, a creative form of change. It is one form of development (Vesterby, 2007). There are many forms or types of development, and understanding the ways in which they all interrelate to create the world we have today results in the universal conceptual mode. The model is formed by way of the connectivity that occurs with all these interrelating types of development. This paper presents the foundational forms of that connectivity.

Connections

Everything is not connected to everything.
Everything is, however, connected to something.

Things exist in space, and they continue to exist with time. Things connect with one another in space, and they connect with one another through time. Everything is connected to something adjacent, either in the three-dimensional place that is space, or sequentially adjacent in the continuously ongoing change that is time. There are the connections things have by way of direct contact with other things. Then, as something that exists continues to exist, as it goes through the change that is continuing-existence, it has both, a connection to its history and a connection to its future, what it is developing from and what it is developing into.

The modern generalist mode of analysis and understanding uses the factors that constitute the intrinsic nature of connectivity to combine all aspects of the nature of reality into a single universal conceptual model. There are seventeen nearly universal fundamental factors that establish connection of one part of reality with another, and thereby provide the breadth and depth of the model. Those seventeen factors are: (1) continuity, (2) adjacent relation, (3) coexistent-sequential-difference, (4) sequential enhancement, (5) extensional development, (6) combinatorial enhancement, (7) consequent-existence, (8) continuing-existence, (9) noncoexistent-sequential-difference (change), (10) change development, (11) self-organization, (12) motion, (13) emergence, (14) contact relation, (15) cause, (16) coherent relation, (17) through-flow situation wherein the flow of energy alters the organization of matter and the organization of matter alters the flow of energy. These factors are themselves the functional tool kit of the mental model that when applied, reveal the foundational attributes and the connectivity of the system being studied.

Development is universal in that it played a role in every situation that ever existed, plays a role in every situation that now exists, and will play a role in every situation that will ever exist. The term *development* is used in the modern generalist mode to refer to sequential difference where there is a progressive increase in complexity. It can be as simple as the increasing amount of time that has occurred, it can be the increased complexity that results from the creation of a new level of hierarchy, or it can be as great as the complexity of a newly evolved species of animal. All of the fundamental factors of connection are either cases of development or are factors that play roles in development.

Development is also intrinsically oriented by way of the directionality of the adjacent relation, and by the unidirectional nature of continuing existence, motion, emergence, and cause. Development thus provides a universal framework in relation to which all other factors of the existence, organization, change, and consequences of reality can be placed in correct relation one to another in the universal conceptual model. *The organization and content of the model follows the organization and content of reality.*

This model is universal in that it includes (a) everything we know from below the subatomic level to the entire universe, (b) all known that has passed in time, and (c) all of the future that can be accurately predicted. It cannot all be experienced simultaneously, nor even be contained within one mind. It is not meant to be a model of that sort, but rather a model within which the mind can travel from one part to another by way of the factors of connection, by way of following the development. Because the factors of development are universal, they provide orientation, guidance, and facilitate learning as one leaves familiar territory and ventures into the unknown.

Material reality is composed of elementary particles, which are in large part organized into populations of interactive units, or into objects and systems. The main difference between these populations, objects, and systems, and between the various hierarchic levels that occur with them, is the pattern of organization of elementary particles that gives each of them its intrinsic identity. Each of these patterns of organization comes into existence by way of development. Each individual occurrence of a pattern is created by processes of development. A pattern comes into existence, undergoes changes, and has consequences that are due to its intrinsic nature. This occurs by way of the seventeen fundamental factors of connection in interrelation with diverse other factors that play roles in the intrinsic nature of the various patterns of organization. To understand why a particular pattern of organization exists, and why it has the particular qualities it has, it is necessary to follow the developments of its origin and transformation. To do this it is necessary to understand the intrinsic nature of the seventeen factors and their interrelations with one another. An analysis which omits any of these factors will result in an incomplete understanding.

There are two fundamental pathways of development. One is an aspect of the extension of spatial place, and is due to the difference from one part of space to another part. The other occurs as an aspect of the sequential nature of continuing-existence, and is due to the difference from one part of ongoing existence to another part. With the form of development that occurs with spatial extension, there is a role for difference, but not for change. This is *extensional development.* With the form of development that occurs with continuing-existence, there are roles for both difference and change—*change development.* These two foundational forms of development become interrelated when motion plays a role in a situation.

Factors of the foundational development of the connectivity of reality

In order to make use of development as a factor tool, it is necessary to explore and understand the core attributes of development itself. The foundational development of reality has six major stages, each of which has multiple lesser stages. Those major stages are based on (1) space, (2) continuing-existence, (3) matter, (4) motion, (5) contact, and (6) coherence. Several of the fundamental factors, such as emergence and cause, that establish connections from one part of reality with another originate with the lesser stages. At each of the six major stages of the foundational development of reality, some factors play contextual or constitutive roles in the occurrence of the factors that play connective roles.

The existence of space

There are eighteen aspects of the existence of space (*in italics*) that play roles in connectivity. Spatial place is *immaterial, continuous, three-dimensional, extension.* To exist as continuous extension is to have *parts,* (a) which are *locationally different* and thereby have intrinsic *self-identity,* (b) which are *coexistent* and *adjacent* and thereby occur *sequentially* to one another, and (c) which together constitute spatial *coexistent-sequential-difference.* Along a sequence of coexistent-sequential-difference there is a progressive increase in the amount of difference, which constitutes *sequential enhancement*, and the foundational form of *extensional development*.

The coexistent-sequential-difference of spatial extension is continuous. There is, then, an aspect of continuity to the associated sequential enhancement and extensional development. There are no breaks or interruptions. The existence of one part is connected to the existence of the locationally different sequentially adjacent parts. This constitutes *extensional existential-pathway-development*, an intrinsic quality of reality that provides a continuous pathway of exploration, and a foundational feature of continuous connection for the model.

If there is coexistence, there is relation, minimally that of *distance* and *direction*. The occurrence of relation as an aspect of a coexistence situation is an enhancement of the situation due to the combination of whatever is coexistent—*combinatorial enhancement*. While combinatorial enhancement occurs with the adjacent relation, it also takes connection beyond adjacent relation by way of mediated connection, wherein two things are connected through the role of something else (a) that is adjacent to both (a gate latch connecting a gate to the gate post), or (b) that is in some manner a relation between them (e.g. the space or distance from one to the other). Parts, distance, and direction constitute *pattern of organization*, a major factor of orientation of connective relations.

Three examples of continuously connected development that are due to the intrinsic nature of space itself are (1) the greater the extension, the greater the sequential difference, (2) with two lines extending from a single point, the greater their extension, the further apart they are, and (3) the surface of an expanding sphere increases faster than the increase in its radius.

The continuing existence of space

There are eleven additional factors of connectivity (*in italics*) that are aspects of the *continuing-existence* of space. Space exists, and it continues to exist. Space continues to exist because it exists. Continuing-existence is a consequence of existence. This is connection by way of *consequent-existence*, the existence of something as a consequence of the existence of something else. Consequent-existence is a universal core factor of change development.

Continuing-existence is continuous, has parts, which are adjacent with sequential relations, and thus occurs as a form of sequential-difference. Each part of continuing-existence, as it occurs, is *newly existent*, with *specific sequential location*, occurring after the part that has gone before and before the part that will follow. This is *sequential enhancement by way of creating new part*.

Of continuing-existence only the current part exists, the past parts having ceased to exist and the future parts having not yet come into existence. The parts of continuing-existence are *not coexistent*, and are thereby different from one another, existentially distinct, with unique *individual self-identity*. The sequential-difference of continuing-existence occurs as *noncoexistent-sequential-difference*. Noncoexistent-sequential-difference is change. *Change development* is the progressive sequential-difference that occurs with noncoexistent-sequential-difference.

The continuing-existence of space is a consequence of the existence of space. The change, the noncoexistent-sequential-difference that is continuing-existence is a consequence of the existence of space. The existence of space initiates continuing-existence. It initiates noncoexistent-sequential-difference. It initiates change. *Initiation* is the consequent-existence of change.

Spatial continuing-existence is the ongoing existence of space, of space itself, of what space is. It is the ongoing existence of the self-identity of space. Because it is simply a continuance of the being of space, each part of the change of ongoing existence develops directly from the prior part. Even though continuing-existence is a form of noncoexistent-sequential-difference, the parts are developmentally existentially connected because one part develops directly from the prior part. Continuing-existence is a form of *change existential-pathway-development*, and by way of continuance of self-identity from what has gone before to what follows it constitutes a pathway of connection.

The existence of matter

There are six additional factors of connectivity (*in italics*) that occur with the existence of matter. Matter is discontinuous, occurring as units of various sizes and compositions. Matter exists in space, which provides a *place-to-be existential context* for matter. A unit of matter has an *occupation relation* with the specific spatial place in which it exists, and distance, direction, and *positional orientation* relations with all other spatial place.

The infinite, extensionally three-dimensional, immaterial place of space is all the spatial place there is. To not exist in space is to not exist. There is a *place-to-be existential-dependency relation* between matter and the space it occupies. The occupation relation, place-to-be existential context, and place-to-be existential-dependency are all oriented relations of connection of extensional development.

Matter exists, and it continues to exist. Because to exist is to exist in space, to continue to exist is to do so with the continuing-existence of space. The continuing-existence of space provides a *continuance-of-being existential context* for the continuing-existence of matter. To not continue to exist with the continuing-existence of space is to not exist. The continuing-existence of matter has a *continuance-of-being existential-dependency relation* with the continuing-existence of space. Continuance-of-being existential context and continuance-of-being existential-dependency are oriented relations of connection of change development. Context, occupation, and dependency relations of matter with space provide orientation of understanding within the universal conceptual model.

The existence of motion

There are twelve additional factors of connectivity that occur with the existence of motion. *Motion* is matter passing through space. Motion has the same context and dependency relations with space as does matter, and because it is matter that moves, motion has an existential-dependency relation with matter. The parts of a motion, such as the first, middle, and final parts, occur sequentially and noncoexistently. The parts of a motion are different, existentially distinct, because they are noncoexistent—*motion noncoexistent-sequential-difference.* When it is occurring, motion is continuous and unidirectional. Motion is a form of change, with *change existential context* and *change existential-dependency* relations with spatial continuing-existence. As a motion continues to exist, the continuance of its self-identity initiates new part of change, new part of noncoexistent-sequential-difference, new part of motion. Motion initiates change by continuing to be itself. This is sequential enhancement by way of creating new part.

Because one part of motion is a direct development from the prior part by way of continuance of self-identity, the parts of motion are existentially adjacent to one another. This is *motion existential-pathway-development.* It provides the conceptual model a form of connection that involves changing relations.

There are two forms of change initiated by motion. First is the ongoing change that is the motion itself. And second, because motion is matter passing through space, motion, in a continuous and sequential manner, *changes the extensional relations of matter with space,* the occupation, distance, direction, and positional orientation relations. When there is a *group* of other units present, the motion *changes the extensional relations between the units.* The group of units and the relations between them constitute a *pattern of organization,* and when motion changes the extensional relations between the units, that pattern is changed and a new pattern emerges. Because motion is sequential in nature, and because the changes in extensional relations between the units occur sequentially, this foundational form of emergence is based on sequential enhancement. When a moving unit joins a group of units, and alters the composition of the group by the addition of a unit—*sequential enhancement by way of adding units*—the pattern of organization of the group is changed by way of the combination of the additional unit with the others of the group. A new pattern of organization comes into existence, a new pattern emerges, and this second foundational form of emergence is based on combinatorial enhancement. *Emergence by way of sequential enhancement* and *emergence by way of combinatorial enhancement* are both pathways of change and creation of material pattern of organization that serve in the conceptual model as pathways of connection.

The occurrence of the contact relation

There are four additional factors of connectivity that occur with the contact relation. Matter is *substantial.* Something is-there. Units of matter in adjacent relation, that is, where there is no space between them, are up against one another—they are in *contact.*

Contact is an emergent factor. Movement of a unit in relation to other units results in emergence of new pattern of organization by way of sequential enhancement. It is developmental connection by way of emergence through sequential enhancement. The coming together of units such that in combination they form a group, a new pattern of organization and a new level of hierarchic organization, is emergence by way of combinatorial enhancement. It is developmental connection by way of emergence through combinatorial enhancement.

When motion brings together units of a group into adjacent relation, the contact relation comes into existence. Group and adjacent relation are organizational factors. Contact, while it is existentially-dependent on group and adjacent relation, is something more than organizational in nature. This is developmental connection by way of emergence through combinatorial enhancement that includes the role of substantiality in adjacent relation, resulting in the emergence of contact, a supraorganizational factor.

Contact is an extensional pathway of connection based on the supraorganizational nature of substantiality. It is also a required precursor factor for further developments of connectivity based on the direct interrelations of matter with matter.

In a collision situation, when a moving unit makes contact with a blocking unit, the moving unit pushes against the blocking unit. The moving unit loses some of its motion, and the blocking unit begins to move. A transfer occurs between the units by way of the push. The push causes the blocking unit to move. *Cause* is push, goes with the flow of dissipating energy, and is unidirectional. Cause is a form of developmental connection, is oriented, is a form of existential-pathway-development, and thus provides the conceptual model with another form of change connection—causal connection.

The collision situation is the development-of-origin of the *open/through-flow situation*. Here a flow of energy alters the organization of a situation and the organization of the situation alters the flow of energy. Matter in motion constitutes a flow of energy, and another unit in the path of the motion constitutes a primitive form of organization in that it has extensional relations with spatial place. In a collision, the position of the blocking unit is changed by way of the transfer, the through-flow, of energy from the moving unit to the blocking unit, and the motion of the other unit is slowed and usually deflected.

Open/through-flow situations are in large part characterized by the flow. To follow this pathway of connection—follow the flow. All the organizational factors will be found along the way. This applies from the existing fields and the elementary particles of physics, through all of geology, through biology from cells to social systems and ecosystems, to stars and their planetary systems, to galaxies, and to the universe as a whole. The flow of energy in relation to the organization of matter provides a dynamic map of the universe.

The coherent relation

There is a multitude of additional factors of connectivity that occur with the coherent relation. Matter bonds with matter, which forms coherent structure. There are a variety of ways in which matter bonds with matter from the forces involved with the joining of elementary particles, atoms, and molecules, to structural/mechanical connections, such as the dovetail joints at the corners of wooden boxes, botanical holdfasts such as tendrils, and moveable connections such as the knee joint and clockworks. All of these diverse types of connection are pathways of relation that provide understanding of the connectivity of reality. A particularly significant consequence of coherence is the tremendous development that occurs with through-flow. Coherence results in a virtually limitless variety of forms that redirect the flow of energy in diverse ways—with diverse reorganizations of the patterns of material organization. This consequence of coherence is critical to the development of the types of complexity that occur with geology and all the stages and levels of biological development from the molecular biology of the cell to ecosystems.

Conclusion

This paper introduces the foundations of a universal conceptual model that provides a way for the mind to achieve an understanding of the big picture. It provides a tool that can enable a specialist to explore beyond the boundaries of a particular discipline, and a way to participate effectively in transdisciplinary projects.

References

Brooks, Rodney. (2007a). "Beyond computation: A talk with Rodney Brooks," http://www.edge.org/3rd_culture/brooks_beyond/beyond_p2.html

Brooks, Rodney. (2007b). "The deep question: A talk with Rodney Brooks," http://www.edge.org/3rd_culture/brooks/brooks_p2.html

Mayr, Ernst. (1988). *Toward a New Philosophy of Biology: Observations of an Evolutionist*, ISBN 0-674-89666-1.

Stewart, Ian. (2002). "The Mathematics of 2050," in John Brockman (ed.), *The Next Fifty Years*, ISBN 0-375-71342-5.

Vesterby, Vincent. (2007). "The Modern Generalist, Glossary," http://www.themoderngeneralist.com/glossary.htm

Wilson, Edward O. (1999). *Consilience: The Unity of Knowledge*, ISBN 0-679-76867-x.

Theme 3: Conceptual Modelling

9. Research Methods for Systems Engineering

Timothy L.J. Ferris, Stephen C. Cook, and Elena Sitnikova
Defence and Systems Institute, University of South Australia, USA

Courses on research methods are now commonplace in the postgraduate education. Such courses describe many different methods that can be applied to research problems pertinent to a field of endeavour. When reviewing research methods courses that could be incorporated into systems engineering programs, it became clear that contemporary approaches have a discipline-centric view of research methodology. We argue that systems engineering is a meta-methodology that harnesses many systems-related and engineering disciplines and, in common with other authors, we recognise the need for both quantitative and qualitative research approaches to advance systems engineering knowledge and practice. Furthermore, we recognise that in common with engineering, architecture, and art there is another fundamental approach that applies to systems engineering research: design as a research method. We conclude that a multi-methodological research methods course is necessary, based on the findings described in this paper, to adequately prepare students for research in systems engineering.

Introduction

A review of programs and courses that many universities offer in their curriculum clearly shows that research methodology courses are now commonplace in many disciplines, usually offered in masters and doctoral level programs. Closer inspection of the course outlines indicates that the majority are offered in discipline specific contexts, and that the courses reveal several categories of objectives. It appears that the research methods course taught in any program will have different content and objectives than the courses in all other programs of the same university. The diversity of aims includes courses seeking to introduce students to exactly the current research methodology of the discipline, contrasting, at the other extreme, with those seeking to introduce students to a broad range of methodologies which might reasonably be applied to in the field. There are courses which present research methodology as primarily a study of statistics, and others emphasizing the insight generation objective of research. In the course structure different objectives are also evident. Some courses seek to develop students' ability with respect to the elemental skills of research, taught and assessed separately, whereas others seek to guide students through a small task conducted as a research project to give experience of the end-to-end process of doing research. Some other courses seek to develop the ability of the student to plan a piece of research by writing a research proposal.

Each approach to teaching research methods has advantages and disadvantages and presents distinctive challenges within the course and in the gap between skills gained in the course and a real research project. A tightly controlled single method approach may lead to the take-away message that research must conform to the discipline 'approved' method and thus that research is a formulaic process to generate 'acceptable' results in the academic community. In contrast, multi-methodological approaches result in students willing to use diverse methods, and to choose a research method to suit the question addressed, rather than to adjust the formal research question to fit the methodology. The broad-based approach provides the sense that research is an activity focused on gaining insight into the matter at hand, even at the expense of methodological purity. Students studying research methods must also learn a new way of thinking about learning. The student must learn that research is about finding something new to all people, not just new to the student. This is a fundamental intellectual challenge for students requiring considerable instructor effort.

A multi-methodology course is unsuitable for students researching in fields which demand that 'proper' research be conducted according to a fixed format. In such fields, only the well-respected senior researchers are permitted the license to methods which challenge the methodological orthodoxy, and even the permission is more as a toleration of the respected person than a desirable approach. Conversely, a field permitting methodological diversity would be poorly served by a research methods course which develops a single method, even if other methods are permitted. Therefore the diversity of research methods courses is justified.

The choice of kind of research methodology course follows from the purpose of the research work for which the student is to be trained. Research methods courses for research degree students are normally narrower in scope. In contrast, a course provided for staff of an organization providing applied research services across a broad range of fields has been specifically, at the request of the sponsoring organization, developed to present a range of methods, and to emphasize the insight generation role of research[1].

The model of a discipline promoted by Kline (1995) and described in Cook and Ferris (2007) demands the following elements for an activity to be considered a discipline; a framework of ideas, and area of concern, a methodology for applying the framework of ideas to the area of concern, a methodology for improving the framework of ideas, a community of practitioners and a community of paid scholars. The relationship between these elements is given in Figure 1 extracted from Cook and Ferris (2007).

The paper is organized as follows. Firstly, the paper presents concepts of systems engineering as a discipline including a description of areas of concern, a framework of ideas and methodologies applicable for systems engineering. Secondly, key research approaches – qualitative and quantitative relating to systems engineering multidisciplinary research are identified, analyzed and discussed;

1. This course is EEET 5108 Research Methods in a Multidisciplinary Environment, in the Defence Science and Technology Organization sponsored Continuing Education Initiative, which provides Masters programs offered by various universities in a wide range of fields of interest to the Australian Department of Defence.

and a new approach: design as a research method is introduced. Thirdly, the paper describes some implications for research methods courses within University of South Australia.

Nature of Systems Engineering

We describe systems engineering using Kline's definition of a discipline and explore the implications this has for research method selection for both practice and discipline development.

After World War II systems engineering emerged in response to the increasing cost and technical complexity of development programs in the 1950s and 1960s (Hall, 1962; M'Pherson, 1980; DSMC, 1983) and the difficulties in achieving the objectives of ambitious projects (Ferris, 2007a; Ferris, 2007b). As such, it grew out of other engineering fields and was practiced by engineers educated in particular fields of engineering. Thus, the pragmatic drive of engineers motivated the development of systems engineering, as a field engineering systems in multiple technologies and involving human components. The general concern of engineers is the achievement of goals, not methodological purity. This is well expressed: "Engineering is not a science, but a practice of the necessary to achieve a given goal" (Cripps, 1991).

Systems engineering has always recognized (Ferris, 2007a), that systems must be viewed holistically and understood at a whole-of-system level as well as at the detail level required for design.

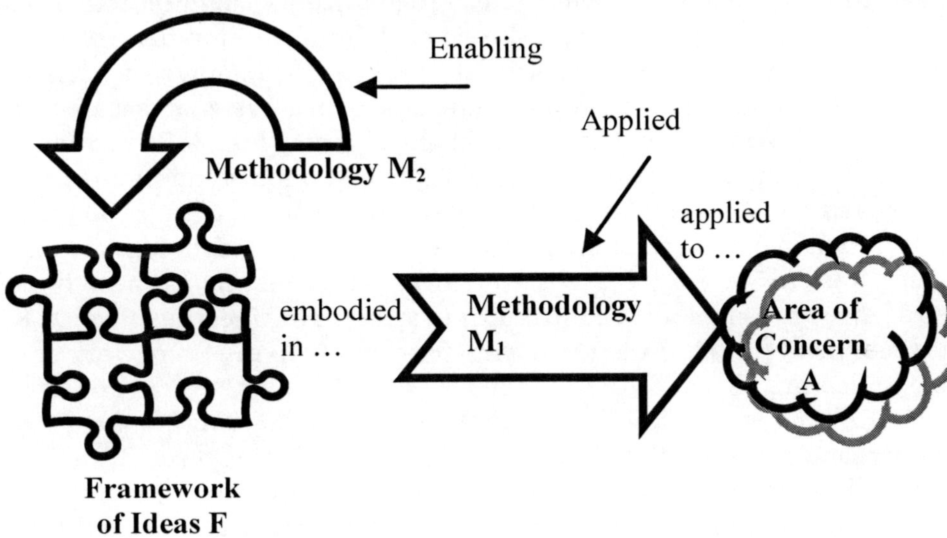

Figure 1 *The relationship of the first three of Kline's (1995) aspects of a discipline*

Areas of Concern for Systems Engineering

Sage (2006) asserts that the current concerns of systems engineering include the technical systems developed, the 'end product systems'; their interaction with human and environmental stakeholders; the support systems, the 'enabling systems'; the development organizations, and the 'process systems'.

A definition in the INCOSE *Technical Vision* (2005) is also helpful in defining what systems engineering is:

"Systems engineering is a professional endeavour that leads to the engineering of a system of humans, organizations and technologies through knowledge management efforts associated with bringing the perspectives of all stakeholders to the associated issues to bear, such as to enable the appropriate: definition of the system to be engineered such as to achieve needed capabilities and fulfil requirements; development of the system through appropriate architecture, design, and integration efforts; and ultimate deployment of the system in an operational environment and associated maintenance and reengineering of it throughout a useful lifetime of trustworthy service to these stakeholders."

The breadth of systems engineering as currently understood, and the growth of interest in the context of systems engineering work, is shown by the ISO/IEC 15288 (2002) view of systems engineering, Table 1, and *Systems Engineering Handbook* version 3 (INCOSE, 2006).

Towards a Framework of Ideas for Systems Engineering

About sixty years ago it became clear that a multidisciplinary approach to ambitious engineering projects was necessary. Initially this was manifest in methods to address the overall project and product system as opposed to individual equipment items. Progressively system objectives have become more ambitious, and have broadened from development of technical solutions to means to address broader problems through well-understood, socio-technical solutions. The result has been technical systems that are deeply embedded in the operational processes of the organizations in which they are deployed, resulting in a need for a broader range of understanding than previously. Systems engineers have always drawn from systems theory and practice for inspiration in dealing with the problems presented by technological systems although it is only recently that systems theory and thinking has been broadly acknowledged as a significant contributor to systems engineering practice. Systems theory and thinking are important contributors to the framework of systems engineering.

Cook and Ferris (2007) argue that systems engineering is a meta-methodology that can tackle both pluralist and unitary problems through an examination of three key components of the conceptual framework: the philosophy of engineering, the philosophy of systems engineering, and systems thinking. As such we assert that the research methods for systems engineering practice will need to cover those from engineering and systems practice, yielding Table 2, as a variation of the categorizations provided by Jackson (2000) and Neuman (2000).

Methodologies Employed in Systems Engineering

It is generally recognized that systems engineering can be regarded as a generic problem-solving methodology (Hall, 1989; Hitchins, 2003; INCOSE, 2000;

Enterprise Processes	Agreement Processes	Project Processes	Technical Processes
Enterprise Environment Management Process	Acquisition Process	Project Planning Process	Stakeholder Requirements Definition Process
Investment Management Process	Supply Process	Project Assessment Process	Requirements Analysis Process
System Life Cycle Management Process		Project Control Process	Architectural Design Process
Resource Management Process		Decision-making Process	Implementation Process
		Risk Management Process	Integration Process
		Configuration Management Process	Verification Process
		Information Management Process	Transition Process
			Validation Process
			Operation Process
			Maintenance Process
			Disposal Process

Table 1 *The systems life cycle processes (ISO/IEC, 2002; 61)*

Stevens, *et al.*, 1998) and Hitchins (2005) says that many would recognize it as similar to the Soft Systems Methodology (Checkland, 1981). Hitchins' describes the activities that are performed from the very beginning: the very fuzzy commencement stage that transforms the initial recognition of a need to a particular solution proposal. In systems engineering much of this work may be performed before it is clear what the solution involves. The method used is essentially a design process as described by Finkelstein and Finkelstein (1983) in their review of design methodologies, which demonstrates that systems engineering is a design discipline.

In this paper we posit that viewing systems engineering as a problem-solving paradigm obscures the true nature of systems engineering: an activity conforming to the design tradition. Such a thought exposes the need for deeper thinking about the range of research methods needed to conduct systems engineering practice and to develop the field.

Discussion of Research Approaches for Systems Engineering

Scientific/Quantitative Tradition

Philosophers of science debate what constitutes the scientific method. The issues concern matters of how observation or experiment should be conducted, such as whether the purpose of experiment is to explore the properties of the observed or to refute hypotheses. Regardless of the position one holds with respect to these debates the scientific method concerns the process of finding out through an empirical process is and what happens under specified conditions.

The scientific process seeks dispassionate observation and inter-observer reliability in the belief that true knowledge of the world is an objective constant. This dispassionate investigation must be balanced against the presence of a theory which both guides the observation and the interpretation of the observations following the argument of Ferris (1997). The scientific process presupposes that there is an external objectively knowable reality and that there is a means to knowledge of it through a rigorous observation processes. The process of observation involves organizing the observational situation according to an underlying theory that the observer holds.

Cropley and Harris (2007) state that the scientific tradition forms the basis for much research practice in systems engineering, for example technical testing, quantitative assessment of systems engineering processes, technical modelling and simulation, and financial analysis.

Qualitative Tradition

The qualitative tradition is an approach to research in which data from numerous different angles, dimensions and layers of perception is collected and assembled into a rich and meaningful picture of a complex, multifaceted situation (Leedy & Ormrod, 2005). Qualitative research methods were developed in the social sciences to enable researchers to study social and cultural phenomena. Now qualitative studies are done in many disciplines including sociology, psychology, history, medicine, and education. Examples of qualitative methods are: ethnography, hermeneutics, case studies, action research, cultural critique, phenomenological studies, and grounded theory. Despite the many different qualitative methods, all apply to situations where research approaches (a) focus on phenomena in "real world" situations; and (b) involve studying these phenomena in all their complexity (Leedy & Ormrod, 2005).

Unlike quantitative research methods, the qualitative tradition relies on understanding and uncovering various aspects of meaningful social behavior or

	Scientific Tradition	Qualitative Tradition	Design Tradition
Basic goal	To establish natural laws so people can predict and control systems	To understand and describe meaningful social action	To imagine *that-which-does-not-yet-exist* and to make it appear in concrete form as a new, purposeful addition to the real world.
Dominant Methods	Analytic scientific methods Problem solving	Ethnography Action research Hermeneutics Cultural critique Case studies	Composition Synthesis Judgement
Research starting point	Hypothesis formation	Research question formation	Identification of a forthcoming situation that requires action
Problems addressed	Systems analysis Performance prediction Optimisation	Understanding and improvement of social systems that create, maintain and operate complex systems	Creation of system solutions to practical needs
Role of common sense	Cleary distinct from and less valid than science	Powerful everyday theories used by ordinary people	Potentially false beliefs that may inhibit creativity Possible inhibitor
Role of theory	That which we are trying demonstrate	That which we are trying to identify	That which we use to inform design
An explanation that is true	Is logically connected to laws and based on facts	Resonates or feels right to those being studied	Is provided by a design that achieve
Good evidence	Is based on precise observations that others can repeat	Is embedded in the context of fluid social interactions	
Place for values	Science is value free, and values have no place except when choosing a topic	Values are an integral part of social life: no group's values are wrong, only different	Values of stakeholders (together with its technical performance) define what is a good system solution
Locus of major creativity	Forming hypotheses	Forming research question	Creating candidate solutions

Table 2 *A summary of the differences between research approaches*

action. If the quantitative research requires answering questions such as "what" "where" and "when", the qualitative approach addresses the questions "why" and "how".

Design as a Research Methodology

The third category of kinds of research which we discuss here is the process of design. This category refers to the act of design as an act of research, not to design as the subject of the research, which could be conducted using any research approach, as appropriate, to particular research questions and objectives. Design is an "activity of making a plan to change an existing situation into a preferred situation" which inherently involves problem solving (Love), and often involves novelty, either because the need or the solution is novel (Guindon, 1990).

There is a difficulty in conceptualizing design as research because design is a general term which spans a broad diversity of situations ranging from the creation of a totally novel product system to address a novel need to the routine application of well established methods to design minor variations in existing products. In addition, traditions of what is normally regarded as research in many disciplines have developed in the academic community. For example, most engineering research in universities follows the quantitative scientific tradition and concerns the scientific investigation of its subject matter. This is reflected in typical PhD regulations which require the candidate "to advance knowledge and/or the application of knowledge through the preparation of a piece of work which represents a significant contribution to a particular field of study" (UniSA, 2007). Thus, in engineering, the design of a solution to a problem is, itself, not normally regarded as research but rather as the application of engineering method. In contrast, disciplines such as art, town planning, architecture, music and industrial design do have a tradition in which the creation of a novel artefact is regarded as an appropriate research activity.

Engineering in general, and systems engineering in particular, concerns the design and realization of solutions to needs rather than the creation of abstracted knowledge, as is the case in many academic disciplines. Design requires the combination of the system needs, knowledge of the potential solution technologies, and understanding of the characteristics of a socially-acceptable solution in order to create a synthesis which satisfies the need. The design process may introduce unanticipated problems, and the need to discover solutions. Regardless of when the unanticipated problems are discovered the outcome of design brought to successful conclusion is the situationally specific knowledge that a particular design is a satisfactory solution to the need. This is new knowledge, albeit of a specific scope. Therefore this discovery of the means to solve the practical problems of implementing a solution to the need is a process of research, an activity of addressing a question: "How can I solve this problem?" and finding an answer, knowledge that did not exist at the start of the process.

However, the narrowness of the scope of the knowledge is a constraint on the interest of the work as "research". Minor design variations on an existing product, whilst commercially significant are generally not particularly novel, nor particularly important in the broader field. In contrast, the design of novel solutions to problems, or the design of a solution to a novel need are more profoundly novel and may be more significant in the field. Contributions in the latter class provide interesting research outcomes because they indicate what can be done where it was previously not known. In this sense design is research and the establishment of precedents is what distinguishes design as research from design which is not research.

Since systems engineering is the engineering discipline specifically concerned with the design and development of solutions to complex systems needs using any technological or non-technological components that are appropriate for the solution design is an appropriate research method to be included in the set of research methods accepted within systems engineering.

Implications for Research Methods Courses

Two of the authors, Ferris and Sitnikova, have taught a research methods course, Engineering Research Practice, at University of South Australia. This course was designed for the needs of students in the whole range of engineering disciplines offered in our university, including systems engineering. The reality and that there is a means to knowledge of it through a rigorous observation processes. The process of observation involves organizing the observational situation according to an underlying theory that the observer holds. The range of fields is broad, but the entire range is within engineering. Therefore the fundamental perspective of the disciplines is to use knowledge to effect solutions to needs. The test of success is the question: "Does it work?"; in contrast with the test of scientific work: "Is it right?" or "Did we learn something?" The difference of discipline emphasis results in different approaches to research.

In engineering, since the objective is to make products which work there is a need for a research paradigm different than the scientific discovery of knowledge for its own interest: design. The quantitative and qualitative traditions of research, in their various manifestations of particular research methodologies, are the subject of most research methods courses. Such courses either teach across a broad range of research methods or address the set most frequently used in the discipline which hosts the teaching of the course. However, even in engineering faculties the existence and methodology of design as a research methodology is almost always omitted. (The authors are unaware of any counter-example to this statement, but cautiously do not wish to make a general assertion). There are some disciplines, notably art, architecture and design, in which there is an academic tradition of recognizing certain classes of creative design work as research. Since the core concern of the engineering disciplines, and most obviously systems engineering, is the design of suitable product entities it is necessary to explore the nature of design as a research methodology in engineering. In a research methods course students should be introduced to this possibility, with careful instruction to ensure that they distinguish between the routine design process in well precedented areas and design research which breaks new ground in the kind of product system or need addressed.

Conclusions

This paper has discussed the nature of three traditions of research work, the quantitative and qualitative traditions and design. These three traditions have been demonstrated to be distinct from each other. We have also shown that in systems engineering much research fits within the quantitative tradition but with some recognition of the value of the qualitative tradition for informing systems engineering related knowledge. The contribution of the third tradition, design, used in some other disciplines, has not been recognized and developed in systems engineering. This paper has contributed an argument for the importance of exploring the nature of design as a research methodology in systems engineering. We have shown that it is necessary for engineering research methods courses to develop student understanding across the three traditions. We have also demonstrated that the introduction to design as a research methodology in engineering, whilst applicable to all engineering disciplines, is particularly demanded by systems engineering.

References

Checkland, P. (1981). *Systems thinking, systems practice*, ISBN 0471279110.

Cook, S.C. and Ferris, T.L.J.(2007)Re-evaluating systems engineering as a framework for tackling systems issues, 24, 169-181, ISSN 1092-7026.

Cripps,S. C. (1991).Old fashioned remedies for GaAsFET power amplifier designers, *IEEE society on microwave theory and techniques newsletter*, Summer, 13-17.

DSMC (1983).*Systems engineering management guide,* Defense Systems Management College, Fort Belvoir, Virginia, USA.

Ferris, T. L. J. (1997).The concept of leap in measurement interpretation, 21, 137-146, ISSN 0263-2241.

Ferris, T. L. J. (2007a).Some early history of systems engineering - 1950's in IRE publications (part 1): the problem, ISBN 0-9720562-5-4.

Ferris, T. L. J. (2007b)Some early history of systems engineering - 1950's in IRE publications (part 2): the solution, ISBN 0-9720562-5-4.

Finkelstein, L. and Finkelstein, A. C. W.(1983).Review of design methodology, 130, part A, 213-222, 0143-702X.

Guindon, R.(1990).Designing the design process: exploiting opportunistic thoughts, 5, 305-344, 0737-0024.

Hall, A. D.(1962). *A methodology for systems engineering,* D. Van Nostrand Company, Inc., Princeton, New Jersey.

Hall, A. D.(1989) *Metasystems methodology*, ISBN 0080369561.

Hitchins, D. K.(2003) *Advanced systems thinking, engineering, and management*, ISBN 1-58053-619-0.

Hitchins, D. K.(2005). Systems methodology, *Conference on systems engineering research*, Stevens Institute of Technology, Hoboken, New Jersey, pp. 19pp.

INCOSE(2000) *Systems engineering handbook, version 2.0.*

INCOSE(2005). *INCOSE Technical Vision, Version 1.1, May.*

INCOSE(2006). *Systems engineering handbook, version 3.0.*

ISO/IEC(2002). *ISO 15288 systems engineering - system life cycle processes,* ISO/IEC.

Jackson,M. C. (2000). *Systems approaches to management*, ISBN 0-306-46506-X.

Kline,S.J.(1995). *Conceptual Foundations for Multidisciplinary Thinking*, ISBN 0-8407-2409-1.

Leedy,P.D. and Ormrod, J. E. (2005). *Practical research planning and design,* ISBN 0-13-

124720-4.

Love, T., A fork in the road: systems and design, 11pp.

M'Pherson, P. K. (1980). Systems engineering: an approach to whole system design, 50, 545-558, ISSN 0033-7722.

Nelson, H. G. and Stolterman, E. (2003). *The design way : intentional change in an unpredictable world : foundations and fundamentals of design competence*, ISBN 0-87778-305-5.

Neuman, W. L. (2000). The meaning of methodology, *W. L. Neuman, Social research methods: Qualitative and quantitative approaches*, ISBN 0205374077 (pbk) or 0205353118.

Sage, A. P. (2006) In *INCOSE 2006 international workshop*, Scottsdale, Arizona.

Stevens, R. L., Brook, P., Jackson, K. and Arnold, S. (1998). *Systems engineering coping with complexity*, Prentice Hall Europe, ISBN 0-13-095085.

University of South Australia (2007). PhD (communications engineering) http://www.unisanet.unisa.edu.au/programs/program.asp?Program=LPRK

10. Compact Mathematical Models of the World System Development and Their Applicability to the Development of Local Solutions in Third World Countries

Andrey Korotayev
Anthropology of the East Center, Russian State University for the Humanities, RUS

The paper considers applicability of compact mathematical models of the World System evolution that have been elaborated by us earlier (Korotayev, A., A. Malkov, and D. Khaltourina. *Introduction to Social Macrodynamics. Compact Macromodels of the World System Growth.* Moscow: URSS/KomKniga, 2006) to the development of local solutions in the Third World countries. We have shown that the long-term macrodynamics of the World System since the 19th century can be described mathematically in a rather accurate way with the following system of differential equations: dN/dt = aSN(1 – l) (1); dS/dt = blN (2); dl/dt = cSl(1 – l) (3), where N is the World System population, S is the surplus produced, per person, over the amount (m) minimally necessary to reproduce the population with a zero growth rate in a Malthusian system (thus, S = g – m, where g denotes per capita GDP), l is the proportion of the population that is literate; a, b, and c are parameters. Our analysis of the applicability of this model to the development of local solutions in the Third World countries confirms that one of the most effective ways to alleviate local problems in the poorest Third World countries is the acceleration of the development of education (especially, for females) that can both decrease the demographic pressure and promote the economic development.

Introduction

In 1960 von Foerster, Mora, and Amiot published, in the journal *Science*, a striking discovery. They showed that between 1 and 1958 CE the world's population (N) dynamics can be described in an extremely accurate way with an astonishingly simple equation:

(1) $N_t = C/(t_0 - t)$

where N_t is the world population at time t, and C and t_0 are constants, with t_0 corresponding to an absolute limit ("singularity" point) at which N would become infinite.

Parameter t_0 was estimated by von Foerster and his colleagues as 2026.87, which corresponds to November 13, 2006; this made it possible for them to supply their article with a public-relations masterpiece title – "Doomsday: Friday, 13 November, A.D. 2026" (von Foerster, Mora and Amiot, 1960).

Note that the graphic representation of this equation is nothing but a hyperbola; thus, the growth pattern described is denoted as "hyperbolic".

Note that if von Foerster, Mora, and Amiot also had at their disposal, in addition to world population data, data on the world GDP dynamics for 1–1973 (published, however, only in 2001 by Maddison [Maddison, 2001]), they could have made another striking "prediction" – that on Saturday, 23 July, A.D. 2005 an "economic doomsday" would take place; that is, on that day the world GDP would become infinite if the economic growth trend observed in 1–1973 CE continued. They also would have found that in 1–1973 CE the world GDP growth followed a quadratic-hyperbolic rather than simple hyperbolic pattern.

Indeed, Maddison's estimates of the world GDP dynamics for 1–1973 CE are almost perfectly approximated by the following equation:

(2) $G_t = C/(t_0 - t)^2$

where G_t is the world GDP (in billions of 1990 international dollars, in purchasing power parity [PPP]) in year t, C = 17355487.3 and t_0 = 2005.56 (see Figure 1).

Note that the von Foerster equation, $N_t = C/(t_0 - t)$, is just the solution for the following differential equation (see, e.g., Korotayev, *et al.*, 2006a: 119–20):

(3) $dN/dt = N^2/C$

This equation can be also written as:

(4) $dN/dt = aN^2$

where $a = 1/C$.

What is the meaning of this mathematical expression, $dN/dt = aN^2$? In our context dN/dt denotes the absolute population growth rate at some moment of time. Hence, this equation states that the absolute population growth rate at any moment of time should be proportional to the square of population at this moment.

As we showed before (Korotayev, *et al.*, 2006a, 2006b; Korotayev & Khaltourina, 2006), the hyperbolic pattern of the world's population growth could be accounted for by the nonlinear second order positive feedback mechanism that was shown long ago to generate just the hyperbolic growth, known also as the "blow-up regime" (see, e.g., Korotayev, *et al.*, 2006b: 5–36 for more detail). In our case this nonlinear second order positive feedback looks as follows: the more people – the more potential inventors – the faster technological

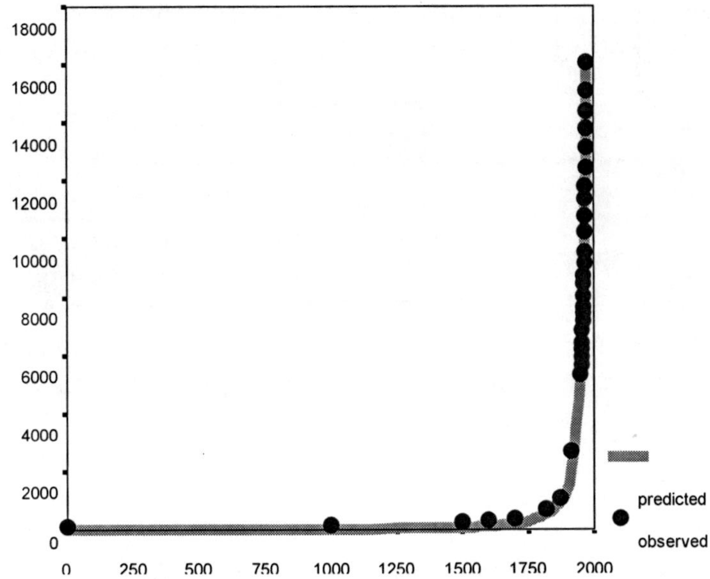

$R = .9993$, $R^2 = .9986$, $p << .0001$. The black markers correspond to Maddison's (2001) estimates. The grey solid line has been generated by the following equation:

$$G=17749573.1/(2006-t)^2$$

Actually, as was mentioned above, the best fit is achieved with $C = 17355487.3$ and $t_0 = 2005.56$ (which gives just the "doomsday Saturday, 23 July, 2005"), but we have decided to keep hereafter to integer numbered years.

Figure 1 *World GDP Dynamics, 1–1973 CE (in billions of 1990 international dollars, PPP): the fit between predictions of a quadratic-hyperbolic model and the observed data*

growth – the faster growth of the Earth's carrying capacity[1] – the faster population growth – with more people you also have more potential inventors – hence, faster technological growth, and so on (see Figure 2).

We have shown (Korotayev, *et al.*, 2006a: 34–66) that for the period prior to the 1970s the World System economic and demographic macrodynamics driven by the above mentioned positive feedback loops can be described mathematically in a rather accurate way with the following extremely simple mathematical model:

---

1. Note that one of the anonymous referees of this paper has suggested that "faster technological growth does not result in faster growth of the Earth's carrying capacity, rather it degrades it faster". However, our analysis of relevant long-term demographic, ecological, and technological data has shown that in long-term perspective all the important increases in the Earth's carrying capacity have been achieved just through the acceleration of technological growth (Korotayev, *et al.*, 2006a, 2006b; Korotayev & Khaltourina, 2006).

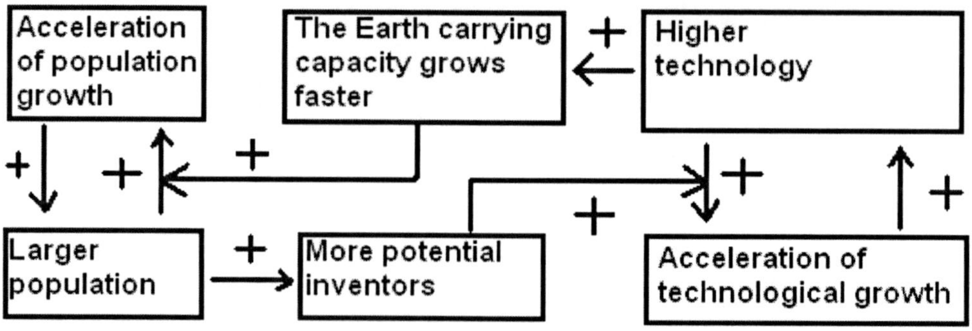

Figure 2 *Block Scheme of the Nonlinear Second Order Positive Feedback between Technological Development and Demographic Growth (version 1)*

(5) $dN/dt=aSN$,

(6) $dS/dt=bNS$,

while the world GDP (G) can be calculated using the following equation:

(7) $G = mN + SN$,

where G is the world GDP, N is population, and S is the surplus produced, per person, over the amount (m) minimally necessary to reproduce the population with a zero growth rate in a Malthusian system (thus, $S = g - m$, where g denotes per capita GDP); a and b are parameters.

Note that the mathematical analysis of the basic model (not described here) suggests that up to the 1970s the amount of S (per capita surplus produced at the given level of World System development) should be proportional, in the long run, to the World System's population: $S = kN$. Our statistical analysis of available empirical data has confirmed this theoretical proportionality (Korotayev, *et al.*, 2006a: 49–50). Thus, in the right-hand side of equation (6) S can be replaced with kN, and as a result we arrive at the following equation:

(4) $dN/dt=kaN^2$

As we remember, the solution of this type of differential equations is:

(1) $N_t=C/(t_0-t)$,

and this produces simply a hyperbolic curve.

As, according to our model, S can be approximated as kN, its long-term dynamics can be approximated with the following equation:

(8) $S=kC/(t_0-t)$.

Thus, the long-term dynamics of the most dynamic component of the world GDP, SN, "the world surplus product ", can be approximated as follows:

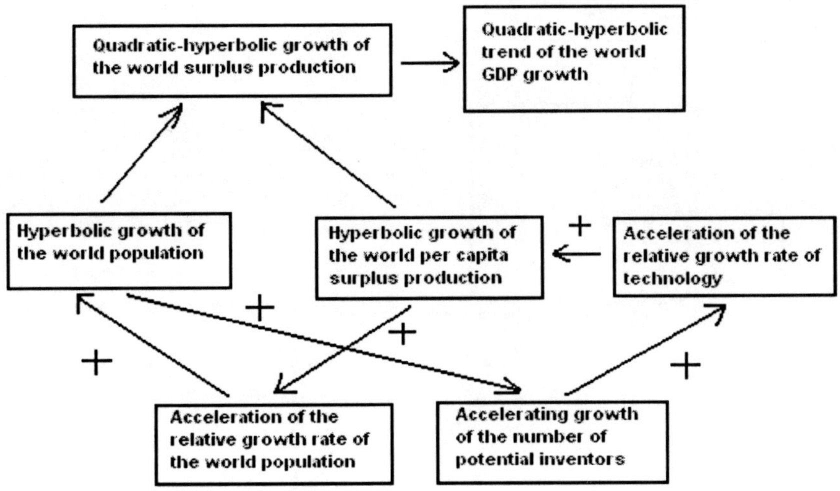

Figure 3 *Block Scheme of the Nonlinear Second Order Positive Feedback between Technological Development and Demographic Growth (version 2)*

(9) $SN=kC^2/(t_0-t)^2$

Of course, this suggests that the long-term world GDP dynamics up to the early 1970s must be approximated better by a quadratic hyperbola than by a simple one; and, as we could see above (see Figure 1), this approximation works very effectively indeed.

Thus, up to the 1970s the hyperbolic growth of the world population was accompanied by the quadratic-hyperbolic growth of the world GDP, just as is suggested by our model. Note that the hyperbolic growth of the world population and the quadratic-hyperbolic growth of the world GDP are very tightly connected processes, actually two sides of the same coin, two dimensions of one process propelled by the nonlinear second order positive feedback loops between the technological development and demographic growth (see Figure 3).

In our special extended macro-model of world economic, cultural, and demographic growth aimed at the mathematical description of both the World System hyperbolic growth (demographically, economically, technologically and culturally) prior to the early 1970s and its withdrawal from the blow-up regime afterwards we make the following additional assumptions: (1) a literate population makes more technological innovations than an illiterate one. Consequently, literacy growth leads to acceleration of technological development. (2) In the Modern era the level of the World System's economic development is determined first of all by the level of development of human capital, which, we believe, can be roughly estimated by the world literacy level for the modernization period. (3) One of the major factors of fertility reduction is the growth of education (especially, female education) (e.g., Cochrane, 1979; Korotayev, *et al.*, 2006a). These assumptions in conjunction with the assumptions of the models presented above suggest the following functional scheme of relationships between modeled subsystems (see Figure 4).

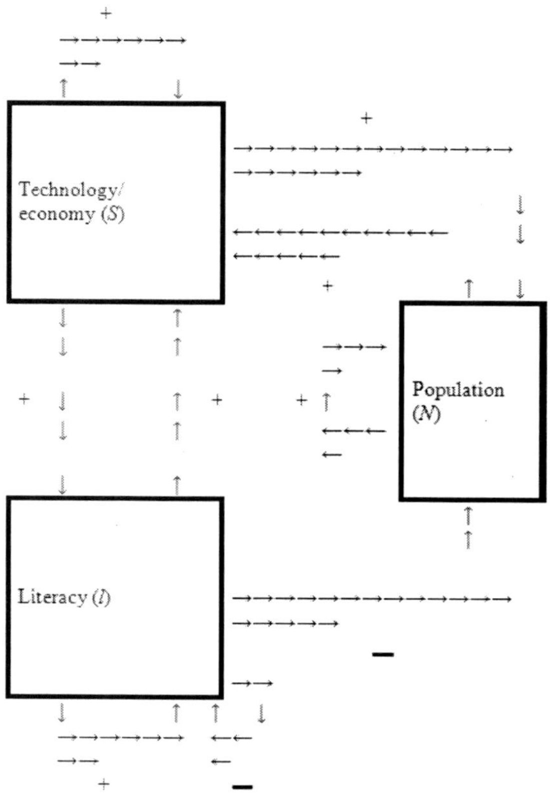

Figure 4 *Functional Scheme of Relationships between Model Subsystems*

The relationships between these three subsystems are modeled using the following set of differential equations:

(10) $dN/dt=aSN(1-l)$,
(11) $dS/dt=blN$,
(12) $dl/dt=CSl(1-l)$,

where l is the proportion of the literate population and a, b, and c are constants. This model generates dynamics shown in Figure 5.

With such a compact model we are able to reproduce rather well both the hyperbolic growth of world population before the 1970s, and the subsequent increasing slow down of world population growth rates ($R^2 > 0.99$, $p << 0.0001$ for all the three variables [Korotayev, *et al.*, 2006a: 83–85]).

Of course, the special macromodel has a much narrower applicability than the general ones. For example, it does not work at all for the preliterate period of human history, as, according to the special macromodel, zero literacy would correspond to a zero rate of techno-economic growth, whereas this does not match the reality at all. On the other hand, the special macromodel describe rather well the modernization period, which appears to reflect the fact that during this period the development of human capital became the most important factor of economic development (see, e.g., Lucas, 1988). Note that

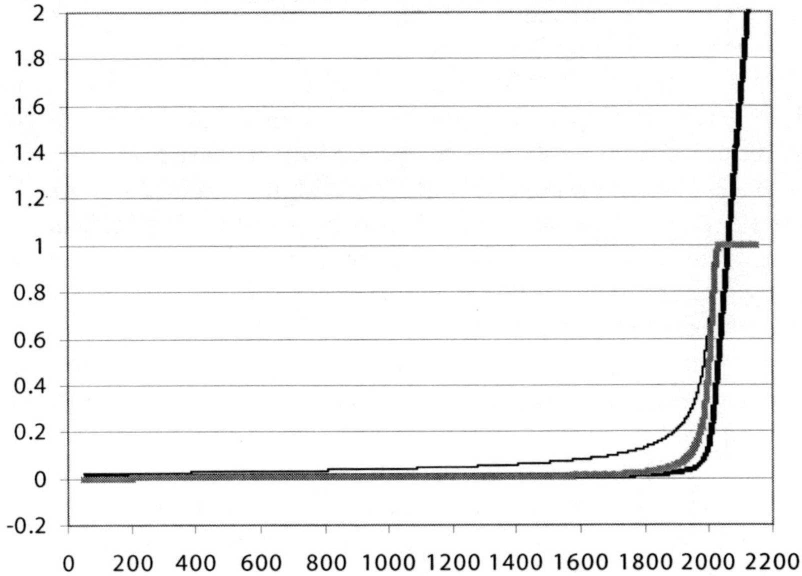

NOTE: thick grey curve – the world population counted as proportion from its size at stabilization level; thin black curve – literacy; thick black curve – level of the World System techno-economic development (S) counted as proportion from its level at world population stabilization point.

Figure 5 *Dynamics Generated by the Model*

for the modernization period the literacy level could serve as a rather sensitive indicator of the overall level of human capital development (Korotayev, *et al.*, 2006a: 92–104). Note also that we have at our disposal some data suggesting that the growth of literacy could serve in itself as a powerful factor of economic development.

Khaltourina's analysis (Korotayev, *et al.*, 2006a: 87–91; note that the principle author of the respective chapter is Daria Khaltourina) indicates that there is a strong and definitely significant linear correlation between the literacy rate in 1800 and GDP per capita at present accounting for 86% of the entire data dispersion.

Therefore, the hypothesis that the spread of literacy was one of the major factors of modern economic growth gains additional support. On the one hand, literate populations have many more opportunities to obtain and utilize the achievements of modernization than illiterate ones. On the other hand, literate people could be characterized by a greater innovative-activity level, which provides opportunities for modernization, development, and economic growth.

Literacy does not simply facilitate the process of perceiving innovation by an individual. It also changes her or his cognition to a certain extent. This problem was studied by Luria, Vygotsky, and Shemiakin, the famous Soviet psychologists, on the basis of the results of their fieldwork in Central Asia in the 1930s. Their study shows that education has a fundamental effect on the formation of cognitive processes (perception, memory, cognition). The researchers found out that illiterate respondents, unlike literate ones, preferred concrete names for colors to abstract ones, and situative groupings of items to categorical ones (note that abstract thinking is based on category cognition). Furthermore, illiterate respondents could not solve syllogistic problems like the following one – "Precious metals do not get rust. Gold is a precious metal. Can gold get rust or not?". These syllogistic problems did not make any sense to illiterate respondents because they were out of the sphere of their practical experience. Literate respondents who had at least minimal formal education solved the suggested syllogistic problems easily (Luria 1976).

Therefore, literate workers, soldiers, inventors and so on turn out to be more effective than illiterate ones not only due to their ability to read instructions, manuals, and textbooks, but also because of the developed skills of abstract thinking.

The ability to read was essential for Protestants (unlike Catholics) to perform their religious duty – to read the Bible. The reading of Holy Scripture was not just unnecessary for Catholic laymen, for a long time it was even prohibited for them. As a result, the level of literacy and education was, in general, higher for Protestants than it was for Catholics and for followers of other confessions that did not provide religious stimuli for learning literacy by commoners (Korotayev, *et al.*, 2006a: 91). In our opinion, this could explain to a considerable extent the differences between economic performance of the Protestants and the Catholics in the late 19th – early 20th centuries in Europe noticed by Weber (2003 [1905]). We do not question that specific features of Protestant ethics could have facilitated economic development. However, we believe that we found another (and probably more powerful) channel of Protestantism's influence on the economic growth of the Western countries.

The findings on the influence of literacy on the economic growth in the contemporary world are very congruent with our findings, e.g., "an increase in schooling has no short-term impact on growth, but a statistically significant effect over the longer term (ten to twenty years)" (UNESCO 2005: 143; see also: Barro, 1991; Coulombe, *et al.*, 2004; Naudé, 2004).

Our own statistical test using the most recent data from the World Bank (2007) and UNESCO confirm those findings (see Tables 1–3 and Figures 6–7).

Indeed, very high levels of adult illiteracy (with less than 30 per cent of adults being literate) turn out to be a very strong and statistically significant inhibitor of any rapid long-term economic growth (Table 2), whereas a very high level of adult literacy (85 percent and more) is an even stronger predictor of positive economic growth in long-term (Table 3).

We believe that the proposed model suggests some concrete ways for the development of long-term local solutions in the poorest Third World countries, especially (but not only) in Sub-Saharan Africa.

Indeed, the most recent long-term projections of the UN Population Division (2004: 12) indicate the overall stabilization of the world population at *c.* 9 billion level by about 2075, that is, incidentally, rather close to the forecast at which we arrived independently on the basis of our mathematical model (Korotayev, *et al.*, 2006a: 112–114). However, what looks as a rather optimistic

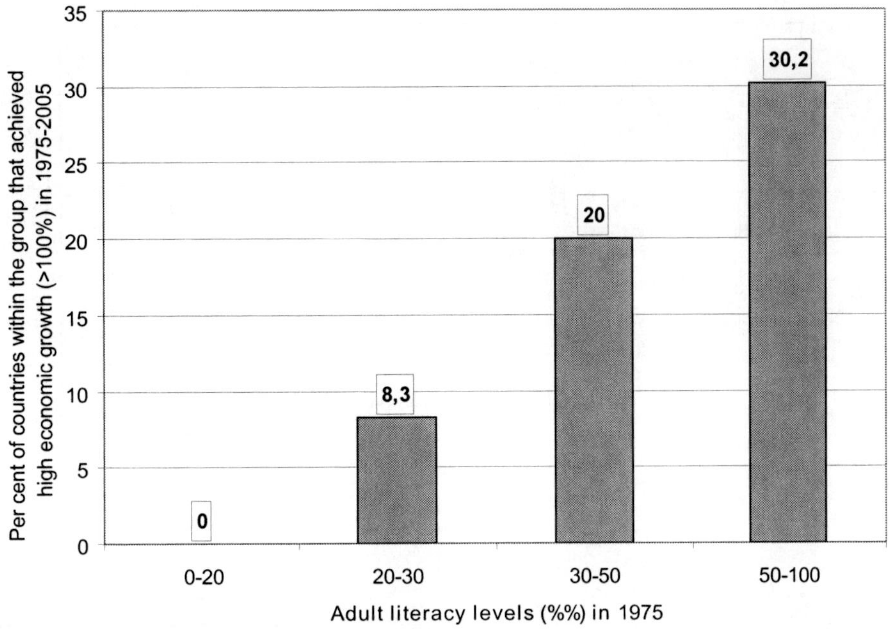

Figure 6 *High Illiteracy Level as an Inhibitor of Fast Economic Growth*

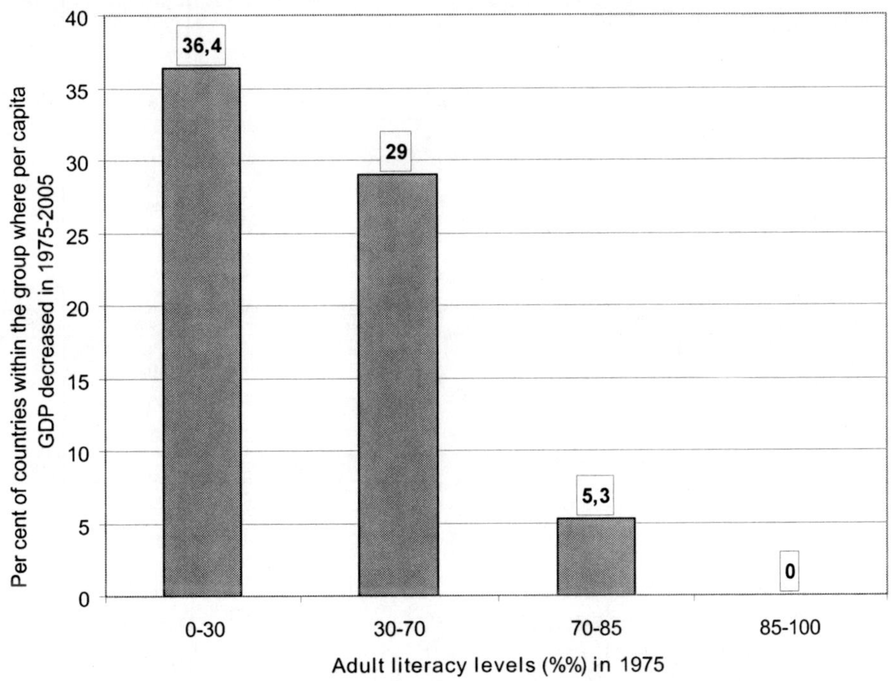

Figure 7 *High Literacy Level as a predictor of Long-Term Positive Economic Growth*

ADULT LITERACY FOR POPULATION AGED 15 YEARS AND ABOVE in 1975	GDP per Capita Growth in 1975–2005						Total
	<0%	0-50%	50-100%	100-150%	150-200%	>200%	
0-20%	3 Centr.Afr. Rep., Guinea Bissau, Niger	6 Benin, Burkina Faso, Chad, Gambia, Mali, Senegal	1 Nepal	0	0	0	10
	30.0%	*60.0%*	*10.0%*	*0%*	*0%*	*0%*	100%
20-30%	5 Burundi, D.R. Congo, Cote d'Ivoire, Haiti, Togo	3 Algeria, Mauritania, Nigeria	3 Bangladesh, Morocco, Sudan	1 Pakistan	0	0	12
	41.7%	*25.0%*	*25.0%*	*8.3%*	*0%*	*0%*	100%
30-50%	3 Iran Madagascar Saudi Arabia	9 Cameroon, Congo, Ghana, Guatemala, Kenya, Malawi, Papua N.Guinea, Rwanda, Syria	0	1 Tunisia	2 Egypt, India	0	15
	20.0%	*60.0%*	*0%*	*6.7%*	*13.3%*	*0%*	100%
50-70%	6 Bolivia, Kuwait, Nicaragua, Un. Arab Emirates, Zambia, Zimbabwe	3 El Salvador Honduras Swaziland	2 Jordan Turkey	0	1 Lesotho	4 Botswana, China, Indonesia, Malaysia	16
	37.5%	*18.8%*	*12.5%*	*0%*	6.3%	*25.0%*	100%
70-85%	1 Venezuela	9 Brazil, Ecuador, Fiji, Jamaica, Mexico, Panama, Paraguay, Peru, South Africa	3 Colombia, Dominican Republic, Israel	1 Belize	1 Sri Lanka	4 Hong Kong, Malta, Singapore, Thailand	19
	5.3%	*47.4%*	*15.8%*	*5.3%*	*5.3%*	*21.1%*	100%
85-100%	0	4 Argentina, Guyana, Philippines, Uruguay	2 Costa Rica, Trinidad and Tobago	0	0	2 Chile, Korea	8
	0%	*50.0%*	*25.0%*	*0%*	*.0%*	*25.0%*	100%
Total	18	34	11	3	4	10	80
	22.5%	42.5%	13.8%	3.8%	5.0%	12.5%	100%

NOTE: The sample includes the countries for both the World Bank (2007) data on per capita GDP (in constant 2000 international $, PPP) dynamics for 1975–2005 and UNESCO (2007) data on adult literacy for population aged 15 years and above for 1975 are available.

Table 1 *Correlation between Adult Literacy in 1975 and Economic Growth in 1975–2005 in the Third World Countries*

		Increase in per capita GDP achieved in 1975–2005		Total
		Less than 100%	*100% and more*	
Adult literacy in 1975	*0-30%*	21	1	22
		95.5%	4.5%	100%
	30-100%	42	16	58
		72.4%	27.6%	100%
Total		63	17	80
		78,8%	21.3%	100%

NOTE: Gamma = 0,778, p = 0,003

Table 2 *High Illiteracy Level as an Inhibitor of Long-Term Fast Economic Growth*

		Change in per capita GDP in 1975–2005		Total
		0% or less	*More than 0%*	
Adult literacy in 1975	*0-85%*	18	54	72
		25%	75%	100%
	85-100%	0	8	8
		0%	100%	100%
Total		63	18	62
		78.8%	22.5%	77.5%

NOTE: Gamma = 1.0, p = 0.006

Table 3 *High Literacy Level as a predictor of Long-Term Positive Economic Growth*

scenario at the global level, does not appear quite as such at the level of some individual countries. For example, the same source indicates that if the current trends continue, the population of Uganda will grow from 23.5 million in the year 2000 to 97.8 million in 2050 and will only stabilize about 2115 at around 170 million level, reaching 167.1 million in 2100; the population of Yemen will grow from 18 million in the year 2000 to 84.4 million in 2050 and will only stabilize about 2115 at around 147.2 level, reaching 144.2 million in 2100; the population of Ethiopia will grow from 65.6 million in the year 2000 to 171 million in 2050 and will reach 222.2 million in 2100 before its projected stabilization in 2105 (UN Population Division 2004: 42, 47, 49–50).

Thus, if the current trends continue, already by 2050 the population of Ethiopia will by far exceed the present-day population of the Russian Federation, which is in fact a catastrophic scenario (for a mathematical model describing such a scenario see Korotayev & Khaltourina, 2006: 92–115), as Ethiopia has by an order of magnitude less natural resources than Russia (for example, the area of Russia fertile "black-soil" lands alone by far exceeds the whole territory of Ethiopia, most of which is not suitable for agriculture). Very soon after 2050 Ethiopia is projected to be joined by Uganda and Yemen. The total inad-

Country	*Risk level*	*Population in 2000 (millions)*	*UN population projection for 2100*	*Projected relative population growth in 2000–2100 (%%)*
Afghanistan	Extremely high	21.4	90.3	322
Angola		12.4	63.0	409
Burkina Faso		11.9	65.2	447
Burundi		6.3	27.6	341
Chad		7.9	34.6	340
Congo		3.4	14.6	322
Dem. Rep. of the Congo		48.6	203.3	319
Guinea-Bissau		1.4	7.0	410
Liberia		2.9	13.5	359
Mali		11.9	70.5	492
Niger		10.7	98.6	818
Palestinian Territory		3.2	14.9	368
Somalia		8.7	66.1	658
Benin	Very high	6.2	18.7	201
Bhutan		2.1	6.4	211
Comoros		0.7	2.2	211
Eritrea		3.7	12.9	248
Iraq		23.2	68.0	193
Madagascar		16.0	61.6	286
Mauritania		2.6	9.8	269
Oman		2.6	8.2	214

Source – UN Population Division 2004: 46–50.

Table 4 *List of "High-Risk" Countries (in addition to Ethiopia, Uganda, and Yemen)*

equacy of Yemeni natural resources for the support of the projected population is noted even by the authors of *World Population to 2300* (who generally avoid such comments):

"*Yemen is probably the extreme case, where 2100 density of 273 [persons per sq. km.] would instead be estimated as 17,071 [person per sq. km.] in relation to potential cropland. Whether potential cropland may be much more productive by 2100 or possibly more degraded, or somehow much less relevant, one cannot say. Many complications of this sort will have to be addressed in working out consequences of these projections*" (UN Population Division 2004).

The other high-risk countries are listed in Table 4.

Note that in all the high-risk countries (with a notable exception of the Palestinian Autonomy that deserves a separate treatment [see it in Korotayev & Khaltourina 2006: 115]) we observe very high levels of adult illiteracy, and especially female illiteracy (e.g., 66.2% in Ethiopia; 71.5% in Yemen; 87.3% in Chad; 88.1% in Mali; 90.6% in Niger; 91.9% in Burkina Faso etc. [UNESCO 2005: 280–286]). Our mathematical model suggests that in order to avoid the catastrophic scenarios in the high-risk countries the adult illiteracy should be totally (or almost totally) eliminated within 10–15 forthcoming years (at least among the reproductive age adults). This would provide a stable long-term relief of the demographic pressure in the respective countries in two ways – both through an adequate reduction of the fertility rates and the long-term promotion of the economic growth. Note that the present-day aims of UNESCO turn out to be clearly inadequate. The 2000 Dakar Framework for Action set up as one of its aims for the 2000–2015 period the reduction of the illiteracy rate by 50% (UNESCO 2005: 29–30), which, for example, with respect to Niger implies the reduction of female illiteracy just to 46% level that is clearly not sufficient for the avoidance of a catastrophic scenario. Note that even this rather modest (against the background of the imminent humanitarian catastrophe in the high-risk countries) aim is considered by the UNESCO experts themselves as highly unlikely to be achieved with respect to the majority of the high-risk countries (UNESCO 2005: 70–71).

This implies the necessity of a radical increase in the literacy growth rates in the high-risk countries, in general; and in particular – the necessity of a radical increase in amounts of the international aid aimed at the elimination of the illiteracy in the high-risk countries (note that at the moment, e.g., very high-risk Ethiopia gets only $0.7 a year of per capita international aid for the development of education, whereas even zero-risk Slovenia gets a more than twice higher amount of such international aid [UNESCO 2005: 414, 416]).

References

Barro, R. (1991). "Economic growth in a cross-section of countries," *Quarterly Journal of Economics*, ISSN 0033-5533, 106: 407–443.

Cochrane, S. H. (1979). *Fertility and Education: What Do We Really Know?* ISBN 0801821401.

Coulombe, S., Tremblay, J. F. and Marchand, S. (2004). *Literacy Scores, Human Capital and Growth Across Fourteen OECD Countries*, ISBN 9780662374565.

Foerster, H. von, Mora, P. and Amiot, L. (1960). "Doomsday: Friday, 13 November, A.D. 2026," *Science*, ISSN 0036-8075, 132: 1291–1295.

Korotayev, A. and Khaltourina, D. (2006). *Introduction to Social Macrodynamics: Secular Cycles and Millennial Trends in Africa*, ISBN 5484005604.

Korotayev, A., Malkov, A. and Khaltourina, D. (2006a). *Introduction to Social Macrodynamics: Compact Macromodels of the World System Growth*, ISBN 5484004144.

Korotayev, A., Malkov, A. and Khaltourina, D. (2006b). *Introduction to Social Macrodynamics: Secular Cycles and Millennial Trends*, ISBN 5484004144.

Lucas, R. (1988). "On the Mechanisms of Economic Development," *Journal of Monetary Economics*, ISSN 0304-3932, 22: 3–42.

Luria, A. R. (1976). *Cognitive Development.* ISBN 9780674137325.

Maddison, A. (2001). *Monitoring the World Economy: A Millennial Perspective*, ISBN 9264186549.

Naudé, W. A. (2004). "The effects of policy, institutions and geography on economic growth in Africa: an econometric study based on cross-section and panel data," *Journal of International Development*, ISSN 0954-1748, 16: 821–849.

U.S. Bureau of the Census. (2007). *World Population Information* http://www.census.gov/ipc/www/world.html.

UN Population Division. (2004). *World Population to 2300*, ISBN 9211514010.

UNESCO. (2005). *Education for All. Literacy for Life. EFA Global Monitoring Report – 2006.* ISBN 9231040081.

UNESCO. (2007). *Estimates and Projections of Adult Illiteracy for Population Aged 15 Years and above, by Country and by Gender 1970-2015.* http://www.uis.unesco.org/en/stats/statistics/literacy2000.htm.

Weber, M. (1905). *The Protestant Ethic and the Spirit of Capitalism.* ISBN 9780486427034 (2003).

World Bank. (2007). *World Development Indicators Online.* Washington, DC: World Bank, http://web.worldbank.org/WBSITE/EXTERNAL/DATASTATISTICS/0,,contentMDK:20398986~pagePK:64133150~piPK:64133175~theSitePK:239419,00.html.

11. Successful Activism Strategies: Five New Extensions to Ashby

PLENARY PAPER

Terence Love[1] and **T. Cooper**[2]
[1]Curtin University, AUS; Lancaster University, ENG; IADE/UNIDCOM, Portugal
[2] Edith Cowan University, AUS

This paper reports two outcomes of research undertaken by the authors. These comprise an extension to Ashby's Law of Requisite Variety and the application of the five extensions to Ashby's Law derived so far by the authors to the complex socio-technical problems associated with developing successful activism strategies and resisting them. These new extensions reposition Ashby's Law of Requisite Variety as a tool of politics and power.

Extending Ashby's Law of Requisite Variety

William Ross Ashby widely influenced researchers involved in systemic analysis and system design, particularly through his Law of Requisite Variety (LoRV) (Ashby, 1956); perhaps the only 'Law' held true across the diverse disciplines of informatics, system design cybernetics, communications systems and information systems. The LoRV is stated in short form in many different ways, e.g., 'only variety can destroy variety' and 'every good regulator of a system must be a model of that system'. The LoRV means that to control any system, the amount of variety (the number of possible states) of the controlling process has to be at least the amount of variety that the system is capable of exhibiting.

This paper describes outcomes of the authors' research in the area of complex socio-technical systems that include significant political and economic considerations such as:

- Civil complex socio-technical systems involving multiple competing stakeholders/constituencies (e.g., infrastructures; built environments with complex socio-environmental behaviors; software development; socio-technical electronic systems such as ticketing, payment and information access systems);
- Military socio-technical systems that involve multiple players (anti-terrorism, situation control, and war-faring systems);
- Politically driven socio-technical systems involving multiple competing interests (e.g., international standards setting and conformance processes;

treaty writing such as European Union and similar international agreements; processes for implementing multi-lateral technical, economic and political agreements; and technology-transfer systems).

The research has resulted in the authors' development of five extensions to Ashby's LoRV that focus on the consequences in terms of power and value distribution, of the effects of dynamic shifts in the different forms of variety and its ownership in ways that over time change the structure of a designed socio-technical system and its locus of control. Four extensions have been reported in earlier publications (Love and Cooper, 2006, Cooper and Love, 2006, and Love, 2007 forthcoming). This paper describes the fifth extension, and the application of all five extensions of Ashby's LoRV to the design of activism strategies and resisting them.

Activism and Systems

Activists persuade institutions to act in particular ways, in spite of the fact that activists do not have the formal power and more frequently belong to constituencies not part of the formal decision-making stakeholder groups. Sometimes activists win and sometimes the institutions win. Why?

Conventionally, successes and failures of activism are analyzed using critical analytical tools of the power situation and the negotiation processes. Geopolitical analysts such as Stratfor (Friedman, 2007) have professionalized these skills and techniques into tools for planning strategies to achieve preferred outcomes.

At heart, the traditional approaches to developing activism strategies have five components:

- Environmental scanning;
- Advice of 'experts';
- Simulation and modelling;
- Critical analysis (thinking situations through in terms of all the dimensions of power, resources, timing etc);
- Scenario-building.

These are supported by a raft of systems tools such as VSM, System Dynamics, Critical Systems Heuristics and second order Cybernetics.

This paper focuses on exploring the role of Ashby's Law of Variety, often claimed to be the only law that is adopted unquestioningly across all systems domains, in terms of the dynamics of power relations in complex socio-technical systems. These involve:

- Multiple constituencies – changing over time;
- Multiple sub-systems;
- Mixed ownership of sub-systems;
- Varying purposes and roles of system and sub-systems;

- Complex and dynamic distribution of formal and informal power and control.

Examples of complex socio-technical systems include: media, transport systems, retail, manufacturing, construction, religion, political systems, education, computerised information systems, design activities, and legal systems. So far we have derived five extensions to Ashby's Law of Requisite Variety that extend its role in terms of power and control in complex socio-technical environments.

These five extensions provide a simple way of understanding the structural dynamics by which power operates in very complex scenarios. From an activism perspective, the use of these extensions to Ashby's Law of Requisite Variety offer the basis for strategies in which apparently obscure or innocuous actions undertaken at one time can create changes in power relationships later, regardless of whether the initiators are in formal power positions or not.

Application of the five extensions requires thinking several levels of abstraction above the usual approach to analyzing power and political situations. Conceptualization can be viewed as 8 levels:

1. Level at which things happen;
2. Level at which people ordinarily plan what happens;
3. Level at which people analyze how people ordinarily plan what happens;
4. Level of systems models and systems thinking (situations are seen as systems and systems thinking and analysis tools are applied);
5. Level of thinking about the variety in systems and the balance between control variety, system variety and environment variety;
6. Level of thinking about the distribution of control, system and environment variety across sub-systems and their conceptual representations (especially important in terms of thinking about information systems);
7. Level of thinking about the time and location distributions of control, system and environment varieties;
8. Level of thinking about the dynamic shifts in power and control that result from the dynamics of change in the time and location distributions of control, system and environment varieties.

Level 8 is the focus of the authors' research in which the five extensions to Ashby's Law of Requisite Variety are derived and applied. The effects, however, drive down through the levels to changing practical outcomes. At other levels, the five extensions offer insights into strategies to reduce de-facto power and to modify system characteristics in ways that will modify power relations over time.

Five new extensions to Ashby's Law of Requisite Variety

The authors research has resulted in them deriving five new extensions to Ashby's LoRV that provide increased understanding of power-related development of complex socio-technical systems and new approaches for designing such systems. Four of the extensions have been reported elsewhere (Love and Cooper, 2007a, 2007b and 2007c (in press). The fifth extension is reported here for the first time. The five extensions to LoRV are:

1. For complex, layered and hierarchical systems involving multiple constituencies in which the distribution of variety generation and control is uneven across the system THEN the differing distributions of generated and controlling variety result in a structural basis for differing amounts of power and hegemonic control over the structure, evolution and distribution of benefits and costs of the system by particular constituencies.
2. For complex, layered and hierarchical systems that have a variety of typical stable states of system structure, THEN the structural system state that the system will evolve into will depend on the relative locations of subsystems generating variety and the control subsystems able to use variety to control overall system variety.
3. Where differing sub-systems of control are involved in the management of a system and some sources of control are able to increase their variety to accommodate a shortfall of requisite variety in other control systems THEN the overall distribution of control between sub-systems and constituencies will be shaped by the amount and distribution of transfer of control to the accommodating control system and its owners.
4. In complex systems in which multiple sources of variety generation and variety control interact THEN the relative effect of different forms of system variety and control variety on system behavior and system control are typically dependent on their relative transaction costs.
5. In complex systems in which multiple variable sources of variety generation and variety control interact and in which control varieties are generated dynamically to respond to changes in system varieties THEN relative control of the feedback loops driving control varieties shapes the future distribution of power and hegemonic control between sub-systems and constituencies over the structure, evolution and distribution of benefits and costs of the system.

Review of previously successful activist situations suggest that success in activism requires acting in alignment with the insights provided by the above extensions. We suggest that activists fail when they undertake activities and strategies that go against the above extensions. Success, however, requires persistence through the time for the changes in system external behaviors and shifts in power and control to occur, AND for the shifts in power and control to be sufficient.

Example of a complex socio-technical system – airports

The case below (see, also Love & Cooper, 2007) illustrates the application of the five extensions in a mixed hierarchical and non-hierarchical complex socio-technical system – an airport. The study demonstrates insights gained about the flow of power and control between the many constituencies involved.

Airports are a typical example of a complex socio-technical system. They involve people and technology. They have multiple subsystems, many of which overlap and are capable of fulfilling similar roles. For example, passengers and guests can be directed round the buildings and environs by ticket staff, security, signage, building structures etc. Airports have multiple constituencies with differing amounts of power distributed over a large number of interdependent subsystems. Distributions of power and constituencies change over time.

Airport systems involve a combination of intelligent, active and passive electronic, physical, human and animal (quarantine and security checking) systems with many processes crossing system and subsystem boundaries. Sub-systems can be outsourced so that control of some sub-systems (and intention to locally suboptimize) potentially lies outside the system in focus. System characteristics, functions and loci of control are both changing and emergent. This latter can perhaps best be seen in times of civil unrest in which external agencies (e.g., army, police, medical experts, engineering systems designers, information systems designers, security experts) can strongly shape internal system functioning and structures in ways that can shift the locus and balance of power and the ways in which benefits are distributed to constituencies.

Extension 1 to Ashby's Law: *The distribution of variety and controlling variety across constituencies shapes power relationships and distribution of benefits.* Airports are organizationally complex with a wide range of services being voluntarily and involuntarily available and used on the site. These are usually associated with specific constituencies each with their own internal management including: ticketing; passenger, luggage and freight logistics; general security; plane-related (anti-terrorism) security; quarantine services; retail and food services; parking services; customs services; immigration management; building services; engineering services relating to airport and environs; health and safety; medical services provision; religious services; engineering services relating to aircraft; engineering services relating to flying infrastructure; coordinating management groups and air traffic control. As the system evolves or is subject to internal or external changes, the amount and distribution of generated variety changes. Planned or unplanned, controlling variety dynamically changes to match the amount and distribution of generated variety. System regulation always occurs, regardless of the provision of explicit control variety and its locations. The system functions in whatever way it functions unless failure is catastrophic. The necessary implicit unintentional controlling variety results from multiple sources including relative transaction costs, system constraints, timing and sequencing issues, unplanned aspects of system structure etc. Thus, the provision of control variety does not necessarily occur in a rational way in which there is a matching between new generated variety in an area for which a subsystem is responsible and the provision of new control variety in that subsystem. For example, if there is a security problem and internal security cannot respond sufficiently, then it becomes a matter for other security systems such as police or the military. Other changes in the distribution of variety may be more prosaic. For example, if retail processes began to dominate an airport's commercial activity then the constituencies associated with retail activity would likely increase their controlling variety and in parallel, there would be a shift in the power balances. If, however, the additional controlling variety were to be supplied by another constituency or group of constituencies, e.g., those charged with expediting passenger movement to planes or those responsible for minimizing carry on luggage (both of which impact on retail activity), the outcomes and balance of power relations are likely to be different. In both cases, the benefits to passengers and other constituencies are likely to change.

Extension 2 to Ashby's Law: *In a system that can have multiple stable configurations/structures, the relative location in the system of variety generators and suppliers of control variety will influence the choice of system structure.*
In airports, management of access is a key issue for many constituencies. Access control crucially depends on accurate identification and information. The physical control of access after the usual processes of personal identification and information gathering is most easily done with physical restraints such as walls and doors. Choice of information gathering technology dominates access design. For some of the constituencies involved in access management, their primary controlling variety is related to direct inspection of an individual for identification and for gathering information about them. For other constituencies, control variety can be exerted via surrogates such as identity cards, radio frequency identification devices, luggage smell (via dogs) and uniforms. Airports can manage access in several ways. The choice of configuration is dependent on the relational positioning and ability of constituencies controlling variety to use their control variety to influence overall system variety. An example of this is the way that airlines are now managing passenger variety associated with check in processes by moving these processes earlier in the system timeline. In some cases, it is possible to 'check in' for the flight before leaving a hotel or 'check in' 'online' at home or at the airport. This is possible because airlines' contact with the variety-generating passenger is closer to the start of processes. In turn, these control variety interventions shape overall system configuration in terms of managing luggage and security and the distribution of space and logistics round the site. Contrast, for example, some small European provincial airports in the 1980s with all luggage handling, customs, and security management happening on the tarmac next to the plane. Another contrasting example is the now defunct People's Express airline, which managed ticketing variety issues by selling tickets in flight and dealing with payment defaults using the police and conventional legal processes on landing, rather than controlling access to passengers before take off.

Extension 3 to Ashby's Law: *Where shortfall in controlling variety by one constituency group or sub-system is accommodated by increase in controlling variety by another constituency/sub-system then power and control tends to be redistributed to the constituency(ies)/sub-systems(s) providing the necessary additional controlling variety.*

An example already mentioned is when one security constituency is limited in the control variety it can provide to respond to a security problem and the additional generated variety is 'mopped up' by increase in control variety of other security constituencies. Alternatively, the mopping up of excess variety can occur through actions of other constituencies. For example, the additional variety from techniques of plane hijacking was matched by engineering services' increasing their controlling variety through their design of secure cockpit doors. In these cases, there is an increased access to power and control of the distribution of benefits and to shaping the system structure by the constituencies providing the additional controlling variety.

Another example is airport design processes. The more variety is controlled in the earlier stages of airport system design, the more the outcome is likely to be similar to what was conceived and intended. Typical variety-controlling activities used by design teams include using well-tested design processes, applying design checking and validation, utilizing construction and engineering research and experience, market research, prototyping and user testing. Any outstanding variety, however, will be accommodated through alternative variety control mechanisms such as repairs, building and infrastructure design modifications (often incorporated into a later 'refurbishment' schedule), and litigation leading to compensation. These latter methods 'mop up' excess variety to result in the intended output of an airport system that functions as expected by all constituencies, particularly stakeholders. Each time variety is 'mopped up' in an unplanned way through sub-systems outside the design process, the balance between constituencies in control of the system is changed. Power becomes transferred to constituencies in different ways from those planned during the design process.

Extension 4 to Ashby's Law: *Relative effects of elements of controlling variety are dependent in a Coasian sense on their relative transaction cost.*

Recently, it was proposed security personnel who have national security clearances (e.g., FBI, CIA staff) should have expedited passage through airport security systems because their provenance has already been checked by a higher level security agency (Schneier, 2006b). In this case, the additional generating variety individuals arriving with different security status and needing security clearance can be matched by several modes of controlling variety. There are several possibilities. For example, personnel with national security clearances could be security checked the same as anyone else. They could be given free passage. They could have a special process that took into account that their clearance must be especially well checked because it is of more value to falsify. Alternatively, they could be given additional privileges and authority over and above existing airport security staff in respect of their national security clearances. In terms of systems outcomes, all of these appear to make good sense. Viewing the choices in terms of 'transaction costs', however, factors in the 'costs' of establishing and running the alternative systems along with the potentially significant additional costs associated with failure of the security system (e.g., if a terrorist obtained airport security privileges by obtaining or falsifying national security identification). In real life, the outcome was that all personnel have to pass through the standard system of airport security and undertake normal passenger security assessment regardless of their other security clearances. The reason is the relative transaction costs: the current system minimizes transaction costs overall. This situation contrasts with an alternative in which passengers can elect to be security checked by an approved external private security organization and given an individual security threat assessment and a 'registered traveller' ID that enables them to bypass the initial airport security assessment processes (New York Times News Service, 2006). This reduces a passenger's time spent in security assessment processes at the airport by about 90%, with a cost to the traveller of around $80 per year. The alternative security assessment processes, both remote and within airports, are expected to be undertaken by approved external organizations. The reasons for the viability of this change also depend on changes to transaction costs. The balance of transaction costs has shifted with the changes in the variety mix. Participating passenger's shoulder some of the transaction costs. There is a redistribution of benefits via reduced costs for the existing security providers at the airport. 'Registered Travellers' benefit by jumping the security queue. There are slightly reduced queue lines for ordinary passengers; and there is a new revenue stream for the constituencies providing the new security services. There are also likely variety changes in relation to management of airport space and passenger logistics. Again, in terms of the variety underpinning system design, all of these changes are likely to affect the relative balances of power and control in an airport ways described by the three earlier extensions to Ashby's Law.

Extension 5 to Ashby's Law: *control of the feedback loops driving control varieties shapes the future distribution of power and hegemonic control.*
Examples of feedback loops are airport management procedures, security response procedures, and airport internal and external planning such as for retail expansion, parking or new runways. Obtaining power by influencing control and ownership of feedback loops can be effective in changing the paradigms within which 'problems' are viewed. Take for example security. Passengers, airport workers and families living near an airport are concerned that security is real and effective. In contrast, for airport management, airline marketing specialists, investors and government, security considerations may be strongly influenced by concerns about maximizing profits or staying in government and thus tend towards security theatre rather than real security (Schneier, 2003, 2006a). Establishing influence in the feedback loops by which control variety such as security or airport planning are actualized results in a shift of power and control over the whole system behaviors. There are three levels at which influence over feedback loops can be undertaken. The first is direct participation in

the feedback loop process, e.g., by membership of the appropriate committees. The second is at a higher level, by influencing the processes by which feedback processes are established. This is becoming more important as feedback loops are becoming automated via artificial intelligence or algorithms. The third approach is conventional by creating additional information paths via media and lobbying to influence the actions of feedback loops.

Implications for activist strategy-making

For activists working in complex situations, the first concern is to identify whether it is layered and hierarchical. It is not only in terms of conventional hierarchical authority involving bosses and sub-ordinates that is of interest, there are many systemic aspects of hierarchy. For example, in the case of learning object systems, there are hierarchies in software and hardware subsystems (Love and Cooper, 2007). If a complex subsystem is hierarchical, the next step is to identify the distribution and 'ownership' of those subsystems creating system variety and the relative amount of variety they create – not only as a snapshot, also changing over time. In parallel, is to identify the distribution and 'ownership' of those subsystems creating control variety and the relative amount of variety they create, again as an understanding of the way these change over time. At that point, it is possible to infer from this structural information, what changes in the distribution of variety will result in changes in the balance of control.

Activists can then attempt to shift the distribution of control and system variety with subsequent shifts in the balance of control. Note: this is a much easier job than fighting for control or increasing power to the level that dominance over the other parties is possible

Learning object systems (LOS) provide a good example. The original military drivers of LOS based them directly on XML as if they were business systems. This made good sense in the highly controlled military environment. Extended into general education it became problematic – in ways that offered large commercial companies the opportunities to control the e-learning economy through proprietary middleware. In effect, control variety was being exerted at the bottom of the hierarchy and couldn't address variety emerging higher in the system. Its failure offered opportunity for a shift in power to those who could provide control variety (Extension 3). This reduced the power and influence of the free-thinking activists and those teaching and producing educational material relative to the commercial concerns. A successful activist strategy, currently being followed, is to participate in the ownership of control variety further up the hierarchy. In this case, it involves a drive for the adoption of RDF as the standardization mechanism, rather than XML. RDF provides an internationally defined top down framework. Its effect is to minimise the need for proprietary intermediate systems. Thus reduces the power and control of commercial and government institutions and redistributes some power and control of benefits to teachers, the creators of the value of the educational material.

Where complex layered hierarchical systems can have different discrete states (such as learning object systems) then activism efforts can be efficiently directed into adjusting the relative distributions and amounts of system and control varieties to trigger a change in system state (Extension 2)

An alternative activist approach is to a) identify weaknesses in control variety in situations in which activist 'owned' sub-systems can expand to fulfil any shortfalls in controlling variety, b) undertake acts that will overload existing control variety, and c) use 'owned' sub-system control variety to stabilise the system. This results in a shift of power towards the activist position (Extension 3)

An example is unions offering to undertake some of the management in complex organizations. Organizations providing outsourcing services have similar potential in arranging a shift in power and control. This latter is recognized by Japanese car companies who in response bring first tier suppliers 'into the family'.

A second order effect is when there are multiple ways of creating system variety and control variety and thus multiple ways that the system can behave and evolve. Extension 4 predicts that the system response and evolution will depend on the relative costs between alternatives of small step changes (i.e. their transaction costs). This is relatively easy to see in competition for different approaches to the provision of banking and eCommerce services. There were a large number of different potential approaches to providing, for example, online banking and its security. Each approach had different relative costs for each element of transaction for each of the constituencies (banks, tellers, administrators, service providers, customers, system designers, etc). The shakeout was to minimise overall transaction costs to create maximum sum of benefits available to constituencies. In practical terms, the relative power and control distributions meant that the banks were able to allocate most of the benefits to themselves and even increase real transaction costs to customers!

Extension 5 points to a wide variety of potential activism strategies. It describes one of the most common activist approaches. Extension 5 proposes that change in the relative balance of control of system behavior can be influenced by affecting the feedback loops by which control variety is modulated to respond to changes in system variety. Activist can influence many of these loops through approaches such as lobbying, increasing public awareness, consciousness raising, deliberately increasing system variety, increasing the need for high level control variety (laws and standards) etc.

An example of this approach is the recent activist activities in the US relating to vehicle carbon emissions by which activists acting to secure differing standards at State level resulted in requests by vehicle manufacturers to the Federal government to set national standards. The pressure was done in effect via extension 4 modality – increasing the transaction costs. Transactions costs would be increased for vehicle manufacturers if they had to satisfy different standards in different states. The upshot of the increase in system variety at state level (from the point of view of the vehicle manufacturing sub systems) was an effect on the feedback loop to increase control variety higher in the system.

Conclusion

This paper described an approach based on five extensions to Ashby's Law of Requisite Variety for gaining additional insights into the redirection of power and control in complex socio-technical systems. This fifth extension is described for the first time in this paper.

The paper illustrated the more general application of each of the five extensions to Ashby's Law of Requisite Variety via a case study of airports. It then pointed to ways similar techniques can be used in developing successful activist strategies.

References

Ashby, W. R. (1956). *An Introduction to Cybernetics* (Vol. 2nd impression). London: Chapman Hall.

Friedman, G. (2007). Stratfor. from http://www.stratfor.com/

Love, T., & Cooper, T. (2007a). Digital Eco-systems Pre-Design: Variety Analyses, System Viability and Tacit System Control Mechanisms. In E. Chang & F. K. Hussain (Eds.), *2007 Inaugural IEEE International Conference on Digital Ecosystems and Technologies 21-23 February 2007 Cairns, Australia* (pp. 452-457). Los Alamitos, CA: IEEE.

Love, T., & Cooper, T. (2007b in press forthcoming). Complex built-environment design: Four extensions to Ashby, Kybernetes.

New York Times News Service. (2006). Airport security: Buy ID card and forget the line. *New York Times News Service.*

Schneier, B. (2003). Flying on Someone Else's Airplane Ticket. *Crypto-gram Newsletter* 15 Aug 2003. Retrieved 9/8/07, 2007, from http://www.schneier.com/crypto-gram-0308.html#6

Schneier, B. (2006a, 13/8/06). Last Week's Terrorism Arrests. Retrieved 9/8/07, 2007, from http://www.schneier.com/blog/archives/2006/08/terrorism_secur.html

Schneier, B. (2006b). Screening People with Clearances. *Crypto-gram* (Oct 15 2006).

12. Systemic Scenarios: A Logical Marriage of Foresight and Systems Thinking for Organizations Entering the 'Conceptual Age'

Rod Sarah
Melbourne, AUS

Steve Tighe
Chasing Sunrises, Melbourne, AUS

For business organizations, the desire and search for competitive advantage is never ending. In the past 'information age', the purchase and use of more information earlier has been seen to provide an advantage. Today however, many organizations receive the same industry data from the same sources at the same time. In the search for competitive advantage the time is now ripe for organizations to embrace foresight. This paper proposes that in business, the 'conceptual age' is about to dawn where success will go to those organizations that can employ practices allowing them to make decisions earlier, based upon rich images of the future – the practice of foresight. If organizations are to adopt foresight then they need to begin thinking systemically. The paper outlines an approach to systemic scenarios - combining the process of scenario planning and systems thinking to deliver a logical, disciplined process for learning from the future.

Background Context

Business organizations operate within environments where the desire and search for competitive advantage is never ending and in order to survive and remain competitive organizations must anticipate and seek feedback about the changes that occur in their business environment. In the language of systems thinking, business organizations, conceptualized as a system, do not operate in a vacuum detached from the rest of the world (Flood, 1988). They are therefore not closed but operate as 'open systems' in that they are open to and exchange energy with their environments (Flood & Jackson, 1991).

Background

"Systems theorists" have been long aware of the concept of open systems theory (Emery, 1999) and the centrality of the relationship between the organization and its environment Over recent years organizations have tried to fulfil this desire for a fit between the business and its environment, and the need to learn, via the purchase and use of historical information. So much so that the Australian Market and Social Research Society claims that the industry in 2002 employed 'some 12,300 people and generated an income of A$587 million' (www.amsrs.com.au, 2007). In effect, business has been in the midst of a sort of *information age*, an age where the race has been to purchase more information and to receive the information earlier than your competitors as a source of competitive advantage. A dominant mindset has been that more and more information creates knowledge, which viewed as a source of competitive advantage.

Much has been written about the 'industrial age' and the move to an 'information age' however like previous ages or phases throughout history, perhaps the sun is about to set on the information age and usher in a new age – the conceptual age (Pink, 2005). Advancements in technology have made this traditional information as a source of competitive advantage less effective. In the interconnected world of 2007, many large organizations receive the same industry data from the same sources at the same time. In the search for competitive advantage the time is now ripe for organizations to learn from the future and to embrace foresight.

Foresight can be described as "*a universal human capacity which allows people to think ahead and consider, model, create and respond to future eventualities.*" In business, this *conceptual age* is about to dawn where success will go to those organizations that can employ practices and processes allowing them to make decisions earlier, based upon creation and recreation of *rich* images of the future – systemic scenarios. If the 'information age' was about knowledge workers, the Conceptual Age is about creators and empathizers'. The creators and empathizers of the future will be those who bring together foresight and systems thinking.

However, whilst the business environment might be right for systemic scenarios to be embraced, many challenges still lay ahead for this emerging field. The onus will be on the systems thinker to become a 'futurist' - to prove that they can evoke *rich* images of the future that provide the platform for future decisions and innovation.

It is this onus which provides the opportunity for futurists and systems thinkers to introduce the concept of systemic scenarios to the business world. Systemic scenarios combine the process of scenario planning with elements of systems thinking to deliver a logical, disciplined process for learning from the future.

Integrating Systems Thinking and Foresight

While foresight and futurists are not new to the ANZSYS community there is much to be done for foresight practitioners and systems thinkers need to embrace each other's approaches. This proposed marriage is consistent with the concept of 'diversity management' (Flood & Romm, 1996) - how we manage the diversity of issues that confront us in contemporary organizational and societal affairs.

Systemic thinking can be a foreign concept to many organizations, where the natural inclination has been to take a myopic perspective, focusing on industry specific data and data tracking. However, to gain longer term competitive advantage the organization should see itself and its industry as part of a larger, social system.

Despite what is written criticizing strategy and strategic management (Mintzberg, 1994; Mintzberg, *et al.*, 1998) many organizations are familiar with the SWOT technique. Looking inside at the organization, the SWOT technique assesses strengths and weaknesses. Looking to the environment, it assesses the opportunities and threats. As a snap-shot static analysis, it provides a perspective of organizations as 'systems in environments', a term coined by the Emery's in framing open systems theory (Emery & Trist, 1965; Emery, 1993; Emery & Purser, 1996; Emery, 1999).

While SWOT is a static analysis, it is the system dynamics methodology that provides early examples of the dynamics of strategy formulation at organizational and societal level. Developed in the late 1950s, by Jay Forrester at MIT , it came to prominence in terms of the future and scenario modelling with Limits to Growth (Meadows, *et al.*, 1972). This was preceded by World Dynamics (Forrester, 1971) and Urban Dynamics (Forrester, 1969). This work was recently updated (Meadows, *et al.*, 2005). These examples of scenario modelling set the agenda for large systems modelling in a variety of applications (Sterman 2000).

Open Systems Theory

We have already defined organizations in their environments as examples of open systems and that work came from early research in General Systems Theory (von Bertalanffy, 1950). This concept however was applied to social setting as Open Systems Theory (OST) - a body of knowledge pioneered and developed at the Tavistock Institute in the 1950s and 60s (Trist & Murray, 1993). In open system theory, organizations as systems operate within a task environment that is contained within a wider contextual environment (see Figure 1 below).

It is the environment where there are currently dramatic and discontinuous shifts in social values and community expectations. *As a consequence people are constantly changing their minds about the decisions they will make.*

Central to this idea is the concept of ecological learning (Emery, 1980) that comes from our inbuilt adaptation to our world, and our ability to extract and make sense of information of it. It is from this methodology and the concept of ecological learning that learning about and from the future can emerge. This insight is arguably central to the integration of systems thinking and foresight practice.

Cybernetics – Viable Systems Theory

Similarly, cybernetics traditions offer business this notion of openness to their environments. For business organizations, the Viable Systems Method (Beer, 1985) proposes a generic and useful framework for understanding information flows in organizations. Beer's Viable Systems Method (VSM) model can be described simply in terms of five main systems (System 3* is an information audit system and is not discussed):

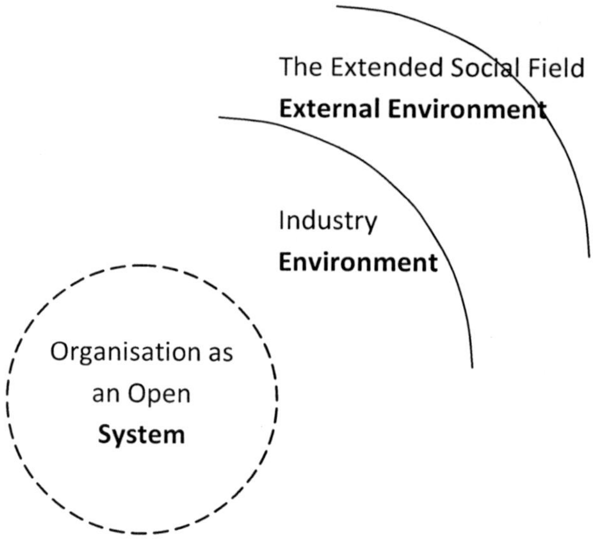

Figure 1 *Open Systems Theory*

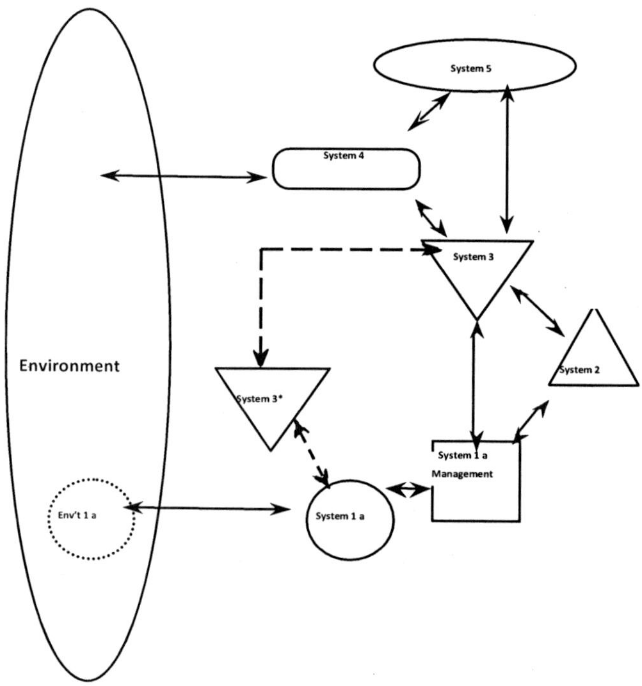

Figure 2 *Viable Systems Model*

System 5:	Policy formulating function
System 4:	Intelligence gathering function
System 3:	Control function
System 2:	Coordination function
System 1:	Operations function

Diagrammatically, it can be represented as Figure 2.

The insight from VSM and our experience in our organizations to date suggests that foresight is a System 4 activity and that the System 3-4-5 dynamic is one that without organizations will not be in-synch with their environments – they will not be viable as they will not be actively adapting to the extended social field – the environment.

Modelling (System Dynamics (SD)

Of the various systems methodologies, it is system dynamics and agent based modelling methodologies that leverage the theory of OST (and the related Search Conference approach) and VSM (the need for a System 4 function for strategic learning), integrates the collaborative and participative learning orientations and offers the practical tool to the foresight practitioner to scenario plan and develop and design ideal futures.

System dynamics adopts a top-down modelling approach whereby we seek to identify the systemic drivers as elements of systemic structure to lead to system behavior. System dynamics looks at macro structures and shifts that model whole of system outcomes and it is this examination of systemic drivers that leads to the practical joining together of the systems thinking and foresight practices and processes.

Integrating Systems Thinking and Foresight

Organizations are successful because the benefits of their goods and services are valued based on a society's existing perceptions - people perceive that the good or service satisfies their existing needs. These perceptions exist at a point in time. They also change over time, influenced by the changes in driving forces which form the elements within a social system.

Typically these driving forces can be grouped into six categories - Values, Social, Technology, Economic, Environment and Politics:

- Values refer to the things that people are attracted to or that they reject. For example, a person may be more pre-disposed towards individual or community-based values;
- Social drivers include health, education and demographic factors such as birth rates and population;
- Technology includes variables such speed, access, cost, and ongoing technology advancements;
- Economic drivers include employment, inflation, wealth, wage rates, and interest rates;
- Environmental drivers include climate, access to natural resources, and environmental damage;
- Political drivers refer to government regulation and legislation.

At the heart of futures thinking is the belief in, and search for, change and uncertainty. Futurists acknowledge two key aspects about the above social system drivers.

System drivers are dynamic

The influence of the system drivers changes over time. At any point in time certain system elements will wield more or less influence. And the outcomes produced by this system will reflect the mix of influence of the system's drivers at that point in time.

For example, in the 1960s, Australian society was dominated by traditional values where many aspects of life in the sixties reflected these values. To conduct a futures exercise to foresee how Australian society might evolve over the next forty years would require an adjustment of the influence of some of the drivers from the sixties, and the creation of scenarios based on a new 'mix' of system drivers.

System drivers are inter-related

The system drivers do not act in isolation. Just as their individual influence within the system may grow or decline, so too will their influence on the other elements within the system. It is this interaction between the system drivers that produces changes in the system (society). And it is this interaction, which gives rise to the systems concept of *emergence.* Emergence occurs when two or more elements are mixed together, and the result is one that could not have been anticipated if the elements were looked at in isolation.

As an example, a rise in the social element of education may have an impact on other elements within the system including people's values, birth rates, marriage rates, travel, legislation, etc.

Systemic Scenarios

Systems produce outcomes at a point in time. They are a reflection of the influence of the system's drivers at a point in time. This is shown visually in Figure 3 below.

Successful organizations thinking systemically will recognise that the perceptions of the dynamic society to which they deliver goods and services are likely to change in the future. We have already alluded to this above in regard to ecological learning and active adaptation. So the challenge is to foresee how these perceptions might change. This is where the role of foresight has a great opportunity to complement and work with systems thinking within business today. For it is futurists who are perhaps best placed to answer the business question: *"What consumer needs will exist in the future, and what will be the perceived benefits that my organization can deliver?"*

There are many commercial references to surveys of CEO's asking *what kept them awake at night*– a popular response is *"What will my customers want tomorrow?"* This is our territory – about searching for desirable futures and looking at the shifts in the extended social field beyond the industry environment. To answer this question, futurists essentially need to imagine into existence a future society based upon a different *mix* of system drivers. This is the role of scenario planning, an approach to learning about the future that looks at plausible, alternative futures for a particular topic based on the interplay of identified driving forces. A visual example of deriving possible needs to drivers is illustrated in Figure 3.

Once the critical driving forces have been identified, the futurist can begin constructing a future scenario world. This can be done by working through the key components of society (work, family, commuting, etc.) and bringing to life a *virtual* future world. Each of these components must be considered from the future perspective, that is, from the perspective of the system drivers wielding different influence to that which they exert today. This should lead to a future scenario that is different to that of today.

To add rigour to this process the futurist should adopt a systemic approach to building a future world. That is, they recognise that the components of the scenario are inter-related. No component of the scenario should be considered in isolation - just as the components of our lives today cannot be viewed in isolation. For example, in 2007 our approach to family life will impact our

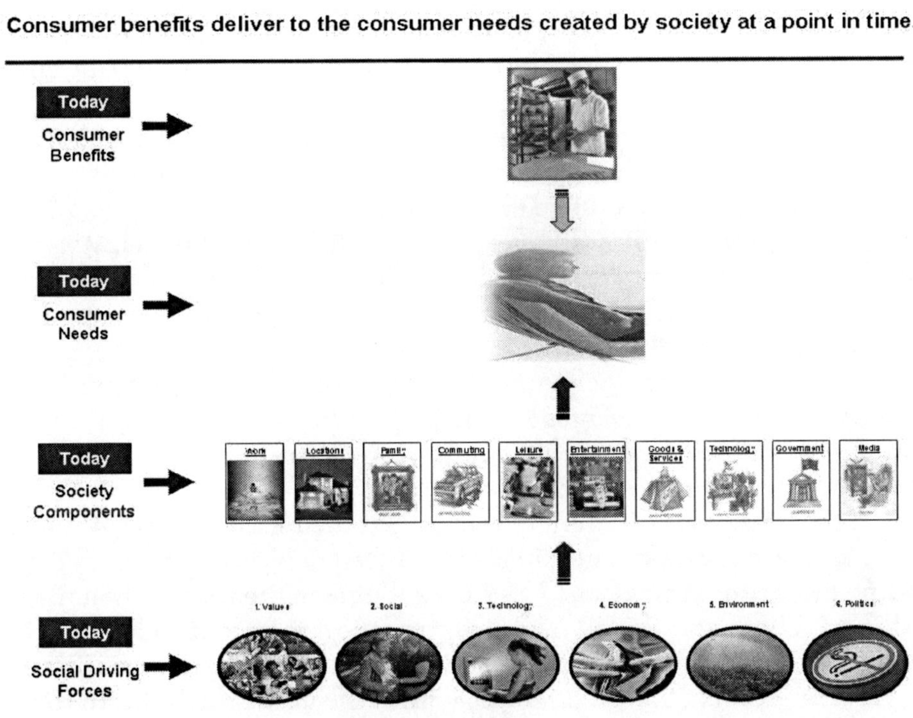

Figure 3 *Social Driving Forces: Matching Consumer Benefits to Needs*

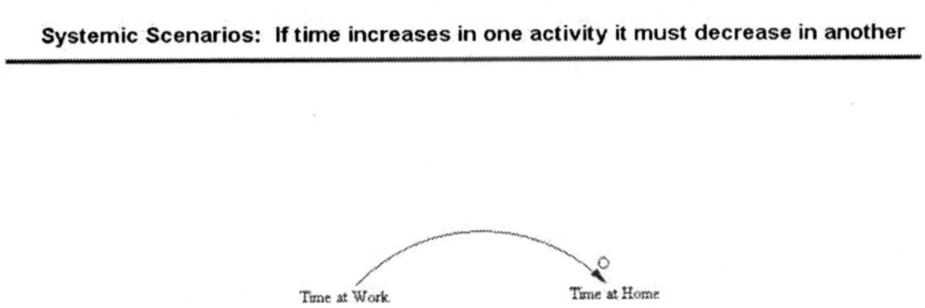

Figure 4 *The Basics of a Systems Map*

working life. And how we decide to commute might be influenced by our attitude towards the environment.

As a simple example, Figure 4 below shows a causal relationship between these two elements to begin what may become a system map – a map of the dynamics of the systemic challenge that the futurist, informed by systems thinking, is seeking to uncover.

Likewise, when constructing future scenarios we need to consider the systemic connections between social components. For example, if people are spending more time doing something in the future relative to today, then they have to be spending less time doing something else compared to today. This is a given since time is a fixed variable. Similarly, if attitudes to the environment are central to how people live in the future, this might be reflected in their means of commuting. So actions in one scenario component will impact outcomes in another component.

By taking a systemic approach the futurist ensures there is a logical consistency throughout the scenario. The futurist can then begin the search for *emergence* within the scenario. It is the concept of emergence that will provide real value for the organization when considering their future operating environment.

Futurist and systems thinker Richard Bawden described *emergence* as occurring when the *'interactions between elements give us surprising outcomes.'* That is, we get emergent properties. To illustrate his point, *'(w)hen you bring hydrogen & oxygen together it's not surprising that you get water. What is real surprising is that you get wet. There is nothing about hydrogen or oxygen that gives the indication of the essence of wetness. The combination produces a surprising outcome* (Bawden 1996).

It's this search for emergence, the search for surprising outcomes, which can surface competitive advantage for an organization. The ability of an organization to see the prospects of emergence earlier than their competitors allows them to prepare and make choices earlier.

If the scenario is different to today, then the relationships that individuals have with each component will also be different. For example, if people are spending more time at work and less time at home in the future, then their relationship with both will evolve. The emergent thinking occurs when we consider the impact of the relationship the individual has with both scenario components. Is it foreseeable that stress levels within the home might begin to rise? Is it foreseeable that divorce rates might rise? Is it foreseeable that office romances might begin to rise? This is an example of multiple perspectives and an example of a simple systems map showing different perspectives is shown as Figure 5.

These are all questions designed to search for emergent properties. As a marriage counsellor in the early eighties, you may have been encouraged to pursue your career by the results of a scenario process that foresaw increasing work hours over the next twenty years.

To assist in the search for emergence within a scenario, the futurist should consider the relationship and worldviews that each player or *actor* within the scenario has with each scenario component. As the future scenario is an adapted version of society today, each *actor* within the scenario will have adapted their behavior in a manner consistent with their worldview.

This is similar to the concept of *unintended consequences.* Unintended consequences occur in a system when an intervention aimed at fixing one *problem*, actually contributes to creating another problem. For example, in a bid to fix traffic congestion, a local council may widen a highway from two lanes to three, only for vehicle travel to become more attractive to commuters and the original problem of traffic congestion to become worse over time. This is illustrated in the scenario archetype below, *Fixes that Fail* as Figure 6.

By considering the role of actors within a scenario, and their worldviews, futurists should be able to foresee the unintended consequences or emergence within a scenario. And it is this approach that can deliver to the client genuine *consumer foresight* about the future of their industry.

The systemic approach to scenario building is but one way that futures work can begin to make a greater impact within the business world. At its core

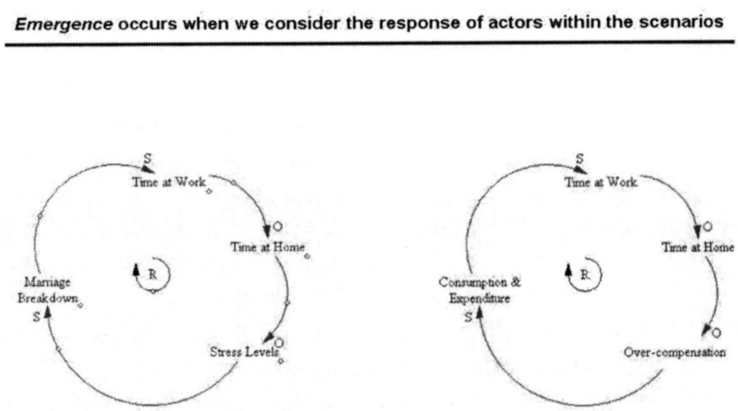

Figure 5 *Multiple Perspectives*

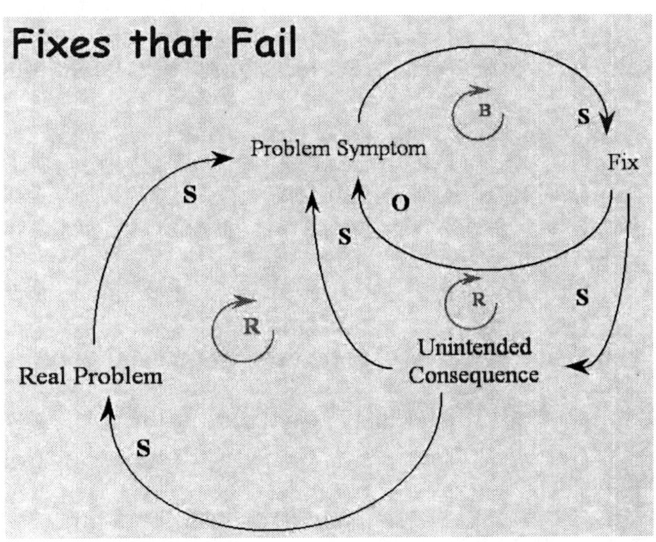

Figure 6 *Fixes that Fail Archetype*

is the recognition that the organization is an element within a broader operating environment, and that consumer change originates at the broader social level. With historical information seemingly providing less and less competitive advantage for organizations, the door that leads to futurists placing a deeper footing within the corporate world is within view. Perhaps it is the methodology of systemic scenarios that holds the key to opening such a door.

Designing Our Way Forward

The theme of the 13th ANZSYS Conference is "systemic development: local solutions in a global environment". To act more effectively locally, what we've proposed in this paper is a more formal and explicit joining together of the systems thinking communities with those of the foresight communities – in a logical marriage of expedience. Together, systems thinking and foresight provide a higher value offer to business as a joint and co-joined contribution to be able to tackle some of the global issues that confront us all. Within this emerging conceptual era, the framework is conceptual and based on systems and foresight principles rather than a mechanistic set of fixed steps which provides an enormous flexibility in its application. The outcomes are to design a more desirable future for all – as the future is unknown and cannot be controlled, what we can control however is our role and behavior in that future. And in behaving in certain ways, we create the future we want – that is, a desired future.

From an open systems perspective, systemic development is the product of the 'system in environment' interaction. The system and the environment constantly redefine each other –as we change, we change the environment. Foresight complements systems thinking and systems thinking complements foresight. It is a logical marriage where systemic scenarios as local solutions not only change the environment, but have the power to create the future we all want. Like any marriage, it is a long-term commitment to a long life together.

References

Bawden, R. (1996). The Future To You, Future of Work Foundation. Audio Tape. February 1996.

Beer, S. (1985). Diagnosing the System for Organizations. ISBN 0-471-95136-6

Emery, F. (1980). Educational Paradigms. In *Participative Design for Participative Democracy* M. Emery ISBN 073-151-484-X.

Emery, F. E. and E. L. Trist (1965). "The causal texture of organizational environments." Human Relations: ISSN 00187267 18(1): pp21-32.

Emery, M., Ed. (1993). Participative Design for Participative Democracy. ISBN 073-151-484-X.

Emery, M. (1999). Searching: The theory and practice of making cultural change. ISBN 90-272-1774-2

Emery, M. and R. Purser (1996). The Search Conference. ISBN 0-7879-0192-X

Flood, R. L. (1988). "Unleashing the "open system" metaphor." Systemic Practice and Action Research: ISSN 1573-9295 Vol 1(3): pp313-318.

Flood, R. L. and M. C. Jackson (1991). Creative Problem Solving - Total Systems Intervention. ISBN 0-471-93052-0

Flood, R. L. and N. R. A. Romm (1996). Diversity Management: triple loop learning. ISBN 0-471-96449-2

Forrester, J. W. (1969). Urban Dynamics ISBN 1-883-82339-0

Forrester, J. W. (1971). World Dynamics ISBN 0-262-56018-6

Meadows, D., Meadows, D., Randers, J. and Behrens III, W. (1972). The Limits To Growth. ISBN 0-85644-008-6

Meadows, D., Randers, J. and Meadows, D. (2005) Limits to Growth: The 30-Year Update. ISBN 1-84407-144-8

Mintzberg, H. (1994). The Rise and Fall of Strategic Planning. ISBN 0-02-921605-2

Mintzberg, H., B. Ahlstrand, et al. (1998). Strategy Safari - The Complete Guide Through the Wilds of Strategic Management. ISBN 0-273-65636-8

Pink, D. H. (2005). A Whole New Mind: Moving from the Information Age to the Conceptual Age. ISBN 1-573-22308-5

Sterman, J. D. (2000). Business Dynamics: Systems Thinking and Modeling for a Complex World. ISBN 0-07-231135-5

Trist, E. and H. Murray, Eds. (1993). The Social Engagement of Social Science. Vol. II. The Socio-Technical Perspective. ISBN 08-1228193-4.

von Bertalanffy, L. (1950). The Theory of Open Systems in Physics and Biology. In *Systems Thinking: Selected Readings*. F. E. Emery. ISBN 0-14-080396-3: pp70-85.

www.amsrs.com.au. (2007). "Australian Market & Social Research Society." Retrieved 13 April 2007.

13. A Categorical Approach to Emergency Conceptual Modeling

Qingquan Wang & Lili Rong
Institute of Systems Engineering, Dalian University of Technology, PRC

Acknowledgement

This work has been funded by the Natural Science Foundation of China (Grant No, 70571011, 70431001), as part of the Emergency Knowledge Decision-making Support project.

Emergency knowledge management is a crucial problem for emergency responses in decision making support; however there has been little guidance as to what makes effective knowledge reorganization. Conceptual modeling has played an important role in such knowledge processing. We have introduced some important notions from the type category theory, and adapted them for use in knowledge piece generation. Object, morphism, type and composition, provide a categorical conceptual model within which the knowledge pieces that form a solution for certain emergency pending problem can be reorganized.

Introduction

Quick and effective decision-making is crucial in emergency responses (Rong, 2005). There are usually improper emergent decisions, detrimental measures, and negligent acts which result in disaster expansion. One of the main factors related with decision-making is the speed and quality of acquiring knowledge, other than the reasons of unsuccessful prevention, communication, resource allocation, cooperation, and systemic limitation. Delayed and inefficacy knowledge acquisition can easily interfere effective decision-making and commanding. Therefore, there exist vital affairs on knowledge management in emergency responses. Furthermore the tendency of emergency management shows more significance and will be inclined to effective emergency knowledge management in such an information society.

Facing emergencies, decision-makers need quick knowledge supply which can make an offer of knowledge support. However in different emergency scenarios, such knowledge is mostly distributed in various emergency departments or documentation. Hence emergency knowledge piece should be collected, represented, selected, matched with requirements and integrated. The whole processing of knowledge reorganization looks as if a kind of special product production. Those emergency departments transferring plentiful emergency knowledge make up of an emergency alliance, emergency knowledge supply chain (Wang & Rong, 2007a).

Effective emergency knowledge management needs sound conceptual models. The conceptual modeling should include a mechanism to capture multidimensional semantic information, including affiliation, time span, etc.. Conceptual model is a representation (typically graphical) constructed by IS professionals of someone's or some group's perception of a real-world domain. It might be used to facilitate the design and implementation of an information system (Shanks, *et al.*, 2003).

Ontology is a description of the concepts in the universe of discourse for the purpose of enabling knowledge sharing and reuses (He & Ling, 2006). Ontology engineering has become very popular and useful in computer science (Chen, *et al.*, 2003), conceptual modeling (Sugumaran & Storey, 2002) and knowledge science (Lu, 2001). Ontology has a substantial connection with conceptual model for its structures of semantics. Effective conceptual modeling should involve the experiential knowledge of domain experts. Reasoning ability provided by ontologies can be used to analyze the relationships in emergency conceptual models. In a narrow sense, there are seldom emergency ontologies used or seldom literatures for emergency responses or decision-making support. Expect for the Crime Emergency Ontology (Wang, *et al.*, 2005). Recent years, there emerge some method researches an some tools of automatic or semi-automatic ontology building, such as TextToOnto (Maedche & Staab, 2000), OntoBuilder (Modica, *et al.*, 2001), OntoLearn (Missikoff, *et al.*, 2002).

Other then the ontology in conceptual model, there has another style of structural knowledge representation in micro-view (Wang & Rong, 2007b), named knowledge piece. With the syncretization between Knowledge piece generation based on type category theory, reviewed in section 2, and ontology engineering, we propose an emergency conceptual model that consists of two main modules, knowledge piece generation and ontology construction. Within the conceptual model, we explore a new way to semi-automatic ontology construction.

In this paper we overview the application of category theory in section 2. In section 3, we analyze the categorical characteristics of knowledge piece and build the emergency conceptual model. In section 4, we apply this model to explore a new way of semi-automatic construction of an emergency ontology. Finally, a summary of this paper is given in section 5.

Overview of Category theory application

Category theory was raised by Lawvere in 1969 on his literature "Conceptual Mathematics - A first introduction to categories". Category theory is a relatively young branch of mathematics designed to describe various structural concepts from different mathematical fields in a uniform way (ter-Hofstede, *et al.*, 1997), as pointed out by Hoare (1989), "Category theory is quite the most general and abstract branch of pure mathematics". The application of category theory has been developed with the improvement of computer science since 1980. Category theory application reached a new milepost with the publication of "Categories and Computer Science" written by Walters (1992). Category theory also has been a mathematical foundation of computer science typically in the fields of computer programming, software engineering, semantics, and artificial intelligence.

Category Theory has been introduced in the relevant fields of conceptual modeling (ter-Hofstede, *et al.*, 1997), and more and more researchers are interested in exploring the application of category theory in conceptual modeling and ontology engineering. For examples, category theory is introduced into object-oriented domain models (DeLoach & Hartrum, 2000), semantics (Lenisa, *et al.*, 2004). In the last several years, category theory has also been introduced in the field of knowledge engineering, especially in ontology engineering, in knowledge representation (Oles, 2000), the IFF category theory (meta) ontology (Kent, 2001), the meta-ontology (Johnson and Dampney, 2001), ontological methodology of domain analysis in (Poli, 2002), the ontology research (Krotzsch, *et al.*,, 2005), the ontology merging with pushout (Hitzler, *et al.*, 2005), the representation of complex data structures using ontologies in the semantic web (Colomb & Dampney, 2005), ACO (structure of meta ontology) (Herre, *et al.*, 2006), mathematical base for ontology structure (Healy & Caudell, 2006) and the geometry of knowledge with category (Brazhnik, 2007). Johnson and Dampney (2001) discussed the application of category theory as a meta-ontology, and they affirmed the semantic power of category theory.

Typed category theory is a new nontraditional category theory proposed by Ruqian Lu (2005). Main contributions of this paper are to introduce category theory into knowledge management and create a mathematic foundation for knowledge science. This improved category theory provides abstract methods of knowledge representation and knowledge processing. Compared to traditional category theory, type category theory ties all morphisms with predefined types and makes the composition of morphisms not necessarily a morphism. This theory can enhance the semantic power of knowledge processing with typed morphisms and their compositions, and can improve the speed and precision of acquiring knowledge. It also can facilitate new approaches of conceptual modeling for its sound structural characteristics.

Conceptual Modeling in Emergency Knowledge Management

Fundamental Definitions of Knowledge Piece

Composites are important phenomena that occur frequently in the real world. A composite is a thing that is composed of other things. Because conceptual models are models of reality and composites are a part of that reality, we must be able to represent composites faithfully as a basis for building databases, knowledge bases, and information systems in general (Shanks, *et al.*, 2004). Linked to the emergency knowledge decision making support, these composites form the process of knowledge reorganization. Emergency knowledge is generally dispersedly stored in emergency documents which are possessed by emergency participators. For example, emergency laws, plans and experiences. The distributed knowledge can be represented with a special structural knowledge representation. So in the emergency responses, knowledge reorganization is defined as the process of integrating knowledge pieces from distributed emergency documentation according to different incident scenarios for decision-makers in emergency responses. And the reorganization is not the processing to focus on the whole document which has been predefined with some structures. Decision-makers can take the reorganized knowledge as references like experiences from domain experts.

Knowledge usually exists with a separated way, when it is associate with a certain problem under a situation, it will be connected. Knowledge piece is a minimized, structural, discrete and indivisible knowledge component contained specific domain meanings in the process of emergency knowledge processing. Losing sight of knowledge granularity in details, knowledge piece may be one paragraph or several sentences connected closely in emergency documentation. See Figure 1. Knowledge is stored in emergency documents with pieces disorderly and unsystematic in the beginning, then it will be conceptualized with structuralized semantic information, finally these conceptualized knowledge pieces will be available to decision makers as a solution.

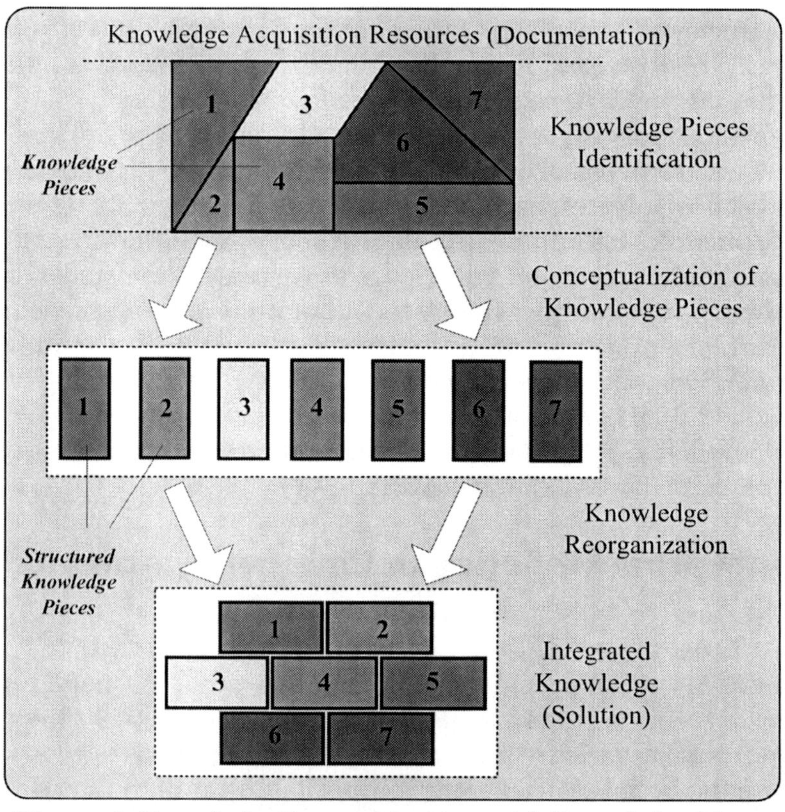

Figure 1 *Knowledge Reorganization with Knowledge Pieces*

Just as nearly 100 chemical elements combined create millions of chemical compounds, and 10 digits combined create infinite numbers; 26 letters combined create hundreds of thousands of words, and these words combined create immeasurable knowledge pieces with semantic information from various fields. Similarly the essence of knowledge management is its connecting mechanisms.

The semantic information in one paragraph is usually insufficient, because we can not obtain the whole connections among concepts in one paragraph only by its words. Therefore the representation of knowledge pieces should acquire semantic information as much as possible from experiences, so that a computer can process a knowledge piece authentically using its concepts, relationships, structures and semantic information like a micro-ontology. Supported by such micro-ontology, domain ontology can be built through the matching and integration of knowledge pieces with implicative semantic information.

We introduce the type category theory, as a universal meta-specification language, for knowledge piece representation and structure based knowledge processing. A knowledge piece is a typed category in the view of category theory. As the main element of category theory is its connection, termed morphism, these categorical knowledge pieces are consist of some classes of objects, morphisms, types, composition rules, and can be an applied bridge from category theory to knowledge science in micro view.

The main reasons for introducing this categorical knowledge pieces follow:

- It puts existing mathematical results into perspective. The geometric properties of category theory are not only in mathematics, but also in knowledge science;
- It has semantic power (Johnson & Dampney, 2001) for knowledge processing;
- It has the ability to map from one knowledge piece category to another;
- It is capable of describing complex relationships in order to avoid losing complexity of relationships (Brazhnik, 2007), i.e., information lost through relationship reduction;
- It can also be a mathematical foundation of knowledge science (Lu, 2005).

Therefore, typed category can be a very formal, structured language to described emergency knowledge.

Problems arise when we want to represent knowledge pieces, define their structures and match them for effective knowledge reorganization. Can really this method bridge the gap between natural language and conceptual model? Can we create a model that makes knowledge pieces a uniform efficient structure, and can this mode be powerful enough to capture the essence of domain concepts and their connections?

Emergency Conceptual Modeling

Facing a certain emergency problem, decision-makers usually have some urgent questions needed to be answered. For example, what is the goal of solving this problem? Which tasks have to be done to achieve the goal? Who can execute these tasks professionally and rapidly? When the executed tasks must come to an end? Where we can obtain relevant resources? How to avoid chain reactions with the occurrence of current incidents?

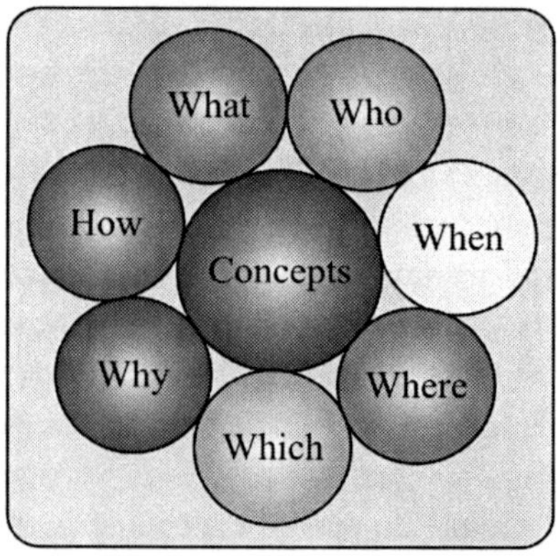

Figure 2 *Concepts Associate with Emergency Problems*

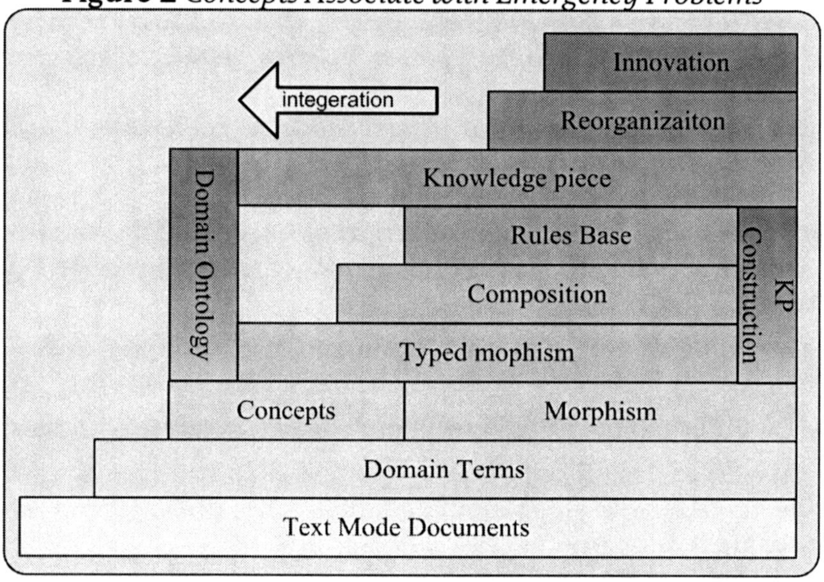

Figure 3 *Emergency Concept Model*

See Figure 2. All these questions associate with domain concepts intuitively. To find the appropriate answers or solutions for them, we obviously need sound conceptual modeling. It is a way to represent and understand the real objects and situations of emergency responses, and a way to connect with emergency documentation or experiential data. Sound conceptual modes facilitate the emergency knowledge resources not only computer-processable but also computer-understandable.

Generally, a way of conceptual modeling includes identifying concepts, descriptions of conceptual properties, identifying relations among concepts, organizing the concepts and relations in a knowledge-base (ontology generation), and then we need some intelligent approaches to retrieval and process based on the definition and syntactic and semantic. Using typed category theory based knowledge piece generation, an emergency conceptual model is proposed in Figure 3.

This conceptual mode is the emergency domain modeling to reorganize emergency knowledge for effective decision making support. It is the process from emergency documentation to integrated knowledge according various scenarios, or even facilitating knowledge innovation. Figure 3 shows that knowledge piece and ontology have similar content, and then knowledge pieces can be integrate to domain ontology with relative precise matching like building block. A knowledge piece, as mini-ontology, is a physical part of domain ontology. The generation of a knowledge piece depends on captured semantic information. In other words, integrating knowledge piece to ontology is the extension from micro semantics to macro semantics. In this model both knowledge piece and domain ontology concerns not only concepts and their relations, but also types of relations and type compositions.

Knowledge piece is consists of some classes: Object class O includes domain concepts, morphism class M the relationships among O; morphism type class T the affiliation restrictions on M; composition rule class R the relationship compositions of M. Hereby the concept set O with defined typed relationships M constitute the intension of knowledge piece, its structure; and the subset of types T and subset of composition rules R form the extension of knowledge piece. See Figure 4, it shows the relationships among these four triples. In this paper, the words of "concept" vs. "Object" and "relation" vs. "morphism" are same, but we still prefer use the word "object" and "morphism" in knowledge pieces, "concept" and "relation" in ontologies by the same token.

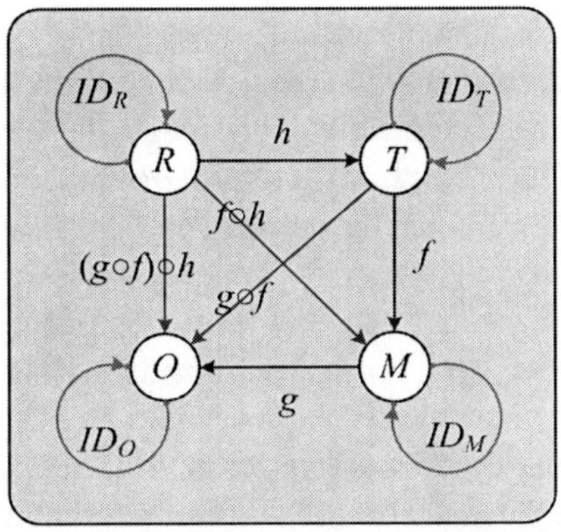

Figure 4 *Four-tuple of Knowledge Piece*

In Figure 4, the morphisms represent the relationships about restriction. Morphism g means M restricts the discrete concept set O for orderly structure of network. Concept set O has its hierarchy independently. Morphism f means T restricts the arbitrary relationships of M to semantic structure. Identity morphism ID represents a can be a reflexive zero-length relationship, like the relationship of "self-imposed". Morphism h means R restricts the attachable types of T to domain knowledge base. Morphism $f \circ h$ restricts relationship composition with experiential knowledge. Morphism $g \circ f$ restricts which pair of objects could have a typed relationship. Morphism $(g \circ f \circ h)$ restricts the concepts from the concept hierarchy.

Morphisms of a knowledge piece in categorical view can be compared to "semantic functions" between concepts. Each morphism has its special definition of type that consists of a triple: value, a domain, and a codomain. For each pair of types, there exist some conditions to combine these types to a rule of composition. Type composition means an indirect relationship about transcendental knowledge or potential relationship as innovated knowledge. Composition rules provide a means for expressing additional, but very important, semantic information in knowledge representation.

This emergency conceptual model can help represent and adjust domain knowledge empirically, create more precise knowledge matching, higher quality knowledge reorganization, facilitate simplified processing of semi-automatic ontology building, and make sense of complex relations in ontologies that need to be maintained effectively. It also allows us to perform quick and accurate retrievals of the existing knowledge pieces with sound semantic power.

Types and Complexity of Relations

Conceptual modeling is supported by defining the objects, their relations or behaviors. These relations usually are abstracted to several typical styles, such as "is-a", "has", "associate with". Condenses of relations among concepts, like over-abstracted concepts, can easily cause information loss and lower knowledge processing precision. Such losses exist in some applications of conceptual modeling and ontology engineering; and a main reason is that relations are limited in the meaning of words, not the situations these relations to be in. i.e. we should know what kinds of situations a relation fits.

Conceptual modeling is also usually confused for the real things. However, within knowledge management, relations between the concepts are also needed to be modeled. Based on the typed category theory, the types of relations and their compositions can make this modeling possible. Domain and codomain are the range appointed for a morphism to special concepts. Types have special hierarchical structures, similar with concept hierarchies, on it values for effective taxonomy. It is obviously that a morphism is an instance of its type.

Such definitions of morphisms are basic structures of knowledge piece generation, and show more characteristics of relations among concepts. With the types of morphisms, we can create a conceptual model with a considerable degree of accuracy and facilitate the automatic generation of knowledge pieces. It is the main reason that we introduce the typed category theory.

In the conceptual model, we can easily find that complexity of relations increased with the categorical definitions of them. The generation of knowledge piece depends on these typed relations more than concept themselves. The number of such morphisms and their types can be used to express similarity or tightness among concepts more precise, or even using to the quantitative knowledge piece matching. Knowledge matching is a basic processing in knowledge management.

Apparently complex relations can raise the precise and speed of emergency knowledge acquisitions, improve the Scalability of knowledge granularity and reduce the complexity in ontology maintain. However, under these type morphisms, there still have some losses or drawbacks. Table 1 shows the comparable analysis of raising complexity of relations in details.

Advantage	Drawback
More expressive and precise	More complex knowledge structures
Reduce complexity of direct links in ontology	Need other storage mode for relations
Quick search and retrieval	*
In capability to create precise models	*
Precise knowledge matching	Great complexity on knowledge matching
Explicit relations	*
Scalability of knowledge granularity	*

Table 1 *Gain from the Increased Complexity of Relation*

Conclusions and Future Work

As we have stated above, Decision-makers usually need enough background knowledge to support their Decision-Making. Most emergency knowledge is distributed in various emergency documentation, or come from different emergency departments. So knowledge needs to be reorganized according to various emergency scenarios. In this paper, a conceptual model for facilitating effective knowledge reorganization in emergency decision-making support has been presented. The conceptual model is based upon prior research on category theory in knowledge science by Ruqian Lu. Following the typed category theory, several elements, object, morphism, type, composition, are combined to the knowledge pieces, a kind of mini-ontology, that achieve relevant sufficient semantic information through morphism compositions. In a micro view, knowledge piece can bridge the gap between knowledge management and its mathematic foundation. Typed category theory help ensure we use the conceptual modeling to produce high quality knowledge integration. It can help guide how the knowledge is representation to achieve high precision of knowledge processing. And it can be used to help make sense of complex relations in ontologies that need to be maintained effectively.

Further work is required to complete the model and incorporate it into an implement station that includes knowledge piece oriented knowledge matching and OWL ontology semi-automatic generation, so that a prototype of emergency knowledge reorganization can be made. Other work dealing with mathematic foundation of knowledge processing and application of categorical constructs needs to be exploited and more knowledge processing methods examined. The research could also be extended to other fields of knowledge science.

References

Brazhnik, O. (2007). "Databases and the geometry of knowledge," *Data & Knowledge Engineering*, ISSN 0169-023X, 61(2): 207-227.

Chen, G., Lu, R.Q. and Jin Z. (2003). "Constructing virtual domain ontologies based on domain knowledge reuse," *Journal of Software*, ISSN 1000-9825, 14: 350-355.

Colomb, R.M. and Dampney, C.N.G. (2005). "An approach to ontology for institutional facts in the semantic web," *Information and Software Technology*, ISSN 0950-

5849, 47(12): 775-783.

DeLoach, S.D. and Hartrum, T.C. (2000). "A theory-based representation for object-oriented domain models," *IEEE Transactions on Software Engineering*, ISSN 0098-5589, 26: 500-517.

He, Q. and Ling, T.W. (2006). "An ontology based approach to the integration of entity-relationship schemas," *Data & Knowledge Engineering*, ISSN 0169-023X, 58: 299-326.

Healy, M. J. and Caudell, T. P. (2006) "Ontologies and worlds in category theory: Implications for neural systems", *Axiomathes*, ISSN 1122-1151, 16:165-214.

Herre, H. and Heller B., Burek P. Hoehndorf, R. Loebe, F. and Michalek, H. (2006). "General formal ontology (GFO) - A foundational ontology integrating objects and processes, Part I: Basic Principles. Onto-Med Report 8," Research Group Ontologies in Medicine, Institute of Medical Informatics, Statistics and Epidemiology, University of Leipzig.

Hitzler P., Krotzsch M., Ehrig M. and Sure Y. (2005). "What is ontology merging - a category-theoretical perspective using pushouts," *American Association for Artificial Intelligence*. ISSN: 0741-9058.

Hoare C.A.R. (1989). "Notes on an approach to category theory for computer scientists," *Constructive Methods in Computing Science*, ISBN: 978-3-540-51369-8, 55: 245-305.

Johnson, M. and Dampney, C.N.G. (2001). "On category theory as a (meta) ontology for information systems research," *ACM*, ISBN: 1-58113-377-4, pp 1-10.

Kent, R. E. (2001). "A KIF formalization of the IFF category theory ontology," *Proceedings of the IJCAI'01 Workshop on the IEEE Standard Upper Ontology*, Seattle, WA, USA.

Krotzsch M., Hitzler P., Ehrig M. and Sure Y. (2005). "Category theory in ontology research: Concrete gain from an abstract approach," http://www.aifb.uni-karlsruhe.de/Publikationen.

Lenisa M., Power J. and Watanabe H. (2004). "Category Theory for Operational Semantics," *Theoretical Computer Science*, ISSN 0304-3975, 327: 135-154.

Lu, R. Q. (2005). "Towards a mathematical theory of knowledge," *Journal of Computer Science and Technology*, ISSN 1000-9000, 20: 751-757.

Lu, R.Q. (2001). *Knowledge Science and Knowledge Engineering at the Turn of the Century*, ISBN 7302044759.

Maedche, A. and Staab, S. (2000). "The Text-To-Onto ontology learning environment," *Software Demonstration at ICCS-2000 - Eight International Conference on Conceptual Structures*, Darmstadt, Germany.

Missikoff, M., Navigli, R. and Velardi P. (2002). "Integrated approach for web ontology learning and engineering". *IEEE Computer*, ISSN 0018-9162. 35(11): 54-57.

Modica, G., Gal, A. and Hasan, M. J. (2001). "The use of machine-generated ontologies in dynamic information seeking," *Proceedings of the 9th International Conference on Cooperative Information Systems*. Heidelberg, Springer Berlin, pp 433-448.

Oles, F. J. (2000). "An application of lattice theory to knowledge representation," *Theoretical Computer Science*, ISSN 0304-3975, 249:163-196.

Poli, R. (2002). "Ontological methodology," *International Journal of Human-Computer Studies*, ISSN 1071-5819, 56: 639-664.

Rong, L. L. (2005). "Reorganizing the knowledge in government documents for quick response". *KSS'2005*, Laxenburg, Austria.

Shanks, G., Tansley, E. and Weber, R. (2003). "Using ontology to validate conceptual models," *Communications of the ACM*, ISSN 0002-0782, 46(10): 85-89.

Shanks, G., Tansley, E. and Weber, R. (2004). "Representing composites in conceptual modeling," *Communications of the ACM*, ISSN 0001-0782, 47(7): 77-80.

Sugumaran, V. and Storey, V.C. (2002). "Ontologies for conceptual modeling their creation use and management," Data & Knowledge Engineering, ISSN 0169-023X, 42: 251-271.

ter-Hofstede A.H.M., Lippe E. and van-der-Weide, T.P. (1997). "Applications of a categorical framework for conceptual data modeling". *Acta Informatica*, ISSN 0001-5903, 34: 927-963.

Walters R. F. C. (1992). Categories and Computer Science, ISBN-13: 9780521419970.

Wang Q.Q. and Rong L.L. (2007a). "Agile knowledge supply chain for emergency decision-making support," *Lecture notes in computer science*, ISSN 0302-9743, 4490: 178-185.

Wang Q.Q. and Rong L.L. (2007b). "Toward an category theoretical approach to structural knowledge representation in real-time emergency decision support system," *ICCS'07*, Beijing, China

Wang, W.J., Guo, W., Luo, Y.W., Wang, X.L. and Xu, Z.Q (2005). "The study and application of crime emergency ontology event model," *Lecture Notes in Artificial Intelligence*, ISSN 0302-9743, 3684: 806-812.

14. Building of Knowledge Organization Model for Complex Knowledge System: Support from a Novel Systemic Solution

Jiangning Wu, Zhongtuo Wang, Yonggui Wang, and **Yanzhong Dang**
Institute of Systems Engineering, Dalian University of Technology, PRC

Acknowledgement:

This work has been funded by the National Natural Science Foundation of China (NSFC) under Grant Nos. 70431001 and 70620140115.

How to organize the knowledge effectively is a key issue for carrying out all sorts of knowledge management activities. The scenario of knowledge organization could affect the performance of knowledge management to a large extent. In this paper, our researches show that the characteristic of the complex knowledge system is consistent with that of super-network model, an existing tool mainly for optimization but a novel systemic solution we contend from the system methodology level. Taking this verdict into consideration, a knowledge organization model based on super-networks for complex knowledge system is proposed. This knowledge organization super-network model integrates four different complex networks, namely, resource network, topic network, concept network and collaboration network. Obviously, the combination of the above four complex networks gets knowledge worker, knowledge object and knowledge carrier involved, which is more harmonious with actual circumstances and further makes a solid foundation for other knowledge management activities.

Introduction

Currently, effective knowledge management system has been an ad hoc focus of organizations in knowledge economic era. Dr. Larry Prusak delivered the second-generation of knowledge management in 2002, which laid emphasis on person's factor in the process of knowledge management. However, the available knowledge systems, the operation objects of knowledge management system, mainly focus on organizing of knowledge resource, namely, knowledge object, and don't take person's factor-knowledge worker into consideration. Some studies have dealt with knowledge organization by means of meta-data (Dublin Core Qualifiers; Wen, 2005). The project of Dublin Core Qualifier built index vocabulary for Web page according to meta-data, which was effective to transform the unstructured or semi-structured Internet resources into structured ones. What it focused on was the external features of the resources. Wen (2005) showed how to extract the knowledge elements from the texts and realize the knowledge organization based on knowledge elements. Knowledge elements mainly reflected the logical structure of the text resources and didn't support semantic issue of heterogeneous resources. Others have tried to solve the knowledge organization by introducing the ontology (Prabowo, *et al.*, 2002; Liu & Li, 2003; Wu, 2001). Probowo *et al.* (2002) presented automatically classified system for Web page according to ontology-based knowledge organization. Liu (2003) adopted the hierarchy and domain concepts of ontology to examine the texts and put forward an approach of multi-level topic classification. Wu (2001) combined ontology and agents to provide solutions for information organization and applications. Besides, still another group (Alexander Sigel, 2000; Bandholtz, 2002; Lavik & Nordeng, 2004; Wang & Fan, 2004) has emphasized the topic-map-based knowledge organization. After analyzing three scenarios, Sigel (2000) put forward the concepts and principles of semantic interoperation for hierarchy model of distributed information resource based on topic map. Bandholtz (2002) proposed the approach for topic map building which included thesaurus and toponymic index, and applied it to environment information network of Germany, which realized the integration of topic map with Web service. Lavik & Nordeng (2004), emphasized that in the process of BrainBank Learning, it was beneficial to introduce the personal topic map to take in the new knowledge and established the relations between knowledge nodes. Besides, Wang & Nordeng (2004) adopted topic map to organize the knowledge for designing the distributed access framework. Topic map, like ontology, aims at examining the essence and regulation of domain knowledge. However, topic map emphasizes particularly on graphic show for large amounts of non-structure information. The topic-map-based knowledge organization owns advantages for the navigation of explicit knowledge, but is lack of support for tacit knowledge.

From the view of system science, there is no doubt that knowledge system is a complex system. However, this perspective has been lost in many knowledge organization systems. The purpose of this paper is to propose a knowledge organization model for complex knowledge systems by introducing super-networks, a novel systemic solution we contend from the system methodology level. This model integrates knowledge worker, knowledge object and knowledge carrier, and will be beneficial to the other knowledge management activities, such as knowledge retrieval and navigation.

The remainder of this paper starts with a discussion of complex knowledge system in Section 2. Section 3 offers a clarification of super-networks definition and its extensive applications, and presents our new opinions on super-networks from system methodology level. Then the knowledge organization super-network model is built and analyzed in Section 4. Finally, Section 5 arrives at the conclusions and explores some possible future works.

Complex Knowledge System

Knowledge systems, as the operation objects of the knowledge management, have great influences on the performance of knowledge management. Knowledge organization system (KOS) is intended to encompass all types of schemes for organizing information and promoting knowledge management. According to the basic components of knowledge systems, we classify the development of KOS into three categories or phases, as is shown in Fig 1. The researches in the first phase focus on two separated dimensions—knowledge object and knowledge carrier. There is almost no attention for knowledge body. In the second phase, researchers and practitioners gradually notice that knowledge body also plays an important role in KOS. Then the dimension has been extended to three, but the three dimensions still keep independent. However, there is no doubt that the three factors are interactive in many knowledge management activities. Then the third phase appears and intends to integrate the knowledge worker, knowledge object and knowledge carrier. The integration of the three dimensions for KOS is the complex KOS we consider.

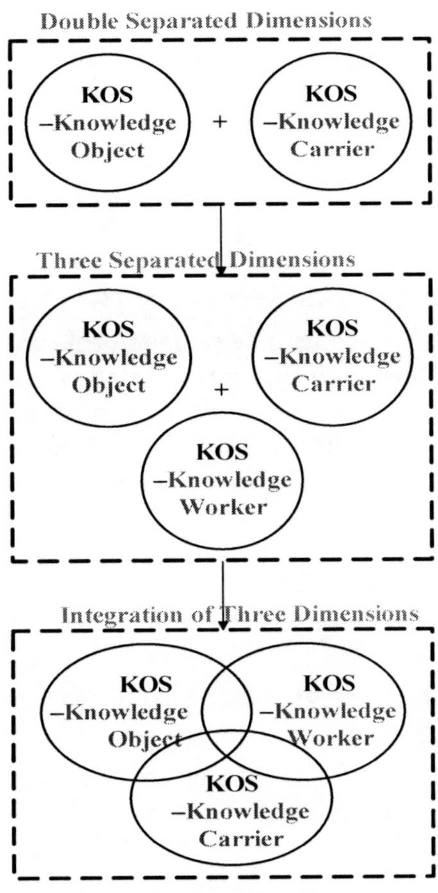

Figure 1 *KOS Development*

According to traditional systemic view, the complexity of KOS lies in the complexities of its unities, that is, the complexity of knowledge worker, knowledge object and knowledge carriers. In other words, the knowledge worker, knowledge object and knowledge carrier, themselves, are also systems. This means that there are many different types of nodes with different properties. Moreover, there are many different types of relationships between those unities, no matter the unities with the same property or different properties. The systemic view has confirmed that networks can also be regarded as a kind of typical systems (Jiang & Liu, 2005). Meanwhile, both the networks and knowledge system can be generalized as sets of nodes and relations. Therefore, networks can be adopted to represent knowledge systems. Likewise, the knowledge worker, the knowledge object and the knowledge carrier can also be transformed into the form of networks. Detailedly speaking, the knowledge worker system can be converted into collaboration network; the knowledge object system can be converted into concept network, topic network, or semantic network; the knowledge carrier system can be converted into resource network, Internet network, or navigation network etc. The corresponding relationship sets contains relationship of recognition, semantic, storage and so on.

Actually, there has been some work done to realize organization of single component of KOS by means of networks. Knowledge network, firstly proposed by Beckmann (1995), means links of organizations and activities motivating knowledge production and diffusion. Naturally, the existing work can be boiled down to the following two categories in terms of focused component:

- Network of knowledge worker. Carley (2002a, 2002b) identified that knowledge network was the linkage of people's belief and concepts. He emphasized that people was the body of the knowledge and knowledge transformation occurred among knowledge bodies.
- Network of knowledge object. The nodes in this work are regarded as concepts, knowledge nodes or discipline domains, while the edges are the relationship of classification among knowledge nodes, or the semantic among concepts etc. (Xu, *et al.*, 2003; Buzan, 1994; Zhao & Lu, 2004; Li & Pang, 2003) are all representatives of such network.

Obviously, the two above traditional networks with single type of nodes or single relationship are no longer valid for the complex knowledge system, which involves several types of nodes and relationships.

Supernetworks: A Novel Systemic View
Definition and Applications

One popular definition for super-networks is Nagurney's (2005), "Super-networks are networks that are 'above and beyond existing networks'". It consists of different types of nodes, links, and flows. Specially in the transportation networks, the nodes, links and flows represent the locations in space, connections in the form of roads, cables etc., and flows to vehicles, data etc respectively. The topological representation of the super-networks is hypergraph, which was first proposed by C. Berge (1973). The difference between the regular graph and the hypergraph lies in the types of the nodes and the properties of the edges among nodes: the regular graph usually includes one type of nodes and the edges which can only connect two nodes, while, the hypergraph contains several types of nodes and the edges which can connect several nodes each time.

Super-networks are conceptual in scope, graphical in perspective, and with the accompanying theory, predicative in nature (Nagurney & Dong, 2002). So they have extensive application prospects. Currently, super-networks with multi-layer and multi-criteria have been applied in supply chain network (Nagurney, 2002a; Stadter & Kilger, 2002; Nagurney & Dong, 2002; Nagurney, 2002b; Nagurney & Toyasaki, 2003), media-based financial networks (Daniele, 2003), multi-criteria traffic network equilibrium model (Nagurney & Dong, 2005) and so on. Besides, the existing researches with super-networks provide strong scenarios for many issues in modern information age, such as telecommunication message and decision, shopping decision etc. Almost all the applications mainly focus on a variety of decision-making problems on network. The probable process of such applications starts with setting some quantitative indexes and several pursuing objectives and then acquires a balance state by solving the corresponding variational inequalities.

A Novel Systemic Solution

Besides focusing on solving the optimization problems about super-networks, system modeling based on super-networks, which we contend from the system methodology level, should also be paid more attention to as a novel systemic view. Traditionally, the approach of system modeling includes discrete system (with lumped parameter) and continuum system (with distributed parameter) in essence, which is shown by Figure 2. The reason is that the discrete system and the continuum system are two states that can be process easily and have strong theoretical supports. Two frequently adopted means are discretization of continuum system which translates the continuous variables into discrete ones or the continuous interval into sets of discrete points, and continuation of discrete system which works in the reverse process of the discretization process.

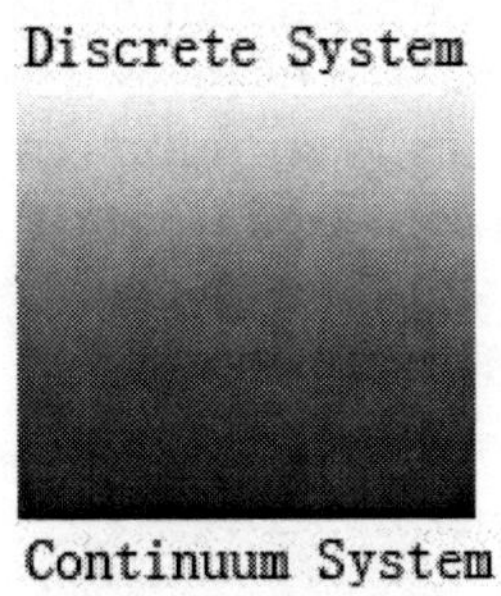

Figure 2 *Traditional System Modeling*

However, although the two extremes of system modeling have gained great achievements and much work has been done for the transformation of the two extremes, the middle state, namely, characteristic and modeling of complex system are still knotty issues. As a matter of fact, both the discretization of continuum system and continuation of discrete system are approximate treatments and will inevitably lose some information. The appearance of complex network, especially the super-networks, provides a possible route to access the modeling of the complex system with information loss as low as possible (Figure 3).

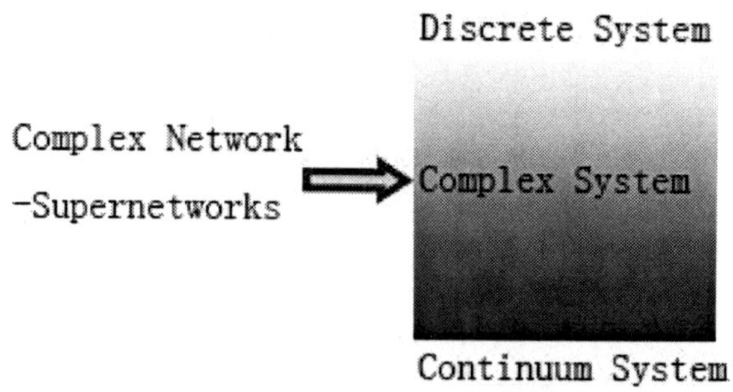

Figure 3 *Super-networks for Complex System*

The fundamental premise of systems theory or the systems approach is that systems, regardless of their specific context, share a common set of elements (Churchman, 1968; Gad & Michael, 1985): *environment, role or function, component, arrangement* and *resources*. The super-network model, derived from systemic view, is also composed of the above several factors. Especially, we give a formal definition in the form of seven-tuple for super-network model:

$$S = (N, R, N', R', F, E, Re)$$

- N is the set of nodes with the characteristic of networks and directly belonging to the whole super-network model. Typically each node also represents a complete network and has the ability to perform effectively a particular and specific task. As a matter of fact, the nodes are the sub-network of the super-networks;
- N' is the set of nodes in each sub-network. All the nodes are confined within the corresponding boundary of sub-network system;
- R is the set of hierarchy relationships among the nodes in different sub-networks. The fundamental concern of these hierarchy relationships is the balance between coordination and autonomy. Generally it is preferable to have the minimum types of relationships among the nodes. The two key dimensions of hierarchy relationships are the configuration or layout of the links among the nodes, actually the sub-networks;
- R' represents the set of all the relationships among the nodes in the same sub-network. Perhaps sometimes there are some nodes belonging to two different sub-networks. The corresponding principle for such circumstances is keeping the minimum of interdependence among the nodes from different sub-networks and the maximum of relevance among the nodes from the same sub-networks;
- The implications of F, E and Re is the same as that of traditional system theory (Churchman, 1968; Gad & Michael, 1985), that is *function, environment* and *resources* respectively: the *function*, or *role* of a system represents its intended impact on its environment. It specifies which services the system is supposed to deliver and what its goals are. It also provides the basis for evaluating the system and thus should be specified in terms that are amenable to

measurement; the *environment* is the set of entities and conditions outside of the system boundary that affects the system or is affected by it. The entities in the environment may be affected by the system, but are not controlled by it; the system *resources* are the elements that used or consumed in building and operating the system. Like the environment, resources exist outside the boundary. Resources are differentiated from the environment in that they are partially controllable. It may include people, raw materials, capital, tools and techniques, etc.

According to the formal definition of super-network model from systems theory, we propose a flow chart for super-network model as Figure 4. This flow actually a reverse process—forward identifications of components and backward building the super-networks. The basic steps can be listed as follows (the implications of N, R, N' and R' are as the aforementioned):

1. Identify the theme of super-network. This is a critical step and should not be ignored. The theme determines the range of system and is also helpful to the following tasks;
2. Identify the nodes (N) directly belonging to the theme acquired from Step 1. It's necessary to get the related experts involved in this step;
3. Identify the hierarchy relationships (R) among the sub-networks;
4. Identify the nodes types and specific representations (N') for each sub-network;
5. For each sub-network, identify all the relationships (R') among the nodes;
6. According to the nodes types and the relationships acquired from step 4 and 5, build the network model for each sub-network;
7. Build the super-network model with the hierarchy relationships R and all the sub-networks model having been built.

Building and Analysis on Knowledge Organization Super-network Model

Through the analysis above, it is obvious to arrive at the conclusion that the characteristic of complex KOS is consistent with that of super-network model. What they focus on are both the complex systems with many different types of components (some components themselves are also complete systems) and relations. This verdict makes it possible to solve the issue of knowledge organization of complex knowledge system by building super-network model. According to the proposed definition and flow chart of super-network model, we build a knowledge organization super-network model, as is illustrated in Figure 5.

This knowledge organization super-network model takes the three components—knowledge worker, knowledge object and knowledge carrier. In particular, the knowledge worker, knowledge object and knowledge carrier are transformed into the collaboration network, concept network and topic network,

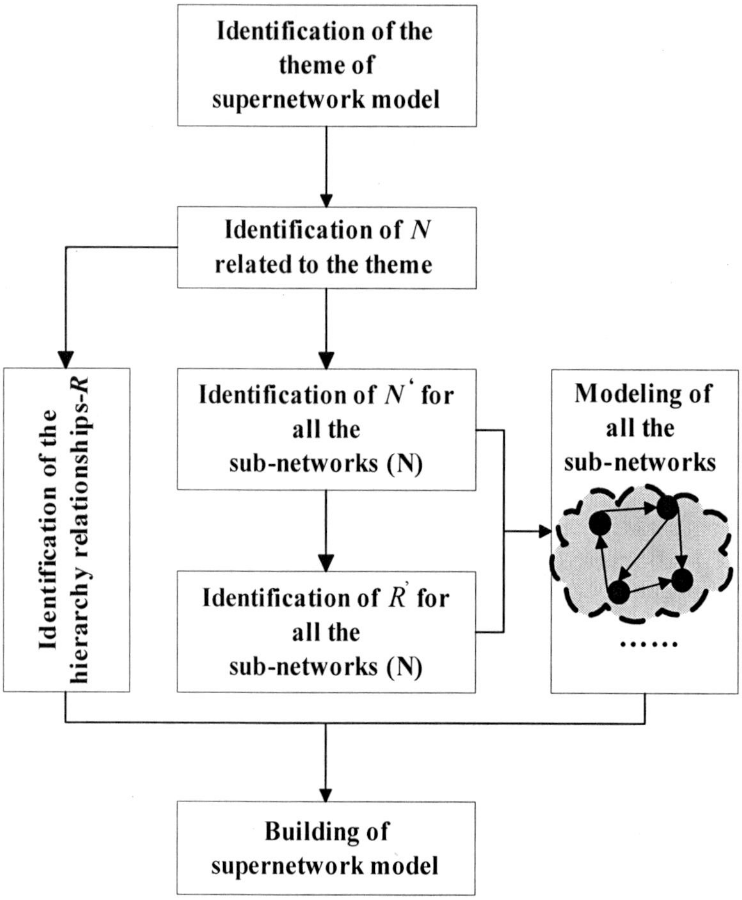

Figure 4 *Flow Chart for Supernetwork Model*

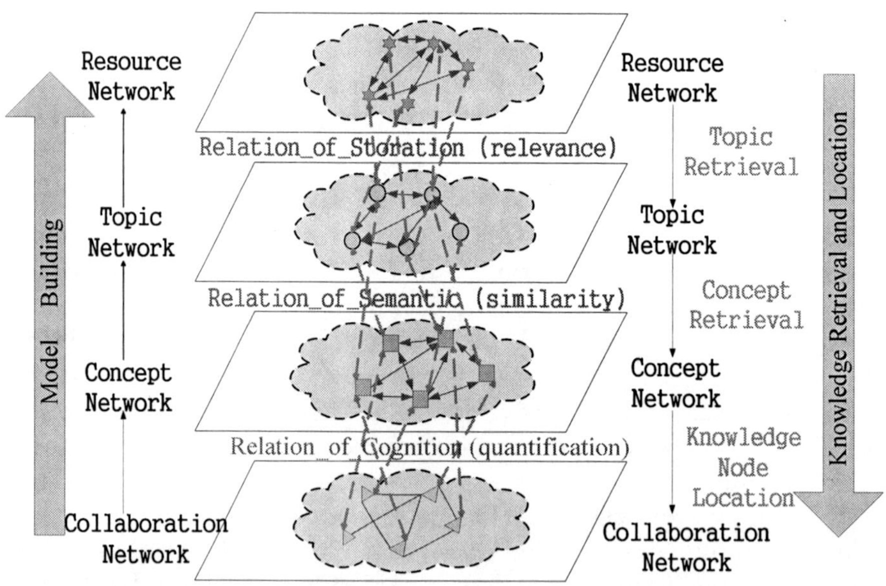

Figure 5 *Knowledge Organization Model Based on Supernetworks*

resource network respectively. The whole process of model building starts with collaboration network, which mainly emphasizes the performances of person's factor, and then integrates the other three networks—concept network, topic network and resource network into one knowledge organization super-network model.

The types of nodes and relationships in the four sub-networks are described as Table 1. The specific nodes types in our model include knowledge personnel, concepts, topics, and knowledge resources. The reason why we take the above four nodes type is that knowledge personnel, concepts, topics and knowledge resources are the reflections of the categorized four kinds of sub-networks. They are the core components in the four sub-networks. What should be pointed out is that the relationships emerged in Table 1 are all include several other sub-relationships. For instance, the relationship "semantic" in the concept network contains sub-relationships of hypernym/hyponym, synonym, part-of and so on. The specific relationships depend on the actual circumstances.

Sub-Networks	Nodes Types	Relationships Types
Collaboration Network	Knowledge Personnel	Collaboration
Concept Network	Concepts	Semantic
Topic Network	Topics	Affiliation
Resource Network	Knowledge Resources	Association

Table 1 *Types of Nodes and Relationships in the Sub-Networks*

Except the building of super-network model, we also examine one of the most important tasks in knowledge management, namely, knowledge retrieval and navigation. Knowledge retrieval intends to search for the proper knowledge object and knowledge carrier, while knowledge navigation purses to locate the knowledge worker. It's not difficult to assume that through the more graphical in perspective and integrated super-network model, many effective knowledge algorithms can be developed because there have been strong supports from well-developed graph and hypergraph theory. Besides, this model also gives possible access to optimize some knowledge management activities by defining some quantitative indexes—semantic similarity, semantic relevance, knowledge quantification etc., as are enlightened in Figure 5.

Summary and Conclusions

In this paper, we discover that the characteristic of complex KOS is consistent with that of super-network model after systemic analysis of KOS, and then based on this verdict a knowledge organization super-network model is presented. The main contributions of this paper can be boiled down to threefold: systemic analysis of the characteristic of complex KOS; emphasis of regarding super-networks as a novel systemic view to model the complex system, and definition and flow chart of super-network model; building of an integrated knowledge organization super-network model combining the three components in complex knowledge system.

For better extension of super-network model approach for complex system and implementation of the presented knowledge organization super-network model, there will be many topics to be looked into but not limited to the following ones: topological parameters of super-networks, such as closeness, residual closeness etc., derived from complex networks; knowledge quantifying approach based on allocating weights value to all the nodes in the super-networks; measurement approach of the importance of nodes in weighted super-networks; specific algorithms of knowledge nodes retrieval in weighted super-networks.

References

Alexander Sigel M.A. (2000). "Towards knowledge organization with topic maps," http://www.gca.org/papers/xmleurope2000/papers/s22-02.html.

Bandholtz T. (2002). "A taxi in knowledge land: A use case that combines topic maps and Web services in a public portal," http://62.231.133.220/idea-eks-nav/papers /03-05-03/03-05-03.html.

Beckmann M.J. (1995). "Economic models of knowledge networks," *Networks in Action*. Berlin, Heidelberg, New York, Tokyo: Springer-Verlag, ISBN-10: 0387589449, pp.159-174.

Berge C. *Graph and Hypergraph*. Amsterdam: North-Holland, ISBN: 0254-05101, 1973.

Carley K.M. (2002a). "Computational organization science: A new frontier," in *Proceedings of the National Academy of Sciences of the United States of America*. America, ISBN: 00278424, 2002(5): pp.7257-7262.

Carley K.M. (2002b). "Information technology and knowledge distribution in C3I teams," in *Proceedings of 2002, Command and Control Research and Technology Symposium*. Vienna.

Churchman C.W., (1968). *The system approach*. Dell, New York.

Daniele P., (2003). "Variational inequalities for evolutionary financial equilibrium," in: A.Nagurney (Ed.), *Innovations in Financial and Economic Networks*, Edward Elgar Publshing, Cheltenham, England, ISBN 9781843764151, pp. 84-108.

Jiang L., Liu Q.H. (2005). "Research on systems science and complex network," in *Journal of Systemic Dialectics*, ISSN 1005-6408, 13(4): pp.14-17.

Dublin Core Qualifiers, http://dublincore.org/documents/2000/07/11/dcmes-qualifiers/.

Gad A., Michael J.G. (1985). "DSS design: A systemic view of decision support," in *Journal of Communications of the ACM*, ISSN 1796-2021, 28 (10): pp.1045-1052.

Lavik S., Nordeng T.W. (2004). "BrainBank Learning - building personal topic maps as a strategy for learning," http://www.idealliance.org/papers/dx_xmle04/ papers/04-02-03 /04-02-03.html.

Li Y., Pang J.A. (2003). "Research on semantic indexing system and semantic retrieval model for Chinese medical information based on multilayer conceptual semantic network structure," in *Journal of The China society for Scientific and Technical Information*, ISSN 1000-0135, 22(4): pp.403-411.

Liu J.J., Li J.H. (2003). "Automatic topic classification of Web texts using ontology," in *Journal of Computer Engineering*, ISSN 1000-3428, 29(11): pp. 95-97.

Nagurney A., Dong J. (2002), *Super-networks: Decision-Making for the information age.*

Edward Elgar Publishers, Cheltenham, England. ISBN 1840649682.

Nagurney A., Dong J., (2005). "Management of knowledge intensive systems as supernetworks: modelling, Analysis, Computations, and Applications," in *Mathematival and Computer Modelling*, ISSN0895-7177, (3): pp.397-417.

Nagurney A., Dong J., Zhang D. (2002a), "*Supply chain network and electronic commerce: A theoretical perspective*", Netnomics, ISSN 1385-9587, 14(4): pp.187-220.

Nagurney A., Dong J., Zhang D., (2002b). "A supply chain network equilibrium model," *Transportation Research E*, ISSN 1366-5545, 38, pp.281-303.

Nagurney A., Ke K., Hancock J., Gruz K., Southwoth F. (2002). "Dynamics of supply chains:A multilevel (Logistical/ Informational/ Financial) netoork perspective," *Environment &Planning B*. ISSN 0265-8135, 29: pp.795-818.

Nagurney A., Toyasaki F. (2003). "Supply chain supernetwoeks and environmental criteria," *Transportation Research D*, ISSN 1361-9209, (8): 185-213.

Nagurney. A., Wakolbinger T. "Super-networks: An introduction to the concept and its applications with a specific focus on knowledge super-networks," *International Journal of Knowledge, Culture and Change Management*, ISSN 1447-9524, 4: pp.1523-1530.

Prabowo R., Jackson M., Burden P., Knoell H.D. (2002). "Ontology-based automatic classification for the Web pages: design, implementation and evaluation," in *Proceedings of the 3rd International Conference on Web Information Systems Engineering*, pp. 182-191.

Stadter H., Kilger C., (2002). *Supply chain management and advanced planning*. Springer-Verlag, Berlin, Germany. ISBN-10: 354043450X.

Tony B. (1994). *Mind Map*, Beijing, China: The Author's Press. ISBN 7560047815.

Wen Y.K. (2005). "Knowledge organization and retrieval based on knowledge elements," in *Journal of Computer Engineering and Applications*, ISSN 1002-8331, vol 1: pp.55-58.

Wang J., Fan Z.P. (2004). "A framework for distributed storage/retrieval of organizational knowledge based on topic maps," in *Journal ofThe China society for Scientific and Technical Information*, ISSN 1000-0135, 23(1): pp.10-14.

Wu C.G., Jiao W.P., Tian Q.J. and Shi Z.Z. (2001). "An information retrieval server based on ontology and multi-agent," in *Journal of Computer Research and Development*, ISSN 1000-1239, 38(6): pp.641-647.

Xu H.L., Kang C.Y., Liu E.SH. (2003). "The review of researches on concept mapping," in *Journal of Subject Education*, ISBN 7561727747, (3): pp.39-43.

Zhao Q.G., Lu ZH.J. (2004). "Discussion for concept map and mind map," in *Journal of CET China Educational Technology*, ISBN 1006-9860, (8): pp.42-45.

Theme 4:
Information Systems

15. A Modularization Approach for Disaster Management Decision Support Models using Agent Technology

Sohail Asghar
Shaheed Zulfikar Ali Bhutto Institute of Science and Technology, Pakistan

Integrated approach towards model management is an increasingly emerging area especially due to the timely nature of the disaster management domain. Although, significant work has been carried out in the area of model management, but there does not exist a comprehensive framework to explain the underlying techniques for model integration in the context of disaster management. Furthermore, hardly any attention has been paid to the modeling of disaster management models required for decision-making. In this paper, we examine the nature of disaster management models in the light of modern information technology techniques and tools. We then concentrate on modularization techniques and argue that these techniques can facilitate integration of models when a disastrous situation is involved. Furthermore, such technique serves as a back-bone for creating a dynamic integrated model for decision support in disaster management. Finally, an algorithm is presented to help clarify modularization techniques and criteria for integrated modeling while mitigating disasters.

Introduction

Model management is one of the most important areas and is widely recognized as a key component of decision support systems. One of the primary tasks of model management is, to perform model integration which consists of combining existing DSS models and components. It involves tasks such as connecting models and formulating composite models from existing models, collection of models, model reuse and analysis. Model integration, over the past two decades, has emerged as one of the most widely researched topics in the field of model management (Asghar, Alahakoon, and Churilov, 2006).

In order to produce effective decision making in disaster management that can also easily maintain adaptiveness, special consideration is given to the modular approach for the development of decision support systems for disaster management.

The purpose of modularization is to provide the flexibility to organize and adapt a tailored DSS model for decision support in disaster management according to the needs of the disaster. The main model is decomposed into smaller sub-routines or loosely coupled (as independent of each other as possible) modules, which are functionally well-defined and self-contained. The main advantage of breaking down a model into a modular structure is, to provide flexibility, reusability and modularization to the field of model management. Using this approach, one can easily determine a particular DSS need for which we might execute a complete model. Instead of that, only one modular routine can be executed to fulfil the desired need. However, the development of this methodology of a "loosely coupled module structure" for DSS models makes it easier to apply to various complex disasters-related issues. Although modularization and object-oriented approach to DSS already exist in the literature, it has not been applied for model integration especially in the field of disaster management. We have shown the basis of modular decomposition in the proposed framework which is a based on the agent technology.

The structure of the paper is as follows: Section 2 discusses the previous work carried out towards the development of A Multi-Layered Architecture for Disaster Management Decision Support Systems – MILD DSS. Section 3 elaborates on the critical components of the proposed framework with special emphases on the characteristics of such components and modules. Section 4 articulates the plug-in and implementation aspects of the proposed framework for modularization and highlighting the role of such plug-in structure to the MILD DSS. Finally, Section 5 concludes the paper and sets the directions for future research.

Overview of Previous Work

In this section, we provide an overview of the integrated model generated by the MILD DSS to gain the understanding of the model which needs to be protected. The Oxford English Dictionary gives several definitions of the word "disaster". First, it is defined as "a sudden accident or a natural catastrophe that causes great damage or loss of life"; second, as "an event or fact leading to ruin or failure". The multidisciplinary nature and increasing complexity of the disaster management area has resulted in the increased use of Decision Support Systems (DSS). The need for decision-making in disaster management often requires a decision support system to fulfil the decision needs. Disaster Management Decision Support Systems (DMDSS) are dedicated to supporting decision-making in disaster management and are considered to be complex applications possibly integrating advanced computing techniques and requiring state-of-the-art research and development efforts. Disaster management issues generally possess the following characteristics:

- A global perspective;
- The uncertainty involved in decision-making;
- A changing nature;
- Dynamic and multi-criteria decision support needs;
- Highly interdisciplinary.

Due to such characteristics, decision support systems for disaster management have gained increased consideration by the research and scientific community. In this context, finding a possible solution to develop an effective and efficient DSS for disaster management is an appalling and challenging area of research. The literature reveals that currently the following problems are associated with the existing DMDSS:

- It is evident from the literature that over the past two decades, a large number of decision support systems have been produced by various developers on the basis of specific needs in specific disaster types (Tufekci, 1995; Pourvakhshouri & Mansor, 2003). The problem in developing DMDSS is that a DSS developed on the basis of specific needs cannot be adapted to handle the various activities of a disaster with different characteristics. Furthermore, these systems cannot be readily modified with the changing needs of disaster management because they are developed to fulfill the specific and targeted needs of decision-making in a particular disaster;
- The traditional DMDSS do not consider common and environmental factors across diverse disasters for effective decision-making in a new disaster situation. In the disaster management domain, a large number of DSS models are available. Such models do not handle mutually exclusive problems and as such much overlap appears in their functionality. It also shows that most of the DMDSS overlap the functionality for example, the simulation model for emergency evacuation (Pidd, De Silva & Eglese, 1993) providing decision support for evacuation planning (Silva, 2001), an integrated emergency model DSS for hurricane;
- Emergencies (Tufekci, 1995), and regional evacuation modeling systems (Tufekci & Kisko, 1991), are all designed for the same functionality (evacuation). Such overlapping of functionality justifies the need for integrating DSS in disaster management;
- Since one disaster may trigger another (for example, a volcanic eruption may lead to forest fires), with the requirement of diverse DSS needs, it is quite possible that a number of different models may have to be used simultaneously;
- There can be certain situations in which user needs can be fulfilled by executing one or more subroutines or modules. Therefore, when a new situation comes along, subroutines can be reused to provide the solution for a new problem. For example, the evacuation planning system (Pidd, De Silva & Eglese, 1993) can be decomposed into modular subroutines; the decision support need in flood management "timely distribution of flood emergency information" can be fulfilled by execution of a few of the subroutine of evacuation DSS system instead of developing the complete DSS model from scratch. The existing DMDSS lacks such functionality;
- Therefore, we raised the above-mentioned problems associated with the existing DMDSS based on the analysis of the previously developed systems. To address these problems, we need a framework which can provide the fol-

lowing functionalities: The framework should not intend to provide decision-making for a only specific decision support need, for example, an evacuation modeling system which is capable of providing decision support to fulfill only the evacuation decision need during a disaster. Rather, we need a DMDSS which can be adaptive and tailored according to the dynamic needs of a disaster (Asghar, Alahakoon & Churilov 2007; Asghar, Alahakoon & Churilov, 2006);

- The framework can easily reuse existing subroutines/DSS models/DSS sub-models to overcome the overlapping problems. The justification for the reusability is an important issue which needs to be addressed due to the fact that different subroutines may serve the same decision support need in spite of the fact that there may be some common needs across different disasters. And more importantly, it is the common environment which becomes the basis for the reusability;
- Because of the large number of activities and issues within disaster management different DSS models were developed to fulfil the decision support needs. Therefore, multiple models are required in order to provide decision-making in disaster management. Model integration is suggested as a better alternative approach. Hence, we need a framework which can support model integration for effective decision-making.

We proposed an architecture which overcomes these limitations of the existing DMDSS and possesses the above-mentioned functionalities. The multi-layered architecture designed for such purposes is called MILD DSS which can improve the efficiency and reusability of traditional DSS developed for disaster management. The objective of the architecture was to enhance the effectiveness of the traditional DMDSS development process by integrating decomposed modular DMDSS subroutines focused on a disaster scenario. Such subroutines are selected on the basis of the needs classification scheme (Alahakoon, and Churilov, 2006). The proposed architecture is adaptive through the selection of subroutines according to the changing needs of decision-makers in the process of decision-making. It produces an integrated model which provides support that fits current user's decision support needs focused on a disaster situation. Therefore, the functionality of the architecture can be summarized as facilitating the DSS developer by selecting functionally -independent modular subroutines from the disaster management domain to produce an integrated model based for a disaster scenario. It is emphasized that the integrated model is not based on a particular decision support need but is developed on the basis of dynamic decision needs of a disaster. The architecture of the MILD DSS is shown in Figure 1 which consists of three layers: independent, dependent and interface.

The functionality of the layers and the components of the proposed architecture are not discussed here as this is beyond the scope of this paper. Further details of the architecture can be found in (Asghar, Alahakoon, and Churilov, 2006). A prototype was developed to validate the conceptual model and tested on the basis of a wild land fire case study known as the Hayman Fire (Graham, 2003). The Hayman Fire is a good source of a large number of decision support needs which can be fed into the MILD DSS to generate a dynamic integrated model based on such decision support needs.

In order to support the decision- making in the disaster management domain, the integrated model achieved using MILD DSS possesses the following characteristics:

- Extensibility, which in a DMDSS refers to the ability to generate new DMDSSs, for new applications by modifying or building upon previous DMDSSs. The obvious advantage of such capability comes in terms of minimal cost and reduced development efforts. We emphasize that MILD DSS is designed to serve the extensibility;
- The knowledge base of the MILD DSS is composed of existing modular subroutines developed for DMDSS (but labeled and grouped according to needs classification scheme). The integrated model is generated using such subroutines for different applications eliminating the need for duplication and reducing the possibility of errors and inconsistencies;
- Previously designed and developed DMDSS models are focused to serve a specific decision task. For example, some DSS models have been developed and are currently used for flood risk assessment and management such as RAMFLOOD (Onate, and Piazzese, 2003). But the MILD DSS is

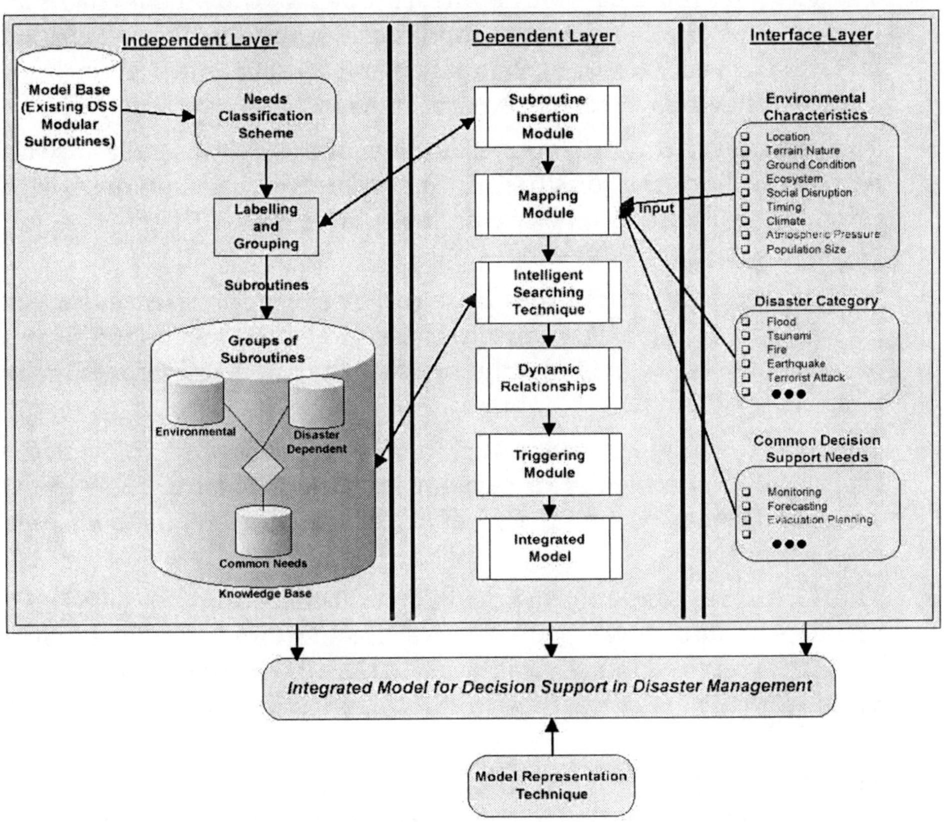

Figure 1 *A Conceptual Architecture of MILDDSS*

not designed to fulfill specific decision support needs and requirements of disaster management but focuses on generating an integrated model based on dynamic decision needs. Therefore, the MILD DSS generates modular subroutines (integrated model) required for decision tasks for different disaster scenario. The concept of an integrated model is not to develop a single DSS model that addresses all decision support needs, but to facilitate the design of such an integrated model;

- The focus of the MILD DSS is to propose an integrated model that effectively supports decision-making. The effectiveness comes with the use of modular DMDSS subroutines achieved on the basis of dynamic decision needs;
- The MILD DSS is easy to use and better addresses user decision support needs for a given scenario;
- The modular subroutine selection criteria, associated with the MILD DSS (based on the needs classification scheme) is a significant contribution towards decision-making and adds more value to traditional decision-making approaches;
- The datasets attached with modular subroutines of the integrated model are available to execute the groups of subroutines, independently, to validate the concept of loosely coupled independent subroutines;
- The MILD is a multi-layered architecture and its knowledge base is a collection of diverse independent modular subroutines. The user interface is crafted in such a way that the analyst or DSS developer has the impression that they are interacting with a single, coherent system;
- To utilize an existing model saves on development time, but it sometimes requires additional efforts to link up existing models. Our approach also provides flexibility to replace existing subroutines with new ones when decision support needs change;
- Had the modular subroutines been run by other approaches (for example, the simple manual approach) these integrated results might not be obtained so readily. It is highlighted that the integrated model makes it possible to obtain new insights;
- The need for an integrated model in disaster management is due to the high level of complexity of decision-making problems, their multiple scales of description, and the diversity of available independent specific models;
- The decision makers and DSS developers are becoming the heaviest user of independently developed DSS models and subroutines. The availability of an integrated model and the MILD DSS framework allows them to profit from the use of existing modular subroutines and to evaluate their appropriateness;
- The MILD DSS is designed to make it easier for DSS developers to develop an integrated model with better outcomes in terms of model adoption, peer review and utilization.

A Proposed Framework for Modular Modelling

Fully automatic modularization techniques are useful for development of integrated model for decision support in disaster management. Such techniques help to improve the design by using modular approaches. Modularity is an approach to break a problem into smaller parts or modules so that the modules put together can perform as a system. With modularity, it is possible that a module may turn out to be a part in another solution to a problem. The major advantage of using a modular approach in DSS development is that modules can be reused in order to develop a hybrid DSS model for new applications. Our approach can be considered a preliminary step before performing model integration and composition. The simplicity and flexibility of the approach assist the process of model integration.

In addition, the modular approach greatly facilitates the integration of existing models. For example, some DSS models have been developed and are currently used for flood forecasting. If we decompose this into smaller modules using our proposed technique, few of these flood forecasting models can be used to establish wild-fire forecasting DSS model. The modularization approach was applied to solve the problem and we find it a promising technique for modeling complex decision support systems. It helps to reduce the complexity of the DSS by decomposing the models into smaller sub-routines at a more detailed level.

Figure 2 shows the framework of proposed modularization for disaster management models. This framework has the following main components:

Model Base: The model based is composed of existing decision support systems models developed for disaster management. For example,

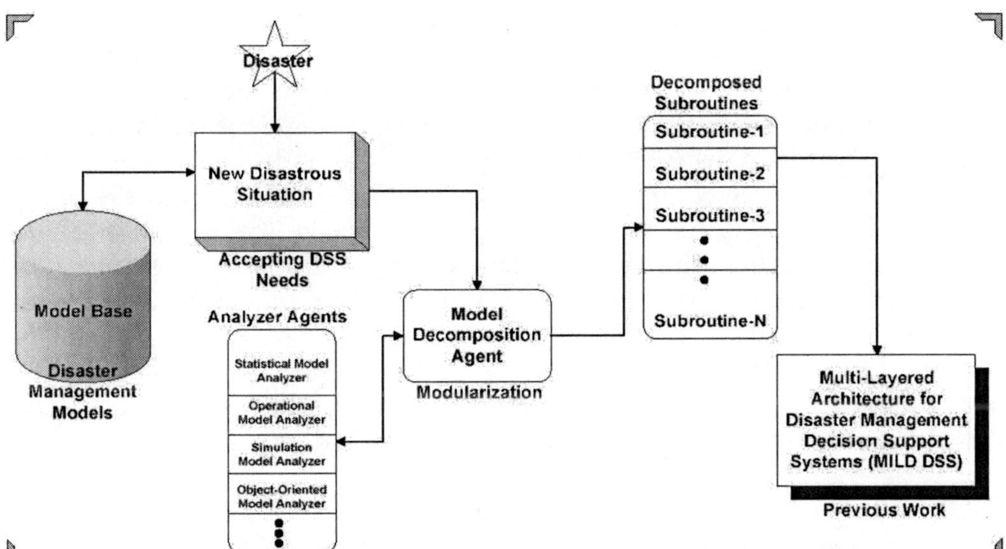

Figure 2 *A Proposed Framework for Modularization of Disaster Management Models using Agents Technology*

$$D_i = R\left(T_i + \frac{e^{-a_a T_i}}{a_a} - \frac{1}{a_a}\right) + D_{i+1}$$

The structure of the model base contains the following:

- The model, for example, equation ;
- Description and brief explanation of a subroutine;
- Description of the parameters of a subroutine (input and output details);
- Reference and source of a subroutine;
- Parent model of a subroutine;
- Analyzer Agents: The decision support models for disaster management are of different categories such as statistical, operational, relational, object-oriented and simulations. We have declared an agent called analyzer agent to represent these different categories of models. The functionality of such an agent would be true representation of these;
- Categories and will further support model decomposition agent. For further reading on agents technology please refer to (Olguin, Delgado, and Ricarte, 2000; Boudaoud, and McCathie-Nevile, 2002).

Model Decomposition Agents: This core agent acts as back-bone of the framework. It performs the actual modularization using the following criteria: There are two levels of modularization: first, we have to decide which modules are disaster dependent and which are disaster independent; the second is the decision to separately identify environment depended and independent modules. As shown in Figure 3, we can emphasize that Model A consists of Module A, which is always a pair of one dependency level and one environmental level. The dependency level consists of disaster independent and dependent modules and the environmental level contains environment dependent and independent modules. Initially, in decision support systems, the traditional needs and environmental needs are combined. By the separation shown in Figure 4, we are trying to segregate traditional and environmental needs. The advantage of such modularization is that different modules, which describe the same functionality, can be reused easily. Therefore it facilitates the development of a new model from existing modular.

Decomposed Subroutines: The decomposed subroutines on the basis of modularization are stored in a database and further fed into the MILD SSS.

MILD DSS: The MILD DSS has already been explained in section 2. It uses the modular decomposed subroutines and then performs selection of the subroutines. Using Employing the core functionality of the architecture it generates the dynamic integrated model for decision support in disaster management.

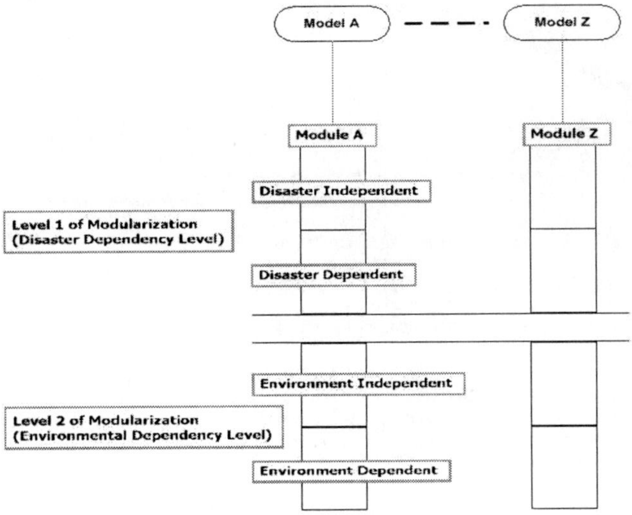

Figure 3 *Domain Independent Modular Decomposition Structure*

Modularization as Plug-in for MILD DSS

The criteria for modularization and major components of the framework are defined. We focus our attention on developing algorithm that makes modularization happen and produces modular subroutines based on the proposed criteria. Figure 4 depicts the algorithm for modularization of decision support model developed for disaster management activities. The algorithm produces the desired results but works for small models only.

The above-mentioned proposed framework for modularization serves as a plug-in which is built on top of the MILD DSS (described in section 2). This extension implements the overall functionality of the MILD DSS. The extended work of modularization is developed using agent technology. Such a plug-in also provides a consolidated view of the overall functionality to generate integrated model for decision support in disaster management.

Conclusions and Future Research Directions

The proposed framework for modularization is very useful and serves as a plug-in to main MILD DSS architecture designed and developed to obtain dynamic integrated model for decision support in disaster management. It comprises of the following main components: (a) model base; (b) analyzer agents; (c) decomposition agents; and (d) decomposed subroutines. The criteria for modularization has been suggested and validated by plugging in the MILD DSS. One of the main algorithms has also been elaborated for completeness. In future, we will demonstrate the usefulness of the complete systems with larger decision support models for disaster management.

References

Dolk, D. and J. Kottermann, Model Integration and a Theory of Models. Decision Support Systems, 1993. 9(1): p. 51-63.

Gagliardi, M. and C. Spera, Towards a Formal Theory of Model Integration. Annals of

```
Initialize global variables DISASTER DEPENDENT AND ENVIRONMENT
DEPENDENT LEVEL
Perform a depth first left most traversal of the tree
itarting at the toplevel node to find the decision support model existence.
:or each node x (
if (x, node-type == DISASTER_DEPENDENT_lEVEL)
COLLECT THE COMPLETE MODEL;
BREAK THE MODEL INTO
DISASTER_DEPENDENT &
DISASTER INDEPENDENT SUBROUTINES;
retum;
else if (x.node-type == ENVIRONMENT_DEPENDENT_LEVEL)
COLLECT THE COMPLETE MODEL;
BREAK THE MODEL INTO ENVIRONMENT_DEPENDENT AND
ENVIRONMENT_INTEPENDENT;
retum;
else
failure-prob = DYNAMIC_MODULAR_SOLVER()
failure-prob = STATIC_MODULAR_SOLVER ();
x.node-type = BASIC_EVENT;
x.inputs.clear(); ))
```

Figure 4 *Algorithm for Modularization Criteria Performed by Modular Decomposition Agent*

Operations Research, 1995. 58: p. 405-440.

Basu, A. and R. Blanning, Model Integration using Meta-graphs. Information Systems Research, 1994. 5: p. 195-218.

Tsai, C., Model Integration using SML. Decision Support Systems, 1998. 22: p. 355-377.

Geoffrion, A. Reusing Structured Models via Model Integration. in Proceedings of Twenty-Second Annual Hawaii International Conference on the System Sciences. 1989. IEEE Computer Society, pp. 601-611, 1989.

Chari, K., Model Composition using Filter Spaces. Information Systems Research, 2002. 13(1): p. 15-35.

Shiba, N., J. Jima, and K. Ohta, Model Integration for Managerial Decision support using a Model Description Language with a Formal Semantics. Cybernetics and Systems: An International Journal, 1999. 30: p. 761-781.

Boardman, Wholes and Parts -A Soft Systems Approach, . IEEE Transactions: Systems Man and Cybernetics, 1995. 25(7).

Tufekci, S., An Integrated Emergency Management Decision Support System for Hurricane Emergencies. Safety Science, 1995. 20: p. 39-48.

Cheng, M. and C. HoKo, Computer-aided DSS for Hillside Safety Monitoring. Automation in Construction, 2002. 11: p. 453-466.

Onate, E. and J. Piazzese, RAMFLOOD Project: Decision Support System for Risk Assessment and Management of Floods. 2005, International Center for Numerical Methods in Engineering (CIMNE), Gran Capitán, s/n, Campus Norte UPC, 08034 Barcelona, Spain. Available: http://www.eu-lat.org/eenviron/Onate.pdf. Accessed: Feb. 2005.

Pourvakhshouri, S. and S. Mansor, Decision Support System in Oil Spill Cases. Disaster Prevention and Management, 2003. 12(3): p. 217-221.

Pidd, M., F. De Silva, and R. Eglese, A Simulation Model for Emergency Evacuation. European Journal of Operational Research, 1996. 90: p. 413-419.

Silva, F.N.d., Providing decision support for evacuation planning: a challenge in integrating technologies. Disaster Prevention and Management, 2001. 10(1): p. 11-20.

Tufekci, S. and T. Kisko, Regional Evacuation Modeling System (REMS): A Decision Support System for Emergency Area Evacuations. Computers and Industrial Engineering, 1991. 21(1-4): p. 89-93.

Asghar, S., D. Alahakoon, and L. Churilov, A Modular Subroutine Selection Process in Disaster Management Based on a Needs Classification Scheme. ACCEPTED for publication in the INTERNATIONAL JOURNAL OF INTERNET AND ENTERPRISE MANAGEMENT, 2007.

Asghar, S., D. Alahakoon, and L. Churilov, Categorization of Disaster Decision Support Needs for the Development of an Integrated Model for DMDSS. Accepted for Publication in the International Journal of Information Technology and Decision Making (IJITDM), 2006.

Asghar S., Alahakoon D., and C. L. A Modular Subroutine Selection Process Based on Needs Classification Scheme. in Proceedings of the11th Annual Conference of Asia-Pacific Decision Science Institute (APDSI 2006). 2006. June 14-18, 2006, Hong Kong.

Asghar S., Alahakoon D., and C. L. A Multi-Layered Architecture for the Decision Support in Disaster Management. in Proceedings of the 4th International Conference on Information Science Technology and Management (CISTM 2006). 2006. July 16-18, 2006, Chandigarh, India.

Graham, R.T., Hayman Fire Case Study. 2003, Gen. Tech. Rep. RMRS-GTR-114. Ogden, UT: U.S. Department of Agriculture, Forest Service, Rocky Mountain Research Station. 396 p.

Martin, M. and B. Gemma, A Multi-agent System for Emergency Decision Support, in Intelligent Data Engineering and Automated Learning. 2003: Springer-Verlag. Lecture Notes in Computer Science 2690. Pág. 43-51. Hong Kong, March 2003. IDEAL.

Olguin, C., Delgado, A., Ricarte, L., An Agent Infrastructure to set Collaborative Environments. Educational Technology & Society, 2000. 3: p. 65-73.

Peña, C.I., Marzo, J.L., & de la Rosa, J.L. . Intelligent Agents in a Teaching and Learning Environment on the Web. . in Proceedings of the 2nd International Conference on Advanced Learning Technologies (ICALT2002). 2002. September 9-12. Kazan, Russia. P. Kommers, V. Petrushin, Kinshuk, & I. Galeev (eds.), IEEE Press.

Boudaoud, K. and C. McCathieNevile. An Intelligent Agent-based Model for Security Management. in Proceedings of the Seventh International Symposium on Computers and Communications (ISCC'02). 2002. IEEE, Computer Society. 1-4 July 2002 Page(s):877 -882

16. Winning the IT Security Battle with Guerilla Tactics

Danuvasin Charoen
National Institute of Development Administration, Bangkok, Thailand

Lorne Olfman and **Terry Ryan**
Claremont Graduate University, USA

We recently completed an action research study in our organization to successfully implement a training program to improve system users' behavior related to security. The study was initiated after we decided to increase the minimum "password" length from 8 to 15 characters. We used a unique approach by designing training for creating passwords to fit with theories pertaining to human memory. In addition, we also created and delivered security awareness training. Most end users who took the training reported that after training they were able to use strong passwords without writing them down. Requests to the help desk for password resets due to forgetting decreased. Most users also reported that they are much more aware of security threats. Another practical outcome of the study was that the training we conducted had a positive organizational impact by increasing awareness of security issues in a short time period and at little cost.

Introduction

At CollIT we provide information technology services to academic institutions, such as universities and colleges. Assuring computer security is a critical strategic issue for us. Providing IT securely is at the heart of our business model, and it is critical to attaining the customer trust we need to be able to renew existing contracts and add new ones. In addition, because we serve many similar customers, we have the opportunity to apply what we learn in working on security with one customer to our work with other customers. We gain economy of scale by sharing knowledge across various IT organizations as we do our work. As a result, we view the development and sharing of computer security knowledge important in gaining and keeping competitive advantage. A breach of security can have disastrous consequences for our customers and for us.

A large number of our clients are small, private institutions that strain to meet the increasing burden posed by information security. It is important to identify low cost, yet effective, tactics to improve security at client sites. We must balance a number of competing priorities during the life of a contract (ERP implementations, network upgrades, etc.). We use these "guerilla" tactics to improve security even with a lack of funding for large-scale security initiatives. In this paper, we report how we implemented a successful security-training action research project at one academic institution. The project improved users' behaviors at this institution, and it provided us with an innovative model that we will be able to apply at other institutions.

Motivation

Partnering with one of the institution's academic departments, we implemented the project to improve users' knowledge and skill in the use of passwords. In May 2005, it became clear that many of the people using the institution's mission-critical systems did not respect the importance of safe password practices. They used passwords that were easy to guess or break, shared passwords with subordinates and colleagues, used passwords across multiple systems, left written notes of passwords in places that others could see, and frequently asked our help desk staff to reset forgotten passwords. The institution, which is located in California, is required by law to notify all individuals from whom it collects information if the information becomes compromised. The costs of such notification, and possible loss of goodwill, can be staggering.

Action Plan

Given this, as well as a number of recent serious security breaches of database systems at other academic institutions, we decided to take action. We immediately implemented a policy requiring system users to use only "strong" passwords, which have a minimum of 15 characters, including two numbers and one symbol (which could be an uppercase letter), and which must be changed every six months. In addition, we initiated the project reported in this paper, to design training that would help users understand the importance of passwords and help them develop skill in making up strong, memorable passwords.

CollIT did not have any training program of this kind, nor were we aware of similar programs elsewhere. Thus, we set about designing a training solution that would be usable and useful for users of the institution's systems. We adopted an action research perspective, which focuses on iterative application of research to practical problems and reflection on results. We drew on existing research from the field of security, which provides knowledge of the positive impacts of safe password practices and the field of psychology, which provides knowledge of how to memorize effectively. We began our research by surveying the users of the institution's mission critical systems (about 200 in total, of which about 135 are very active users) to determine what they knew about security, the use of passwords, and methods for creating passwords. What we learned from the survey from which we received 55 responses, helped to motivate our project, indicated important areas for design of the training program, and provided a baseline for assessment. Responses from users confirmed two expected problems: they have difficulty memorizing passwords, and they have little awareness of IT security. In addition, we also learned that a problem in communication between the users and the IT administration existed in that users misunderstood IT security policies while IT administrators were unaware of the extent of this misunderstanding. Here are some of the results from the survey:

- 22% of the users indicated that they had only lower case letters in their password;
- 72 % of the users reported that they had at least one or more number in their passwords;
- 3% of the users reported that they had only numbers in their password;
- 33% created the passwords by using some name or date that has personal significance for them, such as the name or birth date of a family member;
- 40% created the passwords by combining whole or partial names, dates, words, and numbers to make a string of characters such as "January 2005";
- The users used seven systems (mean=6.85) that require a password;
- The users used four passwords (mean=3.6) for these systems;
- 20% reported that they used their system passwords for other systems such as Yahoo!, AOL, etc.;
- 49% reported that they wrote down their passwords;
- 25% had to refer to the written password when they logged in to the systems;
- 14% reported that they shared their passwords with friends or colleagues;
- 22% believed that it is not important to have a strong password to protect the systems;
- 33% of the users reported that it was difficult to use the current required password.

Training Design

With the insights provided by prior research and our initial survey efforts, we designed and implemented training methods and materials. We initially presented them to a group of lead users in a face-to-face meeting. The feedback from the meeting helped us further refine the methods and materials from which we established a training Website. The Website was implemented utilizing simple, inexpensive techniques by one member of our research group in only a few weeks. The Website made use of scripting and database access tools commonly used in basic Web applications.

We designed the training to include four components:

1. Presentation to each user of five methods for creating strong, memorable passwords;
2. Interactive use of one method of the user's choice to create a password;
3. Retesting after 24 hours of the user's recollection of the password he or she created;
4. Information to enhance the user's security awareness made available after password training was complete.

The five methods, designed using concepts from cognitive psychology, are as follows.

1. FIRST LETTER MNEMONICS: Using the first letters of a favorite quote, poem, song or sentence. For example, given "Red sky at night, sailor's delight; red sky at morning, sailor take warning," the generated password would be "Rsansdrsamstw01";
2. COMBINATION OF MEANINGFUL WORDS, NUMBERS, AND SYMBOLS: Combining related words with a number using a symbol. For example, given "Mammoth", "Big Sur", "Tahoe", "1874", and the symbol "+", the password would be "Mammoth+Bigsur+Tahoe+1874";
3. MEANINGFUL PASS PHRASE: Composing a sentence that includes at least two numerals and one symbol, and then capitalizing each noun. For example, the sentence "I405 traffic was bad for my car!" would become "I405 Traffic was bad for my Car!";
4. SUBSTITUTION: Changing a sentence by replacing characters according to a set of substitution rules. For example, "Did you run 15 miles?" becomes the password "D1d you run 15 m1le5?" by substituting "1" for "i" and "5" for "s";
5. WORDS THAT RHYME WITH NUMBERS: Selecting a 4-digit number, identifying a rhyming word for each digit, and then concatenating the number and these words. For example, given the number "2267," the password might be "2267BlueShoeBricksCoven". (Rhymes don't have to be perfect, just memorable for the user.)

The number of numerals, number of symbols, set of allowable symbols, or capitalization in passwords generated by any of these methods can be changed to conform to specific requirements. We expected that passwords so modified will still be memorable. For all methods, users are encouraged not to use their names, street addresses, telephone numbers, pets' names, or other obvious personal information. Theories and Concepts Supporting the Methods of Constructing Passwords appear in the appendix 1.

Training Implementation

Each user participated in the training according to the following schedule. The typical time to complete the training was between 30 and 45 minutes.

Day 1

1. The user registers at the training Website;
2. The user reads examples of each of the five training methods;
3. The user is asked to select a method for creating a password;
4. The user provides the information and creates the training password;
5. Five "test" Websites allow the user to practice the new password. The user is asked to log into each Website and is notified if he/she types the wrong password;

6. If the user types the wrong password, a pop-up window appears to remind him/her of the password;
7. A few questions are included to distract the user so that he/she does not move too quickly between sites, thus requiring a longer delay between logins;
8. Once the user has successfully logged into five Websites, he/she has completed the training.

Day 2

1. An email was sent automatically one day (24 hours) after the user completed the training;
2. The email asks the user to log into a specific Website;
3. The user has to use the password from training to log into the Website. He/she is given three tries;
4. If the user fails to remember the right password within three attempts, he/she is notified that he/she entered the wrong password;
5. The user has the chance to go back to the training Website if he/she cannot remember the password.

October 2, 2005 was the official launch date for the training Website. December 15, 2005 was its official closing date. The site remained active for a short time after its official closing date.

Results

Based on the database log files, 33 users registered with and visited the training Website. The users were required to create a password with at least 15 characters, two numbers, and one symbol. Eight users chose method 1, five users chose method 2, nine users chose method 3, five users chose method 4, and one user chose method 5, for a total of 28 users who chose a method and created passwords. Five additional users registered on the Website, but did not participate in password creation.

No breach of security at the institution from any source is known to have occurred either before or after the training. Thus, it is difficult for us to quantify directly the value of the project. One indication that the training had a positive impact on password memorability is in the number of registered calls to the help desk asking for password resets. Our data show that there was a significant drop during the time that the password memorization training Website was available compared to the previous year, despite a significant increase in password length and complexity. When the training Website was removed, an even larger spike in requests occurred, compared to previous years' numbers. Post-training interviews and our observations of users' behavior suggest that a significant number of users benefited from the training, as discussed in the following section.

Based on a thorough analysis of the training Website, interviews with trainees, and other information derived from help desk logs and word of mouth, we provide the following "lessons learned".

Lessons Learned

TRAINING IS IMPORTANT, ALTHOUGH IT IS NEITHER A ONE-SHOT SOLUTION NOR A PERFECT ONE.

Our observations of user behavior show that the habit of writing down and sharing passwords seems to have been greatly reduced. This may be due to generally heightened awareness of the importance of passwords and consequences that follow from them being compromised. The majority of users believed that their security awareness had been significantly increased after the training. They felt they had a better understanding of security threats and how to prevent them

The training Website provided users with an opportunity to test the strength of their current passwords. Many stated at the end of training that the first thing they would do when they returned to their desks was to change their passwords from weak to strong ones.

Users who accessed the training Website were generally convinced that the site helped them understand how to create a strong password. Most of these users felt that the strong password creation methods were easy to use. In addition, after learning methods for strong password creation, users were interested in trying to utilize what they had learned.

The users most actively accessed the online training during the first five weeks. This can be explained by the fact that the users received an email from Office of Information Technology and the researchers during the first week of the training. Also, the users were required to change their password at the end of October (Week 4), in order to access the systems.

The online traffic indicates 172 visitors were from southern California. However, there were other users who were not from California. This can be explained by the fact that some users told their friends and family about the Website.

The online training required the users to go over several steps of the training. If the users completed the training, they were asked to come back at the log-in page. In other words, the log-in page should be the last page the users viewed before they exited the online training. The traffic report indicates that only 23% of the users completed the training. In addition to the fact that only a small percentage of users completed the voluntary training, there were other concerns that need to be noted. A few users still felt compelled to write their passwords or some part of them down as memory triggers. Others did not want to take the time to memorize the passwords they created in training. One user noted that it was an inconvenience to have to remember a strong password; on receiving, via an email message, the password that had been created during training, his next step was to copy and paste it into the password dialog box of the training system. Another user said that the strong password was worth remembering, but that this would be the same password that he would use for all systems.

Further, there were a few instances where training may also be shown to be a double-edged sword in that more information about the potential holes in security processes may entice people to consider exploiting these holes. These reactions were not expected.

Repetition should be embedded in the password creation systems

As we would predict, the users reported that the more often they used a password, the less likely they were to forget it or write it down. This finding is congruent with Zviran and Haga's (1999) finding that "the more a password is used, the less difficult it is to remember" and "the more frequently a password is used, the less it is written down". One of the online training program's features was its requirement that users re-type their newly-created password five times. The findings from the online training indicate that this repetition process helped some users increase memorization. The fact that only five repetitions had a positive effect is encouraging.

While ease of typing is still a major issue whenever users need to type a long and complicated password, repetition can reduce this problem. Users need to be encouraged to log on and off of their systems regularly until they have memorized the password completely and can type it correctly.

The purpose of the password policy should be conveyed to the users

Before the study began, most users did not know or understand the security and password policy. Many users questioned why they needed a long and complicated password. They did not really know the reasons behind the policy and were frustrated by the perception that we (IT administrators) only told them what to do, but not why they should do it. This created a misunderstanding. We have learned that policies should be directly communicated and clearly explained to the end users. In the end, this is the responsibility of the institution's administrators.

Prior to our project, there was nothing in the institution's policy concerning passwords indicating a punishment for violations. We have come to realize that policies should make it clear to users that a policy violation will be punished harshly. Making such punishments known should lessen the vulnerability of any organization's information systems and raise the fear of detection among those who might abuse them.

Biometrics identification should be introduced as soon as it becomes cost effective

Every password has its flaw. It does not matter how strong a password policy is; some users will always practice insecure computing. Some will use weak passwords, some will write them down, others will share them, and still others will use the same password with multiple accounts. One of the best emerging solutions to avoid these problems is the use of biometric identification.

Biometric identification is based on physiological or behavioral characteristics unique to individuals (Jain, *et al.*, 2000). These characteristics include face, hand, finger, eye, signature, voice, and key stroke. Because these physiological and/or behavioral characteristics are unique to each individual, these characteristics can uniquely identify a user. However, the key challenges of biometrics at the time of this writing are high cost, lack of standards, user acceptance, and legal ambiguity (Chandra, *et al.*, 2005), thus making the technology beyond the reach of most small and medium sized institutions.

Conclusion

The action research project described above developed and implemented a practical and affordable method for improving the strength and memorability of passwords, while it raised security awareness among system users. Based on our post-training analysis, it appears that the training changed the way in which users come up with passwords and remember them. We found that password training can help to bridge the communication gap between IT administrators and users on this issue.

In the future, with our clients, we will be able to use the results from this study to develop stronger IT security policies regarding password utilization. We also will be able to use what we have learned about the kind of Web training employed in this project to develop successful training methods regarding other system usage practices.

Through this project, we were able to advance the way in which we can help our clients meet their information security needs in a way that balances IT service priorities effectively. We developed a Web-based training method that is effective—users created secure passwords that they were able to remember—as well as low cost—one developer built the training site in a short time and users underwent training over parts of two days.

Being able to improve client security without having to fund large-scale security initiatives constitutes a strategic win for us that we can repeat in future contracts. We have an opportunity to transfer the lessons learned in this project to other clients, in the process making them more secure and making us more valuable to them. Our clients will benefit through increasing the security knowledge of their system users. We will benefit through having an innovation that we can apply at many other institutions. Not a bad way to feel a little more secure. In conclusion, the study provides a complete picture of how the end users utilize their passwords. The findings in this study contradict the findings in the previous literature (Zviran and Haga, 1999) that strong password is necessarily difficult to remember.

References

Anderson, J. R. (1974). Verbatim and propositional representation of sentences in immediate and long-term memory. *Journal ofVerbal Bearning and Verbal Behavior, 13*, 149-162.

Chandra, A., and Calderon, T. "Challenges and constraints to the diffusion of biometrics in information systems," *Communications of the ACM* (48:12) 2005, pp 101-106.

Chase, W., & Ericsson, K. A. (1982). Skilled Memory. In J. R. Anderson (Ed.), *Cognitive skills and their acquisition* (pp. 141-189). Hillsdale, NJ: Erlbaum.

Ericsson, K. (1995). Long-Term Working Memory. *Psychological Review, 102*(2), 211-245.

Jain, A., Hong, L., and Pankanti, S. "Biometric Identification," *Communications of the ACM* (43:2) 2000.

Kintsch, W. (1970). *Models for free recall and recognition.* New York: D.A. Norman (Ed.).

Kintsch, W. (1974). *The representation of meaning in memory.* Hillsdale, NJ: Erlbaum.

Zviran, M., and Haga, W.J. "Password security: An empirical study," *Journal of Management Information Systems* (15:4) 1999, pp 161-186.

Appendix 1
Theories and Concepts Supporting the Methods of Constructing Passwords

Techniques of constructing passwords	Memorization Concepts	Theory
Method 1: First Letter Mnemonics	• Meaningfulness • Familiarity • Organization • Association	• Kintsch's Propositional Theory of Text Memory (Kintsch, 1974) • The generate – recognize theory (Anderson and Bower, 1972; Kintsch, 1970) • Cues retrieval theory (Chase & Ericsson, 1982; Ericsson, 1995)
Method 2: Combination among meaningful words, numbers, and symbols	• Meaningfulness • Familiarity • Pattern • Organization • Association	• Kintsch's Propositional Theory of Text Memory (Kintsch, 1974)
Method 3: Meaningful pass phrase	• Meaningfulness • Familiarity • Association	• Kintsch's Propositional Theory of Text Memory (Kintsch, 1974) • The generate – recognize theory (Anderson and Bower, 1972; Kintsch, 1970)
Method 4: Substitution	• Meaningfulness • Familiarity • Association • Organization	• Kintsch's Propositional Theory of Text Memory (Kintsch, 1974) • The generate – recognize theory (Anderson and Bower, 1972; Kintsch, 1970) • Cues retrieval theory (Chase & Ericsson, 1982; Ericsson, 1995)
Method 5: Using Words that Rhyme with Numbers	• Meaningfulness • Rhymes • Pattern	• Kintsch's Propositional Theory of Text Memory (Kintsch, 1974)

17. Information Infrastructures in the Extended Value Chain of the Food Industry

Jonas Hedman
School of Business and Informatics, University College of Borås, SWE

Stefan Henningsson

During the last decades, organizational boundaries have been blurred and technological innovations has introduced the alternative of integrating business with partners higher up or further down in the value chain. This integration has most often been emphasized as something entirely positive, but the reality shows that many organizations choose not to integrate with their peers. The integration of corporate Information Infrastructure (II) serves as a prerequisite for business integration and also as a reflection of the strategic decisions to integrate with suppliers and customers. We study four product flows (milk, sugar beets, pork, and peas) in the Swedish food industry. The empirical data comes from nine case studies. We address the questions why and why not the information flow is integrated. Based on our findings, we draw conclusions on the central criteria that drive and hamper the evolution of inter-organizational integrated value chains. One key finding is that integration is driven by institutional requirements, such as traceability of products in the value chain, from governmental agencies.

Introduction

Only a decade ago many companies strived for homogenous and standardized enterprise-wide IS. With the result in hand, we can se that the foreseen architecture never was accomplished (Corbitt, *et al.*, 2006). Rather complex information infrastructures (II) emerged as a result of pressure and changes in, to the organization, external and internal context (Hanseth & Braa, 2001).

Nevertheless, the business needs that originally laid the foundation for approaching consolidated large scale systems still prevail. By integrating business processes from the end consumer to original suppliers in terms of products, services and information the participating organization can provide additional value for the consumer and/or supplier. Forward and backward integration enables that higher efficiency and effectiveness in areas such as scheduling, transactions and planning can be leveraged (Lubatkin, 1988).

It is impossible to achieve an effective supply chain without information and communication technology (ICT) (Gunasekaran & Ngai, 2004). The beneficial effects are heavily dependent on the ability to integrate information systems (IS) appropriately (Henningsson, 2007). The development in ICT during last decades has set the ground for global integration initiatives as it is now possible to create the II that are necessary in geographically spread value chains. In this sense, the IS integration reflects the strategic decisions regarding integration in the extended value chain and IS integration initiatives reflects the ambition to integrate with the peers.

Much is written on intra-organizational value chains and internal integration and how to make it work efficiently. Less is known about the extended value chain with focus on the whole chain from initial producers to end consumers (Browne, *et al.*, 1995; Jagdev & Browne, 1998). Methodologies like Business Process Reengineering does not apply well to external business processes as different corporations often operate autonomously: there is no higher authority to orchestrate a top-down approach. In this article we present a study of four product flows (milk, pork, sugar, and peas) involving nine organizations active in the Swedish food industry. Our purpose is to describe how they integrate their II and on which foundation they assumes their strategies. In doing so, we will provide further insight to the understanding of external integration in the extended value chain. We will in the next section present how the study was carried out before turning to the theoretical framework in which our research contribution should be fitted. Further, we present the findings and our theoretically grounded analysis that aims to clarify key criteria for choosing to or not to integrate IS in the extended value chain.

Research Methodology

The empirical phase of the work aimed at collecting data in relation to the theoretical framework. Nine case studies were performed, including three farmers, four food producers, one corporate function of one grocery chain, and one large grocery store and they are:

- Askliden AB is a milk producer, with 250 milk cows;
- Bramstorp Gård AB produces sugar beets and peas;
- Coop Norden is the corporate function of the second largest grocery chain.
- Danisco Sugar's facility at Örtofta refines sugar beets into raw sugar – has a monopoly;
- Findus AB is specialized in frozen food, such as vegetables (illustrated by peas), meat and fish;
- ICA Tuna is a local grocery store and belongs to the ICA group;
- Skånemejerier is a cooperative owned and a leading actor among dairy products;
- Swedish Meats is the leading slaughter house in Sweden and also a cooperative;
- Tygelsjö Mölla is a pig farmer, who delivers 4500 piglets to Swedish meat.

The cases were selected based on the four product flows: milk, pork, sugar, and peas. The products were in turn chosen based on some unique features regarding need for integration along the value chain, e.g., planning horizon and harvesting are critical time constraints for pea farming. A number of actors and products are not included, e.g., end consumers and governmental agencies. However, the phenomenon under investigation is integration mediated through II. Thus, we will not make any claims regarding the individual cases or the products – only towards the information infrastructure integration of the food chain.

Integrating the Extended Value Chain with ICT

Integrated Information Infrastructures

Only a decade ago many companies strived for homogenous and standardized enterprise-wide IS that should be the informational backbone of the corporation and seamlessly integrate business processes and information flows throughout the whole supply chain. With the result in hand, we can se that, in spite of the substantial efforts put into the quest, the foreseen architecture never was realized. Rather complex IIs emerged as a result of pressure and changes in, to the organization, external and internal context (Hanseth & Braa, 1998). Despite the unsuccessfulness of the great enterprise-wide IS in the effort of consolidating IS constituents into one large scale system, the business needs that originally laid the foundation for approaching these systems still prevail.

The II of today's companies consist of a growing pile of systems that specifically target various aspects of the business, including Customer Relationship Management (CRM), Enterprise Resource Planning (ERP), and Supply Chain Management (SCM). The terms of these systems tend to vary as vendors and consultants launch new marketing efforts, and trends come and go. However, the business needs they address tend to show more stability over time.

Information Infrastructures in the Extended Value Chain

Management and coordination of the internal value chain is a well researched topic (Konsynski, 1993). Less is, however, known about the strategy of corporations taking part of a larger chain that spans cross organizational boundaries, the extended value chain (Markus, 2000). The development in ICT, in combination with extended pressure of globalization, environmental consideration and transformation of organizational structures, is said to transform organizational boundaries, blurring the frontiers to customers and suppliers (Browne and Jiangang, 1999). As the technological platform continues to develop, the foundation for extending the corporations business process becomes more and more relevant. Manufacturing companies cannot longer be seen as individual systems, but rather as participators in an extended value chain (Browne and Jiangang, 1999). Establishing the appropriate information infrastructure has been found closely related to many of the potential benefits that can be obtained by combining to organizational units (Henningsson, 2007). Also in the leveraging of potential benefits from integration into an extended value chain creating the integrated information infrastructure is considered a key issue (Gunasekaran & Ngai, 2004).

In order to set the ground for the extended value chain, somehow the II of the organizations have to be integrated. "Surprisingly, very little literature directly defines integration" (Schweiger & Goulet, 2000: 63). Creating an integrated information infrastructure roughly denotes the creation of linkage between to previously separated IS (Markus, 2000) at technical-, business process, and business practice level (Konsynski, 1993). Although IS integration normally is thought of in the context of modern, global corporations doing real-time business with its partners, the idea of IIs is not new. Corporations seek business integration basically because customers and suppliers expect it. For intra-organizational integration the key benefits are often referred to such things as providing the customer with one single interface and harmonize production and logistics throughout the corporation (Markus, 2000). The drivers for external integration higher ability to respond to market change (Konsynski, 1993).

The food industry as extended value chain

The Swedish Food industry

The number of end consumers is just above ten million consumers, whereof one million is Norwegians, who cross the border to Sweden to shop food and alcohol. The Swedish market is dominated by three large retail chains, ICA, Coop, and Axfood, with a total market share of 72%. There are several major food producers in the southern part of Sweden – Skåne, such as Procordia Food AB, and Findus Sverige AB, Skånemejerier. Skåne is the most important agricultural area of Sweden with some 8700 farmers. The main food products from Skåne are different types of crops, dairy products, rape, sugar beats, and meat. In the following sections, we present the empirical data from the nine cases along the four product flows. The focus is on various types of II integration among the actors. The specific information flow and IS of the four products (milk, meat, sugar and peas) from the farmer, through the producer and to the retailer, will also be described.

Milk flow

Milk production at Askliden AB is supported by milk robots and automatic feeding machines, without almost any human interaction. The data collected by the milk robots (amount and quality etc) is linked trough an advanced IS to the Swedish Diary Association (SDA), who makes analysis of data and provides feedback, e.g., what to feed each individual cow. SDA and Askliden also diffuse data and information to other milk producers. In addition, Askliden uses a number of other IS to support their business. For instance, PC-Stall Journal to manage all their live stock and Genvägen which used to pick out the best bull for each cow. The data is not passed to the Skånemejerier.

The entire production is sold to Skånemejerier. The price is based on quality (fat and taste). When the milk arrives from the farmers at the dairy in special halls and checked it is pumped into storage silos. Thereafter it is processed. The milk is cooled down and the cream is separated from the milk. Both products are being pasteurized and mixed together again to meet specific percentages of fat. Before the milk is packed it is being homogenized. To support this Skånemejerier use an ERP-system (Movex) to handle logistics, purchasing, resource management, financial assets, maintenance, supply chain management and data warehousing. A system called EDI/Link-XLM is used to manage the electronic information flow (order, invoicing, and payment) to and from farmers and customers. It is fully integrated with Movex. In the beginning of 2005 the EU passed a law that would make it possible to track the origins of food products. To comply with this law, Skånemejerier implemented a system that could be used for extracting up-to-date packing data. When handling customers, Skånemejerier uses a CRM. The packaged milk is sold to the retail chains in southern part of Sweden.

Pork flow

Tygelsjö Mölla is specialized on pig breeding and has one costumer, namely Swedish Meat. The farmer makes an agreement once year on production quotes. The production quote is 4500 Piggham pigs and delivered on regularly bases. The quality of the pig is based on percentage of fat in the meat. In order to benchmark the individual farmer Swedish Meats provide the farmers' with PIGWIN. Tygelsjö Mölla use PIGWIN to compare their own productivity with other breeders. They also use a web portal supplied by Swedish meats with information such as the quality of the animals they have delivered, and how much they are willing to pay for these.

Swedish Meats is the largest meat producer in Sweden. The information flow starts with the communication between the farmer and Swedish Meats. The farmer notifies Swedish Meats via Internet, SMS or telephone, on how many and what kind of animal that he/she wants to deliver. Swedish Meats uses several different systems to collect data about the animals, for example their weight, age and origin. All of the information from these systems is sent to their ERP system. Swedish Meats uses approximately 4-5 systems when interacting with the farmers for handling payment, butchering notifications and so on. They also use a CRM (Contact Relationship Management) system when collecting the information from the farmers which is used to keep track of all of the 17 000 farmers. Swedish Meats collaborates closely with their customers concerning quality and relevant production information. Even though the system handles the whole process from the farmer until the meat is packaged and delivered, no detailed information is passed on to the customer. It is possible to have a continuous information flow from the origin to the end customer, if requested.

Sugar flow

To grow sugar beets, Bramstorp Gård uses a web portal supplied by Danisco Sugar. All information exchange between the farmer and Danisco is done through the portal. The information consists of for example invoices and dates for seed distribution. The information flow is more or less one-way, from Danisco to the farmer. Danisco, as the leading sugar producer in the region, uses SAP's ERP-system R/3 to cover the IT needs of the entire organization, internally as well as externally. The SAP modules used in the sugar beet information flow are: Agri, Sales & Distribution, and Logistics. The Sales & Distribution module (SD) is used to handle the information exchange between Danisco and their customers, while the Logistics module aids the transportation of the processed product (feed and sugar) stored at Örtofta. Agri is used to control the delivery of beets from farmers by creating delivery plans. The module is connected to the web portal www.sockerbetor.nu. As in the Findus case, Danisco aims to guide the farmer on how to best cultivate sugar beets by providing information, for example appropriate PH levels, protecting against erosion, balanced fertilization and numerous hints and tips on how to protect and salvage parasite infected crops and soil. After the sugar beets have been harvested and transported to Danisco's processing plants the sugar is extracted from the beet and mixed, thus breaking the information chain.

Pea flow

When we investigated the Bramstorp case we found that when growing peas the farmer is not passing on any information in the value chain himself. The pea production process is very dominated by Findus. It is Findus who controls the information gathering, and they more or less tells the farmer what and were to grow the peas. Findus uses ERP-systems from both SAP (administration) and Movex (production). They supply the farmers with information about which fields are suitable for pea cultivation, when to plant seeds, how much and what kind of fertilizing to use as well as when to harvest the crops etc. This information is extracted from Findus's data-bases which are based on soil samples from the farmers' fields. This means that in many cases Findus knows more about a field than the farmer that owns it. In the production at Findus's plant data about peas is gathered, such as quality and origin, so that Findus can provide feedback for the farmer. In the future even the end consumer can take part of this information, i.e. know from which field the peas have been grown. Today the information flow is broken when the peas are packaged for consumers. There is no integration between the Findus production system and the packaging system. Findus also collects a lot of information from the market and competitors, but this is not an issue for the pea information flow.

Summary

The Swedish food industry is to a large extent characterized by a number of oligopolies among the dairy chains, monopolies among the food producers, rigor governmental regulations, and loyal end customers. However the competition has increased over the past years, due to new retail chains, deregulation of the global food market, and increased price sensitive among end customers. Integration takes palace mainly between the farmers and food producers. The key aspect for this integration is who sensitive the product is, cf. sugar beets and peas. Between the food producers and the grocery chains there little integration. The only information given to the food producers is order quantity. They have no or little information regarding sales and stock, which hampers their production planning. At the end of the food chain huge amounts of data is collected through the loyalty cards but it seems that only ICA has the knowledge to use it.

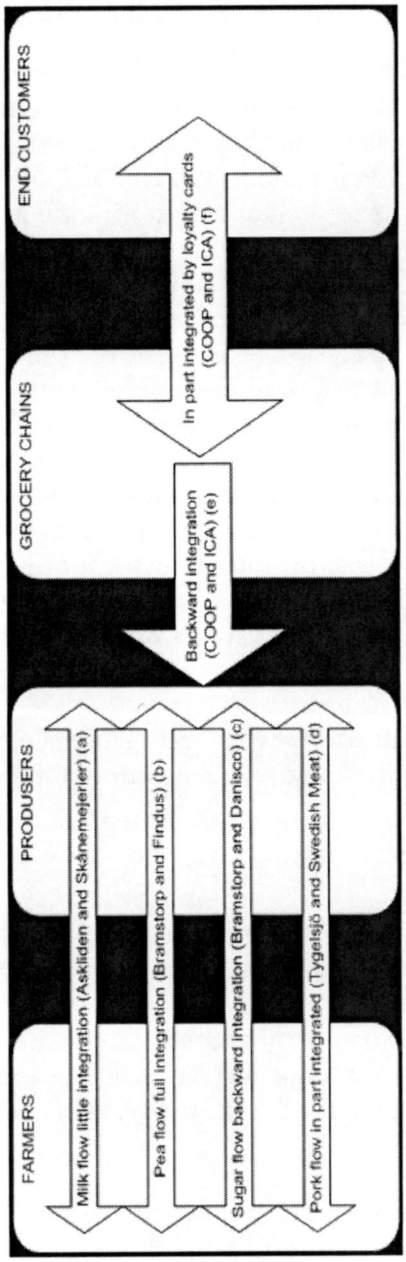

Figure 1 *Integration in the food industry*

Figure 1 shows the four product flows and the cases along the value chain. It also shows the integrated information infrastructure and where it is not integrated. Note that the integration flow converge at the grocery level, indicating that information flows concerning the products is handled in the same way here.

Key criteria for integration choices

With the aid of ICT, detailed information about food products can be collected and distributed throughout the food chain. It is the producers and the retailers who dominate the information flow in the food chain, in large part because of their size. In most cases they control and provide the various systems that are used for data gathering and distribution. Retailers are dominant in terms of controlling the main retail outlets of food products in Sweden and the information concerning the products they sell. They try to influence the producers and the packing industry by pushing for the use of RFID (Radio Frequency Identification) tags on their products as well as added barcode information (EAN 128). The producers aim to control the production process to a large extent because they are responsible for the safety and quality of the food products by law, and at the same time want to maximize the production output of the farmers.

Overall, a lot of information concerning the products that we have studied is collected through out the food chain. However, in most cases a limited amount of information is transferred from one actor to the next in the chain. We can only speculate on the reason for this, but apparently the actors feel that there is no need to relay information that they consider to be of no real practical use to others. There is, for example, no reason for Skånemejerier to collect data on which of the farmer's cows that produces the most milk, since they are only interested in the milk itself. This attitude seems perfectly reasonable in our cases.

In our empirical data three drivers of inter-organizational integration specifically stand out:

- Control – Large organizations with well established brands seeks control over the complete production cycle to ensure stability in quality;
- Legislation and policies – Most of the integration actually stems directly from imposed requirements from authorities or interest groups on order to stay in business;
- Economic use of resources – A limited set of integration initiatives is implemented to enable more efficient use of existing resources.

As can be seen, the drivers are mostly of the character of being "necessity" rather than business strategic. In our empirical data we find a relation to certain hampering condition that seems to hinder the progress of business enhancing initiatives:

- Bargain power – The industry is dominated by a few large key actors that can set the condition for the numerous small producers. This leads to that the larger player can obtain the information they want, but smaller actors have no access to data that would enhance their business;
- Organizational agendas – No common understanding of how to improve the extended value chain.

Regarding the hampering conditions, purely technical factors do not seem to be severe hampers in our empirical material. When the organizations agree upon an integration need, they seem to solve it. The key criteria are more of knowing what is beneficial for business and succeeding to convince stakeholders of the necessity.

Conclusions

ICT has developed to such a level that it is possible to create the extended value chain that integrates all steps in the chain from original produces to end consumer. However, just because it is possible to integrate does not mean companies do so. Our study of nine companies in the Swedish food industry shows that the organizations' own agendas acts as hampering factors and only those companies that are large enough to exercise pressure on its partners manage to leverage the potential benefits of II integration in the extended value chain. The condition that the extended value chain lacks a common owner makes impossible some of the well established success factors for integration projects, such as top-level management support as there, basically, is no top-level management for the extended value chain. Integration is based on mutual benefits and or exercise of barging position of the buyer.

We see that technological innovations may facilitate integration in the future, but still the most outstanding finding from our empirical data is that organizations not seem themselves as an extended value chain that are competing with other value chains. We see that to some extent the individual companies are dependent on the others success, e.g., Findus needs the pea cultivator to be successful in order to continue successful business and even the larger retail chains are dependent on the success of Findus. This finding is also supported in previous research (Jähn, *et al.*, 2006). In some relations, this dependency is well recognized, in others not.

Our findings encourage more studies within the field, not at least action oriented initiatives. The distributed management of extended value chains is an important factor to consider. For example does some combinations of strategic IS planning characteristics seem to be for effective than others (Segars & Grover, 1999), does this imply that integration initiatives directed to the extended value chain should follow a specific path due to their bottom-up nature? Many questions doubtlessly remain unanswered regarding the role of ICT in the extended value chain.

References

Browne, J. and Jiangang, Z. (1999). "Extended and virtual enterprises - similarities and differences," International Journal of Agile Management Systems, ISSN 1465-4652, 1(1): 30-36.

Browne, J., Sockett, P.J. and Wortmann, J.C. (1995). "Future manufacturing systems - Towards the extended enterprise," Computers in Industry, ISSN 0166-3615, 25: 235-254.

Gunasekaran, A. and Ngai, E.W.T. (2004). "Information systems in supply chain integration and management," European Journal of Operational Research, ISSN 0377-2217, 159: 269-295.

Hanseth, O. and Braa, K. (2001). "Hunting for the treasure at the end of the rainbow. Standardizing corporate IT infrastructure," Journal of Collaborative Computing, ISSN 0925-9724. 10(3-4): 261-292.

Henningsson, S. (2007). "The relation between IS integration and M&A as a tool for corporate strategy," In the proceedings of 40th Hawaii International Conference on System Science, Waikoloa, Hawaii, US.

Jagdev, H.S. and Browne, J. (1998). "The extended enterprise - a context for manufacturing," Production Planning & Control, ISSN 1366-5871. 9(3): 216-229.

Jähn, H. et al. (2006). "Performance evaluation as an influence factor for the determination of profit shares of competence cells in non-hierarchical regional networks," Robotics and Computer-Integrated Manufacturing, ISSN 0736-5845, 2: 526-535.

Konsynski, B.R. (1993). "Strategic control in the extended enterprise," IBM Systems Journal, ISSN 0018-8670. 30(1): 111-142.

Lubatkin, M. (1988). "Value-Creating Mergers: Fact or Folklore," The Academy of Management Executive, ISSN 0896-3789, 2(4): 295-302.

Markus, M.L. (2000). "Paradigm shifts - e-business and business/systems integration," Communication of the Association for Information Systems, ISSN 1529-3181, 4(10).

Schweiger, D.M. and Goulet, P.M. (2000). "Integrating mergers and acquisitions: an international research review," Advances in Mergers and Acquisitions, ISSN 1479-361X, 1: 61-92.

Segars, A.H. and Grover, V. (1999). "Profiles of strategic information systems planning," Information Systems Research, ISSN 1526-5536, 10(3): 199-233.

18. SOA to Solve the Post-Acquisition Integration Blues?

Stefan Henningsson, Claes Svensson, Linus Vallén
Department of Informatics, Lund University, SWE

More and more companies are experiencing the post-acquisition backwash when organizations and their information systems (IS) should be integrated in order to leverage the anticipated synergetic effects following a corporate acquisition. However, lately the alternative of Service Oriented Architectures (SOA) has started to rapidly penetrate contemporary business life based on the promise of scalable and flexible information infrastructures. Many questions regarding the consequences of a shift towards this kind of IT architecture still remains unanswered. We study five Nordic companies with the objective to describe and explain which impact SOA have on the post-acquisition integration process. The conclusion is that the use of SOA in many cases facilitates post-acquisition integration, but the advantages are based on certain conditions and a more graded view of SOA's usefulness is asked for.

Introduction

Only a decade ago many companies strived for homogenous and standardized enterprise-wide IS. With the result in hand, we can se that the foreseen architecture never was accomplished (Corbitt, *et al.*, 2006). Rather complex information infrastructures emerged as a result of pressure and changes in, to the organization, external and internal context (Hanseth & Braa, 2001).

Nevertheless, the business needs that originally laid the foundation for approaching consolidated large scale systems still prevail. Managers are still seeking organizational transparency, customers are still demanding one global partner, production and logistics may still be smoother with appropriate coordination, and in addition information and process inconsistencies are lurking across the enterprise (Evgeniou, 2002). As a result there has been an increased focus on ways to make possible coordination and cooperation between the various IS-related components that exists within a global enterprise. IS integration has become one of the major challenges for modern business (CIO-Magazine, 2006).

One major reason why the vision of the fully integrated enterprise-wide IS never become true was due to constant shifts in the organizational boundaries (Evgeniou, 2002; Hanseth & Braa, 2001). For contemporary business, the act of acquisition has been cultivated to a major tool for corporate strategy (Sirower, 2003). In 2005, the worldwide number of completed and pending mergers and acquisitions (M&As) rose to 35 208 (EC, 2005). However, despite the popularity and apparently pursuing attraction of M&A, history tells us that the endeavour is a risky and complicated process (e.g., Giacomazzi, *et al.*, 1997). The failure rates express that many lessons on M&A are still to learn. As modern enterprises are highly dependent on their IS, they cannot function in an integrated manner before the IS are appropriately integrated (Alaranta, 2005; Giacomazzi, *et al.*, 1997; e.g., McKiernan & Merali, 1995; Robbins & Stylianou, 1999). In a recent survey by Accenture, only 40% of 400 interviewed enterprises claimed their last M&A-related IS integration being successful (Accenture, 2006). Whatever "successful" actually means in this context, it is an apparent statement that something does not work in the way it should.

One of today's most topical developments in IS is the transition from the former client-server/database-oriented modules that were used by many enterprise resource planning systems to a more flexible architecture built on software components, the Internet, and a variety of XML- related protocols – commonly referred to as SOA (Duke, *et al.*, 2005). SOA is tempting grace to its potential flexibility and relative easiness in integrating new organizational units. However, little is still known on how the transition to SOA affects business operations. In this article we integrate existing theories of SOA and post-acquisition integration (PAI) into a number of proposition on the relationship between IS integration with SOA and PAI. These propositions are then investigated empirically by data collected from five industrial companies that use SOA in their everyday activities.

Research method

The problem domain of IS integration in PAI is very sparsely treated by existing scientific literature. Nevertheless large amounts of literature and research about the two main areas, SOA and PAI, can be found. We will in this article integrate prior theory in the two domains highlighting potential relationships and implications on the counterpart. These potential relationships are stated as a number of propositions. The propositions where used as guidance when collecting empirical material.

Five Nordic industrial companies participated in this study, here referred to as: Alfa Laval, Dynapac, KCI Koncranes, Sandvik and Volvo CE. Interviews, a combination of face to face and telephone mediated, were carried out with manager in charge of SOA and responsible for IS integration in the M&A act. In all, ten semi-structured interviews were made with IT professionals and IT managers at the companies. Interviews were semi-structured to assure that relevant data was collected in order to being able to cover the theoretically deducted propositions, but at the same time open up for new empirical discoveries as the field being infantile. The analysis was divided into three phases: data reduction, data display, and conclusion drawing and verification.

PAI and SOA – Proposed Relations

Corporate acquisitions is not a new phenomenon, it has been around for almost a century now (Sirower, 2003). Going up and down in waves the movement has at all time been driven by fundamental economic forces.

New technologies, changes in regulations and the reducing of communication/ transportation costs also affect the acquisition activity. This text does not make any claims at being all-covering. Due to limitations in space we consider the room is better used at justifying the particular propositions we make and foremost concentrate on our empirical findings. A more elaborate discussion on the contributing theoretical foundation can be provided upon request. For a more holistic views of IS integration and acquisitions, see e.g., Henningsson & Carlsson (2006).

In integrating existing research on PAI and SOA we arrived at five proposals on how SOA can influence PAI:

Proposal R.1: The relatively low cost and commitment for implementing SOA is of relevance for the outcome of the acquisition.

Motivation: Reduced cost due to increased business agility and reusability in combination with platform independency

Indicative references: (Datz, 2004; Zhu, 2005)

Proposal R.2: The integration of new departments and acquired companies is easier when using SOA than when using centralized system solutions.

Motivation: Loose coupling with SOA makes member addition easier and easier to maintain business support

Indicative references: (Datz, 2004; Gemstone, 2005)

Proposal R.3: When acquired companies can maintain their present system the acceptance against the acquiring company and the commitment among the employees is better.

Motivation: No new system imposed on acquired company should make resistance less sever and eliminates the rejection possibility

Indicative references: (Haspeslagh & Jemison, 1991; Larsson & Lubatkin, 2001)

Proposal R.4: The use of SOA leads to better communication between businesses and IS departments, which facilitates the integration of an acquired company.

Motivation: IS departments are forced to think in terms of business processes. Better communication gives better alignment

Indicative references: (Markus, 2000; Van Der Zee & De Jong, 1999)

Proposal R.5: Use of SOA increases the chance for receiving the expected benefits from an acquisition.

Motivation: SOA makes the integration efforts needed more predictable
Indicative references: (Bekier, *et al.*, 2001; Datz, 2004; Haspeslagh & Jemison, 1991; Zhu, 2005)

SOA and M&A at five companies

We present our study of SOA use at five Nordic companies according to the five proposed relationships as described in the last section. Due to space limitations only a summary of answers can be presented, but a complete coverage is available from the authors upon request.

The companies that have been selected for this research are established in a variety of areas (See Table 1). They all have a long tradition of growth trough acquisitions and frequently acquire smaller units which then are integrated with existing operations. All of them have experienced problems in the past with post-acquisition integration and has thus approached SOA as a promising alternative. Their use is still limited and the data below refers to experiences in initial projects that according to current plans should be extended in a near future. The managers' experiences do not come from any particular, isolated project, but is rather the total experience of their companies' SOA use.

R.1 - The relatively low cost and commitment for implementing SOA is of relevance for the outcome of the acquisition.
All respondents in the research mentioned that use of SOA leads to faster integration and economical advantages when integrating acquired companies. "*The most obvious potential with using SOA is the lower costs and better timeframe.*" (IS Manager, Dynapac) To receive these benefits from integration with SOA the condition was said to be a functioning SOA and a great understanding for the business processes within the organization. All respondents described the first phase of implementing SOA as problematic and most crucial since it involves defining the business processes on which the whole SOA is depending. The respondents described these investments as comparable to a driver's license. When through this phase the costs and commitment related to SOA was relatively low.

R.2 - The integration of new departments and acquired companies is easier when using SOA than when using centralized system solutions.
All respondents replied that SOA makes the integration easier than when using centralized system solutions with the same condition as for the first relationship, that the SOA is well implemented and understood in the organization. The IT manager at Koncranes pointed out that one of the big differences between SOA and centralized system solutions is: "*...the timeframe where the integration with centralized system solutions often takes at least six month, up to a year, but when using SOA can be shorten to two-three month.*". Despite the problems that can be connected to the beginning phase of using SOA all respondents although clearly preferred SOA compared to centralized system solutions. The main reason for their choice of SOA was said to be the possibility to change a system one part at a time, instead of having to change the whole system at the same time, which often is very complex and time consuming. A representative at Sandvik described SOA as a better alternative because of the smoother integration, were it is possible to maintain most of the old system and just add new modules. But even though the use of SOA mediates the possibility to maintain an old system,

	Business	Sales (€)	Empl.' S	IT budget	IT empl.	SOA experience
Alfa Laval	Temperature control equipm.	1 700 M	9 500	2,5 %	250	SOA used in integration of several acquired as well as in-house units.
Dynapac	Road construct.	3 738 M	10 000		125	Use SOA on a regular basis to integrate new units.
KCI Koncra-nes	Heavy lifting equipment	971 M	5 900	2 %	48	Using SOA to arrive at a more centralized structure. SOA used to integrate a few acquired companies.
Sandvik	Materials technology	6 760 M	39 000	5 %	500	Only pilot projects of SOA to integrate acquired companies.
Volvo CE	Compaction equipment	400 M	2 000	3 %	50	Have used SOA to integrate numerous business systems. Pilot studies on how to integrate acquired units.

Table 1 *Participating Companies*

the majority of the respondents mentioned that the old systems often were liquidated due to their poor usability and inefficient functionality which is further described in relationship R.3.

R.3 - When acquired companies can maintain their present system the acceptance against the acquiring company and the commitment among the employees is better.
All respondents meant that the acceptance was better in acquired companies when using SOA for integration compared to their experiences of other solutions. A manager at Alfa Laval said that companies that have continued working with their ERP system without having to change anything have not suffered from any lack of acceptance at all. The reason for the better acceptance was claimed to be the possibility to slowly change a business system one part at a time instead of changing the whole system at a time which was explained to be very problematic. To proceed slowly by doing tests, pilot studies, and by learning along the way was described by Dynapac as the optimal approach for SOA. But although the acceptance could be maintained by leaving the system in the acquired company intact this was not truly the case. A majority of the respondents mentioned that there often was a need for changing the systems used in the acquired companies since they tended to be quite old an inefficient. SOA could in these cases be used to integrate those systems with for example a new simpler user interface which facilitated for the user who instead of having to enter data into several system now could achieve the same thing by entering data into one system. The acceptance was said to be unaffected by the change of the system as long as the new system facilitated the work for the user.

R.4 - The use of SOA leads to better communication between business and IS departments, which facilitates the integration of an acquired company.
The research shows that SOA in some cases can lead to better communication, even though the general experience was that this so far was not fully achieved. Koncranes described that SOA can lead to better communication since it is dependent on proper definitions of business processes, which further requires business people and IS people working together. This might also be the case in some companies according to the other respondents, but that this improved communication would facilitate the integration of an acquired company, is not anything that they mention could be taken for granted, and even though the respondents agreed to that SOA in some cases can lead to better communication between business and IS departments the majority of them described the current situation as lacking from such communication. Sandvik mentioned that the work at the IS departments have not changed very much but was hoping for a change in the future, whereas the IS department focused on buying customized modules instead of dealing with special development.

R.5 - Use of SOA increase chances for receiving the expected benefits from an acquisition.

All respondents agreed to this relationship with the same condition as for relationships one and two, that the SOA is properly implemented in the main organization. The majority of the representatives from the surveyed companies described the benefits from using SOA for integrating acquired companies as being the faster integration of new companies and their products. Another benefit was the increased customer value that SOA often brings. "*One of the advantages for the customers is that they instead of being dependent on what product to order are forced to use a certain order system, can use one unified order system.*" (IT Manager, Volvo CE). Koncranes gave the following example of how SOA can affect the acquisition outcome: *"An acquired company was buying components to a much higher price than the main organization used to do, and since we did not make a fast integration with SOA the acquired company continued to buy the components to over-prices, due to the lack of visibility, for a longer period of time than they would have done if we had used SOA."*

Other relationships (customer related)

The most underlined benefits of using SOA was the faster and less expensive integration, but also the non organizational benefit of the increased value for the customer was considered important. One manager even described it as the most important SOA effect and as the main objective with implementing a SOA solution. The customer value was primarily said to depend on the unification of ordering processes. An example could be the elimination of the need for customers to use several user identities, which facilitates for the customer when doing business with the company. "*One is no longer needed to operate various systems involving green screens with low usability.*" (Sandvik) But as with many of the other relationships between SOA and M&A the increased value for the customer was by the respondents said to be dependent on how well the SOA is implemented in the main organization.

Other relationships (education related)

The whole research was permeated by the respondents discussing the condition for great understanding for, and properly defined business processes, and the outcome of SOA being dependent on this. "If one is unable to map and define the business processes within the organization it is impossible to further discuss SOA, and therefore SOA also tends to turn into a question of education in process thinking." (Dynapac) The overall understanding among the respondents was that educations were a good solution for increasing the consciousness for business processes within the organization. One IT manager further argued that the lack of education and knowledge about SOA also was the reason for the uncertainty about SOA that exists among many companies and managers.

Summary of relationship verification

All five propositions were to some degree confirmed, but in most cases conditioned and dependent on contextual factors (see Table 2). One of the more outstanding conditions is that the SOA is well implemented and understood in the organization. If not the potential advantages cannot be reached. The two new relationships can be formulated as follows:

R.6 – Successful integration of an acquired company using SOA leads to increased value for the customers.
R.7 - Poor understanding for the business processes that SOA depends on leads to reduced chances for succeeding with the integration of an acquired company.

These relationships are empirically grounded based on the existing empirical data and their validity outside the specific contexts needs to be further researched.

Concluding discussion

The use of SOA is rapidly penetrating contemporary business life. For the many companies with corporate acquisitions as a natural part of their growth strategy, SOA is tempting due to its potential flexibility and relative easiness in integrating new organizational units. The purpose of this study was to deepen the understanding of the relationship between SOA and corporate acquisitions. By investigating related literature, we deductively concluded

	Theory	**Finding**
R1	The relatively low cost and commitment for implementing SOA is of relevance for the outcome of the M&A.	Confirmed by all respondents with the condition that business processes are well understood.
R2	The integration of new departments and acquired companies is easier when using SOA than when using centralized system solutions.	The practice is in conformity with existing theory, integration is said being smoother.
R3	When acquired companies can maintain their present system the acceptance against the acquiring company and the commitment among the employees is better.	Replacing existing IS only when needed because of the existing systems inappropriateness avoids many political struggles and cultural clashes.
R4	The use of SOA leads to better communication between business and IS departments, which facilitates the integration of an acquired company.	Respondents see the potential in a future, but disagree on the proposition with regard to the current situation.
R5	Use of SOA increases the chance for receiving the expected benefits from an M&A.	Faster and more predictable integration increase chances for leveraging of expected benefits.

Table 2 *Validation of Relationships*

five potential relationships (R1-R5 below) that was confirmed, but gradated and conditioned, by a study of five Nordic companies. We were also able to reinforce existing theory by identifying two additional relationships (R6 and R7):

R.1: The relatively low cost and commitment for implementing SOA is of relevance for the outcome of the acquisition.

R.2: The integration of new departments and acquired companies is easier when using SOA than when using centralized system solutions.

R.3: When acquired companies can maintain their present system the acceptance against the acquiring company and the commitment among the employees is better.

R.4: The use of SOA leads to better communication between businesses and IS departments, which facilitates the integration of an acquired company.

R.5: Use of SOA increases the chance for receiving the expected benefits from an acquisition.

R.6: Successful integration of an acquired company using SOA leads to increased value for the customers.

R.7: Poor understanding of the business processes that SOA depends on leads to reduced chances for succeeding with the integration of an acquired company.

One condition for successful integration with SOA that were connected to several of the other relationships was mentioned. This condition involves the difficulties of the first phase of implementing SOA and is represented by relationship 7.

The fact that no companies rejecting SOA or opponents of SOA, claiming other alternatives of system integration solutions as being superior to SOA participated in this study could be seen as a weakness. During the pre studies for this research involving companies using other solutions were discussed, but was said to be included in the study only if their representatives considered themselves actively chosen not to use SOA. Since we were unable to find such companies, and our purpose did not demand such involvement, we let it go, but it would be interesting to include these companies in future research.

We believe that this research has deepened the understandings for the relationships between SOA and acquisitions, but there are doubtlessly many more interesting implications of SOA that is not covered in this study.

References

Accenture. (2006). Executives Report that Mergers and Acquisitions Fail to Create Adequate Value. Retrieved 2006-11-11, from http://accenture.tekgroup.com/article_display.cfm?article_id=4364

Alaranta, M. (2005, 29-30 September 2005). *Integrating the Enterprise Systems after a Merger: Managing the Change in a Manufacturing Company.* Thirteenth European Conference on Information Systems, Regensburg, Germany.

Bekier, M. M., Bogardus, A. J., & Oldham, T. (2001). Why Mergers Fail. *McKinsey Quarterly,* 0047-5394 (4).

CIO-Magazine. (2006). The State of the CIO 2006: Your Agenda [Electronic Version]. *CIO Magazine*. Retrieved 2006-10-08 from http://www.cio.com/archive/010106/JAN1SOC.pdf

Corbitt, G., Themistocleous, M., & Irani, Z. (2006). *ERP/EAI System Issues and Answers: A Research Journey.* 39th Hawaii International Conference on System Sciences.

Datz, T. (2004). *Tjänstebaserad arkitektur lovar snabbare utveckling, effektivare arbete och enklare integration – om den installeras rätt.* : IDG.

Duke, A., Davies, J., & Richardson, M. (2005). Enabling a scalable service-oriented architecture with semantic Web Services. *BT Technology Journal* 23(3), 191-201.

EC. (2005). *Mergers & Acquisitions note 2* (No. 2). Brussels: European Commission.

Evgeniou, T. (2002). Information Integration and Information Strategies for Adaptive Enterprises. *European Management Journal,* 0263-2373 20(5), 486-494.

Gemstone. (2005). *GemFire Enterprise Data Fabric for Service-Oriented Architectures* Gemstone.

Giacomazzi, F., Panella, C., Pernici, B., & Sansoni, M. (1997). Information systems integration in mergers and acquisitions: A normative model. *Information & Management,* 0378-7206 32, 289-302.

Hanseth, O., & Braa, K. (2001). Hunting for the treasure at the end of the rainbow. Standardizing corporate IT infrastructure. *Journal of Collaborative Computing,* 0925-9724 10(3-4), 261-292.

Haspeslagh, C., & Jemison, B. (1991). *Managing acquisitions. Creating value through corporate renewal.* New York, Ny: The Free Press.

Henningsson, S., & Carlsson, S. (2006, 15-17 July, 2006). *Governing and Managing Enterprise Systems Integration in Corporate M&A* European Conference on Information Systems 2006, Gothemburg, Sweden.

Larsson, R., & Lubatkin, M. (2001). Achieving acculturation in mergers and acquisitions: An international case survey. *Human Relations,* 0018-7267 54(12), 1573-1607.

Markus, M. L. (2000). Paradigm Shifts - E-Business and Business/Systems Integration. *Communication of the AIS* 4(10), 1-45.

McKiernan, P., & Merali, Y. (1995). Integrating information systems after a merger. *Long Range Planning,* 0024-6301 28(4), 54-62.

Robbins, S. S., & Stylianou, A. C. (1999). Post-merger systems integration: the impact on IS capabilities. *Information & Management,* 0378-7206 36, 205-212.

Sirower, M. L. (2003). Investor Communications; New rules for M&A success. *Financial Executive,* 0883-7481 19(1), 26-30.

Van Der Zee, J., & De Jong, B. (1999). Alignment Is not Enough: Integrating Business and Information Technology Management with the Balanced Business Scorecard. *Journal of Management Information Systems,* 0742-1222 16(2), 137-156.

Zhu, H. (2005, August 15-17). *Building Reusable Components with Service-Oriented Architectures.* 2005 IEEE International Conference on Information Reuse and Integration (IEEE IRI-2005), Las Vegas, Nevada, USA.

19. A Systemic Approach to Usability in Mixed Reality Information Systems

Susanna Nilsson and **Björn J. E. Johansson**
Human-Centered Systems, Institution of Computer and Information Science, SWE

In this paper we describe a systemic approach to usability in information systems, by applying a cognitive systems engineering perspective (CSE) on usability analysis of Mixed Reality (MR) Systems. MR systems are general information systems designed for specific applications. Information systems have a global distribution and usability methods for design of such systems and interfaces are based on traditional human computer interaction theories assuming a decomposed view of the user and interface. CSE approaches system design by viewing the system as a whole, focusing on the goals of the joint cognitive system. CSE is a holistic approach to usability, allowing more flexibility in methodology than traditional HCI guidelines. The conclusion is that CSE is an appropriate foundation for usability analysis and design of information systems such as MR systems, which are global, and general in the technical solution, but local and specific in their real world application.

Introduction

Today many technologies, such as computer software, have global distribution with users all over the world in many different cultures. Technologies developed for specific purposes have also become more widespread and used in different domains by different social and economic groups. When new technologies are introduced into a domain it may affect the user and task on both a practical and a social level. A technical system or interface should have as much positive effect on the user and her/his surroundings as possible, while at the same time minimizing the negative effects of the system both for the user and other individuals, ultimately being beneficial to society in general. Traditional usability guidelines are often restricted to the technical system, ignoring the context in which the system is used, as well as the effect the system or interface may have in shaping the same context. When designing an interface the developer needs a good perception of who the user is and where and how the system can and should affect the user in her tasks.

Mixed Reality (MR, see below) systems are information systems that merge real and virtual information with the purpose of aiding users in different tasks (Azuma, 1997). An MR system is a general system much like a computer is general – it has potential as a tool for many different purposes in many different situations. This means that MR systems should be flexible enough to allow users to define the application to the specific cultural and social context. Seeing that MR systems are as diverse in application as the term information system, studying usability in these systems on a general level is impossible, or at least bound to provide little practical value. The literature on usability in MR systems is limited which makes it interesting to explore new ways of addressing design of MR systems. Traditional human computer interaction (HCI) research makes assumptions about the interaction between user and system that rarely apply to MR systems. Instead we propose using a systemic approach to usability in mixed reality information systems – the Cognitive Systems Engineering (CSE) perspective (Hollnagel & Woods, 1983). The purpose of this paper is to describe how this approach can be used to formulate a general method for studying usability in MR information systems.

Background and related research: Systemic approaches and CSE

Traditional HCI is based on a scientific tradition of hypothesis testing to ensure scientific validity of its claims by allowing repeatability of the results of usability studies. However the repeatability of studies involving human activity has been seriously questioned by among others Simon (1956) as well as in the soft systems methodology (Checkland & Holwell, 1998). The foundation of Soft Systems Methodology is "learning from intervention in real-world problem situations" (*ibid.*) rather than the classical hypothesis testing. In approaching complex socio-technical systems, the basis of CSE does not differ much from the soft systems methodology.

According to Checkland (1999) a systems approach is, much like a scientific approach, a meta discipline. Studying something scientifically implies using a certain paradigm of methods that are based on defined laws of nature. Studying something from a systems approach means assuming that the world contains "structured wholes which can maintain their identity under a certain range of conditions and which exhibit certain general principles of wholeness" (ibid). This mode of thinking is not new, for example, already Carolus Linnæus divided plants and creatures in nature in a systemic fashion based on their characteristics and properties in his 'Systema naturae' (1758, org. 1735). This is just one of many ways of approaching our surrounding world systematically. Numerous ways of decomposing our surrounding world into system components have been developed, all with their own specific purpose. When it concerns information systems, the information processing approach has been, and is, prevailing. From this perspective, a system (human, animal or machine) is divided into a number of components that propagates or processes data. The approach was developed by, among others, Shannon & Weaver (1949). This idea had profound impact, not the least on the Macy conferences (Dupuy, 2000; Heims, 1993), and its long lasting effects on the theoretical foundation of cybernetics, cognitive science, computer science and design cannot be ignored by anyone working in these fields, although often are forgotten in contemporary texts.

The most important consequence of the information processing paradigm is probably that it has focused largely on structural descriptions focusing on what something *is* rather than what it *does*. Although these two directions in many respects are inseparable, the way of approaching a problem, or even defining what the problem is, differs greatly. In 'traditional' HCI, the interface and the user are almost always seen as separate entities that exchange input and output. The focus of design based on this approach has consequently been improving that interaction as much as possible. Little thought is given to the task that is actually going to be performed by the user when using the program/tool beyond the interface. In contrast, a functional perspective would instead begin by asking what the purpose(s) or goal(s) of the system is and what the pre-requisites for achieving that goal(s) are. One approach using this mode of thinking is Cognitive Systems Engineering (Hollnagel & Woods, 1983, 2005). Hollnagel and Woods suggested that a 'cognitive system' should be described in terms of functions rather than hypothetical structures of information processing. By approaching the study of humans and machines from this perspective, CSE avoids the basic problems of detailed modelling of internal structures and can focus on the performance of a controlling system in its context.

"*Instead of viewing an MMS*[1] *as decomposable by mechanistic principles, CSE introduces the concept of a cognitive system: an adaptive system which functions using knowledge about itself and the environment in the planning and modification of actions.*" (Hollnagel & Woods, 1983: 583)

More recently, a systemic approach, Joint Cognitive Systems (Hollnagel & Woods, 2005), has been suggested. The fundament of that approach is functional decomposition, using the cybernetic concept of requisite variety (Ashby, 1956). By 'requisite variety' Ashby refers to the ability of a system to exercise control over another system. According to him, a system can only control another system if it can present a higher degree of variety than the system that it tries to control (only variety can destroy variety). Another way of explaining the concept is that the 'repertoire of performance' that a system can present explains if he/she/it can control a situation. Constraints are also put on the system by the environment, and everything that is beyond the control of the system, but puts constraints on it, is considered to be a part of the environment. The boundaries of a system can thus be defined from the components ability to exercise control over another component, and vice versa from its inability to do so (Hollnagel & Woods, 2005). Hollnagel & Woods uses the example of traffic to illustrate the JCS concept (see Figure 1).

A car and its driver are considered a JCS. The driver-vehicle system can move in itself, but its behavior is constrained by the road (if we assume that it is a normal two-wheel drive with a 'sensible' driver). The road, and the traffic on it, is in turn a part of the traffic infrastructure, which is constrained by the topography in which it is located. Lastly, the weather will affect all of these parts and is also completely beyond driver-vehicle control. There are thus a number of analytical levels that the researcher can chose from depending on what the research focus is. The important thing to remember is that any driver-vehicle system under study is part of a larger context that shapes its behavior. The same conclusion is valid for any user-system configuration. Goals and variability takes place on

1. Man-Machine System, our footnote.

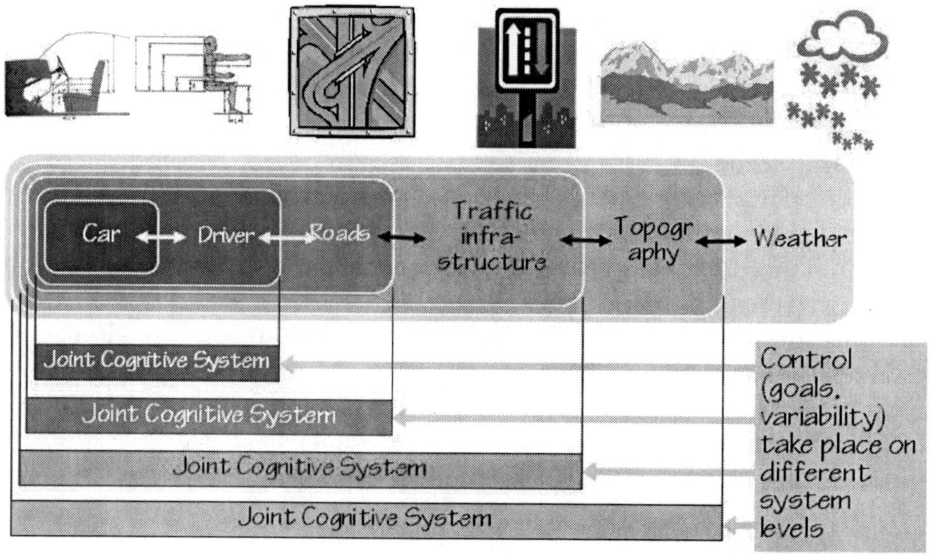

Figure 1 *An example of a Joint Cognitive System in traffic (Hollnagel & Woods 2005)*

several different system levels, and will thus affect and be affected by other levels. Where to begin and end the analysis must be judged both by the purpose of the investigation as well as pragmatic aspects.

A holistic approach to analyzing Mixed Reality Systems

Mixed reality Systems are in general information systems that merge the real world with elements of virtual information to varying extent. Milgram and Kishinos (1994) virtual continuum is often used to describe the relation between augmented reality, virtual reality and the stages in between. Mixed Reality is the collective name for all the stages (see Figure 2). Azuma (1997) mentions three criteria that have to be fulfilled for a system to be classified as a Augmented Reality system: they all combine the real and the virtual, they are supposedly interactive in real time (meaning that the user can interact with the system and get response from it without delay), and they are registered and aligned in three dimensions. Technically, there are two principally different solutions for merging reality and virtuality in real time today – video see-through and optic see-through (Azuma, 1997; Kiyokawa, 2007).

According to the CSE approach, one should look at the goal of completing a task as a joint cognitive system instead of focusing on the merging of the real and the virtual. The task might be repairing an engine – the human is supported by the virtual elements presented by the technology. In this section two different aspects of a JCS approach to MR system are discussed, first the descriptions of MR systems – where the boundaries between system, human and artifacts are drawn, and secondly the use of the MR systems as a tool or a prosthesis.

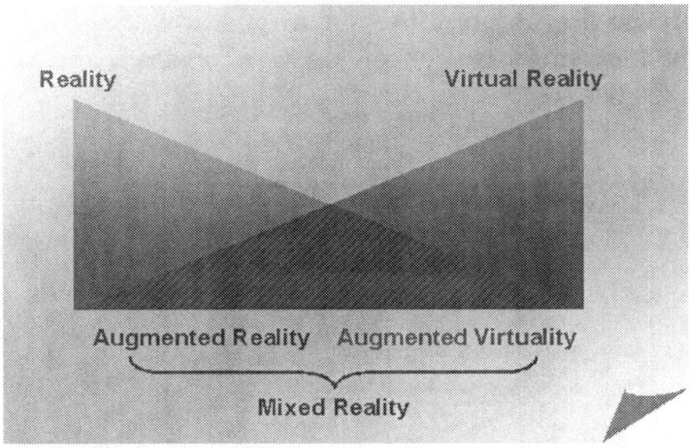

Figure 2: *The Virtual Continuum (figure from Gustafsson et al 2003 after Milgram and Kishino, 1994)*

Describing Mixed Reality systems in relation to usability

The definitions of MR systems found in the literature to date are examples of the natural scientific methodology and this may affect the structural or functional decomposition of MR systems. In general MR systems are described in very technical terms with details of components and their functions (figure 3). Often the hardware and software are described separately which confirms the clear boundaries within the system.

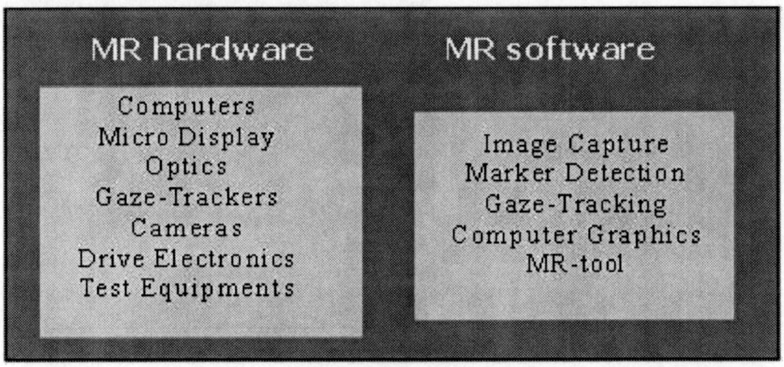

Figure 3 *Decomposing the MRS to hard and software*

The technical description is needed for the repeatability of the studies, but when approaching usability in these information systems other types of descriptions are necessary. Articles from the MIXER 2004 workshop (a part of the larger Intelligent User Interfaces conference) claim to have a usability approach as can be seen from the quotation from this paper:

"*...our research aims at providing elements useful for the design of usable MR systems by focusing on the interaction between the user and the MR system*" (Mansoux, *et al.*, 2004)

Despite this aim the descriptions and decomposition of the MR systems in the articles all make the same distinctions between system and components, but adding the user (figure 4).

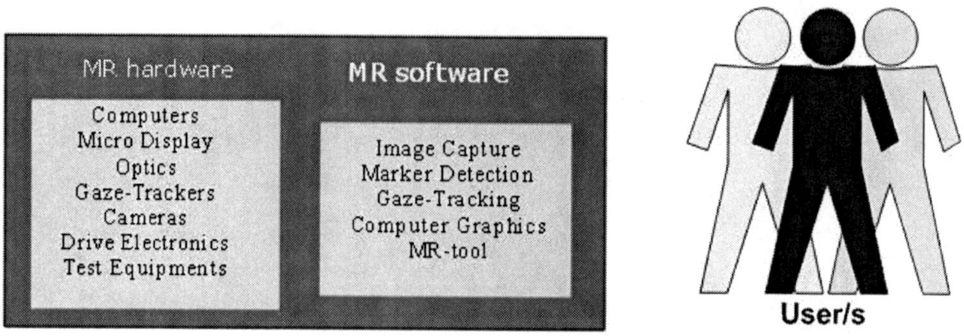

Figure 4 *The user/s separate from the system*

Figure 4 illustrates a traditional usability approach to human-system interaction. The system and the human working with the system are separate entities and are also analyzed separately. The systems output becomes the users input and vice versa, leaving two separate input-output systems that are studied as information processing units (Hollnagel & Woods, 2005). One paper does include a functional, rather than structural decomposition of the MR system but the physical boundaries are still intact (Figure 5).

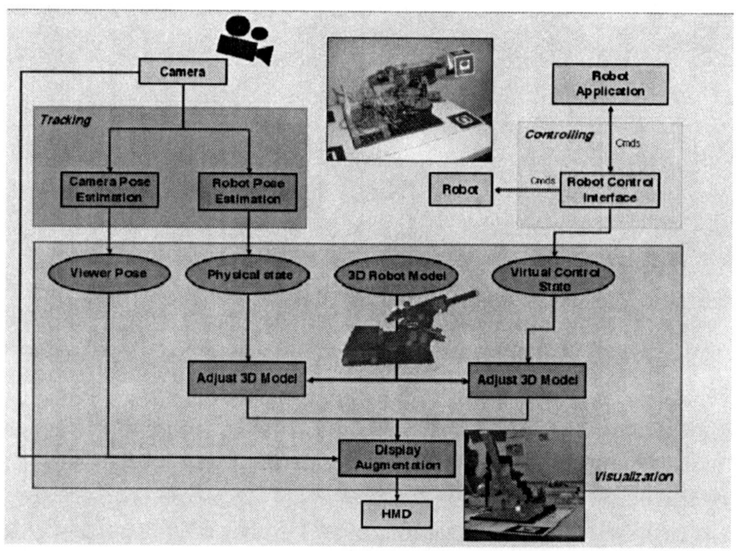

Figure 5 *Decomposition of a MRS with functional division between tracking (upper left rectangle) and visualization (lower rectangle), HMD and robot (upper right square). Still the image shows clear physical boundaries (Klinker, et al., 2004).*

Typical of traditional HCI the context of the system is not included in the MR system description. This excludes discussion on how the environment and experimental setup may have affected the use of the MR system (figure 6). A majority of studies performed on usability of MR systems so far are laboratory or experimental studies, which may be the reason for omitting the context dimension is from the discussion. The focus remains on the individual artifacts and users in the system and their individual performance, not the performance of the system as a whole – the joint cognitive system.

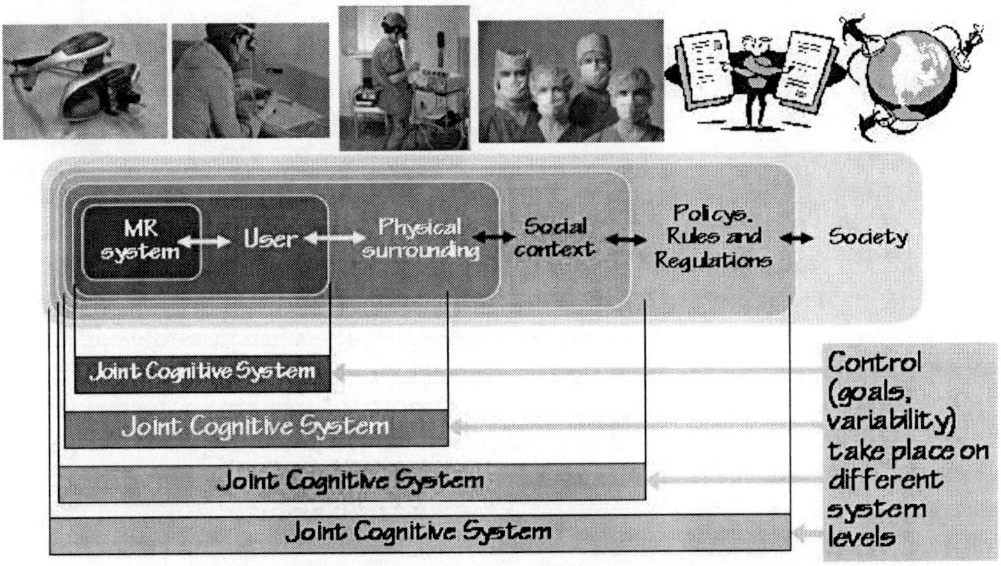

Figure 6 *The MR system as a part of a joint cognitive system (derived from Hollnagel & Woods, 2005)*

Applying a different aggregation level

Analyzing MR systems from a JCS perspective means approaching usability in the system from a different level. In this paper we propose to approach the MR system by defining the system based on the goals of the use and experience of the system as opposed to defining it from its technical and structural components. The terminology used in papers on MR systems is often based on an assumption that the MR system is the 'system' which the user 'interacts with'. However it may be more useful to look at the purpose of the system and the fact that the user is actually interacting *through* the system and not solely *with* the system. If the goal in fact is to interact with the world via the MR system, then one could base the decomposition on the interaction technique, instead of individual technological components (Mackay, 1998).

As seen in figure 4 the boundary between the human user and the artifact is based on the assumption that the human ends where the artificial system begins – there is an obvious division between display and the users' eyes. Even within the artifact the boundary is drawn based on physics – software and hardware (see figure 3). But this does not have to be the case. The boundary could be drawn differently, allowing the camera and display to be part of the human perception, as an extension of the abilities of the user. This boundary also coincides with a boundary drawn when defining the system based on functionality (i e what the system component does) instead of structure (e g hardware and software). The function of the camera, and display in combination with the users visual perception is to convey an image or other virtual information to the user, who then takes action. The function of the computer, processor and code is to generate and execute commands, most often in response to user action, changing the visual appearance in the display and thus the users' perception of the world.

Mixed Reality Systems as artifacts - tool or prosthesis?

In video see through MR the user experiences the world only through the artifact, while the optic see through should have more of an 'embodiment relation', in the same way a pair of glasses act as an extension of our eyes. In a video see through system, the system takes on the so called amplifier hermeneutic relation (Hollnagel & Woods, 2005), where the artifact is an interpreter and takes care of all communication between the operator and the application. The MR system is not transparent to the user, meaning that all information is filtered through the system and then projected on the display, with possible additional information, to the user who has little control over it.

In MR systems used for technical support the system in itself could be viewed upon as a tool for retrieving and presenting information, but if it is used for example as a part of distance expert guidance it can be considered an extension of the expert assistant's eyes and arms when giving instructions in the operator's field of view.

Many of the definitions used to describe MR systems rely on the physical boundaries between the parts of the system which illustrates a tool view on the combined MR system. The person in the system is *using* the system to retrieve information or solve problems. By not focusing on the physical boundaries, but instead using a JCS approach, focusing on the common goals of the system, it can be seen as a prosthesis or an extension of the human system capabilities. The interaction with the environment becomes the tool for achieving the goals, goals such as repairing an engine or starting up complicated technical devices. The MR system can be viewed upon both as a tool and as a prosthesis depending on the context and purpose of using the system. The question is if this affects the development and the design of the system as it very well should.

Concluding Discussion

MR-systems do not always have clearly defined user groups, however they are most often, designed to complete certain tasks in specific situations. This becomes obvious if we consider that two MR systems that are identical in terms of the technical solution (hardware) can be used in very diverse settings like industry, military or healthcare. This makes the CSE approach appropriate for studying usability in MR-systems, since, as in CSE, the task, goals and performance of the user and system are more important than the details of the users' internal processes and interaction with the artifact. Rather, the composition of user and artifact should be studied in relation to the goals of the activity in which they are involved. By applying a systemic perspective based on functional decomposition, these goals become manifest, guiding the designer in his/her quest. The JCS approach helps the designer identify the various levels of analysis in a specific case, which is needed if one is to understand how control relationships are affected by for example the introduction of an MR-system. MR is also particularly challenging because of the tools/prosthesis crux. Since an MR-system provides input directly in the user's perceptual and auditory fields, it both expands and limits the user's capacity. It expands it by directing attention and providing instructions, and it limits it in exactly the same way: when the user is given indications on what to focus on, attention is also taken away from other things. This is also why it is extremely important of a designer to consider the actual use context – a limited understanding of the context may have severe outcomes if the MR-system changes the task at hand in such a way that MR-Human-JCS performs erroneous. This is an apparent risk if a decomposed approach focusing solely on human-MR interaction is applied. The CSE/JCS approach is an effort to avoid this by utilizing a systemic functional analysis of the application domain. Our conclusion is thus that CSE is a useful approach in addressing design and evaluation of information systems and this paper has exemplified this by an analysis of an information system that could be used in a wide range of disciplines.

References

Ashby WR (1956) An introduction to Cybernetics. Chapman & Hall, London.

Azuma, R. (1997) A survey of Augmented Reality. *Presence: Teleoperators and Virtual Environments.* 6 (4), August. p355-385

Checkland, P. and Holwell, S. (1998) *Information, Systems and Information Systems. Making sense of the field.* ISBN 0 471 95820 4

Checkland, P. (1999) *Systems Thinking, Systems Practice.* ISBN 0 471 986062

Dupuy, J-P. (2000) *The Mechanization of the Mind: On the Origins of Cognitive Science,* ISBN-10: 0691025746

Heims, S.J. (1993) *Constructing a Social Science for Postwar America: The Cybernetics Group, 1946 – 1953,* ISBN-10: 026258123X

Hollnagel, E. & Woods, D.D (1983) Cognitive Systems Engineering: New wine in new bottles. *Int. Journal of Human-Computer Studies* 51, p 339-356

Hollnagel, E. & Woods, D.D. (2005) *Joint Cognitive Systems. Foundations of Cognitive Systems Engineering.* ISBN 0 8493 2821 7

Linnæus, C. (1758) *Systema naturæ per regna tria naturæ, secundum classses, ordines, genera, species, cum characteribus, differentiis, synonymis, locis.* 10th edition, Available at: http://dz-srv1.sub.uni-goettingen.de/cache/toc/D265100.html.

Kiyokawa, K. (2007) An Introduction to Head Mounted Displays for Augmented Reality. In Haller, M., Billinghurst, M., Thomas, B. (eds): *Emerging Technologies of Augmented Reality: Interfaces and Design.* ISBN 159904067 0

Klinker, G. et al (2004) FixIt: An approach towards assisting workers in diagnosing machine malfunctions *Proceedings of the IUI-CADUI Workshop on Exploring the Design and Engineering of Mixed Reality Systems (MIXER).* Funchal, Island of Madeira, January 13th

Mackay, W.E. (1998) Augmented Reality: linking real and virtual worlds. *Proceedings of ACM AVI '98, Conference on Advanced Visual Interfaces.* L'Aquila, Italy: ACM. Keynote address. pp. 1-9.

Mansoux, B., Nigay, L. & Traccaz, J. (2004) Abstract and concrete interaction with Mixed Reality systems. The case of the mini-screen, a new interaction device in computer assisted surgery. *Proceedings of the IUI-CADUI Workshop on Exploring the Design and Engineering of Mixed Reality Systems (MIXER)*. Funchal, Island of Madeira, January 13th 2004.

Milgram, P. & Kishino, F. (1994) A taxonomy of mixed reality visual displays. *IEICE Transactions on Information Systems*, Vol E77-D, No 12 December 1994

Nilsson, S. and Johansson, B. A Cognitive Systems Engineering Perspective on the Design of Mixed Reality Systems. *Proceedings of the 13th European Conference on Cognitive Ergonomics* September 20-22, Zürich 2006

Warren Weaver and Claude Elwood Shannon (1963). The Mathematical Theory of Communication. Univ. of Illinois Press. ISBN 0252725484.

Simon, H. A. (1956) Rational Choice and the structure of the Environment, *Psychological Review*, vol 63, pp 129-138

20. An Approach to Sustainability for MIS: Some Recommendations

Craig Standing and **Paul Jackson**
Edith Cowan University, AUS

Because it is intimately bound up with modern business functions and practices, and is pervasive in many business projects, the MIS function is ideally placed to influence the way in which work systems are designed and implemented. In this article we argue that decision making and governance in MIS should identify and apply principles of economic, social and environmental sustainability to its engagement with the business. We demonstrate by showing how at points within the MIS value chain, decisions can be made which enhance the sustainability of the organization.

Introduction

Sustainability burst onto the scene in 1987 with the publication of the Brundtland Commission report (World Commission on Environment and Development, 1987), which defined sustainable development as "development which meets the needs of the present without compromising the ability of future generations to meet their own needs". In this article, we develop a framework for applying the principles of sustainability to decision making and action in the world of Management Information Systems (MIS). We take a general systems perspective and attempt to introduce principles of sustainability into decisions for the design, development, acquisition, maintenance and use of information systems (IS) in the broadest sense. We find that there are several opportunities in the management of IS where decisions are made which could usefully apply sustainability principles. We conclude that the application of these principles at the appropriate point will be of benefit to future and current generations. It may also add greater relevance and attractiveness to the practice of the IS discipline and provide an opportunity for reinvention.

Sustainability

There are many definitions of sustainability and sustainable development, a concept which first emerged in the domain of ecology and environmental protection. Dryzek (Dryzek, 1997) reports that the US Transport Research Board of the US Academy of Sciences spent $1 million to develop a definition - and failed. Therefore we take Brundtland's definition as it is generally understood, meaningful and accessible. It implies collective social responsibility, limits to "the good life" and the moral imperative to think of the impacts of our actions on others, particularly in the future. The importance of sustainable development is fairly self-evident: the unfettered and wasteful consumption of limited resources, such as oil, wood, water and gas, and the destruction of ecosystems is leading to disaster – furthermore when we are denuding rainforests to make veranda furniture or subsidizing European cows for $2.50 per day and 1 billion people live on below $1 per day it leaves many of us feeling that we are doing something *wrong* (Hawkins, 2006).

In the business context, sustainability is seen as a *constraint*. Business survival is predicated upon the generation of value through minimizing costs, maximizing revenue and surviving within hyper-competitive markets. This is the core of the "sustainability paradox": whilst it can tinker around the edges, within capitalist systems there is no "higher authority" to mandate sustainability – profitability is king. As Eckersely (Eckersley, 2006) argues, the "liberal democratic state is not capable of protecting the world's ecosystems...on any *effective* and *systematic* basis". In order to align economic freedom and sustainability, sustainability must be viewed as a *condition* of doing business rather than a constraint. Indeed, it is clear that to the present day, in spite of the overwhelming evidence of waste, destruction and pollution, no country is on a "fully sustainable trajectory", even though some countries are doing far better than others.

In a similar vein, Cartright and Craig (2006) argue that the ethical stance implied by corporate governance as defined by the OECD precludes sustainability from being an important consideration in business: shareholder value, investment protection and legal compliance appear to be the sole criteria for good governance. For example, the precautionary principle is one leitmotif which characterizes ecologically advanced states such as Sweden and Germany: if a development is to be initiated which may harm the environment then this will be constrained until the impact is understood. But Eckersley's words ring in our ears: attempts at introducing sustainability always seem to be confronted with the twin monoliths of profitability and competition. It seems to us that a "higher power" is required to ensure that a sustainable trajectory is followed and this must come either from political authority, the law or an ethical stance that is taken to be self-evident, much as murder is taken to be an unacceptable form of disposing of competition. So although we believe that actions can be initiated which make sense and which are acceptable within current business expectations, we also believe that on occasion a position must be adopted by IS staff and management which derives its strength from its ethical *rightness* with regards to sustainability.

Sustainability has become associated with business, not only through the ecological footprint left by industrial activity, but also in the more general sense of how it is managing its economic, environmental and social impacts. These impacts are reported through performance indicators in Corporate Social Responsibility reports, often as part of a firm's annual report as the "triple bottom line". The actual objective is usually reputation enhancement, although the number using the report to benchmark performance is increasing, so actual sustainable management does not seem to be a prime motivator yet (Centre for Australian Ethical Research, KPMG, & Deni Greene Consulting Services, 2005). Australian business is lagging, with only 18 per cent of S&P/ASX 300 companies producing sustainability reports, about half of that for public and non-listed companies and "the 200 smallest companies within the S&P/ASX 300 have an even lower rate of production of sustainability reports of 8 per cent" (Centre for Australian Ethical Research, *et al.*, 2005: 3).

CSR reports extend ecological sustainability therefore to include social and economic aspects. To function in a sustainable manner requires objectives and policies which have been translated into procedures and principles of operation. At a global level, a system of carbon credits for example should reduce the amount of C02 in the atmosphere. At a firm level, building shopping centres, constructing mines or using heavy haulage in population areas has an impact upon social systems. Comprehensive CSR management requires that policies be operationalized across all three areas of corporate social responsibility. The 2005 Environmental Sustainability Index (Yale Center for Environmental Law and Policy, 2005) identified good governance, that is the development, implementation and monitoring of appropriate policies, as the most significant influence upon good environmental principles. However, the standard texts on Information Systems Governance (e.g., Murphy, 2002; Weill & Ross, 2004) do not explicitly identify sustainability as a goal (although it is implicitly present in the striving for efficiency and reuse).

How is sustainability relevant to information systems?

MIS is existentially dependent upon the success of the firm and the achievement of profit. It is a service designed to increase efficiency, cut costs and promote innovation and market share growth. In spite of this one-dimensional view, we see many opportunities for the MIS function to play a role in pointing the way to sustainability. Some of these result in true savings and benefits: reduction in waste, improved exploitation of materials, reduced travel, more usable, maintainable and long-lived systems and so on. These are the benefits which will have less difficulty being accepted by managers. But other benefits will be based on the judgment that a course of action is wrong, or will make life tougher for those in the future. Whilst such considerations from MIS may not be decisive, until we reach some level of "reflexive modernisation", when sustainability, through institutional evolution or by physical necessity becomes a condition of doing business, one can at least exert some form of influence. There have been ethical-humanist, consensual approaches which provide a precedent for this (Ehn, 1992; Mumford, 1995). The increasing awareness and level of sustainability governance at the corporate level also provides some leverage for IS management and staff to pursue more sustainable practices (Knoepfel, 2001).

Information systems have struggled for years in the face of the "productivity paradox", where overall financial gains from IS investment have appeared dubious, and expensive failures and overruns in development projects have been common (Strassmann, 1997). And yet IT continues to consume the lion's share of capital investment (Carr, 2003). This acknowledges the role that IT plays in maintaining a competitive position, indeed, within the context of the global competitive marketplace, in ensuring the *sustainability* of the business.

We believe this sustainability should be extended to include the ecological and social systems within which the business operates.

Robinson *et al.* (2006) propose a sustainability model for construction which includes dimensions of stakeholder management, investors, environmentally sound projects, safe working conditions, pollution, defects and rework. We can apply a similar approach in MIS if we take a systems view and consider the elements which need to work together to achieve the purpose of information systems (Checkland & Scholes, 1990), but in a sustainable way. Sustainability for MIS means authentic communications and considerate stakeholder relations, the use of technology and systems to support projects which harm neither the environment nor people, systems which are extendable, reusable and which develop user capabilities, databases which are not used for unethical purposes. The following true life vignettes gained in conversation with practitioners demonstrate where sustainability thinking may have made a difference.

A system is implemented which deliberately reduces the amount of knowledge required by users and business staff to perform the work. The personnel are replaced by cheaper, less educated users and the system runs quite well. Two years later, corporate strategy changes and the personnel are required to take on additional duties. However, the less trained and less capable employees are unable to understand and cope with the new demands. They block and prevaricate; hindering the implementation of the strategy... ***The short-sighted reduction of knowledge and capability restricts future growth and prosperity.***

A very large system was developed by contractors, which radically changed how the business was to run. Change management was a major issue and extensive training and consultation done. But the handover of the software was rushed, maintenance resources were scarce, programmers moving to new exciting projects and managers did not consider transferring deep knowledge of the design and intent of the very extensive and complex software. As the system went into maintenance, bug fixes and extensions to function were inappropriate and counter the design intention, and led to the software life being reduced.... ***the handover led to an unsustainable maintenance approach and reduced the life of the software.***

A government agency had to rewrite its system to prepare for the year 2000. They had seven systems responsible for infrastructure construction, maintenance, planning and so on, so they set about rewriting each system. There was no attempt to define common services, common data or a common user interface...until a consultant reviewed the projects and an overall architecture was developed and enforced. If not for this, seven stovepipes would have arisen from the ashes of the previous systems... ***without systems and data architecture, there will be wastage and inflexibility.***

In vignettes like these we see demonstrated several aspects of the Brundtland dictum: we see the wastage and abuse of resources which leads to problems for future programmers, managers and users. The first scenario is a waste of current knowledge and a restriction on future growth, and was a deliberate but ill-conceived decision; the second leads to an early grave for a new, expensive system, but is forced upon decision makers through restrictions in resources and time; the third scenario will lead to wasted development time, difficulties for users and developers and is created through ignorance of the importance of architecture and discipline. They are all erosions of sustainability.

Given that the core mission of MIS staff and management are to be cost-effective and provide solutions and services that contribute to profitability and efficiency, we believe that it is possible to introduce a level of sustainability thinking into the MIS value chain. We describe these in the following sections.

Sustainability Principles to Guide IS Development

The concept of sustainability has different meanings to different groups but we suggest that there are a number of key themes that run through the various interpretations. It is only recently that the importance of sustainability as a business issue has found its way on to boardroom agendas and into business degree curricula. However, there are still problems associated with incorporating sustainable activities in work practices due to a lack of common understanding related to the concept. Our list below of sustainability principles for the IS profession are by no means an exhaustive list but rather an attempt to provide actionable principles that can achieve maximum impact.

1. Be aware of sustainability and how it applies in our work environments: *The starting point for change is awareness and education.*
2. Be aware that business efficiency and cost are not the only criteria for making decisions about IS: *Social and environmental factors need to be considered in the decision making process. In other words, dependence on decision making based upon economic rationality alone is not sustainable.*
3. Use participatory and inclusive approaches to understand how systems interact and coevolve: *There are two points in this the principle. Firstly, that a consideration of the system impact of decision making is important and to achieve this inclusive participatory approaches are required.*
4. Design information systems to maximise the use of resources and minimise wastage: *A "throw away culture" is not sustainable because it wastes resources. The definition of resources should include human effort and knowledge.*
5. Consider the future needs of the organization in acquiring and developing software: *Responsible sustainable behavior should consider the impact of today's decisions on the future.*
6. Learn to recognise and avoid management and technology fads: *Short term solutions that do not align with long term sustainable strategies should be avoided.*
7. Introduce sustainability principles into the governance of your IS: *Sustainability should be incorporated in IS governance plans.*

Using these key themes underlying the concept of sustainability we propose further principles which can be practically applied by the information systems function in organizations. The principles are set within the well established and understood information systems life-cycle and can be used to guide decision making and action.

Strategic planning

- Be aware of sustainability and how it applies in our work environments;
- Develop a sustainability architecture;
- Develop decision making principles which embody sustainability principles;
- Be aware that business efficiency or market expansion are not the only criteria for making decisions about IS;
- Learn to recognise and avoid management and technology fads;
- Infrastructure acquisition;
- Have purchasing guidelines for equipment with a small ecological footprint;
- Minimise waste of software, equipment and knowledge of people;
- Consider ergonomics in infrastructure purchasing guidelines;
- Business analysis and system specification;
- Consider all components of the future system;
- Use participatory and inclusive approaches to understand how systems interact and coevolve.

Feasibility study

- Consider how all components of the system will be affected;
- Consider whether components that are being dispensed with are actually necessary for future growth or operations;
- Consider the new system from the point of view of robustness;
- Implement organizational forms and processes using software which minimizes wastage and use of non-renewable resources;
- Project planning;
- Ensure that project planning guidelines are fair and equitable to participants;
- System design and development;
- Design for the long term;
- Design for re-use;
- Design to minimise waste;
- Consider the role and importance of design and how it impacts on daily life, use of resources, time and effort. Its ability to empower rather than constrain;

- Implementation and change management;
- Minimise risk of failure (waste) in implementation;
- Consult with and communicate with stakeholders.

Discussion and Conclusions

The notion of sustainability and how IS can contribute is not new. Indeed, there are many IS conferences which are now including this as a theme or topic. We argue that the sustainability theme is more than just the addition of a new research direction to sit alongside the more established and accepted research themes within the discipline. It is an example of an opportunity for IS to re-invent itself in terms of relevance. Many IS Departments in Universities are under threat from decreasing enrolments despite apparent shortages of IS professionals. Some fear that the information systems discipline may not survive in academia (Agarwal & Lucas, 2005). In addition, debates still rage over whether a more detailed technical focus aligned to the IT artifact (Benbasat & Zmud, 2003) or a higher level perspective of the organizational and societal implications of IS is more relevant and in the best long term interests of the discipline (Agarwal & Lucas, 2005). We suggest that IS has a pivotal role to play in addressing key global problems and issues; sustainability being one (if not the most important) of those issues.

To re-invent itself the discipline of IS must look beyond its economic rationale to embrace a wider purpose that incorporates social and environmental issues. Social and environmental issues have been a topic of IS research in the past, especially in relation to developing countries (Walsham, Robey & Sundeep, 2007) but these themes still appear to rest firmly on the margins of IS research whereas research linked to "cost savings" and "productivity gains" are perceived as being central (Lee, 2001). If the discipline of information can focus on implementing mindfully (Swanson & Ramiller, 2004) in relation to critical global issues such as sustainability then it is more likely to be seen as relevant and as a consequence have a brighter future. However, this will require a paradigm shift within the IS discipline since the majority of research papers examine the contribution of IS from a purely economic perspective.

Where to now?

In this paper we have argued for the need for the discipline of information systems to debate where it can contribute to sustainability. We have suggested a number of principles which can be amended and extended. In addition, we have presented a number of points in the information systems life-cycle where these principles can be put in to practice. However, if the discipline of IS is to make a major contribution to the sustainability issue then a mindset shift or paradigm shift is required by IS researchers and extensive debate on future directions.

References

Agarwal, R. and Lucas, H. (2005). Information Systems identity Crises: Focusing on High Visibility and High Impact Research. MIS Quarterly, ISSN 0276-7783, (3), 381-398.

Benbasat, I. and Zmud, R. (2003). The Identity Crisis Within the IS Discipline: Defining and Communicating the Discipline's Core Properties. MIS Quarterly, ISSN 0276-7783, 27(2), 183-194.

Carr, N. G. (May, 2003). IT Doesn't Matter. *Harvard Business Review*, ISSN 0017-8012

Cartright, W., & Craig, J. S. (2006) Sustainability: aligning corporate governance, strategy and operations with the planet. *Business Process Management Journal,* ISSN 1463-7154, *12*(6), 741-750.

Centre for Australian Ethical Research, KPMG, & Deni Greene Consulting Services. (2005). *The State of Sustainability Reporting in Australia 2005* (No. http://www.environment.gov.au/settlements/industry/corporate/reporting/pubs/survey2005.pdf). Australian Government: Department of the Environment and Heritage.

Checkland, P., & Scholes, J. (1990). *Soft Systems Methodology in Action.* ISBN 0471986054, Chichester: John Wiley and Sons Ltd.

Dryzek, J. S. (1997). *The Politics of the Earth.* ISBN 0199277397, Oxford: Oxford University Press.

Eckersley, R. (2006). From the liberal to the green democratic state: upholding autonomy *and* sustainability. *Int. J. Innovation and Sustainable Development,* ISSN 1740-8830, (4), 266-283.

Ehn, P. (1992). Scandinavian Design: On Participation and Skill. In P. Adler & T. Winograd (Eds.), *Usability.* ISBN 0195075102, New York: Oxford University Press.

Hawkins, D. E. (2006). *Corporate Social Responsibility.* ISBN 023000220X, Basingstoke: Palgrave Macmillan.

Knoepfel, I. (2001). Dow Jones sustainability group index: a global benchmark for corporate sustainability. *Corporate Environment Strategy,* ISSN 1066-7938, *8*(1), 6-15.

Lee, A. S. (Research in Information Systems: What We Haven't Learned. MIS Quarterly, ISSN 0276-7783, 25(4), V-XV.

Mumford, E. (1995). *Effective Systems Design and Requirements Analysis - The Ethics Approach*, Basingstoke: MacMillan Press.

Murphy, T. (2002). *Achieving business value from technology.* ISBN 0471232300, Hoboken, NJ, John Wiley & Sons.

Robinson, H. S., Anumba, C. J., Carrillo, P. M., & Al-Ghassani, A. M. (2006). STEPS: a knowledge management maturity roadmap for corporate sustainability. *Business Process Management Journal,* ISSN 1463-7154, *12*(6), 793-808.

Strassmann, P. (1997). *The Squandered Computer.* ISBN 0962041319, New Canaan, Conn.: Information Economics Press.

Swanson, E. B. and Ramiller, N. C. (2004). Innovating mindfully with information technology. MIS Quarterly, 28(4), ISSN 0276-7783, 553-584.

Walsham, G., Robey, D., and Sahay, S. (2007). Foreword: Special Issue on Information Systems in Developing Countries, MIS Quarterly, ISSN 0276-7783, 31(2), 317-326.

Weill, P., & Ross, J. W. (2004). *IT Governance: How Top Performers Manage IT decision Rights for Superior Performance.* ISBN 1591392535, Boston: Harvard Business School Press.

World Commission on Environment and Development. (1987). *Our Common Future.*

Oxford: Oxford University Press.

Yale Center for Environmental Law and Policy. (2005). *Environmental Sustainability Index: Benchmarking National environmental Stewardship* (No. http://www.yale.edu/esi/ESI2005_Main_Report.pdf). Columbia University: Yale University and Center for International Earth Science Information Network.

Theme 5: Managing Systemic Development

21. From Sustainable to Systemic Development: An Inquiry into Transformations in Discourse and Praxis

PLENARY PAPER

R.L. Ison[1], **R.J. Bawden**[2], **B. McKenzie**[1], **R.G. Packham**[2], **N. Sriskandarajah**[3] and **R. Armson**[1]
[1] Systemic Development Institute, The Open University, UK
[2] Systemic Development Institute and University of Western Sydney, Australia
[3] Systemic Development Institute and Unit for Environmental Communication, Swedish University of Agricultural Sciences, Uppsala, Sweden

This paper, through a systemic inquiry, explores the context of, and makes the case for systemic development rather than sustainable development. Systemic development is a form of praxis and thus a process rather than an end state. The move from sustainable to systemic development contains conceptual and practical transformations involving discourse (based on changes in understanding) and praxis. In our systemic inquiry we start by analyzing some of the contributions from the 2006 ANZSYS conference that elucidate constraints and possibilities for the transformation we seek. As part of this overall transformation, issues of building institutional and relational capital have to be addressed. We present three vignettes based on our own praxis to elucidate what might be done under the rubric of systemic development, and to highlight the sorts of capacities that need to be built.

1. Exploring the context for systemic development

Our starting point is to congratulate the organizers on selecting the theme of *systemic development*. The theme is topical and germane to contemporary circumstances and provides an opportunity for participants in the 'ANZSYS conversation' to pursue a systemic inquiry commenced at our last conference. In their contribution to the ANZSYS Anniversary Edition of Systems Research & Behavioral Science, Bawden, McKenzie & Packham (2007) examined '*how the emergent notion and practices of systemic development have been taken beyond the academy as* [they] ... *sought to extend* [their] *work as facilitators of learning into different organizations*'. They claimed that their: '*experiences help to shed light on the reasons why systems approaches in total have not become as widespread in the academic and general community as the founders of the modern systems movement, with its origins in the post second world war period, had hoped*'. In this paper we elaborate on this theme, not through any sense of resignation, but because we are collectively embarking on a new phase of activity through which we seek 'situation improvement'.

Our starting point is to build on contributions from the 2006 ANZSYS conference as a means of exploring the context from which a case for systemic development emerges. We then articulate what can be gained from conceptualizing our task as a systemic inquiry, the substance of which is the conceptual and practical transformations needed to move beyond 'sustainable development' to 'systemic development'. As part of this overall transformation, issues of building institutional and relational capital have to be addressed[1]. We explore the challenges of institutionalizing systems thinking and practice and elucidate conceptual and practical challenges that lie ahead.

1.1. Characterizing what is at issue

An analysis of some of the papers presented at the 2006 conference (Table 1) suggests a set of related issues that contribute to this inquiry. In summary these are (Table 1): (i) widespread lack of epistemic awareness in domains of practice and policy development – a crisis of knowing; (ii) lack of awareness of the implications of living in language; (iii) inappropriate measures of system performance (e.g., GDP); (iv) lack of awareness of how objects arise ...and the implications of reification, the creation of 'things' such as the environment, resources etc; (v) lack of congruence between what is espoused and what others experience - 'talking the talk but not walking the walk'; (vi) failures to institutionalize systems understandings and practices in manners that create demand pull and sustain institutionalization, and (vii) a focus on scientism at the expense of design – particularly the praxis associated with the design of learning systems. We expand on these points through our paper.

The issue of the poor institutionalization[2] of systems was a theme manifest in several ways during the 2006 conference: For example, one sub-group explored, as part of a wider 'conversation mapping' exercise, the issue of the place of systems in the academy (Figure 1). From this analysis three themes were then identified:

- The search for viable institutional form(s) for systems studies is not yet over, multiple forms are possible, and we should not expect institutions (organizations) to persist indefinitely.
- Systemic approaches are more than a discipline; they are ways of knowing differently within all disciplines.
- Systems studies do not exhibit the rigor of scholarship or an adequate coherent internal framework to stand alone as an area of study in a University.

1 Relational capital results from the presence and interactions of different elements of the other forms of capital—natural, social, artificial and human through the involvement of citizens, formal groups, enterprises, and institutions sharing the same concerns which only become explicit when these are derived from collaborative knowing (SLIM 2004b).

2 Institutionalisation in the sense used here is the active process of creating an institution and follows the definition of institutions offered by North (1990) of the rules of the game in a society – institutionalisation is thus the process of creating and gaining acceptance of, and organising around, the rules of the game.

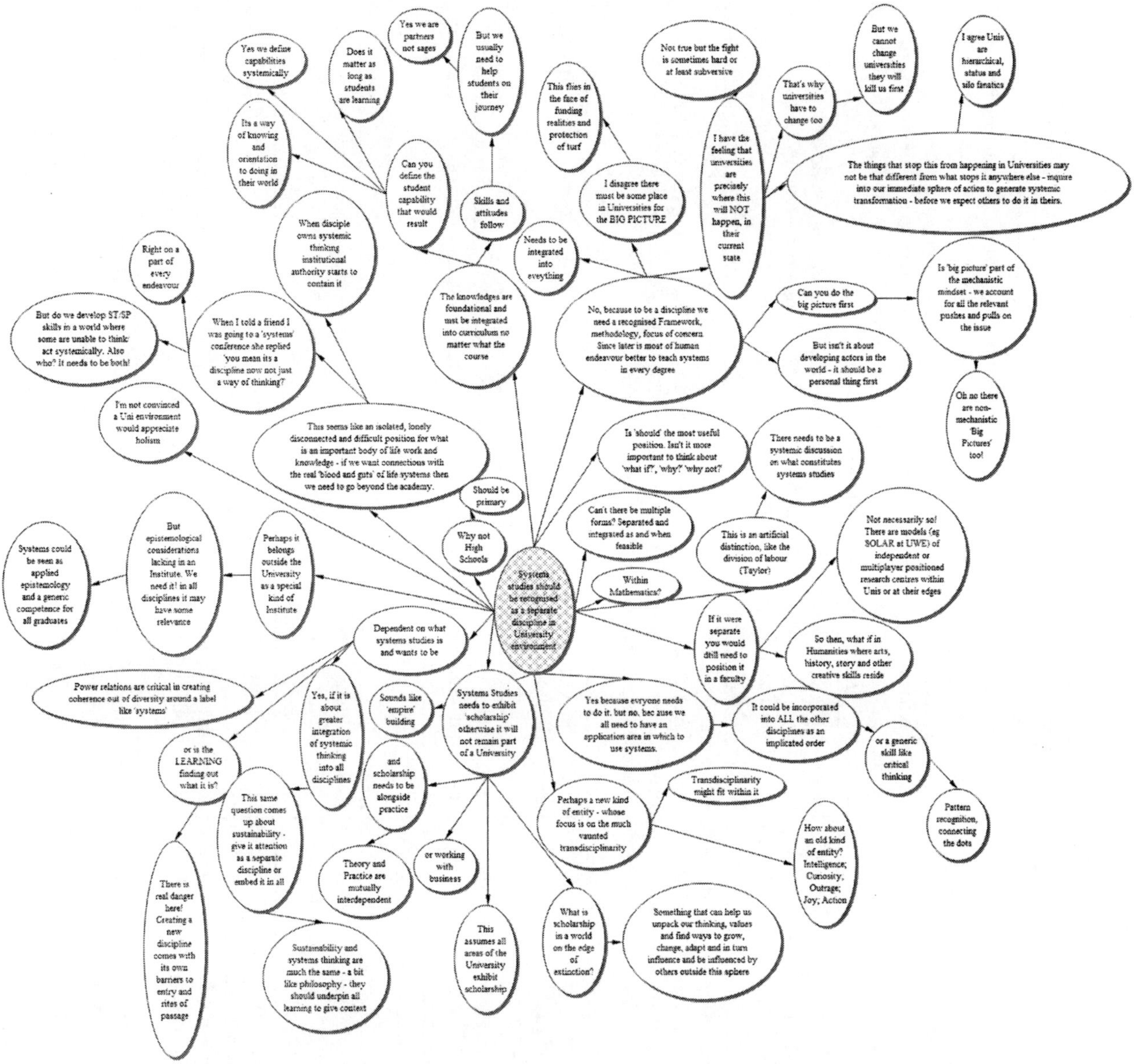

Figure 1 *The output of a conversation map developed by participants in the 2006 ANZSYS conference (Source: collated by Bruce McKenzie)*

The first theme relates to the question of what is the institutional (and organizational) form best suited to conserving over time a vibrant systems conversation?[3] Having named these as themes, it would be possible to further a systemic inquiry by using, say, an SSM approach. Another means of proceeding would be to explore what changes in *understandings* and *practices* might be required to realize the conservation of a vibrant systems conversation. Figure 2 is a heuristic device to help with such an inquiry (Steyaert & Jiggins 2007).

3 Conversation here is in the sense of its Latin roots – *con versare* – meaning to turn together – so conversation is form of doing – a praxis.

Paper Authors	Main issue addressed	Rationale for inclusion
Lamberton	Gross national happiness in Bhutan	A more systemic pathway than GDP which recognises that what is at stake is the ongoing coevolution of *Homo sapiens* with the biophysical world as well as with other species – it is an issue of relationship.
Yalmambirra	What is spoken, and who speaks, on behalf of Wiradjuri peoples?	We live in language mainly without recognition of how language creates us (and others) and what we do – systems approaches often involve a process of 'deconstruction' before engaging in 'reconstruction' – a process that can be unsettling and, in the first instance, seen to be lacking in utilitarian value.
Mize	Efforts to protect ecosystem integrity by "locking up" resources in reserves risk the disruption of traditions compatible with sustainability.	Many current policies and practices are built on understandings based on a paradigm of *resource sufficiency* that conceptualizes elements in ecosystems as 'things' to be conserved. In contrast the paradigm of *functional integrity* presupposes an account of a system having crucial elements that are reproduced over.
Allen & Lang	As new knowledge changes previous maps become transitional objects in the evolution of new perspectives. What dragons (symbols of the unknown) do today's organisational leaders expect to discover at the edge of their worlds?	Policies and practices, including change management strategies are still too often built on outdated concepts of command and control. What is being developed are practices that move towards 'coevolutionary anticipatory action learning.' These will be needed more that ever in a 'climate change world'.
Pamminger & Crawford	Surprisingly, for everything we had done, employees were of the opinion that we were: 'talking the talk but not walking the walk.'	The challenges associated with the design and realisation of learning systems that enable 'walking the walk'
Vargese & Ching	The Queensland Department of Primary Industries and Fisheries (DPI&F) actively uses generative dialogue to enhance inquiry, discovery and collaboration to build social capital and deliver its strategic priorities.	New ways of operating in organisations are required – this example is worthy of further inquiry so as to understand better how systemic and deliberative approaches can be institutionalised.
Sheffield & Lau; Ison & Schlindwein	Being aware of one's epistemic commitments -in relation to knowledge management, complexity, system etc	Lack of epistemological awareness constitutes a trap with practical implications – it can result in project mismanagement, conflict, rejection, lack of valuing of difference, bifurcation into smaller and smaller communities of practice, unethical practice, etc.
Herriman, Willetts & Partridge	Environmental Education must be holistic and about connections. In order to address environmental challenges, people need to think broadly and understand systems, connections, patterns and causes..	Design features for 'learning systems' to deliver the holistic intent of 'environmental education' or 'education for sustainable development' are now recognised and increasingly used. But are these 'learning systems' viable into the long-term, capable of ongoing self-organisation? How can they be best institutionalised?

Table 1 *Selected examples from papers presented at ANZSYS 2006 that address (explicitly or implicitly) the transformation from sustainable to systemic development*

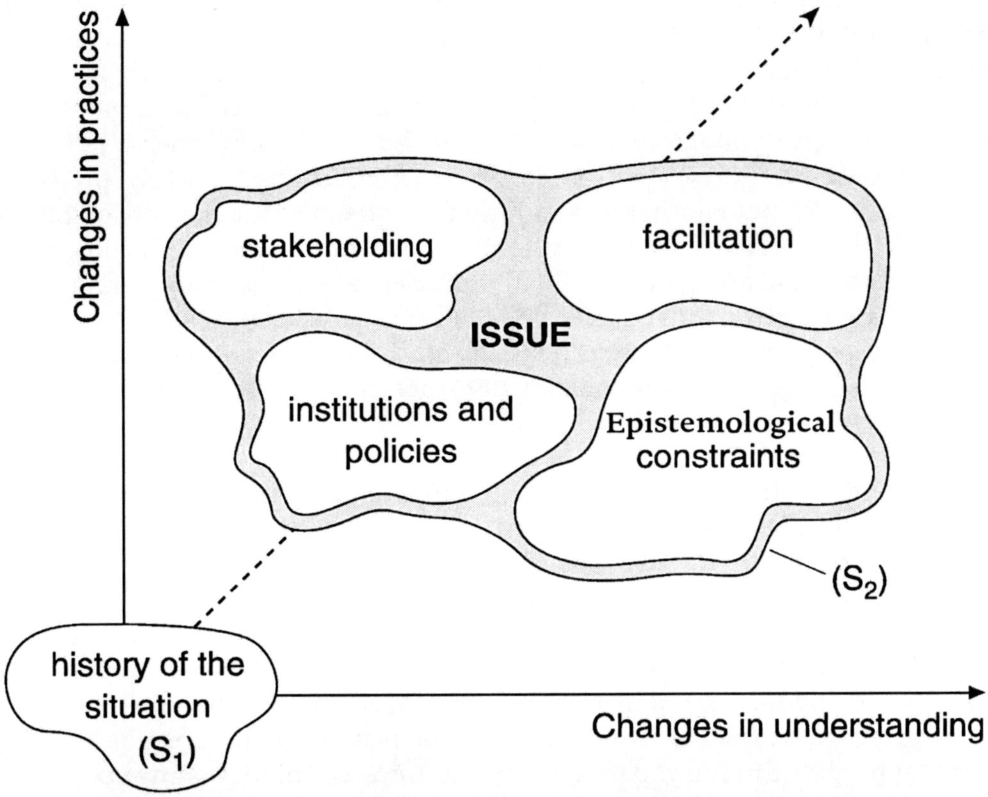

Figure 2 *An heuristic device that can be used to facilitate changes in understanding and practice in situations of complexity and uncertainty. (Source: Adapted from SLIM 2004a).*

1.2. Systemic inquiry

Systemic inquiry is a particular means of facilitating movement towards social learning[4]. It can be seen as a meta-platform or process for 'project or programme managing' in that it has a focus on (i) understanding situations in context and especially the history of the situation (Figure 2); (ii) addressing questions of purpose; (iii) clarifying and distinguishing 'what' from 'how' as well as addressing 'why'; (iv) facilitating action that is purposeful and which is systemically desirable and culturally feasible and (v) developing a means to orchestrate practices across space and time which continue to address a phenomenon or phenomena of social concern when it is unclear at the start as to what would constitute an improvement.

Systemic inquiry builds on, and extends Churchman's (1971) epistemological assumptions; it is concerned with the design of inquiring (or learning) systems and is grounded in various traditions of systems scholarship including second-order cybernetics (von Foerster & Poerkson 2002; Maturana & Poerkson, 2004) and applied systems studies (Open University 1998; Checkland 1999).

4 Understood as concerted action by multiple stakeholders in situations of complexity and uncertainty

Addressing the design of inquiring systems Churchman (1971) reflected that the tendency, then prevalent, was to bolster science and its research as the paradigmatic exemplar of an inquiring system. He rejected this and observed that '*....reflective learning in the literal sense... is the thinking about thinking, doubting about doubting, learning about learning, and (hopefully) knowing about knowing'* (p. 17). He defined 'inquiry' as an activity which produces knowledge (p. 8); put another way inquiry facilitates a particular way of knowing which, when enacted, makes a difference. As Churchman (1971) observed, when exploring the metaphor of a 'library of science', the common definition of science as a systematic collection of knowledge is '*almost entirely useless for the purposes of designing inquiring systems ... in other words knowledge resides in the user not in the collection... it is how the user reacts to the collection ..that matters*' (p.10).

Through empirical and design research members of the SLIM project (see http://slim.open.ac.uk) have found certain 'variables' to enhance or constrain the transformation processes that lead to social learning (Figure 2). Thus *institutional arrangements*, including *policies* may be conducive, or not. How *stakeholding*, an active process, is built is important, as is whether adequate *facilitation* occurs (by people called facilitators as well as through mediating technical objects), or not; *epistemological constraints* are also common and need to be addressed.

In short, issues that are considered to be systemic in nature require some kind of appropriate inquiry to progress them. *Systemic* inquiry is an approach to managing complexity which is adaptive to changing circumstances and which draws explicitly on understandings of systems thinking, action research, cooperative inquiry and adaptive management. It is a key element of doing systemic development through which particular transformations – personal, social, situational – are realized.

2. The emergence of systemic development

2.1 Conceptual issues

Systemic development, essentially a constructivist approach to systemic praxis, arose from our experiences of the mismatch between *what was* and *what could be* in what was then, for most of us, our domain of primary concern – agriculture and rural development, and we have since extended our focus to many other areas of human endeavour. Systemic development builds on what Checkland (1993) had implied with his *Systems thinking: systems practice* – the recognition that *systems* were epistemic devices for learning and change. At that time, as now, we were also frustrated that others did not seem to be open to the cognitive dissonance we were experiencing. In subsequent activity in Australia, the UK, the USA, Denmark, Norway and Sweden as well as consulting assignments in many countries, we have developed differing forms of practice that can all be seen as contributing to *systemic development praxis*.

Those closely associated with the formation of SDI (Systemic Development Institute – see http://www.systemicdevelopment.org) then working from the University of Western Sydney (Hawkesbury) increasingly came to describe systemic development as the need for the *epistemic transformation of the prevailing collective worldview* of agricultural development practitioners in Australian agriculture. Their motivation was to address the paradigmatic challenge of what they perceived as an emerging *Era of Persistence* that would replace the *Era of Productionism* that had long prevailed within modern agriculture (Bawden 1997). They came to select persistence over sustainability because they saw it as a more active term that connoted an evolutionary capacity to persist in the face of change through a combination of adaptive and generative strategies (conceptualized as system-environment coevolution). Later work with other industries focussed attention on *resilience* that enabled *Persistence*. The response they made was to place critically reflexive cognitive development at the centre of their pedagogical and capacity building endeavours and to focus on *Systemic* rather than *Sustainable* Development. From experiences of educating systems thinkers they had concluded that systems thinking was only possible if individuals could be(come) systemic. They chose not to highlight a visionary state but to focus on the inclusive and holistic nature of processes that addressed the nexus between the epistemic development of critically self-reflexive 'actors' and material and social 'acts of development' (or improvement) under complex, often confrontational circumstances. Related pedagogical and capacity building activities were pursued concurrently in the UK (Ison, Blackmore & Armson 2007), in the Nordic countries (Sriskandarajah et al. 2006) and in an increasingly wider array of domains (e.g., Stirling 2001).

The concerns that gave rise to the term 'sustainable development' were not new. Blackmore (2005) argues that Vickers (1980) focused more on our physical, institutional and appreciative (including cultural) bases of existence –for him 'to sustain' meant to keep going, whereas the discourse of the early 1990s around sustainable development was concerned with bringing environmental, economic and social factors together and has been for the most part 'praxis poor'. In the UK High (2002) undertook research to characterise 'sustainable development' in such a way as to justify claims that the systems traditions can inform an effective response to complexity and change. Using the diversity of understandings of sustainable development as a starting point, he showed that this diversity covers a range of rhetorical, theoretical and operational concepts, none of which were universally agreed. His response was to suggest treating sustainable development as an ongoing, 'real-world' discourse characterized by certain events and particular forms of debate and language. Taking such a view allows a pragmatic vision of sustainable development, which does not exclude parties to it on the basis of their beliefs, but rather includes them on the basis of their willingness to engage with others.

Despite the strong emphasis placed on *sustainable regional development* across the EU, recent Swedish evaluations indicate slow progress in integrating sustainable development goals into the work of regional governing bodies. This inertia has been associated with needed capacity building not being in place (Dovlén & Hilding-Rydevik 2007). The significance of the space for discourse and mutual learning across multiple actors and professions responsible for the implementation of sustainable development, transformational change at the individual and organizational level, and indeed the place of systemic competence, are all recognized in the Nordic work, but evidence of any attempts to institutionalize systems thinking to support these changes is lacking.

In the years since High's (2002) work we note the frequency with which the language has moved from *sustainable development*, with its historical roots in the Brundtland (1987) definition to *sustainability*. In this linguistic shift a paradox has emerged – on the one hand a seeming greater social consensus about issues of sustainability whilst at the same time the underlying conceptualizations have diverged so much that it now precludes effective dialogue as to what constitutes 'improvement' as well as the practices needed to move towards 'improvement'.

All of this work invites acceptance of a post-modern perspective relating to *process* rather than a modernist perspective which reifies sustainable development as some *thing*: an endpoint, a target, an indicator etc. All too often the shift of the discourse to *sustainability* has done more to retain the modernist position – *some thing* has to be sustained!! In this paper we seek to move the conversation from one based on *sustainable* development to one based on *systemic* development, recognizing that it ultimately is our own on-going relationship with the Earth, with other species and with each other that is at stake[5].

Recent conceptual strands of our work emphasise the need for dialogue between stakeholders (Kersten & Ison 1998), including making allowances for those who cannot speak for themselves (Midgley, 2000): development in this view needs to be contestable, and not pre-defined by those wanting to "develop". How languaging, particularly the entailments of the metaphors we (often unknowingly) use (McClintock et al. 2004), and emotioning (Russell & Ison 2005) constrain or enhance our understandings and practices are important strands of our inquiries into the nature and facilitation of epistemic shifts. Systemic inquiry is also future orientated and can benefit from practices and techniques that have been developed for *futuring* in SDI projects - exploring plausible future connectivity so that the epistemological and ethical aspects of 'resilience' are incorporated into action strategies. The issue of ethics, and what constitutes ethical practice, are also strongly featured in our work (e.g., Bawden 2000; Packham & Sriskandarajah 2004; Collins, Ison & Blackmore 2005).

2.2. Why epistemological awareness matters

It is no accident that those contributing to systemic development praxis have as a core concern matters of epistemology – elsewhere the challenge of epistemic development as part of educating the systems practitioner has been highlighted (Salner 1986; Bawden & Packham 1993). The significance of this issue arose whilst writing this paper; an email distributed by ISSS (International Society for the Systems Sciences) seeking inputs to an article being prepared to provide 'a summary overview of systems theory' (http://en.citizendium.org/wiki/Systems_theory/Notes).

In what is written thus far, the primary focus is on "science" rather than holism – 'systems seen as a transdisciplinary and multiperspective *scientific in-*

5 The key elements upon which all relational capital is built.

quiry'. We see this as a cultural predisposition entrenched within, particularly, the USA and is a claim often made without a true appreciation of what scientists do. In our arguments for systemic inquiry as part of an overall process of systemic development, the seeking and providing of scientific explanations is a legitimate and often important form of inquiry – but it is not the only form of inquiry needed to engage with and understand complexity and change. An exclusive focus on scientific inquiry avoids any connection with other ways of knowing, such as intuition, spirituality etc. As expressed thus far ISSS is concerned with the dynamics of *the system*, ignoring the *context*, the environment within which the system sits[6]. ISSS's perspective seems to be, implicitly at least, that the system is known and agreed upon, rather than being contestable depending on the purpose. In our view, systemic development is concerned with dealing with these boundary critiques, and how that effects an exploration, a description and an understanding of issues of concern, and above all how one learns participatively to move forward, while reflecting back to check if an 'improvement' has occurred, as the definition of the improvement is contextual and changeable, yet grounded and definable at a particular point in time.

3. Learning by being/doing

In this section we create three vignettes as a means of reflecting on the commonality, yet diversity of our praxis. In our experience, *learning to be systemic* requires the learner to adopt a 'participatory' attitude to learning, develop good listening skills, to suspend judgement, to appreciate the ethical positioning of situations and acknowledge that other participants (or non-participants) have different but valid knowledge that is of value to everyone engaged in a given situation. Without this 'mental model' and the underlying emotioning it is extremely difficult to develop an orientation to learning systems principles - gaining a holistic appreciation of interconnectivity and contextual understanding of 'improvement'. Collectively we have found that didactic means of learning about systems generally fail and whenever possible we choose to start off experientially.

3.1 Recent programs of SDI (Vignette 1)

The general principles listed above are achieved in programs run under the auspices of SDI by creating a series of learning experiences that commence with a focus on ethics, listening and diversity before any attempt is made to introduce the notion of systems or systemic development, and includes the use of:

1. 'Credible sources' (as judged by participants) endorsing the role and value of using systems thinking to address complex issues they regularly encounter;
2. A 'road map' of the learning journey. This aide has proven important for participants who have structured their life (including work life) to avoid acknowledging uncertainty. Although the details of the 'road map' are rarely fully appreciated the fact that there is a framework that is continually re-

6 From our perspective a system is always distinguished by someone and through the distinction that is realised, a system – boundary-environment relationship is produced

ferred to changes the emotional setting. It becomes a useful reference point as the program's critical and systemic thinking activities exposes flaws and limitations in their current 'ways of doing'.

Introducing systems thinking as a form of transformational (change) thinking enables the participants to work through their personal engagement with various forms of thinking - logical, reductionist, problem solving, intuition, transactional and transformational - to discover that they already utilise different forms of thinking to deal with different situations. The goal we share with them is to move from accidental to intentional use of different thinking processes. This approach helps to demystify systems thinking and give the learner a greater sense of control over the learning activities.

Participants find out through various activities that the principles and practice of systems thinking is fundamental to gaining the skills of social enquiry. Each learning experience has been designed on the assumption that the features and practice of being systemic can be learnt through personal discovery, group discussion and inquiry, and designing and implementing systemic activities in the participant's own context (discover – discuss – apply). Participants demonstrate a capacity to move from talking about to doing and thus using new systemic competencies and capacity to gain immediate return on their investment in the learning activities.

In SDI projects experience shows the time allowed for participants to complete learning experiences to be a critical design factor. This applies both to the focussed learning periods (workshops) and the primary experiential learning (between workshops). Three days has been found to be the most effective, long enough to get deeply into material and create a strong bond between learners (essential for managing the emergent uncertainty) while short enough to avoid information overload and the debilitating fatigue that can set in for people unused to ongoing intensive cognition. Six to eight weeks between workshops has been found to be best – shorter than this and learning projects that are embedded in their day-to-day work are usually not sufficiently completed to maximise the learning experience and provide sufficient material to share with other learners in the next workshop. Longer than this period sees a loss of the momentum that has been established in the workshop, particularly for participant's whose work environment is hostile to change. Participants have identified a meeting of about one hour with the facilitator in the middle of this period as the time when breakthroughs in understanding and original insights are gained.

Small group additional learning activities are also considered to be essential to consolidating an individual's confidence in using systemic practices. Here, clusters of learners work together on a complex (intractable) problem suggested by senior management. This gives an organizational focus and urgency to the learning, plus an opportunity to demonstrate at the end of the program the value of systemic practices and participants' ability to use such practices credibility.

3.2 The Open University PersSyst project (Vignette 2)

The PersSyst Project represents an investment of about £1 million over five years by the Open University (OU) to develop systems thinking and practice skills as a basis for 'distributed leadership'. This is a joint project of the Systems Department and the Human Resources Division of the OU with, at inception, the OU's Vice Chancellor chairing the project board. In a recent evaluation, the project was described (van Ameijde 2007) as being:

"set up ... to develop a community of practice around systems thinking and practice. The core activities of PersSyst which aim to fulfil the objective encompass the provision of open workshops and tailored interventions using systems approaches. The workshops aim to facilitate participants in their development of systems thinking and practice using a variety of tools and methods. The interventions aim to help teams, units, and departments to tackle complex issues using a variety of systems tools and methods, and to develop the capacity of the clients for using systemic approaches in subsequent situations. Additional activities include lunchtime sessions, mini-workshops, informal one-on-one sessions and other initiatives."

The project has a number of design features (Ison & Armson 2006):

1. We work within situations that can be characterized as a 'mess' (Ackoff 1974). In our teaching and practice Ackoff's distinction between 'messes' and 'difficulties' consistently helps people to make sense of their situation. We have found that the widespread tendency to treat messes as difficulties often exacerbates complexity and may create the circumstances for systemic failure;
2. The 'project' has not been set up as a traditional project (and thus managed in a typically first-order project managing manner) but rather as a systemic inquiry encompassing action research elements;
3. Consistent with second-order cybernetic understandings we recognise that as researchers, facilitators, etc. we are part of the situation – there is no external 'objective' position;
4. Responsibility replaces objectivity i.e. we take responsibility for what we do and create the circumstances where others can be both response-able and responsible (e.g., we do not consult for, or attempt to resolve messes for those we engage with but create the circumstances for them to do it themselves).

In reflecting on the key aspects of their praxis Ison & Armson (2006) noted that their practice starts with acknowledging the prior experience of those they engaged with in an attempt to create the sense of this being valued. As much as possible they worked by invitation, since an invitation is grounded in a particular emotion that is different to a request or a demand.

Their starting position, and much of their praxis, was grounded in their understanding of the biology of cognition as espoused by Humberto Maturana, where love as an emotion arises when an other arises as a legitimate other (this does not necessarily have to be another person). This is not a romantic notion but quite practical – it can be as simple as acknowledging someone through the act of saying 'good morning' in a manner that creates the experience we associate with authenticity, concern or love.

They go on to say, "*As with Maturana, we appreciate that the operation of love does not require agreement by anyone. In our practice we try to surface difference and avoid premature attempts at agreement. Because the situations we operate in are usually best characterized as messes, we see an ethical responsibility not to press any sense that people should, or ought, to use the systems approaches we offer. Although we experience systems approaches as offering ways forward in the face of complexity, we believe nonetheless that their usefulness is an emergent property of the interaction between the approach, the person and the situation they face. However powerful we believe the systems approach to be, we cannot make claims about the usefulness of them for another. Many of the people we work with experience their work as pressured and stressful and we have no wish to add another 'ought-to' to their workload. We claim only that we and others have found systems approaches to be useful. Thus the invitation to engage with systems ideas is made with recognition that we have to allow the recipient of the invitation the freedom to decline, without prejudice to any existing or future relationship we have with them.*"

This sometimes required a determined stand in an organization accustomed to 'rolling out' staff-development programmes that carry an implied compulsion. Although they chose to frame their approach as an ethical stance, grounded in the biology of love, it was also pedagogically expedient. People learn much faster and more effectively when they have freely chosen to engage. It enabled them to build their work on enthusiasm. They observed that this strategy resulted in the generation of as much demand for development activities as they could meet. Participants self-nominated for workshops based mainly on the experiences of colleagues who had experienced the workshops and were now using the approaches effectively.

Successful outcomes have occurred across most of the activities undertaken within the project (van Ameijde, 2007) but despite an initial conducive institutional and organizational setting (apart perhaps from level of funding) it remains difficult to deal with what many still see as a major limitation - that PersSyst style interventions can not solve problems or offer solutions – instead they provide a framework for individual and collective learning and therefore depend on the commitment of participants in taking ownership of the problems and using the tools and methods in working through issues themselves. This requires a particular set of constantly adapting institutional and organizational settings that it is sometimes difficult to sustain.

3.3. Design of learning systems: agroecology in the Nordic region (Vignette 3)

Learning how to be systemic was a key competence in educational programs at Hawkesbury in the 1980s and 90s. Of the many international collaborations we were part of in the curriculum building area, the work with the Nordic School for Agroecology/ Ecological Agriculture over the past decade or so has been noteworthy (Sriskandarajah et al 2006; see http://www.agroasis.org/).

Organic farming has emerged as an alternative to industrialized modes of food production in Scandinavia in recent decades, and this development has called for a pedagogy capable of equipping learners at universities with systemic capabilities and collaborative competence. An MSc program in Agroecology built on these principles is now offered through the University of Life Sciences in Norway. Agroecology has emerged as the academic field that bridges agriculture, nature and society, thereby supporting the practice of ecological farming, with the ultimate goal of sustaining production, food security, community and environmental health.

All learners in this program spend a compulsory first semester working through a series of experiences on issues with clients in rural communities. Their systemic inquiry begins with the analysis of a farming household and its description as a system, accommodating multiple perspectives. Students then go on to map the complex food system in a community or water catchment and, in collaboration with the local actors, develop proposals for its improvement. Apart from acquiring the knowledge of the special features of ecological agriculture, students in the program also learn to manage their own learning through reflective practice and acquire skills in facilitating learning by others. Evaluation of their performance takes place through demonstration of competence to manage complexity and their ability to link theory to practical situations.

The final semester of the two-year program is devoted to thesis research. Students may choose to pursue their work as facilitators of systemic development initiatives with farming or food enterprises. A recent graduate of the program facilitated agricultural innovation and learning on a farming enterprise in Southern Norway as her thesis research. Through a 'systemic action research' approach, she was able to '*initiate immediate innovation and learning on the farm and also contributed to the long term resilience of the farm system by building its capacity to become a learning system*' (Vaastrøm et al. 2007).

The foundational aspect of the program has been the intensive semester devoted to systemic thinking and its design features as a learning system for around 20 students each year. The dozen or so academics in the region who designed the program have actively collaborated in this project for over a decade and they see themselves as constituting a learning system along with their practitioner counterparts. The program stands out as a model in systems education for sustainable rural development in the region.

These three vignettes reflect commonalities as well as differences in our systemic development praxis. As part of our on-going systemic inquiry within the evolving SDI arrangements we seek to better appreciate and value these commonalities and differences so as to be better positioned to create the circumstances for others to learn with us. We all recognize the challenge faced in finding and conserving conducive institutional settings.

4. Institutionalizing - current challenges

At the last ANZSYS conference a group chose to explore the issues, constraints and opportunities associated with Systems in the academy (Figure 1). Similar issues are associated with education for sustainable development, or in the US 'greening' the curriculum. Bawden (2007) notes that '*to be prepared to pursue the innovative pedagogies that are indicated for education for sustainability is to be prepared to directly confront many academic conventions in a manner that demands profoundly non-conventional academic ways of thinking and acting. Perhaps most significantly of all, it also dictates the unconventional cognitive embrace of ways of valuing and feeling and indeed, of being*'.

Despite findings such as that of Hunting & Tilbury (2006), that a move to systems thinking was one of six key transformations needed for organizational change towards sustainability, there seems limited evidence within and without the academy that such changes are occurring. They also found in their research that '*participants became more aware that sustainability has to not only have a 'whole of institution' approach but also an 'outside institution' approach too. Building this approach required a big change in thinking to create cultural change rather than a merely technical change. Some participants did not realize just how important or challenging this could be*'. The 'outside institution'[7] developments seem more positive in the UK and California than in Australia. The UK now has a whole of government approach to sustainability and there is growing, albeit fragile, recognition that capabilities for implementing sustainability are intimately involved with building capability for systems thinking and practice. At the moment these are under the rubric of 'Skills for Joined-up Government' prompted by recent capability reviews that suggest that cross-government working is a major challenge (A. Robinson pers comm.).

There are macro and micro issues associated with institutionalization. At the macro-level it is worth remembering that many of the innovations that gave rise to the industrial revolution were developed by men (sic) out of sympathy with established organizations such as Universities (Bronowski & Mazlish, 1975). We may be in another such era in which novel organizational forms that combine public good research, 'think and do tanks', philanthropy and entrepreneurial activity within an 'open source' ethos are required to create a strong dialectic with traditional organizations. This is a trajectory that SDI is exploring.

SDI was first established in 1998; it has sustained itself since that time through the maintenance of a network of relationships that had their origins at Hawkesbury, aided by joint projects, some under the SDI banner, some not, and by other facilitative institutional arrangements – appointments as visiting teachers, professors etc. In the past 12 months changing personal circumstances have enabled more face-to-face meetings to critically reflect on the role and nature of SDI and to begin a reorientation process. In this process we have attempted to draw out what we have learned about our own evolving systems praxis as well as exploring and questioning the institutional arrangements that are likely to be most conducive to the transformations we seek to foster.

7 Really 'organization' in the sense used in this paper.

At the micro level many systemic inquiry interventions are commissioned by organizations through the activities of middle management (e.g., Westpac Bank's systemic inquiry into developing an innovation capacity is managed three tiers below board level). This usually requires the neophyte systems practitioners and/or systems consultant to report their experiential learning in traditional propositional form to more senior decision makers. This process is rarely successful and constitutes a major institutional encumbrance for gaining acceptance and action on the basis of systemic development.

Within SDI's suite of projects, the Westpac activities have been largely successful because of the engagement of a senior executive in the experiential aspects of the inquiry (though innovations of this sort are not immune to the departure of key players). Recent work with Maxxium Worldwide was also successful and valued within the organization because senior management chose to engage in their own, albeit limited, systemic inquiry. This experience enabled them to appreciate the holistic nature of the inquiry and its findings. This is a good example of how engaging in systemic inquiry can lead to changes in understandings and practices (Figure 2). In the process significant interconnections and ethical dissonance are generally revealed. Of course people who have experienced systems approaches can gain positions of leadership and then may be in positions to become champions. This leads us to conclude that a major constraint to institutionalization of systemic development praxis rests on the answer to the question: *who participates*?

For senior management the difficulty is their inability to accept that seemingly 'resolved' issues of sustainability are contestable as a bigger picture is created. The notion of continual improvement fundamental to systemic development cannot generally be accommodated by 'business as usual' practices. Hence systemic development is an 'in-your-face' style of challenge to the approach to issues that are complex. The traditional approach of engaging 'expert knowledge' flounders when examination of the complexity demonstrates that the 'expert knowledge' pertains to only a part of the whole. By and large organizations shape their institutional management of complexity from this 'expert' position. Until there is acceptance that such an approach is only applicable to what Snowden (2000) calls 'complicated' issues, where the answer is knowable if you have the appropriate knowledge, proponents of systemic inquiry into issues of sustainability that have no single or continuing answer will find their work blocked by senior management.

If an organization is serious about embracing systemic development and its core practice of systemic inquiry then senior management must be directly involved, have prior experience of systems or be willing to devote some time to participate experientially in a learning system designed by those who have been engaged in the systemic development activity.

The emergence of imperatives for action by governments and business - based on the now almost universal agreement about the need to engage in climate change adaptation, the transition from peak oil and on-going biodiversity destruction - mean that we are entering new, uncharted territory. The territory least explored it seems is the development of novel, viable institutional arrangements as well as praxes to respond to these challenges.

5. Conclusions

Our aim in this paper was to contribute to a systemic inquiry, the substance of which was the conceptual and practical transformations needed to move beyond 'sustainable development' to 'systemic development'. We started our inquiry by drawing out themes arising from the 2006 conference (see Table 1 and section 1.1). We have extended this inquiry by orchestrating reflections on the origins and activities of SDI as practices that can contribute to systemic development praxis and issues of institutionalization.

In our on-going inquiry, we have re-established that *lack of epistemic awareness* (point (i) from section 1.1) is a widespread issue about which it is difficult to speak. By raising it here we hope to bring the issue into greater awareness. Bawden (2007) makes the case for conceptualizing the critical systemic inter-connectivity between the epistemic development of people and the development of the world about them, as *systemic development.* The case has additionally been made here for systemic inquiry as an integral part of this emerging praxis.

In outlining aspects of our praxis we hope to have given some indications of the awareness we have, and responsibility we take, for living in language, a particular aspect being awareness of how language can reify objects and understandings beyond the act of their distinction or the circumstances in which the understanding was valid – sustainable development is a case in point.

Maturana and Varela (1987) argue that the transformation of our way of 'seeing' is a vital prerequisite for 'doing' things differently, because what we *do* in this world essentially reflects the way we '*see*' or construe situations and phenomena in it. The challenge we seek to address is to explore novel institutional arrangements that value the duality at the core of a community of practice – that of participation and reification (Wenger 1998) - such that we and others might one day claim to have experienced a coevolutionary system which has facilitated the conservation of a systemic conversation and, through its actions, meaningful social learning.

6. References

Ackoff, R.L. (1974) *Redesigning the Future,* Wiley, New York.

Allen, Lynn & Lang, Trudi (2006) Here Be Dragons: Mapping future Possibilities Using an Emergent Framework. Proceedings of the 12th ANZSYS conference - *Sustaining our social and natural capital* Katoomba, NSW Australia, 3rd-6th December.

Bawden, R.J. (1997). Learning to Persist: A Systemic View of Development. In *Systems for Sustainability: people, organizations and environments* Stowell, F.A.. Ison, R.L., Armson, R., Holloway, J., Jackson, S., and. McRobb, S.(eds). Plenum Press, New York.

Bawden, R.J. (2000) Valuing the epistemic in the search for betterment. *Cybernetics and Human Knowing* 7: 5-25

Bawden, R.J. (2007) Pedagogies for Persistence: Cognitive Challenges and Collective Competency Development. *International Journal of Innovation and Sustainable Development* (in press)

Bawden, R.J., McKenzie, B. & Packham R.G. (2007) Moving beyond the academy: The intellectual and moral challenges of systemic capabilities. *Systems Research & Be-*

havioral Science **24**, 129-141.

Bawden, R.J. & Packham, R.G. (1993) Systemic Praxis in the Education of the Agricultural Practitioner *Systems Practice* **6**: 7-19.

Blackmore, C.P. (2005) Learning to appreciate learning systems for environmental decision making – a 'work-in-progress' perspective. *Systems Research & Behavioral Science* 22, 329-341

Bronowski, J. & Bruce Mazlish (1975) *Western Intellectual Tradition: From Leonardo to Hegel.* Harpercollins New York.

Brundtland, G.H. (1987). *Our Common Future.* World Commission on Development and the Environment. Oxford University Press. Oxford.

Checkland, P.B. (1993) *Systems Thinking, Systems Practice,* Chichester, John Wiley & Sons. (Published previously in 1981).

Checkland, P. (1999). Soft Systems Methodology. A Thirty Year Retrospective. In Checkland, P. and J. Scholes (1999). *Soft Systems Methodology in Action.* Chichester: John Wiley

Churchman, C. W. (1971) *The Design of Inquiring Systems: Basic Concepts of Systems and Organization.* Basic Books, London.

Collins, K.B., Ison, R.L. & Blackmore, C.P. (2005) *River basin planning project: social learning (Phase 1).* Published by: Environment Agency, Rio House, Waterside Drive, Aztec West, Almondsbury, Bristol.

Dovlén, S & Hilding-Rydevik, T (2007) Sustainable Development in Regional Development Practice: A socio-cultural view of evaluation. In: Khakee, A (Ed.) *New Principles in Planning Evaluation,* Ashgate (in press).

Herriman, Jade Willetts, Juliet & Partridge, Emma (2006) Learning Together for Sustainability: The Value of Group Based Peer Learning. Proceedings of the 12th ANZSYS conference - *Sustaining our social and natural capital* Katoomba, NSW Australia, 3rd-6th December.

High, Chris (2002) *Opening up spaces for learning: A systems approach to sustainable development.* Unpublished PhD Thesis, The Open University, UK.

Hunting, S.A. & Tilbury D. (2006) *Shifting towards sustainability: Six insights into successful organizational change for sustainability,* Australian Research Institute in Education for Sustainability (ARIES) for the Australian Government Department of the Environment and Heritage, Sydney: ARIES.

Ison, R.L. & Schlindwein, S. (2006) History repeats itself: current traps in complexity practice from a systems perspective. Proc. 12th Australia New Zealand Systems Society (ANZSYS) Conference, "*Sustaining our Social and Natural Capital*", 3rd – 6th December.

Ison, R.L. & Armson, R. (2006) Think, Act & Play im *Leadership* der Kybernetik zweiter Ordnung.Lernende Organization. Zeitschrift fur systemishes Management und Organization No 33, September/Oktober (www.lo.isct.net) ISSN 1609-1248 pp. 12-23.

Ison, R.L., Blackmore, C. P. & Armson, R. (2007) Learning participation as systems practice. *Journal of Agricultural Education and Extension.* **13** (3) 209-225.

Kersten, S. & Ison, R.L. (1998) Listening, interpretative cycles and dialogue: Process design for collaborative research and development. *The Journal of Agricultural Education & Extension* **5**, 163-178.

Lamberton, Geoffrey (2006) Bhutan's Gross National Happiness Project: Lessons from the East. Proceedings of the 12th ANZSYS conference - *Sustaining our social and natural capital* Katoomba, NSW Australia, 3rd-6th December.

Maturana, H. & Varela F. (1987) *The Tree of Knowledge: The biological roots of human understanding,* Boston, New Science Library, Shambala Publications.

Maturana, H. & Poerkson, B. (2004) *From Being to Doing. The Origins of the Biology of Cognition.* Carl-Auer , Heidleberg.

McClintock, D., Ison, R.L. & Armson, R. (2004) Conceptual metaphors: a review with implications for human understandings and systems practice. *Cybernetics and Human Knowing* **11**, (1) 25-47.

Midgley, G. (2000) *Systemic Intervention: Philosophy, methodology and practice.* Kluwer Academic/Plenum Publishers, New York.

Mize, James M. (2006) Integrating Indigenous Cultural Traditions in the Management of Protected Marine Resources: The Fiordland example. Proceedings of the 12th ANZSYS conference - *Sustaining our social and natural capital* Katoomba, NSW Australia, 3rd-6th December.

North, D., 1990. *Institutions, Institutional Change and Economic Performance.* Cambridge University Press, Cambridge.

Open University (1998) *Managing Complexity. A systems approach.* (Course Code T306) Open University, Milton Keynes.

Packham, R.G. & Sriskandarajah, N. (2004) Systemic Action Research for Postgraduate education in Agriculture and Rural Development, *Systems Research and Behavioral Science* **22**:119-130.

Pamminger, Francis & Crawford, Julian (2006) Every Journey Starts with a Single Step: Yarra Valley Water's Journey Towards Environmental Sustainability. Proceedings of the 12th ANZSYS conference - *Sustaining our social and natural capital* Katoomba, NSW Australia, 3rd-6th December.

Russell, D.B. & Ison, R.L. (2005) The researcher of human systems is both choreographer and chorographer. *Systems Research and Behavioral Science* **22**, 131-138.

Salner, M. (1986) Adult Cognitive and Epistemological Development in Systems Education. *Systems Research* **3** (4): 225-232

Sheffield, Jim & Lau, Edward (2006) Identifying the Philosophical Assumptions of Knowledge Management Perspectives. Proceedings of the 12th ANZSYS conference - *Sustaining our social and natural capital* Katoomba, NSW Australia, 3rd-6th December.

Snowden, D (2002) Complex Acts of Knowing: Paradox and Descriptive Self awareness, *Journal of Knowledge Management* **6**, 2.

Sriskandarajah. N., Francis, C., Salomonsson, L., Kahiluoto, H., Lieblein, G., Breland, T.A., Geber, U & Helenius j. (2006) Education And Training In Ecological Agriculture: Nordic Region and U.S.A. In: *Organic Farming - Global Perspectives* Taji, A., Kristiansen, P & Reganold, J (ed) CSIRO Publications. pp 385-406.

Steyaert, P., Jiggins, J., 2007. Governance of complex environmental situations through social learning: a synthesis of SLIM's lessons for research, policy and practice. *Environ. Sci. Policy* **10** (6), 575–586.

Stirling, S. (2001) Sustainable Education. Re-visioning Learning and Change. Schumacher Briefings 6, Green Books, Dartington.

van Ameijde, Jitse (2007) *PersSyst Evaluation Report.* Unpublished Report, The Open University May 2007.

Vargese, J. & Ching, G. (2006) Creativity, Complexity and Organization in the DPI&F Ecology. Proceedings of the 12th ANZSYS conference - *Sustaining our social and natural capital* Katoomba, NSW Australia, 3rd-6th December.

Vaasstrøm, M., Christensen, M., Sriskandarajah, N. & Lieblein, G. (2007) *Facilitating Agricultural Innovation and Learning through Systemic Action Research.* 10th annual Conference of the Nordic-Scottish University network for Rural and Regional Development: Innovation Systems and Rural Development. Denmark, March 2007.

Vickers G. 1980 Education in systems thinking. *Journal of Applied Systems Analysis* **7**: 3-10.

von Foerster, H. & Poerkson, B. (2002) *Understanding Systems. Conversations on Epistemology and Ethics.* IFSR International Series on Systems Science and Engineering, 17. Kluwer Academic, New York and Carl-Auer , Heidelberg.

Wenger, E. (1998) *Communities of Practice: Learning Meaning and Identity.* Cambridge University Press, Cambridge.

Yalmambirra (2006) Knowledge and Wiradjuri: Who is telling the truth? A Wiradjuri Perspective. Proceedings of the 12th ANZSYS conference - *Sustaining our social and natural capital* Katoomba, NSW Australia, 3rd-6th December.

Theme 6: Organizational Systems

22. How Do We Know It's Working? Addressing the Evaluation Conundrum

Rosalind Armson
The Open University, ENG

Acknowledgements

The author gratefully acknowledges the support of Jitse van Ameijde in identifying some of the cited literature.

As more and more capacity for change is demanded by employers of their staff evaluation of human-resource development initiatives becomes more pressing. But evaluation is often perceived as missing the point or evaluating the wrong thing. This paper uses systems ideas to explore this conundrum and develops an influence-diagram model of professional practice to make sense of the issues. A theoretical basis is proposed for an evaluation methodology that meets the needs of all the stakeholders; is coherent with a systems approach; and transcends simplistic cause-and-effect models of development.

Introduction: The Conundrum

At a time when the capacity to create and sustain organizational change is a high priority, it is natural for executives and managers to look for evidence that development interventions deliver value for money. This has led to growing need for simple in-house evaluation approaches, capable of enactment by non-experts. However, studies have shown (Ramlall, 2003; Becker, Huselid & Ulrich, 2003) that less than 10 per cent of companies used formal methods of measuring the effectiveness. Where evaluation does occur, it is typically designed to tell senior executives whether a particular training programme, personnel-development programme or cultural change programme has been 'worthwhile'.

It can be argued that evaluation requests are often based on a model in which the results of a development intervention, such as a workshop or training programme, are traceable through a linear chain of causation (intervention leads to improved performance that leads to organizational benefit). Those involved (trainers, participants and others) will understand that the effects of an intervention are much more diverse and that the chain of causes and effects is neither linear nor fully traceable.

A request for data to demonstrate the success of an intervention is not an unreasonable one. Senior executives need timely, validated and rigorous information to formulate strategy but few senior executives have time, energy or enthusiasm for enquiring into the 'swamp' (Schön, 1983) of people's experience. However, as Ulrich (1997) points out, managers have traditionally relied on vague and undefined concepts such as morale, turnover and commitment for assessing the impact of Human Resource activities.

But those engaged in the action know that success or otherwise is not reducible to simple metrics. This is the conundrum of evaluating human activities. The evaluation takes place in a complex situation with multiple and interacting influences, and multiple patterns of causation and yet many stakeholders demand evaluations that present bullet-point conclusions derived from simple metrics.

This paper emerges from the struggle to produce evaluation data that recognizes the needs of senior executives whilst also recognizing the experience and learning of other, often unrecognized, stakeholders. It attempts to explore what an 'ideal' systemic approach to evaluation might do; what a methodology to approach these ideals might look like; and how a systemic view might transcend the difficulties of evaluating human-resource interventions. It is written from a second-order cybernetics perspective (Maturana and Varela, 1988) and builds on the author's experience of trying to meet requirements for self-evaluation, an external evaluation, and supporting others in meeting external demands for self-evaluation. Examples are drawn from the author's experience in the university and in other organizations.

A framework of systems ideas

This section uses a number of systemic ideas and devices to explore why 'simple numbers to measure success' are unsatisfactory on their own. These ideas are not in themselves very complicated but they are nonetheless challenging to apply rigorously and reveal phenomena that managers may not wish to acknowledge.

Many of the systems ideas used in developing this analysis are those taught to undergraduate students at the UK Open University (2000). In recent years, the PersSyst Project, a joint project between the Open University's Systems Department and its Human Resources Division, has been developing the capacity of university staff for systems thinking and practice. In this section a number of key systems ideas are used to identify some features of human-resource interventions not normally addressed by evaluation.

Perceived complexity

The complexity and variety humans perceive in their organizational environments mean that the results of any intervention, including development interventions, are also likely to be complex. Nor will they be limited to those expected or hoped for. The complexity of 'what happened' – the intervention, the participation, the participant and their work situation – cannot be fully represented by a set of metrics. Even well chosen metrics are simply numbers attempting to represent a set of diverse phenomena, even if the numbers represent defensible evidence. At this point it serves simply to note that the intricacy and variety of human behavior is not well represented by numerical data that is unsupported by qualitative narrative. This issue has arisen a number of times in the author's experience when, for example, evaluation addresses the quality of the intervention but fails to note that the benefits are stifled, for example, by structural obstacles or by the participants' work. In one intervention, very little positive benefit had accrued to the organization, even though participants rated the workshops very highly and found them to be useful. The questionnaire had failed to reflect the participants' major complaint. They had not been allowed the opportunities to exercise the new skills acquired in the workshops.

Cause and effect

Systems Thinking recognizes that human phenomena are rarely connected by simple chains of cause and effect. Organization change or improvements in human performances may be triggered by development interventions but many other causal effects will contribute to change and the change itself may not be that anticipated. For example, one intervention resulted in the participants being able to articulate their frustration with management more cogently.

Unintended consequences

A systemic approach to intervention will recognise that intervening in a human situation will have unintended consequences. This does not mean that all unintended consequences will be unwanted. It does mean that the 'success' of an intervention may be realized in unexpected ways or may be undermined by unwanted consequences. One group were so angered by the mismanagement of an intervention that they refused to work with the consultant involved, took responsibility for the process themselves, and delivered a plan for improvement. In the process they had ceased to be the reluctant and passive group they had been assumed to be, and instead became leaders for organizational development in their department.

It is also important to note at this point that notions such as 'success' and 'unwanted consequences' assume an observer who wants and evaluates. Success and 'wanted-ness' are not objective qualities. A systemic approach to evaluation will thus include exploration of unintended consequences, both wanted and unwanted. Its remit will also allow for recognition of success (or failure) realized in ways that were not anticipated in the design of the intervention and allow for different perceptions and valuing of these.

The three Es: systems hierarchy

Checkland and Scholes (1999) make a powerful distinction between Efficacy, Efficiency and Effectiveness and suggest that in Soft Systems Methodology, attention be given to defining criteria for each of three distinct levels in the systems hierarchy. The idea can be extended to prompt exploration of 'success' in other activities.

The first E, Efficacy, asks whether the intervention does what it is supposed to do. At this point there is often an unrecognized issue about *whether* the activity is able to do what it is supposed to do. For example, many human-resource development interventions are designed to develop participants' skills, attitudes or knowledge. Defining criteria for efficacy exposes the assumptions behind such an enterprise. For example, a development workshop is often seen as something 'done to' participants, such that improved performance is an inevitable outcome of participation in a successful workshop. This view neglects the influences of other elements in the participant's practice context (as shown in Figure 1). It is build on a pedagogic model of the participant as passive recipient of skills or knowledge as 'stuff' transferred from the facilitator.

Setting indicators or criteria for Efficiency (the second of Checkland's 3 Es) reveals the costs and the benefits of an intervention. A systemic view would take account of indirect costs as well as direct costs to funders. Costs to other stakeholders are often neglected (the latter is discussed below), even where these are significant. The decision to invest in a development project is a decision that the value of the development will outweigh the money or other costs. Evaluations are thus frequently oriented towards finding out whether the value has been realized. But this is not the same as ascertaining whether it was 'good value for money' in the sense that implies comparison with other offers of varying quality or price. Efficiency criteria, such as the frequently sought 'value for money', neglect an implicit 'compared to what?'. (Monetary language here is a synecdoche for any organizational costs of a development project.)

Evaluation will often look for evidence that developmental activity has been Effective. Effectiveness is the third of Checkland's three Es. This is usually taken to mean that the activity has made a positive difference to the wider system of which it is a part. 'Happy sheets' explore whether the workshop was well run, interesting and relevant. Participants' improved performance is less easy to attribute to the workshop, however. Improved performance is likely to develop over time, as participants become more skilled and only when they have the opportunities to use those skills. Performance improvement may also be blocked by structural arrangements. For example, a department producing products for customers with disabilities could not improve its performance because it was limited to producing last-minute adaptations of the mainstream product instead of designing parallel products alongside the mainstream products.

Boundary judgments

Boundary is a key systems concept and Systems Thinking recognizes that boundaries are identified *by an observer*. Thus boundaries may be contended. A systemic approach to evaluation will thus make the boundaries of the intervention explicit. Evaluations built on a linear cause-and-effect relationship between development intervention and measurable organizational benefit draw a boundary that excludes many effects deemed important by stakeholders directly involved in the intervention.

A systemic approach that recognizes these issues will involve setting the boundaries of the evaluation much wider, looking for impacts over a wider range of time and influence. An evaluation informed by systems thinking is likely to set the boundaries wider than might otherwise be the case, recognizing that unintended consequences are part of the outcome. The evaluation will make clear what was part of the intervention and what was not; and what was part of the outcome and what was not. It will also recognise that these are contended issues and that different stakeholders favour different boundaries, discarding elements outside the boundary as irrelevant or unimportant.

Time is also a dimension of boundary judgment that needs to be explicit. The impacts of a development intervention may be realized over time as skills and confidence increase and work-in-progress makes way for the new approach. This consideration exposes the poverty of the so-called 'happy sheet' that only measures the unreflected-on experience of the workshop. Overall effectiveness will emerge and evolve from the participant's later practice and, if the workshop has indeed been successful, the participant's absorption of new attitudes, skills, and understandings will no longer be credited to the workshop (or other intervention) by the participant. Many systems consultants will recognise that 'If I do this well, they'll think they've done it themselves.' It can be argued that a good intervention will trigger further self-directed development. In deciding how to time evaluation there is thus a balance between 'giving it time to work' and losing any attribution to the workshop.

Multiple stakeholders

An evaluation informed by systems thinking would recognise the needs of all the stakeholders and the potential impact upon each of them of any particular evaluation strategy. It will also recognise that evaluation is a profoundly political process. There are inequities in power in most development situations and the outcomes of an evaluation are likely to influence the future trajectory of activities that have impacts on people's lives in ways that they may not control. This is a major reason why participants and deliverers can be acutely nervous of 'simple metrics' used to judge the worth of an intervention. Checkland (1999) insists that Customers, Actors, and Owners be identified in defining a relevant system. This draws the author's attention to different stakeholder groups for any purposeful activity.

Those who fund or commission the activity are the Owners of the HR development intervention (in Checkland's terms). They are likely to want evidence that the activity has been 'successful'; that it has delivered 'value for money'; and that there are emergent results such as measurable better performance. They need a simple response to the question 'was this successful and value for money?' without being drawn into the minutiae. Funders, perhaps by nature, prefer quantitative data to which they can attribute 'objectivity'. Thus while a systems thinker might espouse a pluralist, constructivist, phenomenological paradigm, addressing the needs of funders involves epistemological awareness (Armson & Ison, 2004) that attends to the needs of those outside that paradigm. Meeting funders 'where they are' requires the language of multiple paradigms. The challenge is to do this with integrity, especially in a project that specifically works to increase systemic awareness. Those who commission development activities may be prepared to engage with the complexities but often have to contend with the need to account themselves for perceived success or failure. They are likely to have a strong interest in demonstrating success or, failing that, evidence of extenuating circumstances. Commissioners may also seek evidence of whether an approach has usefulness for the future. They are, in this sense, likely to be more willing to engage with the complexity of the activity and its context and of the evaluation and its context.

The Customers, the intended beneficiaries of a development initiative are likely to have a very rich model of the impact of the activity, and of its success or otherwise. They will also be among the first to recognise unintended consequences. They will also be more aware than many of the complexities of improving performance in the face of the multiple influences acting upon them. Indeed, if they are not able to orchestrate their work and its context with newly acquired skills, they are likely to experience the intervention as 'malicious development' in the face of pressure to improve performance. The author has repeatedly been told stories that report participants' frustration with development intended to 'fix the people' when their attempts to perform well are frustrated by structures beyond their control.

The Actors, the deliverers of the intervention, are politically vulnerable to the estimation of success or failure but also have a different stakeholding. They will often be very aware of the constraints on an intervention and of the circumstances that limit its success. They may, however, also be looking to an evaluation to build an understanding of how future interventions might be designed to build on the experience and learning of both themselves and the participants. They may also wish the 'Owners' of the intervention to become aware of the complexities of the situation and of changes that can be made to the work and its context if improvements are to be achieved. The Actors, along with the Customers, are likely to be frustrated and misrepresented by a quantitative evaluation that does not recognise the complexity of the situation in which they are working.

Third party stakeholders often have the most contested stakeholdings, precisely because they are outside the design of the intervention and beyond the boundaries of the evaluation. They are not, however, outside the range of unintended consequences. Given that many interventions succeed or fail in unexpected ways it is important to design third parties into the evaluation. Third parties hold much of the evidence as to the form that success or failure took. For example, a development activity that succeeded in achieving most of its objectives was nonetheless the source of much discontent and was widely thought by the department concerned to have been 'a waste of time'. The cause of this discontent, not detected by the initial evaluation, was that non-participating department members were covering, without much acknowledgement or thanks, for their absent colleagues for one day a week over ten weeks. Attending to the needs of non-attending participants in subsequent interventions markedly improved the success perceived by departments involved. Owners often exclude third parties from the evaluation. Indeed, without their evidence, those who commission the intervention will be left exposed if the success is less than expected.

Performance as an emergent property of a system of influences

With a multiplicity of perspectives and the lack of clear chains of causation, evaluation that takes account of the systemicity of impacts needs a model of how success or failure emerges. This section proposes a sense-making model that can be used to develop an evaluation methodology that takes account of the differing needs of stakeholders, their differing epistemologies and the lack of auditable trails of cause and effect.

A person working in an organization can be seen as part of a system of influences. That person's perceived performance in their role is an emergent property of this system of influences. Performance emerges from the interaction of:

- The person, doing whatever they do;
- Their skills, experience and dispositions;
- The context within which they work, including their boss, their colleagues, their tools, environment and resources;
- The task the person is trying to do.

These constitute a mutually interconnected system of influences within which each element influences each of the other elements. This system of influences is the 'practice' of this individual shown in Figure 1. The extent to which the

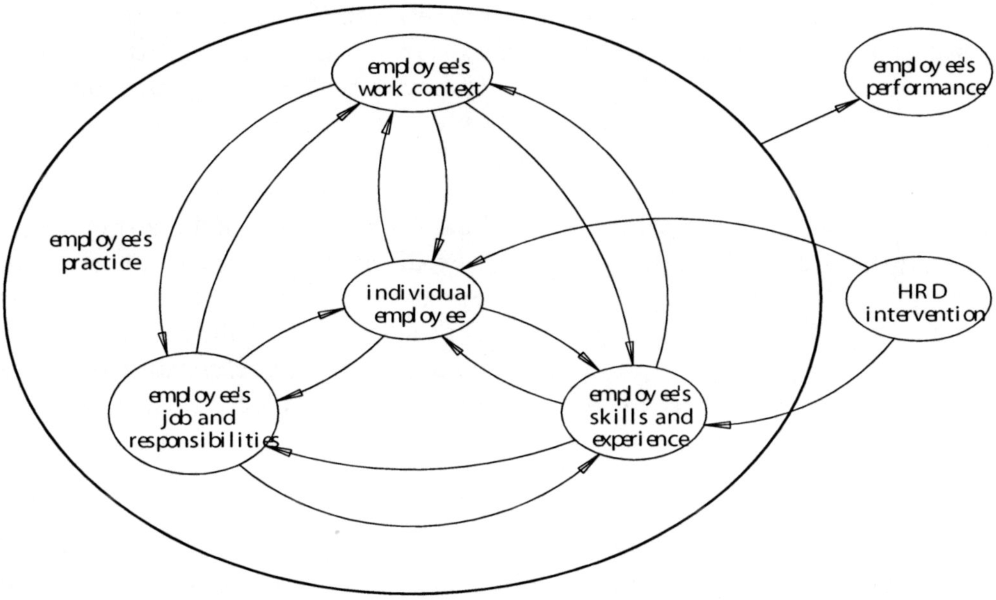

Influence diagram of the impact of an HRD intervention on the employee's system of practice

Figure 1 *An influence diagram of the impact of an HRD intervention on the employee's system of practice*

employee is able to orchestrate these influences depends on the extent of their autonomy.

'Performance' emerges as a property of the individual's practice. Human-resource development (HRD) interventions are usually designed to develop the individual and their skills, experience, understanding and disposition. Impacts on the work context and on the work itself are less often addressed. The model shown in Figure 1 has profound implications for the evaluation of HRD interventions. The intervention itself has no *direct* influence on the employee's performance. Thus, as observed by the author, attempts to improve the performance of an employee can be frustrated if, for example, the employee's line manager does not create the space and opportunity for enhanced performance; or where the job remains the same despite the employee's enhanced capacities; or where the employee has inadequate resources.

This model has proved to be powerful in a number of ways. First, it has helped to make sense of the mismatch between the paradigms of those who commission the evaluation and those who have participated in the intervention. The expectation of the former that an intervention will (or should) improve performance takes no account of the different systemic levels at which these phenomena occur. It locates the cry of participants and developers that 'it's much more complicated than that' in the interactions that lead to performance as an emergent phenomenon.

The model shown in Figure 1 carries the clear implication that individual employees are the only stakeholders who can attribute a connection between the intervention and improved performance. They are the only stakeholders engaged at the systemic level from which performance emerges.

The conundrum of evaluating HR interventions - or other interventions in situations perceived as complex – emerges from the encounter between two essentially incompatible paradigms. This results for a demand for 'objective' and probably quantitative data that is independent of the researcher-evaluator. This demand is situated firmly in a positivist paradigm. As such, it may be perceived as hopelessly inappropriate and impossible-to-comply-with by development practitioners, participants and third parties because it neglects their experience of the complexities that are the very stuff of success or failure. Systems Thinking, with a constructivist-pluralist epistemology is able to recognise, and contend with, this clash. The systems thinking alluded to above is able to accommodate the positivist paradigm as one of the pluralities of multiple stakeholding. This enables the demand for quantitative and objective data to be seen simply as a customer need that can be met by finding accommodations between the needs of all the stakeholders (Checkland, 1999).

The lack of a direct connection between performance and intervention suggests that participants have an important role in evaluation, not only as stakeholders but as the legitimate attributors of the connection between the intervention and the performance outcome. Leaving this attribution to participants also has implications for coherence and for ethicality, especially if the intervention is designed to build leadership capacity, autonomy or personal responsibility. It makes no sense, nor would it be ethical for developers to claim improved performance as a direct result of the intervention. To do so cuts out the participants and is inconsistent with enabling them to take responsibility for their own performance.

It should also be noted that the link between intervention and improved performance, even when attributed by participants, may not be a causal one since development interventions may serve as triggers for, rather than causes of, change. The example cited above where a team was so enraged by a development activity that they had seized control of their own development is an example of this.

The theoretical basis for a methodology

The discussion above provides the basis for the design of an evaluation methodology. The evaluation methodology must take account of the different stakeholdings and values. This means that there are unlikely to be agreed criteria for 'success'. It must also recognise that different stakeholders have different needs from the evaluation and will have different paradigms for understanding and recognizing success. Accommodating these differing needs and paradigms means recognizing that these are legitimate, even if incommensurable.

A systemic evaluation methodology will also need to address the intervention at three different systemic levels: the intervention itself; its contribution to the wider purpose it is serving; and the way in which it was carried out. Boundaries will be set to include unintended and other consequences, and 'success' realized in unexpected ways. It will also contain easily identifiable indicators that senior executives will recognise as representing simple indicators or measures of success.

The resulting methodology, described elsewhere, elicits success criteria from a wide variety of stakeholders at three different systemic levels to create questionnaires that then generate both quantitative and qualitative data (Armson and Meynell, forthcoming). These are then presented in ways that allow all the participants to make sense of the evaluation, in ways that meet their separate needs. Initial indications are that the approach has been useful and welcomed by those using it and commissioning evaluation since the approach is able to provide simple "success or failure" indicators as well as detailed learning that supports "doing it better next time".

References

Armson, R. and Ison, R. L. (2004). *Juggling with Complexity: searching for system* ISBN 0749258241.

Becker, B., Huselid, M., & Ulrich, D. (2001). *The HR Scorecard: Linking People, Strategy, and Performance,* ISBN 1578511364.

Checkland. P. and Scholes, J. (1999). *Soft Systems Methodology in Action,* ISBN 0471986054.

Maturana, H. & Varela, F., (1980) *Autopoiesis and Cognition: The realization of the living,* ISBN 9027710163

Open University Systems Group, (2000), *T551 Systems Thinking: a primer*, ISBN 074928403X

Ramlall, S. (2003). Measuring human resource management's effectiveness in improving performance. *Human Resource Planning*, ISSN 0199-8986, 26, 51-63.
Schön, D., (1983), *The Reflective Practitioner*, ISBN 0465068782
Ulrich, D. (1997). Measuring human resources: an overview of practice and prescription for results. *Human Resource Management*, ISSN 0958-5192, 36, 303-320.

23. Worker Endurance Management in the 21st Century

Carlos A. Comperatore
The Johns Hopkins University Applied Physics Laboratory, USA

Pik Kwan Rivera
Engineering Psychologist, US Coast Headquarters, USA

While work environments devoid of stressors are a rarity in the twenty-first century, it is also difficult to find employers who deliberately identify and manage these stressors. Personnel work embedded in a complex system of stressors that affects their health and ability to maintain performance efficiency. Unfortunately, what is more common in civilized twenty-first century work environments is that workers are left to their own devices to mitigate the impact of endemic stressors. In this paper, we offer the use of a systems approach to develop systemic organizational changes to protect workers' health and performance. This systems approach is derived from the US Coast Crew Endurance Management system currently under implementation in Coast Guard maritime work environments. The purpose of this work is to provide the means for both workers and managers alike to identify and control job specific stressors and prevent long-term adverse effects on worker health and well being.

Stressors Form Endemic Complexes in the Work Environment

No matter where people work (e.g., airports, command centers, refineries, commercial and military airplanes, commercial and military afloat platforms, offices, nuclear power plants, etc.), they do so embedded in a complex of stressors that chronically tax their physical and mental resources (Comperatore, Rivera *et al.*, 2005). In this context, we employ the term stressor as a stimulus that causes stress to an organism.

Stressors often occur concurrently in work environments (e.g., high workload tempo, frequent exposure to customers, long work hours, etc.), simultaneously impacting workers' physiology and psychological well being. In general, workplace stressors organize into a complex system of interacting elements (Comperatore, 1990, 1993, 1994, 1996, 1999, 2001, 2003; Guastello, 1995). As stressors incidence increases in daily work routines, their combined impact on worker health and performance is augmented (see Figure 1).

Reducing the incidence of workplace stressors requires a systems approach because of the need to identify industry traditions (e.g., commercial maritime, military), employee behaviors, and organizational management

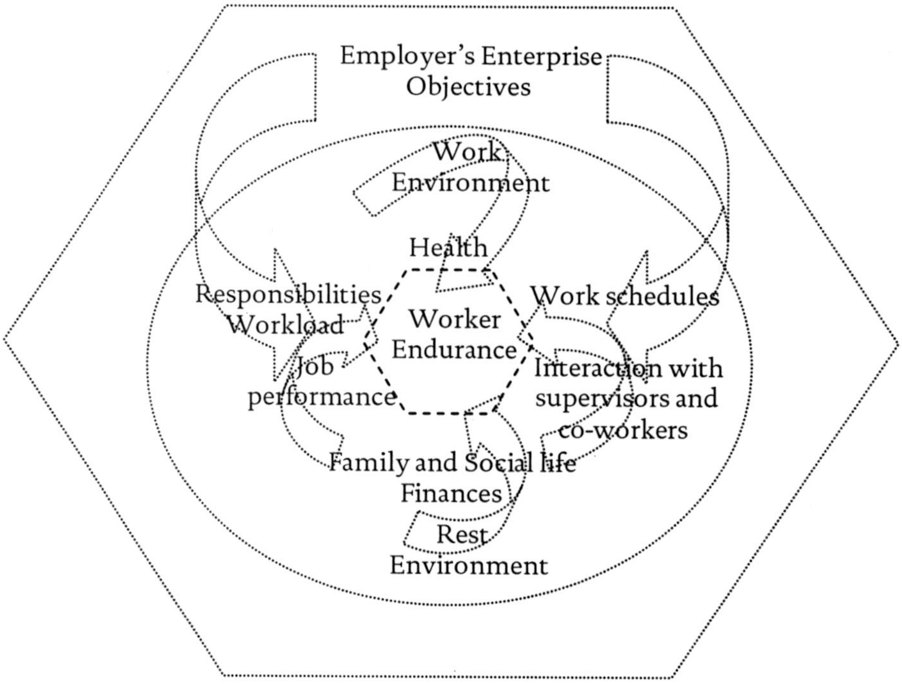

Figure 1 *Worker Stressor Complex. Interaction of stressors impacting physical and psychological resources. Controls to mitigate the impact of this stressor complex must go beyond quick fixes, such as sleeping pills, stimulants, or work schedules formulas (after Comperatore and Rivera, 2005).*

culture and attitudes that contribute to the formation of the stressors complex (Comperatore & Rivera, 2005).

Currently, an endurance management program designed to preserve crewmember health and performance in maritime environments employs a systems approach to decompose the stressor complex into, among others, individual behaviors, organizational practices, regulations, industry culture, and environmental conditions. In practice, USCG officers and crewmembers use a software tool, developed by the USCG Crew Endurance program, to identify high incidence endurance risk factors and to develop a mitigation plan that reduces the combined effects of endemic stressors on crewmember health and performance. The tool is the product of many years of research on methods to manage crew endurance in military missions that began in 1990 under the Crew Endurance program developed for the Army Safety Center (Comperatore, 1996; Comperatore, Carvalhais & Della Rocco, 1998; Comperatore, Bloch & Ferry, 1999; Comperatore & Rivera, 2003). Today, a similar program is the vehicle to implement practices that control stressors in commercial maritime work environments.

Following, we will review evidence of the impact of modern 24 hour operations on human health and performance and offer a theoretical adaptation of the Crew Endurance Management program as a potential means to protect workers health and performance in other than maritime operations.

Modern Society's Endemic Risk Factor: Twenty-four Hours Operations

Twenty-four operations require workers to function during times of the day when their internal physiology is attempting to restore energy resources. Unless a well planned method to re-adapt workers to spend energy during the night and sleep during daytime is in place, workers experience not only sleep restriction, but also challenges to their internal biological clock responsible for regulating critical physiological systems such as sleep and cellular energy restoration.

Work Schedules That Compete With Family Time: A Daily Trade Off

Consider a worker whose family responsibilities require that she spends time with her children in the evening. Daily shifts greater than 8 hours (e.g., 12 hour shifts) combined with long commuting times will interact with evening family time and result in the daily restriction of sleep duration (e.g., less than 6 or 5 hours) throughout the work week. If long sleep periods are possible during days-off, fatigue grows over the work week only and peaks towards the last two days of work. If weekend work is also part of job requirements, then fatigue is likely to become chronic and its effects on health and performance will not subside until a prolonged period of restorative sleep is possible (e.g., approximately 1 week with daily sleep periods of 7-8 hours in duration). This ensemble of stressors, namely shiftwork, duty duration, commuting time, and family time (in this case the need for family time becomes a stressor), concurrently maintain a steady pressure on the individual to trade sleep for family time (Comperatore, Rivera, *et al.*, 2005).

Throughout the world, rotating work schedules combined with long work hours affect, among others, railroad conductors and engineers, law enforcements officers, security specialists, security and intelligence analysts, air traffic controllers, airport passenger screeners, airport baggage handlers, nurses and doctors in hospitals and clinics, truck drivers, and crewmembers throughout diverse segments of the commercial maritime industry.

Rotating Reporting Times, Long Work Hours, Naps, and Caffeine Dependence

Another example of stressors synergistically taxing workers' energy levels day by day can be found in work environments requiring long work hours (12 hours per day) and rotation of starting times (e.g., 0230, 0430, 0500, 0600). Initially the work schedule restricts workers to less than 7-8 hours of uninterrupted sleep per day. This situation emerges as personnel balance social and family life with a work schedule that demands that they retire in the early evening hours. For instance, if one is to sleep 7-8 hours per day, reporting times at 0430 require sleep to begin at approximately 1900, to wake up at 0300, dress, eat breakfast, and travel to work (provided a short duration commute). The early bedtime is difficult to accomplish for personnel who have young families. In their case, personnel must use time in the evening to interact with a day-oriented family living in a day- oriented society. Upon return from the work day, particularly after a 12 hour work day, some people may choose to nap for a short period of time, sometimes beyond 2 hours. This is a good practice, but it may cause a delay in bedtime during the evening. In other words, it is difficult to retire at 1900 if one naps for more than 30 minutes during the afternoon. Thus, personnel who nap in the afternoon may not retire earlier than 2100-2200, restricting the second sleep period to approximately 5 hours. While one may obtain eight or more hours of cumulative sleep per day, each period is too short to supply sufficient restorative sleep. Napping can help reduce the experience of fatigue after work; however, if not managed properly it will not help reduce fatigue during the work period.

In addition to daily sleep debt, workers will also experience the desynchronization of physiological energy cycles from their work and rest cycle. This is evident, in some cases, as personnel work during the night in dimly lit environments. Bright light, whether artificial or natural, is required to synchronize peak energy availability with work periods. The light that workers see throughout the day becomes a crucial element that, if not managed properly, can cause the experience of jet lag symptoms. During the night as the biological clock is set to restore energy (attempting to sleep), workers try to carry out complex cognitive and decision making tasks. Combining this physiological confusion with increasing daily sleep debt results in well documented performance degradation until the vicious cycle is broken and only after the mounting nocturnal sleep-debt is settled (e.g., several nights of uninterrupted 8-hour sleep periods).

Daytime sleepiness sets in within few days of exposure to these and similar work schedules. In many cases, personnel may habitually consume stimulants such as caffeine, available in soft drinks, coffee, and in over the counter formulations, to combat daytime sleepiness during work periods. Adverse health effects of caffeine addiction range from cardiovascular disorders to, paradoxically, chronic fatigue.

Caffeine dependence has been shown to disrupt the architecture of sleep, degrading its daily restorative value, particularly when caffeine consumption occurs within 4 hours or less of bedtime. Thus, the very coping strategy used to maintain alertness during work periods sabotages the daily restoration of alertness, increasing the experience of fatigue, even after waking from long periods of sleep (e.g., 8 hours). The experience of daytime sleepiness forces personnel into a vicious recurrent behavioral pattern (Figure 2 below).

Health Conditions and Job Related Stressors

The adverse impact of endemic stressors on health and performance is augmented when workers battle health conditions (e.g., apnea, high blood pressure, type II diabetes), experience disrupted sleep due to unmanaged stress or chronic anxiety, lead a sedentary life style (e.g., lack of exercise), and/ or make poor daily diet choices (e.g., emphasis on consuming foods high in fat content, processed sugar, caffeine, starch). The aggregate effect of these stressors on the ability to stay alert and be mentally sharp is difficult to accurately calculate. Yet, although

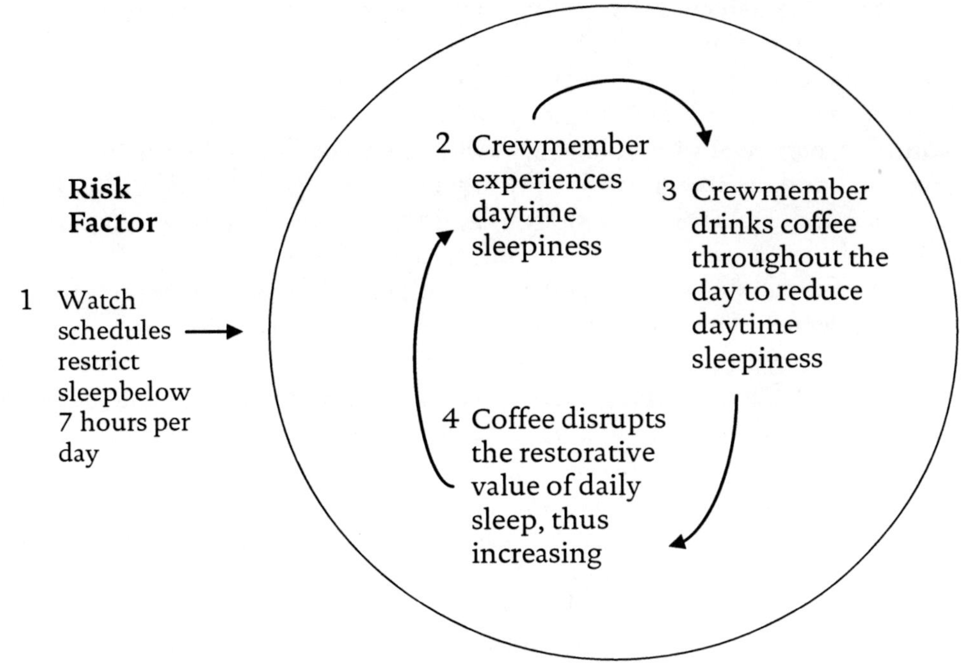

Figure 2 *System Limit Cycle. Depiction of a recurrent vicious feedback pattern: watch schedule structure restricts daily sleep below 7 uninterrupted hours, crewmember experiences cumulative sleep deprivation, thus drinks coffee throughout the day to reduce daytime sleepiness, Coffee reduces restorative value of daily sleep, thus crewmember resorts to daily caffeine consumption to reduce sleepiness.*

conservative, we can safely assume that under these circumstances workers' experience of fatigue will be pervasive throughout the work week and that work performance is likely to degrade daily during the latter half of the work day (OTA report, 1991). While the human brain is a complex system with incredible adaptability, it is also a machine with stiff energy requirements. Less than 7-8 hours of uninterrupted sleep per day are not sufficient to restore biochemical resources necessary to maintain cognitive performance no matter how simple the job. Most notably, inadequate sleep is particularly damaging to cognitive abilities in jobs where decision making, safety and/ or security may go hand in hand.

Systems Analysis Requirements

Managing worker endurance requires a thorough understanding of the many contributing elements that form the stressor ensemble (Comperatore & Rivera, 2005). In many work environments, endemic stressors are often tied to tradition and local culture. For any change to have an impact on individual behavior or choice, or organizational philosophy, there is a need for a well established set of practices ensuring that changes remain in effect long enough to be measured. Without presenting value to the individual and organization, any behavioral or policy improvement is likely to de-evolve due to cultural and practical pressures.

In the concept presented here, a systems approach is used to identify and understand the influences among the various elements forming the stressor complex, namely, individual behaviors and choices, organizational practices and policies, and environmental conditions (see Figure 3). We propose the use of a system model to depict descriptions and associations among interacting elements within and among layers of hierarchical influence.

The first analysis requirement is to identify system elements and their corresponding functionalities. Second, it is necessary to describe the organization of elements within a model comprised of hierarchical layers that aids to conceptualize the influence among sets of elements, grouped according to common attributes. The third requirement is to characterize the interaction and feedback loops among elements within layers, and fourth is the depiction of influence networks among elements between layers. These observations are conducted with the purpose to detect emerging synergistic interaction. Influence networks can provide insights on which stressors combine to affect worker health and performance. Once a vicious network of stressors is identified, it is then possible to design a comprehensive systemic plan to reduce the daily incidence of specific key noxious stressors.

The following data gathering activities support the analytical requirements presented here:

- Conduct a functional task analysis to understand worker responsibilities, workload, and work environment;
- Identify and describe stressors present in the work environment that impact individual workers as they discharge their duties;
- Analyze stressors with high daily incidence describing their combined effect on worker health and performance;
- Identify the dependencies among organizational goals, operating costs, staffing numbers, and work schedules required to meet daily operational objectives;
- Study patterns of sick-call with the purpose to identify illnesses or health complains that are frequently reported among workers sharing similar duties;
- Produce system diagrams showing the dependencies among duties, stressors, health complains, and productivity for each departmental segment within the organization;
- Identify high yield systemic controls that can significantly mitigate the impact of the stressor complex on personnel.

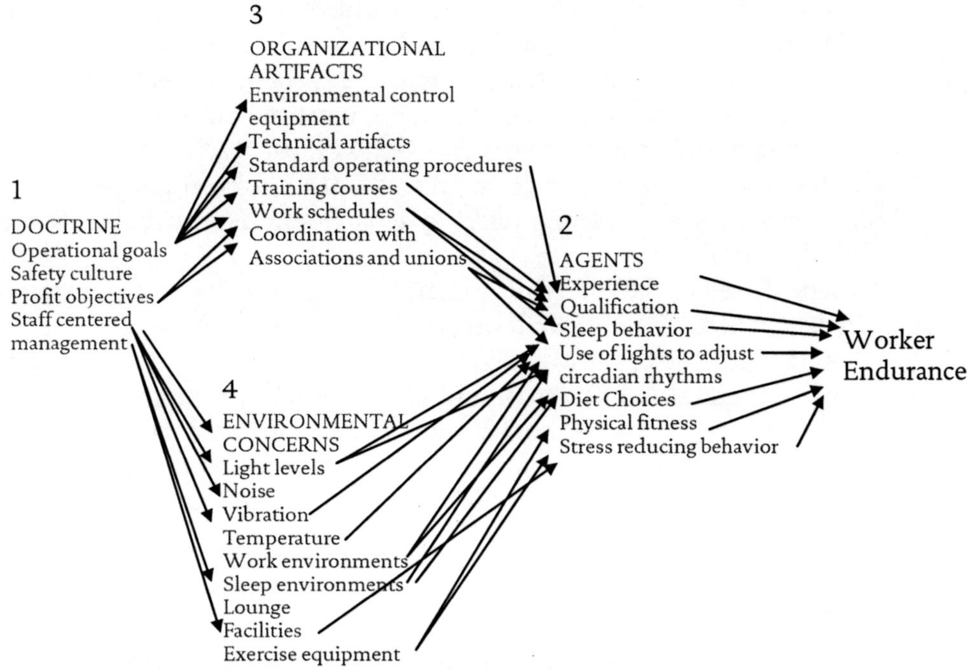

Figure 3 *Interdependent Worker Endurance Elements. This is an example of the various dependencies that originate under three domain categories, namely Doctrine, Agents, and Organizational Artifacts. Elements in the Agents and Organizational Artifact domains combine to generate endurance, while elements in the doctrine domain contain requirements, and environmental conditions further challenge personnel's endurance.*

The Worker Endurance Management System (WEMS): Description and Implementation

Once the analytical requirements are met, we propose the use of a multi-layer model using domains that describe organizational complex adaptive systems (Axelrod & Cohen, 2001), namely artifacts, agents or personnel, and organizational doctrine. For instance, from functional task analysis and workload assessments, information on workload and work schedules is placed under the organizational doctrine category. Information on personnel behavior (e.g., choices during leisure time, preferred daily bedtime, diet choices, preferred mealtimes, etc.), staffing numbers, and personnel training, on the other hand, is parceled to the agent or personnel domain. Details on technology, available automation, control of environmental lighting and temperature, and other artifacts necessary for workers to carry out job related duties are listed under the artifact or technology domain. Dependencies are then drawn among the various elements under each domain with the purpose to identify potential modifications in the relationship among elements or in the nature of some of the elements themselves that will yield adaptive systemic performance improvements.

At the very foundation of the model the first level includes doctrine that is immutable and critical for the survival and growth of the organization, the second level includes all elements that characterize agents or personnel, and the third level includes artifacts such as technology, work schedules, policies, and business processes that agents use to discharge their duties. A fourth level in the model includes environmental concerns in the work environment (e.g., noise and ambient temperature in the engineering department near turbines) that affect agent's health and performance.

Elements listed in the Doctrine domain affect elements in other levels directly, but received little or no modulating feedback from other levels. Doctrine reflects the major purpose of the organization's very existence and it is most difficult to change. Agent actions to maintain endurance and mitigate the impact of workplace stressors constitute the second or Personnel level of the endurance system. Personnel actions help to manage human endurance limits, specifically physiological limits. Examples of second-level system elements are:

- Consuming a proper diet;
- Reducing daily caffeine intake;
- Taking the opportunity to sleep 7-8 hours per day when available;
- Avoiding heavy meals before bedtime, etc.;
- Seeking training;
- Improving job qualifications.

Agents modify behavior in response to guidance originating from the Doctrine domain, and use Organizational Artifacts to discharge job related duties. Organizational actions and technology artifacts that facilitate workers' efforts to carry out job related activities could, if well guided, mitigate the effects of workplace stressors.

The Organizational Artifact level constitutes the third system level of the model. Examples of Organizational Artifacts are:

- Policies supporting the use of watch schedules that ensure sleep and watch schedule stability;
- Improvements to workplace meal choices;
- Habitability improvements to the work and sleep environments;
- Modification of traditional policies that disrupt sleep, for instance use of 12-hour rotating shifts.

A High Leverage System Pivot

The first organizational action requires the formation of a local working group. The composition of this team requires experienced personnel that are respected by both peers and supervisors. Members must be personnel with administrative responsibilities and able to train workers. The working group's goals are to identify and implement potential changes in the execution of duties, environmental improvements, policies, and workplace practices that may protect and improve personnel health and performance. Their objective is to find the relationships among elements in the model that result in the formation of a stressor complex. Specifically, the working group endeavors to identify the influence of doctrine and organizational practices, regulations, beliefs, worker choices, and attitudes that together increase the incidence of various stressors concurrently and that result in inescapable adverse health effects.

- Personnel efficiency in taking advantage of rest opportunities.

Worker Endurance Education

In addition to the formation of a local working group, the successful implementation of the WEMS requires the implementation of an aggressive education program to provide managers and personnel a clear understanding of their contribution to the management of workplace stressors. Local working group members, management, and personnel at large must share the same critical information on human physiology and endurance limits. Through participation in the education program, each individual learns his or her role in the process of developing and implementing practices that prevent the unnecessary disruption of personnel's efforts to obtain sufficient rest, exercise, proper diet, and sufficient daily leisure time. Coordination and execution of workplace management practices that support and maintain good endurance requires the participation of all management levels of an organization.

A good example of education programs in support of worker endurance management is provided by the U.S. Coast Guard (CG) at the Leadership Development Center in New London, CT. The USCG trains prospective commanding and executive officers as well as operations officers on good crew endurance (CE) management practices. In addition to the CG Leadership Development Center CE training, the CG Office of Health and Environmental Safety trains CG safety and health specialist on endurance management science. This training provides specific information on how to design work schedules that support crew readiness and appropriate rest during time off periods. Also, the use of practices to prevent the desynchronization of personnel' biological clock during shiftwork rotations is encouraged. In addition, personnel learn specifics on how to manage caffeine intake, appropriate hydration practices, diet requirements, and control of environmental stressors in the work environments. CG Safety and Health specialists are well versed in the use of CE educational software to help train workplace personnel. This community provides direct support to workplace crew endurance working groups and to personnel working on designing work and watch schedules to provide appropriate crew rest and operational readiness.

Conclusions

The WEM system prescribes that organizations' management and leadership develop a thorough understanding of the debilitating effects of workplace stressors, relevant to their organizations' specific operations, and work environments. Safety managers can provide key contributions to the WEM system if they understand what specific environmental improvements (e.g., endurance education, modifications to work environments such as proper temperature regulation, lighting, etc.) personnel require to mitigate the adverse effects of the workplace stressor complex on performance. Just as important is the need for personnel to obtain proven training on how to cope with job related stressors and to be able to trust that leaders, managers, and supervisors will support their daily efforts to maintain a healthy lifestyle.

The success of the WEM system lies on its emphasis to ensure that organizations support the implementation of a set of practices that protect personnel' s endurance restoration during time-off. These practices include not only modification of watch schedules, workplace policies, or work and rest environments, but also the development and implementation of enterprise-wide policies. Without clear and tangible support from management throughout the organization, the disparity between managers' practices and worker training will quickly result in reduced program credibility among workers. Workers at large will become skeptical as to the intent of the program and withdraw their commitment to make changes in their daily practices. Widespread cynicism leaves workers feeling alienated from the very resources that are intended to support them in the daily grind to cope with the adverse impact of workplace stressors on health and performance.

References

Comperatore, C.A., Rivera, P.K. et al., (2005). Enduring the shipboard stressor complex: A systems approach. Aviation, Space, and Environmental Medicine, 76(6), 108-118.

Comperatore, C.A. (1996). The Systems Approach to Crew Rest, in Crowley, Newton, Davidson, Newton, Lindsey, and Marcum (Eds.), Leader's Guide to Crew Endurance, (pp 21-25). Fort Rucker, AL: U.S. Army Aeromedical Research laboratory and U.S. Army Safety Center.

Comperatore, C.A., Bloch, C., and Ferry, C. (1999). Incidence of Sleep Loss and Wakefulness Degradation on a U.S. Coast Guard Cutter under Exemplar Crewing Limits. U.S. Coast Guard Research and Development Center Technical Report R&DC 03/99.

Comperatore, C.A., Carvalhais, A.; Della Rocco, P.; Schaab, B; Bloch, C. (1998). Development of Crew Endurance Plans for USCG Air Stations- Phase I. U.S. Coast Guard Research and Development Center Technical Report RDC 14/98, Government Assession Number AD-A 358396.

Comperatore, C. A., & Chairamonte, J. A. 1993. Implementation of a shift lag coping strategy at the Eastern Army Aviation Training Site during NVG training. (USAARL Report 93-24) Fort Rucker, AL: U.S. Army Aeromedical Research Laboratory.

Comperatore, C. A., Chairamonte, J. A., Lawhorn, K. L., & Allan, L. W. (1994). Unit specific crew rest strategies: phase 1 evaluation of the 1/212th aviation battalion during shift-work transitions (USAARL Report 94-3) Fort Rucker, AL: U.S. Army Aeromedical Research Laboratory.

Comperatore C. A., & Krueger G. P. (1990). Circadian rhythm desynchronosis, jet lag, shift lag, and coping strategies. In: Scott I, (Eds.), Occupational Medicine: State of the art reviews, vol. 5. (pp. 323-342). Philadelphia, PA: Hanley & Belfus, Inc.

Gustello, Stephen J. (1995). Chaos, Catastrophe, and Human Affairs : Applications of Nonlinear Dynamics to Work, Organization, and Social Evolution. Lawrence Earlbaum Associates, Mahwah, New Jersey..

Office of Technology Assessment, Biological Rhythms: Implications for the Worker, (1991), (Report OTA-BA-463), Washington, DC: U.S. Government Printing Office.

Smolensky, M., and Lamberg, L. (2001). The Body Clock Guide to Better Health. Henry Holt and Company, LLC. New York, New York

24. Complexity in Acquisition Systems: A Framework to Monitor Trade-offs and Their Impact on Capability Emergence

Carlos A. Comperatore
The Johns Hopkins University Applied Physics Laboratory, USA

Bryan Bender
Office of Maritime Domain Awareness Systems and Architecture, United States Coast Guard, USA

Large acquisitions are complex systems that usually employ linear processes to monitor the effectiveness of contract teams. As a complex adaptive system, acquisitions seek to field capabilities that emerge from an intricate balance between technology, agents and doctrine. These domains evolve independently and often outside the direct purview of the acquisition team. In practice, acquisition managers review technology efforts alone to measure progress toward the desired end state. Without the benefit of a complexity-based review, managers often face high-consequence decisions without time to quantify the state of capability emergence and project the impact of changes in any one domain. This paper presents a framework to monitor an acquisition's developmental progress, determining future capability emergence from the present-day state of technology, agents and doctrine. Borrowing heavily from nonlinear dynamics, the framework treats acquisitions as complex adaptive systems, where estimating developmental stability and near-term unexpected outcomes are the means to ensure capability emergence.

Complex Acquisition Systems

In this work we advance the notion that large acquisitions create environments reflecting specific characteristics of complex adaptive systems (CAS), and that undesirable and unexpected consequences often result from undetected inherent nonlinear dynamics. This paper presents a hypothetical framework designed as a tool for the acquisition manager to monitor the complex system dynamics that results from the rich interaction among agent populations (e.g., management, technical, and contracting).

Observable acquisition characteristics map to the elements of CAS described in definitions focusing on dynamic networks of agents, their coherent behaviors, and system outcomes emerging from innumerable decisions throughout the life of the acquisition (Waldrop, 2002). In many acquisition environments, populations of agents are engaged in a host of parallel activities with the purpose to develop new artifacts (e.g., ships, aircraft, technology, etc.) necessary to improve operational efficiency and organizational performance (e.g., staff reductions to increased force projection capacities). Competition and cooperation among agents (e.g., contractors and management team) result in decisions, actions, reactions, and ultimately self-organizing coherent behavior, if adaptive. The acquisition system is complex because interaction among agents, expressed in decisions and activities, even early in the life of the acquisition have great influence over the probability of desired outcomes (Axelrod & Cohen, 2000).

In many acquisitions the objective is to field new operational capabilities that depend on the intricate balance among innovative technology, corresponding changes in doctrine as well as the development of new agent types. The acquisition evolutionary process injects developmental changes in these major domains, namely technology innovation, operational doctrine, and agent populations. Often these domains evolve independently and away from the direct purview of the acquisition management team. Because acquisitions exist in a "natural" environment, shaped by iteration, replication and feedback (Axelrod & Cohen, 2000), the interactions among agents have a nonlinear impact on the eventual outcomes. Critical operational requirements (mission objectives) form the center of gravity attracting behaviors, technology development, and strategies that evolve with the purpose to bridge operational and performance gaps. We postulate here that operational requirements form an attractor that supports the formation of a complex adaptive system (CAS) evolving from an environment where agents interact, exchange information, copy and modify successful strategies, and learn adaptive behaviors.

In the natural acquisition environment, the operational requirements form a common objective that unites large numbers of agents. The interaction between two primary agent types, acquisition managers (AMs) and contractor teams (CTs) is highly dependent on efficient information exchange. Information flow is the lifeblood of the acquisition "organism." Fluctuations in this flow can profoundly impact decision making, particularly when feasibility and/or cost concerns trigger trade-offs in system design and specifications. During these sensitive periods, information exchanges tend to become less efficient as CTs seek alternatives to the original design before sharing information regarding potential performance failures.

Inefficient information flow forces very big decisions through very small windows in time. Maintaining awareness of the present and future state of capability evolution and analyzing the interdependencies among the domains of technology, agents and doctrine is critical and difficult to achieve. Without the benefit of simultaneous review of the developmental status in the three domains, AMs often face high-consequence decisions without time to evaluate and accurately project the impact of changes in the realization of acquisition-defined requirements.

In this paper, we offer a framework to monitor an acquisition's developmental progress, determining future capability emergence from the present-day state of technology, agents and doctrine. The framework treats acquisitions as complex adaptive systems, where estimating developmental stability and near-term unexpected outcomes are the means to ensure capability emergence.

Capability Emergence through Acquisition

Emergence

Capability emergence depends on the timely and appropriate evolution of doctrine, agents and technology. Capability emerges from an acquisition when effective technology is fielded to qualified agents in order to execute an strategy. Specific information from each of these three basic elements shapes the evolutionary development of each other. Agent training depends on the technology that applies to a given operational capability; the technical specifications of the technology artifact depend on the Operational Requirements Document's (ORD's) description of how agents will use the technology to support a strategy. Agents, technology, and strategy each contribute unique capacities to the system that, in the aggregate, yield capability emergence.

A Systems Framework to Maintain Awareness of Acquisition Progress

Tracking System Design Changes in Acquisition Domains

In the course of an acquisition, AMs must constantly assess the impact of specification trade-offs. This vital activity must follow a clear and consistent methodology to determine the impact of the modification or loss of a single specification on the emergence of specific capabilities. Without a view toward emergence, AMs often remain unaware of trade-off decisions or their impact during Usability Tests (UTs) or design reviews unless disclosed by the CT. With a complexity-based review, AMs can improve their change-analysis and better calibrate the objectives of UTs and design reviews to detect specification trade-offs and determine the real state of capacity development.

Capacity development yields capability emergence

Capability emergence depends on the realization of system capacities and each capacity depends on a set of specifications that should map to system requirements derived from a strategy. The word "capacity" is used in this context as referring to quantifiable development of specifications, within the agent, technology, or doctrine domain. These system specifications develop as the CT works to meet project milestones. Capacities are realized when a collection of interdependent system specifications have reached developmental thresholds, then, the system exhibits testable functionalities.

For instance, a strategy for an early weather warning capability might include a weather watch center staffed with personnel that employ sensors to detect the formation of dangerous weather patterns and alert the public in the event of threatening storms. Clearly this capability cannot emerge from the technology domain alone. Capacity developments in the agent and doctrine domains are just as critical. Consequently, capability emerges when qualified agents employ effective technology in the execution of well-formed strategy.

In this case, the capacity to train personnel on the of use radar to detect the formation of a storm depends on specific objectives offered in a program of training courses, the curriculum for each course, and the specific technical material covered in each course. In addition to training courses, qualification standards also are necessary to ensure that personnel can demonstrate the ability to use technology and procedures to conduct mission related activities during real-world scenarios. Capacity developments in the technology and doctrine domains also are just as critical as in the agent domain. More specifically, weather sensor technology (sensor, software, and human computer interface) must develop sufficiently to meet ORD requirements (e.g., detect conditions that predict the formation of a severe storm 1-3 hours before it actually develops). Lastly, emergency procedures are needed to provide early storm warning to the population at large. Appropriate instructions are necessary to guide personnel in the use of the sensors and communications systems not only to detect and identify weather threats, but also to efficiently and timely warn the population at-large of impending threats. The desired capability emergence is a function of capacity development under each domain.

Estimating Acquisition Stability State

The formula below is proposed to estimate system developmental stability by comparing the current state of capacity development against the expected state of unique ORD capabilities. Considering a single capability (e.g., early detection of threatening weather patterns and prediction of trajectory, speed, and duration within 10 % error), AMs must first determine the threshold of evolutionary development, as a function of time, for each capacity associated with the chosen domain capability (namely, agents, technology, or doctrine). A team of technical experts, working for AMs, estimates the time required and the developmental thresholds (h) needed for each capacity such that each domain will be sufficiently mature to yield capability emergence. In our example acquisition, for instance, the capacities needed in the agent domain, n, involve staffing, training, and qualification standards. The Acquisition Technical Team (ATT) must identify the specifications under each capacity. For example, capacities for staff training would specify training objectives that must be met in each required course to provide adequate knowledge, skills, and abilities (KSAs) for agents to use the new technology and operational procedures.

Setting Capacity Performance Thresholds and Tolerance Levels

The ATT plays a crucial role in determining the developmental threshold for capacities across domains. Before any determination of capacity development can be reached, it is necessary to establish developmental thresholds and tolerance levels. An expert ATT, proficient in the domain of the subject capacity, must analyze each specification and estimate the expected rate of development as a function of time, as well as establish the thresholds and tolerances necessary for system functionality emergence (capacity). The ATT's expertise must be compatible with each system capacity under examination. The ATT's job is to analyze each specification and determine the expected rate of development as a function of time, as well as thresholds and tolerances necessary for system functionality emergence (capacity). Developmental thresholds pertain to a critical point in development. Once several specifications reach these developmental thresholds, system capacities begin to emerge and functionalities can then be observed and their performance tested. System capacities emerge as sufficient system specifications reach their developmental thresholds.

Detecting Potential Trade-offs and Estimating the Impact on Capability Emergence

Once the expected developmental functions and thresholds are set, the ATT then carries out periodic assessments of the developmental state by reviewing project plans, achieved milestones, usability test results and available progress reports with the CT. The ATT's objective is to determine as early as possible the actual shape of each critical system specification's developmental function. This analysis allows the ATT to estimate whether critical developmental thresholds will be reached in time (Figure 1 – panels B, E, and F), as well as to identify speci-

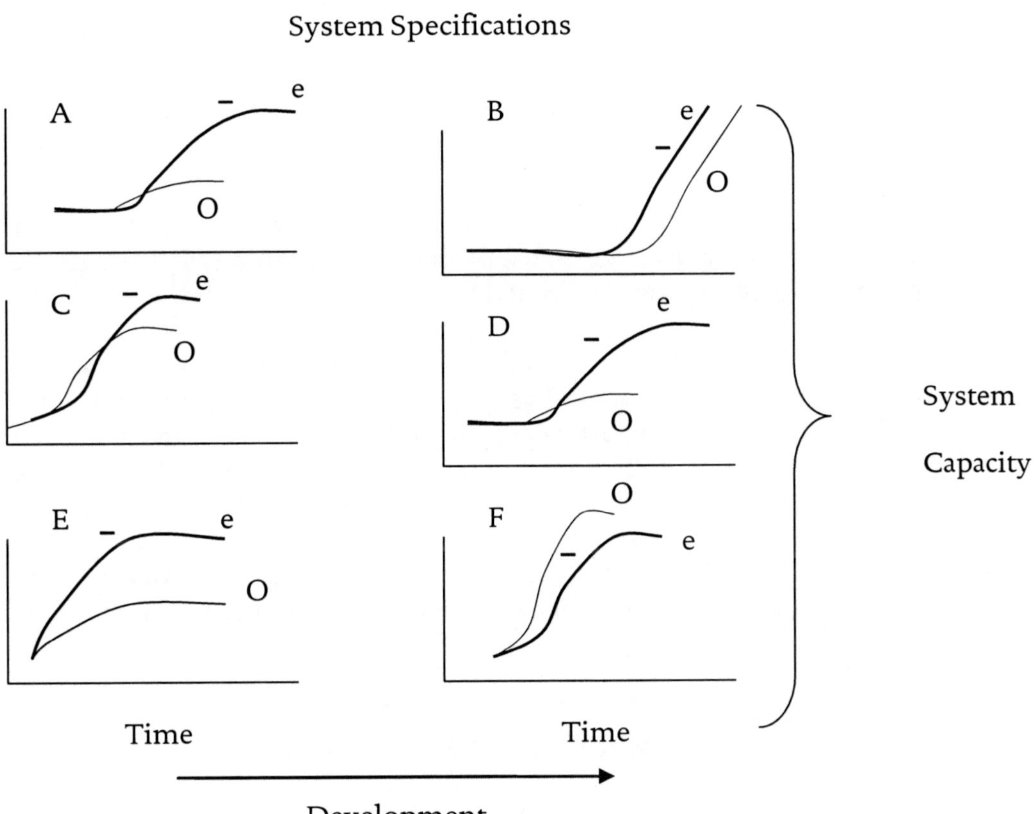

Figure 1 *Developmental Patterns of System Specifications. This illustration depicts developmental patterns of system specifications. This example shows the analytical products of the ATT, initially identifying the critical system specifications, the expected (e) developmental rate for each specification as well as appropriate thresholds and tolerances (thicker lines and dashes) necessary for system capacity emergence. The observed (o) function (thinner line) depicts the actual developmental function that ATT observes during a "current-state" analysis.*

fications that will not reach their corresponding thresholds within the contract's period of performance (Figure 1 – panels A, D, and C). Identifying system capacities that will not emerge within the acquisition's period of performance will allow the ATT to forewarn AMs of capabilities that are unlikely to be realized as expected, thus minimizing the incidence of unexpected outcomes. This process provides AMs with sufficient time to carry out alternative analyses, review and research new CT proposals designed to compensate for system specification trade-offs, and make informed decisions on cost-overruns and trade-offs.

Quantifying Capability Emergence

In this section we use the example in Figure 3 to focus on analyzing a single ORD derived capability, the corresponding system capacities within the agent domain, and corresponding system specification to illustrate how to quantify developmental progress at a given point in time. The developmental threshold for each capacity can be determined as follows under the agent domain asking the following questions:

- Do training objectives express ORD derived capabilities enduring that personnel will be trained to employ new technology and doctrinal artifacts and carry out activities ORD capability in the operational environment?
- Do system specifications map to training capacities that in turn ensure that training objectives are realized? What percentage of training requirements is met by system capacities in the agent domain?

In this case, the ATT task is to determine the level of correspondence among training objectives offered in basic and advance schools, and KSAs prescribed in the ORD. Thus, in a perfect *happy path*, both the basic and advanced schools (see Figure 3) will yield a 100% KSA index, or a KSAi of 1. In a more realistic world the ATT assessment of both schools would yield some percentage of desired KSA yield, for instance, .7 (basic training school) and .5 (advanced school), thus yielding a KSA index of .35. This index will be used in combination with the staffing index to further calibrate the agent domain state value.

Basic Course KSAi = NKSAsO / NKSAsR
Advanced Course KSAi = NKSAsO / NKSAsR
Total Course KSAi = Adv Coursei * Bas Coursei

NKSAsR : Number of KSAs prescribed in the ORD that prepare personnel to use technology and doctrinal elements for early warning
NKSAsO : Number of KSAs that map directly to training objectives within courses offered in enterprise training system

Following with this example, the ATT must use the ORD specifications to determine the threshold and tolerances for the staffing requirement system specifications. How many operators the ORD prescribes and how many operators are required as a function of task analyses conducted after system design.

Operational Performance Gap

Lack of Capability to Provide Early Warning to the Population at-large of Impending Severe Storm Threat

New Capability Requirements: Sufficiently early detection of threatening weather patterns and prediction of trajectory, speed, and duration of storm.

System Requirements

Agent Capacities

Staffing requirements:

- Emergency Operations Center 24/7 watch
- 25 staff members / 4 positions/ 6 staff members per position/ 1 department head

Training requirements:

- 1 Basic Training School/ Radar Operation Tracking/ Response Operations
- 1 Advanced Training School/ Data Fusion/ Sensor Correlation/ De-conflicting tracks/Use of simulation tools

Qualifications requirements:

- Two years field experience detecting, tracking, estimating storm's paths

Doctrine Capacities

- Operational objectives document / Concept of Operations/ Field tactics/ Technical procedures/

Technology Capacities

Detection Requirements

Figure 2 *In this example, a single ORD derived capability is presented in contrast to an operational performance gap in the field of emergency operations and early warning. Corresponding capacities and system requirements are listed across acquisition domains. Development of system specifications are critical to meet each stated requirements (not shown on this figure).*

The ORD provides thresholds for these values, thus staffing specifications are part of the design, but are dependent on technology evolution, particularly in promised automation capacities. A *happy path* staffing index of 1 indicates that system designs in the technology and doctrinal domains meet ORD personnel requirements. The ATT, however, assesses whether technology and doctrinal developments support the ORD's staffing thresholds. The percent error relative to the ORD's thresholds is calculated by:

$$\text{Staffing } i = |NOR - NOA / NOR|$$

NOR: Number of operators required per ORD
NOA : number of operators required as a function of technology development and CT's system design

The agent domain state index then provides an indication of the current state of this domain at the time of the assessment as shown in Figure 4.

System Specifications

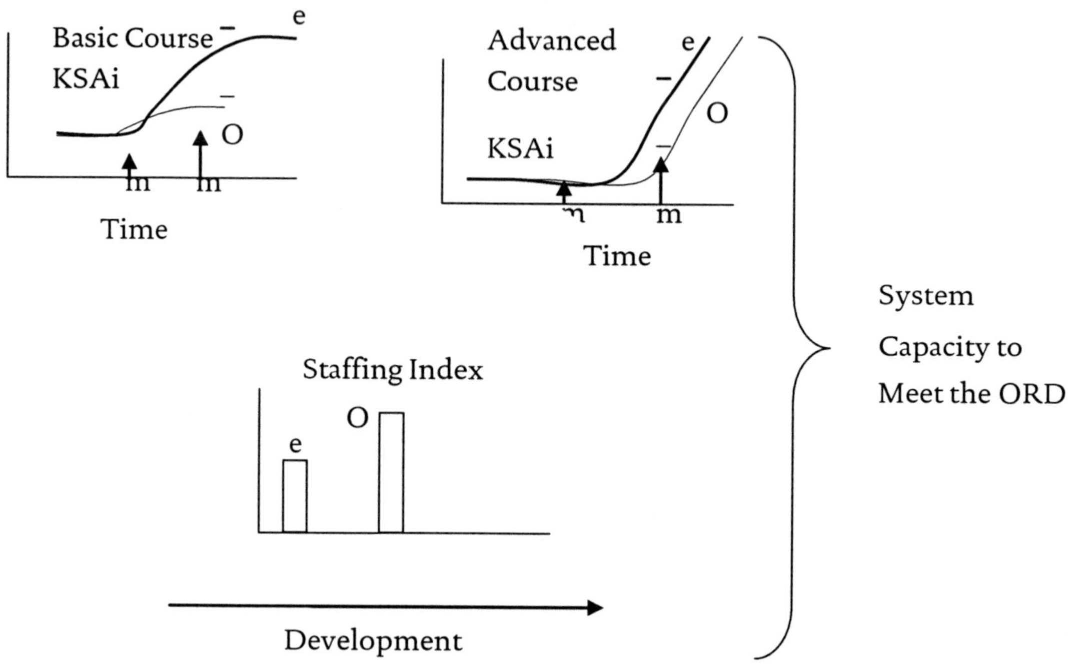

Figure 3 *Staffing System Specifications. This example depicts the usefulness of current state assessments. In the case of the basic course, KSA indices indicate that if the developmental progress remains the same relative to the measurements (m), then this course will fall short of the expected development, thus suggesting that specification trade offs are taking place. In contrast, there are no concerns with trade-offs in the case of the advanced course, other than development is slow. The estimation of the staffing index indicates that more personnel than prescribed in the ORD will be required to operate the early warning system.*

In this example, the ATT deduces that potential cost overruns are not only possible with respect to course development, but also with expected life cycle costs. Impacts on capability emergence can be deduced from the fact that sufficient trained and qualified personnel will not be available upon delivery should developmental progress occur as estimated. Early warning capability will not be available 24 hours per day, seven days per week as required in the ORD.

The agent domain state index (Δa) below illustrates the current state of development in contrast to the desired state of development as indicated by the ATT.

$\Delta_{\text{agents : Total Courses KSAi or}}$
Δ_{agents}: Adv Coursei * Bas Coursei

Similarly, in other domains, as in the case of technology and doctrine, the ATT determines the actual thresholds in the evolutionary development of each capacity and calculates a percent index indicating the number of capacities within each domain that reached maturity at the time of the assessment. For each capacity, the ATT determines the threshold of development for system specifications that are crucial for the emergence of functionality and reviews the current state of development by examining the actual work being conducted by the CT, results from prototype performance and usability assessments, and system design reviews. A percent score is determined for each capacity and then all capacities are aggregated as indicated below:

Technology Capacity i = CnO / CnR

CnR : Required specification (n) development for the realization of the specific capacity
CnO : ATT's assessment of the observed development state of the capacity's specifications

In the aggregate of capacities under the technology domain, the technology domain status index is calculated as follows :

Δt: (CnO/CnR) *(C1O/CrR) *(CsO/CsR)* ....(CzO / CzR-))

On the best of circumstances the total value of Δt will be equal to 1 or 100% specification maturity under each capacity. A similar logic is followed for the determination of the doctrine domain status index:

Δd: (CnO/CnR) *(C1O/CrR) * (CsO/CsR) ....(CzO/CzR)

In the case of the doctrine domain the ATT determines the information necessary to provide doctrinal artifacts to personnel in order to realize the capability requirements determined in the ORD. Once the doctrine domain developmental threshold is determined the ATT calculates the current state of the domain by calculating the percent index, as indicated above, for each doctrinal artifact, namely CONOPs, SOPs, and Qualification standards.

Domain Maturity Thresholds and Capability Emergence

Assigning maturity thresholds to each domain requires the estimation of the number of capacities that must be realized for the domain to reach maturity. Once the domain index is calculated then monitoring the domain throughout developmental time requires iterative assessments of the current state of evolution (Figure 5). Once the three domains reach maturity, a nonlinear jump in system performance improvement will be measurable, but not before. The ATT must remind AMs that as long as one of the three domains remains below the maturity threshold, capability emergence will not take place as expected and system performance will exhibit significant deficits.

The ATT's role in determining a domain's maturity threshold in terms of capacity realizations requires technical expertise relevant to the domain, the

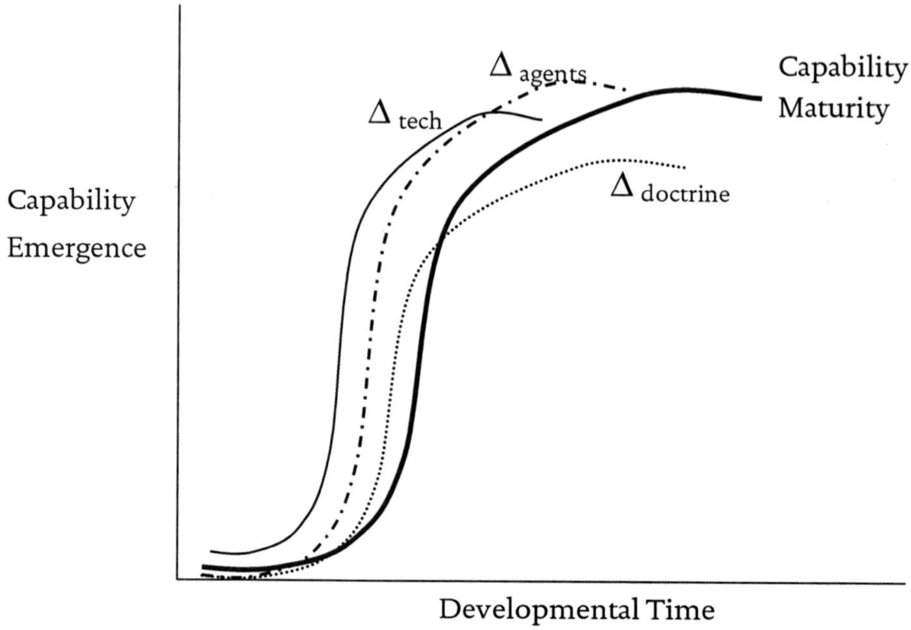

Figure 4 *This illustration depicts the dependence of capability emergence on capacity domain maturity. The nonlinear leap in capability maturity occurs as a function of the synergy among inter-domain system capacities.*

capacities, and systems specifications. As it is evident, a critical ATT role is to trace the dependencies among ORD capability requirements, system specifications, system capacities, domains, and ultimately capability emergence. This information must be developed for each capability, a daunting task when considering the number of capabilities associated with large acquisition efforts.

Conclusion

The analytical products of the ATT initially involve identifying critical system specifications, the expected developmental rate for each specification, as well as the appropriate thresholds and tolerances necessary for system capacity emergence. Once the expected developmental patterns are elucidated, ATT members must concentrate their efforts on collecting evidence of actual developmental rates, calculating the resulting rate of maturity, and estimating the ultimate effects on capability emergence at the time of delivery. These analyses are possible only if the ATT uses a systematic method to document capacity realizations in each domain. The results of analytical efforts contrasting expected versus observed developmental rates allows AMs to anticipate capacity changes and impacts on capability emergence throughout the acquisition's developmental phase.

In the absence of a systematic methodology, the delays in information updates during periods when the CT engages in trade-off decisions will result in a situation picture characterized by information limit cycles and analytical happy paths. Under these conditions, AMs will be unable to anticipate trade-offs and ultimately experience frequent crucial decisions involving loss of capability, cost overruns, or both.

This framework applies CAS theories to provide a mental model that, while theoretical, can illuminate trade-off activities and maintain reasonable information update rates, thus allowing the formation of a realistic acquisition situation picture that does not obscure critical issues.

References

Axelrod, Robert and Cohen, Michael D. (2000). Harnessing Complexity : Organizational Implications of a Scientific Frontier, ISBN 0-465-00550-0.

Guastello, Stephen J. (2006). Human Factors Engineering and Ergonomics: A Systems Approach, ISBN 0-8058-5006-6.

Guastello, Stephen J. (1995). Chaos, Catastrophe, and Human Affairs: Applications of Nonlinear Dynamics to Work, Organization, and Social Evolution, ISBN 0-8058-3163-0.

Olson, Edwin E. and Eoyang, Glenda H. (2001). Facilitating Organization Change, Lessons from Complexity Science, ISBN 0-7879-5330-X.

Waldrop, Mitchell M. Complexity: The Emerging Science at the Edge of order and Chaos. Touchstone, New York, NY.

25. Towards an Analytical Framework Supporting Defence Strategic Planning

Andrew Gill, Wayne Hobbs, David B. Matthews & Greg Newbold
Strategy and Capability Integration Group, Defence Systems Analysis Division, Defence Science and Technology Organization, AUS

The Australian Department of Defence recently articulated a Strategy Planning Framework that sets forth a suite of strategic-level documents that aim to support informed and balanced decision-making for the Australian Defence Force of today and for the future. To support this, an Analytical Framework is being developed by the Defence Science and Technology Organization and will consist of a Process Component – to capture the inputs, outputs and transformations of the underlying processes, a Methodological Component – to identify appropriate analytical methods to support the transformation functions, and a Validity Component – to form an improved understanding of what constitutes valid Defence strategic planning. This paper presents initial demonstrations of each component of the Analytical Framework on a selected case-study.

Introduction

The Australian Department of Defence recently published a handbook, the Strategy Planning Framework Handbook (SPFH), which describes a Strategy Planning Framework (SPF), to support the conduct of Defence strategic planning (Department of Defence, 2006). Before the publication of the SPFH, critique of Defence strategic planning was conducted by the Defence Science and Technology Organization (Hibberd *et al.*, 2003; Keir *et al.*, 2004). Of particular concern, at the time, were criticisms of 'strategy staff not sufficiently educated in strategy-making', due to 'staff rotation and shortages flowing from the high tempo of operations' (Keir *et al.*, 2004). Similarly, the operational tempo tended to focus the mind on 'pressing events and issues rather than shaping and hedging Defence's strategic policy' (Keir *et al.*, 2004).

After the publication of the SPFH, a proposal for an Analytical Framework was put forth since while it 'does attempt to link documents internal to each of the three components, it is not clear how they are supposed to inform each other nor take the appropriate inputs and transform them into the outputs' (Keir *et al.*, 2006). Various analytical methods were suggested but noted that 'such an Analytical Framework would develop over time to define the purpose of the various elements (including documents), the links between them, and their analysis requirements'.

The aim of this paper is to continue that initial effort towards an Analytical Framework and will explore the broad characteristics of a Process Component, a Methodological Component, and a Validity Component. Given the nature of the complexity of the problem, ideas and tools from relevant systems theory frameworks, including Systems Engineering (Blanchard and Fabrycky, 1998), Critical Systems Thinking (Jackson, 2000), and Habermas's theory of knowledge-constitutive interests will be used (Habermas, 1968).

Defence Strategic Planning

What is Defence Strategic Planning?

The key elements of the Australian Defence Glossary definition for strategy include the notions of; goals or objectives – that is, the ends that are sought; options or actions – that is, the ways these ends may be pursued; and of choice or design – that is, the decision on which specific way to purse these ends. These elements also map onto the 'necessary and sufficient conditions for the existence of a problem' (Ackoff, 1962).

Strategy, then, is the end-product of a process of decision-making which involve the resolution of problems. Strategy concerns itself with two sets of processes, in each of which problems can occur. In the planning process, strategy focuses on the 'innovative, creative, exploratory and intuitive activity' of deciding on sought ends and possible ways (Keir et at, 2004), while in the control process, strategy focuses on the 'activities undertaken to translate that into action' (Keir *et al.*, 2004).

Defence strategic planning is therefore the resolution of problems to enable decision-making in both the planning and control processes which underpin the development and implementation of strategy.

How is Defence Strategic Planning Done?

As a framework, the SPF should be concerned with 'putting into place processes, organizational structures and conducive environments that will result in the smooth production of useful, relevant, insightful strategic plans for Defence' (Keir *et al.*, 2004). The high-level objectives of the framework should therefore be to 'broaden and deepen the knowledge-base from which decision-makers can draw; to develop programs and plans to achieve set goals; and to communicate that direction to the rest of the organization' (Hibberd *et al.*, 2003).

In pursuing these objectives the SPF comprises three components – Strategy Development (concerned with planning); Deliberate Planning for Operations (concerned with control) and Capability Development (also concerned with control) – the latter two being differentiated by the time-frame of interest (respectively, the Force-in-Being and the Future-Force).

The Strategy Development component 'analyses Australia's strategic environment in both the near and far term, identifies and prioritizes threats and opportunities, and formulates policy consistent with the Government's current and future National Security Objectives, which subsequently shapes both the employment of the ADF for current operations and the form, size and strength of the future force' (Department of Defence, 2006).

The Deliberate Planning for Operations component considers the above policy advice and decides upon both the 'defence international engagement operations the ADO conducts in order to shape the strategic environment to favorable ends' and the appropriate preparedness levels of the non-committed elements of the ADF for 'anticipated military operations' (Department of Defence, 2006).

The Capability Development component considers the above policy advice and decides upon the capabilities to acquire, enhance, maintain, reduce or dispose of so as to 'minimize strategic risk and exploit strategic opportunities while being consistent with Government priorities and within resource constraints' (Department of Defence, 2006).

A Supporting Analytical Framework

Process Component

The SPF seeks to unify these components to provide a congruent, coherent and comprehensive set of documents and processes. However, it is beyond the scope of the SPFH to give a detailed description of the process whereby the documents are formulated, which defers responsibility for form, content and derivation to separate drafting groups (Department of Defence, 2006: 3). Since Defence strategic planning is not a pure, linear, top-down process and that a constant, interactive dialogue between all components is desirable (Department of Defence, 2006: 8), it is therefore important that the many functions (at the subsystem level) of Defence strategic planning be clearly identified.

From a process perspective, while the Analytical Framework proposed by Keir *et al.* (2006) successfully articulates the relationships between documents, it does so without explicitly determining the functions underpinning them or identifying their inputs, outputs and linkages. This paper makes use of the recent publication of the SPFH to begin to produce such a process map of Defence strategic planning. The framework of documents is functionally decomposed using the principles and ideas from Systems Engineering (Blanchard & Fabrycky, 1998: 1-4) to identify the inputs, outputs, transformations and relationships within the SPF.

Methodological Component

A great strength of the Analytical Framework proposed by Keir *et al.* (2006) is that it comprehensively considered the three components of Defence strategic planning and attempted to suggest specific methods, tools or techniques for particular problems. With this focus, it therefore naturally devoted relatively less attention to describing relevant methodological issues and solutions. Methodologies – or the principles of method use – are important as they enable one to learn about the success, or otherwise, of method use by the ability to critically reflect that use upon the relevant methodological presuppositions. The choice of methodology (and methods within it) is also important and should be related to the inherent problem types associated with each document. Finally, the potential benefit and/or conflictions of using multiple methods or methodologies is an issue that deserves consideration.

This paper applies the principles and ideas from Critical Systems Thinking (Jackson, 2000; Ulrich, 1983) to the problem of Defence strategic planning in an attempt to place the Keir *et al.* (2006) Analytical Framework within a larger, and hopefully more considered methodological framework. In particular, it sets out to achieve three specific objectives: (1) to classify various Defence strategic planning activities using the System of Systems Methodology (SoSM) problem-context classification scheme (Jackson, 2000: 357) to determine and describe relevant methodologies; (2) to place the various methods, tools and techniques suggested in Keir *et al.* (2006) within this framework of methodologies; and (3) to expose alternative methods and methodologies which might usefully be brought to bear.

Validity Component

Finally, a vexed question often associated with any framework developed to assist decision making is that of providing a set of criteria for assessing the validity of the results generated by using methods from that framework (irrespective of the 'right' methods being suggested by the Methodological Component). This compels one to consider the question of what constitutes the basis for the legitimacy of the results of various methods. This is essentially a normative activity, as the validity of the results of specific methods is a relation between the manner in which the methods were employed and the norms of reasoning (or standards of rationality) applicable to the particular problem-contexts under consideration.

This paper attempts to tackle this problem by tracing the forms of rationality associated with the different problem-contexts and through the relevant systems methodologies, (developed in the Methodological Component), to their foundations in relevant social theory. For the SoSM, this is critical theory and one of its most influential proponents is Habermas and his theory of knowledge-constitutive interests (Habermas, 1968). These foundations, in turn, allow useful definitions for validity to begin to be offered as well as developing initial criteria for assessing validity claims made on the results of specific method use for resolving problems in the various Defence strategic planning activities.

Case-Study Demonstrations

Illustrative Example

Here, the three components of the Analytical Framework are explored through the Strategy Development component of Defence strategic planning, since this generally receives the least amount of analytical support in practice. Three key Strategic Development documents, and their development processes, are examined from the perspectives of process, methodology and validity.

The Defence Planning Guidance (DPG) is the 'ADO's lead strategy document' (Department of Defence, 2006: 13) and analyses the future strategic environment to identify the contingencies Australia might face. The analysis makes judgements about the likely future states of strategic variables as well as their strategic dynamics. Against the backdrop of Australia's strategic interests, the DPG provides planning guidance in managing the risk these contingencies pose in both the current and future strategic environments.

Australia's Military Strategy (AMS) describes 'how the military power of the nation might be applied to achieve the Government's national security policy objectives within a whole of government framework, crafted to the particular contingencies in the DPG' (Department of Defence, 2006: 14). The AMS articulates the types of operations the ADF must prosecute, the military effects required in these operations, and the military response options which enable these effects to be produced.

The Future Joint Operating Concept (FJOC) articulates the future roles, missions and methods for the ADF and describes 'how the ADF of the future might fight at the operational level of war to achieve the objectives of the strategies from the AMS' (Department of Defence, 2006: 15).

Process Component

The above documents are defined in relation to a number of characteristics including intent, expected outcomes, and predecessor, partner and successor relationships (Department of Defence, 2006: 39-70). A high level systems view of the DPG, AMS and FJOC documents may be developed, using these interrelationships. Furthermore, it is then possible to functionally decompose this high level systems view into a functional framework, through the intent statements and interrelationships explicitly contained within, or deducible from, each document or document description, provided within the SPFH. These functions, and the relationships between them, can be represented in a process map, showing the inputs, outputs and transformations. Figure 1 provides an illustration of the process map underlying the key elements of the Strategy Development component, where transformations are represented by the arrows, and the inputs and outputs are attached to the tail and head of the arrow, respectively.

This illustration, even at this low level of functional decomposition, begins to highlight a number of important observations from a process perspective. First, that the Strategy Development documents may (and often do) encapsulate multiple functions (e.g., the DPG includes the functions of *determining strategic priorities*, *analyzing the Future Strategic Environment*, and *identifying contingencies*). Second, that the output of some functions may be the input to multiple other functions but have differing resolution requirements placed upon it (e.g., the DPG output of *contingencies* feeds into two other functions).

What the illustration doesn't show, but may become apparent on finer functional decomposition, are the following. First, that responsibility for performing some functions may be unclear, as the output of that function may be encapsulated in multiple documents but not clearly labelled as inputs (e.g., both the DPG and FJOC appear to contain data related to the output of the *analyzing the Future Strategic Environment* function). Second, that the intent statements and interrelationships explicit in, or deducible from, the SPFH are insufficient to correctly, or uniquely, determine the underlying functional structure.

The process map above perhaps implies that Strategy Development is a top-down flow of strategic guidance – it is not. Rather the process map is intended to promote understanding of the underlying process and to provide an auditable path of the influence of defence decisions on Defence strategic planning.

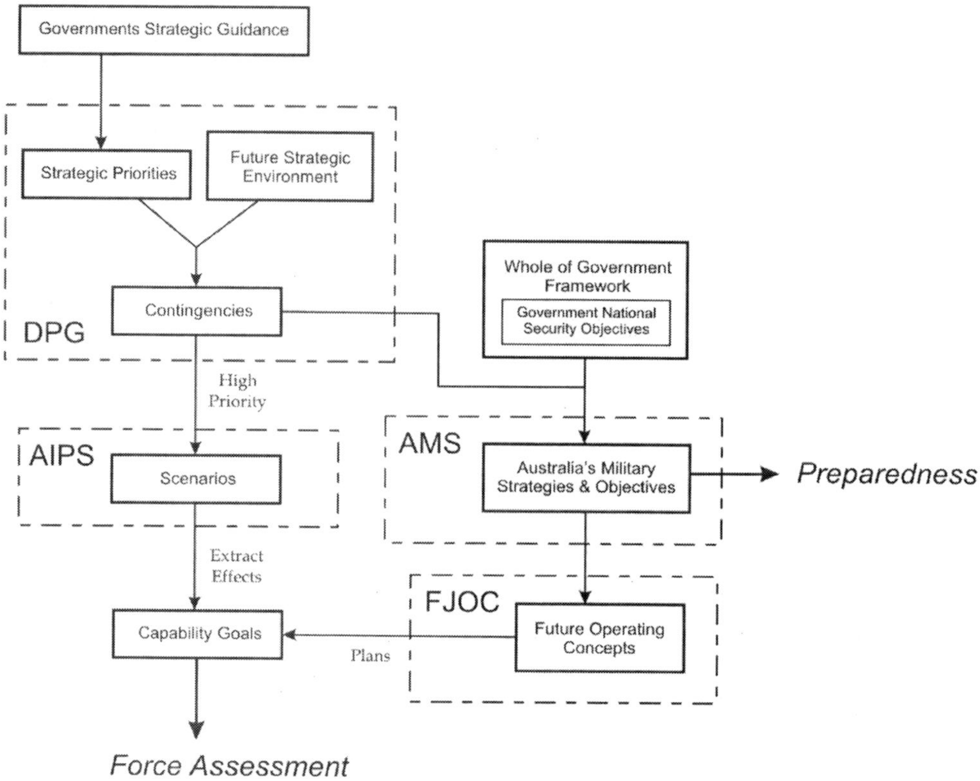

Figure 1 *Illustrative Process map of key Strategy Development Functions*

Understanding the transformation involved in each function will also guide the nature of the analytical support that is appropriate (i.e. the granularity or resolution of results required).

Methodological Component

The SoSM is a classification scheme of problem contexts (and associated systems methodologies) for the complementary and informed use of methods. The schema makes distinctions based on two facets where most complications seem to arise – the complexity (simple or complex) of the nature of the system of interest within which the problem lies; and the nature (unitary, pluralist or coercive) of the relationship between stakeholders.

Here we use a modified SoSM, adopted from Matthews (2007), which focuses on aligning the two Habermasian human conditions of 'interaction' and 'work' (Habermas, 1974) with the two archetypal Defence strategic planning problem types (planning process and control process problems, respectively). Out of this alignment specific methodologies can be identified. According to Habermas (1968) a third condition arises in pursuing the 'success of interaction'. Two risks to this success exist. First, power relations (e.g., rank or superiority) may lead to non-ideal conditions for generating consensus. Second, instrumental (not communicative) forms of reasoning may infiltrate the quest for a solution and therefore solve the wrong problem. The key characteristics of these three systems methodologies – communicative, instrumental and critical - are described in Table 1 (adopted from Matthews (2007)).

The hierarchical nature (DPG → AMS → FJOC) of the Strategy Development documents suggest a distinction whereby the DPG has an interest with 'what to do' in terms of the set of planning contingencies to prepare for and thus deserves a communicative systems methodology, while both the AMS and FJOC interest themselves with 'how to do it' in terms of an appropriate strategy and method of warfare for these contingencies and thus a instrumental systems methodology is pertinent.

Indeed, Keir *et al.* (2006), in discussing the analytical support available for the DPG, AMS and FJOC, appear to take this latter methodological perspective. For example, for the DPG the Soft OR method of Futures Analysis is offered, and for the AMS and FJOC the Hard OR method of Experimentation is discussed.

However, on close inspection, each document can be seen to have elements of the 'other' problem-context as well. For example, the DPG has the stated problem of needing to provide guidance for the management of risk in the future security environment; while both the AMS and FJOC have needed to generate consensus among key single-service stakeholders. This prospect was also illuminated via the Process Component which indicated documents encapsulating multiple functions. Therefore problem associated with the production

Fundamental Condition	Interaction	Work	Success of Interaction
Cognitive Interest	What to do?	How to do it?	Why do it?
Goal	To develop, maintain and extend consensus in regard to appropriate action	To achieve technical efficiency in achieving set goals	To critique what is thought to be objective
Form of Reasoning	Communicative	Instrumental	Critical
Method of Inquiry	Consensus Generating	Answer Generating	Assumptions Surfacing
Examples of Techniques within the Management, Planning & Decision Sciences	Soft OR, e.g. SSM Requirements Engineering Problem Structuring Methods Group Decision & Negotiation Techniques	Hard OR, e.g. Decision Theory Modelling & Simulation Experimentation Systems Analysis Policy Analysis	Critical OR, e.g. Strategic Assumption Surfacing & Testing Critical Systems Heuristics Psychology (sensemaking) Philosophy (epistemology, ontology)

Table 1 *Key Characteristics of System Methodologies*

of each document should be viewed from both perspectives and the imperatives of both 'dominant and dependent' systems methodologies be given due consideration.

This, and Table 1, allow us to say more about the analytical situation than that offered in Keir *et al.* (2006). First, that there exist other specific methods (consistent with the dominant methodology) that might be usefully applied to the problem, as an adjunct to those stated in Keir *et al.* (2006) or as alternatives (e.g., for the DPG other Soft OR methods such as Soft Systems Methodology (SSM)).

Second, that each document has a secondary problem-context to which a range of methods (consistent with their parent dependent methodology) might usefully be brought to bear (e.g., for the AMS methods such as Group Decision & Negotiation within a communicative systems methodology for the generation of consensus among key single-service stakeholders).

Finally, when viewed from the perspective of the communicative systems methodology (whether dominant or dependent), a critical systems methodology should be also be employed to deal with the role-specific-concerns of the stakeholder community, including clients, decision-makers, experts and those affected by the decisions but not involved in their making. For example, for the FJOC, the single-services and enabling concept developers (e.g. NCW or logistics) require that their role-specific concerns are heard and considered appropriately. The use of Critical OR methods, such as Critical Systems Heuristics (Ulrich, 1983) may be appropriate.

Validity Component

Drawing upon Wiggershaus (1986), one can begin to provide a set of criteria for assessing the validity of the results of any of the methods selected according to the Methodological Component, as summarized in Table 2.

Unfortunately, within the analytical community there is a tendency to rely solely on instrumental forms of reasoning (as evidenced by a proportion of techniques offered in Keir *et al.* (2006)). However, this distorts our view of the cognitive interests embedded within plans and decisions and reduces all to the 'technocratic' one of how to make the existing system function better. Moreover, it opens the analyst up to the charge of advocacy analysis by limiting the boundary of the planning or decision making problem to the imperatives of the client of the day.

In contrast, the authors suggest that validity is found through acknowledging the different forms of cognitive interest at work in every problem and harnessing appropriate forms of reasoning for each embedded cognitive interest in order to provide valid applied scientific advice at each stage in the Defence strategic planning process.

Summary

The objective of this paper was to improve upon the fine beginnings of an Analytical Framework, proposed by Keir *et al.* (2006), to support Defence strategic planning. A review of that framework suggested that it

Form of Reasoning	Valid when	Assessment Criteria
Communicative	they succeed in developing, preserving or extending consensus on appropriate action	they have survived robust encounters with alternative perspectives within an *ideal speech situation*
Instrumental	they succeed in achieving technical control over objectified processes	they are logically deducible from axioms that have been verified within the problem situation at hand
Critical	they are able to render explicit presuppositions that have been hitherto unacknowledged	the presuppositions are criticized immanently (by making use of existing organizational norms, values or interest), transcendentally (by making use of new or hitherto suppressed norms, values or interests) or empirically (if the presupposition is not normative and if it is possible to design a *crucial experiment* which takes the presupposition to the tribunal of observation in isolation from other auxiliary hypotheses)

Table 2 *Validity Assessment Criteria*

may benefit from the development of additional Process, Methodological and Validity Components. These components were developed using ideas from relevant systems theory and subsequently explored in relation to the problem of the Strategy Development component of the SPF. With respect to this problem, the Process Component developed a process map from functionally decomposing Strategy Development documents and identifies relationships, transformational processes, inputs and outputs. The Methodological Component classified the various Defence strategic planning activities within a modified SoSM so as to determine relevant methodologies and expose alternative methods which might usefully be brought to bear. Finally, the Validity Component traced this modified SoSM to its origins in Habermasian social epistemology so as to describe the forms of reasoning (with associated epistemic norms of validity) applicable within each of the problem-contexts, and argued that in order to be valid, analysis needs to harness all three forms of reasoning, which demands a pluralistic perspective be taken, in each of the Defence strategic planning activities described in this paper.

The ultimate goal of this Analytical Framework is to be able to resolve complex planning and decision-making problems by conceptualizing the interrelationship between different documents, inputs, outputs, functions and cognitive interests at work within Defence strategic planning by acknowledging and understanding the different forms of reasoning they require; and finally, to appropriately select and apply different methods to these problems. The ideas expressed here are the first tentative steps, in a series or cycle of many steps, toward that goal.

References

Ackoff, R. L. (1962). *Scientific Method*, Wiley, New York.

Blanchard, B.S. and Fabrycky, W.J. (1998). *Systems Engineering and Analysis*, Prentice Hall, USA, 3rd Edition.

Department of Defence, Director Strategic Guidance. (2006). *Strategy Planning Framework Handbook*, Defence Publishing Service, Canberra.

Habermas, J. (1968) *Knowledge and Human Interest.* Translated by Shapiro, J. Beacon Press, new York, USA.

Habermas, J. (1974). *Theory and Praxis*, Heinemann, London, UK.

Habermas, J. (1981). *The Theory of Communicative Action Volume 2 Lifeworld and System: A Critique of Instrumental Reason.* Translated by McCarthy, T, Beacon Press, Boston, USA.

Hibberd, T., Brown, T., Barkley, H., Ng, S. and Keir, R. (2003). *Objectives for the Strategic Planning Framework*, Client Report 316, Defence Science and Technology Organization

Jackson, M. C. (2000). *Systems Approaches to Management*, Klewer Academic / Plennum Publishers, New York.

Keir, R., Hibbert, T. and Ennett, J. (2006). *Analytical Framework for the Strategy Planning Framework*, Client Report 245, Defence Science and Technology Organization

Keir, R., Hibbert, T. and Barkley, H. (2004). *The Strategic Planning Framework within Defence*, Client Report 365, Defence Science and Technology Organization

Matthews, D. (2007) *Planning and Decision Making in an Interconnected World.* DSTO Research Report. In Draft.

Ulrich, W. (1983). *Critical Heuristics of Social Planning: A New Approach to Practical Philosophy*, Haupt, Bern.

Wiggershaus, R. (1986) *The Frankfurt School: Its History, Theories and Political Significance.* Translated by Robertson, M. MIT Press, USA.

26. Applying Resonance Metaphor to Understand Communication in the Participatory Design of a Hospital Information System

Salesio M. Kiura
Nairobi, Kenya

In this paper we are using the resonance metaphor as a lens to further our understanding of interaction that we had with project partners as we sought to develop a Hospital Information system. We describe four approaches that we used as means to promote understanding between the project stakeholders who have diverse domain expertise. These methodologies are: holding informal sessions that promote preparedness and freedom of expression, alignment of the design process to what is familiar and experienced to the participants, dedication of ample time for the process and lastly use of a shared graphical representation in the process. We present a discussion of our experience and propose that such an approach, centered around the project participants achieving resonance can help improve quality of deliverables necessary in an information system development project.

Introduction

Application of information technology in health is an established phenomenon. By its nature, health services provision is a socially oriented undertaking, with practitioners relating directly to the social aspects of the society. The implication is that information technology applications in the health care systems are not only technological systems but also the so-called socio-technical systems. The design and development of these systems take socio-technical approaches as well. Participatory Design (PD) of information systems is one broad methodological approach that recognizes this socio-technical aspect of systems development, not only in health but also in general systems' design and development. In PD the potential users of the system under development take center stage in the design process with active roles in related decision-making processes.

Participation

Our view of participation is the ways in which people take an active role in shaping decisions that affect their lives especially workplace processes, culture and structural setup. This view has its origins in Scandinavian initiatives in computer systems design, which sought increased worker involvement in processes of technical change and innovation. We subscribe to the Scandinavian collective resources approach that recognizes the importance of perspectives, interests, conflicts and participation among multiple expertise standpoints for a certain social objective pooling the various forms of specialized and situated expertise to increase the collective understanding of a given situation (Ehn & Kyng, 1987).

In this light, development of a hospital information system is approached from a collaboration effort of all stakeholders. The result is cooperation between the information system designers/developers (whom we henceforth simply refer to as designers) and the workers at the hospital (henceforth simply referred to as users).

Communication

Interaction of PD project stakeholders is paramount to the success or failure of the project. Through communication the various expertise groups seek to narrow the divide between their views of the world as defined by their specific domains of expertise. They especially achieve this by learning from each other (Floyd, 1993). Through communication the two groups learn from each other, negotiate positions, get comfortable with changes of attitudes, ways of working and workplace (re) organization. The users communicate about their domain and the foreseen features to be considered in the design while the designers communicate the ways in which technology can be used to alleviate the identified domain problems. Communication between the two leads to a mutual understanding in which as much as users remain domain experts and designers remain experts in design and development, the two get to appreciate the other's point of departure in the ensuing interaction as the project unfolds. We analogically describe this by stating that a designer's submission will resonate with the user's domain knowledge and vice versa. By resonance we mean that interaction of the two will find meaning in each other and set in motion a combined effort towards finding a solution to the domain problem. The two groups will initiate, reinforce and maintain each other's efforts in addressing the problem. This is analogous to physical resonance during which a system tends to oscillate with high amplitude when excited by energy at a certain frequency (Billah & Scanlan, 1991).

Resonance metaphor

The various approaches that encourage close cooperation between designers and users mainly differ in terms of their definition of user roles in the cooperation and the goals that act as the driving force behind the push for cooperation. Irrespective of their differing perspectives these approaches converge on shared concerns that current and potential users be integrated into the assessment, design and development of systems that have impact on their workplaces (Asaro, 1996). Participatory methodologies such as ETHICS (Mumford, 1983), STEPS (Floyd, *et al.*, 1989) and MUST (Kensing, *et al.*, 1998) have their main essence in the support for a wider inclusion of the user community in the design. Results of interaction between users and designers communities determine the success or failure of the process. In a setting with diverse expert groups, the interactions will be fruitful when the expert groups find harmony not only with the subject of interaction but also with their counterpart project partners. Achieving this harmony calls for a process that supports each participant to identify with the other to an extent that what one contributes in the interaction evokes prior residual knowledge about the domain or information about the contributor. The resonance metaphor view of communication and information exchange argues that the essence of communication is to find resonance between communication partners. Resonance in the sense that for parties A and B engaged in communication, each party must identify with the other for effective communication. This resonance can take the form of appreciating the other's view of the subject domain, from connecting diverse revelations or elements of knowledge about the context. Once these connections are synthesized, it will enable users and designers identify with the wisdom of the others (including experiences and associated emotions specific to a domain). (Gärdenfors, 1996).

This paper's contribution is attempts to address the question of how to enhance a process for attaining resonance between the parties in a PD project. We highlight experiences with PD approaches and explain the results of our interactions in light of attaining resonance among the project partners. We advance our view that communication in a PD informed project should take this view of finding resonance between the stakeholders as represented by different expert groups.

Communication and Resonance Metaphor

The essence of communication

The main tenets of PD practice are learning from each other and collaboratively carrying out a design process (Floyd, 1993). This to occur, PD project stakeholders interact with one another by various ways such as observations, communiqué documents, taking part in the execution of a task, workshops, seminars, etc.

We base our view of communication on the view advanced by Rogers *et al.* that *"communication is a process in which participants create and share information with one another in order to reach mutual understanding"* (Rogers & Agarwala-Rogers, 1976). We extend this view to include the view that communication must not always be directed to another person or entity but also there are cases of intra-personal communication, when the source doubles as the receiver and the effects of communication apply (viz. change of behavior, attitudes, views, etc). With this extended view, the focus changes from transferring an idea (as was the emphasis of Rogers *et al.*) to the essence of communication being to extend or shape the idea and its impact when applied or followed. Our focus is about communication in a (design) team for informing the design process consequently influencing the design results.

We further extend our view of communication based on the views of Gärdenfors (1996) who starts off with the assertion that information exists in two worlds: the world of technology and the world of humans. Artifacts such as computers, telephones, telegraphs, radios, videos, etc symbolize the world of technology. Emphasis of communication is about 'channeling' information from one party to the other. Gärdenfors contrasts this with a human world of information where communication is more about assimilation, understanding and seeing effects (or consequences) of communication. In the two worlds there is the similarity of a general communication model that involves a message's creation, transmission, reception, interpretation and response. However, the emphasis, especially during interpretation is different in the two worlds. The extra supportive information available in the human world can be summarized as the contextual consequences that are accessible because of some kind of relation between the message, the medium, and the receiver that consequently relates directly to the interpretation and the action or response. A PD project scenario is more of the human world as differing domain experts interact. The determinant factor in the interaction for successful communication is the extent to which participants identify with the information interchanged. This identity will be supported by interpretation and engagement not only between the participants but also intra-personal as exemplified by individual participant's reflection on prior knowledge that shapes the meaning of messages exchanged.

The resonance metaphor in communication

One way to describe communication between two people is "ways in which we exchange information" (I send you information, you receive it and you send me back information, which I consequently receive). The ways in which people carry out this exchange are channels that humans have to one another. The essence of the exchange is to "put across a message". This gives the sense of "message conduction" and is referred to as the conduit metaphor described by Reddy (1979). According to Reddy this view of communication has its roots in the information theory (Shannon & Weaver, 1964). The underpinning of information theory is *the transmission of signals from a sender in channels of communication to a receiver.* In this view, combining a number of symbols forms a message that is channeled to the receiver in one way or another. In a language-based communication, the symbols are language artifacts (letters, words, sentences etc) and the channels can be seen as speaking and writings (Linell, 1982). This conduit metaphor view of communication would view the participants of communication as passive objects (a transmitter and a receiver) where human communication consists largely of established forms, patterns and structures.

An alternative to describe communication as advanced by Gärdenfors (1996) is ways in which partners establish states of resonance between themselves. When two people communicate the receiver of the information responds in a way to reinforce the information from the other. Responding and reinforcing will lead to establishment of some kind of 'common grounds'. Identifiable consequences of communication are exemplified by the responses. According to this view of Gärdenfors, communication is not passive and isolated but that any new information evokes old information just as a source's vibration frequency that is equal to or nearly equal to another's resonant frequency will cause resonance (Billah & Scanlan, 1991).

Partners in communication achieve some harmony (resonates) with one another and understanding another means an individual is able to resonate with the contributions of others.

When applied to PD, information about the contextual ramifications of the area, organization or environment under study does not exist by itself in forms, reports, descriptive analysis texts, etc but emerges only when the non-experts in the domain area resonate with the material. What users tell designers or the designers tell the users remain tokens (physical tokens when written down or recorded) until interpretation and resonance in the two 'communities' is achieved.

For effective communication in PD, the listener must not be a passive receiver of a ready-packaged message, but active participant in creating the information. The more similar experiences and background the communicators have, the less time they need to establish resonance. We hence propose that the endeavor in a PD encounter should result in a co-construction of knowledge as the different partners' views intercourse. Teamwork and feedback are resonance-seeking approaches. Teamwork rich in feedback is a necessary approach to interaction for a meaningful communication (Grice, 1957).

Case study

Our study is in the context of a project to develop a Hospital Information System (HIS) for a medium size district hospital in a developing country. The system crosscuts various departments of the hospital. The community that forms the project partners has a diverse representation including medical doctors, clinical officers, nurses, and medical information officers. These users with their specific set of skills and performing specific tasks at the hospital represent experts informing design decisions in the project.

The work reported in this paper refers to a revisit of the case study in which after an initial project establishment exercise, the revisit is done to further elicit the requirements for the project. The requirements elicitation process took the form of interviews, individual meetings, workshops, observations and participation in the execution of tasks hitherto performed manually. Case study methodology is used with the goal of studying the contemporary work of the hospital in its real life context (Yin, 1989). Previous computerization efforts failed partly because the users weren't consulted widely. We used a participative approach to transverse technological aspects of the system to the social implications for sustainability, social economical justification and ownership.

Discussion and examples from the case study

We argue that communication in PD is only effective in the situation that the designers and the users achieve resonance.

Building on the philosophies and objectives of PD, we planned our engagement with the users to achieve mutual learning. We applied tools and methods that were familiar to the users. Furthermore, we grounded our design work on the users practice (work tasks and settings) and supported anticipation of future work situations. We held a workshop with all the project stakeholders where we centered our discussion on the users' work scenarios with an aim to get the requirements embodied on their daily tasks. We adopted graphical representation of the processes and possible scenarios at the hospital on a common board visible to all workshop participants for their input and critique. This was effective in describing and exemplifying user practices. The interactions were informal and flexible enough to allow differing levels of detail that evoked reflection (as exemplified by suggestions for more details and possible scenarios). This contributed to communication overboard amongst group members of diverse roles at the hospital. To avoid distractions by work demands and the hospital environment, we held the workshop outside the hospital.

In the workshop we set 'department sessions' where each department would in a scenario-based way explain to the rest about their work. 'Records people' represented the tasks of the health records and information department, 'wards people' represented tasks in medical information gathering from wards and 'consultancy/diagnosis people' represented expertise on information relating to direct interaction with patients. As each of these expert groups presented their work scenarios, interrelationships between the various departments came out, each understanding the other's work, and how someone's tasks relate to the other's tasks.

As a preparation for this workshop, we held 'phased interviews' with the users. Phased to mean we had interviews and extensive informal discussions with the users first as individuals, then as a group. We found that sessions with individuals, especially those of the lower cadres gave them a space to express themselves in unprecedented ways such that they felt prepared when they met in groups (both departmental meetings and all departments together at the workshop). The space for self-expression that such designed interview provided was an indication that such an approach promoted sharing of information and hence communicating. (See also Kiura, 2006)

We propose that the participants had an opportunity to experience resonance at three levels: with one-self (reflection as they tried to describe and present their tasks); with colleagues (as in a group setting they cooperated in contributing to the analysis of their departmental tasks) and with designers (with external entities). In these interactions, and especially in the context of discussing the possible software solutions that could be mapped to their work processes, anticipation and future projections of their work settings were visible. Discussions transposed the status quo of their work organization and processes to the expected possible changes because of a HIS.

From this discussion, we identify four approaches for a methodology that promotes communication resonance during an empirical phase of a PD:

1. Informal sessions that promote preparedness and freedom of expression. Our interviews at individual, departmental and group levels denote a kind of coaching experience. It took the form of a process through which the users were facilitated to unlock their potential and expand their views about their own work. Individual convictions and believes especially for low cadre workers was developed. The lower cadre staff felt that the prospective sys-

tem was recognizing their work experiences and developed a sense of ownership to the solution as opposed to viewing the exercise as a corrective measure from their seniors (Kiura, 2006);

2. Alignment to what is familiar and experienced. Our decision to work with the users' practices and processes promoted bonding (establishment of relationships) to the extent that project participants, irrespective of areas of expertise, felt as sharing a common fate: success of the project. Using tools and methods familiar to them, we tapped to existing competencies and feeling of continuity and gradual change. Gradual as the users identified their status quo as the point of departure for proposed changes. This promoted identity by the users, enriched their contribution, engagement, satisfaction and articulation in the whole process;
3. Dedication of ample time (for the process). The workshop setting freed the minds of users (and designers alike) from feelings of rushed understanding of what is presented, reaching an informed decision and being required to respond. Our workshop aspects and setting that contributed to this included having it as a full day session holding it outside the hospital setting;
4. Shared graphical representation that although initiated by a single participant, developed into a creation of the whole group. We adopted scenario based representation of work processes to differing amounts of details. These were extended through contributions from the group. In instances of differing views about a given representation, patience, moderation and reflection in 'time-out' periods promoted compromise and identity with changes.

Promoting attitude changes in the design process

The four approaches we have described were helpful to us by assisting participants achieve some kind of harmony. Moreover, the approaches enhanced their absorption into the situation – the workshop tasks. Our project can be considered a social phenomenon involving people, their context of time, events and attitudes resulting in own social meaning. In a social phenomenon, a dominant factor is the individual as well as the collective attitude framework of the actors. In our case, these attitudes were reflected in the positions, expectations and understanding of tasks. Our approach can be understood as a cyclic process that affected the project participants in reconciling their attitudes both as individuals and as a group. All participants started with own attitudes about the context and the need for an information system at the hospital. These attitudes shaped the design process by influencing all activities and tasks carried out. Consequently, participants' attitudes were influenced and their positions and judgments shifted as represented in Figure 1.

Contributions of our view to the design process

Attitudinal transformations that project participants undergo as described above influences the results of the design. In the requirements analysis phase, we sought to identify features and objects to create a representation of the problem and the accompanying solution at the hospital. The representation sought

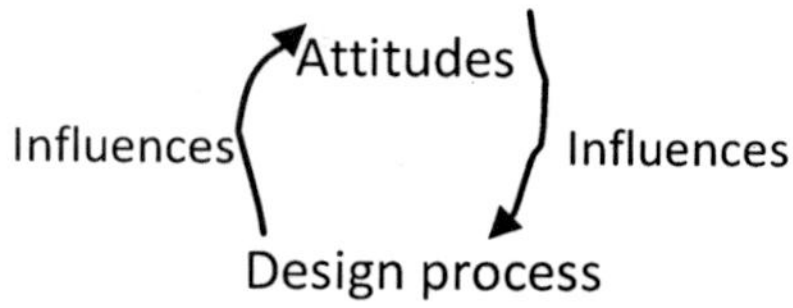

Figure 1 *Attitudes influence the design process that consequently influences the attitudes*

was one that's not only agreeable to both the users and the designers but one that as much as possible reflects the hospital's 'real world'. However, given the cyclic nature of the process, any such artifact representation is dynamic. Changes in the participants' understanding of the problem domain and conceptualizations of the problem domain have direct impact on any representation that is created. The representations of the hospital environment, processes at the hospital and general workplace structuring will vary as attitudes, perceptions and interpretations change. These changes are inevitable as the participants' understandings get clearer from mutual learning. Figure 2 below demonstrates the creation of the analysis objects and features in the context of the interplay between the attitudes and the design process.

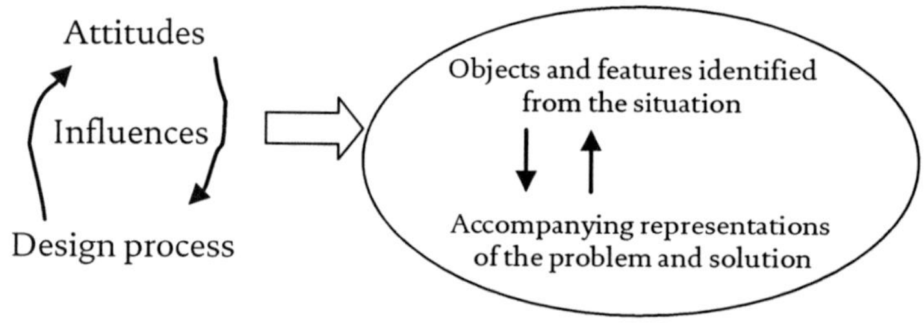

Figure 2 *Results of a cyclic interplay between the attitudes and the design process in a project affects the statement of the problem and conceptualized solution*

An example of objects, features and problem-solution representations is a requirements document from the requirements analysis phase. Figure 3 below, represents the iterative development of the deliverables from the requirements phase in a continued process. The doted lines represent the extents to which the contents of the deliverables have been agreed upon as 'real world representations'. These also signify the level to which the participants are finding identity with each other and thereby assuming states of resonance with the each other and the project situation.

At the end of the requirements identification and analysis, a requirements specification document is expected. In each iteration, the inter play between the attitudes and the adopted process will evolve an instance representation of the project setting. During each iteration the requirements are fine-tuned. It has been noted that individuals arrive at solutions by iteratively reframing the problem (Rittel, 1984).

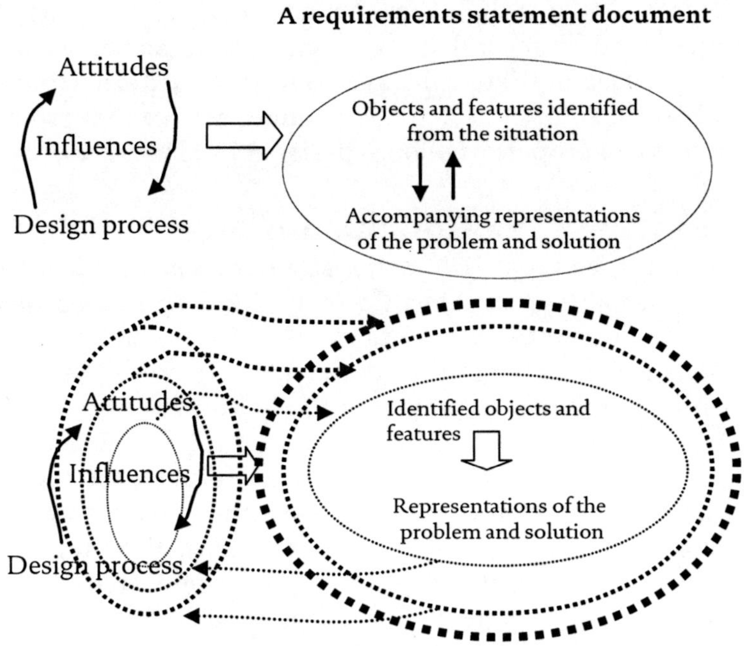

Figure 3 *An iterative interplay of the attitudes and the process itself reflects the building of harmony and hence resonance as reflected in the continued improvement of the systems design*

In a group work situation, as group members bring different perspectives to the problem solving process, each begins to understand the problem and conceive a possible solution. The risk is that with diverse understandings, perceptions, interpretations, etc the group ends up with different problems and consequently different solutions as represented by identified objects and features. The challenge is to coordinate the evolving problem understanding, considering others' understandings of the problem for an effective commonly agreed upon design document. The process leads to a solution that is not biased towards anyone expert group. This is the goal of PD and our approach sought to reinforce it. Designers will not implement a pre-conceived understanding of the domain. The domain experts will enrich that as the situational context is understood and considered. The users don't end up with a replication of current problematic situations, transfer of bottlenecks from the manual system to the computerized solution since the designers' influence and own understanding will have been considered.

Another observation is that when project participants attain resonance in communication, bonding occurs. As a thrust of our findings we argue that PD approaches should seek as much as possible to support communication between stakeholders; leading to stakeholders identifying with each other. This ought to be analogous to how a source frequency matches the resonance frequency of the second object (Billah & Scanlan, 1991). The approaches address expression problems, unfamiliarity of tools and methods, rushed decisions and they promote teamwork through shared creation of artifacts (such as graphical representation of a work process). As is the case with resonance where an interaction between two factors determines the resonance (external forces and properties of the object itself), PD approaches should be those that promote making explicit the forces and properties of both designers and users' views.

Conclusion

We have argued that PD practice approaches should seek to go beyond the formally presented information but seek deep meanings, invite opportunities to identity with the users in a way analogous to achieving resonance. In a PD project, interaction is in our understanding about exploring feelings, emotions, experiences and wisdom of users in their areas of expertise while users unfold the designers' attitudes, experiences and wisdom as represented by their technical competence. Eventually the team establishes common views of the problem and consequently the two reinforce each other in a manner analogous to principles of physical resonance. We have outlined experiences with four approaches that in our experience reinforced communication to establish resonance. We argue that as project stakeholders' attitudes change towards a common understanding and perception, requirements identified are iteratively fine-tuned to represent the project's real world.

References

Asaro, P. M. (1996). *Transforming Society by Transforming Technology: The Science and Politics of Participatory Design.* Urbana, University of Illinois Press.

Billah K., and Scanlan R., (1991). *Resonance, Tacoma Narrows Bridge Failure, and Undergraduate Physics Textbooks*, American Journal of Physics, 59(2), 118-124 Available online at: http://www.ketchum.org/billah/Billah-Scanlan.pdf

Ehn, P. and Kyng, M. (1987). 'The Collective Resource Approach to Systems Design', in G Bjerknes, P Ehn, and M Kyng, *Computers and Democracy: A Scandinavian Challenge*, Brookfield, VT: Avebury, pp. 17-57.

Floyd, C. (1993). "STEPS –A Methodical Approach to PD", in Communications of the ACM June 1993, vol. 36 No. 4, pp. 83.

Floyd, C., Mehl, M., Reisin, F-M., Schmidt, G., Wolf, G., (1989). "Out of Scandinavia: Alternative Software Design and Development in Scandinavia." In: Journal for Human-Computer-Interaction. Vol.4 pp. S. 253-380, Lawrence Erlbaum Ass, Hillsdale, N.J, 1989.

Gärdenfors P., (1996). Human communication - what happens? In: The Contribution of Science and Technology to the Development of Human Society, edited by B. Reichert (ECSC-EC-EAEC, Brussels, 1996).

Grice, P. (1957). 'Meaning' Philosophical Review 66, 377-388.

Kensing F., Simosen J., Boedker K., (1998) "*MUST- a method for participatory Design*" in: *Human Computer Interaction.* Vol. 13, No. 2, 1998.

Kiura, S.M. (2006*)*. Project Establishment in the Context of Participatory Design: Experience from a Hospital Information System Development Project in a Developing Countr*y*. Proceedings of the 39th Annual Hawaii International Conference on Volume 5, Issue, 04-07 Jan. 2006 Page(s): 96a.

Linell, P. (1982). *The written language bias in linguistics, Studies in communication 2 Department of Communication Studies*, Linköping University.

Mumford E., (1983). *Designing Human Systems for New Technology - The ETHICS Method* [online], Available at: http://www.enid.u-net.com/C1book1.htm
Rogers, Everett M.; Agarwala-Rogers, Rekha (1976), Communication in Organizations, New York: Free Press.
Reddy M., (1979). "The Conduit Metaphor", in: Metaphor and Thought ed. A Ortony, Cambridge University Press, pp 284 – 324.
Rittel, H. W. J. (1984). Second-generation design methods In: Cross, N. (Ed.), *Developments in Design Methodology* (pp. 317-327). New York: Wiley
Shannon,C.E ., Weaver,W (1964) *"The Mathematical Theory of Communication"* University of Illinois Press, Urbana.
Yin, R. K. (1989). *Case Study Research: Design and Methods.* Beverly Hills, CA: Sage.

27. A Systemic Application of User-Based Design

John Molineux
Murrumbeena, AUS

The paper describes a systemic approach to the application of Integrated Administrative Design, a user-based design methodology which enables stakeholder group participation in the design of administrative processes. The paper outlines the application of the process to redesign an employment health and safety system within a large government agency. It shows how the tool can be used in a systemic way to enable its application in administrative systems design in a nested system. Included in this approach is the creation of user pathways, which describe how the various user groups interact with the system. It concludes with an assessment of the methodology and recommends its potential application for use in other organizations.

Organizational context

This administrative design process took place in the Compliance division of the Australian Taxation Office (ATO). The ATO is a large government agency employing around 22000 people, of which around 10000 people are employed within the Compliance division. This division consisted of ten separate business lines and each line had a separate Health and Safety Committee, set up under the requirements of the Occupational Health and Safety Act 1991. The Committees were supported by line-based human resource (HR) practitioners.

A series of internal audits carried out on the health and safety (H&S) systems within the Compliance division's business lines found a wide range of inconsistencies and problems with these systems, with only two of the lines receiving favorable ratings for meeting H&S regulatory requirements.

In September 2006, a restructure of support functions (the 'Plan and Manage Review') occurred, aimed at obtaining a more consistent approach, and improving the efficiency and effectiveness of the HR, finance and business support functions. One of the functions integrated was the H&S function, and the change involved a proposal to replace the ten line-based Committees with one Committee.

The author's responsibility was to put this change into action, as part of his management role in HR. In October 2006, the author and the manager of H&S for the Compliance division decided that it would be best to engage stakeholders and re-design the system using an internal ATO methodology titled *Integrated Administrative Design* (IAD).

Design of administrative systems

The IAD process was developed in the ATO in 2000 and was originally titled Integrated Tax Design, for the purpose of developing taxation administrative systems. It was later further developed in 2002 and renamed IAD, to enable the design of other administrative systems.

Simon (1996) states that design involves human beings using knowledge to create what should be, things that do not yet exist. He notes that design "is the principal mark that distinguishes the professions from the sciences" (p. 111).

Principles around design have been proposed by Romme (2003: 562-3), who combines his work with that of Nadler and Hibinio (1990) and outlines three values and ideas that define the content dimension of design inquiry: (1) each situation is unique; (2) focus on purposes and ideal solutions; and (3) apply systems thinking. Romme also puts forward four other ideas that define the values and ideas regarding the process of design. The first, *limited information*, guards against excessive data gathering in that "too much focus on the existing situation may prevent people from recognizing new ideas and seeing new ways to solve the problem" (p. 563). The second, *participation* is crucial as "Involvement in making decisions about solutions and their implementation leads to acceptance and commitment". The third, *discourse* is important as "the design process should initiate and involve dialogue and discourse aimed at defining and assessing changes in organizational systems and practices". The fourth, *pragmatic experimentation* is "essential for designing and developing new artifacts" (p. 563).

IAD is a design methodology that is very much aligned to the thinking outlined in Romme's (2003) article, as IAD is based on a philosophy that representative groups of users of an administrative system should be involved in the design of the system. Also, the ATO's IAD process has design principles, which are aligned to Romme's six values/ideas on design:

1. Each project under IAD is seen as a *unique* situation within a particular context, and so requires a design process that takes this into account;
2. Each project is very much driven by the intent or *purpose* of the proposed change and attempts to design an *ideal solution*;
3. The IAD methodology pulls in *systems thinking* about the context of the situation, its potential impact on other systems and uses systems techniques in the design process;
4. The IAD process uses *limited information*, so as not to overwhelm new and innovative thinking with old patterns of behavior;
5. IAD uses extensive *discourse* in the workshops with user groups and other stakeholders;
6. IAD is involved in considerable *pragmatic experimentation* and testing.

The IAD process is outlined in the ATO's Design Guide (2004) and consists of six major steps. The first stage is *intent formulation,* which is a "living, ongoing process, potentially extending through all stages" (ATO, 2004: 0.9).

It is important that the original intent is understood, shared and explicitly articulated at the start of the project. The second stage is *blueprinting*, which is a "process the design team undertakes to develop a high level design of the entire change they are intending to make" (p. 0.9). The design is informed by the experience of the designers working with user groups impacted by the intended change. Emerging from these discussions are designs of user pathways, which are shown as diagrams "as a sequence of interactions the user will have...in both transitioning with the change and in their ongoing interactions with the change" (p 2.16). The third stage is to *design products*, which includes designing specific services for communities and user groups. It uses design workshops to translate the conceptual design and prototyping of products identified to deliver the user pathways mapped in the blueprinting process. The fourth stage is to *build products*, which may involve a range of support systems, information products, training of staff and detailed process maps and guides. The fifth stage is to *test user pathways*, which is where testing occurs to assess the interaction of all the products and services to understand the combined impact on user groups, and to iron out any problems before the change is implemented. The final stage is to *implement change*, where the system is handed over to the administrators and community to use and evaluation occurs to find any emerging problems so that final corrections can be made.

In setting up a design team, it is important to have the distinctive contribution of three 'voices' of design. The first of these is the *voice of intent*, a person who is usually the project sponsor. It is their role to see that the design realizes its intent. The second is the *voice of experience*, a person who brings a practical and focussed view on the design intent. This voice speaks of practicality and feasibility, and understands impacts and consequences on the existing systems. The third is the *voice of design*, a person who can provide expertise in the IAD process, and who can concentrate on building openness, flexibility and adaptability, and can challenge existing thinking and promote discovery.

The IAD process has been used successfully in the ATO over the last few years, particularly in the design of new or revised taxation administration systems, in response to government legislative and policy changes. Its internal use in HR management to design a health and safety system had not been tried before.

Health and safety systems

Health and safety systems are created in organizations to prevent work-related injury and illness of employees. Zink (2005: 543-4) recommends that there are critical components that will be success factors for an organizational H&S system, including the need for health to be "part of the company's policy and strategy", requiring "strong support by top management" and "sufficient broad basis of health dimensions and health indicators as control systems". Importantly, he recommends that the health system needs to be "integrated into existing management systems". This latter point was one of the key problems of the preceding H&S system in the ATO.

The ATO system, however, is generally in line with successful H&S structures internationally, such as in Scandanavia, where they have three different collaborating structures: Safety Committees; independent and autonomous safety representatives; and experts on H&S (Lindøe & Olsen, 2004). The overall ATO system has all of these structures in place. However, its safety committees were somewhat fragmented, and communication within the system needed significant improvement. Many of the line-based committees were operating at a level that was too low to influence behavior change within the workforce, and many of the employee representatives focused on site issues, rather than work system improvements.

In this context, Hall, *et al.* (2006) stress the importance of the involvement of employee representatives that are knowledge activists. They found that those employee representatives that sought external knowledge about work safe processes and actively persuaded management to accept changes, gained more improvements to H&S in the workplace than those looking narrowly at just the 'shop-floor' type of safety issues. This was an aim of the ATO change, to lift the committees from local to systemic issues such as risk assessments, work processes and safe work systems. The ATO already had in place site safety forums and employee H&S representatives to look after those local issues, such as faulty equipment.

In redesigning the ATO system to become more effective, one of the indicators would be a reduction in risks. Mearns and Håvold (2003: 410) have stressed that H&S risks can "only be managed and never entirely eliminated", implying that organizations "have to keep constant vigil to determine potential weaknesses in their health and safety management systems, in order to keep risks as low as reasonably practicable". In this context, the redesign needed to address the minimisation and mitigation of health risks.

Other factors to be considered in the redesign are outlined by Mearns and Håvold (2003: 422), who noted from their research that there were certain leading indicators that improved safety performance and reduced accident and incidents rates. These were the installation of a safety climate and health and safety management practice, and strong communication, health surveillance, health promotion, management commitment and workforce involvement. They also found strong auditing practices reduced hazards.

In designing the new system, all of these factors became critical considerations. The new system needed to build a climate of H&S management practice, improve communication, management commitment and workforce involvement, focus around the impacts of auditing, and enhance intelligence pathways and health promotion activities.

Systemic thinking

In using IAD in a systemic way, it was important for the designers to understand the system in its context. This is where systemic thinking is useful.

In discussing the various systems techniques, Flood (1999: 129) notes that systemic thinking offers "a particularly profitable way of gaining meaningful insights into things that are local to us in space and time" and "deepening systemic appreciation facilitates construction of incisive insights into each viewpoint". Systemic thinking uses synthesis, in addition to analysis, in understanding the complex nature of the world and its problems. Bawden, *et al.* (2007: 131) suggest that it involves "learning how to deal with complex situations in a systemic manner" and Johannessen and Olaisen (2005: 1261) feel that systemic thinking is "oriented towards deeper contexts and therefore, the construction of new patterns". Maani and Maharaj (2004: 33) have found that systemic thinking "does not affect performance directly, but it rather affects *understanding*, which can then lead to better task performance." It is this understanding or insight into complex systems that can enable better or more informed decision-making.

In looking at levels of systems, Bawden, *et al.* (2007: 130) discuss three dimensions of sub-system, system and suprasystem in a complex they title "The Development Holon", and note that "developments or improvements at any one of 'the levels' had the potential to both influence and be influenced by changes in the others". They find that (p. 132) participants who have "developed systemic competencies" are able to re-conceptualize logic "from a systemic perspective", which allows them to see learning "as a critical, self-reflective, self-organizing learning system of nested cognitive subsystems in three dimensions from which meaning and action are continually emergent". It is this form of systemic thinking that has emerged in the IAD design process.

The ATO's H&S system had three major components, each operating fairly autonomously. The highest level system was the national ATO H&S system, under the coordination of the National Executive Health, Safety and Wellbeing (NEHSW), set up under the OH&S Act. The next level system consisted of line-based Committees established under the direction of the NESHW. The final layer consisted of site-based Site Safety Forums (SSFs), which obtained input from the employee Health and Safety Representatives (HSRs) based at those sites. In a complication, the HSRs were selected and coordinated on a line basis, even though their work was site based. In all there were around twenty line-based H&S Committees and twenty-six SSFs. Some four hundred HSRs and deputy HSRs were coordinated through line-based HR officers, but were required to attend the site-based SSFs.

The changes to the OH&S Act enabled a rethink in the way the whole system was structured. Given this opportunity, the author intended to use it to advantage the Plan and Manage Review process by using it as a catalyst for change.

The revised system reorganized responsibilities under the OH&S Act. The National level system was largely maintained, except for the way employee representatives were appointed. The major changes were made to the other two layers. The second layer was reorganized based around the major ATO divisions, of which there were five. The site based layer was to be coordinated through the Site Leadership Forums, as HSRs' primary role was site-based. The new Compliance H&S system was designed around the three layers. It fitted in the context of its ATO-wide suprasystem, and contained five working parties and other networks, which operate as sub-systems of the Compliance system.

Designing the new system

The design work was commissioned in October 2006, and responsibility for its implementation was given to the author, as HR manager for the Compliance division. A small design group was formed in November 2006, who would lead the design of the new system. The small group included the author, the H&S manager, one H&S coordinator, and an information designer. The author took on the role of the *voice of intent*, the H&S manager and coordinator took on the role of the *voice of experience*, and the information designer took on the role of the *voice of design*.

The author established a reference group, the Health and Safety Coordinators Network, which consisted of the author's H&S team, HR practitioners from several Compliance lines, and two ATO H&S Advisers. This group commenced in November 2006, and would meet weekly by phone hook-up. It became a key body to discuss ideas, evaluate proposals, and obtain quick communication across the Compliance division of the ATO.

The design team then set out to map the different user groups of the system, and develop a process to work with representative user groups. It also decided to hold a two day workshop in December 2006, where various representatives of the user-groups would come together to explore the issues and come up with some alternative design models.

The author established the intent at the outset of the first workshop, but reiterated to the workshop attendees that all design options were open within the parameters of the intent of the Plan and Manage Review. This initial workshop was quite exploratory, and four different design models were suggested, along with the reasons for each model and sets of advantages and disadvantages. It was agreed the models would be referred to the Compliance Executive Team and the NEHSW for a decision on a preferred model, which would then proceed to more detailed design.

During this time, the design team met with various user groups to establish user pathways under the proposed changes. Some of these pathways involved significant changes to the current state, whereas others required minimal change. It was noted at these meetings that the three *voices* needed to be evident. The *intent* often needed to be clarified up front by the author, so that the users worked within the parameters set by the Plan and Manage Review. The voices of *experience* came out from the user groups as they put forward their ideas and discussed problems under the existing system, and identified potential problems and issues with the new system. At these workshops, the *voice of design* challenged thinking, sought clarification, and asked difficult questions. This proved invaluable, as it helped the users see through the existing system and help them release into thinking about how it could be better with the new system. Various *user pathways* were developed and appeared in diagrammatic form and were added to the blueprint, which was gradually being written. One of these pathways is included as Figure 1.

The blueprint document, which arose out of these discussions, contained the complete design, including the various user pathways interacting with the new system, project risks and mitigation strategies, and connections with other systems.

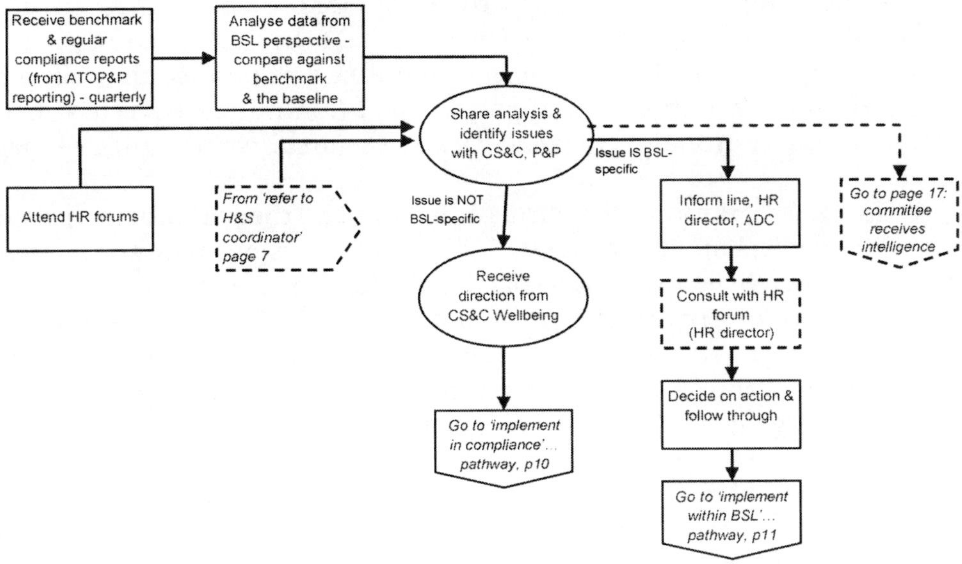

Figure 1 *User pathway for line health & safety professionals to identify and escalate an issue*

Following the writing of the blueprint, the author's H&S team had moved into the *design products* stage, including developing key documents for the new forum. A draft three-year plan was developed, as was a draft Charter for the proposed Committee.

The author prepared a proposal for consideration at a senior executive discussion forum, prior to the proposal and recommendation to the Compliance Executive. The proposal outlined the various options, but recommended that one Committee be formed with working parties based around specific topics and issues to support it, based on the understanding that it was the closest option to the original intent. The proposal outlined the concerns of various stakeholders about each of the models. It was then referred to the Compliance Executive, who requested further design work on the preferred option, whilst endorsing a proposal to set up an interim Committee who would undertake ongoing planning for the proposed changes.

More detailed design work commenced in February 2007, following reflection on the direction provided by the Compliance Executive. Coincidentally, there was an opportunity to undertake further changes, as changes to the OH&S Act became effective from March 2007. One of these changes was that H&S committees needed to contain at least as many employee representatives as management representatives. The author suggested that the interim Committee be established in the same manner as that intended by the changes to the Act, to ensure goodwill with union representatives, and to achieve engagement of senior management representatives. The Compliance Executive agreed with this, and the first planning workshop was held in March 2007. This workshop was attended by six management and six union representatives, as well as the design team, and progressed work on the blueprint, plan and Charter. Further work was commissioned and another workshop was planned.

Another report was written by the author for the Compliance Executive and the NEHSW, who approved the new design. At the next workshop in May, it was clear that the transition to a new Committee was proceeding well, and a Chair for the new Committee was appointed. The Committee requested further design work, with proposals to come back to the first 'live' Committee meeting.

The new Committee met formally in June, and the IAD process had now moved into the *build products* stage. Following discussions with the reference group, the author developed a proposal that the Committee accomplish its work through five working parties, based around specific H&S topics: (1) health and safety audits; (2) risk management; (3) communication; (4) education and product development; and (5) issues management. The Committee agreed and allocated one management and one employee representative to each of the working parties, supported by members of the H&S network. The following day, the network members met and further designed the processes and parameters for these working parties. The new system was ready to be fully tested with its pathways established. Following this meeting, an e-mail was sent to all Compliance division staff, informing them of the changes and inviting comment on the draft plan and blueprint. Responses were collated by the H&S team and suggested changes were discussed and evaluated at the network meeting, with some incorporated into revisions of the plan.

The project was then ready to enter the *implementation* stage, as the design had largely been completed and built, feedback had been sought, prototypes had been trialled through the Committee, and users informed.

Using IAD to design occupational health and safety systems

The author's positive experience in this process has led to the recommendation of this paper that IAD should be used to design other H&S systems. Its systemic use led to broader thinking about the system in its context, and systemic solutions were embedded into the design of the new system. The new system immediately generated a higher level of management commitment and involvement, and improved the focus around the minimisation of risks, as well as improvements in safe work systems. However, it still remains to be seen as to whether the new system, once fully implemented, actually reduces accident rates or time-off-work rates. As these rates are lag indicators, no conclusive outcomes will be known before about mid-2008.

What is clear is that the rigorous process involved in IAD imposes a methodology that is thorough and highly engaging. Its use of participation builds community support and goodwill. Feedback from stakeholders indicates that it is highly successful at involving various user groups. It makes implementation much easier, as it enables up front evaluation of user engagement, so there should be less resistance to change, less errors and 'workarounds', and fewer implementation surprises.

It is recommended for future research that IAD be implemented in other organizations for a variety of administrative design processes. It has potential to be used in other parts of the public sector, and in some service sector industries. It is a methodology grounded in the principles of design and participatory action research.

References

Australian Taxation Office. 2004. *The Design Guide.* Unpublished internal paper.

Bawden, R, McKenzie, B. and Packham, R. 2007. Moving Beyond the Academy: A Commentary on Extra-Mural Initiatives in Systemic Development. *Systemic Practice and Action Research,* 24 ( ): 129-141. ISSN 1094429X.

Flood, R.L. 1999. *Rethinking the Fifth Discipline.* Routledge, London. ISBN 041518530.

Hall, A., Forrest, A., Sears, A. and Carlan, N. 2006. Making a Difference:

Knowledge Activism and Worker Representation in Joint OHS Committees. *Relations Industrielles / Industrial Relations,* 61 (3): 408-436. ISSN 1703-8138.

Johanssen, J-A and Olaisen, J. 2005. Systemic philosophy and the philosophy of social science—part I: transcendence of the naturalistic and the anti-naturalistic position in the philosophy of social science. *Kybernetes,* 34 (7/8): 1261–1277. ISSN 0368-492X

Lindøe, P.H. and Olsen, O.E. 2004. Implementing Quality and Health/Safety Systems in the Hospitality Industry. A Comparison with the Aluminium Industry in Norway. *Scandinavian Journal of Hospitality and Tourism,* 4 (2): 154-172. ISSN 1502-2250.

Maani, K.E. and Maharaj, V. 2004. Systems Thinking and Complex Decision Making. *System Dynamics Review,* 20 (1): 21–48. ISSN 08837066.

Mearns, K. and Håvold, J.I. 2003. Occupational Health and Safety and the Balanced Scorecard. *The TQM Magazine,* 15 (6): 408-423. ISSN 0954-4786.

Nadler, G. and Hibino, S. 1990. *Breakthrough Thinking.* Prima, Rocklin, CA. ISBN: 10:0761506489.

Romme, A.G.L. 2003. Organization as design. *Organization Science,* 14 (5): 558-573. ISSN 1047-7039.

Simon, H.A. 1996. *The Sciences of the Artificial,* 3rd ed. MIT Press, Cambridge, MA. ISBN: 10:0262691914.

Zink, K.J. 2005. From industrial safety to corporate health management. *Ergonomics,* 48 (5): 534-546. ISSN 0014-0139.

28. It Takes Three to Tango: The Role of Process Development in NPD

Lincoln Wood
Department of Information Systems and Operations Management,
The University of Auckland, NZ

Acknowledgements

The author would like to acknowledge the anonymous reviewers for their useful feedback and critiques which have improved the content and outlay of this paper. Also of critical importance are the numerous academic mentors that have contributed to this research.

New product development (NPD) is a subsystem of the firm as a whole and contains interactions between three distinct functions: product design, process design, and production. The interrelationship between the functions within the NPD subsystem and between the NPD subsystem and the firm are critical to successful product launches. Boundaries and information flows between the functions will be explored. Developing an understanding the strategic objectives of the organization allow modifications within the NPD subsystem to increase the overall effectiveness in meeting corporate objectives. Points of intervention may be more readily identified and leveraged.

Introduction

The traditional view of a *design - production* interface in manufacturing organizations has been investigated previously, but when process design is also considered as a separate function, other interfaces must also be investigated (Lu & Wood, 2006). This article seeks to understand how NZ high tech manufacturing organizations have structured the functions involved in the new product development (NPD) process to meet their corporate objectives.

Literature Review

Lu & Wood (2006) highlight the fact that there are three separate functions in the process realization process in NZ high tech organizations, and that they each have different responsibilities. The three functions are: product designers, process design, and process realization (production). Together they work towards generating a fast time to market (Pawar, *et al.*, 1994; Burchill & Fine, 1997; Wheelwright & Clark, 1994), improving productivity and throughput (Terwiesch & Bohn, 2001; Lager, 2002); generating a smooth production ramp-up period (Billington, *et al.*, 1998, Terwiesch & Bohn, 2001); and ensuring customer acceptance of the new product (Lemon & Carl, 1991). With a current drive towards product diversity and variety of offerings on the market, one of the most critical objectives is time to market (Stalk, 1988; among others).

Each of the functions uses different information as input into their jobs and they frequently have differing objectives. Pisano (1997: ix, Preface) noted that, "... process development involved specific technical and managerial challenges that remained unaddressed by the existing bodies of literature." Thus while product design and process execution (production) are relatively well studied, the importance of the process design, and the interactions between this function and the other two, are not as well understood.

The product designers will use customer requirements as an input, with the objectives of incorporating as many of these as possible. Commonly over the past few decades they have also been influenced by the disciplines of Design For Manufacture (DFM) and have designed the products in such as way as they are easily assembled or manufactured by production teams. The concept referred to a dyadic split between the design function and the production function; the role of process development is largely ignored. Much of the extant literature is based on studies of machining or assembly plants (Whitney, 1995; Nevins & Whitney, 1989; Whitney, 1988; among others), which perhaps explains this.

Process design is the task of creating the manufacturing processes so that production is able to manufacture the designed product. While the product designers may perform this task, it is possible to have a separate and technologically competent process design team (Lu & Wood, 2006). In these circumstances the separate function interacts with product design and production teams, translating the product requirements into process requirements and designing or adapting process equipment accordingly for use by the production team, then facilitating transfer to the factory floor. It involves a plan for the entire execution system, drilling down to detailed plans for individual processes and details, such as the outfitting of tools and equipment on the floor, and conducting pilot runs (Clark & Fujimoto, 1991).

Upon completion of the product design and process design the production team is required to produce the product as an on-going task. The process settings and process equipment designed by the process design team is a critical input, as is the manufacturing requirements of the production planning team – to meet the market demand.

The product designers have the objective of designing a product with specifications that will meet the customer requirements. The process designers transform the product requirements into process requirements and then design the processes and process settings to run smoothly to meet these needs. The production team transforms the process settings, raw materials, and production planning inputs, into the physical output of the organization.

Each of the functions utilizes different types of information from different parts of the organization, works on different processes, towards different objectives. While they seek a local optimum within each function they must also be aware of the organizations imperatives and work cooperatively in order that the NPD meets the objectives of the firm.

Research Methods

The case study method was used to address the gap in knowledge concerning process design and the interaction between the functions due to the exploratory nature of the research. Initially reviewing issues relevant to the product realization chain and techniques existing in relevant literature provided a theoretical background. Key informants in exemplar firms were selected and interviewed, along with other participants where more detailed information was required. Resulting transcriptions were analyzed using techniques of qualitative data analysis (Strauss & Corbin, 1998). The following description is an elaboration of the major concepts that emerged from the data collection and analysis. This study was an exploratory investigation of the phenomena in their natural setting, which was hoped to result in a good understanding of the context (Eisenhardt, 1989). The two NZ cases used for this research were MedCom1 and MedCom2.

MedCom1 faces strict market requirements yet has become the market leader in an international niche medical devices market. They use leaps in technology for radically new products, yet similarity between successive products is high. Existing architecture is reused to reduce development times, making use of parts and process commonality and advantages to production workers, smoothing ramp-up production runs.

Another medical product is produced by MedCom2 using two distinctive components allowing targeting of niche markets using the consumable component. The design for the consumable component is inexpensive and rapid, leading to rapid development and introduction to satisfy variety requirements. Parallel development can proceed on the capital-intensive base component where much of the existing architecture is maintained when possible.

Discussion

Lu & Wood (2006) postulated that the process design function is able to exist separately and generate new interactions with the product design and production functions. The example used was from a Singapore printed circuit board assembly plant. In Wood & Lu (2007) similar demarcation in functions was studied in the NZ context of high technology manufacturers. The treatment of the process design function as a separate function in the NZ context was not constant and clearly not as straightforward as it appeared in the Singapore context. There were several critical strategic considerations in the NZ cases:

1. They are export orientated organizations that do not compete on cost, but on functionality and product variety – seeking to fill market niches, and;
2. Product innovation and rapid change is necessary.

This study looks at the way in which these successful NZ cases structured their NPD subsystems to generate meet these requirements. Adjustment of the boundaries and responsibilities amongst the functions involved with NPD reveals the methods used by these NZ cases to meet their strategic considerations, which differs slightly from the approach outlined by Lu & Wood (2006).

A critical component of their competitiveness is through releasing a flood of products to the market, products that are innovative and meet the customer requirements. They compete either in a niche market, or niches market segments, where their output can meet the global demand and it is small enough not to be targeted by major international players. Meanwhile, manufacturing of older products, and support for older products, often continues – creating a huge amount of product variation in production.

For the product realization process these NZ cases identify several key objectives (Wood, 2005):

- They must be able to translate customer requirements into product functionality;
- New products must be designed rapidly;
- New products must be released constantly;
- Support for products is continued, creating extensive product variety on the floor.

Ashby's Law of Requisite Variety states that only variety may destroy variety (Ashby, 1956); in this case, only by having the ability to generate a variety of different outcomes in production can they cope with the variety of work representing the large product variety and production requirements. As Beer (1979: 89) notes, "ONLY variety absorbs variety," and he considers, "that this law stands in the same relation to management as the law of gravity stands to Newtonian physics." A workforce in the factory must therefore be able to generate an equivalent amount of variety in their processing to that of the work schedules comprised of various distinct and complex products. Production staff must be able to cope with this variety with either of two methods: they must either be highly skilled, or, they must have equipment that is able to generate the requisite variety to cope with the variety of production work they face. While many organizations employ low-skilled labour in production, this requisite variety obviously does not enter the NPD process at this point. Instead the NZ cases opted to reduce the variety in the work schedules through re-arranging the NPD sub-system to better meet the strategic objectives of the firm.

With the importance of the products and product innovation to the organizations, the product designers frequently exercise significant authority over the NPD process. At times they are in direct control and retain full responsibility for the product from conception through to death (in both MedCom1 and MedCom2 cases). The product designers must approve changes as they maintain ultimate authority for the product throughout the lifecycle.

In the NZ cases this means that for the traditional NPD subsystem of the firm (comprising of product design, process design, and production) there are three information inputs that were identified by Wood & Lu (2007):

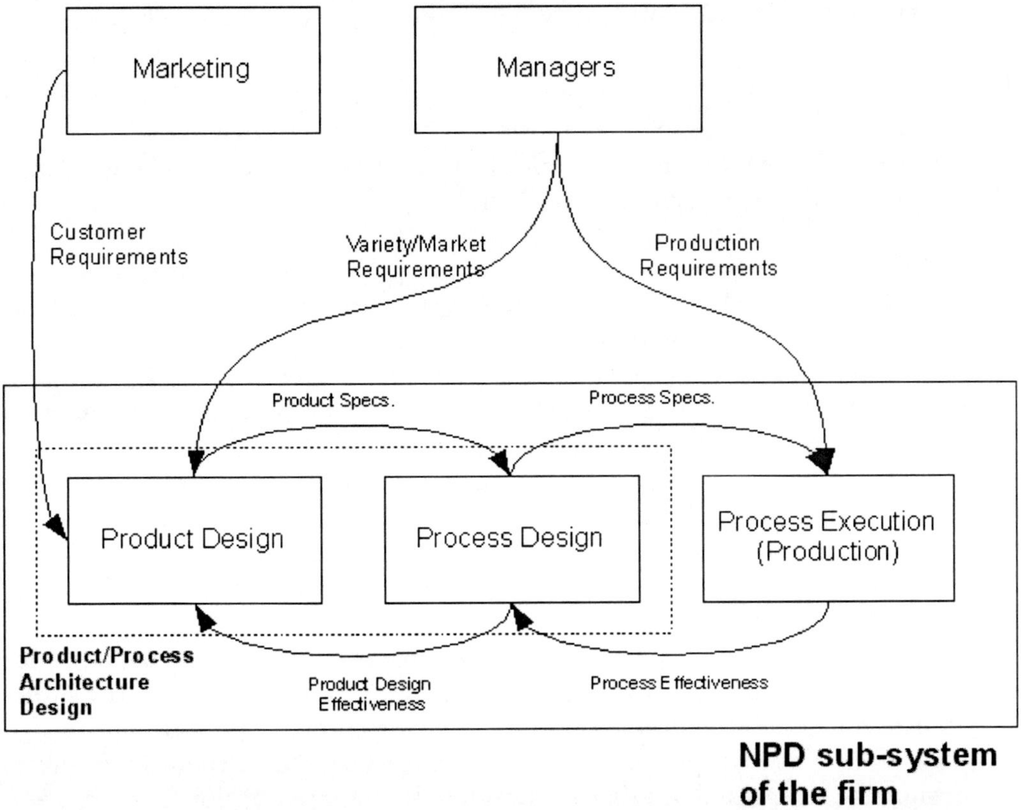

Figure 1 *Traditional NPD sub-system of the firm; product/process architecture jointly developed by the product design and process design functions, with a triadic NPD sub-system representative of that illustrated by Lu & Wood (2006).*

1. Customer requirements;
2. Strategic objectives (the variety/market requirements – the range of products and market niches that are to be targeted), and;
3. Production requirements.

These are illustrated in Figure 1 in relation to the functions involved in NPD, with the NPD sub-system based on the triadic relationship between functions - the basic relationship discussed by Lu & Wood (2006). The first two are direct inputs to the product designers. A trade-off frequently exists: more products released rapidly should mean less development time per product, incorporating fewer features. Moreover, more product variety means that the job of production becomes more difficult. The product designers are required to balance these competing objectives to align the NPD process with the firm's objectives. In these traditional cases of NPD the interaction between the product design and process design functions generates the product and process architecture for the products. Part of the role of the process design function is to mediate between the process requirements of the production function with the more technically orientated product design function (Lu & Wood, 2006).

Wood & Lu (2007) outline two different types of NPD projects:

1. A highly novel project that includes a radical adjustments of process design (a leap between an old generation and a new generation), and;
2. A less novel project that incrementally evolves an old product design, holding process design as constant as possible.

Carefully fluctuating between these two options, with the vast bulk of projects lying on the less novel end of the spectrum, the product designers are able to better meet these competing objectives.

Through generating product designs where successive designs retain existing product architecture as much as is feasible, the process design work is eased, as the processes are frequently identical or very similar. Existing equipment may be re-used, or adjusted to compensate, with a small amount of work required. Furthermore, when the processes are introduced to the production function, they are already familiar with these processes and so less training and learning time (learning curve) is required to get production 'up to speed' to meet the firm's objectives for production.

Under these circumstances the role of process design, as a separate function, may appear to be diminished, however when they are aware of the product architecture, the upcoming projects, they can prepare process options in advance, so that as firm product specifications are passed to them from product designers they are able to discard previously prepared options, and narrow down to a tight range of prepared options. This speeds the process design work. Under these circumstances where the product architecture is held constant the situation is illustrated in Figure 2.

Information from the production function on the effectiveness of processes can be passed to the process designers. In this case it may be that the glue required for a certain step is messy and is causing too many problems. With this information as an input the process designers may not be able to directly change the process without a change of the product design. As such they present a mediating influence in the NPD process; they are able to translate the (frequently) less technical complaints of production into the more technical language of the engineers for communication to the product designers. As Clark & Fujimoto (1991: 123) note: "effectiveness of process engineering depends as much on the ability to interact with product designers and the factory as it does on technical skills."

However, for any given product architecture there comes a time where no more innovation or functionality can be incorporated into the basic design. At this point there is a need to have a leap in the underlying architecture – it must totally change in order to be able to incorporate new innovations and functions. Such a change may be required due to the physical limitations of older technology. For these situations a full product development team is used. This will incorporate product designers, process designers, and production staff (as in Figure 1). Under these circumstances the product design team have much greater say. They are required to be familiar with the processes that will be used.

In MedCom1 the product designers will often be the process designers as well, for small niche products, often to the extent that they will manufacture the first batches themselves before handing off to production. In these cases the manufacturing processes are very similar to previous products.

As a result the coordination between the three functions changes, depending on the nature of the NPD project. Through holding the product architecture constant for an extended period, introducing new products that involve only minor product design changes, with the flow-on effect of minor process design changes, it is possible to reduce the time taken during the NPD project. As the role of process design is essentially a "problem-solving process that attempts to narrow the gap between what is known about the process and its likely performance and what needs to be known in order for the process to perform as desired" (Hayes, *et al.*, 2005), effective process design is critical to rapid time to market. Through retention of product architecture the existing process architecture can be largely re-used, reducing need for extra work. Furthermore, it enables *process design for product design* (Wood & Lu, 2007) to take place, and enables set-based engineering to occur. As the process designers are familiar with the basic product and process parameters that will be used, in advance they can prepare a set of possible parameters. When they have more certain information, they can discard some of these previously prepared options and plough on ahead, picking up where they had left off their work with less information.

With the changing role of product designers comes the critical responsibility for the product throughout the lifecycle. With higher levels of commonal-

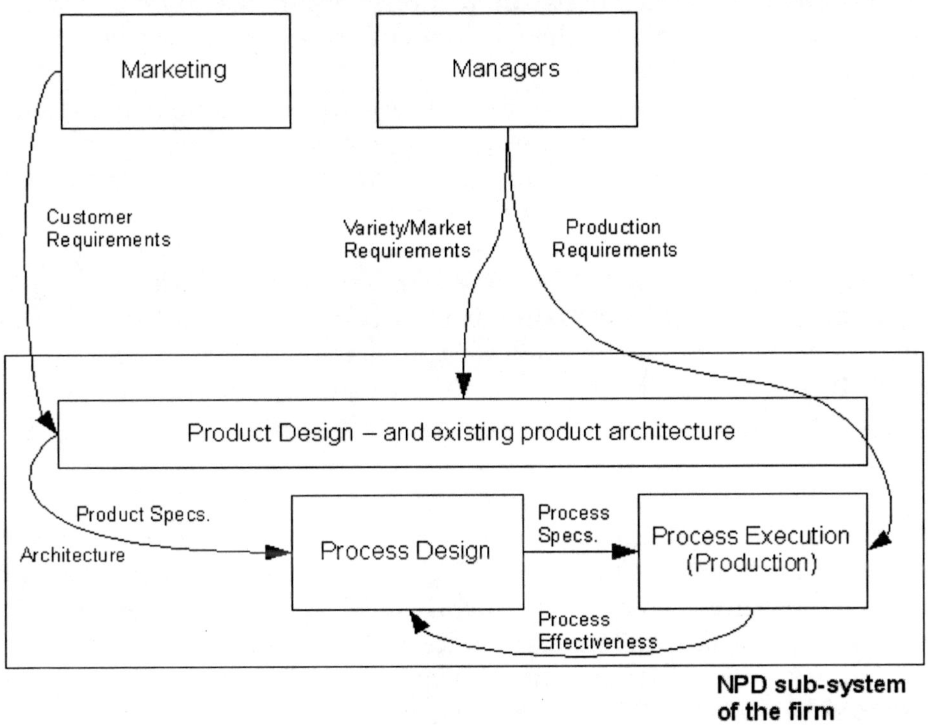

Figure 2 *NPD with pre-existing product architecture to speed NPD; existing product architecture used as a basis for the process design.*

ity between the product architectures and process architectures within product families a larger number of new products can be introduced with lower levels of design work. When the process design work revolves around a well understood product architecture options can be prepared in advance of provision of firm specifications, allowing a previously prepared option to be utilized as a base for further development – reducing overall process development time. With strategic requirements to rapidly introduce large varieties of products, re-arranging the functions and responsibilities of the NPD sub-system in the manner of Figure 2 can aid over-all organizational effectiveness. However with a more novel project (or a leap in technology or incorporation of new technologies) a reversion to the more traditional structuring of the NPD sub-system as illustrated in Figure 1 may be more appropriate.

When there is a need for product variety it is sensible to bestow the product design function with the authority to implement a consistent architecture. Through prudent planning the architecture design can withstand multiple small changes in the future to generate a wealth of product varieties with small amounts of work to then be completed in the process design and production functions. In this manner the product design team absorb the requirements for variety imposed on the NPD sub-system, instead of using skilled-flexible labour or flexible processes. Thus rather than using highly skilled production staff, or extremely flexible or complex processing equipment, product variety can be absorbed by the product designers through careful design and maintenance of product/process architectures – and not passed to the production function. This represents a shift in the functional interactions within the NPD sub-system and a change in the information exchange, particularly between the product design and the process design functions.

NPD projects lies along a continuum and the arrangement of the subsystems involved in NPD will alter based on the positioning of the project. Thus an appropriate arrangement of the subsystems may be selected (with the correct boundary specifications between the functions) along with the appropriate mix of projects, to meet the organizations strategic imperatives. The arrangement of the subsystems involved will determine who has more authority in the project and will impact on the expected interactions, responsibilities, and information flows amongst the functions. Not all NPD projects are created equal; using input from the firm's strategic objectives can inform an appropriate arrangement of subsystems to effectively meet the firm's goals.

Conclusion

Based on the requirements of the organization the structuring of the subsystem responsible for NPD can be of critical importance. Presented are two structures, which are frequently used in the NZ context in order to meet differing objectives. The reasons for the selection of each are outlined, along with the shifts in information flows and product/process architectures that should be expected. This correct demarcation of the boundaries between the functions involved in NPD and the responsibilities of each can force alignment with the corporate objectives for product variety through clearer allocation of responsibilities.

Further research is required to provide more empirical evidence for the existence of the two methods of organization of the NPD sub-systems discussed, and the reasons propelling the use of each. Study of a range of manufacturing contexts would also provide increased generalization of the concept.

References

Ashby, W. R. (1956), An introduction to cybernetics, London: Chapman and Hall.

Billington, C., Lee, H.L, Tang, C.S. (1998) "Successful Strategies for Product Rollovers", Sloan Management Review, ISSN 1532-9194, Vol 39 No 3, pp. 23-30.

Burchill, G. and Fine, C.H. (1997) "Time versus Market Orientation in Product Concept Development: Empirically-Based Theory Generation", Management Science, ISSN: 1526-5501, Vol 43 No 4, pp. 465-478.

Clark, K.B. and Fujimoto, T. (1991), Product Development Performance: Strategy, Organization, and Management in the World Auto Industry, Harvard Business School Press, Boston, MA.

Hayes, R., Pisano, G., Upton, D. and Wheelwright, S. (2005), Pursuing the Competitive Edge, John Wiley, New York.

Lager, T. (2002) "A structural analysis of process development in process industry", R&D Management, ISSN: 0033-6807 , Vol 32 No 1, pp. 87-95.

Lemon, J.R. and Carl, E.J. (1991) "A Structured Approach to Concurrent Product/Process Development", Manufacturing Systems, Vol 9 No 6, pp. 32-39.

Lu, Q. & Wood, L. C. (2006) "International Journal of Operations & Production Management", International Journal of Operations and Production Management, Vol 6, No 10, pp. 1123-1145.

Nevins, J. L., Whitney, D.E. (1989), Concurrent Design of Products and Processes: a Strategy for the Next Generation in Manufacturing, McGraw-Hill, New York.

Pawar, K.S., Menon, U. and Riedel, J. (1994) "Time to Market", Integrated Manufacturing Systems, ISSN: 0957-6061, Vol 5 No 1, pp. 14-22.

Pisano, G. P. (1997), The Development Factory: Unlocking the Potential of Process Innovation, Harvard Business School Press, Boston.

Stalk, G. (1988) "Time: The next source of competitive advantage", Harvard Business Review, ISSN: 0017-8012, Vol 66 No 4, pp. 39-60.

Terwiesch, C. & Bohn, R. (2001) "Learning and Process improvement during production ramp up", International Journal of Production Economics, ISSN: 0925-5273, Vol 70 No 1, pp. 1-19.

Wheelwright, S.C. and Clark, K.B. (1994) "Accelerating the Design-build-test Cycle for Effective Product Development", International Marketing Review, ISSN: 0265-1335, Vol 11 No 1, pp. 32-46.

Whitney, D. E. (1988) "Manufacturing by design", Harvard Business Review, ISSN: 0017-8012, Vol 66 No 4, pp. 83-91

Whitney, D. E. (1995), "Nippondenso, Co. Ltd.: A case study of strategic product design", in Liker, J.K., Ettlie, J.E. and Campbell, J.C. (Ed.) Engineered in Japan: Japanese Technology-management Practices, Oxford University Press, New York, pp. 115-151.

Wood, L. C. (2005), "Functional interactions for product realization", Unpublished Masters Thesis, The University of Auckland.

Wood, L. C. & Lu, Q. (2007), "Process management within high Tech NZ firms", *under review: International Journal of Innovation and Technology Management*

Theme 7:
Regional and Environmental Systems

29. On Becoming Mainstream: Perspectives on Regional and Environmental Systems

PLENARY PAPER

Roger Attwater
Capital Works & Facilities, University of Western Sydney;
Graduate Research Program in Environment and Policy,
University of New South Wales

The intent of this paper is to describe the range of concepts and tools of a systemic and integrative nature which are becoming part of mainstream approaches to regional and environmental management. Fundamental challenges in relation to connectivity, scale and environmental governance include the structure of overarching statutory frameworks, and a crisis of ability to translate sophisticated scientific knowledge into pragmatic guidance for policy and management. Useful integrative and systemic frameworks are those which are both robust and able to be broadly communicated. Frameworks discussed include: those relating to state of the environment reporting and sustainability auditing such as the urban metabolism model; regional integration through integrated catchment management, and water sensitive urban design; organizational initiatives based upon environmental management systems; and emerging conceptual foundations around the notion of resilience. Issues around the dynamics of learning and participative engagement are also discussed.

Introduction

Regional and environmental systems are characterized by layers of complexity and multiple drivers interacting at different scales and timeframes. Both the natural systems and the organizational and institutional systems show complex arrangements of global and large scale drivers (such as climate change and international treaties), regional contexts (e.g., landscapes and government structures), and diverse local adaptive strategies and responses (e.g., ecosystem health, sustainable communities and local governance).

Our history of attempts at effective policy and management are littered with the results of treating aspects of our environment in isolation. It is also a litany of partial solutions given the ideological and political context of the day. Given the highly political nature of regional and environmental governance, workable integrative and systemic frameworks need to be highly robust, and operate in a highly contestable domain. The focus of this paper is on the broad range of frameworks which continue to show utility and flexibility in engaging issues of regional and environmental contexts.

Connectivity, Scale and Environmental Governance

At a scale of State and nation, international dialogues relating to sustainable development and climate change continue to drive some connectivity between statutory frameworks which guide our formal systems of governance. While some situations, such as New Zealand, have been able to apply an overarching statutory framework for natural resources, in the majority of cases these are still fragmented, though with increasing cross reference to overarching principles such as sustainable development.

At the level of States in Australia, where operational governance of environment and natural resource is situated, innovation in formal institutional tools have been occurring,. This has included a move beyond regulatory tools to incorporate economic incentives and participatory approaches for environmental management and stewardship. In New South Wales, the Protection of the Environment Operation Act is founded on incentives enabling organizations to determine their own least cost solution to reduce environmental pollution. The NSW Total Catchment Management Act relies upon participatory methods to achieve environmental stewardship. Fragmentation, duplication, and competition for regulatory roles are still common in institutional arrangements, though overarching reforms seek to rationalize and combine critical thematic areas with emerging policy tools. In response to international drivers, problems of fragmentation at State levels, and critical issues of resource scarcity, institutional reform led from a National level has been fundamental. In commenting on the case of water reform in Australia, Crawford (2007) clearly states the need for national initiatives which enable careful contextual and participative analysis, and move towards a systems approach in approaching the issues of scale and complexity.

Challenges of Interpretation: An Example of Environmental Risk Management

Given that in Australia the legislative responsibility falls to State governments, the Commonwealth has focused on broad ranging environmental audits, and the development of guidelines. One of the most well developed areas are those developed as part of the National Water Quality Strategy. Particularly for the values associated with the protection of aquatic ecosystem, a very detailed, scientific and systematic approach to risk management was developed (ANZECC 2000). These utilize decision trees to determine 'trigger values' for problematic parameters, and comprehensive monitoring strategies. While elegant and sophisticated in design, these guidelines were written up in a manner that is difficult to interpret and most managers in local government situations have found these too difficult to understand and use.

This reflects a common crisis in the way in which our science is interpreted into guidance for policy and management, and communicated to local managers and the community. The more sophisticated the science the greater the challenge becomes. This reinforces the need for simple and robust frameworks to assist in communicating between these knowledge systems – a clear case for the role of systems thinking and practice. A related need is for facilitated communication between different communities of practice, stakeholders, scientists and policy makers regarding perceived risks and environmental concerns. While often left to the media and political means, more structured roles for systemic inquiry and action research are clear (e.g., Attwater and Derry 2005).

The State of Our Environment

A fundamental challenge is in meshing strategic and broader scale drivers with opportunities for regional and local governance. Over the past few decades key drivers have included the global discourse on sustainable development and the way in which these principles have been written into international treaties and agreements, and national and State legislation. Through these discourses a number of useful robust frameworks have emerged, such as those relating to State of the Environment Reporting.

In Australia, the 1996 State of the Environment (SoE) Report (SOEAC 1996) was a landmark publication. Two key frameworks utilized in this were the Pressure-State-Response (PSR) model for environmental indicators, and the Urban Metabolism Model. Building upon a framework developed for OECD countries, the PSR Model provides a simple and robust model for considering what we are trying to monitor through indicator systems. The Pressures are defined as all human-induced factors contributing to deleterious impacts on the condition of our environment. The State is the current condition of the environment. Responses are the individual behaviors and organizational policies which contribute to reducing the Pressures and improving the condition or state of the environment. While this has been adapted and added to, it is fundamentally a very robust framework of interpretation for considering the complexity of environmental indicators.

Another very useful integrative framework which was used in the 1996 SoE Report was that of the Urban Metabolism Model. This provides a simple framework for considering not just the resources used by a city and forms of wastes generated, but also the emergent properties of livability generated by these resource transformations (Newman 1996, 1999)

"*Sustainability for a city is thus not only a reduction in metabolic flows (resource inputs and waste outputs, it must also be about increasing human livability (social amenity and health*" (Newman 1999).

Along with use as a reporting framework for Australian urban environments, this framework has been used with materials flow analyses of regions such as the ACT (Birkeland and Schooneveldt 2003) and for investigating aspects such as the CO_2 implications of the way we move water through our cities (Kenway 2007). This model also has possible potential for scaling down for investigating embedded components of our urban landscapes. For example, in my role as Environmental Manager at the University of Western Sydney I am faced with 6 campuses embedded in different parts of the Western Sydney urban landscape. I hope this framework and related methods can help guide some integrated sustainability audits of UWS.

Integration for Natural Resource Management

A recent forum organized by Land and Water Australia has focused on questions of integration in natural resource management. Bammer (*et al.* 2005) suggests the following ways of thinking about integration:

- "re-engagement of fragments that have been intensively studied by reductionist methods;
- Beginning with and studying whole system contexts, using a plurality of approaches. In the case of NRM, landscape context including people, place and resource base, is essential;
- As an approach of practice inherent or developed in individuals and organizations.

These three forms of integration are not interchangeable. All are necessary and require intellectual and practical development, as well as supportive institutional structures" (Bammer, *et al.* 2005, p. 5)

Regional Integration

At a regional scale, one of the most challenging aspects are the range of roles, ideologies, and perspectives, even just within formal governance structures of government agencies. In this domain, frameworks building upon contestable concepts have tended to emerge, i.e., those that can be defined according to very different perspectives. This case will be developed for one such example, that of integrated catchment management, though is common of other 'integrated' conceptions for water resource, natural resource, or environmental management.

The Example of Integrated Catchment Management

In a broad ranging review of integrated catchment in the mid 1990s, Cameron, *et al.* (1996) described literature on the subject tended to show that definitions of ICM tended to be limited by disciplinary backgrounds, rather than reflecting the full scope of issues allegedly being integrated. Three key concerns were identified as drivers which continue to work in dynamic juxtaposition: administrative accountability, public participation, and Aldo Leopold's 'land ethic'. These partially incompatible concerns may perhaps operate as in tension, with the particular forms of ICM at a particular time reflecting this mix.

Perception of issues, and potential tools available, are heavily dependent upon the scale of view relating to personal or professional praxis. Dynamics occurring at local, regional and larger scales certainly operate at different frequencies and in response to very different drivers. As posed by the author previously (Attwater 2005) one view of integrated catchment management is as a role in translation and advocacy across these scales and perspectives.

A growing area of interest is in consideration of distributed systems of management and technology, linking critical characteristics at different scales rather than just a focus on either centralized or decentralized approaches (e.g., Attwater, *et al.* 2007). The mechanisms required include diverse and varied 'meso-scale' arrangements to enable connections between regulatory oversight, management processes and inclusive localized solutions. These include formal organizational partnerships and offset arrangements for investment. These can be driven by transformations of waste streams into valued resources, such as recycled water in a total water cycle perspective, or industrial wastes reused through industrial ecology.

Design as Integration: The Case of Water Sensitive Urban Design

Another key opportunity for integration is through critical design elements which can be interpreted differently according to scale and context. An emerging case example of this for our urban environments is that of Water Sensitive Urban Design (WSUD). WSUD seeks to achieve multiple outcomes regarding the role of water movement in our urban landscape, and commonly builds on a combination of engineered structures which mimic the cascades and transformations of energy and material carried by water through a landscape. Key objectives include: protecting and enhancing natural water systems within urban development, integrating stormwater treatment in multiple use corridors in the landscape; protecting water quality from drainage inputs derived from urban areas; reducing run-off and peak flows from the impervious surface of urban areas; and adding value through cost-effective drainage strategies (CSIRO 1999)

Depending upon perspective, WSUD can also be considered as one nested aspect within a hierarchy of management practices (CSIRO 1999). Effective design needs to be underpinned by land-use planning controls, and effectiveness will be enhanced through source controls (operational and behavioral). Only with this hierarchy in place can engineering / structural works for stormwater treatment and flow management be effectively established.

Organizational Systems

In the case of businesses and industries, environmental management systems and risk management systems are becoming more common as a means of accountability to environmental and public health risks. These can provide a robust logic for linking a range of tools and approaches to deal with complex contextual issues such as those relating to water recycling (e.g., Attwater, *et al.* 2006), going beyond a systematic guide to becoming a robust systemic framework for sustainability initiatives.

New Conceptual Foundations

An exciting area of development has been that of innovative conceptual schemas developed to engage the fundamental interactions between governance processes and the dynamics of environmental systems. A very important area of conceptual development has been that of resilience management and socio-ecological systems (e.g., Gunderson and Holling 2002). Through a worldwide network called the Resilience Network, the concepts of adaptive management developed by Holling were expanded to address issues of resilience in social, institutional and environmental systems. As part of this network, CSIRO Wildlife and Ecology have developed and tested these concepts against a number of regional situations in Australia (e.g., Walker and Salt 2006). This framework has also been drawn upon in work addressing the landscape role of agricultural systems neighboring world heritage (Attwater and Merson 2007).

The Dynamics of Learning and Participative Engagement

The inherent nature of learning involved in engaging new issues and situations is a truism, though the means for explicitly incorporating these aspects in inquiry and management continue to be a challenge. Since the late 1970s, a learning approach has been fundamental to mainstream rural development (e.g., Korten 1980), with the rhetoric of participatory development becoming a worldwide phenomena through the 1980s and 1990s. During this time a vast literature emerged on various methods of participatory appraisal (e.g., Chambers 1983, 1994) and methods and concepts to support environmental and social change (e.g., Scoones and Thomson 1994, Slocum *et al.* 1995), reflecting substantial lessons learned. Eventually, these concepts and language began showing up in publications from institutions such as the World Bank and the Asian Development Bank. This followed on into recent literature supporting decentralization, though I'd suggest as a very contestable concept underpinned by a range of ideologies.

Landcare in Australia and New Zealand

In Australian and New Zealand, landcare emerged as our local version of this global participatory phenomena, and eventually a social movement in its own right. With both government recognition of resources to be harnessed, real opportunity for government-community partnerships, and local diversification of interests, this led to numerous variants such as bushcare, dunecare, etc. Alongside this movement was the increasing engagement of school children in local environmental studies of an experiential nature, such as waterwatch. These groups and the issues they faced were often varied and emergent, and reflected dynamic of the group's energy resources and focus. Attempts by agencies to provide structured support led to some successes, though also the varied and emergent nature of these groups often became somewhat institutionalized as attempts were made to scale up the growing successes of particular local initiatives.

Changing Nature of Communities

A fundamental challenge still remains as to how to engage communities. This has, in my view, two major dimensions. Firstly, the very notion of community is changing, with locality-based communities being subsumed under more complex communities of practice and related networks. To engage these more complex and dynamic structures, fluid notions and methods are necessary. Secondly, community voices have tended to rely on a small committed number of people. Institutional requirements for consultation in particular time frames, and an increasingly seen need to consult often results in over consultation or fall back positions of 'proxy' voices by particular interest groups on behalf of sections of the community. A challenge is to provide processes of action learning and engagement which ebb and flow with people's availability, dynamics of their issues of concern. This is commonly difficult for agencies and researchers with deadlines and budgets. This is a clear and ongoing need for systemic practice, and seeking to embed this in support structures.

Engaging Disciplinary Perspectives

Another area of participative engagement is with scientists, cultural researchers, engineers and the plethora of disciplinary perspectives which contribute to regional and environmental management. Rather than setting themselves up as a separate 'meta-discipline' and comparison with simplistic 'positivist' strawmen, systems thinkers and practitioners need to engage other forms of inquiry with respect and recognition of opportunity to contribute. A separate paper at this conference addresses the need for pluralist inquiry to engage issues of validity common to all rigorous inquiry, along with broader issues from action research and related perspectives (Attwater 2007). Greater acceptance of what systems practitioners can offer can only come through developing mutual respect and evidence of effective complementarity in methods, not mere rhetoric.

References

Attwater, R. Booth, S., Davey, P., Guthrie, A. (2002) "Opportunities for investment in stormwater and wastewater in the Hawkesbury-Nepean", Australian Journal of Environmental Management, ISSN: 1448-6563, 9(3): 169-184

Attwater, R., Derry, C. (2005) "Engaging communities of practice for risk communication in the Hawkesbury Water Recycling Scheme", Action Research, ISSN: 1476-7503, 3(2): 193-209.

Attwater, R.. Booth, S., Guthrie, A. (2005) "The role of contestable concepts in transdisciplinary management of water in the landscape", Systems Research and Behavioral Science, ISSN: 0005-7940, 22: 185-192.

Attwater, R., Aiken, J., Beveridge, G., Booth, C.A. (Sandy), Derry, C., Shams, R., Stewart, J. (2006) "An adaptive systems toolkit for managing the Hawkesbury recycling scheme", Desalination, ISSN: 0011-9164, 188(1-3): 21-30.

Attwater, R., Merson, J. (2007) "Resilience of agri-industries neighboring the Blue Mountains World Heritage Area", *Systems Research and Behavioral Science,* ISSN: 0005-7940, 24(2): 249-252.

Attwater, R., Aiken, J., Derry, C. (2007) "Diversity and decentralisation for water cycle management: reflections from the Hawkesbury Water Recycling Scheme", in: Khan, S.J., Stuetz, R.M., Anderson, J.M. (eds.) *Water reuse and recycling,* ISBN 978 0 7334 2517 2, pp. 49-56.

Attwater (forthcoming) "Methodological cascades for pluralist inquiry: some case examples of environmental governance" paper for ANZSYS'07 Systemic development: local solutions in a global environment, Auckland, New Zealand.

Birkeland, J., Schooneveldt, J. (2003) *Mapping regional metabolism: a decision-support tool for natural resource management,* ISBN 0 642 76102 7.

Cameron, J. Gomez-Fort, R., Macpherson, D. (1996) *Integrated catchment management as communicative rationality: the case of the Hawkesbury-Nepean.* Report on the project "Innovative approaches to environmental valuation in integrated catchment management funded by LWRRDC, School of Social Ecology, University of Western Sydney.

Chambers, R. (1983) *Rural development: putting the last first*, ISBN: 05826644437.

Chambers, R. (1994) "Participatory rural appraisal (PRA): challenges, potentials and paradigm", *World Development*, ISSN: 0305-750X, 22(10): 1437-1454.

Crawford, P. (2007) What is missing in national water reforms ? ATSE Focus http://www.atse.org,au/index.php?sectionid=1000, Australian Academy of Technological Sciences and Engineering

CSIRO (1999) *Urban stormwater: best practice environmental management guidelines*, ISBN: 0 643 06453 2.

Gunderson, L.H., Holling, C.S. (2002) *Panarchy: understanding transformations in human and natural systems*, ISBN: 1-55963-856-7.

Kenway, S. (2007) "Future cities and water – a systems view" *Ozwater 2007*, Australian Water Association, Sydney.

Newman, P., Birrell, B., Holmes, D., Mathers, C., Newton, P., Oakley, G., O'Connor, A., Walker, B., Spessa, A., Tait, D. (1996) "Human settlements", in: State of the Environment Advisory Council (SOEAC) *Australia: State of the environment 1996*, ISBN: 0642553009, Chapter 3.

Newman, P.W,G. (1999) "Sustainability and cities: extending the metabolism model" *Landscape and Urban Planning*, ISSN: 0169-2046, 44: 219-226.

Scoones, I., Thomson, J. (1994) *Beyond farmer first: rural people's knowledge, agricultural research and extension practice*, ISBN: 1853392375.

Slocum, R., Wichhart, L., Rocheleau, D., Thomas-Slayter, B. (1995) *Power, process and participation – tools for change*, ISBN: 1 85339 303 7.

State of the Environment Advisory Council (SOEAC) (1996) *Australia: State of the environment 1996*, ISBN: 0642553009.

Walker, B., Salt, D. (2006) *Sustaining ecosystems and people in a changing world*, ISBN: 1-59726-092-4.

30. Methodological Cascades for Pluralist Inquiry: Some Case Examples of Environmental Governance

Roger Attwater
Blue Mountains World Heritage Institute;
Graduate Research Program in Environmental Policy and Management, University of New South Wales

With an increasing interest in adaptive and integrative governance, approaches to inquiry need to maintain internal rigour while embracing a broader systemic and pluralist context. This paper reflects upon the adaptive methodological approaches taken in three different inquiries in relation to the metaphor of a methodological cascade. The first case is that of investment in stormwater and wastewater management in the Hawkesbury-Nepean River Basin, Sydney. The second case example is risk communication relating to a range of communities of practice utilizing recycled water as part of the Hawkesbury Water Recycling Scheme. The third case example is an ongoing project investigating the role of agri-industries as a landscape buffer between the Blue Mountains World Heritage Area, and the encroaching urban sprawl of Sydney. The issues of validity discussed here are potentially very important to the broader integration of systemic perspectives alongside disciplinary inquiry.

Introduction

Methodological pluralism has been a common theme of interest in the systems literature. Following broad ranging debate following the development of the 'system of systems methodologies' by Jackson and Keyes (1984) methodological pluralism continued to be recognized as a core value of critical systems thinking and practice, along with improvement and critical awareness (Midgley, 1996, 1997). Other perspectives reflecting the importance of informed and pluralist methodological practice includes 'total systems intervention' (Flood & Jackson, 1991) and multimethodology (Mingers & Gill, 1997). The author has previously sought to contribute to the ongoing conceptual discussion of methodological pluralism through investigating the philosophical underpinnings and methodological implications of different economic perspectives, attempting to map these onto a SOSM-like typology (Attwater, 2000).

The approach developed in this paper attempts to address issues of validity and rigour in relation to both qualitative and quantitative information which may be collected as part of a systemic inquiry. It is proposed that systemic inquiry, either as a mixture of methods or as an application of an established systems methodology, must still address these basic issues in the way in which they deal with core information upon which interpretations are made. Criticisms of systems research by disciplinary perspectives often reflect a perceived lack of traditional rigour. Moreover, systemic inquiry must address broader ethical criteria, though this may be undermined if not enough attention is paid to basic issues. This paper builds upon constructivist criteria and action research, though other broader ethical and systemic perspectives could be drawn upon.

The applications discussed here are from a domain of environmental governance, though these issues are certainly not limited to this domain. Environmental governance is an area of inquiry and adaptive management which clearly requires different forms of inquiry for different contextual dimensions. Issues of environmental governance commonly involve a range of agents, organizations, and instruments interacting at different scales. Given an increasing interest in adaptive and integrative policy and management, approaches to inquiry need to be able to maintain internal rigour while embracing a broader systemic and pluralist context.

Post-Positivism, Constructivism and Action Research

The first section of this paper briefly provides an overview of epistemological issues relevant to inquiry into biophysical and institutional dimensions of environmental governance. These include post-positivist approaches to biophysical dimensions, interpretive and constructivist approaches to organizational initiatives, and action research perspectives for participative inquiry.

Post-positivism extends the key attributes of positivist inquiry to embrace uncertainty. It still holds to the ideals of objectivity and validity in inquiring into an external reality, but recognizes the difficulty in grasping that reality. Objectivity is interpreted as the extent to which multiple observers can agree on a phenomenon. This is generally sought through recourse to the reliability to which measurement procedures yield the same answers however and whenever they are carried out, and validity in terms of the extent to which a measurement procedure gives a correct answer (Kirk & Miller, 1986). Engagement with phenomena through a post-positivist epistemology requires the researcher to be precise, un-biased, open, honest, and receptive to criticism (Smith, 1990).

In seeking to incorporate subjectivity, constructivism views reality as multiple mental constructions. Inquiry is seen as interaction, with the aim being to reflect the multiple realities according to participant's views. The 'goodness' of the inquiry relates how clearly and objectively the range of beliefs is presented (Lincoln, 1990; Marshall, 1990). Building upon this basis, criteria of research 'trustworthiness' have been developed. These include questions as to: 'have the people been changed by the process?; have they a heightened sense of their own constructed realities ?; do they have an increased awareness of the constructions of other stakeholders?; and to what extent did the investigation prompt action ?' (Lincoln, 1990).

There are numerous areas of inquiry which have sought to mould these aspects of post-positivist and constructivist inquiry. Given the authors background an area of familiarity is that of rural development and sustainable agriculture. Building upon decades of previous work on these and related matters Pretty (1994) summarized the following aspects as key dimensions of inquiry for sustainable agriculture:

- "Prolonged or intense engagement of various actors, to build trust, rapport, and become open to multiple influences;
- Persistent and parallel observation of the phenomena and its context, to increase depth and breadth of perspective;
- Triangulation of sources, methods, and investigators, to cross-check;
- Analysis and expression of difference of perspectives of a wide range of actors, accurately represented and not resolved into a single consensus;
- Negative case analysis, or sequential revision of working hypotheses;
- Peer checking by those not involved in inquiry, to explore implicit biases held by single investigator;
- Participant checking of data, interpretation, and conclusions, particularly if researcher is claiming to represent participant's views;
- Reports with working hypotheses and contextual descriptions and visualizations;
- Parallel investigation and team communication, for potential demonstration of replicability;
- Reflexive journals by researchers on feelings and methodological decisions;
- Inquiry audit, so that there is enough information for a disinterested person to examine the processes and products;
- Impact on stakeholders' capacity to know and act, through demonstrated impact on increased sense of own constructed reality, other stakeholders' constructions, and understanding of the range of possible activities". (Pretty, 1994)

Pretty (1994) provides an incorporation of attributes of inquiry more likely to address issues of validity from post-positivist and constructivist, and the ethical and participative aspects have been addressed further in the field of action research. Rather than a rather constrained view of action research as reflective practice, Bradbury and Reason (2001) provided examples of broad ranging forms of action research, and summarized this diversity in terms of 'broadening the bandwidth of validity. They expressed validity in action research as the practical and reflexive concerns which emerge from a pluralist and participatory worldview. Reflecting upon a broad range of case examples, Bradbury and Reason discussed a range of dimensions of quality in action research, including:

- Relational praxis (concepts and application);
- Reflexive and practical outcomes;

- Range of dimensions of knowing;
- Conceptual-theoretical integrity;
- Extending ways of knowing;
- Methodological appropriateness;
- Engaging in significant work;
- Purpose through emergent inquiry towards enduring outcomes and consequences.

This clearly indicates that researchers who utilise action research as a broad rationale of their practice have in fact broad ranging challenges in how they legitimise their work. It is the authors view that to ensure that research based upon systems thinking and action research is recognized in traditional university situations, not only is it important that critical peer review is utilized, but that also systems researchers show respect for, and incorporate issues of validity across relevant traditions.

Case Examples of Methodological Cascades

Three different case examples of research recently undertaken are discussed below in terms of the logic used to adaptively develop methodological cascades relevant to each inquiry. Each of these provides a very different means of methodological development, reflecting pluralism in meta-methodological approach as well as in the mixing of methods.

Case 1. Investment in Stormwater and Wastewater

This case was established as commissioned research for the Hawkesbury Nepean Catchment Management Authority in western Sydney, with the issue being to address both the point source pollutants involved with wastewater treatment and diffuse source pollutants from stormwater (Attwater *et al.*, 2002). Two major strategies influenced the methodological streams presented in Figure 1. Firstly a broad and embracing definition of investment was used, in relation to 'investing in the future' rather than limiting the scope to cost-benefit or financial tangibles. This was supported by international literature, particularly from the OECD which critically addressed the successes of economic incentives compared to the neoclassical theoretical conceptualizations. The second key strategy was developed from an interest in developing upon the system of systems methodologies (Jackson & Keyes, 1984) in relation to philosophical assumptions and methodological implications and economic methodologies in general (Attwater, 2000). Complementary methods of an analytical, interpretive and critical nature were utilized in a complementary fashion.

Based upon rigorous baseline data, cost-effectiveness analyses were undertaken, along with semi-structured interviews relating to opportunities for organizational and institutional leverage. Issues of validity for the analytical component were addressed through building upon rigorous baseline data, with a workshop of experts in the field to reconsider the assumptions inherent in the analysis. In the interpretive analysis of organizational leverage, hermeneutic

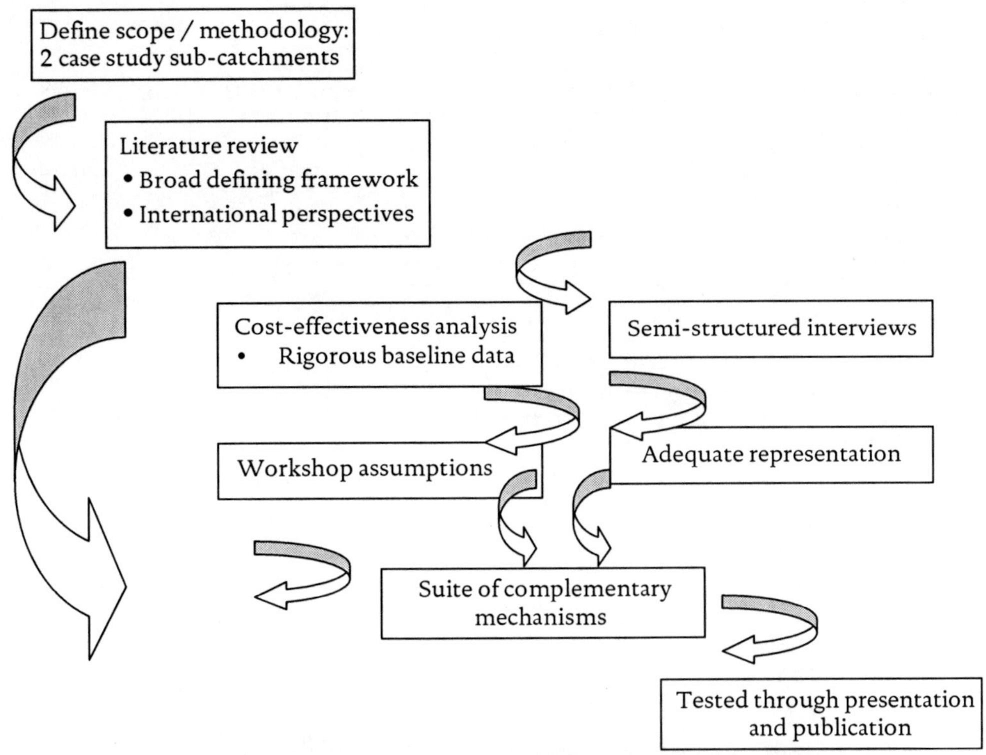

Figure 1 *Methodological Cascade of Investment Study*

cycles of checking interpretation were undertaken, along with attempting to ensure adequate representation of views in case study situations.

These were then framed in a broader critical framework, building upon a broad problem framing through an embracing definition and review outlined above, and followed by adaptive methods to check the assumptions and interpretations developed within each methodological stream. These provided feedback to support the valid outcomes of each stream, strengthening confidence in the integrative analysis which incorporated a suite of complementary mechanisms. These recommendations were then further tested through presentation to key audiences and broad peer review (Figure 1). As short and sharp commissioned research, unfortunately there was limited opportunity to pursue ongoing co-construction of implications with participants.

Case study 2. Risk Communication and Water Recycling

The second case study emerged during the development of an environmental management system for the Hawkesbury Water Recycling Scheme. Challenges involved in differing awareness and views as to risks associated with the use of recycled water became apparent, along with the need to engage a broad range of groups in actively managing the risks involved. An attempt was made to go beyond traditional stakeholder type analysis for focus on the range of 'communities of practice' each with their particular networks of involvement, values and behaviors. These included active water users such as workers on dairy, horticultural and agricultural technical staff, and passive users of nearby facilities such

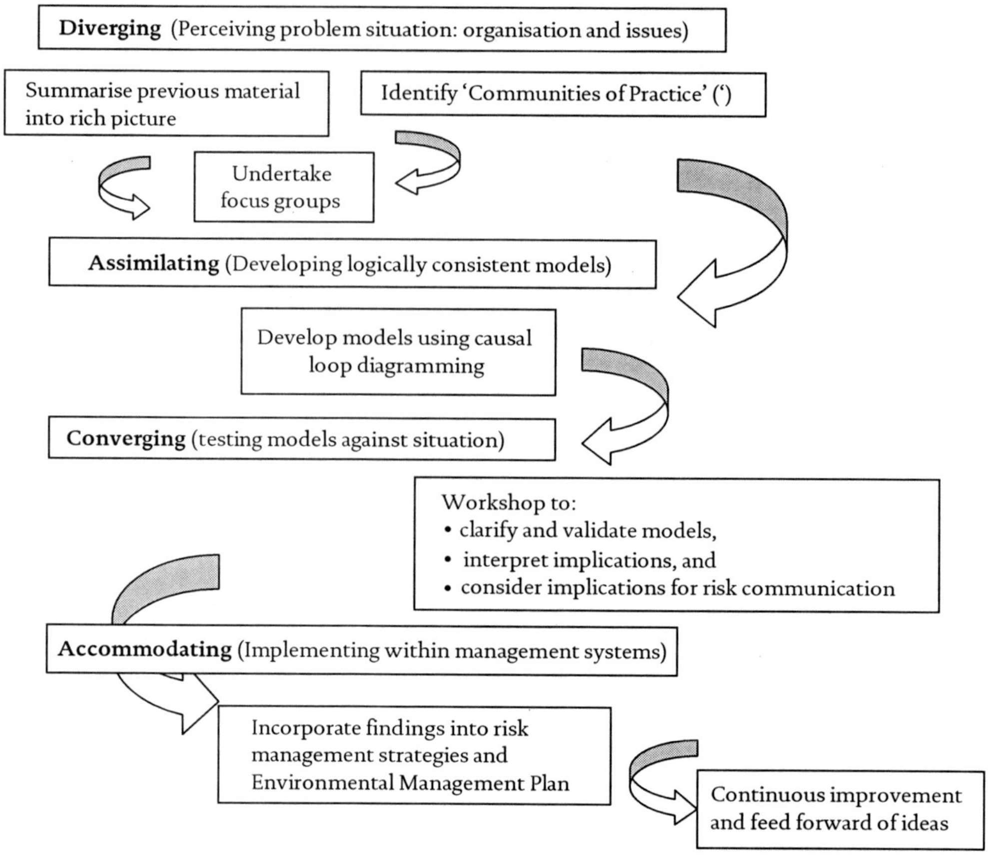

Figure 2 *Methodological cascade for risk communication study*

as childcare workers. Fundamental to the methodology developed was an intent to respect and document the views held by these differing groups, attempt to translate the implications of scientific monitoring to their situation, and attempt to co-construct ways of sharing knowledge and information. In this case, a meta-methodological guide based upon Kolb's learning cycle was utilized (Kolb, 1984) (Figure 2).

In this case, issues of validity had two aspects, firstly hermeneutic cycles of interpretation and discussion to develop simple diagrams representing issues perceived, and information strategies required to address these. At a much broader scale, issues of validity as action research were sought in relation to the 1st, second and third person strategies, which are discussed in detail in Attwater and Derry (2005). First person strategies were about why we as researchers engaged with these issues in these ways; our interests in engaging the community within the university, and in broaching both science and systems methods. Second person strategies are about how we saw the role of the research participants – representatives of our communities of practice. This included the importance of dialogue on issues of common concern, and their role as integral managers of associated risks. Third person strategies related to broader processes of social inquiry, surfacing and communicating perceptions, co-constructing intersubjective rules, contributing to collective behavior and the emergence of workable common property.

Case Study 3: Sustainability, Agri-industries and World Heritage

The third case study is a project which is nearing completion which has been undertaken for the Blue Mountains World Heritage Institute. The intent of this project is to provide a grounded basis for advocating the value of current horticultural activities as a landscape buffer between encroaching land use change around the Blue Mountains World Heritage Institute. The logic of the methods used has followed an adaptive response to the outcomes of each step of engagement. Initially, semi-structured interviews were undertaken with a range of different primary producers in a case study area. Discussions were interpreted through trying to utilise a conceptual framework of resilience and panarchy (Gunderson & Holling, 2002) and these interpretations have been presented elsewhere (Attwater & Campbell, 2005; Attwater & Merson, 2007). This was only a preliminary step, as from this a subset of primary producers were approached to help develop a range of methods focusing on a subset of types of production and marketing strategies. Underpinned by concepts of ecosystem services and agro-ecology, a range of approaches have been tested. These include: the application of landscape function assessment as a semi-quantitative assessment of ecosystem services in orchard situations, and the collaborative testing of saleable fungal products from local organic wastes. Also, these specific cases are being generalized through the use of geographic information systems to inform discussions about regional scenarios (Figure 3).

For this study, each component of the inquiry had different needs in terms of validation. The preliminary discussions of issues perceived needed to be rechecked through ongoing engagement and summarized in relation to groupings of perspectives which emerged. The interpretations in relation to concepts of resilience and ecosystem services needs to be broadly tested and this is ongoing as implications in relation to regional scenarios are juxtaposed against these frameworks of interpretation. The participative testing of microbial initiatives and water conservation emerged from interests expressed, and required particular scientific input relevant to these areas. The testing of landscape function analysis as a quantitative measure of ecosystem services was undertaken by drawing upon people who had applied these methods elsewhere. The broader logic of how these methods complemented one another continues to be tested through review workshops, discussions with participating landholders, and presentation at forums like this one. Ultimately, the test of this mix of methods will be as a well-grounded study which can be provide a basis for policy advocacy by the Blue Mountains World Heritage Institute.

Concluding Comments

Each of these studies reflects a different meta-methodological arrangement of component methodologies, with both the overarching logics and component methodologies tailored for the particular focus of the inquiry. Traditionally, validity and rigorous inquiry is undertaken by researchers developing an expertise in a particular set of methodological tools. In cases of environmental governance, it has been well recognized that interdisciplinary or multidisciplinary teams be formed to ensure both internally rigorous contributions and

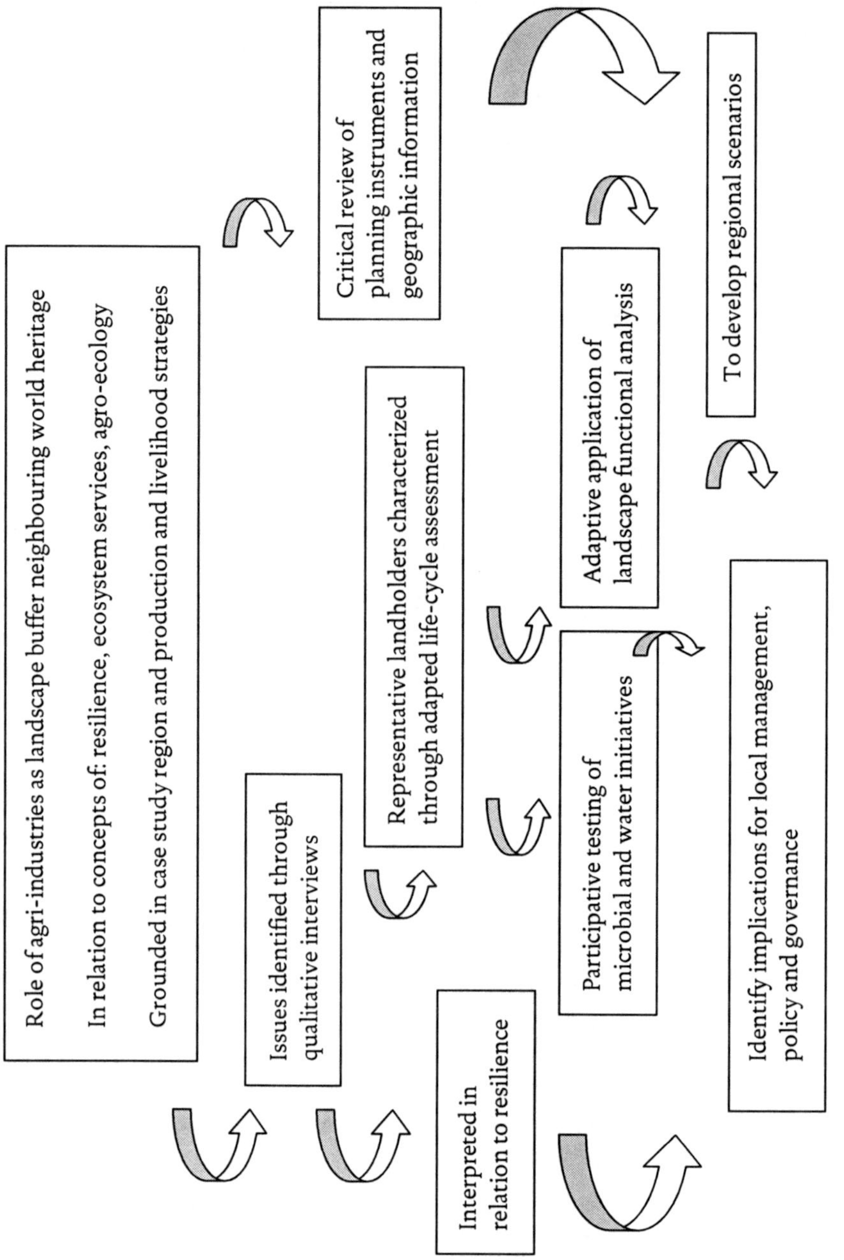

Figure 3 *Methodological Cascade for Agri-industry Project*

a mix of perspectives. The challenge comes when individuals seek to continue to broaden their competencies and draw upon different mixes of methods. The same logic of seeking teams of researchers is a sound strategy. It is suggested here that while continuing to try to extend mixes of methods reflecting upon core issues of validity and rigor are always important, both in the case of the types of analytical and interpretive information utilized, and broader systemic or participative ideals.

References

Attwater, R. (2000). "Pluralism, economic rhetoric and common property", *Systemic Practice and Action Research,* ISSN: 1094-429X, 13(4): 543-557.

Attwater, R. Booth, S., Davey, A., Guthrie, A. (2002). "Opportunities for investment in stormwater and wastewater in the Hawkesbury Nepean", *Australian Journal of Environmental Management,* ISSN: 1448-6563, 9(3): 169-184.

Attwater, R., Campbell, M. (2005). "Managing resilience in landscapes and personal praxis", in: Richardson, K.A., Gregory, W.J., Midgley, G. (eds.) *Systems thinking and complexity science: insights for action* – Proceedings of the 11th ANZSYS / Managing the Complex V Conference, ISBN: 0976681498.

Attwater, R., Derry, C. (2005). "Engaging communities of practice for risk communication in the Hawkesbury Water Recycling Scheme", *Action Research,* ISSN: 1476-7503, 3(2): 193-209.

Attwater, R., Merson, J. (2007). "Resilience of agri-industries neighbouring the Blue Mountains World Heritage Area", *Systems Research and Behavioural Science,* ISSN: 0005-7940, 24: 249-252.

Bradbury, H, Reason, P. (2001). "Conclusion: broadening the bandwidth of validity: issues and choice points for improving the quality of action research", in: Reason, P., Bradbury, H., (eds.) *Handbook of action research: participative inquiry and practice,* ISBN: 0761966455.

Gunderson, L.H., Holling, C.S. (2002) *Panarchy: understanding transformations in human and natural systems,* ISBN: 1-55963-856-7.

Jackson, M.C., and Keys, P. (1984). Toward a system of systems methodologies, *Journal of the Operational Research Society,* ISSN: 0160-5682, 35, 473-486.

Kirk, J. Miller, M.L. (1986) *Reliability and validity in qualitative research,* ISBN: 9780803924703.

Kolb, D.A. (1984). *Experiential learning: experience as the source of learning and development,* ISBN-10: 0132952610.

Lincoln, Y.S. (1990). "The making of a constructivist: a remembrance of transformations past", in: Guba, E.G. (ed.) *The paradigm dialogue,* ISBN: 0803938233.

Marshall, C. (1990). "Goodness criteria: are they objective or judgement calls?", in: Guba, E.G. (ed.) *The paradigm dialogue,* ISBN: 0803938233.

Midgley, G. (1996). "What is this thing called CST?" In: Flood, R.L. and Romm, N.R.A. (eds) *Critical Systems Thinking: Current Research and Practice,* ISBN: 0306454513.

Midgley, G. (1997). "Mixing methods: developing systemic intervention" in: Mingers, A., and Gill, A. (eds.) *Multimethodology: the theory and practice of combining management science methodologies,* ISBN: 0471974900.

Pretty, J. (1994). "Alternative systems of inquiry for a sustainable agriculture", *IDS Bulletin, ISSN:* 0265-5012, 25(2): 37-48.

Smith, J.K. (1990). "Alternative research paradigms and the problem of criteria", in: Guba, E.G. (ed.) *The paradigm dialogue,* ISBN: 0803938233.

31. Landscape Systems Modelling A Disturbance Ecology Approach

Jacqueline Margetts, Rod Barnett and **Nikolay Popov**
School of Architecture and Landscape Architecture, Unitec, NZ

Acknowledgement

We would like to acknowledge Unitec for assistance with a research grant for this project.

This paper reports on research which explores the modelling of landscape systems over time using multi-agent simulation (MAS) software called NetLogo. Two case studies investigate a disturbance ecology approach to the recovery of Pacific Island settlements after cyclonic events. First, the natural tropical forest sequence of colonization-succession-disturbance which operates on Pacific Islands subject to frequent cyclonic events is modelled according to the rules of forest recovery. Then, rules derived from the tropical forest model are applied to a Pacific resort to explore design possibilities as the resort responds to cyclonic disturbance. There are two useful outcomes: the possible impact of a cyclone on a resort is modelled, and new patterns of resort design emerge. The research shows that MAS can not only model natural landscape systems but also be used to explore an infinite number of 'what-if' design scenarios. The results show the potential for MAS in landscape architectural practice.

Introduction

Landscapes are complex adaptive systems. They are created and shaped by dynamic processes which interact with each other in a myriad unpredictable ways. Landscape systems evolve and adapt in response to the forces and flows of energy and material within them. A coastline or beach, a national park, an urban precinct, a suburban street; each of these is to be understood as, among other things, a landscape system, and each has its unique patterns of organization, boundary conditions and ecologies. Most significantly they are all self-organizing systems.

The move from considering landscape as a static canvas to conceiving it as a dynamic set of systems is relatively recent. The systems approach, imported partially from ecology and partially from nonlinear dynamical theory, has been investigated by a number of landscape architects and allied researchers over the last ten years, particularly in the fields of urban studies and catchment management (e.g., Corner, 1999; Waldheim, 2006; Berger, 2006). Landscape architects now recognise that it is critical to understand landscape systems and to work with them to ensure that their design interventions reflect the complexity and dynamism of the systems with which they engage.

The growing emphasis on landscape systems has precipitated a need to re-think the way that landscape is depicted. Landscape architects conventionally draw plans, maps and diagrams both to represent the terrain they are working with, and to illustrate their design intent. These techniques are poorly equipped, however, to represent the manifestation of multiple landscape processes occurring over time. The complex adaptive systems inherent in landscapes elude easy capture in two dimensional graphic form. How can these complex processes which interact, change and evolve be represented when they are so difficult to depict by means of conventional techniques? The issue, in fact, is not simply one of graphic representation of dynamic processes, but of dealing with open-endedness and unpredictability in the design process. There is a larger question then: how is it possible to work with these systems in more interactive ways? Representing landscape process entails not only a move from two-dimensional mapping to three-dimensional modelling, but to modelling in time, that is to say, by means of animation. If the nonlinear characteristics of landscape systems can be modelled and design interventions introduced into the models, then alternative outcomes can be tracked and evaluated, and the best schema selected for development.

The most basic model of an environment is the map. Cartography is universally used as a representational tool to enable landscape interventions to be formulated and depicted graphically. Maps can be extremely sophisticated, as Graphical Information Systems (GIS) data maps demonstrate. GIS captures multiple layers of information and displays it at a wide scale-range in very sophisticated forms. Crucial elements missing from GIS data maps however are the feedback loops that drive self-organizing systems. Positive and negative feedback loops are of central importance in all living systems (Capra, 1997). Landscape systems are no exception; they regulate the biotic and abiotic elements present within them at all scales, including the planetary scale (Lovelock, 1979). It is the presence of these two forms of circular causality that makes systems dynamic and unpredictable, but it is this that is missing in conventional ways of representing, and therefore thinking about, landscapes.

Feedback loops

In the 1960s chemist Ilya Prigogine developed an influential theory about self-organization while studying systems under conditions of non-equilibrium. According to Prigogine nonlinear systems not only maintain themselves in a stable state far-from-equilibrium, but may actually evolve. When the flow of matter-energy through them increases, they may go through new instabilities and transform themselves into structures of increased complexity. These structures were termed 'dissipative structures' (Prigogine & Stengers, 1984). Prigogine showed that the instabilities and jumps to new forms of organization that characterise these systems are the result of fluctuations amplified by positive feedback loops.

Feedback is a characteristic of any system in which the output, or result, affects the input of the system, thus altering its operation. Positive feedback (known as auotcatalysis) is a property of dissipative structures (or nonlinear systems). The study of feedback loops has enabled researchers to distinguish between the pattern of organization of a system and its physical structure. A system may be chaotic, but not random.

Such systems have three main features. First, they are open and part of their environment, and yet they can attain a structure and maintain it in far-from-equilibrium conditions. These systems run contrary to the second law of thermodynamics, which states that such systems move towards disorder rather than order. Second, the flow of energy in these systems allows them spontaneously to self-organise by developing novel structures and new modes of behavior. Self-organizing systems are therefore said to be 'creative'. Third, dissipative structures are complex. Their parts are so numerous that there is no way a causal relationship between them can be established. Instead, their components are connected by networks of feedback loops operating at different levels, different scales and different rhythms.

Landscape systems, we suggest, are dissipative structures. This paper outlines current work that is been undertaken by a group of Unitec researchers who are modelling landscape systems and evaluating the effectiveness of this modelling for design. The research centres on a series of studies undertaken in Pacific island countries. It uses disturbance ecology as a theoretical driver for the development of a new approach to the design and planning of Pacific Island settlements subject to periodic devastation by cyclones.

Tropical Forest Disturbance Dynamics in the Pacific

In a move away from Clemensian ecological theory many ecologists see disturbance as a necessary part of landscape development. Clements viewed ecosystems as closed, stable, self-regulating systems, which develop relatively enduring ecological communities with a defined climax community (Clements, 1936). There is now a general consensus among ecologists that vital, stable ecosystems are open systems which are in a constant state of flux, operating at the edge of equilibrium (Keller & Golley, 1999; Odum, 1997). This flux is due to disturbance, both natural and human-induced, which is now understood as a key factor in the maintenance of ecosystem health.

Accordingly, the disruption of Pacific ecosystems by cyclones can be seen as essential to the health of those ecosystems – they *require* disturbance to maintain their vitality and integrity. In Pacific environments both marine and land-based ecosystems recover remarkably quickly from even quite devastating natural events. Their health and resilience are as much products of the ability to reorganize after catastrophic change (positive feedback) as they are effects of preservative (or negative) feedback systems.

The ability of ecosystems to recover quickly after extremes of damage can be clearly seen in Niue, which was struck by tropical cyclone Heta on January 5th 2004. The cyclone was of such force that the whole southern part of the capital Alofi was completely devastated. The damage included the complete destruction of the southern part of the town and its entire associated infrastructure. What was most extraordinary about the extent of the damage was that it was so unexpected. Alofi is perched at the top of a sheer cliff over 28m above sea level, seemingly far above the worst storm waves. The force of cyclone Heta was such that it pushed huge quantities of water before it, causing localized sea-level rise. Massive waves then surfed on the top of the elevated sea, crushing everything before them. The entire coastal edge was stripped of vegetation, and huge quantities of rock and topsoil were dragged by waves into the sea. Wind speeds exceeding 300km per hour caused extensive damage over the whole island. The forest, even on the leeward side of the island, was completely stripped of leaves, and vegetation over the entire island was either wind-burnt, salt-burnt or snapped off. The destruction was seemingly complete.

About three months after the cyclone, while the community was still in a state of shock, and the massive job of cleaning up was still a long way from completion, it was interesting to note that the vegetation, even in the most affected areas, was beginning to recover. Plants were re-sprouting and seeds were germinating. Plants regenerated not only from snapped off stems but also from root fragments lodged in rock – all that remained of the extensive coastal vegetation. Leaves reappeared on trees and grass began to re-grow in the salt-drenched soils.

It was this systemic landscape resilience which first suggested to us the possibility of using disturbance theory as a generator for developing a model for Pacific settlement design. If ecological systems can self-organise after disturbance events, why can't this same model be applied to the recovery of human settlements? Alofi has struggled to recover after Cyclone Heta. The rebuilding has been fraught with difficulties, the most prominent being economic; Niue has a very small population (approximately 1500) and a fragile economy which is heavily reliant on aid and remittances. The economic burden of re-establishing Niue's infrastructure is enormous, and aid has been difficult to secure. It was clear from the outset that it would not be possible to simply rebuild what was lost in the cyclone. Also, it may not be desirable. Pre-cyclone Alofi, while tiny in population, sprawled along five and a half kilometers of road and was without a discernible centre (Riddell, 1992).

The research team postulates that Pacific islands require urban infrastructures that can operate under dynamic, fluctuating conditions. If they were conceived as socio-spatial patterns that can evolve and change, rather than as ordered, rigid distributions of architectural objects, then cyclone-devastated urban areas might self-organise into resilient urban ecologies. The colonization-succession-disturbance process offers a way of responding positively to the process of evolutionary change – an alternative to the model of formal intervention-based cultural aesthetic models which are currently the norm. Instead of seeing cyclones as a necessary part of the system and therefore to be assimilated, typical urban settlements attempt to resist cyclonic events. The system tries to expel them.

In a previous paper (Barnett & Margetts, 2005) we outlined what was required in order to test whether the colonization-succession-disturbance model is a useful and generative approach to this problem. In that paper we suggested that a first step would be the modelling of a traditional Niue village. This would describe housing typologies, linkages between activities and spatial patterns, the point centres of village life (market, church, clinic, chief's dwelling, etc) and the relationships between these and the natural ecologies that constitute the larger morphological patterns and networks of Niue settlement. A model of traditional village structure would also show the patterns of social, economic and cultural flows in which the codes of Pacific life are embedded, and the limits imposed on development by traditional land tenure systems.

While all this information was considered essential to the development of a robust model, we quickly realized that not only was such fine-grained information going to be quite difficult to obtain, but that its inherent complexity was beyond our current skill level to model. We needed to find a more simplified 'village' to work with first, which we could then use as a basis for more complex modelling. It occurred to us that tourist resorts fitted our criteria quite well. They are subject to the same cyclonic disturbance as villages, but operate in a comparatively simplified manner. Resort communities organise around fairly well-defined patterns according to rules associated with tourism, and it can be argued that they are essentially consumption-based systems. Pacific island tourist resorts operate without the additional complexities of land tenure, chiefly systems, religious structures and so on that are present in many Pacific villages. Even though resorts are relatively simplified community systems, there are still a great number of interactions to deal with. Importantly for our research, Pacific island tourist resorts almost always instantiate the resistance model – the settlement system does not include the cyclone.

Modelling Landscape Systems

Models are abstractions or simplifications of reality, used to gain insights into how a particular 'world' operates (Batty, 2007). Digital modelling has become relatively widespread in a number of disciplines in recent years, brought about by advances in computer technology. Batty suggests that 'in terms of many systems that exist in the real world, the only kind of experimentation that is possible is through computer simulation' (Batty, 2007: 8). Models are tools for looking into the future; they are able to answer multiple 'what if' questions about the system of interest. Most real world systems, of course, are infinitely complex and are subject to multiple subtle and unpredictable interactions that are impossible to identify in their totality. Despite the fact that models must necessarily be gross simplifications of any given system, they nevertheless have been shown to be useful tools to identify emergent properties of complex systems.

Multi-Agent Simulation (MAS) techniques are currently considered one of the more effective methods for modelling complex systems, and have been used extensively in large-scale urban planning. MAS are capable of modelling the collective dynamics of interacting objects in both space and time. They are particularly useful for constructing dynamic simulations at different time-scales. Much of the current research using spatial simulation technology is occurring in fields such as computer science, physics, chemistry, ecology, biology, mathematics and urban planning, but there is none that we can identify in landscape architecture. While translating work undertaken in other discipline areas for application into landscape architecture is not without difficulty, this research project demonstrates that it is possible and useful results can be obtained.

To commence the experimental modelling of landscape systems, an appropriate computer modelling environment had to be identified. Since most modelling software packages are products of research institutions and universities, they frequently require advanced computer programme skills. However, of the environments in the public domain, NetLogo was selected for use in this project as it is relatively easy to learn (an important consideration given that the research team are landscape architects, not computer programmers), and has a large model library (much of which is based in ecology) that we considered could be used or adapted in our particular project. NetLogo is a multi-agent programming language and modelling environment for simulating natural and social phenomena. It is particularly well suited for modelling complex systems evolving over time.

After developing some initial models to gain confidence with the software and explore NetLogo's potential in landscape architecture, a tropical forest model was constructed. This model created a simplified tropical forest, comprising soil with variable suitability for tree growth and two types of trees, one whose seeds are distributed by wind and another by birds. Three sets of rules were developed. The first were those that govern tree growth, distribution and interactions with the environment. When the model was run, the development of the forest could be observed over time. Trees would grow, reproduce, interact with their environment, and die. NetLogo allows for each of the variables to be changed, for example the number of seeds produced by trees, their rate of growth and so on. Second, rules for the effect of cyclonic damage and subsequent recovery were introduced into this model. These rules governed a variety of factors such as the force of the cyclone, the extent of damage that trees suffer, the effect of wave damage, and the change of environment after inundation by salt water. Finally, recovery rules were developed. Trees could recover not only by normal reproductive strategies to do with seed distribution, but also by plant fragments and re-growth of damaged trees. Again, each of these variables was adjustable so damage and recovery could be observed according, for example, to different cyclone strengths.

While in many respects quite simplified, this model did show that it is possible to simulate a landscape system and to show how it reacts to disturbance. One of the key observations made was that each time the model was run, even under identical conditions, the outcome was somewhat different. The outputs of the model are emergent patterns, rather than predictable, reproducible outcomes. This result coincides with our understanding of landscapes as autocatalytic systems in which non-linear interactions occur.

Having established that NetLogo can be used to model natural landscape dynamics the next task was to apply the model to a resort. An opportunity arose to work in conjunction with a developer who was planning a resort in Fiji. The developer, Krukziener Properties Ltd, provided their plans and designs for the proposed resort at Sovi Bay and a small research team went to Fiji, accompanied by a number of fourth-year Unitec Bachelor of Landscape Architecture students and a representative from the development firm. The students were directed to undertake a number of surveys and analyses of the landscape conditions in place there, including a catchment survey, ecological analyses, tree surveys, a hydrological analysis and a survey of comparative resorts in similar coastal conditions.

The Sovi Bay resort design appears to follow the same basic pattern as similar developments in Fiji. The underlying system based on consumption is evident. Villas (bures) are located in gradated proximity to the beach, while service and entertainment hubs such as pools, bars and restaurants are designed to meet a range of criteria for maximum patronage. The proposal for the Sovi Bay resort is formulated to fulfil certain underlying requirements of both the visitor and the operator, and is arranged in a fairly standard way when compared to similar resorts examined along the same coast.

The first step in the modelling process was to build the resort site in NetLogo by importing GIS data and input physical data gathered by the research team and students. The proposed resort design was then located on the site, rules were developed to guide the response of the built structures to wind and wave damage, and the cyclone destruction model was run. After this, a recovery model (based on the tropical forest colonization-succession-disturbance rules re-worked to fit a resort context) was introduced to see what would happen if the resort were allowed to re-configure to these rules subsequent to cyclonic intervention.

The resort model's central components are villas (accommodation) and hubs (activity centres such as restaurant, bar, swimming pool, kids club and so on). Rules were developed around proximity to beach, the popularity of hubs, movement patterns and tree reproduction (which were governed by 'gardener' rules, rather than by natural system rules). Again, as in the tropical forest model, the outcomes of the resort model were general patterns, rather than a single new resort design. The rules which governed the various interactions taking place within the model were formulated to satisfy a set of objectives, and these objectives would be the same however the designer approached the design. They include aspects such as the minimum distance that a villa can be located near a hub, the maximum distance a villa can be away from the beach, the location of paths with respect to both villas (not too close) and hubs (easy access). The model shows us in a systematic way that these requirements can be met by many means, and when variables change, such as environmental change due to cyclonic disturbance, new patterns of possibility emerge for the design of the resort. Running the model with periodic cyclonic events shows an interesting response to changing conditions. Instead of simply rebuilding what has been destroyed, the model demonstrates that the resort can adapt and respond to the changing conditions. Dynamic qualities emerge as a direct response to disturbance, while still seeking to satisfy the predetermined set of 'consumption' objectives.

Conclusion

When the results for the tropical forest and the resort are taken together they show us that natural landscape systems *can* be modelled and these models can respond to disturbance events. Human systems can also be modelled, although the unpredictability of human behavior limits the degree of complexity of the rule-based interactions. Having said this, it is important to note that the resulting outcomes of the models are not designs, but open up new ways of thinking about the design possibilities. In the Pacific resort situation, widely predicted increases in sea-level rise and an associated increase in cyclones means that resorts which can be more responsive to these events will have an advantage. Critically, and most usefully, possible new resort forms emerge from the complex interaction of the feedback loops operating within the NetLogo model. Multiple what-if scenarios can be explored in the initial stages of the resort design, and the outcomes of such explorations can not only help to inform the final resort design, but also to plan reconstruction scenarios after cyclonic damage occurs. This result indicates to us that it may be possible now to extend the model to account for the more complex interactions occurring in Pacific villages.

In a more general sense we have demonstrated that the modelling of landscape systems can play a useful and hitherto unexplored role in planning and design. We realize that this is just the beginning of the research required to investigate the possibilities of multi-agent simulation modelling in the discipline of landscape architecture, but the work we have undertaken to date indicates its potential to work directly with complex systems.

References

Barnett, R. and J. Margetts (2005). "A Disturbance Ecology Model for Pacific Urbanism: Education at the Sustainable Edge". *Indigenous Technologies and Sustainable Development,* http://www.esc.auckland.ac.nz/People/Staff/smit023/SPPEEX/#2005Wananga.

Batty, M. (2007). *Model Cities.* CASA Working Paper Series, ISSN 1467-1298. http://www.casa.ucl.ac.uk/working_papers/paper113.pdf

Berger, A. (2006). *Drosscape: Wasting Land in Urban America,* ISBN 978-1568987132

Capra, F. (1997). *The Web of Life,* ISBN 0 00 654751 6

Clements, F. E. (1936). "Nature and Structure of the Climax." in *Foundations of Ecology: Classic papers with commentaries* (1991) Real, L. and Brown, J. H. (eds) ISBN: 978-0-226-70594-1.

Corner, J. (1999). *Recovering Landscape: Essays in Contemporary Landscape Architecture.* ISBN 978-1568981796

Keller, D. and Golley, F. (1999). *The Philosophy of Ecology: From Science to Synthesis.* ISBN 978-0820322209

Lovelock, J. E. (1979). *Gaia: A New Look at Life on Earth.* ISBN 978-0192862181

NetLogo, http://ccl.northwestern.edu/

Odum, E. (1997) *Ecology: A Bridge Between Science and Society,* ISBN 978-0878936304

Prigogine, I. and Stengers, I. (1984). *Order Out of Chaos: Man's New Dialogue with Nature,* ISBN 978-0394542041

Riddell, R. (1992). *Urban Planning Need for a Capital Centre at Alofi with Emphasis on a Retail Centre,* Suva, South Pacific Bureau for Economic Cooperation.
Waldheim, C. (2006). *The Landscape Urbanism Reader,* ISBN 978-1568984391

32. Local Sustainability Advances with Metropolitan and Global Advantages

PLENARY PAPER

Jack Meek
Department of Public and Health Administration, University of La Verne, USA

Acknowledgements

I wish to extend my appreciation to conference chairs Professor Kay Fielden and Professor Jim Sheffield who encouraged me to prepare this plenary paper for the ANZSYS 2007 Conference on "Systemic Development: Local Solutions in a Global Environment," Auckland, New Zealand, December 2-5, 2007.

This paper reflects on the growing recognition of local interdependencies and the inadequacies of the current administrative state to respond to cross-jurisdictional issues such as environmental management. The paper reviews four kinds of locally derived approaches and their potential for both expanding participation in solution making as well as providing system-wide benefits or global advantages. While locally focused, these advances are viewed as "adaptive" structures that add to metropolitan system complexity with system-wide effects.

Introduction

It has become more apparent that many of our human problems are complex and cross-jurisdictional in nature, requiring interdisciplinary approaches and research (Meek, 2001; Meek & Newell, 2005) as well as cross-jurisdictional administrative collaboration. This understanding means that traditional forms of inquiry and administration alone are not likely to fully address current issues by themselves. There is a need for continuously innovative forms of interaction. These innovative forms are likely to evolve as networks and operate alongside the existing traditional more formal and bureaucratic structures, adding complexity to our current patterns of interaction.

With the advancement of technology and communications, we more easily recognize our interconnections and interdependencies (Friedman, 2005). How well Brazil manages its rain forests and how the United States manages its consumptive practices in energy affects the world. Events that used to seem far away and distant are now very close, or what James Rosenau (2003) refers to as "distant proximities." How well we manage our resources and our environment does not only affect our local quality of life but will also influence the quality of life of other, even distant, lands and people. These themes reflect a kind of interdependence that our existing governmental systems find difficult to respond to because of their jurisdictional and representation limitations.

The argument advanced in this paper is that locally derived environmental solutions offer enormous potential for contextualizing solutions that can involve deeper participation than existing institutions while at the same time promoting system-wide beneficial effects. After a comment on the current nature of the administrative state, the paper summarizes four kinds of metropolitan system adaptations: conjunction, citizen-centered public management, local strategy development and the creation of intermediate (third-party) structures. The potential of these "adaptive" approaches to expand participation in environmental solution, and to generate system-wide benefits and global advantage, is briefly examined.

The Disarticulated State

Environmental management presents a complex condition for us to study and to administer. In the political response to the environmental challenge, we rely on a species of representative public systems that are designed to be responsive only to electoral feedback and representative directives. Yet, these structures are often characterized by narrow participation and limited discourse. In addition, the bureaucratic systems, designed to implement decisions based upon this narrowed representation, lack the ability to adjust to cross-jurisdictional or cross-bureaucratic territories for various reasons. They lack the ability to collaborate, to adjust, and to re-organize to address problems that cut across boundaries. The prominent scholar H.G. Frederickson (1999) refers to this condition as the "disarticulated state."

The central assumption behind the emergence of innovative structures is that our current representative governmental systems (republics) and their corresponding administrative systems, by themselves, may not be the best or only mechanisms for generating good practices for environmental management. Our current forms of representation are characterized by narrowed participation and influence (Fox and Miller, 1995) and our major bureaucratic systems are viewed as powerful units of enforcement that are unresponsive to citizens (Kathi & Cooper, 2005). As a result, a "crisis" of democracy is apparent (Macedo *et al.*, 2005) with the declining levels of citizen participation, confidence and trust in government (Putnam, 2000).

The Adaptive Local System

This paper reviews four kinds of local adaptive practices that are characteristic of metropolitan initiatives responding to various forms of interdependencies: administrative conjunction, citizen-centered public management, the construction of locally-focused strategies, and the use of intermediate structures.

1. Administrative Conjunction

The challenges of environmental governance places demands on governmental systems to "learn" how to facilitate public interests and demands and to be more inclusive in the design and delivery of coordinated public responses. While some may consider this a normative position on governance, it is also one that will likely be pragmatic, functional and effective.

Public administrative systems are evolving into a more connective, or "conjunctive" state in approaching common problems. In his famous declaration of the "repositioning of public administration," H. George Frederickson indicates that the field is moving away from the favorite theories of political scientists, "theories and concepts of the clash of interests, have electoral and interest group competition, of games, and of winners and losers" towards "theories of cooperation, networking, governance, and institution building" (Frederickson, 1999: 702). Indeed, to address problems of complexity, our urban systems are adjusting, in part, through administrative conjunctive activities (Meek, Schildt & Witt, 2002).

Administrative conjunction remains a key component to administrative responsiveness and adaptation. As one example of local administrative connectivity, it was found that sub-regional associations and collaborations within metropolitan jurisdictions offer participants benefits that they are unlikely to find in broader region-wide settings (Hubler & Meek, 2006). In environmental affairs, regional agreements among local governments are emerging, such as the recent "Regional Greenhouse Gas Initiative" (RGGI) that caps emission levels among nine states in the Northeastern United States (Regional Greenhouse Initiative 2007). In the area of metropolitan public safety issues, a uniquely joint (or conjunctive) administrative "adaptive" response designed to facilitate jurisdictional interdependences (Meek, Newell & DeLadurantey, 2007) has been observed. These findings support the notion that administrative and community leaders recognize the limits of their own local jurisdictions and seek collaborative (conjunctive) solutions to commonly viewed interdependent conditions (Newell & Meek, 2005).

2. Citizen-Centered Public Management

In the area of civic engagement, Cooper, Bryer and Meek (2006) review relationships between the citizens and government including agencies. The focus of this discussion is placed on various kinds of civic engagement ranging from adversarial to citizen-centered. The central argument advanced is that "citizen centered public management" offers the most potential in expanding both citizen trust and governmental responsiveness, but it is likely to be the most difficult to achieve.

Public participation can take on various forms and should be considered as multi dimensional. Indeed, there are many participatory solution alternatives that can address metropolitan and environmental management problems. In the examination of various kinds of public participation in environmental management, the promise of expanded participation coordinated with an open and capable administrative system can produce relevant beneficial environmental management solutions. In this manner, a methodology of citizen engagement can create a mutual learning environment (Maxwell & Yin, 2006) that can sort out local environmental practices promoting a new pattern of relationships among citizens, governmental officials and the environment (Meek, 2007). Some of these patterns are discussed in the paragraphs that follow.

3. The Construction of Local Strategies

There is a family of locally designed strategies that can influence environmental outcomes. For example, despite the fact that the United States has not signed the 1998 Kyoto Protocol, some 418 cities in the United States, including Los Angeles, have adopted the Kyoto guidelines. Decentralized and local responses to environmental management have had much attention and seem to be the more responsive than national policies to environmental challenges recognized as a global threat. Here is a brief comment on two recent examples that show promise.

The City of Claremont - one among 184 cities in the Southern California region - has developed local solutions that confront the challenges of urban sprawl. First, the citizens of Claremont, as a collective, decided to purchase an adjacent parcel of land (Johnson's Pasture) for preservation and park use in order to keep the land from being converted into housing. Second, over a decade ago, the city initiated a long-term and visionary design of a transit village. The transit village is now a reality where citizens can enjoy local services as well as commute via train to areas in the Southern California region. Third, citizens and city officials that reflect contextually relevant environmental solutions that have metropolitan and global advantages have involved community leaders in the design and implementation of various local sustainable projects through actions. These actions can be interpreted as a systems understanding of environmental management that reflects knowledge that local solutions are not only possible but can also contribute to both regional and global environmental sustainability. The Claremont strategies can be viewed within a larger paradigm of environmental management strategies in the evolution toward sustainability beyond "environmental protectionism" and "recognizes long-term sustainability as a constraint to economic growth (Randolf, 2004: 11). For Randolf, local approaches such as these "...aim to modify traditional economic accounts to include environmental values by internalizing externalities" (Randolf, 2004: 12).

Also located in Southern California, the City of Santa Monica has developed a rather sophisticated approach to sustainable development that includes a mix of quantitative and participatory designs. The overall approach is approved by the city council and is monitored by a citizen commission where sustainable concepts are designed and, after data is gathered, where citizens monitor the results of various strategies designed to influence sustainable outcomes. These indices are reexamined as useful concepts on a periodic basis. (Sustainable Santa Monica, 2007).

4. Intermediate Structures as Adaptation

There are "third-party" collectivities or networks emerging in metropolitan governance that facilitate connections among citizens and other collective interests. These networks include traditional forms of government as participants and often require governmental authority to operate. These third party structures are examples of "intermediate structures" that allow for citizen collectives to interact with existing power systems in different ways. Intermediate structures are additive elements to the local metropolitan system and add to system complexity. With system complexity, new patterns of relationship are identifiable that are both beneficial to and supportive of contextually driven values.

Intermediate structures have various features (formal and informal, regional and local, narrowly and broadly focused) and can be described as collective action approaches that offer connections between the social, civic, economic, administrative and political spheres. They are forms of self-organization that reflect adaptive capacities that may be more resilient than traditional representative systems. Intermediate structures influence traditional governmental deliberations in both direct and indirect ways. What follows are some examples of the affect of intermediate structures on governance and environment regimes in different locales. Because our current traditional jurisdictionally-based governmental units are limited, intermediate structures offer some optimism in advancing governance that is more responsive to citizen interests, more contextually relevant and provide system-wide environmental benefits.

Conservancies-California [1]

The use of third party (quasi-governmental, non-profit and perhaps private) structures as land use options in metropolitan areas is quite common. The California State Legislature has established nine (9) conservancies with jurisdiction over specific areas in the State. The Santa Monica Mountains Conservancy (SMMC) and the San Gabriel & Lower Los Angeles Rivers and Mountains Conservancy are two of these nine. The other seven are the following: Baldwin Hills Conservancy; California Tahoe Conservancy; Coachella Valley Mountains Conservancy; San Diego River Conservancy; San Joaquin River Conservancy; Sierra Nevada Conservancy; and State Coastal Conservancy. An example of a private non-profit conservancy is the Claremont Wildland Conservancy (CWC).

The Santa Monica Mountains Conservancy (SMMC) owns land - 55,000 acres whereas the Claremont Wildland Conservancy (CWC) is an educational and lobbying organization geared toward facilitating preservation of open space. Some motivated citizens formed the CWC without help from the municipal entity. The City of Claremont and CWC have formed a loose partnership and are cooperating with each other to achieve the mutual goals of implementing the public's desire for greater open space preservation. Between the state-established conservancies and local conservancies are regional conservancies such as The San Gabriel Mountains Regional Conservancy is kind of umbrella for the local conservancies and addresses watershed and open space issues in the broader region.[2]

1 The author owes a special thanks to Tony Witt, Director of Community Services, City of Claremont and to Steve Harding, Deputy City Manager, City of Santa Ana for assistance with this section.

2 In addition to open space preservation conservancies there are historic presentation groups that call themselves Conservancies such as The Los Angeles Conservancy. Most, if not all of the historic conservancies focused on preservation are locally generated private non-profits that lobby and educate about the value of preserving historic

Conservation Units-Brazil [3]

Another potentially promising environmental management strategy is the use of "conservation units" in the rain forests of Brazil. Conservation Units or *unidades de conservacao* (CUs) are legally enabled jurisdictional units created to address the significant deforestation trends in evidence in the state of Rondonia, Brazil. Pedlowski *et al.* (2005) trace the history of these units to the 1990s created by federal and state agencies to reduce the rate of deforestation, becoming law in 2000. Supported by a World Bank loan to consolidate 51 CUs into a network of national, state and municipal entities, these units represent a remarkable achievement local, state, national and international institutional collaboration. Pedlowski *et al.* (2005) report mixed findings with regard to the implementation utility, namely the conservation units have "been useful in curbing deforestation within their boundaries; however, many CUs face pressure from the combined activities of illegal farmers seeking new sources of timber and agricultural land" (p. 149). One central finding of the authors is that despite World Bank and federal funding, the CUs lack permanent staff and only "sporadic protective measures have been taken to enforce their (CU) limits" (p.150). In short, the CUs lack "sufficient institutional capacity to manage protected resources" and there is a need for broader stakeholder participation, "including local, state, and federal agencies, as well as private logging firms and local communities in formulating management plans for all CUs" (p. 154).

Special Improvement Districts

Another kind of approach to environmental management includes land management strategies in the design of special improvement districts. These approaches reflect the momentum toward an on-going and significant rise in the privatization of public space. Research conducted by Jeff Pompe (2006) focuses on the developing phenomenon of gated communities that are island or coastally based. The paper highlights how those who benefit from the access and aesthetic value of a pristine environment should also pay the costs of securing the coastal surrounds that they enjoy. Looking at the role of private neighborhood associations (PNAs) in sustaining the natural ecosystems, the author shows how premiums for gated communities can assist with this and highlights the fairer distribution of costs for costal protection by allocating these to those who benefit most from the enhanced natural environment. While there are a number of concerns with regard to the use of PNAs (including inequities in housing and land access) the paper also reveals inequities in wealth accumulation. The implications of these findings for shared contributions to sustaining common shorelines and for sustaining and integrating communities are apparent but emerge in a more hidden and evolutionary form.

---

buildings.

3 The following three sections that discuss conservation units, special improvement districts and planning areas are slightly revised versions from that previously published by Jack W. Meek (2007).

Protected Areas-- New Zealand

Protected Areas (PAs) like Conservation Units are newly formed entities that deal with biodiversity conservation and have great promise, but there is need for continuous and sustained dialogue among stakeholders as to what is meant by biodiversity conservation how it is mutually managed. One finding in a study of a national park (protected area) is that there is a need for consistent representation of park use for residents (Ormsby & Kaplin, 2005). Ormsby and Kaplin argue, "understanding people-PA (protected area) interactions and perceptions can help guide future PA management strategies to increase conservation effectiveness, through efforts such as environmental education and communication programs" (p. 156).

Intermediate Structures and Complex Metropolitan Systems

Locally derived strategies and intermediate structures offer enormous benefits for expanded local participation (Fung, 2006) and have real possibilities for regional and global environmental advantages. In terms of kinds of intermediate structures, deliberative bureaucratic approaches, such as the use of conservation units or protected areas incorporate citizen engagement and have similar positive outcomes to report with regard to decision-making (with representative stakeholders included) and management implementation (curbing deforestation).

The use of special improvement districts provide for a unique mix of stakeholder consensus, self-assessed financing and service implementation. These projects are not possible without stakeholder agreement and the resultant service is narrowly focused around agreed upon objectives. However, many of the jurisdictions that seek self-assessment are also accessible by additional stakeholders (these jurisdictions are public space) and it is not clear as to the assessment of added services reduces the overall service capacity that could be available system wide. For financing environmental management strategies, these types of financial tools may reduce the financial burden on the general public, but at the possible expense of reduced access to public space.

More research is needed with regard to the legal parameters of intermediate structures as well as actual levels of participation. In regard to the latter, Thomas has found a varied level of public participation among conservancies despite the promise of their participatory potential (Thomas, 2003). In addition, we need to examine the implications of the overall benefits of these structures as they may preserve existing land-use patterns that freeze wealth patterns for the sake of environmental benefits at the expense land access for increasing and diverse populations.

With respect to the main theme of this conference, "Systemic Development" Local Solutions in a Global Environment," this paper has attempted to demonstrate that a family of locally designed responses has implications for contributing environmental benefits beyond local benefits. Some of these local responses (intermediate structures) are designed within jurisdictional boundaries (such as special improvement districts or some kinds of conservancies) while others represent partnerships that cross inter-jurisdictional boundaries. Because these responses represent locally designed strategies, they are likely to be contextually relevant, more easily understood by local stakeholders and more likely to be viewed a legitimate and sustainable.

It is the recognition of complex relationship between environmental interdependencies and geographic jurisdictions that form the basis for creating intermediate structures that respond to cross-jurisdictional concerns. One implication of these approaches is the understanding is that policy directives designed from control-centered administrative units (or national units) are likely to fail on their own. In addition, the complexity literature teaches us about non-linearity, about how dynamic our social systems are and how social contexts change, how local systems of unique and diverse. The key to each of these examples reviewed in the paper is the process by which local leaders and citizens made decisions on local sustainable strategies. This avenue of inquiry offers a difficult challenge for rationally conceived, linear-based approaches that are designed on assumptions about a system that is linear in behavior, predictable, and contains undifferentiated units of analysis. Locally designed strategies have the potential for creating contextual meaning.

With the emergence of localized intermediate structures, however, our metropolitan systems become more complex. These new structures do not replace existing political and economic systems but add interactions to the system. It is very possible these new patterns may take the form of positive enforcements and recursive patterns that can influence patters of interaction that bring about negative environmental influences. Clearly our metropolitan systems, with increased forms of participation will become more complex and this outcome may be very welcome, as the patterns of interaction can be more contextually relevant and locally responsive, while at the same time offer system wide benefits.

References

Cooper, T.L., Bryer, T. and Meek, J.W. (2006) "Citizen-Centered Collaborative Public Management." *Public Administration Review,* ISSN 0033-3352, 66 (December): 76-88.

Fox, C. J. and Miller, H.T. (1995). *Postmodern Public Administration: Toward Discourse,* ISBN 13: 978-0-7656-1704-0 (2007).

Frederickson, H. G. (1999) "The Repositioning of American Public Administration." *Policy Science and Politics* P.S., ISSN 1049-0965, 32(4): 701-711.

Friedman, T. (2005). *The World is Flat: A Brief History of the Twenty-first Century,* ISBN: 0-374-29288-4.

Fung, A. (2006) *Empowered Participation: Reinventing Urban Democracy,* ISBN: 0-691-11535-4.

Hubler, P. and Meek, J.W. (2005) "Sub-regional Transportation Initiatives: Implications for Governance," *Journal of International Public Administration,* ISSN: 0190-0692, 28: 1081-1094.

Kathi, P. C., & Cooper, T.C. (2005). Democratizing the Administrative State--Connecting Neighborhood Councils and City Agencies. *Public Administration Review,* ISSN 0033-3352, 65(5): 559-567.

Macedo, S., *et al.* (2005) *Democracy at Risk: How Political Choices Undermine Citizen*

Participation, and What We Can Do About It, ISBN: 13: 978-0-8157-5404-6.

Maxwell, Bronen and Lin Yo, C., (2006) "The Value of Community Participation," paper presented at the Australia-New Zealand Systems (ANZSYS) Conference on "Sustaining Our Social and Natural Capital," Katoomba, Australia, December 3-6, 2006

Meek, J.W. (2001)"The Practice of Interdisciplinarity: Complex Conditions and the Potential of Interdisciplinary Theory," *Issues in Integrative Studies*, ISSN 1081-4760, 19: 123-136.

Meek, J.W. (2007), Participation Approaches to Governance: Implications for Environmental Management Enfoques participativos da governabilidade: Implicações no gerenciamento ambiental. *Agenda Social: Revista do Programa de Pos-Graduacao em Politicas Sociais, UENF. Campos dos Aoytacazes, n.0, pp. 17-36,jan/abr/2007.* Accessed July 6, 2007, http://www.uenf.br/Uenf/Pages/CCH/Agenda_Social

Meek, J.W., De Ladurantey, J and Newell, W.H. (2007) "Complex Systems, Governance and Policy Administration Consequences," *Emergence: Complexity and Organization,* ISSN: 1521-3250, 9(1-2): 24-36.

Meek, J.W. and Hubler P. (2006) "Business Improvement Districts (BIDs) in Southern California: Implications for Local Governance" *International Journal of Public Administration*, ISSN: 0190-0692, 29 (1-3): 31-52.

Meek, J.W. and Newell W. H. (2005) "Complexity, Interdisciplinarity and Public Administration: Implications for Integrating Communities," *Public Administration Quarterly*, ISSN 0734-9149, 3: 321-349.

Meek, J.W., Schildt K. and Witt, M. (2002) "Local Public Administration in the Metropolitan Context," in H. George Frederickson and John Nalbandian (eds). *The Future of Local Government Administration: The Hansell Symposium,* ISBN: 0-87326-130-5.

Ormsby, A. and Kaplin, B.A. (2005) "A Framework for Understanding Community Resident Perceptions of Masoala National Park, Madagascar." Environmental Conservation, ISSN: 0376-8929, 32(2): 156-164.

Pedlowski, M, Matricardi A. E.A.T., Skole D., Cameron S.R., Chomentowski W., Fernandes C. and Lisboa, A. (2005) "Conservation Units: A New Deforestation Frontier in the Amazonian State of Rondonia, Brazil." *Environmental Conservation,* ISSN: 0376-8929, 32(2): 149-155.

Pompe, J. (2006) "Residential Property Values in Gated and Nongated Barrier Island Communities," paper presented at the Australia-New Zealand Systems (ANZSYS) Conference on "Sustaining Our Social and Natural Capital," held in Katoomba, Australia, December 3-6, 2006.

Putnam, R. D. (2000). *Bowling Alone: The Collapse and Revival of American Community*, ISBN: 0-684-83283-6.

Randolph, J. (2004) *Environmental Land Use Planning and Management*, ISBN 1-55963-948-2

Regional Greenhouse Initiative. www.rggi.org Accessed June 27, 2007.

Rosenau, J. (2003) *Distant Proximities: Dynamics Beyond Globalization in a Turbulent World,* ISBN: 0-691-09524-8.

Sustainable Santa Monica (2007) Accessed September 1, 2007. http://www.smgov.net/epd/scp/

Thomas, C. W. (2003). "Habitat Conservation Planning," in Archon Fung and Erik Olin Wright (eds.) *Deepening Democracy: Institutional Innovations in Empowered Participatory Governance,* ISBN: 1-85984-466-9.

33. A Systems Approach to Building Resilience to Natural Disasters at a Local Level in Pacific Island Nations

Stephen C. Russell
Defence and Systems Institute, University of South Australia, AUS

This paper uses systems methodology to examine how risks from natural disasters are addressed in Pacific Island Nations, particularly those risks from storm related hazards. It is argued that the common top-down approach to dealing with risk in these communities using vulnerability analyses is not effective, and that a bottom-up approach may be preferable. While such an approach is not new, it is considered important to highlight the need for such communities to take possession of the problem of reducing risk, and it is suggested that the means for reducing risk should be sought not just in modern technologies, but in a systems based blend of modern and traditional methodologies.

Introduction

Vulnerability of Pacific Island Nations to weather & climate change

While Pacific island nations are vulnerable to many kinds of natural disasters, they are particularly vulnerable to weather related events, such as cyclones and droughts. Their close association with a highly dynamic ocean-atmosphere interface and their high ratio of shoreline to land area mean that the impacts of storms can be especially severe. The low topography of Pacific atoll states, such as Kiribati and Tuvalu, means that they are at exceptional risk from a rise in sea-level due to the effects of global warming (Brookfield, 1989, Nurse, *et al.*, 1998).

Most models of global warming predict an increased risk of more extreme weather events, including more persistent droughts, and higher intensity wind storms. As the destructive power of wind storms is very sensitive to the peak wind velocity (SwissRe, 1997), the effects on Pacific Island Nations are likely to become more and more severe as global warming takes effect.

Typically, Pacific Island Nations are resource poor, have narrow economic bases that depend on primary production, and are sensitive to global markets for attracting foreign exchange. The fragility of these economies is illustrated by noting that the inflation-adjusted agricultural commodity prices (in a sample of 18 major export commodities that are important in Asia and the Pacific) decreased by an average of 57% over the period from 1980 to 2004 (quoted in Dawe, 2006, based on data from IMF, 2006).

Russell (2007) notes that, while some of the more populous countries in the World have suffered losses equivalent to 10% of their Gross Domestic Product (GDP) from extreme disasters, Pacific Island Nations have sometimes suffered losses of more than 100% of their GDP. Similarly, the percentages of the populations affected by disasters in the Pacific region have been far greater than in most other countries of the world. The nations themselves typically have tenuous central control, poor communications and limited infrastructure. It is not surprising, therefore, to find that the capacities of Pacific Islands to cope with disasters are limited.

How they became vulnerable

Ever since the Pacific islands were colonized by Europeans, the islanders' reliance on traditional knowledge and coping mechanisms have been degraded. The European focus on making profits has resulted in unsustainable developments of cash crops, loss of forest cover, massive soil erosion and other forms of environmental degradation (Clarke & Thaman, 1993). Forests continue to be degraded today through rising urbanization and population growth, local demands for building timber and fire wood, new agricultural developments, growing industrialization and the global demand for commercial logging.

A survey of beach mining on South Tarawa, Kiribati (Webb, 2005), for instance, shows that nearly all of South Tarawa's present erosion problems could have been avoided if humans had not altered or destroyed the natural defence systems of the land. These human activities include beach mining, poorly located or conceived coastal development, reclamation, and causeway construction.

Critically, the responsibility for most of the infrastructure in Pacific Island Nations belongs to the central governments (Freeman & Warner, 2001). In normal circumstances they often have more immediate priorities than reducing the vulnerabilities of distant communities. However, in times of emergency it is often impossible for them to cope with the scale of a disaster and they turn to the international community for aid. Foreign aid agencies are mainly interested in relieving the immediate threats to human life, and don't see it as their responsibility to stay with the communities to build their capacities over the long term. "Humanitarian assistance grants generally have short time limits and strict criteria that do not allow expenditure on anything other than meeting urgent needs" (Twigg, 2004). This means that the long term coping capacities of the islanders are not improved through disaster relief, and indeed they are often eroded further. As the costs for dealing with disasters escalates, in an environment of relatively flat economic growth in funding, fewer dollars are available for reducing the vulnerabilities and increasing the resilience of the communities of the Pacific Islands to natural hazards (Shah, 2007).

Much has been written on the need for consultation in assessing hazards and vulnerabilities to disasters at all levels, however, engagement with the people at risk is still minimal (Pelesikoti, 2007). There is a lack of quality information about hazards, a lack of the means for communicating information, and a lack of emergency plans and coordination of actions to be taken in the event of a hazard event.

Different Viewpoints

The top-down view

While it is not the intention here to discuss the politics of aid and development in Pacific Island Nations, it is important to understand the context. According to Sydee (2004) current strategies for dealing with the effects of climate change emphasise adaptation and sustainable development. While these objectives form the basis for much needed monetary assistance from aid agencies, they support a top-down model for development. In effect, the donor countries influence the course of development in the developing countries through their vetting of the projects that will be funded. Donor countries perpetuate the myth that any growth in monetary wealth facilitates adaptive capacity. Barnett (2001), however, argues that the social policies that result from aid packages and unequal trading arrangements "undermine adaptive capacity rather than fostering it." Fry (1997) argues that the offers of aid to the Pacific Island Nations are often inappropriate to the Island people's needs, and are perhaps "outright damaging to the coping capacity of the people."

According to Sydee (2004) the traditional strengths in Island communities, such as kinship structures, reciprocity, migration, and the financial remittances from extended ex-patriot communities abroad, are under-recognized in scientific assessments and policy development. In addition, the whole concept of treating Pacific Island Nations as "vulnerable" communities tends to work against their cause. Foreign investors are loath to commit resources to such countries, and the islanders themselves are not persuaded to work towards sustainable development if they believe they might ultimately have to leave their homes when the islands are consumed by the sea. Campbell (2003) argues that a 'vulnerability label' indicates a weakness within communities, and while their natural resilience is left unrecognized, the vulnerable entity itself becomes identified as the problem.

The bottom-up view

This dilemma was discussed by Russell (2007) in an attempt to understand the main issues for rural communities in Pacific Island Nations facing increasing risks from hydro-meteorological (weather related) hazards. As a first step, Russell drew a 'rich picture' diagram (in the terminology of Checkland, 1981) of a rural community, reproduced in Figure 1. This picture suggests that the remoteness of the community from the central government, and the providers of infrastructure and other social benefits, means that the central governments do not see the resilience of their distant rural communities as 'their problem'. The only other option is for the communities themselves to take possession of the problem. This supports a bottom-up view of building resilience, rather than the more common top-down approach.

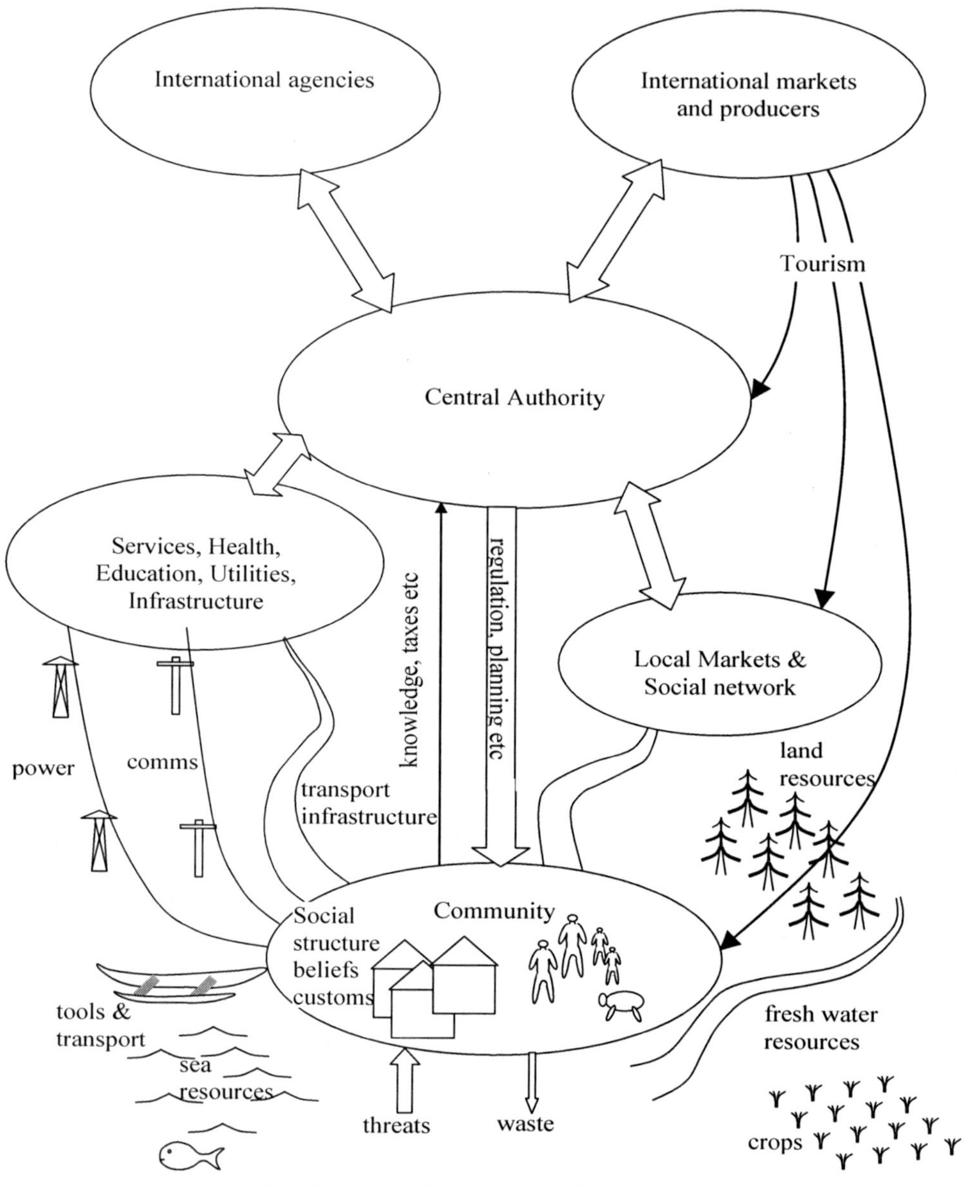

Figure 1 *'Rich Picture' diagram of a rural community in a Pacific Island Nation, from Russell (2007)*

Traditional Resilience

The potential for traditional resilience

Campbell (2006) showed that traditional communities were able to deal with natural hazards before the intrusion of European influences. They satisfied all the elements of resiliency proposed by Wildavsky (1988), including fragmented land use, to ensure that the loss of any one piece of land did not mean the total failure of crops; a diversity of cropping, both within a single island, and between different islands; the tending of forest gardens that were protected from strong winds by the surrounding trees; the maintenance of strong contacts with other communities on the island and on neighboring islands through familial connections, celebrations, and feasts; and the storage and preservation of excess food in times of plenty against times of want. The houses they built were more resilient to cyclones than present day houses, as they avoided the gaps and windows that allowed a dangerous build-up of pressure between the inside and outside of a house.

Mercer (2005) suggests that many of the traditional methods for building resilience may still be relevant in the environments of today. The knowledge of specific coping strategies may be kept alive through spoken histories, and still be known to a knowledgeable few. If the knowledge could be recovered, perhaps through semi-structured interviews or eliciting the oral histories, not only would it be a valuable resource for increasing resilience in communities, but it would add to the cultural heritage of the community, the nation, and ultimately the world.

Before such steps are carried out, it is necessary to determine the potential for improving resilience through the elicitation of suitable traditional practices. It is by no means certain that traditional practices would be of benefit to the communities themselves. For instance, the environment may be too different from the past; modern technologies may render the traditional methods obsolete; there may be impediments from current land ownership regulations; it may be difficult to work within the confines of the rules and practices of the central administrations and aid agencies; or the youth who currently see urban environments as their only hope for a future, may see no value in implementing traditional methods in the rural community. Moreover, the knowledge holders may not be willing to pass on their knowledge.

Traditional agroforestry

Agroforestry is considered here as an example of the contrast between modern and traditional practices, and the state of the environment that most Pacific Island Nations face. According to the FAO (the United Nations Food and Agricultural Organization – Clarke and Thaman, 1993) "*agroforestry* is a collective name for all land-use systems and practices in which woody perennials are deliberately grown on the same land management unit as crops and/or animals."

There are two approaches to *agroforestry* – modern and traditional. Modern practices rely on field experimentation in crops, trees and animals in various combinations and conditions to determine the highest overall yields. Traditional approaches rely on native trees and familiar combinations that have been worked out over hundreds of years of experimentation. While the traditional methods may not return maximum yields, they are adapted to local conditions and promise more dependable yields.

In the opinion of Campbell (1985), the most significant modifications to the social, economic and political cultures of Pacific Island Nations have been the 'replacement of resilient and diverse agro-ecosystems with mono-cropping for commercial agriculture'. Thaman (1989) argues that the institution of government sponsored coconut plantations in Kiribati has lead to the gradual elimination of a wide range of culturally important tree species. Clarke and Thaman (1993) say that the fixation of governments on mono-cultural cash crops has meant that most indigenous wild species and the wide range of *cultivars* (plants cultivated for their useful properties) have received little attention. Many of those that survive today do so in small niche environments or in household gardens. There is so little knowledge of these crops that nobody has the basis for promoting their expansion or maintenance.

This goes to the heart of the problem, as the belief in the central authority is so pervasive that even the bearers of traditional knowledge tend to believe their knowledge is inferior (Sillitoe, 1998). This attitude is extremely dangerous, since it puts at risk the vast bodies of traditional knowledge acquired by indigenous populations over the centuries, not just about crops, but about all ways of coping with hazards (Rouhban, 1999). Indeed, it is still rare today to find instances of the actual transfer of traditional knowledge and understanding of risks and hazards from indigenous communities to the developed world (Quarantelli, 1992).

That is not to say that there is no value in modern methods and technologies. However, the focus on modern solutions needs to shift towards giving due consideration to traditional methods. There needs to be a blending of modern and traditional methodologies, and a disentanglement of what is sustainable in the long term from what is profitable in the short term.

Systems Methodology

The Livelihood Model

In terms of a systems methodology, it is necessary to understand the actual needs of the communities and the stakeholders involved, including the central governments, and determine the requirements that will satisfy those needs. This can be approached through the 'Livelihoods Model' of Blaikie, *et al.* (1994), where individuals in each household have access to various resources and assets (e.g., land, water, fauna and flora, labour etc), choose from possible income opportunities according to their 'access qualifications' (money, resources, skills, knowledge, health etc), and decide how to apportion the income between consumption, storage and investment. This occurs within an environment (including risk factors), with inputs from social relations (group, network etc) and inputs from the 'structure of dominance' (class, gender, ethnicity, age, disability, power, politics, international influences).

A simplified version of the model of Blaike, *et al.* is shown in Figure 2 (from Russell, 2007).

However, this only represents 'normal life'. When a hazard event strikes the communities must cope using resources they have available or which become available. This applies not only to the immediate concerns of the emergency, but well into the future until a new equilibrium is established.

Human coping strategies can be viewed in terms of Maslow's (1970) hierarchy of human needs – where the needs that are higher up the hierarchy, like love and self determination, must wait for the satisfaction of needs lower down, such as food, water, shelter and sleep (Wisner, *et al.*, 2004). Indeed, in the International Karakoram Project, Miller (1981) discovered that villagers in the area of study in Pakistan, "whilst totally aware of the hazardous environment

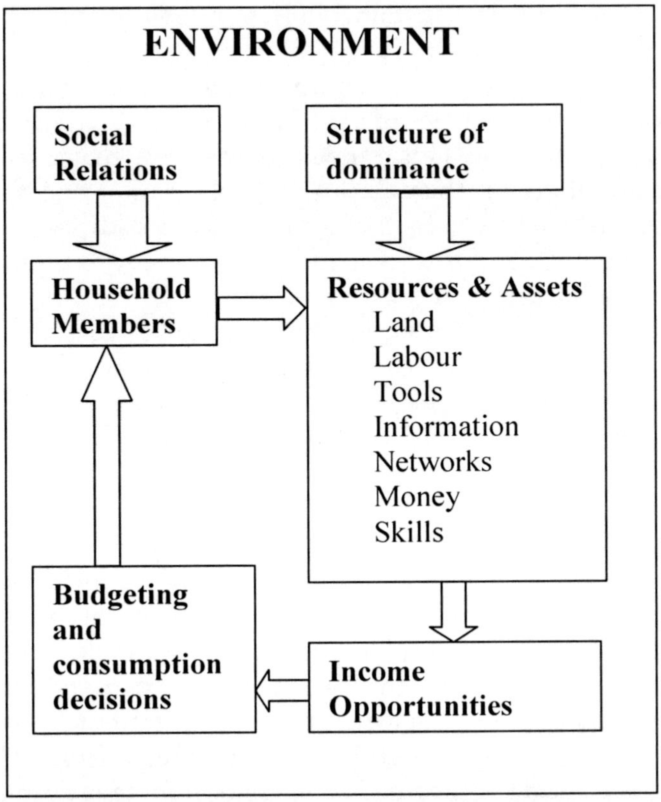

Figure 2 *A simplified version of the livelihood model of Blaike et al. (1994)*

that surrounded them, knew that they could do nothing to control floods, mud flashes and avalanches and consequently were prepared to build their homes on the worst land, however dangerously situated, so that the best land could be cultivated."

Communities adapt to hazards as best they can, and it is important to understand their perspectives. Local tracks, for instance, are often seen as more important by communities than the main roads provided by the government. Women, in particular, use the tracks for hours each day fetching and carrying water and fuel. Tracks and bridges can be severely disrupted even by small hazard events, affecting the wellbeing of the whole community, so assistance in maintaining or improving local-level transport infrastructure is important, but often overlooked (Twigg, 2004).

In the sustainable livelihoods analysis of (Ashley & Carney, 1999), people rather than resources, facilities or services, are the main concern. This means identifying livelihood-related constraints and opportunities across all sectors, areas, and social groups; recognizing how the various factors change with time; understanding the factors that influence people; recognizing and including the relevant stakeholders (from individuals, to community based organizations, to international bodies); and acknowledging the strategies that people and the various groups adopt to achieve the goals that they pursue.

The goal of achieving sustainable livelihoods involves building livelihoods that are sustainable in the face of shocks and stresses, independently of unsustainable external support. If a community is to be sustainable, it must base its livelihood on the maintenance of the long-term productivity of available resources, natural or otherwise. This implies, for instance, that any dependence on cash crops that are subject to the vagaries of global market prices, are in the end, unsustainable. Dependence on cash crops results in steadily decreasing income with time for a given effort, as well as the displacement of traditional land use patterns to achieve the diminishing returns.

Also, it is vital that no one community achieves sustainable livelihoods at the expense of another. Water resources, for instance, will become a more important issue with time, as global climate change causes more droughts. It is, therefore, not sustainable for one community to take all water resources upstream, leaving none for those lower down.

A comparison with vulnerability analysis

Sustainable livelihood analysis has some overlaps with local-level vulnerability analysis (Twigg, 2004), however their goals are different. With vulnerability analysis, the goal is to gather an understanding of what vulnerabilities exist, and reach consensus on how to reduce the highest priority vulnerabilities. It involves using modern technologies in the form of mapping technologies, but also seeks to derive advice from locals through interviews or recording oral histories and stories. Ideally, the knowledge gained is used not only to reduce vulnerabilities by taking concrete action (as in literally pouring concrete), but also to advise the communities on how they should act before, during and after times of emergency.

While many of the outcomes from vulnerability analyses can be highly beneficial, they focus on the 'vulnerability' as the object of analysis. If the behavior of the community members is not changed, then all the good intentions may be for nothing. It is precisely at this point that sustainable livelihoods analysis may assist in achieving better outcomes.

Moving towards resilience

In the sustainable livelihood model the focus is to change the behavior of the community members to achieve more resilient practices and ways of life. Just as short term diets for overweight adults don't tend to lead to long term weight loss, so too in the case of communities the focus needs to be on long term changes to livelihoods to achieve resilience.

The process for achieving change, while it is not prescribed here, can be judged against three criteria (Checkland & Scholes, 1990): its efficacy (whether it actually works); efficiency (whether it uses least resources); and effectiveness (whether it achieves the longer term aims of the government). Any analysis needs to show that the chosen methods work (whether they are traditional, modern or a combination of both); that they use fewer resources than other methods; and that by achieving more sustainable livelihoods in individual communities in a Pacific Island Nation, the whole nation benefits.

The intention is not to prove or enhance the model, but to improve the problem situation. As human activity systems are complex, there will never be total agreement between all parties, so the objective is to seek an accommodation between different interests.

Conclusion

In conclusion, it is suggested that it is not effective for Pacific Island Nation communities to depend on central governments and foreign aid agencies to mitigate the risks they face from natural hazards. These hazards, particularly weather related hazards, are only likely to increase in the future due to global warming. It is essential, therefore, to empower the communities to take possession of the problem of risk mitigation for themselves.

The means of reducing risks in relatively isolated communities should not focus just on applying modern technologies, nor on simply reducing vulnerabilities. The means should involve the application of traditional methods in combination with appropriate modern technologies to encourage community members to change their lifestyles in ways that will improve their long term resilience to natural hazards.

References

Ashley C. & Carney D. (1999). *Sustainable Livelihoods: Lessons from Early Experience*, Department for International Development, ISBN 0850034141, London, UK.

Barnett, J. (2001). "Adapting To Climate Change In Pacific Island Countries: The Problem Of Uncertainty", in *World Development*, ISSN 0305-750X , 29(6): 977-993

Blaikie, P., Cannon T., Davis I. and Wisner B. (1994). *At Risk: Natural Hazards, People"s Vulnerability and Disasters,* ISBN 0415084776

Brookfield, H. (1989). "Global Change and the Pacific: Problems for the Coming Half-Century," The Contemporary Pacific, ISSN 1527-9464, 1&2, 1-17.

Campbell, J. (2006). "Traditional disaster reduction in Pacific Island communities" ISSN 1177-2425, GNS Science Report 2006/038.

Campbell, J. (2003). "Geography, Vulnerability and Nature," Paper presented at the New Zealand Geographical Society Annual Conference, Auckland, July 6-11, 2003.

Campbell, J. (1985). *Dealing With Disaster: Hurricane Response in Fiji,* ISBN 0866380582.

Checkland, P. (1981). *Systems Thinking, Systems Practice,* ISBN 0471279110.

Checkland, P. and Scholes, J. (1990). *Soft systems methodology in action,* ISBN 0471927686.

Dawe D. (2006). "The State of Food and Agriculture in Asia and the Pacific 2006," RAP Publication 2006/03, FAO, Bangkok.

Clarke W. and Thaman R. (eds.) (1993). "Agroforestry in the Pacific Islands: Systems for Sustainability" FAO, ISBN 9280808249.

Freeman P. and Warner K. (2001). "Vulnerability of Infrastructure to Climate Variability: How Does This Affect Infrastructure Lending Policies?" Report Commissioned by the Disaster Management Facility of The World Bank and the ProVention Consortium Washington, October 2001

Fry, G. (1997). "Framing the Islands: Knowledge and Power in Changing Australian Images of the South Pacific." The Contemporary Pacific, ISSN 1527-9464, 9(2): pp. 305-344.

IMF (International Monetary Fund) (2006). "International Financial Statistics online database," (available at http://ifs.apdi.net/imf/about.asp).

Maslow, A. (1970). *Motivation and Personality*, 2nd edn, ISBN 9780060419875.

Mercer, J. (2005). "Reducing vulnerability in South Pacific Small Island Developing States: The indigenous or modern way?" Coventry Centre for Disaster Management, Coventry University.

Miller, K. (1981). "The International Karakoram Project, 1980: A First Report," The Geographical Journal, ISSN 0016-7398, Vol. 147, No. 2, July 1981, pp. 153-163.

Nurse, L., McLean, R., Suarez, A., with Ali, M., Hay, J., Maul, G, & Sem, G. (1998). "Small island states," in T. Watson, M. Zinyowera & R. Moss (Eds.), "*The regional impacts of climate change: An assessment of vulnerability*," ISBN 0521634555 (pp 333-354).

Pelesikoti, N. (2007). "Disaster risk reduction and disaster management national action plan (2006-2016), of the Government of the Republic of Vanuatu," Pacific Islands Applied Geoscience Commission, Suva, Fiji.

Quarantelli, E. (1992). "Can and should social science research knowledge and findings from developed societies be applied in developing societies," University of Delaware Disaster Research Centre, Preliminary Paper 178.

Rouhban, (1999). "Scientific Knowledge, Technical Experience and Traditional Wisdom," in Ingleton, J. (Ed) *Natural Disaster Management: A Presentation to Commemorate the International Decade for Natural Disaster Reduction (IDNDR)*, pp164-165, Leicester: Tudor Rose.

Russell, S. (2007). "A Systems Approach for Dealing with Natural Disasters in Pacific Island Nations," proceedings from the Systems Evaluation and Test and Evaluation Conference, *Complex Systems and Sustainability*, Sydney, Australia, 24-27 Sept 2007.

Shah, A. (2007). *US and Foreign Aid Assistance*, GlobalIssues.org, Last updated: Sunday, April 08, 2007

Sillitoe, (1998). "The Development of Indigenous Knowledge," Current Anthropology, ISSN 0011-3204 , Vol. 39, No.2: pp223-251

SwissRe. (1997). "Tropical Cyclones" 201_9678, Swiss Reinsurance Company, Zurich.

Sydee, J. (2004). "How Are the Pacific Island Countries Attempting to Fight Global Warming?" University of Wollongong, Australia – available on e-Journal http://www.uow.edu.au/arts/research/ejournal/archives/jun04/jsarticle.pdf

Thaman, R. (1989). "Applied Atoll Research for Development: Proceedings of the Kiribati Applied Atoll Research for Development Consultation", Tarawa, 27 February to 2 March, 1989. Ministry for Natural Resource Development, Bairiki, Tarawa, Kiribati

Twigg, J. (2004). "Disaster risk reduction - Mitigation and preparedness in development and emergency programming," Humanitarian Practice Network at Overseas Development Institute, London, UK, No. 9, Mar. 2004

Webb, A. (2005). "Technical Report – An assessment of coastal processes, impacts, erosion mitigation options and beach mining," EU EDF – SOPAC Project Report 46, *Reducing Vulnerability of Pacific ACP States*, Suva, Fiji.

Wildavsky, A. (1988). *Searching for Safety*. ISBN 0887387144.

Wisner B., Blaikie, P., Cannon, T., and Davis, I. (2004). *At Risk*, 2nd ed. ISBN 0415252164.

34. Generating Policy Relevant Knowledge: How and Why?

J.P. Kropp, K. Eisenack and **M.K.B. Lüdeke**
Potsdam Institute for Climate Impact Research, GER

Global society faces new types of environmental problems. Today civilization is a significant factor of interference in the global ecosphere. The variety of involved mechanisms is characterized by trans-sectoral interdependencies and interrelationships. This makes it very difficult to design adequate intervention strategies. New techniques therefore are needed at the science-stakeholder interface in order to learn from each other, but also to structure complex problems in an adequate manner. In this article we present the archetype approach for this task. It can be used as a formal as well as a qualitative approach. The power of this approach is illustrated by examples from current research.

Introduction: Ways to cope with complexity

Our understanding of the coupled human-environment system is blurred by a variety of facets. A key characteristics of the entire earth system that it often exhibits an exceptional dynamics involving innumerable system parts and a multitude of (non)linear interrelations. Despite this science tended to a further division of disciplines trying to answer sectoral questions. The next step emerging was the systems view, originally focussing on whole ecosystems. During this phase it was often argued that by just increasing the detail of the analysis more successful utilization and control strategies for our natural environment could be provided. Indeed, this was an undertaking that was bound to fail. A rigorous assessment of micro-scale processes has been possible so far only for significantly simplified systems. Thus, a bunch of examples (e.g. as for marine capture fisheries, cf. Eisenack & Kropp 2001, Eisenack et al 2006a) has shown that this was not sufficient. With the increasing awareness that humankind unfolds the major pressure on the natural environment more holistic and integrated approaches are propagated. These efforts, however, were as well embossed by the problem of complexity, but had additionally to cope with knowledge of different quality (quantitative/qualitative). The problem is now that - on the one hand - it is impossible to explicitly analyze the human-environment interface in all details while - on the other hand - it is a necessary to examine complex mechanisms and their interplay to avoid potential management failures (cf. Kropp, *et al.*, 2002). In such a complex world the challenge is not to analyze more and more details formally, but follow an approach allowing to identify the general functionalities of a system. From the point of view of a systems analyst such an approach should include the identification of potential precursor signals indicating critical events or should at least supply a weak prognosis of a system's potential development paths.

In such a case two problems arise. The first is related to the foundation of a theoretical concept. This is often difficult to understand by policymakers. Therefore science has the duty to translate this knowledge to concrete policy options. This includes that also the basic assumptions, e.g. the concrete definitions or relationship between variables, of the theoretical basis are accepted and translated adequately. The second problem is often formulated by the decision makers. They often argue that scientific information is insufficient or too weak to allow the implementation of adequate interventions or management strategies. But regardless which strategy policy-makers choose when facing threats, as e.g., marine overexploitation or global warming, there is a considerable uncertainty about the outcome of applied management strategies. This is not related to the input provided by science, but to the variety of additional effects related to institutional barriers, binding and legal concepts, and administrative settings. Looking on these facets in more detail it becomes obvious that policy making is mostly not based on quantitative scientific findings. Illustrative examples are, e.g., budgeting or cost-benefit analyses for large investment projects which are ignored when not appropriate. Thus, in their own field policy makers widely accept uncertain and even intransparent situations. On the other hand they demand more quantifiable information from science. Despite these facts we have to establish a new paradigm in policy making, i.e., it must be understood that science often has to deal with weak and soft prognoses only and that this cannot be an argument for non-action.

In this paper we will discuss strategies of knowledge generation in an uncertain and complex environment. We will make clear that in spite of indeterminacies it is possible for policy making to choose judicious measures and exemplify our approach by the discussion of examples from the management of renewable resources and adaptation to climate change.

The Pattern Approach

Pattern recognition is powerful technique to cope with complex situations and it is an essential component of the learning process in human–environment interaction. For example, the brain of mammals is most efficient in reconstructing fragmentary information and providing solutions for unknown situations by referring to analogous cases. During the second half of the 20th century, neuroscience discovered and described the underlying mechanisms of these processes.

Subsequently, a variety of artificial neural network methodologies have been developed to make use of these features (cf. Kohonen, 2001; Kropp & Schellnhuber, 2007). Compared to the efficiency of brains, artificial neural networks have several shortcomings; for example, they need a huge amount of input data and do not explain how they achieve results. Thus, they have a limited suitability to deduce knowledge from qualitative and uncertain situations that are common in our daily life.

This is related to several crucial barriers undermining systematic examinations of man-environment interactions, as non-linearities or the complexity of multi-cause–multi-effect processes. In face of these discouraging features, the questions is how to provide policy-relevant knowledge that would help decision-makers to approach safe-limits for a selected task. Here we propose as the pattern approach, but in a more general manner. We understand a "pattern" as an archetype which is representative for a typical combination of society-environment interactions which brings about facets of global environmental change and/or being a response to such changes. The basic assumption behind this concept is that there are typical mechanisms of socio-ecological interaction that reappear at different places around the world. Starting from this premise it is clear that such a description needs a sufficient level abstraction. It should be general enough to be potentially found in more in than cases, but not too general. In the latter case explanatory power is lost by ignoring important differences in mechanisms and their conditions. Even if the definition of the pattern or archetype is weak (in a mathematical sense) should allow for policy and decision-makers two things: in case successful strategies (management, adaptation, etc.) are determined in one particular situation they can transferred to other situations belonging to the same archetype. This constrains the space of potential action schemes generally, a demand often formulated by policy makers. Secondly, the structuring of complex knowledge is as well a learning, i.e., pattern building process. It allows to achieve for an overview about a certain problem without going lost in too much details.

At this point the question arises how to establish these archetypes. In principal this is possible in different ways, from formal to non-formal, by evaluating narratives (e.g., by case study evaluation based on articles, cf. Petschel-Held and Lüdeke 2001) or quantitatively (e.g., by neural network approaches). At the end this depends on the objective of the analysis. But in principle we understand an archetype as a cognition component of arbitrary complexity (cf. Kelso, 1997). With regard to this openness is essential for a transdisciplinary approach to find a common ground acceptable for all involved scientists and stakeholders. In the following section we will introduce some examples and show how they are used in the decision making process.

The Syndrome Approach

An early example of such an approach was introduced by the German Advisory Council on Global Change (WBGU 1993). In a more general context of global change research, the approach was suggested as an instrument to analyze complex transsectoral phenomena. It was inspired by medical sciences where typical symptoms of pertinent cofactors constitute hazardous patterns (causal typologies), so-called syndromes (cf. Schellnhuber, *et al.*, 1997). It provides a semi-quantitative and transsectoral overview of the 'dynamical degradation patterns' that characterize contemporary human–environment interactions across the planet (cf. Figure 1) (Schellnhuber, *et al.*, 2002). The names (Figure 1, left hand side) are chosen either to sketch the main processes or to represent a paradigmatic area, where the respective processes can be observed

Utilization syndromes: pattern resulting from inappropriate use of natural resources	
Sahel syndrome	Overcultivation of marginal land
Overexploitation syndrome	Overexploitation of natural ecosystems
Rural Exodus syndrome	Environmental degradation through abandonment of traditional agricultural practices
Dust Bowl syndrome	Unsustainable agro-industrial use of soils and water
Katanga syndrome	Environmental degradation through depletion of non-renewable resources
Mass tourism syndrome	Development and destruction of nature for recreational ends
Scorched earth syndrome	Environmental destruction through war and military action
Development syndromes: man environment problems arising from unsustainable development	
Aral Sea syndrome	Environmental damage of natural landscapes as a result of large-scale projects
Green revolution syndrome	Environmental degradation through the adoption of inappropriate farming methods
Asian tiger syndrome	Disregard for environmental standards in the context of rapid economic growth
Favela syndrome	Environmental degradation through uncontrolled urban growth
Urban sprawl syndrome	Destruction of landscapes through planned expansion of urban infrastructures
Disaster syndrome	Singular anthropogenic environmental disasters with long-term impacts
Sink syndromes: environmental degradation through non-adapted disposal systems	
Smokestack syndrome	Environmental degradation through large-scale dispersion of emissions
Waste dumping syndrome	Environmental degradation through controlled and uncontrolled waste disposal
Contaminated land syndrome	Local contamination of environmental assets at industrial locations

Figure 1 *List of 16 Syndromes as Proposed by the WBGU (1993)*

(Figure 1, right hand side). Note that syndromes are non-exclusive, i.e., distinct syndromes can occur simultaneously at the same location and they can be coupled, for example, by symptoms belonging to different syndrome pattern. The approach seeks for typical functional patterns of human–environment interactions by defining their essential mechanisms (cf. Boardman, 1995). In any case, this is a formidable task, since it implies an extensive evaluation of case studies, expert elicitations, and field work. The essential elements of this approach are *symptoms* (approximately 80). They are the basic entities for the description of the earth system with respect to problematic developments. A symptom is a functional aggregate of detailed variables describing a single sub-process of global change closely related to the human–environment interface. Examples are the loss of species diversity, urbanization, or freshwater scarcity The other component focus on the *interrelations,* i.e., the connecting elements for the symptoms and specify the causal relations. They are defined as monotonic relations, i.e., with increasing (enforcing) or decreasing (mitigating) effect.

This concept was used to inform the Federal Government of Germany how the exceptional dynamics on our entire planet evolve and which role humanity plays in this planetary super game. But this was not the end of the story. The symptoms in this concept are not only system states, but could also be a change of a state. Together with the arrows between them makes such a pattern dynamic. Thus it is not only a diagnosis of the present state but allows also for prognosis.

An Example: The Marine Overexploitation Syndrome

A formal dynamic description of marine overexploitation on an integrated and intermediate functional scale is provided to assess the general development paths in fisheries. Major symptoms are, for example, degradation of ecosystems, policy failure, or expansion of infrastructure. The problematic development pattern is specified by the syndrome-specific network of interrelations (Figure 2) which is based on a case study survey examining the general processes in fisheries. (cf., for example, Harris, 1999; Charles, 2001 for an overview). This means we have identified symptoms and interrelations which are at least necessary, but - possibly - not sufficient for the occurrence of the syndrome core (cf. Figure 2, for details cf. Kropp, *et al.*, 2006 and the references therein).

Based on the introduced qualitative analysis and a review of the state-of-the-art bio-economic modelling, a model approach was developed which integrates the main system parts and could help to anticipate the future development in fisheries. As indicated in Figure 2, fisheries can be characterized as

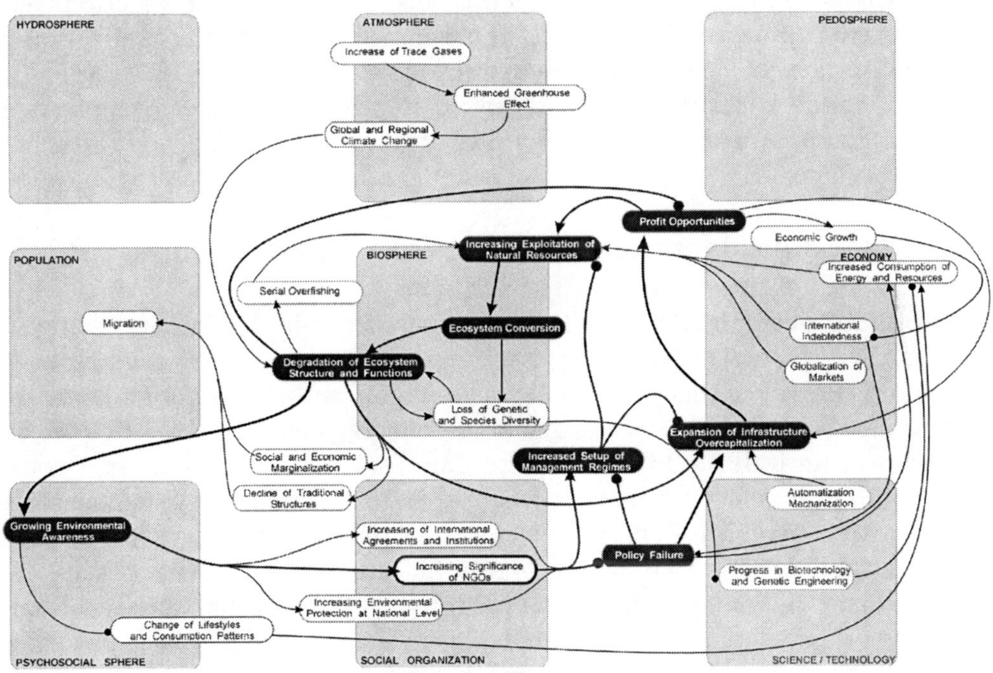

Figure 2 *Network of specific interrelations of the marine overexploitation syndrome. The symptoms in the black ellipses and their interrelations are the necessary ones designating the so-called core of the syndrome. The other symptoms generate specific expressions of the syndrome.*

a coevolutionary system which consists of an economic and a natural systems part. If we are focussing on the core of the syndromatic pattern, it becomes clear that this system is far from being fair and effective. It constitutes a vicious cycle, characterized by market mechanisms and policy constraints which have set the optimization paradigm (cf. Schellnhuber & Kropp, 1998) in industrial fisheries into force. Consequently, economic pressure on marine renewable resources has been a major topic discussed in environmental economics over the last two decades. One of the key characteristics in this context is the highly specialized capital stock (ships, gear), which cannot readily be converted to other uses, i.e., fisheries are characterized by some kind of indolence which inhibits capital reduction. But despite recent efforts, intrinsic system properties (uncertainty) have led to a situation in which current modelling approaches are still rudimentary and deal with unsuitable simplifications (for example, equilibrium solutions, linear assumptions), because vagueness seems to be an obstacle for improved models.

A qualitative differential equation (QDE) model (cf. Kuipers, 1994) based only on trends and thresholds of qualitative variables and monotonicity relationships between them can be formulated more easily as a quantitative model which needs concrete parametrizations, which are often unknown, at least for the module representing economic decisions of market competitors (cf. Eisenack, *et al.*, 2006 and the references therein). A QDE can be considered as a generalization of an ordinary differential equation (ODE). Same holds true for the results. While an ODE provides only a single development path, a QDE supplies a set of trajectories, embracing all possible developments (evolution tree). Each of them can be understood as a representation of a specific realization of an ODE which is consistent with the definitions of the above QDE. By applying graph theoretical methodologies, this set of solutions is structured in a state-transition graph representing the dynamics of fisheries according to the qualitative model (Figure 3).

Developing Adaptation Strategies to Climate Change in the Baltic Sea Area

The project "Developing Policies & Adaptation Strategies to Climate Change in the Baltic Sea Region" (ASTRA) assesses regional impacts and raises awareness of ongoing climate change and develops strategies and policies for adaptation. Stakeholders from municipal and regional planning authorities participate together with a multidisciplinary scientific team (more than 40 partners, 7 countries). Although the occurrence of climate change is similar in the whole study region impacts may differ among the countries or sub-regions. Furthermore it might be possible that each city or region has particularities that precludes a simple transfer of strategies from one community to the other. Other difficulties might be associated with different frameworks for legal planning or administrative settings. In order to assess this, a semi-structured questionnaire was send to all partners. The qualitative research design of the study took advantage from a modified grounded theory approach (e.g., Strauss & Corbin, 1990) and was created for multiple purposes. The main objective was to establish a basis

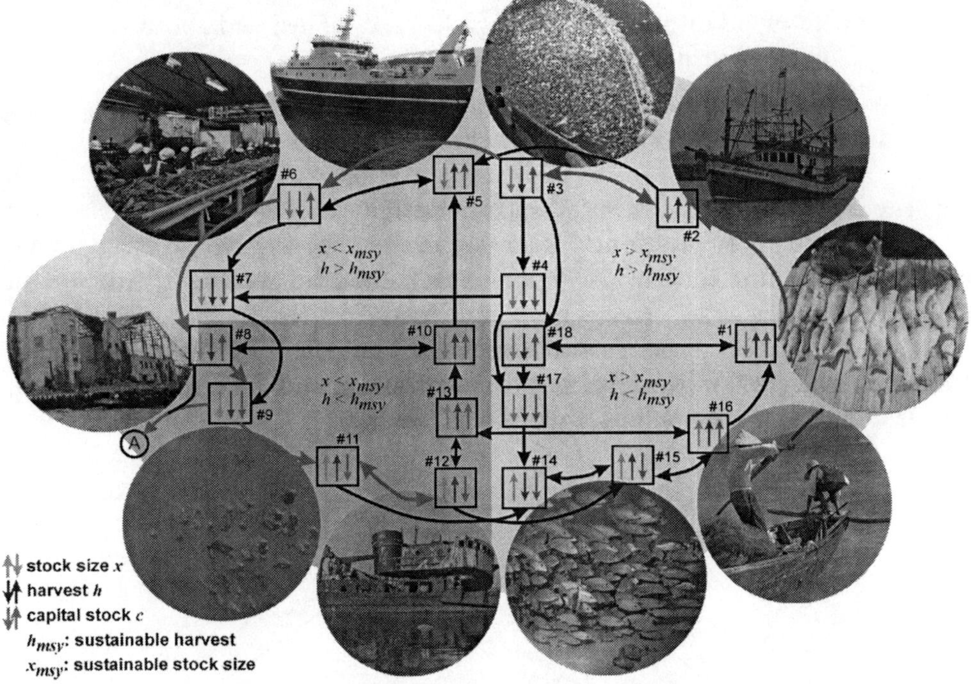

Figure 3 *State transition graph of a less supervised fishery. The arrows in the boxes label the direction of change of stock, harvest, and capital. The colored sectors depict the level of criticality in fisheries. Here e.g. $x > x_{msy}$ (stock above sustainable level). Only in the green and yellow sectors, the fisheries are approximately in safe limits. Ⓐ indicates the total breakdown of both fisheries and resource, the red arrows represents a development observed for blue whale hunting during the last 60 years. It is very critical, for example, when a system enters state #3 or #2. Than transitions to serious developments are almost unavoidable. It is also visible that arbitrary turning points are also impossible. This shows that boom and bust cycles , expressed by a potentially (vicious) cyclic development, is a major feature or marine capture fisheries. This graph shows also that any fishery can analyzed qualitatively with regard to its current state although we have only weak knowledge on hand. This implies that concrete action can be taken in order to avoid irreversible transitions (cf. Kropp, et al., 2006).*

for the development of adaptation strategies by assessing the state-of-the-art in local climate protection, stakeholder problem framing and knowledge on climate change. It should identify basic adaptation needs in the study region in an explorative style and aimed to formulate working hypotheses and entry points for further planning and further scientific work. The systematic assessment of stakeholder views and framing is considered important for three reasons:

1. Adaptation strategies evolve from regional experience - their implementation therefore would rather be feasible and assessable at regional than at global level;

2. We expected that there is a very diverse knowledge about climate change impacts, about adaptation and mitigation strategies, and about the (un)certainty of climate projections, and;
3. We wanted to evaluate what stakeholder demand from science regarding a sustainable planning in the light of climate change.

Since the questionnaire was semantically designed some kind of systematization was needed for evaluation. This was done by applying AtlasTI©, a software that allows to define semantic categories and a coding system. It further automatically identifies relationships between them (Figure 4).

Similar archetypes of problems were identified for the exposed units, supporting and constraining factors for adaptation, and for climate change impacts as well. The major results were the following:

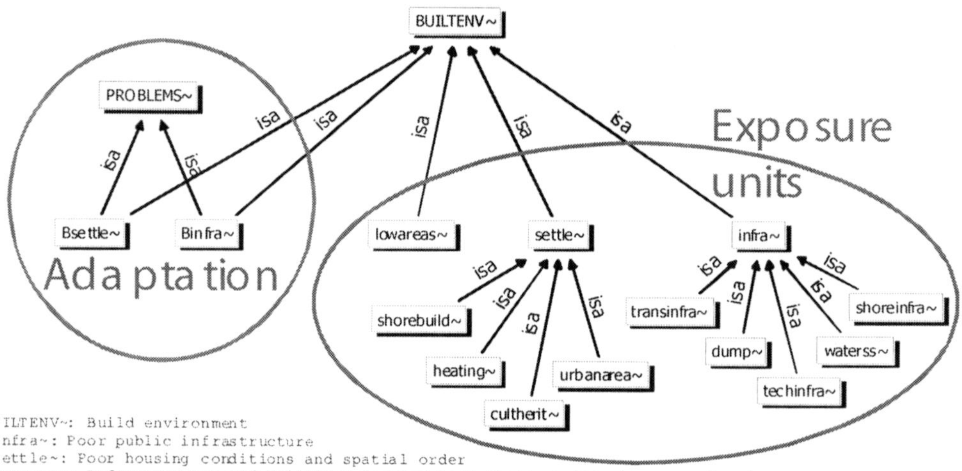

BUILTENV~: Build environment
Binfra~: Poor public infrastructure
Bsettle~: Poor housing conditions and spatial order
lowareas~: Infrastructure and buildings located near shore on low above sea level
settle~: Buildings in general
shorebuild~: Buildings near shore
heating~: Heating of houses
cultherit~: Cultural heritage
urbanarea~: Urban area in general
infra~: Infrastructure in general
transinfra~: Transportation infrastructure, places
dump~: Landfill dumps
techinfra~: Technical and communication infrastructure
waterss~: Water supply system infrastructure, sewage plants
shoreinfra~: Infrastructure near shore
PROBLEMS~: General meta-category for problems

Figure 4 *Example of the schematic structuring of the answers of the questionnaire, here for the build environment. Each mentioned answer where either associated to a problem class or to sub-clusters (patterns) belonging to settlements or infrastructure which itself on the end are part of build environment .From the form of the answer can be derived the awareness of the respondent, i.e. she either sees a systems part as a threatened entity (exposed unit) or she tries to associate some concrete problems to it (adaptation is needed). This structuring helps to obtain a general overview how the problem framing among the stakeholders is constituted. The study suggests that besides awareness raising and coordinative efforts it may be important how local and national institutional levels interact such that the supportive capacity of higher levels is complemented with detailed knowledge from lower levels.*

- Problem awareness is primarily framed by potential impacts in the case study regions. There is little attention for vulnerable exposure units and little explicit knowledge on policy responses. In many cases exposure units are only described in a very vague or general way. Climate change is mainly seen as mitigation problem (reduction of greenhouse gases), while adaptation issues are vague, unclear, difficult to structure. Climate change is not a priority on the local or regional level, and lack of financial resources hinders adaptation.
- Many constraining institutional arrangements are seen as informal. They have the form of complaints about "soft factors" as missing knowledge and citizens' awareness, inadequate education, political inaction and bad coordination of diverse institutions. Problems are found more on the local scale, while enabling institutions and actors are seen on higher levels. It is likely that there is a shift of responsibilities to higher institutional scales (mitigation?). Most existing climate change policies are related to natural hazards (event related), or national greenhouse gas mitigation strategies

The results are partly disappointing, in particular considering that climate change is now longer avoidable. The current situation may be characterized as being on the threshold between a "pre-learning" and a learning phase of the involved institutions - an intermediate period between recognition of the scope of the problem and steps towards more concrete policy frames. Whether or how this threshold is passed is likely to depend on the next actions to take. Nevertheless this stage provides good opportunities to define entry points for concrete planning and adaptation in the Baltic Sea Region.

Conclusion

Starting from the assumption that an integrated analysis of the coupled social and natural processes is necessary to solve problems of global environmental change, we resolve this dichotomy to open up the field for diversity of methods. Currently we have the impression that research as well as policy making does not take full advantage of formal methods yet. In this paper we focussed mainly on the scientific side of the problem, i.e., we want to deduce knowledge on complex phenomena either with or without stakeholder participation. What we found is that the archetype approach is a very beneficial approach in this context, since it can structure complex knowledge, but can be also used a learning concept, since it allows to present complex mechanism in a simplified manner. A further advantage is that we can combine knowledge of different quality in the presented approach. This in general opens a promising road on the analysis of socio-ecological systems.

References

Boardman JT (1995). Wholes and parts – a systems approach *IEEE Transactions on Systems, Man and Cybernetics* 25 (7): 1150–1161

Cassel-Gintz M and Petschel-Held G. (2000): GIS-based assessment of the threat to world forests by patterns of unsustainable civilization nature interaction. *Journal of*

Environmental Management 59: 279-298

Charles A. (2001): *Sustainable Fishery Systems.* Oxford: Blackwell, 384 pp.

Eisenack K and Kropp JP (2001): Assessment of management options in marine fisheries by qualitative modeling techniques. *Marine Pollution Bulletin* 43 (7–12): 215–224

Eisenack K, Tekken V, and Kropp JP (2007): Stakeholders' Perceptions of Climate Change in the Baltic Sea Region. *Coastline Report*, in press.

Eisenack K, Welsch H, and Kropp JP. (2006a): A qualitative dynamical modelling approach to capital accumulation in unregulated fisheries *Journal of Economic Dynamics and Control.* 30: 2613-2636.

Eisenack K, Lüdeke MKB, Petschel-Held G, Scheffran J and Kropp JP. (2007): Qualitative Modelling techniques to Assess Pattern of Global Change. In: *Decision Making and Risk Management in Sustainability Science: Advanced Methods*, edited by JP Kropp and J Scheffran. New York: Nova Science Publishers, Chapt. 3, pp. 83-127. ISBN 978-1-60021-427-1

Harris M. (1999): *Lament for an Ocean. The Collapse of the Atlantic Cod Fishery: A True Crime Story* Toronto: McClelland and Steward Inc., 389 pp.

Kelso JAS (1997): *Dynamic Patterns.* MIT Press: Cambridge.

Kohonen T. (2001): *Self-Organising Maps* Berlin: Springer, 362 pp.

Kropp JP and Schellnhuber H J. (2007): Prototyping broad-scale climate and ecosystem classes by means of self-organising maps. In *Self-Organising Maps: Applications in Geographical Information Sciences*, edited by P Agarwal and A Skupin. London: Wiley & Sons (ISBN: 0-470-02167-5).

Kropp JP, Eisenack K, and Scheffran J (2006): Marine overexploitation: a syndrome of global change. In: Multiple Dimensions of Global Environmental Change (ed. S. Sonak), Chapt. 15, p. 257-284. TERI Press, New Dehli.

Kropp J, Reusswig F, and Lüdeke M K B. (2001) Global analysis and distribution of unbalanced urbanization processes: the Favela syndrome. *GAIA* 10 (2): 109–120

Kropp JP, Zickfeld K, and Eisenack K. (2002): Management of critical events: the breakdown of marine fisheries and the North Atlantic thermohaline circulation In: *The Science of Disasters: Climate Disruptions, Heart Attacks, and Market Crashes*, pp. 192-216, edited by A Bunde, JP Kropp, and H J Schellnhuber Berlin: Springer, 453 pp.

Kuipers B. (1994) *Qualitative reasoning: modeling and simulation with incomplete knowledge.* Cambridge: MIT Press, 418 pp.

Lüdeke M K B, Petschel-Held G, and Schellnhuber H J. (2004): Syndromes of global change: the first panoramic view. *GAIA* 13 (1): 42–49

Petschel-Held G and Lüdeke M K B. (2001): Integration of case studies on global change by means of artificial intelligence *Integrated Assessment* 2 (3): 123–138

Petschel-Held G, Block A, Cassel-Gintz M, Kropp J, Lüdeke M K B, Moldenhauer O, Reusswig F, Schellnhuber H J. (1999): Syndromes of global change: a qualitative modeling approach to support global environmental management *Environmental Modeling and Assessment* 4 (4): 295–314

Schellnhuber H J and Kropp J. (1998): Geocybernetics: controlling a complex dynamical system under uncertainty. *Naturwissenschaften* 85 (9): 411–425

Schellnhuber H J, Lüdeke M K B, and Petschel-Held. (2002): The syndrome approach to scaling: describing global change on an intermediate functional scale. *Integrated Assessment* 3 (2–3): 201–219

Schellnhuber H J, Block A, Cassel-Gintz M, Kropp J, Lammel G, Lass W, Lienenkamp R, Loose C, Lüdeke M K B, Moldenhauer O, Petschel-Held G, Plöchl M, Reusswig F. (1997): Syndromes of global change *GAIA* 6: 19–34

Sietz D, Untied B, Walkenhorst O, Lüdeke MKB, Mertins G, Petschel-Held G, Schellnhuber HJ (2006): Smallholder agriculture in NE Brazil: Assessing heterogeneous human-environmental dynamics. Regional Environmental Change 6: 132-146.

Strauss, A. and J. Corbin (1990): Basics of Qualitative Research. Grounded Theory Procedures and Techniques. Sage, Newbury Park.

WBGU (1993): World in Transition: Basic Structure of Global People-Environment Interactions. Economica, Bonn.

35. Application of Soft Systems Methodology in Planning: A Case of Integrated Natural Hazards Risk Management

Ljubica Mamula-Seadon
Ministry of Civil Defence and Emergency Management

Acknowledgements

I would like to thank Associate Professor Tom Fookes from the School of Architecture and Planning, Auckland University for his challenging contribution to this work. I have learnt a lot from Tom about a 'weird and wonderful' world of the New Zealand planning. I am also grateful to GNS Science, Geohazards project, Objective 1, for providing financial support that made it so much easier to concentrate on the research.

This paper addresses the topic of integrated environmental planning and environmental risk management, with particular focus on risks from natural hazards, within the context of the New Zealand cooperative, decentralised planning regime for sustainability. The paper identifies major shortcomings in the practice of planning and natural hazards risk management. It is proposed that the interpretative systems thinking paradigm, presented in the Soft Systems Methodology, offers an alternative approach to current practice, allowing for coalescence of the positivist and post-positivist in a structured, purpose oriented manner, yet in the tradition of communicative, participatory planning. Through application of Soft Systems Methodology to structuring a debate about desirable and feasible changes to practice of integrated environmental planning and risk management for natural hazards, adjustments to the current statutory and non-statutory framework were suggested and a conceptual model of this, improved framework developed; specific strategies for achievement of integration in practice identified and modes of implementation suggested; specific strengths and weaknesses of the system highlighted, and a number of future actions recommended.

Context

The magnitude and possible irreversible environmental change induced by environmental risks have created an unprecedented interest in this topic in the late 20th century. Recently the issue of climate change and resulting exacerbation of risks from natural hazards is the focus of many debates, both for the general public and the politicians, as the latest severe weather examples from

New Zealand testify. Solutions are urgently sought to address the consequences of those events. However, at the same time the validity of a purely scientific, rational approach to risk assessment and management has been continuously contested. The perceived transformation of the political environmental problems into the technical 'factual' questions that could be decided by technical experts in the environmental agencies divorced from social reality for excluding values and value judgments from the environmental decision-making process, has been strongly challenged in the last few decades (for example, Mergolis, 1996; Brown, 1990; Fischer, 1996; Jeager, *et al.*, 2001). Compounded with dynamic, complex and multifaceted requirements that numerous sustainability programmes introduced to redress some of the deficiencies of earlier environmental policy approaches to planning, including planning for risk reduction, complexities that were problematic under earlier regulatory mandates became even more pronounced (Mazmanian & Kraft, 1999).

Since the 1992 Rio Earth Summit adopted Agenda 21, integrated planning has been accepted internationally as an essential tool for achieving sustainable development. Cousin (2002) defines integrated planning as effective multi-disciplinary, whole of government planning, applying broad means for implementation of plans, which requires vertical and horizontal integration. Vertical integration is strategic and policy driven whereas horizontal integration is achieved through cooperative action within and between spheres of government, best reflected in shared governance. The integration needs to be maintained over time. It relies upon strategic, spatial and corporate planning within the legislative framework of the planning system and the local government system (Cousins, 2002).

With the passing of the Resource Management Act 1991 New Zealand became one of the first countries to incorporate the concept of sustainable management in mainstream legislation, with integrated national framework and goals for resource and environmental management. In this regime, environmental risks are managed as elements of environmental planning and development management within local councils (May, *et al.*, 1996). The Resource Management Act 1991, as the core legislation which integrates environmental planning in the country, specifically prescribes that environmental risks are dealt with through the functions and duties required of relevant agencies and the mechanisms specified for carrying out these duties. The RMA integrated model of planning is reflected in the Civil Defence and Emergency Management (CDEM) Act 2002, that encourages an integrated approach to hazard management at a local authority level, to link land use management with risk reduction. The mechanism for achieving this in the field is through Civil Defence Emergency Management Groups, which are a consortia of local authorities based on existing regional council boundaries, working in partnership with emergency services.

However, both the integrated, cooperative environmental planning regime and the environmental risk management regime as its sub-set, have proven to be highly complex, and controversial, political and management issues. In the last fifteen years a significant body of research has been generated on the topic, with particular accent been placed on natural hazards, since a number of reports (May, *et al.*, 1996; PCE, 2000; Johnston & Becker, 2001; Kerr, *et al.*, 2002; Ericksen, *et al.*, 2003) drew attention to shortcomings in practice, while recent extreme events caused major disruptions in public domain. In relation to natural hazards, most planning instruments across the country with a few limited exceptions, scored poorly for the *interpretation of the purpose* principle. This was mainly because they did not provide clear explanations and links of how the legislation purpose is translated to the local physical and social conditions. Planning instruments and practice also showed a poor inter and intra-organizational co-ordination, either for lack of clear linkages between these documents and the policies included in the plan or for deficiences in practice due to capability issues. In short, whereas significant general advances have been made in planning and efficiency in the institutional processes now in place, effectiveness from a natural hazard risk perspective is still a distant goal (May, *et al.*, 1996; PCE, 2000; Johnston & Becker, 2001; Kerr, *et al.*,2002; Ericksen, *et al.*,2003). This reflects a more general conclusion elsewhere that New Zealand suffers from poor policy implementation (PCE, 2004). The additional difficulties are the ever-changing requirements on practice. Adaptivity and change are required in evolving systems like the New Zealand one (CAE, 2004; the author, 2006). In addition, requirements for negotiated outcomes are essential if sustainable development principles are to be implemented, as is the relationship management, transparency and inclusiveness of the processes (CAE, 2004; PCE, 2004; the author, 2005).

This leads to the challenge of improving the quality of policy and decision-making in the face of uncertainty and complexity. The challenge here is to find ways to integrate technical and social data more comprehensively and meaningfully in both analytical inquiry and public discussion. Interest in integrating social learning and goal-oriented decision making is pertinent to the realm of planning because the post-modern landscape urges confronting the challenge of continuous change, not by creating blueprints or rigid regulatory regimes, but by trying to influence its direction and preparing to meet uncertainty, making connections among ideas and among people, setting in motion joint learning and coordinating among interests and players and, generally, finding new ways to work on the most challenging tasks (Innes, 1997).

In practice, procedures for citizen participation that help build community acceptance of planning decisions are often built into a traditional 'rational-adaptive' model (Kaiser, *et al.*, 1996), in the sense of preventing governmental decisions from being made on the basis of habit and intuition only, while enhancing the structured application of knowledge and methodology in order to stimulate more explicit and open argumentation based on credible information. This is particularly well reflected in a cooperative approach to planning, as advocated in Europe and other developed nations, including New Zealand, where various kinds of rationality are combined. This cooperative model takes a positive approach to complexity and uncertainty, defining them not as obstacles, but as a part of the challenge (Glasbergen, 2003).

One of the ways both environmental planning and risk management have embraced this challenge is through a renewed interest in complexity and systems theory. This provides a possible vehicle for coalescence of positivist and rational thinking on the one hand, and post-positivist and constructivist thinking on the other, allowing for integration of science with the social practice of planning as a dialogical process (Byrne, 2003). The argument here is that complexity science, understood as integrative and dialectical, offers a way out of the impasse that integrates expert and lay knowledge and intentions in that complexity allows for agreed descriptions of context and potential, but delimits the range in time and space of that understanding, as a synthesis (*ibid.*). The preferred method of engagement here is *action research* (Byrne, 2003).

Within this context, it was proposed that the application of systems theory to improving environmental risk management, within the context of cooperative and collaborative planning in New Zealand, would lead to an improved practice. Soft Systems Methodology (SSM), with its emphasis on people and purposeful actions and its *action research* method, was seen as a potentially suitable vehicle for this task.

Methodology

The interpretative systems approach, or 'soft systems thinking' (Jackson, 2001), based on Habermasian communicative theory so often referred to in planning, was applied to structure a debate about the state of natural hazards risk management practice and to seek desirable and feasible changes. In Checkland's Soft Systems Methodology (SSM) systemicity is transferred from the world to the process of inquiry into the world. It combines a cyclic learning process with the use of systems models within that process. This facilitates dealing with complex social processes, by identifying alternatives, and seeking accommodations which allow change to happen (Checkland & Scholes, 1990; Checkland, 1999; Jackson, 2001; Lendington, 1999). A detailed discussion about the methodology can be found elsewhere in literature and will not be addressed here.

In this research, the overall approach to investigation of the state of practice of natural hazards risk management and improvements followed the approach of SSM by:

1. Establishing a 'rich picture' of the situation (i.e. current state of practice)
This was achieved by a number of means: an extensive research into the relevant literature, statutory and non-statutory planning and risk management instruments, questionnaires and interviews with practitioners and stakeholders, and local case studies.

An overview of literature and unstructured preliminary interviews teased out whether there was a perception amongst practitioners that improvements of current practice were needed; an overview of relevant statutory and non-statutory instruments and initiatives at the national and regional levels helped develop a framework for analysis; structured questionnaires and interviews assisted in detailing components and processes of the framework, and teased out stakeholders and their corresponding roles, as well as some aspects of power. Local case studies on management of risks from natural hazards further detailed the state of practice. The evaluation of practice was done in terms of its 'systemicity': its unity/conformity of purpose and objectives with components and processes of the risk management /environmental planning framework. Through those investigations stakeholders of the risk management 'system' were identified in terms of their roles in the 'system'.

2. Modelling and facilitation of debate

A number of conceptual systemic models of environmental risk management frameworks for natural hazards were developed, from an explicit point of view and with an explicit purpose, and desirable and feasible changes were sought through facilitated interaction among stakeholders, in an iterative fashion, until a consensus was achieved. This was done in workshops and individual or small group sessions, as pragmatically feasible. The role of the author here was as the initiator and synthesiser of ideas, as well as the one of facilitator, or agent of change. An example of the models used to facilitate the discussions is shown in Fig. 1.

It needs to be re-iterated here that using the conceptual model had a two-fold purpose: to improve practice by introducing desirable and feasible changes to the components and processes of the practice, using the conceptual model as a benchmark; and to facilitate learning about the practice. Centering the discussion and learning around a proposed conceptual model based on agreed principles allows for trans-boundary approach and adaptivity, and makes the process of enquiry transparent. This reflects the principle that the quality of process is as important as the outcomes. It also allows for (re)negotiated outcomes. Importantly, it enables all stakeholders in the SSM process, regardless of their place in the institutional matrix of the regime reflected in the model, to understand the whole matrix as a system with all its critical elements and relationships.

Over one hundred stakeholders took part in the research nationally, with thirty two stakeholders (planners, scientists, emergency managers, engineers, urban designers, risk managers and community members) ranging from senior strategic to the level of resource consent processing, being directly involved in the meetings and workshops in the two main centres, Auckland and Wellington.

Findings

As the research into applicability of systems approaches to structuring a debate about integrated planning and natural hazards risk management progressed, it was gradually revealed that the nature of the New Zealand planning and risk management regime is fundamentally systemic (the author, 2006). However, out of over one hundred stakeholders who took part in questionnaires, conference workshops and general discussion about the integrated planning and risk management framework only four were familiar with systems approaches. None of the stakeholders involved in workshops was familiar with systems approaches, and none had previously looked at the natural hazards risk management regime in systemic terms. All the workshop participants, therefore, had an opportunity to look at the regime they operate within from a new angle, and the one very much reflective of its original intent. All of them identified learning, either from the model or, and often more so, from discussion within the group, as one of the important outcomes of the exercise. All participants found the use of a model to explore the situation useful. However, they were not so comfortable with consensus building approach because they were not sure that the genuine consensus was reached. It is important to note that they were not uncomfortable with this approach either. Those who most readily responded because they found the approach attractive and useful were senior policy planners, some spatial urban designers and regional and local council civil defence managers – all practitioners, in the Auckland (largest urban) region. Some, for example, printed the model as a poster for use in everyday situations. Some participants intended to use it for development of management strategies. Those who less readily responded to the approach appeared to be scientists and social scientists from a research institution. It was interesting that the systemic model was seen by them as 'too idealistic'.

The above situation was also reflected in how the participants saw the usefulness of the approach. Whereas senior policy and emergency planners, community leaders, Maori and spatial urban planners saw the approach as very useful and worthwhile pursuing (although they doubted the capacity for implementation and logistic problems involved when a large number of representatives across wide spectrum is to be assembled), the social scientists and scientists were more sceptical - or less familiar with the theoretical background to complexity management?

All participants suggested that more detail about components and processes would be useful for understanding the model, and the risk management regime in general. It was strongly suggested that an interactive model based on the conceptual model discussed be made available to all practitioners.

All participants saw the main importance of systems approach at a strategic level and in initial phases of policy development.

Interestingly, quite a few participants iterated that the approach be translated into specific practices at an everyday level which would not require an understanding of the whole system. This, of course, is at odds with the approach. One of the key requirements for a successful implementation of systemic (integrated) approaches is that each stakeholder, regardless of their place in the institutional matrix of the regime, understands the matrix as a system with all its critical elements and relationships. Considering the complexity of the regime and probable pressures that practitioners are under it is not surprising that there may be resistance to 'having to understand the whole system'. However, the danger inherent in translating a complex approach into simple practices cannot be underestimated. Therefore, finding the ways of being specific at the level of everyday practice, while retaining larger picture, appears to be the immediate challenge here.

One particularly interesting, and heartening, outcome of these workshops was a recognition of the Auckland group that resilience is not only about community participation, but is an emergent property that manifests itself when all components and processes of the system work in balance with each other and with the purpose of the system.

Was the approach useful, then? All participants felt that, in the process, they have learnt more about the regime they operate within. The meetings also created opportunities for future collaboration among the participants. A number of strengths and weaknesses of the regime were identified and improvements suggested. The groups agreed on proposed improvements and strategies for improvements. Therefore, it can be said that, from the point of view of usefulness of the approach to structuring a debate and enabling learning, as well as identifying desirable and feasible changes to practice and strategies for implementation, the SSM approach proved useful.

To gain a full picture, however, it is necessary to say that most participants did feel that the approach is complex, and doubted it's suitability from the logistics point of view.

In addition, it is necessary to consider the requirements on the SSM 'user' or 'primary problem solver'. In other words, the SSM researcher's perspective needs to be taken into consideration, as well.

Soft Systems Methodology approach to structuring a debate and seeking improvements to the practice of natural hazards risk management in New Zealand involved a few important requirements on the SSM investigator/researcher (user or problem solver in SSM terminology):

- Risk management expertise: In order to fully appreciate a 'rich picture' of the practice it was necessary for the Problem Solver / Investigator to have a thorough, detailed understanding of the risk management theory and practice, both at the general theoretical level and a specific level of investigation (in this case natural hazards risks), as well as at the level of the larger immediate system (in this case the environmental risk management system).
- Environmental planning expertise: In integrated environmental management systems like the New Zealand one, where risks are managed as a part of the planning regime, it was necessary for the investigator to have a thorough understanding of the theory (worldview) of planning that underpins this regime, as well as the regime itself – planning instruments, processes, issues and trends in everyday practice. Also, in order to be able to create a common platform for the two practices – the one of planning and the one of risk management – the epistemologies of both need to be grasped.
- Systems expertise, including facilitation and mediation skills: In order to successfully facilitate learning and deliberating on changes, the investigator has to develop defendable, healthy systems models based on sound logic and appropriate for the task at hand. In other words, the investigator needs sound systems knowledge and skills. The investigator also has to be skilled in bringing together different (and often adversarial) stakeholders and mediate acceptable outcomes. The task involves ensuring transparency of the processes, but also generosity in sharing insights and knowledge, while been prepared to deal with patch protection, personal professional sensitivities and criticism, refusal, and sometimes even the loss of intellectual property.

Obviously, the skills required constitute a 'boundary' case of professional endeavour, a whole new 'expertise' that has to be developed. To make things more complex, this new expertise may or may not be appreciated, or may even be seen as threatening by the established professions. The task, on the other hand, is formidable, and requires a broad set of skills, in-depth specialist knowledge, and a considerable investment of time and energy.

These consideration need to be taken into account, together with the earlier mentioned issues of overall capacity and commitment of the stakeholders in complex systems like the New Zealand integrated environmental planning and risk management, when systems approaches to seeking improvements in practice are sought. Whereas the overall conclusion about the suitability of SSM approach to structuring a debate and improving environmental risk / natural hazards risk management practice remains a positive one, particularly bearing in mind the systemicity of this practice, there needs to be an awareness of complexities and demands on expertise and resources needed when complex management systems are introduced.

Conclusion

In conclusion, the Soft Systems Methodology (SSM) applied to structuring a debate and identifying strategies for improvement of the complex practice of natural hazards risk management in New Zealand, provided for structured relationship management, coherence, both internal and with the purpose, adaptivity, trans-boundary approach, focus on process and its quality and transparency, and accent on dialogue and mediation, with allowance for constant re-negotiation of outcomes. Those elements deliver on the key reference beacons for this research in terms of requirements on complexity management.

The approach also resulted in concrete recommendations for changes to the framework and practice, as well as strategies for implementation, in relation to the shortcomings identified earlier (the author, 2006).

The weaknesses of the approach were identified as well, as discussed in the previous paragraph.

In delivering on those objectives SSM has addressed most of the weaknesses of the integrated environmental risk management for natural hazards identified previously. Moreover, in the course of its implementation it has provided learning for all involved, thus doubly strengthening the resilience of the management system.

Application of SSM in this case has also opened up planning processes to greater participation by a variety of stakeholders, in a structured and consistent manner. The methodology delivered on the requirements for environmental governance characterized by the wider involvement of interested parties, both in policy formulation and in implementation processes. It allowed for transparency and consistency, within the legislative framework of the planning system. Those are principles central to integrated planning that form a basis for sustainable management.

In addition, the methodology has delivered on requirements for effective integrated and adaptive management and capacity building, by enabling each participant/stakeholder in the exercise to understand the whole IERM management regime, with all its critical elements and relationships, regardless of their particular place in the matrix of this regime, while primarily managing relationships, in an adaptive and transparent manner.

It has also provided a blueprint/model for management of risks from natural hazards.

In terms of SSM methodology as an analytical approach, no specific adjustments to methodology as such were required. However, time and other work related pressures on participants dictated that a pragmatic approach be taken and a number of models to be used in final workshops reduced to one. Generally, the approach requires a substantial commitment of time and energy of the participants, a very rare commodity in the present day workplace climate. This may prove to be its major shortcoming. However, the usefulness of the results achieved by the truncated, one model, approach suggests that it can be adjusted to fit in with time and other constraints.

In addition to the above, as a part of its discourse, the thesis argued for a 'middle of the road, or 'boundary' approach, in an effort to bridge the gap created in the last 30 years between positivist and post-modern currents in theory and practice. It is often argued that this led to the situation in which process planning substituted spatial, physical planning and the object of planning – human settlement – became neglected. This also led to a planning profession been challenged in terms of what constitutes its 'expertise'. The focus of planning on process solely is present in New Zealand. One of the examples of its impact is reflected in the critique often laid against the RMA and its emphasis on cumbersome processes vs. resource management efficiency. This work introduces a possibility for the planner to re-claim expertise, while still remaining a participatory process facilitator. It does, however, pose a challenge to planning education in terms of fostering managers of change that can successfully, and consistently, deal with complexity.

This conclusion is even more pertinent considering that the research has revealed a New Zealand environmental planning and risk management regime as being fundamentally systemic, as are, indeed, the generic requirements for any planning regime for sustainability. In that respect the thesis has drawn attention to the need for caution when transformative frameworks and processes of land use planning for natural hazards are argued for at this hour. It was demonstrated that the New Zealand planning regime, including provisions for management of risks from natural hazards, fundamentally has all of the necessary characteristics to deliver on integrated management. It is the *implementation* and *capacity* that were identified as the core issues.

The research has identified mainly senior, strategic level planning and policy oriented participants as being really responsive to systems approaches. It was observed that, generally, the higher the strategic level a person is operating at, the more sympathetic they were towards systems approaches. They were also more knowledgeable of the framework as the whole. Considering that, if a systemic regime is to function, an understanding of its purpose, components and processes has to exist at all levels this is of concern. The least familiar with the systemic nature of the planning and risk management regime appeared to be scientists and social scientists in a crown research institution, and some risk managers.

The above reflects an indication that, if integrated approaches are to be operationalised, it is necessary to provide senior level, strategic leadership across the spectrum, including traditionally 'reductionist' areas such as science and science-based institutions. However, this would have to be only a transitional step toward permeating the whole practice with systems knowledge and skills. In effect, applying systems approach in practice would mean, in many cases, a *redesign of research strategies and projects*, as well as project teams, on a consistent and long-term basis.

This means, that, effectively, a new type of expertise is required. Building the capacity for this is a formidable task. However, as the research has demonstrated, if sustainable outcomes are indeed to be achieved, complexity and integrative management systems are here to stay.

References

Brown, D. 1990, Integrating Environmental Ethics with Science and Law, *The Environmental Professional*, Vol. 12, NAEP, pp. 344-350

Byrne, D., 2003 Complexity Theory and Planning Theory: a Necessary Encounter, *Planning Theory*, vol 2(3): 171–178

Centre for Advanced Engineering, 2004, *Planning for Natural Hazard Risk in the Built Environment*, CAE, Christchurch

Checkland, P., 2000, Soft Systems Methodology: A Thirty Year Retrospective, *Systems Research and Behavioral Science*, Syst. Res. 17, pg. 11-58

Checkland, P. 1999, *Soft Systems Methodology: A Thirty Year Retrospective*, John Wiley & Sons, Chichester, England

Checkland, P.1981, *Systems Thinking, Systems Practice*. Jn Wiley & Sons, Chichester, Sussex, UK.

Checkland P, Holwell S. 1998. *Information, Systems and Information Systems: Making Sense of the Field*. Wiley: Chichester

Ericksen, N., Berke, P., Crawford. J. and J. Dixon (2003). *Plan-Making for Sustainability: New Zealand Under the RMA*. Hamilton: International GlobalChange Institute, University of Waikato. (Also published for international market by Ashgate, 350 pp.)

Fischer, F., 1996, Risk Assessment and Environmental Crisis: Toward an Integration of science and Participation, in Campbell, S. and Fainstain, S. (Eds.), *Readings in Planning Theory*, Blackwell Publishers, Oxford, pp. 485-506

Glasbergen, P. (edit.) 1998, *Co-operative Environmental Governance*, Kluwer Academic Publishers, Dordrecht

Innes, J., 1997, The Planners' Century, *Journal of Planning Education and Research*, Vol. 16, No 3, p. 227

Jackson, M. C., 2001. Critical Systems Thinking and Practice. *European Journal of Operational Research* 128: 233-244

Jaeger, C., Ortwin, R., Rosa, E. And Webler, T. 2001, *Risk, Uncertainty, and Rational Action*, EarthscanPublications Ltd, London, pp.320

Kerr, J., Nathan, S., Van Dissen, R., Webb, P., Brunsdon, D. and King, A., 2003, *Planning for Development on Land on or Close to Active Faults: An interim guideline to assist resource management planners in New Zealand*, Ministry for the environment and institute of Geological and Nuclear sciences, Wellington, pp. 58

Ledington PWJ, Ledington J. 1999. The Problem of Comparison in Soft Systems Methodology. *Systems Research and Behavioral Science* 16: 329-339

Margolis, H. 1996, *Dealing with Risk: Why the Public and the Experts Disagree on Environmental Issues*, The University of Chicago Press, Chicago, pp. 227

May, P., Burby, R.J., Ericksen, N., Handmer, J.W., Dixon, J.E., Michaels, S. and Smith, I., 1996, *Environmental Management and Governance: Intergovernmental approaches to hazards and Sustainability,* Routledge, London/New York, pp. 254

Mazmanian, D. A., and Kraft, M. E., (Eds.), 1999, *Toward Sustainable Communities: Transition and Transformation in Environmental Policy*, MIT Press, Cambridge, Mass.

Parliamentary Commissioner for the Environment, 2001, *Building on the Edge – The Use and Development of Land On or Close to Fault Lines*, Ministry for the Environment, Wellington

Parliamentary Commissioner for the Environment, 2004, *Missing Links:*
Connecting Science with Environmental Policy, Office of the Parliamentary Commissioner for the Environment, Wellington

Theme 8:
Social Systems

36. The Theory and Practice of Boundary Critique: An Application to Community Involvement in Water Conservation

PLENARY PAPER

Jeffrey L. Foote[1], Jan E. Gregor[1], Maria C. Hepi[1], Virginia E. Baker[1], Don J. Houston[2], Gerald Midgley[1,3-6]
[1]Institute of Environmental Science and Research (ESR) Ltd., NZ
[2]Institute of Technology and Engineering, Massey University, NZ
[3]School of Management, Victoria University of Wellington, NZ;
[4]School of Sociology and Anthropology, University of Canterbury, NZ
[5]Centre for Systems Studies, Business School, University of Hull, UK
[6]School of Natural and Rural Systems Management, University of Queensland, AUS

Boundary critique is a theory and set of methodological ideas for exploring the inclusion, exclusion and marginalization of both people and issues. This paper argues that boundary critique can enhance systemic intervention. An application of boundary critique is presented to illustrate the argument, focusing on community participation in the management of ongoing water shortages in a small seaside town in New Zealand. The theory of boundary critique helped to reframe people's understanding of a thirty-year conflict between the District Council and community. This led to the design of a participative workshop, and a way forward was identified that both the District Council and community could accept. Feedback from the workshop participants suggested that the intervention generated valuable results for all the parties involved.

Introduction

This paper describes the theory of *boundary critique*, which is a key aspect of the methodology of systemic intervention (Midgley, 2000). Systemic intervention asks practitioners to work with stakeholders to explore the issues of relevance to them prior to creatively designing or mixing methods. As part of this exploration, boundary critique offers practitioners a set of ideas to inform the *systemic* exploration of issues. A core concern in being systemic is to explore what, and whose views, should be included in, or excluded from, an intervention (Churchman, 1970; Ulrich, 1983; Midgley, 2000). We support our theoretical and methodological argument with a practical example of how boundary critique informed the selection and mixing of collaborative methods to structure community involvement in an evaluation of a water supply strategy for a small seaside community facing ongoing water shortages.

In the systemic intervention described in this paper, boundary critique was pivotal in building stakeholders' understandings of the problematic situation and guiding the team's selection of an appropriate mix of methods to systemically deal with a long-term and ingrained value conflict over the community's water supply. Specifically, we used boundary critique to make definitions of the problem context explicit from a variety of different points of view. Using it, we argue that we were able to identify important areas of agreement and disagreement between stakeholders, as well as the dynamics of marginalization that were critical in preventing the on-going conflict from being satisfactorily resolved. We also argue that boundary critique was instrumental in enabling the team to consider, in advance of implementation, how specific methods might impact on the situation of concern. Thus it was useful in guiding the selection of those methods that the team thought would be most likely to produce meaningful participation and allow a successful and sustainable systemic intervention to be undertaken.

Below, we outline the theory of boundary critique before illustrating how this informed our choice of a variety of methods for use in our water management intervention.

The Theory of Boundary Critique

The term 'boundary critique' was first coined by Ulrich (1996) and was then used by Midgley, *et al.* (1998) to consolidate various writings (e.g., Churchman, 1970; Ulrich, 1983; Midgley, 1992) on how value and boundary judgements should be made during interventions. Only a brief overview of boundary critique is offered here. For more details see Midgley, *et al.* (1998) and Midgley (2000).

Churchman (1970) notes that where the boundaries of analysis are placed in systems projects has important consequences, given that these boundaries determine how improvement is defined and problems are managed. Boundaries indicate what information is considered relevant and what is considered superfluous, and are the result of value judgements. Churchman (1970) recommends that the boundaries of an analysis should be pushed out to 'sweep in' as much information as possible (without making the analysis incomprehensible), to test the adequacy of the intended improvement in the light of alternative perspectives.

Ulrich (1983) takes this work a stage further by discussing how the exploration and setting of boundaries can be undertaken through dialogue between stakeholders, making boundary judgements more 'rational' and robust than if simply imposed by planners or external researchers in the absence of meaningful community participation (see Ulrich, 1983, for details of what it means to him to undertake 'rational analysis'). The implication here is that the most 'rational' boundary is not necessarily the widest possible, but the one that is agreed to be most ethical and useful by those involved in and affected by an intervention (the meaningful participation of the affected being crucial).

Midgley (1992, 2000) then builds on Ulrich's work by arguing that there is often more going on in projects than just the inclusion or exclusion of stakeholders and issues: it is not uncommon to find particular groups and the issues that concern them becoming *marginalized* – neither fully included nor excluded from the system, and subject to strong labelling and ritual treatment. Midgley (2000) talks about marginalized people and issues being made 'sacred' or 'profane' to indicate the potency of the valuing or devaluing that they are subject to. He also offers two models of marginalization processes, demonstrating how marginalization comes about through conflicts between groups making different value and boundary judgements, and how it can become entrenched in institutional arrangements. One of these models proved to be particularly useful in our intervention to address the ingrained conflict around water shortages (see later in this paper).

Additionally, Midgley (2000) argues that boundary critique can support the practice of methodological pluralism (drawing upon methods from a variety of paradigmatic sources to enhance flexibility and responsiveness) by being explicit about values and power relations and requiring more penetrating explorations of problematic situations than most systems methodologies ask for. Midgley suggests that explorations informed by the theory of boundary critique almost always result in the design of multi-layered interventions, involving the creative mixing of methods, which is in marked contrast to some other pluralist methodologies where more superficial diagnostic strategies tend to result in simple choices between 'off-the-shelf' methods. The implication is that systemic intervention informed by boundary critique is more flexible and responsive than these other methodologies. The means by which boundary critique feeds into the creative design/mixing of methods has been illustrated through a number of case studies (e.g., Midgley, *et al.*, 1998; Midgley, 2000; Boyd, *et al.*, 2004; Córdoba & Midgley, 2006), and can also be demonstrated through reflection on our water management intervention (detailed below).

The Local Context

Our intervention took place in a seaside township – a small but popular tourist destination in New Zealand. It has a permanent population of just 800 people that swells to an estimated 5,000 with an influx of non-permanent residents and tourists during peak holiday seasons. The land pattern in the harbour catchment area is steeply sloping and relatively barren. Unlike other New Zealand cities and towns that have access to major rivers or underground aquifers, only three small streams supply water to the township. Rainfall patterns make the stream volumes highly variable and greatly reduced in the summer months or in times of drought, which can last several months. Drought conditions tend to coincide with the greatest influx of holiday-makers to the area.

Although the township has long been a popular tourist destination, the decline of the agricultural sector since the 1980s has seen its survival increasingly depend upon economic contributions made by growing numbers of non-resident ratepayers and tourists. At the time we entered the picture, the town's small rating base and limited access to water sources had put the District Council (the local government body with responsibility for urban water services) in a challenging position to provide the community with a constant high quality water supply at an acceptable cost. Furthermore, issues around water scarcity and conservation had been a long-standing point of contention between the District Council and the permanent resident community. Prior to our involvement, successive political administrations had failed to reach a satisfactory solution to the ongoing water shortages despite growing expressions of concern by the community. Council officers indicated that the issues had at least a thirty-year history, with one person suggesting that they were first recognized as long ago as the 1950s. More recently, however, the District Council had adopted a ten-year water supply strategy. This had been approved in principle but had not yet been enacted. It consisted of long-term infrastructure upgrades, as well as short-term water conservation initiatives, including universal water metering. The short-term measures were intended as a stopgap and were seen as instrumental in reducing the likely cost of the longer-term infrastructure upgrades.

Anticipating a particularly dry summer, the District Council initiated a save-water campaign building on existing water restrictions, including alternative-day hosing bans and bylaws requiring the installation of water-efficient appliances in new property developments. Various save-water initiatives were proposed (with advice from a public relations company), ranging from door-to-door visits to poster displays of water conservation measures. However, budgetary pressures meant that the only initiatives actually implemented were (i) newspaper advertising to raise residents' awareness of water scarcity and conservation; and (ii) signs to inform residents and tourists that water restrictions were in force.

Our team engaged with the District Council's Water Supply Committee to evaluate the water conservation campaign. The District Council was keen to adopt a participatory systemic intervention approach (Midgley, 2000) to engage with the community over the issue of water scarcity in recognition of the fact that the effectiveness of the water conservation campaign depended on the cooperation of all users in the watershed. However, communication with the community was problematic for the District Council. First, it lacked expertise and resources for in-depth consultation; second, it was unsure how to best negotiate competing social, economic, environmental and cultural concerns; and third, the community, frustrated with previous consultation exercises (which were seen as either pre-determined, or evidence of the District Council's inability to reach a decision), were deemed 'difficult' to work with. In this context, the ability of our team to intervene as a relatively 'independent' third party was highly valued.

For the purposes of this paper we will set aside any further discussion of the issue of 'independence', which is inevitably problematic in interventions – but it is sufficient to note that the local stakeholders *viewed* us as independent, in the sense that we were not 'captured' by any single agency agenda. In particular, we were not paid by the District Council: financial support for the intervention came from the Foundation for Research, Science and Technology, as it was part of a larger research programme to develop and test systems methodology for water management.

The work was planned in three parts, each shaped by aspects of systemic intervention (Midgley, 2000) – including boundary critique, methodological pluralism and reflections on various understandings of improvement in the local situation. First, the evaluation would start with the team interviewing a variety of stakeholders to surface issues relating to water conservation. Second, we would produce reflections on the water conservation campaign, although just how this was to be done was left open pending the findings from the interviews. Third, we would facilitate a stakeholder workshop to (i) assist the District Council with community involvement, and (ii) improve the water conservation campaign for the summer. Thus the stakeholder interviews/evaluation would inform the boundary critique, which would in turn guide the team in selecting the most appropriate methods for the workshop.

Boundary Critique for Evaluation and Intervention

The District Council agreed to sponsor the research with the understanding that a diverse range of people would be interviewed, including those not considered key audiences in the District Council's water conservation campaign – e.g., property developers and Māori (the indigenous people of New Zealand). Interviewees were asked to recommend others with different viewpoints to their own, as well as those that might be involved in or affected by the water conservation strategy. The boundaries of participation in the evaluation were finalized when interviewees stopped suggesting new names and conceptual saturation occurred, indicating that most (if not all) key issues were surfaced. Interviews were chosen as an appropriate way to surface stakeholder viewpoints as they enabled the team to uncover a range of stakeholder perspectives, as well as providing a confidential space to discuss difficult issues which stakeholders may not have felt comfortable raising in a workshop setting.

In total, 40 individuals (including councillors, council staff, business owners, permanent and non-permanent residents) were interviewed. The interviews explored perceptions of water scarcity, and comment was specifically sought on the District Council's ten-year water supply strategy. Interviews were tape-recorded for later transcription, and were analyzed using the grounded theory procedure of open coding (Strauss & Corbin, 1999). This approach helped to identify and develop emerging concepts that accounted for stakeholder viewpoints, building a rich description of the issues characterizing the management of the watershed.

Given difficulties in recruiting a sufficient number of non-permanent resident interviewees, and the risk of marginalizing these perspectives, a survey was sent out to 600 of the township's 724 non-resident ratepayers. A total of 326 responses were received and analyzed using simple exploratory data analysis techniques including descriptive statistics and box-plots (Erickson & Nosanchuk, 1979). The 40 stakeholder interviews and survey data surfaced a variety of issues, and our analysis of these fed into the production of an evaluation report.

Evaluation Findings

Our findings are presented briefly below, organized into stakeholder perspectives. This way of structuring the material enabled us to conduct a marginalization analysis (an aspect of boundary critique discussed later).

Permanent and non-permanent resident viewpoints

Resident rate payers were generally supportive of the water conservation messages, but opinion was split amongst the permanent and non-permanent residents over which group was responsible for excessive demands made on the water supply, and accordingly, who should bear the burden of responsibility for curtailing water-dependent activities.

Non-permanent residents were critical of permanent residents with flourishing flower and vegetable gardens. However, these permanent residents regarded themselves as conservation minded. Many were senior citizens and depended on their vegetable gardens to subsidise limited incomes, and thus they felt that they only broke the water restrictions out of necessity. In contrast, they claimed that the non-permanent residents knowingly ignored the water restrictions while flushing out speedboat motors and watering flower gardens and lawns. Some permanent residents expressed concern that the township had become a 'playground' for non-permanent residents and tourists who engaged in water-dependent activities at times when the water shortages were the most acute. Indeed, some permanent residents were adamant that the existing water supply was sufficient to support the town's 800 permanent residents, if only the non-permanent residents would go away.

The non-permanent residents tended to respond to these criticisms by arguing that they paid the same rates as permanent residents yet used less water in total per annum than their permanent neighbors. For this reason many non-permanent residents reasoned that they had a right to use as much water as they wanted, irrespective that the town's reservoir could only store two to three days of treated drinking water.

However, the permanent and non-permanent residents both agreed that having to connect new properties to the town's water supply served to aggravate the existing water shortages. Therefore, a number of residents expressed a reluctance to conserve water, perceiving that any individual effort to save water was a poor guarantee of future surety for the town's supply, given the perception that any individual savings would be negated by the impacts of further housing developments.

Business viewpoints

Businesses in the area depend on tourists and non-permanent residents. Business owners were interested in solving the water problem because water is crucial to the survival of most of their enterprises. Nevertheless, whilst agreeing to conservation in principle, business owners were concerned about how visible the crisis ought to be. Many thought the prominent water restriction sign on entering the township was inappropriate, feeling that a positive image was important for the tourism industry: for example, a Business Promoter said that it was 'not good for tourists to be reminded of all the negative things'. Overall this group expressed a strong preference that the crisis be managed 'invisibly' so as not to impinge on the activities of the transient visitors.

District Council viewpoints

A zoning decision taken in the early 1980s meant that the District Council had little option but to connect new households to the town water supply. If they failed to do so, the District Council risked litigation from landowners wanting to subdivide existing properties.

A number of councillors, real estate owners and business owners saw further development as having an important part to play in funding future infrastructure upgrades, given the District Council's small rating base. For these reasons, the District Council had resisted the attempts of permanent and non-permanent residents to reframe the water scarcity problem in terms of the consequences of development.

Boundary Critique for the Identification and Depiction of Tensions and Conflicts

Van Vugt (2002) identifies a number of factors that undermine the effectiveness of water conservation initiatives. Namely, people are unlikely to conserve water if they (i) perceive the cause of the water scarcity to be due to the activities of self-interested individuals; (ii) perceive a lack of personal benefit; or (iii) have questions over the efficacy of water conserving actions. The themes identified through the interviews suggested that *all* these conditions were present, indicating a number of weaknesses with the District Council's short-term water conservation campaign that would also be likely to undermine the ten-year water supply strategy.

In addition, it was discovered that underlying the visible water scarcity debate was a conflict between two values: an anti-development (or limited development) value which sought to preserve the heritage and integrity of the township, and a pro-development value where residential expansion and the promotion of tourism were perceived to be vital to building the township's economic and rating base. This conflict is depicted in Figure 1. It should be noted, however, that Figure 1 represents just one of several conflicts in the watershed that were addressed through our research – it was by no means the sole focus. Nevertheless, giving a single concrete example is useful in terms of illustrating the value of boundary critique.

While the two groups with different values shared an interest in maintaining the integrity of the township's water supply, the conflicts over strategy remained highly charged. At the time of the research, the District Council afforded primacy to economic development. Nevertheless, they had found themselves in a precarious position in their attempts to balance competing economic, environmental and social concerns. In this respect it is significant that the save-water campaign targeted existing residents, and not tourists or even future residents. Addressing concerns about subdivisions and increased tourist numbers would have required a political solution: the transcendence of some

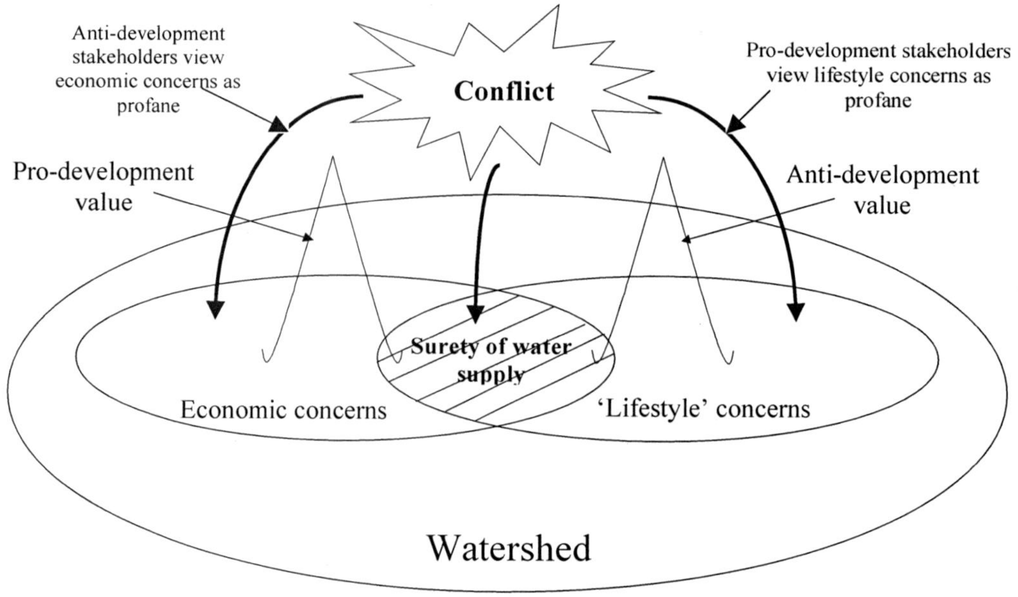

Figure 1 *Conflict in the watershed, depicted using the boundary critique diagramming conventions developed by Midgley (2000) and Yolles (2001).*

existing interests, and a widening of the boundaries to include discussion about the nature and role of development within the township. Indeed, the focus of the save-water campaign on providing individual households with information about water conservation depoliticized the water scarcity issue and decoupled the save-water campaign from the debate about economic development. Given the inherent difficulty in ensuring a secure water supply in light of ongoing development, the save-water campaign can be viewed from this perspective as an attempt to *contain* or *stabilise* the conflict generated by the two values, rather than provide any sustainable resolution.

While conflicts like this can indeed be stabilized rather than resolved, the theory of boundary critique proposes that this is often achieved by processes of marginalization where some people and/or issues are devalued and derogated (regarded as profane) by those who work in, or can command the support of, the key institutions of authority (Midgley, 1992, 2000). The result is likely to be a dismissive attitude towards alternative perspectives, leading to mutual distrust. Constructive dialogue becomes difficult and strategic battles ensue where each side uses whatever means it has at its disposal to either enforce its own preferred strategy (in the case of an institution of authority), or to resist this enforcement (in the case of people who find themselves marginalized). In the case of a water conservation campaign, where the acceptance and involvement of the population is crucial to success, strategic battles of this kind will most likely have a fatal impact on the campaign.

From this analysis, in our evaluation report and in our discussions with Council officers, we challenged the District Council's position that water conservation should be decoupled from the broader debate on the desirability of economic development. This was problematic for a number of people. From the standpoint of the District Council, the issue of economic development was deemed to lie outside the boundary of the problem. Indeed, from their perspective, its continued resurgence had long frustrated their attempts to gain feedback on the proposed strategy to reduce ongoing water shortages. While the District Council saw merit in involving the community, previous attempts at consultation had proven problematic for all parties. Community members who attended earlier Council workshops had seen the consultation as either too prescriptive, or evidence of the District Council's inability to reach a decision and display strong leadership. The council engineers also found the workshops unhelpful. In their view, some community members hijacked the process by raising issues beyond the remit of the water supply strategy (concerning economic development), meaning that incorporating community feedback into the strategy was difficult at best. The result was a situation characterized by ill feeling and mistrust. The District Council therefore perceived consultation as 'high risk', holding the potential to cloud the main issues with what were perceived as 'extraneous' concerns, and creating a vicious cycle where existing interests would become further entrenched, making the resolution of the ongoing water shortages unlikely.

A Community Workshop to Renegotiate the Boundaries

Despite these reservations, the District Council went ahead with the third aspect of our intervention. They organized a community workshop for our team to present the findings from the evaluation of the water conservation campaign and for the council engineers and their technical consultants to consult with the community over the ten-year water supply strategy. Wanting to avoid a repetition of some of the problems mentioned above, we worked with a representative of the District Council to design the workshop using a mix of different systems methods.

In the run-up to designing this workshop, we explained to the council engineers that decoupling the water scarcity problem from issues of economic development only served to frustrate attempts to manage the ongoing water shortages. For this reason we suggested that, instead of viewing community concerns about economic development as intrusions into the Council's definition of the problem, they could more positively be regarded as valid and useful feedback for improving the effectiveness of the water conservation strategy. Unless some existing interests could be transcended, and for a organization to constructively debate the desirability of economic development, the water supply strategy would most likely continue to be undermined by conflict between pro- and anti-development values. In structuring our discussions with Council officers and engineers, we found the diagramming conventions of boundary critique (e.g., Figure 1) very useful. The engineers clearly understood the problem when we discussed it with them in these terms.

Nevertheless, although the boundary critique enhanced understanding of the issues, the council engineers and the Water Supply Committee initially disagreed with our conclusion that the Council would need to discuss the desirability of economic development with the community. Since housing and subdivisions (a key aspect of economic development) were governed by the District Plan, the District Council saw the issue as being more appropriately debated as part of the district planning process, and not during consultation about the water supply strategy.

This continuing reluctance to include the economic development issue in the workshop agenda posed an ethical dilemma for our team. Would it be better to accept the constraint being imposed on us, or withdraw our services? We clearly had credibility as a relatively 'independent' third party, so to accept the constraint could have further marginalized community perspectives, making the workshop little more than a sophisticated public relations exercise. However, if we could continue our engagements, we might be able to reintroduce the development issue at a later date, enabling more meaningful community involvement. Eventually, we decided to remain engaged on the grounds that we could do more of value by continuing to communicate with the Council than by withdrawing. We had three reasons for making this judgement. First, all the stakeholders agreed that the ongoing water shortages were undesirable and needed to be managed, although existing residents expressed concern that property developers and/or future residents needed to take more responsibility for managing the water scarcity problem. Second, the District Council and its engineers saw community ownership as critical: a ten year plan would cut across approximately four council terms, making it important that community support was robust and enduring. Third, from an activity theory perspective (Engeström, 2000), contradictions can act as springboards to generate new tools and understandings, which can shift existing patterns of control, expertise and legitimacy. It was therefore hoped that, when the District Council were engaged with the community using systems methods, and the community representatives raised their concerns in this context, the District Council would begin to see the value of allowing economic development to be put on the agenda.

As well as providing a way to critique the District Council's approach to community involvement, the analysis depicted in Figure 1 suggested a way forward that would allow community viewpoints to be incorporated into the water supply strategy. We designed the workshop to enable feedback on our evaluation as well as critical and creative reflection on the ten-year water supply strategy. Whilst economic development was not mentioned *explicitly* as a boundary issue, the format of the workshop would allow the researchers to present the data using the community's voices in the form of quotations to make the broader social and political context clear.

Additionally, the boundary critique and subsequent negotiations with the District Council guided the team in selecting a combination of methods that would be both acceptable to the Council and encourage a broad 'sweep in' of issues, including previously marginalized viewpoints. The key question coming out of our boundary critique that we needed to address through the choice of an appropriate set of methods was, 'how can we ensure that the Council is able to consult on its technical proposals (their primary concern) *and* allow the development issue to emerge, but in a manner that is closely *connected* with the

Council's proposals?' We hypothesized that only by enabling such a connection to be made would the Council be able to fully appreciate the importance of the development issue to their agenda. Essentially, we needed *systemic* methods, able to support the participants in learning how issues interacted across their boundaries of concern.

The methods we chose were a combination of 'scenario building' (e.g., Andrews, 1992; Ravetz, 2000), to enable the production of best and worst case scenarios related to the Council's predefined technological proposals; and 'rich picturing' (Checkland, 1981; Checkland & Scholes, 1990), a method which encourages participants to co-create a visual representation of an issue. Rich pictures usually take the form of cartoon-like drawings with arrows denoting interactions and relationships. While Checkland (1981) prefers to limit rich picturing to the representation of 'real world' problem situations, we adapted the technique to support participants in constructing visual portrayals of possible future scenarios.

We anticipated that this scenario building approach would enable the participants to connect the development issue to the evaluation of the Council's technical proposals. These proposals were to be used as the primary focus, but in constructing best and worst case future scenarios for the technological solutions, the participants would be required to think about the environment (including the potential scope of residential and economic development) which made the future appear desirable or not. In particular, the participants would have to think through how the technological solutions might enable or constrain the emergence of desirable and undesirable futures, taking into account different viewpoints on desirability.

In addition, we thought that the use of rich pictures would add value by facilitating creative exploration and the co-construction of understandings; allow the representation of different viewpoints; and (with facilitation) support the identification of underlying conflicts and values.

The Workshop

Our use of boundary critique had given us good knowledge of the stakeholder and community demographics. In applying our methods, we were therefore careful to ensure that the physical layout of the workshop would enable meaningful participation. For instance, many of our community participants were at retirement age, including several who were hard of hearing. This made it important to have separate spaces for the breakout groups so people did not have to struggle to hear each other over the noise being created by other groups. We also provided both easels and tables for the flipcharts so that people could choose to stand or sit according to their needs and preferences.

Approximately 50 permanent and non-permanent residents, the Mayor, the Water Supply Committee, council engineers and their technical consultants attended the workshop. It began with the team presenting the findings from the evaluation of the water conservation campaign along with community impressions about the ten-year water supply strategy. Community concerns were mirrored back to the District Council using quotations from our interviews. This process helped the workshop participants to distance themselves from the conflicts expressed, and to recognise community concerns as evidence of contradictions in how the watershed was managed rather than seeing them as personal faults (Engeström, 2000). For the council engineers, engaging with the quotations and responses of the workshop participants helped them realize the significance of the fact that the water scarcity issue existed in a broader social and political context. Even at this early stage in the workshop they began to accept that this needed to be taken into account before the community could commit to the water supply strategy.

After discussions of the evaluation findings, the council engineers and their technical consultants made presentations about the ten-year water supply strategy. Following these, our team facilitated the scenario building exercise to draw out the community expectations and concerns surrounding the implementation of various elements of the strategy. The workshop participants broke into six small groups and were instructed to construct either a best case or worse case scenario associated with the water conservation campaign, universal water metering, and planned infrastructure upgrade projects. As discussed earlier, each scenario was captured by workshop participants in the form of a rich picture (Checkland, 1981; Checkland & Scholes, 1990), which was then presented back to the wider group.

Each group was also asked to identify (i) a key positive expectation, and (ii) a concern for comment or response in the workshop. For the District Council, the positive expectations suggested performance measures of the water supply strategy, while the community concerns signalled possible implementation barriers that would need to be addressed as part of the strategy development process. With consent from the workshop participants, the discussion was tape-recorded.

Outcomes

While previous workshop discussions between the District Council and the community had been polarized, in this case the evaluation results, quotations and scenario building exercise helped mediate between the diverse viewpoints held by the District Council and the other workshop participants. In a subsequent workshop with the Water Supply Committee, the community's concerns and expectations were further deliberated with a recommendation made to full Council that their universal water-metering project should stay in the budget, and the council engineers should continue with the implementation of this aspect of their strategy. Community concerns over the fairness and equity of the charging regime, originally expressed in our workshop, prompted the Water Supply Committee to recommend that a representative group of water users in the community should help develop a metering policy and charging regime using data from a full year of 'dummy' meter readings. Possibilities for the charging regime would include that each property be allocated a daily water allowance (attracting a uniform annual charge), with only 'excess' consumption charged at a higher rate, and that monthly meter readings would be taken during times of water scarcity.

A key outcome from our own workshop was community support or 'buy in' for the water conservation strategy and water metering, provided that the charging regime could be accepted as equitable. In addition, constructive feedback on our approach was received from the workshop attendees, with one long time community activist commenting in a tape recorded discussion at the end of the workshop that in 'six years of meetings' with the council on the water issue, this was 'one of the more positive'. Council engineers also found the meeting 'fun', in contrast to some previous exchanges with the community. Other council members noted that the workshop forum achieved 'good results' and generated 'worthwhile discussion without getting at each other's throats'.

For both our team and the community, the workshop was successful in allowing the broader concerns around development to be articulated and acknowledged by the District Council. The facilitated forum was equally valuable for the District Council in that they were able (despite their initial reservations) to link the concerns over development and equitable charging to their immediate agenda, thereby ensuring that the ten-year supply and water conservation strategies achieved community consent. In feedback following the intervention, the council engineer with responsibility for the water supply strategy wrote:

'The decision-making tools ... have allowed a wide range of stakeholders to be actively involved in the decision-making process. The methods employed have provided a non-threatening environment for stakeholders to express their views and this participation has led to general acceptance of the consultation outcomes' (Council Engineer)

Reflections

Below we provide some general reflections on the intervention before drawing some conclusions on the value of boundary critique to systemic intervention.

Overall, the systemic intervention resulted in good local outcomes as perceived by the various people involved: there was significant learning, exchanges of ideas, and increased understanding amongst the various stakeholders of others' positions and values. Factors contributing to the success of this work, aside from the use of boundary critique, included the intersecting interests of the District Council and our team, and the perception that we constituted a relatively 'independent' third party. This third party involvement was important for legitimacy, and also because the Council engineers were not comfortable using systems methods on their own. The ability of the team to negotiate on behalf of the community, explore community dynamics with the District Council, and broker the diverse stakeholder interests (both informally and in the formal workshop), was also an important factor in making the intervention successful.

However, some cautionary points are worth noting. Systemic intervention can establish sound process, as can other participative and pluralist approaches (e.g., Mingers & Gill, 1997; Rosenhead & Mingers, 2001), but it cannot *guarantee* win-win outcomes for all. Ultimately, transcending narrow interests is dependent on the willingness of key players to participate. Pressure for participation can be exerted by building strategic alliances (Vega-Romero,

1999), and by encouraging mutual learning (Midgley, 2000), but there can never be iron-clad guarantees. In our view, however, this should not be regarded as a weakness of systemic intervention and boundary critique. The days when researchers tried to engage in social engineering, believing that they had the ability (and the right) to produce pre-planned outcomes, are long gone (White & Taket, 1993; Midgley, 2003). Today, a more realistic understanding pervades that systems practitioners are players in the game, not observers transcending and manipulating it.

Another issue is that project opportunities often come with inherent risks of client capture. Were it not for the eventual willingness of the District Council to genuinely explore and address the community's concerns, our final workshop could easily have become a slickly managed package to soften up the community and smooth the implementation of technical solutions (e.g., water metering) within a strategy that remained contentious. In this instance the District Council was the manager of the problem and the gatekeeper. Criticism could be levelled at us that the intervention left many aspects of the underlying economic/lifestyle tension unchallenged due to the focus of the research on decision-making for water, and the need for our team to build its reputation and signal to potential clients that it is a useful rather than unruly agent. From this position, it could be claimed that we were overly instrumental, taking for granted the pre-defined end of addressing the water scarcity issue. Indeed, it is possible that some community members secretly *welcomed* ongoing water shortages, since this placed physical limits on housing, subdivisions and tourist numbers, and reminded the District Council that the desirability of economic development is contested:

"*If we were terribly successful [in addressing the water scarcity issue] then we may get even more development here and tourists may overrun us.... We would destroy the nature, the character and the very fabric of the community – the things we love about the place.*" (Comment from the Community Workshop)

The possibility of such a future consequence raises the issue of whether our team had actually been 'captured' by the District Council, despite the wide spread perception that this was not the case. This is a matter for judgement. Ours is that we were *not* captured. We have two reasons for saying this: first, the integrity of the water supply was recognized as an issue by all the stakeholders, including those opposed to further development; and second, we sought to overcome the District Council's resistance to incorporating people's concerns about economic development. Whilst there was more to the development issue than was dealt with in our project, it was at least put on the agenda in a meaningful way.

Related to this, a further power dynamic is noted. The Māori (local indigenous) representatives we interviewed decided not to be actively involved in the community workshop on the grounds that they had a separate water supply to their township, and therefore did not need to negotiate with mainstream authorities in this instance. However, the interdependencies within a watershed or catchment area mean that this position could change in the future. The invitation to be involved in the evaluation of the District Council's ten-year water supply strategy may have been too narrow, with issues significant to the urban water cycle that might have engaged Māori in ongoing dialogue remaining outside the scope of inquiry. This is something for us (and others seeking to engage Māori in systemic intervention projects) to bear in mind for the future, and it signals something that the literature on boundary critique (Ulrich, 1983; Midgley, 2000) is quite clear about: boundary critique can help people explore issues of inclusion, exclusion and marginalization, but it cannot make analyses truly comprehensive – there will inevitably be issues beyond the focus of the exploration, simply because it is impossible for any individual or group to have a 'God's eye view' of the 'whole system'. Nevertheless, by recognizing the impossibility of genuine comprehensiveness, and by making explorations of boundaries and values a focus of inquiry, boundary critique enables *greater* comprehensive than simply taking boundaries and values for granted (Ulrich, 1983; Midgley, 2000; Midgley & Ochoa-Arias, 2004).

These concerns noted, this paper has focused on how boundary critique was used as a means for theoretical reflection to successfully build greater understanding and dialogue between the District Council and the wider community it served, as well as to enhance the effectiveness of their ten-year water supply strategy. We conclude, based on the evidence from this environmental management case study – and various applications to social issues reported in the literature also support this conclusion (e.g., Cohen & Midgley, 1994; Midgley, *et al.*, 1998; Midgley, 2000; Yolles, 2001; Foote, *et al.*, 2002; Boyd, *et al.*, 2004; Córdoba & Midgley, 2006) – that boundary critique can be a useful lead-in to systemic intervention, and can ultimately enable decision makers to make robust policy choices that are more inclusive of political, social, environmental and economic concerns than they might otherwise be.

Conclusion

This paper has presented a case study of how systemic intervention was used to support community involvement in water management, and how the methodological language of boundary critique enabled the team to conceptualise a long-term and ingrained conflict and creatively mix several systems methods to resolve it. Our experience with assisting the District Council to meaningfully involve the community shows that boundary critique can help make the processes of choosing and applying methods more systemic than they might otherwise be, in the sense that it can aid detailed reflection on boundaries for purposeful action.

Acknowledgements

We wish to acknowledge the assistance of Ann Winstanley and Alistair Sheat (ESR); Roberta Hill (WEBResearch Ltd); and Gail Tipa (Te Rūnanga o Moeraki, Te Rūnanga o Ngāi Tahu). Thanks are also due to the District Council and community members involved in the project we have reported. Finally, we acknowledge the financial support provided by the Foundation for Research, Science and Technology (FRST): contract C03X0304.

References

Andrews, C. J. (1992). "Sorting out a consensus: Analysis in support of multiparty decisions," *Environment and Planning B*, ISSN 0265-8135, 19: 189-204

Boyd, A., Brown, M. and Midgley, G. (2004). "Systemic intervention for community OR: Developing services with young people (under 16) living on the streets," in, G. Midgley and Ochoa-Arias A. E. (eds.), *Community Operational Research: OR and Systems Thinking for Community Development*, ISBN 0-306-48335, pp. 203-252.

Checkland, P. (1981). *Systems Theory, Systems Practice*, ISBN 0-471-27911-0.

Checkland, P. and Scholes, J. (1990). *Soft Systems Methodology in Action*, ISBN 0-471-92768-6.

Churchman, C. W. (1970). "Operations research as a profession," *Management Science*, ISSN 0025-1909, 17: B37-B53.

Cohen, C. and Midgley, G. (1994). *The North Humberside Diversion from Custody Project for Mentally Disordered Offenders: Research Report*, ISBN 0-85958-842-4.

Córdoba, J-R. and Midgley, G. (2006). "Broadening the Boundaries: An Application of Critical Systems Thinking to IS Planning in Colombia," *Journal of the Operational Research Society*, ISSN 0160-5682, 57: 1064-1080.

Engeström, Y. (2000). "Activity theory as a framework for analyzing and redesigning work," *Ergonomics*, ISSN 0014-0139, 43: 960–974.

Erickson, B. and Nosanchuk, T. (1979). *Understanding Data: An Introduction to Exploratory and Confirmatory Data Analysis for Students in the Social Sciences*, ISBN 0802073824.

Foote, J. L., Houston, D. J. and North, N. H. (2002). "Betwixt and between: Ritual and the management of an ultrasound waiting list," *Health Care Analysis*, ISSN 1065-3058, 10: 357–377.

Midgley, G. (1992). "The sacred and profane in critical systems thinking," *Systems Practice*, ISSN 0894-9859, 5: 5-16.

Midgley, G. (2000). *Systemic Intervention: Philosophy, Methodology and Practice*, ISBN 0-306-46488-8.

Midgley, G. (2003). "Systems thinking: an introduction and overview," in, G. Midgley (ed.), *Systems Thinking, Volume I: General Systems Theory, Cybernetics and Complexity*, ISBN 0-7619-4959-3.

Midgley, G., Munlo, I. and Brown, M. (1998). "The theory and practice of boundary critique: Developing housing services for older people," *Journal of the Operational Research Society*, ISSN 0160-5682, 49: 467-478.

Midgley, G. and Ochoa-Arias, A. E. (2004). "An introduction to community operational research," in, G. Midgley and A. E. Ochoa-Arias (eds.), *Community Operational Research: OR and Systems Thinking for Community Development*, ISBN 0-306-48335, pp. 1-36.

Mingers, J. and Gill, A. (eds.) (1997). *Multimethodology: The Theory and Practice of Combining Management Science Methodologies*, ISBN 0-471-97490-0.

Ravetz, J. (2000). *City Region 2020: Integrated Planning for a Sustainable Environment*, ISBN 1-8538-3606-0.

Rosenhead, J. and Mingers, J. (2001). *Rational Analysis for a Problematic World Revisited: Problem Structuring Methods for Complexity, Uncertainty and Conflict* (2nd ed.), ISBN 0-471-49523-9.

Strauss, A. and Corbin, J. (1999). *Basics of Qualitative Research: Grounded Theory Pro-*

cedures and Techniques, ISBN 0803959400.

Ulrich, W. (1983). *Critical Heuristics of Social Planning: A New Approach to Practical Philosophy*, ISBN 3-258-03219-X.

Ulrich, W. (1996). *Critical Systems Thinking for Citizens: A Research Proposal.* Centre for Systems Studies Research Memorandum #10. Centre for Systems Studies, University of Hull: Hull.

Van Vugt, M. (2002). "Community identification moderating the impact of financial incentives in a natural social dilemma: water conservation," *Personality and Social Psychology Bulletin*, ISSN 0146-1672, 27: 1440-1449.

Vega-Romero, R. (1999). *Health Care and Social Justice Evaluation: A Critical and Pluralist Approach.* PhD Thesis, University of Hull, UK.

White, L. and Taket, A. (1993). "The death of the expert," *Journal of the Operational Research Society*, ISSN 0160-5682, 45: 733-748.

Yolles, M. (2001). "Viable boundary critique," *Journal of the Operational Research Society*, ISSN 0160-5682, 52: 35–47.

37. Organizational Systems: Why Emotions Should be Taken into Account

Julia Göbel
Carrick Institute for Teaching and Learning in Higher Education, AUS

Kevin Laws
Faculty of Education and Social Work, The University of Sydney, AUS

It is common to think of organizations as comprised of systems and subsystems, interconnected in a variety of ways. Management is seen as a matter of ensuring that the systems operate effectively and efficiently. However, to ignore the human element in organizations often leads to the downfall of managers, and maybe the collapse of the organization, for without people there are no organizations. People have values and feelings, and experience emotions while at work and in the other aspects of their lives. Human emotions must be acknowledged, especially in times of change. This paper proposes a model that takes account of emotions within organizations.

Introduction

Danny is a committed and experienced motor technician working for a well-known car dealership. He always tries to improve work processes in order to become more efficient. An ineffective computer system has resulted in technicians needing more than double the time for a particular service leaving them, and customers, frustrated. The company's structure and inadequate communication channels make it difficult to disseminate the problem to people in charge.

One day when the work atmosphere was very strained and the computer system was not working properly, Danny's workshop boss complained about the "incredible slowness" of the technicians. Danny's anger boiled over, he slammed the door of the car he was working on and inwardly damned the job. "I've just had enough. If they won't listen to me, they're on their own."

Mary is leaving the principal's office with a bright smile. "I have waited for such a long time and now, finally, all my hard work has paid off." She has just been promoted me to a head teacher. "I am so relieved and happy."

An hour later, Mary is on her lunch break and reflects upon her achievement. "I feel really good about the recognition of my hard work and value to the school. But am I actually the right person for this? It will mean a lot more work and responsibilities for me. I'm not sure whether I can live up to everyone's expectations."

Everyday scenarios like these are all too familiar. We all deal with hassles, anger, joy, excitement and satisfaction at work. People are not isolated 'emotional islands' (Barsade & Gibson, 2007: 54). Consciously and unconsciously they take all sorts of emotions to work with them. Emotions are a normal part of being human.

"That organizations are emotional places is a truism. It arises from the simple fact that organizations rely on human beings to function and human beings are emotional animals: loving, hating, fearing, envying, prone to pleasure and pain."

(Armstrong, 2000: 1)

Although there is no argument that organizations are "emotional cauldrons" (Albrow, 1992: 313), organizational theory has all too often neglected emotions as an integral part in understanding organizational life. Research, however, has repeatedly shown that emotions influence performance, decision-making, staff turnover, conflict resolution behavior and leadership (Barsade & Gibson, 2007). Emotions in organizations not only affect organizational learning and change, they are also an intrinsic feature of learning and change.

In this paper we place emphasis on emotions that occur within an organizational context. We are concerned with the social role of emotions and their effect on structures and power relations within an organization. The paper proposes the inclusion of emotions within systems models of organizations in order to more closely reflect the reality of life within them.

Emotions in organizations

Emotions are seen as short-lived reactions to particular people or events. Emotions are highly contextual and social, and play an important role in social interactions and communication. Differing from feelings, which occur in private, emotional display depends on an audience where emotional performance is often used for strategic effects (Antonacopoulou & Gabriel, 2001; Callahan & McCollum, 2002). The social and cultural dimensions of emotions impact greatly upon organizational social systems.

Hochschild's work (1983) on *emotional labour* marks the beginning of more recent interest in emotion at work (Briner & Kiefer, 2005). Emotional labour involves workers' efforts to consciously control their feelings according to the requirements of their work. Managing and regulating emotional display is something we do all the time. Cultural conventions often prevent us from showing our real emotions. Fineman (1993) challenged the view of organizations as rational places and brought the topic of emotions back to the organizational agenda.

The *circumplex model of affect,* originally proposed by Schlosberg (1952), argues that any kind of emotion falls within the categories of arousal, excitement, pleasure, contentment, sleepiness, depression, misery and distress. The model has had a strong influence on research concerned with organizational change in terms of effects of particular emotions (or the interplay of emotions)

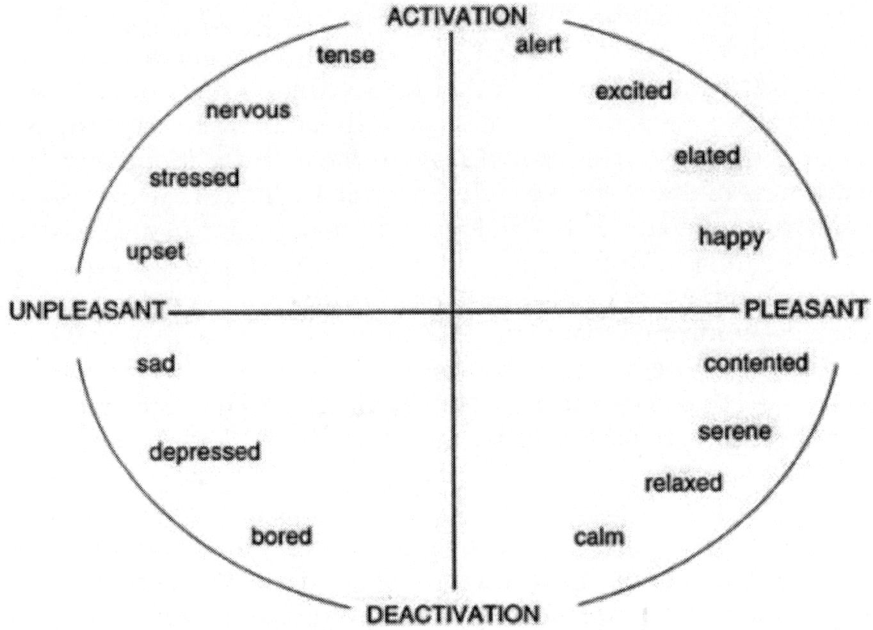

Figure 1 *A Graphical Representation of the Circumplex Model of Affect*
Source: Posner, Russell & Peterson (2005: 716)

on change implementation and its success (Russell, 1980; Larsen & Diener, 1992; Huy, 2002). Posner, Russell and Peterson (2005) devised a graphical representation of the circumplex model by utilizing two continua: 'unpleasant' and 'pleasant 'on the horizontal axis, and 'activation' (arousal) and 'deactivation' on the vertical axis (see Figure 1).

The notion of *Emotional Intelligence (EI),* popularized by Goleman (1995), has had a great influence on the study of emotions at work. EI was originally defined as the "ability to monitor one's own and others feelings and emotions, to discriminate among them and to use this information to guide one's thinking and action" (Salovey & Mayer, 1990: 189). The core message of this concept is that the appropriate utilisation, regulation and appraisal of emotions is critical in terms of organizational effectiveness. Emotional intelligence is seen as a vital component of management and work (Zeidner, *et al.*, 2004).

Another significant influence on research on emotions at work was *Affective Events Theory (AET)* (Weiss & Cropanzano, 1996) which provided an explanation of the role of emotions in worksettings and employee behavior (Ashton-James & Ashkanasy, 2005). AET suggests that environmental conditions within the organization result in particular work events. Depending on the nature of these "events", positive or negative work attitudes such as commitment, satisfaction, disloyalty and dissatisfaction may result.

Systems approaches and models: Do emotions play a significant role?

From the mid-1960s onwards, organizations have been increasingly investigated using a social systems approach. An elementary systems model includes *inputs* (capital, information, human resources), the *transformation process* (labour, management, operations) and *outputs* (products and services, financial, human output, information). Ideally, a feedback loop links outputs to inputs and informs about the appropriateness of outputs, processes and inputs (Robbins, *et al.*, 1997: 55). At the heart of systems theory is the interdependence and interrelatedness of the *parts* to produce a unified whole. However 'parts' such as management, operations, technology or human resources are constructs associated with humans. Human interaction is a necessary condition for organizational functioning. At their heart, organizations are *social* systems and research has repeatedly confirmed that social interactions involve a display of emotions, which in turn have effects on organizational functioning. Therefore, we want to propose a model that takes the importance of emotions into account.

In the field with which we are most familiar, education, Hoy and Miskel (2001) have long advocated a social systems model for understanding schools (see Figure 2). They adopt an open systems model to illustrate how external forces beyond the school influence the internal components of the school. At the same time the school impacts upon the community to provide graduates who have been transformed into something of greater value than when they entered the system. At the heart of an educational organization is a transformation process where the institutions convert inputs (e.g., human resources) into outcomes. Four subsystems are involved in this process: the structural subsystem, the political subsystem, the individual subsystem, and the cultural system. These subsystems support the technical core of the organization where teaching and learning occurs. This model has long been recognized as providing a useful framework for understanding how the subsytems interact to produce the whole educational organization.

However, in spite of the acknowledgement of human beings within this model there is no explicit statement concerning the emotions of individuals and groups involved. We consider that such models undervalue the importance of the people as human beings in the organization.

While Hoy and Miskel's model indicates the interrelationships and interconnectedness of the subsystems it omits any reference to the part that emotions play within an organization. Human beings at work will have emotional responses in relation to the adequacy, inadequacy and quality of the Inputs noted in the model. Emotions will play a part in how those working in an organization, regardless of their level of responsibility, feel and respond to the four subsystems. For example, the power relations evident in an organization's Political System will generate both positive and negative emotions in those who work there, regardless of their level or status. There will be various levels of shared orientations to the Cultural System among management and different groups of staff. There will be a variety of emotional responses to the Structural System, and the Individual System acknowledges that the levels of understanding, knowledge and motivation among all those working in the organization will vary. Emotions also will play an important part in overall feelings of all to the Outputs of the organization.

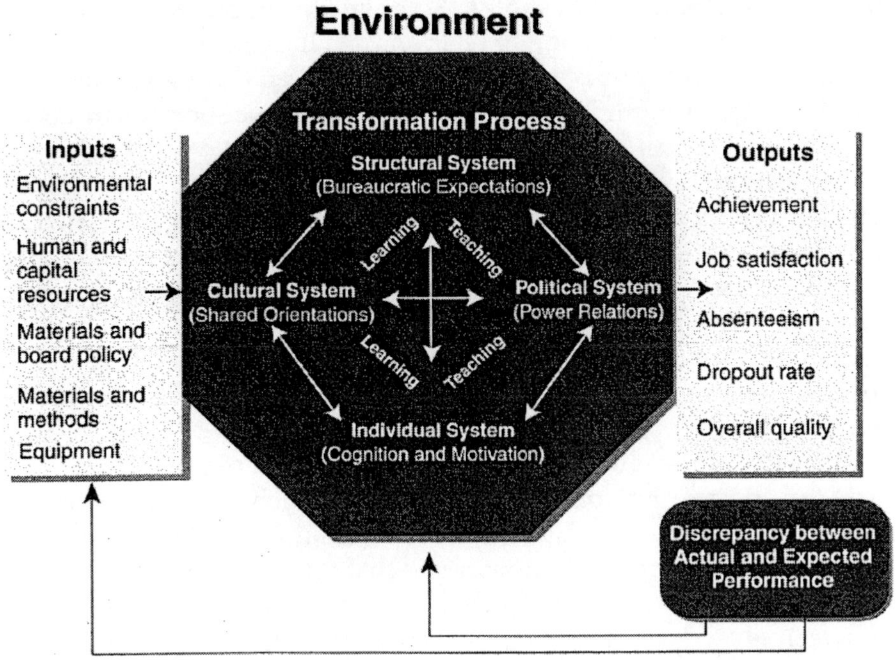

Source: Wayne K. Hoy & Cecil G. Miskel (2001) *Educational Administration: Theory, Research, and Practice.* 6th ed. (p.31)

Figure 2 *Social Systems Model of a School*

Emotions in organizations: An emergent force or a force to be managed?

Callahan & McCollum (2002) have presented a useful framework for conceptualizing the study of emotions in organizations. They describe four perspectives of emotions which are not mutually exclusive but represent different approaches. These are: the "Power Approach", where emotions are seen as a force that affords organizational change; the "Structure Approach" which is concerned with how structures are influenced by emotions; the "Function Approach" which is involved with how to manage and utilise emotions as some may be potentially disruptive; and the "Interpretation Approach" which is concerned with how organizational members interpret emotions and why they interpret them in that way. We will focus largely upon the 'power approach' in our efforts to illustrate the importance of taking emotions into consideration.

Earlier writing in the field of organizational learning and change was primarily concerned with the effective acquisition, dissemination and utilization in order to become a learning organization (Nevis, *et al.*, 1995; Romme, 1997).More recently, there has been a shift towards a rather "social perspective" (Vince, 2001: 1329). This shift contributes to the view that sees power relations and politics as a natural and necessary part of learning and change within organizations (Vince, 2001). Therefore, learning and change in organizations takes place within a social context and is determined through the complex interactions of its members. Vince (2001) argues that individual and collective emotions are not merely a side-effect of this kind of learning but they influence organizational change to a great extent. Since within an organization there exist complex socially constructed power relations it is necessary to understand how information and knowledge is expressed and mediated through these power relations and how learning and change occurs within these social relations (Vince, 2001).

One useful framework in this context, in order to understand how emotions affect (and are affected by) organizational systems and structures, is "Emotion Structuration". In developing this concept Callahan (2004) draws on Giddens' "Structuration Theory" (1979) and argues that the emotions of organizational members structure and are structured by social systems. Power relations are one feature constructed through these systems; the question is: How do emotions affect these relations, how do these relations affect emotions, and what does that mean for organizational change?

Vince (2001) was able to show that the neglect of how power relations are enacted in an organization and how emotions such as defensiveness, anger and anxiety influence these relations, prevent and limit organizational learning and change efforts. The study demonstrated that established political and power relations resulted in the failure to foster learning at an organizational level. Tensions between several subgroups with very different aims made it impossible to actually implement the goals of the learning and change initiative.

Acknowledging that organizations consist of interrelated social webs and, more importantly, of human beings, means that emotions are always involved in learning and organizing. Learning and organizing are not simply rational processes but emotional ones as well. Vince and Broussine (1995) argue that many approaches to organizational learning and change overemphasize the rational and neglect the emotional reactions. However, they claim that these "paradoxical tensions" are fundamental to organizing, learning and change. Based on this we argue that reflection on emotions are an essential feature in the process of organizational learning. If emotions have such powerful effects on successful organizational functioning, systems models should be broadened towards the inclusion of an emotional dimension.

Studies concerned with emotions and organizational change have had many different foci, largely directed at negative processes such as 'downsizing' (Beylerian & Kleiner, 2002; Blau, 2006) and 'resistance to change' (Atkinson, 2005; Bovey & Hede, 2001; Piderit, 2000). Vince and Broussine (1996) have argued that these approaches are often limited in a way that change is associated with 'problems' that can be strategically managed in the form of planned change. Problem-based models of change neglect the complexity of organizational systems and the various emotional aspects inherent within and among different organizational parts. Vince and Broussine emphasise that this is often due to the way organizational systems or cultures work. Various explicit and implicit rules and regulations make it difficult for members to express their feelings as well as to understand and reflect on their own and others' emotions. In attempting to build a framework for change by integrating both emotional and rational factors they propose:

"Change does not only occur as a result of outlining a set of problems to diagnose and solve. It can also be approached through identifying patterns of relatedness and through containing the paradoxical emotions and relations that challenge the way we think about ourselves and others" (Vince & Broussine, 1996: 4).

Furthermore, they argue that emotions and tension between members and groups need to be viewed as an important component of organizational change. In practice these tensions often occur in the form of defense mechanisms or resistance, yet, depending on how they are utilized they can be used facilitate organizational change (Vince & Broussine, 1996).

Antonacopoulou & Gabriel (2001) note that resistance can be seen as a strategy to recover meaning within a change process or to preserve what has worked in the past. Furthermore, they emphasise that there is not much known about positive emotions to change. Change does not necessarily result in resistance, threat and uncertainty. It can also be experienced as growth, learning, hope, stimulation and excitement. Individuals experience change in very different ways: from viewing it as a learning opportunity, to accepting it as inevitable, to denying change altogether. In order to foster change processes successfully, research must explore the variety of emotional reactions to change. A process systems model may assist in this regard.

Roberto and Levesque (2005) emphasise that it is the *emotional* commitment to change initiatives that is most critical. Dissatisfaction with the status quo can be a stimulating and vital catalyst for becoming excited and committed about tackling change. Their research suggests that in order for change initiatives "to stick" (p. 60), managers need to engage emotions of organizational members from the very beginning, rather than trying to deal with and manage randomly occurring emotions after the initiative has been implemented.

Emotions as a fundamental part of organizational functioning: A revised model

Based on research and the fundamental principles and conditions underlying the success of organizational learning and change, we have shown that emotions play a major role in organizational functioning. They mediate and often determine success or failure of improvement initiatives. Therefore, we propose a process social systems model of organizations by adding the emotional factor.

Note that in the revised model emotions are not only brought into organizational settings (input), they are at the heart of every transformation process, influencing and controlling the various inherent systems. Moreover, emotions are also part of outputs / outcomes of organizational processes; they could be positive in nature (in the form of satisfaction or joy) but also negative (in the form of frustration or anger). Either way, all emotions that arise will have the power to inform organizational processes, through feedback loops. Therefore, there is not only a need to recognise and appreciate the potential of emotions for an organization's success, but also a necessity to uncover emotions underlying

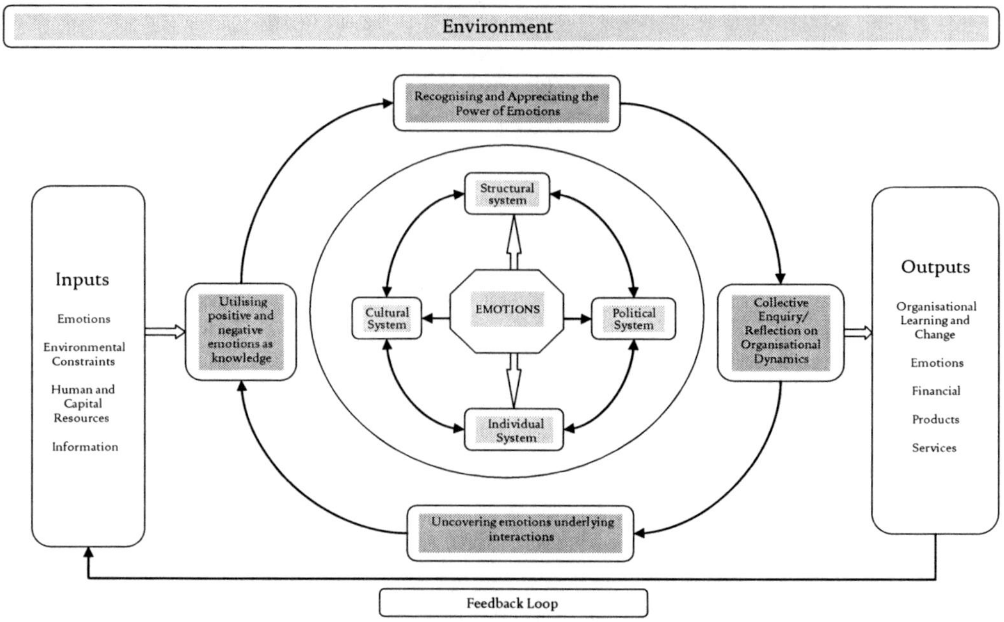

Figure 3 *A Process Model of a Social System Including Emotions*

interactions, to then reflect on these dynamics collectively, and to utilise both positive and negative emotions as knowledge.

In the revised model emotions are seen not only as the central core of the transformation phase, also are acknowledged as an important part of the input and output phases. We emphasise emotions because, not only are they part of every human being, but because workers, being human, bring their emotions to the workplace, experience emotions while in the workplace, and generate emotions through the outputs of the organization.

References

Albrow, M. (1992). Sine ira et studio – or do organizations have feelings? *Organization Studies,* 13(3), ISSN 0170-8406: 313-329.

Antonacopoulou, E. P. & Gabriel, Y. (2001). Emotion, learning and organizational change. Towards an integration of psychoanalytic and other perspectives. *Journal of Organizational Change Management,* 14(5), ISSN 0953-4814: 435-451.

Armstrong, D. (2000). *Emotions in organizations: Disturbance or intelligence?* Paper presented at the Annual Symposium of the International Society for the Psychoanalytic Study of Organizations, London, June. Retrieved June 30, 2007 from: http://www.ispso.org/Symposia/London/2000armstrong.htm

Ashton-James, C. E. & Ashkanasy, N. M. (2005). What lies beneath? A process analysis of affective events theory. In: N. M. Ashkanasy, W. J. Zerbe & C. E. J. Härtel (Eds.), *The Effect of Affect in Organizational Settings Vol.1 (Research on Emotion in Organizations),* ISBN 0762312343, pp. 23-46.

Atkinson, P. (2005). Managing resistance to change. *Management Services,* 49(1), ISSN 0307-6768: 14-19.

Barsade, S. G. & Gibson, D. E. (2007). Why does affect matter in organizations ? *Academy of Management Perspectives, 21* (1), ISSN 1558-9080: 36-59.

Beylerian, M. & Kleiner, B. H. (2002). The downsized workplace. *Nonprofit World,*

20(3), ISSN 8755-7614: 30-32.

Blau, G. (2006). A process model for understanding victim responses to worksite/function closure. *Human Resource Management Review,* 16(1), ISSN 1053-4822: 12-28.

Bovey, W. H. & Hede, A. (2001). Resistance to organizational change: the role of cognitive and affective processes. *Leadership & Organization Development Journal,* 22(7/8), ISSN 0143-7739: 372-382.

Briner, R. B. & Kiefer, T. (2005). Psychological research into the experience of emotion at work: Definitely older, but are we any wiser? In: N. M. Ashkanasy, W. J. Zerbe & C. E. J. Härtel (Eds.), *The Effect of Affect in Organizational Settings Vol.1 (Research on Emotion in Organizations),* ISBN 0762312343, pp.281-307.

Callahan, J. L. (2004). Reversing a conspicious absence: Mindful inclusion of emotion in structuration theory. Human Relations, 57(11), ISSN 0018-7267: 1427-1448.

Callahan, J. L. & McCollum, E. (2002). Conceptualizations of emotion research in organizational contexts. *Advances in Developing Human Resources.* 4(1), ISSN 1523-4223: 4-21.

Fineman, S. (1993). *Emotion in Organizations.* ISBN 0803987331 .

Giddens, A. (1979). *Central Problems in Social Theory: Action, Structure and Contradiction in Social Analysis.* ISBN 0520039750.

Goleman, D. (1995). *Emotional Intelligence: Why it can matter more than IQ.* ISBN 0-553-09503-X.

Hochschild, A. R. (1983). *The Managed Heart: The Commercialization of Human Feeling.* ISBN 0520239334 (2003 edition).

Hoy, W. K. & Miskel, C. G. (2001). *Educational Administration: Theory, Research and Practice (6th Ed.),* ISBN 0072322896.

Huy, Q. N. (2002). Emotional balancing of organizational continuity and radical change: The contribution of middle managers. *Administrative Science Quarterly,* 47(1): ISSN 0001-8392, 31-69.

Larsen, R. J. & Diener, E. E. (1992). Promises and problems with the circumplex model of emotions. In M. S. Clark (Ed.) *Review of Personality and Social Psychology: Emotion and Social Behavior,*.ISSN 0270-1987, *114*: 25-95.

Nevis, E. C., DiBella, A. J. & Gould, J. M. (1995). Understanding organizations as learning systems. MIT *Sloan Management Review,* 36(2), ISSN 1532-9194: 73-85.

Piderit, S. K. (2000). Rethinking resistance and recognizing ambivalence: A multidimensional view of attitudes toward an organizational change. *Academy of Management Review,* 25(4), ISSN 0363-7425: 783-794.

Posner, J., Russell, J.A. & Peterson, B.S. (2005) The circumflex model of affect: An integrative approach to affective neuroscience, cognitive development and psychopathology. *Development and Psychopathology,* 17, ISSN 0954-5794: 715-734.

Roberto, M. A. & Levesque, L. C. (2005). The art of making change initiatives stick. MIT *Sloan Management Review,* 46 (4), ISSN 1532-9194: 53-60.

Robbins, S., Bergman, R. & Stagg, I. (1997). *Management.* ISBN 0724808787.

Romme, G. (1997). Mapping the landscape of organizational learning. *European Management Journal,* 15(1), ISSN 0263-2373: 68-78.

Russell, J. A. (1980). A circumflex model of affect. *Journal of Personality and Social Psychology, 39* (6), ISSN 0022-3514: 1161-1178.

Salovey, P. & Meyer, J. (1990). Emotional Intelligence. *Imagination, Cognition and Personality, 9,* ISSN 0276-2366: 185-211.

Schlosberg, H. (1952). The description of facial expressions. *Journal of Experimental Psychology, 44,* ISSN 0096-3445: 229-237.

Vince, R. (2001). Power and emotion in organizational learning. *Human Relations,*

54(10), ISSN 0018-7267: 1325-1351.

Vince, R. & Broussine, M. (1996). Paradox, defense and attachment : Accessing and working with emotions and relations underlying organizational change. *Organization Studies,* 17(1), ISSN 0170-8406: 1-21.

Weiss, H. M. & Cropanzano, R. (1996). Affective events theory: A theoretical discussion of the structure, causes and consequences of affective experiences at work. *Research in Organizational Behavior, 18* (1), ISSN 0191-3085: 1-74.

Zeidner, M., Matthews, G. & Roberts, R. D. (2004). Emotional intelligence in the workplace: A critical review. *Applied Psychology,* 53 (3), ISSN 1464-0597: 371-399

38. Systems, Structure and Agency: A Contribution to the Theory of Social Emergence and Methods for its Study

PLENARY PAPER

Chris Goldspink[1] and **Robert Kay**[2]
[1]Centre for Research in Social Simulation, University of Surrey, UK
[2]Westpac Banking Corporation, Sydney, AUS

In this paper we reflect on the conference theme 'Systemic Development: Local Solutions in a Global Environment' noting that this echoes sentiments captured in the slogans 'Think global, act local' and the complement 'Think local, act global'. We argue that these slogans embrace inherently systemic insights, but insights which current social and organizational theory, including that inspired by systems thinking, cannot adequately underpin. It is argued that a failure to establish an adequate understanding of the interplay between agency and structure is at the heart of the problem. In this paper we outline our theoretical and empirical collaboration exploring this issue. We draw on the theory of autopoietic systems to argue that social systems are complex systems of a particular class and that what distinguishes them as a class is the reflexive capacity of the constituent agents. Reflexivity happens in and through language and provides a capacity to distinguish macro structure and relate it to 'self 'and thus to change micro behavior, and in so doing contribute to the generation of new emergent pattern. We explore this through two case examples. The first addresses issues affecting innovation within a senior management team in Westpac Bank. The second addresses self-organizing normative processes within the global network institution Wikipedia. Links are drawn between the cases and the theoretical framework advanced in the first section. The cases serve to illustrate how methods which are normally associated with either micro or macro behavior can be combined to help with research into the interplay between the two.

Introduction

The theme of this conference *'Systemic Development: Local Solutions in a Global Environment'* appears to echo two reciprocal insights into the effect of systematicity. The first is captured by the slogan 'Think global, act local' which grew from environmental and social activism (Fisher, n.d). It reinforces that small local changes can propagate and have system wide effects and conveys messages about how individuals may try to effect change with a reminder of the ethical implications (responsibilities) of so doing. The second slogan 'Think local, act global' also rooted in activist practice, reflects how, through new technology, local solutions can be produced by harnessing wide spread active contribution from disparate global resources. These two slogans capture, in a very parsimonious way, what we take to be the implications of highly connected global ecological and social systems. Systems theory has been good at informing this type of insight. It has been significantly less good at supporting a clear explication of how and why such phenomena are possible and the conditions under which they may be realized: it suffers from excessive generality and a concern with macro order at the expense of the generative processes which produce that order.

Returning to the slogans and indeed the theme, at first glance both appear to point to issues of scope (local vs. global), but look more closely and there is an implied issue of level: Both suggest that individual agency (changes in thinking and acting) can have large scale social consequences by which we might read a change at the level of collectives – or of institutions. But here we confront what Keith Sawyer has recently described as *'a fundamental intellectual problem'* (2001; 2003). When we posit the possibility of individuals using their agency (to act out of free will) to effect change on institutions we imply an understanding of the reciprocal relationship between the micro level (agent) and the macro level (social structure). The problem is that we lack such an understanding.

This lack, referred to in the social and philosophy of science literature as the problem of structure and agency or the micro-macro problem, is perhaps more familiar to this audience as the problem of *emergence*. It is of long standing. We argue that without an adequate account of the interpenetration of micro and macro process, we cannot explain the intrinsic nature of sociality and we cannot say much about how and when individuals acting locally may have wider effects nor how disparate individual contributions may be effectively harnessed so as to generate coherent solutions to local problems. Yet, as the appeal of such slogans reveals, to have some understanding of such phenomena would seem important.

The fact that such a fundamental problem remains unsolved should not be taken to imply that it has received no attention: It has received a great deal. That it remains unresolved is more a reflection of how intellectually formidable the problem is.

Wrestling with the micro-macro problem has provided a core to our collaboration over the past eight years. Our concern with it arose from our experience as practitioners it was and remains grounded in our attempt to effect change within organizational and social systems. It is not, therefore, an exercise in theoretical navel-gazing. That said it does not appear to lend itself to a purely empirical treatment.

In this paper we briefly identify the main strands of the theoretical debate around this problem. We then present a theoretical framework which we advance as an attempt to resolve it. Following this we discuss how we are continuing to research the issue using two case studies. These cases serve to ground the discussion and to illustrate ways for furthering our understanding. We also use the cases to illustrate some of the methods we are finding useful.

What is the problem?

The problem is that contemporary approaches to social and organizational science, including those derived from systems thinking, fail adequately to address, either theoretically or methodologically, the reciprocal interplay between macro and micro phenomena. There have been two recent attempts to provide a meta-view of the problem as it applies to understanding social systems: That of Elke Weik (2006) and that of Christian Fuchs & Wolkgang Hofkirchner (2005: 33). Both conclude that existing social theory falls short of providing an adequate account of this relationship. Fuchs *et al.* place systems theory in with other macro focused theories under the heading of *sociologism*. This is consistent with Burrell and Morgan's (1994) argument that it belongs to the functionalist paradigm and as such is poorly placed to understand processes of change – focusing instead on processes of order. This criticism is probably fair if by systems theory, they are referring to the body of work which came out of the attempt at a General Systems Theory or the cybernetics tradition. The associated 'black box' approach clearly masks the relationship between micro and macro. As a body of work, however, systems thinking does support an exploration of the difference made to system level behavior as a consequence of how elements are bounded and connected. Application of the concept to social science, in particular through social cybernetics (Keeney, 1987), and soft systems approaches (Checkland, 1999) also confronted macro theorists with the need to deal with the role of the observer and the role of observation when studying social dynamics. More recently the development of complex systems has provided a better foundation for understanding the macro-micro interplay and for understanding the mechanisms and pre-conditions for emergence.

The concept of emergence has long been central to systems theory: It is implicit to the concept of holism. Unfortunately the concept remains problematic and has arguably brought as much confusion as it has clarity (for recent overviews of the state of play see Achim, 2004; Clayton & Davies, 2006; Sawyer, 2001, 2005).

One of the issues which has bedevilled the debate about emergence is what ontological status to attribute to 'emergent' structures – are they simply 'epiphenomenal' or do they have causal effect? Within social science this problem is manifest by two fundamental questions:

1. Ontologically, what is the origin or nature of (macro) social phenomena and how do they emerge from the (micro) actions of individuals in particular contexts of action?
2. Epistemologically, how is it that we can come to know about social phenomena?

Some useful advances have been made. The critical Realists argue convincingly that previous attempts to answer such questions have suffered from an inappropriate 'bundling' of ontological and epistemic assumptions (Archer, 1998; Bhaskar, 1998). Typically, realism is bundled with objectivism and idealism is bundled with relativism. We agree with Bhaskar that if an emergent structure can be seen to have causal effect then it should be awarded some ontological status.

From Complexity theory we take the understanding that what makes emergent properties irreducible in principle (and hence subject to emergence) is the presence of non-linearity at some level within the systems operation (Bak, 1996; Holland, 1998; Kauffman, 2000; Stewart, 1990). This results in one or both of the following conditions being present:

- Deterministic Chaos (Lorenz, 2001; Williams, 1997);
- Equifinality (Richardson, 2002b) or 'wild disjunction' (Fodor, 1974).

Equifinality as it is known within systems theory or the principle of 'wild disjunction' as it is known in philosophy, refers to a system where a single high level property may be realized by more than one set of micro-states which have no lawful relationship between them (Richardson, 2002a, 2002b; Sawyer, 2001). As there is no *a priori* basis by which the likely micro-state can be determined, such systems are irreducible and unpredictable in principle. From this we can conclude that there are systems which:

- Are inherently analytically reducible (to which the concept of emergence does not apply);
- Are analytically reducible in principle but difficult to reduce in practice and/or where an advance in science/knowledge is needed for reduction to be possible because the results were 'unexpected' (Chalmers, 2006) (to which the concept of 'weak' emergence can be applied);
- Are not reducible in principle (to which the principle of 'strong' emergence is relevant).

To which of these three classes do social systems belong? We argue it is *always* the latter and this has a number of significant implications. The possible presence of non-linearity prepares us not to expect that social phenomena can necessarily be reduced to explanations at the level of physics, biology or individual psychology or behavior even if it is dependent on them. We anticipate and expect that properties particular to the social level may be exhibited, that they may be novel, and that they could well be unpredictable in principle. What is missing, however, is a logically internally consistent theory which explicates the mechanism by which qualitatively distinct social phenomena emerge from the biological micro-processes which underpin it–from human agents. What might such a theory look like?

A possible theoretical treatment

In our view, any theory of sociality needs to be grounded in a biological theory which gives an account of the origins and fundamental characteristics of human social agents: In the case of human social systems this includes cognition and language. We argue that a suitable foundation is present to a large degree in

Maturana and Varela's (1980) theory of autopoiesis. This theory embraces what we know about human cognition in a manner that is epistemologically and ontologically consistent with a complex systems view. Bringing these two views together furnishes significant advantages in that each serves to extend the other. In short, we argue that autopoiesis provides a logical and internally consistent account of what we consider to be:

- The fundamental mechanism of sociality – structural coupling;
- The consequence of language, and;
- A means of dealing with the (reflexive) observer within the generative process of sociality.

When combined with Complexity theory, these concepts potentially allow us to fully describe the interpenetration between structure and agency in human social systems. We have set out the basis of this approach in more detail elsewhere (Goldspink & Kay, 2003; Goldspink & Kay, 2004). Specifically we state:

"*Humans exist in and through domains, which are the product of their structural coupling with an environment. This environment is the world around them including other humans .... The domain is a complex product of the context and time-specific interactions into which the individual enters. Included in this are the linguistic interactions that arise as individuals generate linguistic distinctions about that environment. As humans enter into reciprocal interaction over time, there emerges, as a consequence of structural coupling, a certain alignment of their behaviors, including their linguistic behaviors. Hence we can refer to the resulting domain as a consensual domain. This domain now forms the basic unit of social analysis, and exists in a causal sense but not a physical one*" (Goldspink & Kay, 2004: 605).

It is the mechanisms described above that provide for the emergent phenomena we describe as social. The resulting structurally coupled networks of heterogeneous agents can be expected to be intrinsically (indeed relentlessly) non-linear and hence subject to Chaos and equifinality. It is here that Complexity theory provides a suite of concepts and tools with which to explain and study the dynamic properties. However, autopoiesis also extends Complexity theory. Contemporary approaches to Complexity have failed to come to terms with the implications of the reflexive nature of human agents. To date the concern has been to understand the processes by which order emerges bottom up. Natural complex systems involve agents affecting one another only through local interaction – natural agents cannot observe macro consequences and change their behavior accordingly – human agents, however, can and do. Social systems are complex systems of a particular class and with distinct characteristics. We need to come to terms with the consequence reflexivity has for social emergence.

Reflexive Emergence

What are the emergent mechanisms that generate *human* social phenomena? We have recently described these in some detail at the Fall Symposium of the Association for the Advancement of Artificial Intelligence in Washington (Goldspink & Kay, 2007), the key points are summarized here.

To distinguish natural complex systems from human complex systems we have suggested the need to consider two sets of generative mechanisms – pre-reflexive and reflexive. Linking this back to the theory of autopoietic systems, the pre-reflexive mode operates through structural coupling of behaviors. Specifically we state:

Structural coupling will arise between biological (autopoietic) agents which have sufficient cognitive range (behavioral repertoire) and if they are located in a common environment. Assuming that their phylogeny and ontogeny is such that they can coexist, through the process of recurrent mutual perturbation, each will adjust its structure so as to accommodate the other - their structures will become mutually aligned or structurally coupled.

This is the mode with which complexity theorists and social simulators are familiar. What is missing from it is what Gilbert (2002) has referred to as second-order emergence. This is emergence which arises from the fact that agents are capable of language.

Language radically increases the behavioral plasticity of agents and has significant implications for the dimensionality of the phase space and of the resulting higher order structures it can generate and support. This is because language makes possible the emergence of domains of interaction which can themselves become the target for further linguistic distinction and hence new domains. An appreciation of this was clearly evident in the social constructionism of Berger and Luckmann (1972) but has since been largely ignored. Linking this back to the theory of autopoiesis, Maturana and Varela's (1980) notion of consensual domains giving rise to linguistic domains and linguistic domains supporting the development of further linguistic domains, reflects this bootstrapping of levels possible in human social systems. It makes possible a range of behavioral unparalleled in non-linguistic systems.

More than this, the advent of language means that another completely new source of pattern arises. Language allows the agent to make distinctions on prior distinctions. This capacity greatly expand the structural flexibility of the agent – the agent can now invent worlds or epistemic domains to use Luhmann's (1990; 1995) terminology. One of the abilities which appear to co-occur with language is the capacity to distinguish 'self' from 'other' (Gardenfors, 2006). Agents can then create epistemic worlds and locate 'self' within them. Self narrative also appears to play a role in this and may be fundamental to it (Ezzy, 1998). Narrative appears to arise as a cognitive capability before language albeit in more limited form (Dautenhahn, 2002).

The effect of the emergence of these capabilities is that the phase space of any system comprising such agents is now based partly on ontogenetic variables rather than only phylogenetic (as with non-linguistic/reflexive animals) and is hence subject to influence by the agents in and through their collective action. Furthermore as the agent can now differentiate itself from the environment, it can entertain itself as a causal agent and change its behavior based on what it perceives as emergent social patterns. This suggests, for example, that an agent can form hypotheses about the relationship between a macro structural aspect of the social system in which it is a participant and then act on that hypothesis, potentially changing the structure which it participates in generating. This gives rise to a feedback path between macro and micro phenomena that is not present in any other natural phenomena. It is this that allows us to assert that human social systems are will, of necessity, be non-linear.

How are we working with this in practice?

We mentioned that our interest in this issue was born of practice. Advancement has, however, involved praxis. The theoretical work remains important and necessary as it helps us to successively distinguish more rather than less helpful areas in our practice. Conversely, we have been able to make advances in the theory only as and when we stretch our understanding of the implications through practice. In this section we discuss two practical projects and link them to the ideas presented so far. The first approach addresses the systemic origins of particular social patterns within Westpac Banking Corporation. The second is an empirical and computer simulation case study being conducted as a part of the EU funded project Emergence in the Loop (EMIL) to support the development and understanding of self-organization within global network organizations including, as with this case, Wikipedia. In both cases we had to address a fundamental gap in the literature relating to autopoiesis and Complexity when it comes to social systems – the basic lack of associated method. The cases serve, therefore, to illustrate methods relevant to the study of the interplay between micro and macro process.

Case Study One: Westpac Trust and Innovation

This case study is concerned with the need to plan and give effect to local interventions which have some chance of changing global organizational culture. Some senior managers in the organization have a sense of what broad cultural patterns they *believe* are required for the organization to remain viable within its context and these are *not* the patterns currently observed. The purpose of the case study was to gain insight into processes which generate and maintain those undesired patterns in order to design interventions which had a chance of disrupting them and which might support the emergence of alternative and more desirable patterns. This is, of course, a common enough challenge in organizational change and so the case has wide potential relevance. The detailed results of this study form the basis of a forthcoming publication and are beyond the scope of this paper. Here we focus on the degree to which this approach has been helpful in expanding our understanding of the dynamics associated with micro to macro emergence.

The case has involved two related data collection cycles both using a similar methodology. In both cases the cycles were aimed at collecting data relevant to understanding:

The existing patterns of behavior in relation to 1) collaboration and 2) innovation).

The impact of existing formal and informal structures on the reciprocal interplay between individual sense-making and macro level behavior.

We assumed that we needed three forms of data: 1) an account of an actual series of events that individuals in the social system had experienced and how it was that they saw them as related; 2) how each individual construed those events; 3) a group (macro-level) view of the degree and depth of sharing across the group of alternative construal. The first of these data provide a diachronic (historical narrative) account from an individual and collective perspective: The second provided information on the granularity and heterogeneity of sense-making around that event and: The third told us of the extent to which the individual construal had converged to form a consensual linguistic domain – including which constructs formed the core of that domain.

For the first data set, we chose the method of narrative. The use of narrative within Complexity has grown in popularity, within social research and organizational study over the past few decades (Rhodes & Brown, 2005). We are assuming that a set of shared events will be alternatively construed. It is this difference that contributes to the emergent pattern at the macro-level– each individual acts to extend his/her historical account – to continue the narrative as he/she sees it. Narrative provided the individual's account of how a particular event unfolded – based on their current sense-making and of their role within it.

For the second data set, that pertaining to the individual sense-making of the participants, we chose the repertory grid technique. Repertory grid is derived from George Kelly's Personal Construct Theory (Kelly, 1963), has a constructivist basis and is somewhat epistemologically consistent with autopoietic theory. The approach provides insight into which constructs in each individual's meaning-system primarily orientate their behavior. In addition, measures such as *intensity* and *ordination* generated within Idiogrid (Grice, 2002) reveal how tightly held and therefore subject to change these constructs are. Intensity measures the correlation between constructs in a respondent's grid. Respondents with high *intensity* scores tend to have fewer alternative ways of construing events (Fransella *et al.*, 2004). The *ordination* scores reveal the location of a construct within the respondents construct hierarchy, with higher scores suggesting higher ordination or more meaningful (and abstract) constructs (Landfield & Cannell, 1988). Individuals are less likely to be willing to change higher order constructs as they have significant implications for how they makes sense of their world (Bannister & Fransella, 1989; Kelly, 1963). In combination these scores provide an indication of the level of flexibility the respondents have when it comes to changing the way they perceive events. This willingness to change, as will be discussed below, is extremely important in terms of understanding the emergent dynamics of a social system.

The third data set, the group level construal, was also derived from the individual repertory grids. We conducted a thematic analysis across the constructs of the entire group (see Jankowics, 2004 for a systematic process for doing this). This analysis revealed the degree to which there were commonalities to the sense-making among respondents.

From the combined analysis of the three data sets it was possible to discern three primary distinctions that orientated respondents toward one another and influenced their willingness to collaborate:

- Not in my team / haven't worked with them vs In my team/worked with them before.
- Different knowledge base / perceived as specialized vs Same knowledge base as me / more of a generalist.
- New to the bank vs long time bank employee.

Approximately two thirds of the respondents had one or more of the above as key characteristics in the way they distinguished collaboration between members of the group. These three distinctions appear to form the basis for the creation of sub-groups within the broader team, where people of like characteristics have a much higher propensity to trust and collaborate with each other rather than those they perceived as being different.

The combination of depth with which these constructs were held and the degree to which they were shared across the group strongly drove the eventual outcome of the particular activity we studied. For example, a group that was supposed to be collaborating on a set task instead split to create sub-groups closely aligned to the constructs described above. What is interesting here is that overtly, all the participants wanted to collaborate, and indeed initially did collaborate around the problem they had been set, thus creating a new pattern of interaction that had not existed before. However, over a relatively short period, this new pattern broke down with a slightly modified version of the pre-existing pattern of interaction emerging and conforming to the pattern predictable from the identification of these primary orientating constructs.

Mapping these three data sets together allowed us to identify what we refer to as the key drivers of the emergent pattern. It also provided an appreciation of which drivers could be easily changed and which could not. The results showed quite clearly that, where certain constructs were both deeply held by an individual **and** strongly shared by the group, these constructs would drive the emergent pattern of activity despite a change to the environment of the system.

These observations have lead us to propose the following model (see Figure One) as a way of informing any proposed attempt to change existing organizational patterns. The simple two by two matrix places the depth with which a construct is held on one dimension and the level to which it is shared on another. By mapping the constructs onto this matrix it becomes very clear very quickly which constructs or drivers will be difficult to address, and indeed if not addressed, will work against any proposed change. It also helps with the identification of the characteristics of the social system which are trivial and will

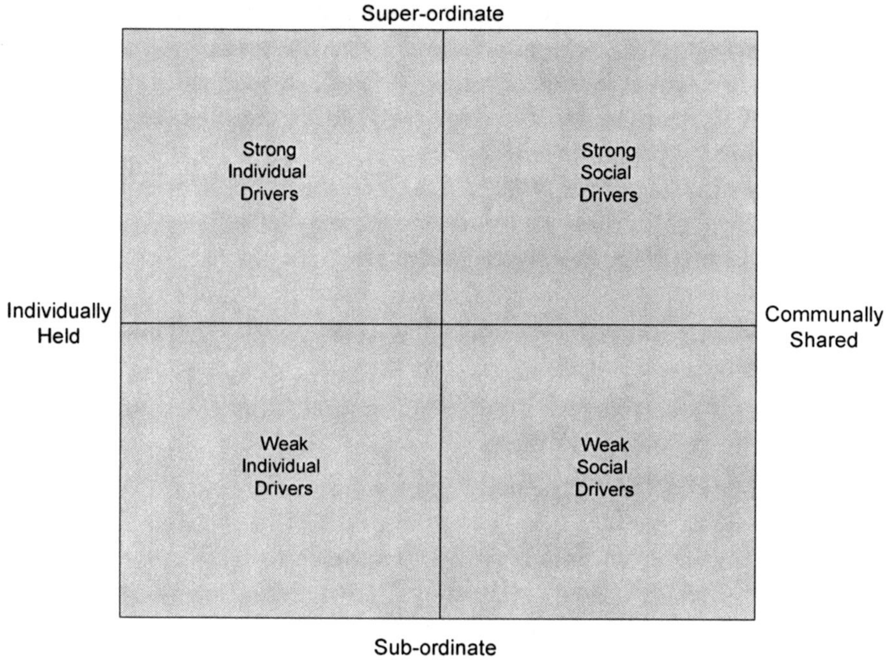

Figure 1 *Proposed model*

have very little impact on the dynamics of the social system.

Importantly, in terms of our broader research program, these observations provide us with a perspective on the way in which the micro level and macro level interact. It provides a guide to intervention – identifying those constructs which are a) most influential on the emergent dynamics and b) those which are most amenable and least amenable to change.

Case Two – Wikipedia

In this case the concern is to understand how widely dispersed and heterogeneous (in terms of having different skills, knowledge, goals and resources) agents can be brought together to produce precise, accurate, well crafted information resources in the form of encyclopaedic articles on a wide range of specific and tightly framed topics.

This case is being undertaken as a part of the EU funded research project titled Emergence in the Loop (EMIL). EMIL is explicitly concerned with the micro-macro problem and is using both empirical and computer simulation methods to advance our understanding of it. The insight behind the EMIL project is that this two-way interpenetration of micro and macro levels is fundamental to 'normative action' in social systems. Agents perceive higher order social structures (norms) and (perhaps) change their (micro) behavior in response, thus at the same time acting on the norm (perhaps reinforcing it or diminishing it). The case studies chosen therefore involve the study of the emergence of social norms. First among the cases to be used in EMIL is that of Wikipedia.

Wikipedia is of interest as the individuals that have participated in creating it have, through their collective action, emerged a set of permissions, obligations, rules and norms which arguably serve to bring it into being and to maintain it as a social system. Significantly, this was not intended or foreseen by those who initiated it (Sanger, 2005). From a governance perspective there are very few means within Wikipedia by which formal control can be exercised and it therefore relies on this emergent normative self-regulation to function despite significant perturbation from 'vandals' (task saboteurs), 'trolls' (social saboteurs), and turnover of contributors in the context of a task which may require the resolution of emotionally and value based conflict.

Normative theory reflects the confusion surrounding the macro-micro problem. There remains considerable confusion, for example, as to whether 'norms' are best ascribed as 'in' the environment or 'in' the agent. There is debate also as to whether normative order is the result of agents applying rules or reflects pattern which appears 'as though' it is rule based. Wikipedia can therefore help us to understand:

- How people influence one another and converge on common expected patterns of behavior;
- The emergence and role of explicit rules and norms in self-regulation of open volunteer communities where there is little to no hierarchy and limited capacity for formal sanction;
- How these norms and rules are invoked and maintained through communicative and administrative acts;
- The relationship between goal, technical artefacts and social structures and the exercise of individual agency.

This case is the subject of a paper being presented in one of the stream sessions of this conference (Goldspink, 2007) so we won't detail it here but again will simply reflect on its place within the development of our thinking.
In Wikipedia there are two classes of activity:

- Editing activity, and;
- Conversation about editing activity.

As this study was not concerned with the productive activity but with the self-organizing and self-regulating phenomena which make it possible, the Discussion pages of a sample of controversial articles were analyzed. Controversial articles were chosen as they were more likely to involve the need to resolve conflict and hence place greater demand on effective normative regulation.

The activity on the Discussion pages comprises a series of 'utterances' or speech acts between contributors about editing activity and the quality of product. The only means for editors to influence one another's behavior is through these utterances. On the face of it then, these pages should provide a fertile source to support analysis of how social norms operate. It was anticipated, however, that the process may involve quite subtle use of linguistic cues.

The pages were coded to a high level of resolution using the Verbal Response Mode (VRM) taxonomy (Stiles, 1992). VRM is very attractive where there is a need (as in this case) to capture many of the subtleties of natural language use that derive from and rely on the intrinsic flexibility and ambiguity of natural language yet map them to a more formal or axiomatic system needed for computer simulation. A range of additional codes were applied, including whether a listener accepted or 'validated' an utterance, the explicit invocation of norms or rules and the associated deontic, and the style and focus of the utterance.

The results of the analysis revealed the following.

- The more detailed and specific behavioral etiquette which has emerged and been formalized within wikipedia over some years seems to have little influence on the overall character and style of interaction within the Discussion pages of the controversial articles.
- The overall quality of interaction of editors falls short of the range and quality of communicative style characteristic of a 'community' and is inconsistent with what one would expect given the demanding nature of the task (they are superficial and non-discursive).
- Most regulation is achieved without the need for frequent explicit invocation of rules or norms. Rather, behavior seems to accord to a convention which editors quickly recognise and conform to and which minimally accommodates what needs to be done to satisfy the task in a context of somewhat heterogeneous personal goals.

Overall then there was a lack of evidence of active negotiation of expectations and standards and convergence of behavior towards a norm. Within the discussion pages there appeared to be an accommodation of a set of conventions and little obvious norm innovation, evolution, adaptation or extension. This suggests that on first encounter with Wikipedia, editors read a set of cues as to what constitutes appropriate or acceptable behavior and then make operational a script which accommodates it and stays relatively constant. This suggests complex cognitive processes and is not consistent with a 'norm as rule following' behavior but rather involves agents noticing emergent pattern and then adjusting their behavior accordingly. This is suggestive of analogical reasoning rather than deductive reasoning of simple rule following. It also suggests a very direct path between macro observation of emergent pattern and micro behavior.

The next stage is to model this process using computer simulation. This is, however, a non-trivial task. In the recent past a great deal has been made of the potential for social simulation. As Sawyer (2003) notes, however, to date most projects have involved emerging macro structure from local micro interactions or building in macro structures and allowing them to impinge on micro processes – none have involved both. One of the goals of the EMIL project is to build a simulator which can help us come to terms with the micro-macro interplay by building a simulator which can support the reciprocal process of bottom up and top down simultaneously. The capability for such a simulator has been determined but not yet implemented.

Reflections and Conclusions

There is a long way to go in resolving the long term problem pertaining to the interplay between micro and macro level social phenomena. However, over the recent couple of decades two important changes have occurred 1) we have begun to take seriously the extent and implications of non-linearity and its consequences for our understanding of natural and social phenomena through the conceptual tools developing under the banner of complex systems 2) we have begin to build the tools needed to explore such systems, in particular the technique of multi-agent modelling. This allows us to revisit and reapply more established methods for the study of situated dynamics in real social systems, beyond the constraints of micro-macro discipline specific boundaries.

Based on our past experience as practitioners and a wide reading of the literature we have outlined an approach which we believe at the very least models some of the characteristics essential to an effective theoretical solution and at best provides a platform upon which one might be based. It is designed to support naturalistic enquiry as well as systematic exploration using the formalisms of multi-agent simulation. While still very much 'under development' and by no means the only possible way forward, it helps to contrast the limitations of many existing theoretical approaches. It serves also to bring some new clarity to some of the perennial dimensions of debate – in particular that around the concept of emergence.

We have argued that systems science does not take us far due in part to its generality and to its intrinsic bias towards the macro perspective. Useful insights can be taken from Complex systems but it needs to be recognized that social systems are complex systems of a particular class and the class specific characteristics have yet to be fully come to terms with. In particular we have highlighted that the study of non-reflexive emergence does not take us very far toward understanding social emergence in human systems.

It is important that future work not only be philosophical but that theoretical advance go hand in hand with empirical work. While the theoretical framework we suggest has no associated methods, we demonstrate through the case studies that often there are a range of existing methods which can be used in the exploration of the relationship between micro and macro but that this generally entails a creative blending of techniques outside of the traditional discipline or paradigm specific environments in which they were developed.

Acknowledgements

One of the authors is involved with the project EMIL, "Emergence In the Loop: simulating the two way dynamics of norm innovation", a three-year EU funded project (Sixth Framework Programme -Information Society and Technologies-Citizens and Governance in the Knowledge Based Society. The views expressed are the authors and do not necessarily reflect those of the Partners to this project.

References

Achim, S.; Phenomenal Emergence; 4, 3, www.swif.uniba.it/lei/ai/networks/

Archer, M. 1998. Realism in the Social Sciences. In M. Archer & R. Bhaskar & A. Collier & T. Lawson & A. Norrie (Eds.), Critical Realism: Essential Readings. London: Routledge.

Bak, P. 1996. How Nature Works: The Science of Self-Organized criticality. New York: Copurnicus. ISBN: 0-387-94791-4

Bannister, D. & Fransella, F. 1989. Inquiring Man: The Psychology of Personal Constructs. London: Routledge. ISBN: 0415034604

Berger, P. L. & Luckman, T. 1972. The Social Construction of Reality: Penguin. ISBN: 0140600019

Bhaskar, R. 1998. The Possibility of Naturalism. London: Routledge. ISBN: 0-415-19874-7

Burrell, G. & Morgan, G. 1994. Sociological Paradigms and Organizational Analysis. London: Virago. ISBN: 1-85742-114-0

Chalmers, D. J. 2006. Strong and Weak Emergence. Canberra: Research School of Social Sciences, Australian National University.

Checkland, P. 1999. Systems Thinking Systems Practice. G.B.: John Wiley. ISBN: 0471986062

Clayton, P. & Davies, P. 2006. The Re-Emergence of Emergence: The Emergentist Hypothesis from Science to Religion. Oxford: Oxford University Press. ISBN: 0199287147

Dautenhahn, K. 2002. The Origins of Narrative. International Journal of Cognition and Technology, 1(1), ISSN: 1569-2167: 97-123.

Ezzy, D. 1998. Theorizing Narrative Identity: Symbolic Interactionism and Hermeneutics. The Sociological Quarterly, 39(2): 239-252.

Fisher, D. B.; Think Local Act Global!; 28 August, 2007, http://www.origin.to/global.html

Fodor, J. A. 1974. Special; Sciences or The Disunity of Science as a Working Hypothesis. Synthese, 28, ISSN: 1573-0964: 18.

Fransella, F., Bell, R., & Bannister, D. 2004. A Manual for Reportory Grid Technique: Second Edition. Chichester: John Wiley & Sons. ISBN: 0-470-85489-8

Fuchs, C. & Hofkirchner, W. 2005. The Dialectic of Bottom-up and Top-down Emergence in Social Systems. tripleC 1(1), ISSN 1726-670X: 22.

Gardenfors, P. 2006. How Homo became Sapiens: On the evolution of Thinking. Oxford: Oxford University Press. ISBN: 0198528515

Gilbert, N. 2002. Varieties of Emergence. Paper presented at the Social Agents: Ecology, Exchange, and Evolution Conference Chicago.

Goldspink, C. & Kay, R. 2003. Organizations as Self Organizing and Sustaining Systems: A Complex and Autopoietic Systems Perspective. International Journal General Systems, 32(5), ISSN: 0308-1079: 459-474.

Goldspink, C. & Kay, R. 2004. Bridging the Micro-Macro Divide: a new basis for social science. Human Relations, 57 (5), ISSN: 0018-7267: 597-618.

Goldspink, C. 2007. Normative self-regulation in the emergence of global network institutions: The Case of Wikipedia. , ANZSYS07. Auckland, New Zealand.

Goldspink, C. & Kay, R. 2007. Emergence in Social Systems: Distinguishing Reflexive and Non-reflexive modes, AAAI Fall Symposium: Emergent Agents and Socialities: Social and Organizational Aspects of Intelligence. Washington.

Grice, J. W. 2002. Idiogrid: Software for the management and analysis of repertory grids. Behavior Research Methods, Instruments, & Computers, 34: 3.

Holland, J. H. 1998. Emergence: from chaos to order. Ma.: Addison Wesley. ISBN

0-201-14943-5
Jankowics, D. 2004. The Easy Guide to Repertory Grids. London: Wiley. ISBN: 0-470-85404-9
Kauffman, S. 2000. Investigations. New York: Oxford. ISBN: 0-19-512104-x
Keeney, B. P. 1987. Aesthetics of Change: Guilford. ISBN: 1572308303
Kelly, G. A. 1963. A Theory of Personality. New Yorke: Norton. ISBN: 0-393-00152-0
Landfield, A. W. & Cannell, J. E. 1988. Ways of assessing functionally independent construction, meaningfulness, and construction in hierarchy. In J. C. M. M. L. Shaw (Ed.), Cognition and personal structure: 67-90. New York: Praeger ISBN: 0275926060.
Lorenz, E. N. 2001. The Essence of Chaos (4 ed.). Seattle: University of Washington Press. ISBN: 0-295-97514-8
Luhmann, N. 1990. Essays on Self Reference. New York: Columbia University Press. ISBN: 0231063687
Luhmann, N. 1995. Social Systems. Stanford: Stanford University Press. ISBN: 0804726256
Maturana, H. & Varela, F. 1980. Autopoiesis and Cognition: The Realization of the Living. Boston: D. Reidel. ISBN: 90-277-1016-3
Rhodes, C. & Brown, A. D. 2005. Narrative Organizations and Research. International Journal of Management Review, 7(3), ISSN: 1468-2370: 167-188.
Richardson, K. A. 2002a. Methodological Implications of a Complex Systems Approach to Sociality: Some further remarks. Journal of Artificial Societies and Social Simulation, 5(2), ISSN: 1460-7425.
Richardson, K. A. 2002b. On the Limits of Bottom Up Computer Simulation: Towards a Non-linear Modeling Culture. Paper presented at the 36th Hawaii International Conference on Systems Science, Hawaii.
Sanger, L.; The Early History of Nupedia and Wikipedia: A Memoir, file:///C:/data/surrey/Case%20Studies/wikipedia/early%20history%20of%20nupedia%20and%20wikipedia.htm
Sawyer, K. R. 2001. Emergence in Sociology: Contemporary Philosophy of Mind and Some Implications for Sociology Theory. American Journal of Sociology, 107(3), ISSN: 0002-9602: 551-585.
Sawyer, K. R. 2003. Artificial Societies: Multiagent Systems and the Micro-macro Link in Sociological Theory. Sociological Methods & Research, 31, ISSN: 0049-1241: 38.
Sawyer, K. R. 2005. Social Emergence: Societies as Complex Systems. Cambridge, UK: Cambridge University Press. ISBN: 0521606373
Stewart, I. 1990. Does God Play Dice - The New Mathematics of Chaos: Penguin. ISBN: 0631232516
Stiles, W. B. 1992. Describing Talk: A Taxonomy of Verbal Response Modes: Sage. ISBN 0803944659
Weik, E.; Working Relationships, A Meta view on Structure and Agency; 1, 7, http://theoryandscience.icaap.org/content/vol7.1/weik.html
Williams, G. P. 1997. Chaos Theory Tamed. Washington D.C: Joseph Henry Press. ISBN: 0-309-06351-5

39. An Exploration of Social Uncertainty in Complex Systems

Ivan Jensen
Metamanagement, DEN

Paul Jackson
Edith Cowan University, AUS

In this paper, we inductively develop a theory of the constituent elements of social uncertainty, based on managerial and consulting experience and informed by the results of a major research project. Theory formation is driven by the tenet that social uncertainty leads to reduction or avoidance behavior. The theory predicts that, with the organization as the level of analysis, social uncertainty is constituted by four conceptual elements: concurrence, coherence, cognition and conformance. The theory is expressed in formal, symbolic notation to aid its experimental verification. The formula is then embedded within the topological mapping of complex systems theory (Juarrero, 2002) to demonstrate how the formula may be used to understand and ameliorate social uncertainty in times of organizational transformation or volatility.

Introduction

Whatever the world is *now*, it is definitely not what it *was* – and the change from now to next seems to take place at an accelerating rate. In the words of Tom Peters (1993) "[the] world is going bonkers. And it is going to get more bonkers; bonkers squared in a few years with bonkers cubed on the way" (see also e.g. Toffler, 1980; Naisbitt, 1984; Giddens, 1991; 1999; Negroponte, 1995; Stacey, 2002; Hedberg, *et al.*, 2000). The way we perceive this increase in complexity - its extent, rate, desirability and how profoundly it affects us - varies tremendously from person to person. One consequence of rapid and significant change, however, is undisputed: it leads to a loss of predictability. This reduced predictability, or uncertainty, is the result of incomplete information about the future and, in turn, leads to the perception that the future is fraught with risk (Giddens, 1999).

In conjunction with a major research project – longitudinally following an organization that is engaged in a process of deliberate, strategically anchored virtualization – we have become increasingly aware of some of the forces that influence actors in a field which is incrementally being stripped of its brick-and-mortar structure and predictability (Klobas & Jackson, 2007). We posit that as social and organizational systems become more complex, human beings generally strive to avoid or reduce unpredictability and uncertainty and that the need to do so is a deeply rooted driving force, both individually and collectively.

We predict that the need to manage social uncertainty will become more pronounced, as relentlessly increasing rates of change drive us towards volatile, complex and virtual environments. "All that is solid melts into air", as hierarchies collapse, organizational boundaries become porous and firms develop novel and ephemeral forms and structures. The corollary to this axiom is that organizational leaders who are confronted with complexity, discontinuity and instability need conceptual tools with which to first understand the influences upon social uncertainty and secondly how to develop appropriate managerial responses. Accordingly, we embed our observations within the theory of complex systems, which are collections of multiple, interacting agents in which order emerges from the behavior and interaction of (often intentional) agents, rather then being predetermined. The history of the system and the system itself play roles in co-causing the behavior of agents, but causation in such systems is often non-linear and unpredictable.

Webster's unabridged dictionary defines uncertainty as "the state of being uncertain, doubt, hesitancy…vague or indistinct, not perfectly apprehended...ambiguous, unreliable, undependable, dependent upon chance...unforeseeable outcome or affect.... That which is uncertain is doubtful or problematical; it often involves danger through an inability to predict or place confidence in the unknown". Uncertainty is thus caused by incomplete information, as discussed by Galbraith (1973) in a task-related, organizational context; conversely, certainty is related to complete information. Uncertainty is an important concept because of its relation to perceptions of risk (Giddens, 1999).

Social uncertainty, then, is uncertainty related to or located in the social field, where hesitancy, vagueness, ambiguity or lack of confidence are reflexive characteristics of social objects or actors in a community. It should be noted that 'social uncertainty' is predominantly a cognitive concept, caused by incomplete information about the social field, which may well be but is not necessarily associated with any emotional manifestations.

Our unit of analysis is the organization and we seek to understand the impact of social uncertainty upon organizations, rather than at the intrapsychic or interpersonal level. We take Scott's definition of an organization as an open system: *organizations are systems of interdependent activities linking shifting coalitions of participants; the systems are embedded in – dependent upon continuing exchanges with and constituted by – the environments in which they operate* (Scott, 1998: 25). Thus, some of the social uncertainty within organizations may originate in their environment.

Social uncertainty will influence the effectiveness of an organization (Zand, 1972); when levels of social uncertainty increase, members collectively react in ways so as to actively reduce or avoid that uncertainty. This will cause participants to spend more time making sense and evaluating risks (Weick, 1979). Managers, who need to maintain productive momentum, must anticipate and minimise the impact of these diversions. Even at the organizational level, higher social uncertainty may well lead to anxiety which, if prolonged, inevitably induces stress and somatic or psychological dysfunction or overt disease. Managers therefore have both an operational and an ethical obligation to attend to social uncertainty and its consequences. Uncertainty *reduction* can be achieved through im- or exlicit manipulation of the constituent variables. Where this is not possible, uncertainty *avoidance* is typically attempted through a move (metaphorically or factually) away from the larger, high social uncertainty context towards sequentially smaller constellations of actors with a lower social uncertainty (larger or smaller groups, triads, dyads, or, ultimately, monads). In an organizational context, such constellations may be, e.g., teams, networks, communities of practice, groups etc.

A certain amount of social uncertainty, however, may be a necessary condition for desired outcomes such as an innovation or high performance. In the face of complete information, writes Stacey, the consequence is the maintenance of the status quo through "ordinary management". Conversely, incomplete information requires "extraordinary management" (Stacey, 2002). For every organization at any point in time there is thus a level of social uncertainty which represents an optimum equilibrium between innovation, openness, order and self-assurance, rigidity, impenetrability, chaos and anxiety or even withdrawal of commitment. The point is not to eradicate the latter, but to find a point in the scale which represents optimal positioning for the particular requirements of an organization. The conceptual framework developed in this paper will help managers to make more informed decisions about the social landscape of their organizations.

In order to gain intellectual control over the factors which influence or are associated with social uncertainty, we reduce the participating variables to abstractions from which background noise has been filtered and which are condensed to give a distinct idea of their role and impact. The formulation should be able to be understood and interpreted 'at a glance'. Therefore in the tradition of Lewin (1997), we present our framework in formal, symbolic notation. The result of the formula is a 'social uncertainty index', which is determined by the contributing variables and their interaction. The symbolic form is dense and generative, permitting the derivation of heuristics and quantifiable hypotheses. To take a simple example, the variable 'Trust' is inversely related to social uncertainty: the higher the trust, the lower the social uncertainty. In the following sections we first define each contributing factor as a variable and declare the relationship of the variables to social uncertainty before combining them into an overall formula.

Variable Definition

Although this is a conceptual paper, the following constructs have been derived through the authors' observations, reflections and abstractions. The individual variables of the conceptual framework we present are ontologically distinct but partially interdependent in organizations. Some of the variables are easily quantifiable whereas others can only be measured or visualized qualitatively or by proxy.

Dispersion Index - DI

The dispersion index measures the degree of physical separation between members of the organization, simply expressed as the sum of the spatial distances. Physical separation generally decreases the regularity and richness of communication and interaction. The greater the dispersion index, the greater the social uncertainty. In the formula, we use $\sum_1^N DI_{ij}$ to denote the sum of the spatial distances between individuals i and j.

Collocation Index - CI

The collocation index measures the proportion of time spent by members of the organization in face-to-face contact, e.g., expressed as a percentage of the total available time. Face-to-face contact improves the construction of common mental models, the building of trust, the clarity of communication and helps reduce ambiguity. The greater the collocation index, the lower the social uncertainty of the organization. In the formula, we use $\sum_1^N CI_{ij}$ to denote total time spent by individuals in the same place, expressed as a proportion of the total available work time.

Individual Identity - I_i

Individual identity is a complex and controversial construct with some theorists such as Goffman (1959), asserting there is in fact no such thing as a 'real self'. We take a pragmatic view that identity is a valid construct which is related to and drives attitudes, traits and behavior. Sedikides and Brewer (2001: 1) write: "... persons seek to achieve self-definition and self-interpretation (i.e. identity) in three fundamental ways: (a) in terms of their unique traits (b) in terms of dyadic relationships, and (c) in terms of group membership". The greater the strength of individual identity, the lower the commitment of group members to group identity and the concomitant standardised behavioral patterns: this increases social uncertainty (Whetten & Godfrey, 1998; Leary & Tangney, 2003). In the formula, we use $\sum_1^N I_i$ to denote the summation of the relative strengths of individual identity components across organizational members, e.g. as measured by the proportion of statements from the Twenty Statement Test that are coded as 'individual'.

Collective Ontology – Sharedness and stability - O_c

This variable describes the degree to which an organization's members have a coherent and shared ontology, or common view of the organization and its underpinning social reality (Hatch & Schultz, 2004). The more shared this view, the lower the social uncertainty (Berreby, 2005). However, the rate at which this understanding changes over time will also influence social uncertainty, such that the greater the rate of change, the higher the levels of uncertainty. It is possible that the mechanism through which a collective ontology is created and maintained is equivalent to that of 'social categorisation' (Hogg & Terry, 2001);

i.e., striving to maximise the distance between self and out-group prototype(s) while, at the same time, minimizing the distance between self and in-group prototype(s).

Epistemology - Ratio of information to knowledge - INF/KN

These variables are necessary to capture the complex relationship between the information which is available to an organization and the explanatory power of the knowledge within the organization to give structure to that information (Devlin, 2001). The greater the ratio of knowledge to information, corresponding to the 'codification' and 'abstraction' of Boisot (1998), the easier it is for an organization to make sense of its environment, the available data, and therefore the lower the social uncertainty. In the formula, this is denoted by INF/KN.

Available and Requisite variety - V

The principle of requisite variety states that there must be as much diversity or complexity inside an organization as in its environment for the organization to be able to deal with complexity (Ashby, 1963; Weick, 1979). Adequate available variety, e.g., when ($V_{avail} \geq V_{req}$), enables organizational responsiveness and self-determination and will therefore reduce social uncertainty. An unfavorable ratio between information and knowledge (which leads to high social uncertainty) can be attenuated by high requisite variety. That is to say, where an organization has sufficient internal mechanisms to identify and then process and react to relevant social stimuli, this will enhance confidence and certainty in the organization's ability to cope. In the formula, V_{avail}/V_{req} indicates the ratio between the available and the requisite variety.

Authority and formal legitimation - S

This variable describes the clarity and acceptance of modes of influence and control within an organization, which are usually, but not always, embodied within managerial or supervisory functions. Where power structures are not explicit or legitimated, there will be greater social uncertainty; in the formula this is indicated by the expression (1 – S), which may vary between 0 ('crystalline order') and 1 ('total anarchy').

Trust - T

Webster's unabridged dictionary defines trust as "a reliance on the integrity, strength, ability, surety, etc. of a person or thing ... trust implies instinctive unquestioning belief in and reliance upon something". In keeping with this Luhmann (1979) defines trust as a mechanism for the reduction of social complexity, which in turn reduces the cognitive load needed for constant checking, control and monitoring. The greater the trust existing in an organization, the lower will be the need for time and energy to be expended in pursuit of more complete information (Kramer & Cook, 2004). In the formula, we use:

$$\sum_{1}^{N} T_{ij}$$

to denote the summation of trust between individuals *i* and *j*. Trust in an organization can be measured, e.g., as described in (Kramer & Cook, 2004).

The Formula

Social Uncertainty (SU), we postulate, is a function of the behavior and interaction of the constituent variables described in the previous sections. We have grouped those variables which appear to amplify or attenuate one another. This adds to the conceptual clarity of the equation and suggests four major categories of influence upon social uncertainty.

Concurrence – the spatial distance between organization members as expressed by the ratio between dispersion and collocation;

Coherence – the consistency in perceptions and self-perceptions between members of an organization as expressed by the prominence of individual identity components and consistency of worldview;

Cognition – the information processing level of the organization as expressed by the ratio of information to knowledge. This is further ameliorated by the organization's capability to ingest and process information to the level required;

Conformance – the degree to which behaviors are legitimated, assertions are accepted on trust, and individuals subject themselves to the requirements of the organization as expressed by the ratio between authority and trust.

The higher each of these categories, the lower will be the social uncertainty. The variables are, however, somewhat interdependent and may well influence, and be influenced by, variables in any of the other categories. For example, whilst high trust reduces the need for explicit power structures, it will also reduce the demand for exhaustive or complete information. In its abbreviated form, the formula for social uncertainty is described in Figure 1.

$$SU = \mathbf{F}\left[Concurrence, Coherence, Cognition, Conformance\right]$$

Figure 1 *Abbreviated formula for Social Uncertainty*

Figure 2 describes in extended form the formula for social uncertainty. The power term, $N(dO_c/dt)$, reflects our belief that social uncertainty increases as a non-trivial function of both the number of actors in the organization (N) and the rate of change of the shared ontology (dO_c/dt). If, for example, the organization is large and the rate of change is negligible, i.e. dO_c/dt is close to zero, then social uncertainty will be very low. An illustration of this constellation could be a peacetime Army. When, on the other hand, the rate of change of the shared ontology is high due to internal and/or external influences then social uncertainty will increase very significantly. This constellation can be found, e.g. with start-up companies, in mergers, with significant changes in strategy, or potentially disruptive/destructive perturbations in the organization's markets or environment.

$$SU = \mathrm{F}\left[\left(\frac{\sum_1^N DI_{ij}}{\sum_1^N CI_{ij}}\right), \left(\frac{\sum_1^N I_i}{O_c}\right), \left(\frac{\frac{INF}{KN}}{\frac{V_{avail}}{V_{req}}}\right), \left(\frac{1-S}{\sum_1^N T_{ij}}\right)\right]^{N\frac{dO_c}{dt}}$$

Figure 2 *The full formula for Social Uncertainty*

In developing this formula, we have constantly conducted thought experiments using a variety of historical and contemporary organizational phenomena to test its face validity. For example, the tactic of some political groupings (usually extreme conservatives) is to present solutions which reduce social uncertainty (this is often after having created that very sense of uncertainty and threat as a platform for the ideological message). They profess strong leadership, clear, traditional values, rejection of internationalism and globalization, and implacable opposition to the national-cultural dilution by immigrants or 'others'. Some people support such policies because they are fearful and uncertain about the risks and dangers they perceive in chaos and lack of rule. Those people come together in large meetings and demonstrations and the coherence of perceptions and self-identity in such groups provides a sense of continuity and uniformity. Modalities for cognition are limited, usually with a single source of information; messages are consistent, digestible and limited and the knowledge to process these messages is simple, self-contained and self-referential. Conformance is manifest in the promise of authority and clear power structures. High concurrence, high coherence, high shared cognition and high conformance act to directly reduce social uncertainty and gain the loyalty of the anxious.

Social Uncertainty and Complex Systems

Social uncertainty is a cognitive, not an emotional state, propagated from judgment rather than sentiment. As a cognitive state, it belongs not to any individual but to the system from which it emerges; it is collectively co-created by all the actors in that system. Thus, social uncertainty is the dynamic result of situated processing of social information and will co-determine future behavior and decision making by the actors in the system. We therefore embed the following observations about social uncertainty in an overall context of complex responsive systems (Juarrero, 2002; Stacey, 2001).

If we are to manage social uncertainty, to minimise its deleterious effects, for example upon decisions to share knowledge or commit to an organization, we need to understand how actors perceive the constituent elements of social uncertainty and develop intentions (Juarrero, 2002: 151). Intentions are directly formed through social institutions which exist within a defined semantic space and constitute "dynamical attractors" which may alter the trajectory of the action. The semantic space provides a contextual constraint which can itself change the action (Juarrero, 2002: 178). A constraint can function as a cause, by creating a field or chronological dependence: the possibility of "what happens next" is co-caused not only by antecedent "billiard balls", or efficient causes, but also by contextual elements.

Figure 3 demonstrates how we have embedded the ontology of social uncertainty into the general framework of complex systems. Each element is placed in an institutional corridor. As we move through time, the intensity of the element changes within the position in the corridor, depending upon the existence and intensity of other institutions in other corridors. The degree of intensity "i" of perceived institutions "c" at any time "t" is a function of the real world (are people really dispersed) and the actors' perception of that dispersion (some people may not even notice). The semantic space is given by the ontology of social uncertainty and determines the trajectory of action for responding to SU. The theory of complex systems allows us to explain how many, but not all, people perceive and respond to social uncertainty in organizations.

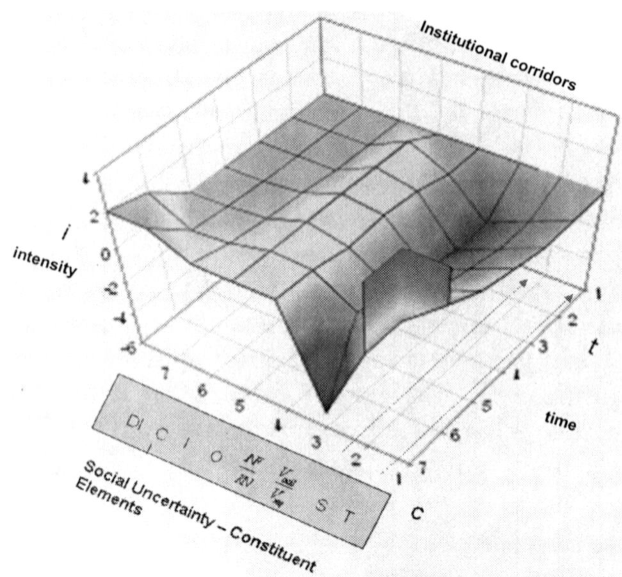

Figure 3 *Mapping the Topology of Social Uncertainty as a Complex System*

Mapping the constituent elements within the theoretical framework of complex systems has potential practical benefits. It may allow us to anticipate and plan for actor responses during periods of organizational transformation and disruption. For example, the topological representation could be a change management tool when developing and implementing information systems for work dispersion or distribution. Or we could map the expected responses of participants to outsourcing or virtual partnerships. The visual nature of the topographical representation would indicate clearly where there are "mountains" of resistance which need to be addressed.

Conclusion

This is a conceptual paper, derived from literature review, personal management experience and partly grounded in the longitudinal study of an organization which is in the process of become distributed and 'virtual'. The concept of social uncertainty seems useful and the notion that reducing social uncertainty, particularly under conditions such as geographical dispersal and disciplinary or cultural diversity, is intuitively appealing. The formula we have developed is a first step in trying to gather and combine the contributing variables; it is compact and transparent, allowing simple heuristics or complex hypotheses to be derived. It can be extended and enriched as research reveals new insights and relationships. The subsequent mapping of the constituent elements of the ontology onto a complex systems topology may lead towards management tools in which the landscape of uncertainty can be anticipated and management strategies developed.

References

Ashby, W. R. (1956). *An introduction to Cybernetics.* ISBN 0416683002, London: Chapman & Hall.

Bar-Tal, Y. (1994). Uncertainty and the perception of sufficiency of social support, control,

and information. *The Psychological Record,* ISSN 0033-2933, *44.*

Berreby, D. (2005). *Us and Them: Understanding Your Tribal Mind.* ISBN 0091801117, New York: Little, Brown & Company.

Boisot, M. (1998). *Knowledge Assets: Securing Competitive Advantage in the Information Economy,* ISBN 0198290861, Oxford University Press.

Clampitt, P. G., & Williams, M. L. (2007). Managing Organizational Uncertainty: Conceptualization and Measurement [Electronic Version]. Retrieved 14th January 2007 from http://www.imetacomm.com/otherpubs/research/UMMCommReports.html.

Devlin, K. (2001). *Infosense: Turning Information into Knowledge.* ISBN 0716741644, New York: W.H. Freeman & Company.

Fields, D. L. (2002). *Taking the Measure of Work: A Guide to Validated Scales for Organizational Research and Diagnosis.* ISBN 0761924256, Thousand Oaks, CA: Sage.

Galbraith, J. (1973). *Designing Complex Organizations.* ISBN 0201025590, Reading: Addison-Wesley.

Giddens, A. (1991). *Modernity and Self-Identity.* ISBN 0804719446, Cambridge: Polity Press.

Giddens, A. (1999). *Runaway World: How Globalization is Reshaping our Lives.* ISBN 0415944872, London: Profile Books.

Goffman, E. (1990). *The presentation of self in everyday life.* ISBN 0844670170, New York: Anchor Books.

Grace, S. L., & Cramer, K. L. (2003). The Elusive Nature of Self-Measurement: The Self-Construal Scale Versus the Twenty Statements Test. *The Journal of Social Psychology,* ISSN 1367-2223, *143*(5), 649-668.

Hatch, M. J., & Schultz, M. (2004). *Organizational Identity.* ISBN 0199269475, Oxford University Press.

Hedberg, B., Dahlgren, G., Hansson, J., & Olve, N.-G. (2000). *Virtual Organizations and beyond: Discovering Imaginary Systems.* ISBN 0471499951, Chichester: John Wiley & Sons.

John, O. P., Kramer, R. M., & Tyler, T. R. (Eds.). (1999). *The Psychology of the Social Self.* ISBN 0805828508, Mahwah: Lawrence Erlbaum Associates.

Juarrero, A. (2002). *Dynamics in action: intentional behavior as a complex system.* ISBN 0262600471, Cambridge, Massachusetts: The MIT Press.

Klein, H. K., & Myers, M. D. (1999). A Set of Principles for Conducting and Evaluating Interpretive Field Studies in Information Systems. *MIS Quarterly,*ISSN 0276-778, *23*(1), 67-94.

Klobas, J. & Jackson, P. (Eds.). (2007 (in press)). *Becoming virtual: Knowledge management and transformation of the distributed organization.* ISBN 3790819573, Berlin: Springer Verlag.

Kramer, R. M., & Cook, K. S. (Eds.). (2004). *Trust and Distrust in Organizations: Dilemmas and Approaches.* ISBN 0871544865, Washington: Russell Sage Foundation.

Kuhn, M., & & McPartland, T. (1954). An empirical investigation of self-attitudes. *American Sociological Review,* ISSN 0003-1224, *19*, 68-76.

Leary, M. R., & Tangney, J. P. (Eds.). (2003). *Handbook of Self and Identity.* ISBN 1593852371, London: The Guildford Press.

Lewin, K. (1997). *Field Theory in Social Science.* Washington: American Psychological Association.

Luhmann, N. (1979). *Trust and Power.* ISBN 0471997587, New York: John Wiley & Sons.

Naisbitt, J. (1984). *Megatrends: Ten New Directions Transforming Our Lives.* ISBN 0446329223, New York: Warner Books Inc.

Negroponte, N. (1995). *Being Digital.* ISBN 0679768378, New York: Vintage Books.

Peters, T. (March 29, 1993). Interview *Forbes ASAP.*

Peters, T. (March 29, 1993). Interview. *Forbes ASAP.*

Peters, T. I. p. i. F. A., March 29, 1993. (1993).

Scott, W. R. (1998). *Organizations: Rational, Natural and Open Systems* (4 ed.). ISBN 013016559X, Upper Saddle River: Prentice Hall.

Sedikides, C., & Brewer, M. B. (2002). *Individual Self, Relational Self, Collective Self.* ISBN 1841690430, Philadelphia: Psychology Press.

Stacey, R. (2001). *Complex Responsive Processes in Organizations: Learning and Knowledge Creation.* ISBN 0415249198, London: Routledge.

Stacey, R. D. (2002). *Strategic Management and Organizational Dynamics: The Challenge of Complexity* (4 ed.). ISBN 0273708112, Upper Saddle River: Prentice Hall.

Toffler, A. (1980). *The third Wave.* ISBN 0517327198, New York: William Morrow.

Weick, K. E. (1979). *The social psychology of organizing* (2 ed.). ISBN 0201085917, Reading: Addison-Wesley.

Whetten, A., & Godfrey, P. C. (1998). *Identity in Organizations: Building Theory Through Conversations.* ISBN 0761909486, Thousand Oaks: SAGE Publications.

Zand, D. E. (1972). Trust and Managerial Problem Solving. . *Administrative Science Quarterly,* ISSN 0001-8392, *17*(2), 229-239.

Zolin, R., Hinds, P., Fruchter, R., & Levitt, R. (2004). Interpersonal trust in cross-functional, geographically distributed work: A longitudinal study. *Information & Organizations,* ISSN 1471-7727, *14*, 1-26.

40. Ethics, Boundaries and Sustainable Futures

PLENARY PAPER

Janet McIntyre-Mills
Flinders Institute of Public Policy and Management, Flinders University, AUS

The paper discusses the way in which a design of inquiring system can be used to address areas of concern that span conceptual and spatial boundaries. Ethical literacy for a sustainable future is assisted by matching knowledge domains to areas of concern by testing out ideas with those who are to be at the receiving end of the decisions and with future generations in mind. The challenge is to find ways to enhance both representation and accountability.

"*...The systems approach begins when first you see the world through the eyes of another*" (C. West Churchman, 1979: 231-232).

"*Ethics is an eternal conversation. The reason that ethical relativism (different strokes for different people") is so bad is that it stops conversation. Relativists are only sure of one thing, their relativism. They actually think that ethics is a search for absolute values, and since it is, it is a hopeless enterprise. Since ethics is an eternal conversation, its conversation retains its aesthetic quality if human values are regarded as neither relative nor absolute*" (Churchman, 1982: 57 and cited in Banathy, 1996: 187).

Introduction

As Barry Jones said in '*Sleepers Awake*', the challenge is to be able 'to hold in mind more than one big idea at any one time!" This is a theme that has been raised by policy makers, ethicists and those who are concerned about sustainability.

The discussion is premised on the idea that many bodies of knowledge exist and that the challenge is to ask questions that will enable the appropriate knowledge to be matched contextually to a task, challenge or problem.

As West Churchman (1982) stresses, all decisions "make cuts" and leave out parts of the whole system. Instead accountable policy making needs to consider the consequences for those will be at the receiving end of the decision. Democratic freedom and diversity need to be fostered through openness to continuous dialogue and listening. We can be free to the extent that we do not limit the freedoms of others. It is at this point that we need to draw boundaries. Two-way communication is needed to test out ideas and to build relationships. The central paradox for democracy is that trust is a risk for people who make themselves vulnerable to others (Warren, 1999); but without trust that is developed through *hospitable rather than merely respectful communication* (Borradori in conversation with Habermas & Derrida, 2003) democracy is unsustainable. Derrida stresses that cold tolerance is insufficient for building relationships.

Understanding the role of values, emotions and consciousness is vital for democracy and the process of making accountable policy. Making connections is the basis for consciousness (Greenfield, 2000). The more connections we can make, the better our thinking, our policy processes and our governance outcomes will be.

A process that helps to enhance policy making and democratic governance is adapted from Ashby's Law (1956) of socio-cybernetics and the principle of subsidiarity (namely that policy needs to be made at the lowest level possible and by those who are to be at the receiving end of the decision, see for example McIntyre *et al.*, 2005, 2006). The complexity of the decision needs to match the complexity of the people who will be at the receiving end of the decision. The elegance and simplicity of this argument is that it is based on systemic, feedback logic that tests out ideas in such a way that the experts are those who actually have lived experience of what works, why and how!

This could be the way forward to enhance complex policy making. It is the subject of a current Australian Research Council Linkage Grant between an Aboriginal NGO and the South Australian Dept of Health, but it has much wider governance implications. Seeing the world in bounded conceptual (disciplinary) and spatial (organizational and geographical) silos supports limited, compartmentalized thinking and practice.

Accountability is about the big picture, not the interests of one department or organization at the expense of others. The old fragmentation approach is 'divide and rule'. The new systemic approach is based on 'link and thrive'.

Responsibility and blame can be apportioned to others. It is very useful for powerful decision makers in the public and private sectors who think merely in terms of the next board meeting, the next election or only in terms of the economic bottom line (at the expense of environmental and social considerations). Consciousness of the opportunity costs of these decisions could lead to more systemic policy decisions. The bureaucrats and CEOs who can think systemically will shape the future in a more positive manner.

Once we are mindful that the consequences of our actions cannot be quarantined we become systemic practitioners.

Feedback or the 'boomerang affect' (See Ulrich Beck in "*Risk Society*" 1992) stresses that pollution, poverty and social injustice do not respect national boundaries.

Even if we could protect ourselves through national boundaries and the barriers of class or privilege-eventually the impact of our social and environmental actions will affect us. Payback or feedback cannot be ruled out of policy decisions. Social and environmental pollution spreads and affects us (eventually) irrespective of our socio-economic power or where we are located. Similarly (and this is our hope for the future) understanding the opportunity costs of not living sustainably on the next generation of life can make a difference.

As Ulrich Beck, Tim Flannery and Sir Nicholas Stern have stressed in "*Risk Society*"," *The Weather Makers" and "The Economics of Climate Change', respectively, we the people* can make a difference through our daily choices as to whether we:

- Make the cultural choice to live in sustainable ways.
- Choose to use and compete for the last of the non renewables – oil and uranium.

The Design of Inquiring Systems

The volumes in the C. West Churchman Legacy and Related Works on "*Rescuing the enlightenment and democracy from itself*" and "*Systemic Governance and Accountability*" make the case for using C. West Churchman's 'Design of Inquiring Systems' as the basis for testing out ideas using 'logic, empiricism, idealism, the dialectic (which includes subjective ideas in the process of dialogue) and pragmatism'.

The "Design of Inquiring Systems" is not only for self reflection, but for engaging with others to achieve 'best matches' and better decision making that is mindful of perceptions, values and emotions.

Systemic approaches (drawing on and adapting Churchman, 1979a, 1982) strive to match areas of concern to policy and practice by considering the following:

1. Subjective ideas that are brought into intersubjective processes;
2. Logical relationships across ideas;
3. Empirical data for the big (broad) and small (detailed) picture;
4. Idealism (not thinking about the consequences), because the moral law states we need to treat people as ends in themselves and not a means to an end;
5. Dialectical relationships that explore one argument versus another antithetical argument and then co-create shared meaning based on dialogue within context;
6. Pragmatic contextual considerations based on considering the consequences.

Initially that sounds contradictory. You may ask how both idealism and pragmatism could be considered at the same time. How can these questions help better decision making?

Ethical Literacy

Ethical literacy for a sustainable future is assisted by matching knowledge domains to areas of concern and needs to take into account the following:

1. **Idealism** which is a *non consequentialist and deontological* or duty based approach, based on taking decisions based on a moral law. It is a priori, because the moral law sets out one's duty, based on prior decisions on what constitutes ethical behavior. The test for the moral law is the being prepared to

live with the decisions if they were to be applied to oneself and one's own children. John Rawls (1999) explains in "The Law of Peoples" that this veil of ignorance approach is the basis for liberal democracy. But he argues that as a basis for democracy across nation states it is problematic as space has to be made for 'decent hierarchical nations' that do not accept democracy.

2. **Narrow pragmatism** is a consequentialist approach based on considering the meanings of the ideas and practices for the majority of stakeholders. It is *a posteriori* approach and it takes into account the points of view of the stakeholders in specific contexts. Pragmatism can be divided into narrow pragmatism that considers the majority, but not all stakeholders. At the other end of the continuum of pragmatism is *'expanded pragmatism'* that considers the consequences for all life.
3. **Expanded pragmatism** is thus based on caretaking for this generation of life and the next. It strives to consider self, other (including sentient beings) and the environment. Its aim is to support social and environmental justice for this generation and the next, based on recognition of connections and relationships extending across all forms of life. Expanded pragmatism advocates and applies the process of ensuring that those who are to be at the receiving end of a decision should be party to the decision making process or at least very well represented, so that decisions are not imposed in a top down manner and so that the wellbeing and interests (a life that is meaningful and free of pain) for the voiceless are considered. These include children, the disabled, asylum seekers and the powerless sentient being or animal. Beings (human and animal) need respect as consciousness is a continuum and human beings share the majority of their DNA with other life forms (Greenfield 2000). As caretakers we have the responsibility to act respectfully to other beings (to the extent that their diversity and freedom does not impinge on others, they should be accorded freedom to be), not merely because they are useful, but because they *are* beings. From this perspective decisions are made with or on behalf of those who are to be affected by the decisions. A range of conceptual tools ranging from narratives, questions, scenarios and models of 'if then' considerations can be used to enable decisions that 'unfold' values and 'sweep in' social, cultural, political and environmental considerations when considering the consequences for this generation of life and the next.
4. **Virtue based approach** is based on the qualities of thinking and practice that make up or constitute an ethical life. It is based on the work of Aristotle. He believed that inner virtue was the result of careful thinking and that eudaimonia (pronounced you-dye-monia) (see O'Grady, 2005: 154) was the goal of reasoning and that it would lead to happiness of the individual and society. Aristotle stressed the importance of phronesis1 or matching the right knowledge to an issue based on a) experiential wisdom, b) an appreciation of the many different kinds of knowledge and c) the ability to apply the right knowledge to an issue based on dialogue. The work of Aristotle stresses the importance of narrative and context for understanding and decision

making. The challenge posed by theorists, feminists and critical theorists is who decides on what constitutes knowledge and its implications for ethical decision making? Each of these need to be understood in detail (see Preston *et al.*, 2002 for *"A framework for Public Sector Ethics").*

We can use idealism as a basis for decision making and be guided by moral laws; this is a non consequentialist approach. If we can consider the consequences this is a pragmatic approach. But if we develop an expanded pragmatism to include all the stakeholders who are to be affected by the consequences of our actions, we move closer to idealism. If we regard the list of considerations above we are likely to make more connections and to be more mindful and much happier as a result. Aristotle stressed this in 'Nicomachean ethics' as a goal for humanity. Thinking brings inner virtue which brings about more accountable practice.

Bateson's approach outlined in 'The ecology of mind' is helpful for achieving mindfulness in that we can think within frameworks at level 1, think about frameworks at level 2 or at level 3 we can leap beyond our frameworks.

Let us think of our choices of energy use as an example of risk management and accountability that is uppermost in our minds. If we think of it in terms of many dimensions and 'unfold values' of stakeholders within and across nation states and 'sweep in' the social, cultural, political, economic and environmental domains then we are likely to have a better understanding of the issues that need to be considered systemically.

We are part of our environment and we shape it by our thinking and our practice.

If we consider the evidence (Stern Review, 2007) we will realize that with a rise in temperature of about 2 degrees Celsius we can expect an extensive impact within the Asia Pacific Region resulting in loss of species diversity, increased vulnerability to drought and low agricultural yields, higher living costs, increased environmental refugees and increased vulnerability of the poor.

Thinking in terms of one political term is absurd when generational futures are at stake. Thinking in terms of the nation state and citizenship is equally absurd when planetary futures are at stake.

We can redress hierarchy within and across nation states by arguing that "A is better off if B is better off". Humanity and the environment could be regarded as a mathematical Eigenform.

"*that is, the dynamic interrelationship of humanity and environment can be regarded as a complex dance or recursion where the two sides co-create one another (within the priority of omnipresent physical conditions*" (to cite Kauffman, 2007, pers comm2.).

At best we can strive to consider social, economic and environmental indicators that show we are destroying the environment and considering options within 'if then' scenarios from the point of view of future users. Vignettes and detailed narratives provide a means to explore complex challenges and enable us to understand the role of values, emotions and consciousness is vital for teaching accountable policy and practice.

Policy and Evidence, What is the Connection?

Two–way, hospitable communication is central to better research and better representation in society.

We need the will to do things differently. Policy change only happens if people can influence policy makers and if they can persuade them that it is in their interests to change. If people are able to think through the implications of their decisions, it could make a difference. This is important for ethics and governance.

Evidence can be put forward by researchers concerning sustainable futures, but without the 'political will' policy does not change. Therefore the most important issue for those who wish to shape policy through dialogue (Dryzek, 1999, 2000) is to help policy makers make the connection that bad policy and practice does not hurt others, it hurts us- if not today or tomorrow certainly within a generation , if not sooner .

Emotions, values and perceptions are central to our humanity. They underpin the so-called 'enemies within' (Churchman, 1979), namely 'religion, morality, aesthetics and politics', the human paradox of our potential for passion and compassion. The more connections we can make, the better our thinking, our policy processes and our governance outcomes will be (see White, 2001, 2002). This point is also made by Baroness Prof Susan Greenfield (2002) in her work '*The Private Life of the Brain*'. I adapt Greenfield (2002) and Cornelius (2005) and concentrate on ways to expand consciousness or mindfulness. Consciousness is based on connections across matter, mind and emotion in environmental context (Greenfield, 2000, McLuhan & Powers, 1989). Making connections is the basis for consciousness. The less connections we make, the less conscious we are (Greenfield, 2000). Consciousness is a continuum.

Because emotions are a major filter of perceptions we need to acknowledge emotions through encouraging people to express their perceived needs in rich stories and pictures. Emotions can limit our consciousness, but they can also alert us to issues that we need to think about. Passion and compassion are the flip sides of one another.

The challenge is to develop a process that is able to engage participation without lapsing into mob irrationality (Fishkin, 2000, Fishkin & Laslett, 2003).

Recognizing overlapping identities and connections can help rescue democracy from its failings. A study of genealogies of migrants in South Australia and of genealogies of Aboriginal Australians in Alice Springs in the NT, for example shows that we are joined through genealogies of connection (Young, McIntyre & Drummond, 2007 forthcoming).

"In this post 9/11 era we need to look for new understandings of national security and safety. We are all, whether newly arrived or 7th generation "white" Australian, of migrant extraction and we have close links with those we colonized. The

histories of chosen and forced heritage are written elsewhere and should not be forgotten (Atkinson, 2002; McIntyre-Mills, 2003) as it has implications for the way in which we understand ourselves and others."

By enabling people to make sense of their own experiences and to communicate this sense making (based on making connections across patterns) to others we can help them to build connections and to establish rapport with each other. Culture and politics are linked constructs that can and do change! The geographical continuity of "One World" (Singer, 2002) is an alternative to conceptualizing separate states and regions and the implications for nationality, race, culture, citizenship and democracy (Beck, 1992, 1998; McIntyre-Mills, 2000; Grugel, 1999). Understanding the "boomerang affect" or the social and environmental "payback" is pragmatic. Idealistically, the more we are able to hold in mind diverse viewpoints (Churchman, 1979 a, b, 1982) the better we will be able to appreciate complex risks and what accountably based on 'feeding forward' (or giving in an hospitable way) ought to entail. It is based on the idea "A is better off when B is better off" (Von Foerster, 1995: 494).

Representation and Accountability

Closed oppositional thinking in science (including economics and religion) is defined as fundamentalism (adapted from Kung and Moltmann 1992). Volume 3 of the C. West Churchman Series argues that *closed paradigms* that are oppositionally *opposed to revision* and reflection (based on criticism) are more likely to lead to *bad decisions* than *open paradigms* that are iteratively tested by diverse stakeholders.

Falsification has implications for ethics. If testing is done by the people at the receiving end of decisions it leads to a better match of services to needs. This wise matching process, based on experience is called *phronesis* by Aristotle in Nicomachean Ethics, as detailed below.

Phronesis as a basis for accountable decisions draws on diverse stakeholders inputs and is pragmatically good for risk management, because people are less likely to be critical of policies that they have helped to construct and which they own. Openness to ideas is vital for:

- Rescuing the enlightenment from itself by embracing paradox and thus relieving it from its potential for exclusivity and non –representation and;
- Enhancing democracy to make it more inclusive and representative (by taking into account the balance between the human desire for individualism and for collectivism).

Two-way communication (that is respectful of diverse ideas and helps to build relationships that span the landscape from local to international governance) is needed in a globalized world. This is the key point made by Berger (1976) and also by both Devji (2005) and Pape (2005) who studied Islamic fundamentalism.

Habermas and Derrida (2003) (in their conversation with Borradori about public philosophy, despite their different perspectives on the nature of representation) both agreed that engagement can prevent alienation and terrorism. They raised concerns about the need for respectful versus hospitable dialogue and recently by Gore in his book "*The Assault on Reason*" (2007), makes the case (based on research and evidence drawn from his own experience) that the lack of public engagement in dialogue and one-way communication raises many problems for democracy.

Decades ago McLuhan and Powers (1989) made the point that "the medium is the message" and that communication technology can have many unexpected impacts, such as dumbing down thinking, because watching TV can be a very passive experience that does not require conceptualisation through reading and thinking. Alternative ways of using communication technology (including TV) in a more interactive way are raised by Banathy (2000).

Systemic Governance and Accountability (vol. 3. of the C. West Churchman series) summarizes some of my own program of research with colleagues from a wide range of disciplines, members of the public and post graduates on participatory approaches focuses on an exploration of interorganisational decision making and policy networks as a way to engage citizens and to make governance ethical and accountable.

Democracy is currently increasingly criticized for not representing the interests of citizens (Institute of Governance 2005) or not taking into account the social justice and environmental concerns that span national boundaries (Singer, 2002), but balance is needed across the institutions of the state, the market and society, not a post Westphalian state (Bowden, 2006).

The challenge for *traditional liberal democracy* was to ensure that government organizations acted as accountable agents for the principles (de Tocqueville, 1945), namely the people they serve. Voting in elected members who represent the people was considered to be both necessary and sufficient. *New Democracy* requires more than social choices made by voting within national boundaries, it requires processes that are responsive to ongoing socio-political, economic and environmental changes and the identity shifts that occur (McIntyre, 2005, a, b; Pape, 2005; Devji, 2005; Giddens, 1991; Bogue, 1989; Eisenstein, 2004).

It requires accountability through deliberation to achieve better decision making, based on testing out the ideas (not only by experts) but by people who have lived experience of issues (McIntyre-Mills, 2003, 2005, 2006; McIntyre-Mills, *et al.*, 2006; Edgar, 1992; Polanyi, 1962). This is essential to address the interests of the less powerful, but also to ensure that the ideas of what works, why and how as far (as the principals are concerned) is addressed in the interests of environmental sustainability, accountability and socio-economic wellbeing (National Economics, 2002, 2003; Edgar, 1992; Cox, 1995).

So I will tell you a little bit about the Neporendi project which draws together my two main interests, namely participatory governance for social and environmental justice, based on testing out ideas and considering 'if-then' scenarios.

Then I will tell you about how what we have learned could be useful for enhancing policy making and for ensuring that people are more ethical.

My current research in progress is funded by an ARC Linkage grant. The pilot of *the knowledge management software system* has been tested out successfully by De Vries and McIntyre as a paper-based model and is currently being developed by De Vries into software. Confidentiality and respect for the rights of the participants is central. A holistic approach to wellbeing and social inclusion is understood as a central value of Neporendi Forum Inc. The aim of the current project is to match the perceived needs of users to the services provided. In the research program the service users are the capacity builders, not the other way around. The research has been conducted by a diverse multidisciplinary team who communicate respectfully with one another as co-researchers and critical friends. The *Industry Partners* include participants from Neporendi Forum Inc, members of the community from the Southern Region. The participants are from the South Australian Health Department with contributions from Anglicare. Together we have explored our understanding of what works, why and how. In so doing we have created the community of inquiry. The team comprises a range of academics that span the social and natural sciences covering the following areas: cultural studies, critical systemic thinking informatics and modelling, sociology and public policy, public health, governance and management. It tests out the principle of subsidiarity and the notion that complex decisions are best made by people who have experience of the issue so that the complexity of the decision matches the complexity of the decision maker. It also argues that if people can see the implications of their decisions and that the decisions about social, economic and environmental matters are linked, they will not think that they can make decisions in isolation. This of course has implications for ethics and for governance. So how can this be achieved? I make the case that it is by enabling people within local communities nested within their regions to have a say. This means that the experts and those with lived experience need to engage in dialogue. They need to think in terms of 'if then' scenarios, in order to think about the short, medium and long term. The aim of the program of research on participatory democracy is to a) build policy from below and across conceptual and spatial boundaries; b) address the increasingly conservative local and international policy environment.

Common Bonds

"*The dream of the Enlightenment was the recognitions of a common bond among all humans that surpassed religious, cultural, and political differences, and to these we now add racial, ethnic, and lifestyle differences. Darwin and his followers have taught us how strong and deep that bond is, it is up to us to recognize it*" (Cornelius, 1996: 218).

I wish to address the knot of essentialism versus non essentialism and its implications for being members of one planet and one species at the moment! Greenfield (2000), a neuroscientist has made the point that consciousness is a continuum in organic life and that alarmingly we share 98 % of the genetic make up of laboratory rats! You are encouraged to laugh and then to think about the implications of this statement for personal morality and public ethics.

The need for an idealistic 'global covenant' based on social democratic ideology is made by David Held (2004), Peter Singer also makes a powerful pragmatic argument about socio-environmental consequences in "One World" and Nussbaum (2006) argues unlike Singer or Rawls, for ethical consideration to be given *irrespective of reciprocal benefit and the notion of reciprocity (linked with veil of ignorance)* or *consequences* and to consider the needs of the disabled, weak and voiceless. This is taken up by Lynne Sharpe (2005) who argues in her recent book '*Creatures like us*' promoted by the Journal 'Cybernetics and Human Knowing' that instead of considering the *right to a life free of pain and a life that is worth living* in *terms of reciprocity and the public good,* as argued by Rawls in 'the Law of People's- that we should think in terms *of relationships* and a *continuum of consciousness* with animals.

At most it means that we need to ensure an environment that accommodates other forms of life. *At the very least* it means that living creatures should not be unnecessarily commodified in cruel , unnecessary experiments, confined or transported in appalling conditions. The Cormo Express (carrying rejected, diseased sheep to the Middle East but dumped in Eritrea)4 is example of so-called live meat cargo trade.

We do not need to choose to be vegetarians to be compassionate - despite its being a rational choice for sustainable futures- because domestic farm animals take more energy to sustain than crops. Farmed animals, however, argues Singer (2002) have the right as sentient beings to a life free of pain. Nussbaum (2007) takes this further and argues that living creatures have a right to fulfill their capabilities or to have 'quality of life'.

If we find this hard to accept in idealistic terms or the expanded pragmatic terms of Singer (based on their being sentient beings) then make the connection (based on narrow pragmatism) that poor quality of life leads to sick animals who are likely to make us sick.

"A is better off when B is better off" (Von Foerster 1995: 494). We only have to think of SARS and the sicknesses of caged birds, pigs and cattle to realize that it is in our interests to be compassionate! Saul Alinsky's (1972) "low road to morality" could bridge the moral divide in contexts where we cannot see eye to eye.

Gore (2007) writes about the way in which two way communication is vital for building relationships and creating attachments between people at the individual level and also at the societal level. Participation is inextricably bound to wellbeing and democracy.

"*Attachment theory is an interesting new branch of developmental psychology that sheds light on the importance of consistent, appropriate and responsive two-way communication- and why it is essential for an individual's feeling empowered... First developed by John Bowlby ..., attachment theory was developed by... Ainsworth... Although it applies to individuals, attachment theory is , in my view, a metaphor that illuminates the significance of authentic free flowing communication in any relationship that requires trust...*" (Gore, 2007: 246).

Developing Systemic Ethics in Our Time

Developing systemic ethics in our time is possible by means of 'unfolding values' and 'sweeping in' social, cultural, political and environmental factors in ongoing cycles of dialogue (see Churchman 1982)

To cite Margaret Somerville (2000: x) we need to consider ethical canaries, in other words the issues of the day which give us an idea of how well or badly we are doing. If the canaries are affected by the social and environmental pollution and sing then we know that we face difficulties.

Unlike Somerville (2006) I do not believe that one shared set of ethics is essential to preserve the sacred. Instead I believe that G.O.D. the generator of diversity (to follow West Churchman 1982) needs to be respected and decisions need to be made on the basis of careful testing with those who are to be affected by our decisions.

We need a process to engage and build shared sense of hospitality to strangers (Derrida in Borradori, Habermas & Derrida, 2003) and a shared sense of concern for the next generation of life. We need to embrace diversity to the extent that diversity does not undermine freedom of others.

Fortunately today mapping can help us to make sense of more than a few variables simultaneously when we make decisions on where to draw boundaries -based on 'if then' scenarios within context. The modeling processes should be used to support dialogue and contextual decisions, because it could help us to be more mindful of 'the enemies within –religion, politics, morality and aesthetics' (Christakis & Bausch, 2006; McIntyre-Mills ,2006a, b).

The dialogical process is in itself an answer. This is what Aristotle meant by dialogue to support wisdom of experience phronesis or matching the appropriate response to a specific issue.

Seeing the connection across greed, lack of planning for the future, investment in conflict rather than building a shared future is vital for developing

	Systemic change		
	Radical humanist approaches to redesign our future	Radical structuralist approaches to redesign the future.	
Subjective-ideographic			Objective - nomothetic
	Interpretive approaches that emphasize culture as the basis for maintaining the status quo	Functionalist – billiard ball approaches	
	Systemic regulation		

Table 1 *A Systemic view of governance and international relations derived from Burrell and Morgan's Grid (1979). (Source: Volume 1 of C. West Churchman Series: 354.)*

sustainable ethics in our time. Future research directions in public policy require collaborative decision making across local and state government, universities, non government, business and the community. Communication processes are needed to match perceptions to outcomes.

We can be free (to reconceptualize and reconstruct categories) to the extent that we respect the freedoms of others. At this point the line needs to be drawn and at this point essentialism and rationalism overlap.

Drawing on volume 1 of the C. West Churchman series, I argue that Fukuyama (1992: 337) stresses that culture and meaning making are perhaps one of the most important dimensions of humanity. Kaplan is cited by Flood and Carson (1993: 142) as introducing cybernetic concepts. He argued that states could be seen in terms of 6 basic patterns5 of relationships. The work of Kaplan and Rosencrance (cited by Flood & Carson, 1992: 145 in volume 1) is also functionalist, takes a deterministic view and uses only positivist methods. The simulations and models used in functionalist terms do not take into account human nature, emotions and meaning. Huntington (1996) comes up with four patterns of relationships, namely:

1. Universal harmony;
2. Multipolar billiard ball of cause and effect;
3. Cold war bipolar, and;
4. Chaos where mutual destruction is possible (as a result of the nuclear weapons of mass destruction owned by hegemonic states and coalitions).

Huntington does not consider human capability to reconstruct the way they see the world and the possibility of systemic governance in the interests of social and environmental sustainability that spans international, regional and national boundaries in a new kind of federalism based on subsidiarity as suggested by Singer (2002).6

Flood and Carson stress that if these writers had looked at the work of West Churchman they would have found a useful source of ideas. Churchman (1979) made it very clear that he did not believe it possible to comprehend a total system and that we always need to be mindful of the so-called 'enemies within', religion, morality, politics and aesthetics'. In the C. West Churchman Legacy and Related works series we argue that these dimensions need to be embraced, because they are the qualities and capabilities that make us human.

Conclusion

Systemic ethics could help us to appreciate "why A is better off when B is better off". Seeing the connection across greed, lack of planning for the future, investment in conflict rather than building a shared future is vital. Public policy requires collaborative decision making across national boundaries in the interests not merely of citizenship rights and the social contract, but in the sustaining life for this generation and the next.

Acknowledgement

My thanks to Professor Louis Kauffman for his comments on sections of an earlier draft

References

Alinsky, S., 1972, *Rules for Radicals: A Practical Primer for Realistic Radicals,* Vintage Books, New York.

Ashby, W.R., 1956, An introduction to Cybernetics, Chapman and Hall, London.

Atkinson, J. 2002. *Trauma trails, recreating song lines: the transgenerational effects of trauma in Indigenous Australia.* Spinifex. Melbourne.

Banathy, B., 1996, *Designing Social Systems in a Changing World*, Plenum, New York.

Banathy, B., 2000, *Guided Evolution of Society: A Systems View*, Kluwer/Plenum, London.

Bateson, G.1972. *Steps to ecology of mind: a revolutionary approach to man's understanding of himself.* New York: Ballantine.

Bausch, K., 2006, 'Be your enemy : The Contributions of West Churchman to Doing Better Governance and International Relations" in McIntyre-Mills, J., *Rescuing the Enlightenment from Itself: Critical and Systemic Implications for Democracy,* C.West Churchman Series, Vol. 1, Springer, New York, Boston, London.

Beck, U., 1992, *Risk Society Towards a New Modernity*, Sage, London.

Beck, U., 1998, *Democracy Without Enemies*, Polity, Cambridge.

Beer, A. Maude,A. Pritchard,B 2003.*Developing Australia's regions: theory and practice.* Sydney. University of New South Wales

Beer, S., 1974, *Designing Freedom,* Wiley, London.

Beer, S., 1994, *Beyond Dispute. The Invention of Team Syntegrity,* Wiley. New York.

Berger, P., 1976, *Pyramids of Sacrifice: Political Ethics and Social Change,* Penguin, Harmonsworth.

Bhabha, H.K. 1994 *The location of culture.* Routledge, London.

Bogue, R., 1989, *Deleuze and Guattari*, Routledge, London.

Borradori, G, 2003, *Philosophy in an Age of Terror: Dialogues with Jurgen Habermas and Jacques Derrida* interviewed by Borradori Giovanna, University of Chicago Press, Chicago

Bowden 2006 Civil society, the state and the limits of global civil society, Global society, vol. 20, No 2, April, pp 155-178.

Brewer, M. and Hewstone, M. 2004.Eds *Social cognition.* Blackwell, Oxford.

Chomsky, N., 2003, *Hegemony or Survival: America's Quest for Global Dominance,* Allen and Unwin, Crows Nest, NSW.

Christakis, A., with Bausch, K.C., 2006, *How People Harness their Collective Wisdom and Power* Information Age Publishing, Greenwich.

Churchman, C. West., 1971, *The Design of Inquiring Systems. Basic Concepts of Systems and Organization*, Basic Books, New York.

Churchman, C. West, 1979, *The Systems Approach*, Delta, New York.

Churchman, C. West, 1982, *Thought and Wisdom*, Intersystems Publications, California.

Cornelius, R. 1996, *The science of emotion: The research and tradition in the psychology of emotion.* Prentice Hall. New Jersey.

Cox, E., 1995, *A Truly Civil Society*, Boyer Lectures, ABC Books, Sydney, NSW.

de Vries, D., The Case for Mesodata: An Empirical Investigation of an Evolving Database System. *Journal of Information and Software* Technology, 2007. To Appear.

Devji, F., 2005, *Landscapes of the Jihad: militancy, morality and modernity*, Hurst and

Company, London.

Dryzek, J., 1999, *Democratizing rationality in Discursive Democracy* Cambridge University Press.

Dryzek, J., 2000, *Deliberative democracy and beyond: liberals, critics, contestations*, Oxford University Press, Oxford

Eisenstein, Z. *Against Empire: feminisms, racism and the west.* Spinifex Press.

Edgar, D., 2001, *The Patchwork Nation: Rethinking Government-Rebuilding Community*, Harper, Sydney.

Edwards, M., and Gaventa, J., 2001, *Global Citizen Action*, Boulder, Colorado.

Encarnacion, O. G. 2006 Civil Society Reconsidered Comparative *Politics* : 257-273.

Fishkin ,J. 2000 The Filter, the Mirror and the Mob: reflections on deliberative democracy. Paper presented at " Deliberating about Deliberative Democracy. February 4-6 , University of Texas at Austin. http://scholar.google.com/scholar?q=Fishkin%2C+J.S+2000+The+filter%2C+the+mirror+and+the+mob&hl=en&lr=&btnG=Search accessed 20 /03/2007

Fishkin, J.S. and Laslett, P., 2003, *Debating deliberative democracy*, Blackwell Publishing, Oxford.

Flannery, T. 2005.*The Weather Makers. The History and Future impact of climate change.* Text Publishing. Melbourne.

Flood , R. and Carson, R. 1993. *Dealing with complexity: An introduction to the theory and application of Systems Science.* Plenum. London.

Flood, R., and Romm, N., 1996, *Diversity Management: Triple Loop Learning,* John Wiley & Sons, New York.

Florini, A., 2003, *The Coming Democracy: New Rules for Running a New World,* Island Press, Washington DC.

Freire, P., 1982, 'Creating alternative research methods: learning to do it', in: Hall, B., Gillette, A. and Tandon, R., 'Creating knowledge: a monopoly?' Society for Participatory Research in Asia, New Delhi: 29-37, in: *The Action Research Reader,* Deakin University Publication, Victoria.

Fukuyama, F. 1999 *The great disruption: Human Nature and the reconstitution of Social Order.* London. Free Press. Get thus

Fukuyama, F. 2006 ed., *Nation Building Beyond Afghanistan and Iraq*, Johns Hopkins University Press, Baltimore.

Fukuyama, F., 2004, *State Building: Governance and World Order in the 21st Century, Cornell University Press*, New York, Ithaca.

Gallhofer, S., and Chew, A., 2000, "Introduction: accounting and indigenous peoples", Accounting, Auditing and Accountability Journal, 13(3):256-267.

Gallhofer, S., and Chew, A., 2000, "Introduction: accounting and indigenous peoples", *Accounting, Auditing and Accountability Journal*, 13(3):256-267.

Geertz, C., 1975, "Thick description: towards an interpretive theory of culture", in Geertz, C., *The Interpretation of Cultures*, Selected Essays, Basic Books, New York.

Gibbons, M., Limoges, C., Nowotny, H., Schwartzman, S., Scott, P., and Trow, M., 1994, *The New Productions of Knowledge: The Dynamics of Science and Research* in Contemporary Societies, Sage, London.

Giddens, A., 1998, *The Third Way: The Social Renewal of Democracy*, Polity, Cambridge.

Giddens, A., 2001, *The Global Thirdway Debate*, Polity, Blackwell.

Gore,Al 2007. *Assault on Reason.* Bloomsbury.London.

Greenfield, S., 2000, *The Private Life of the Brain: Emotions, Consciousness and the Secret of the Self,* John Wiley and Sons, New York.

Grugel, J., 1999, *Democracy without Borders: Transnationalization and Conditionality in New Democracies*, Routledge, London.

Habermas, J., 1984, *The Theory of Communicative Action: Reason and the Rationalization of Society*, Beacon, Boston.

Haraway, D. *Simians, Cyborgs and Women. The Reinvention of Nature* Free Association Books, London.

Held,D. 2004. *Global covenant: The social democratic alliterative to the Washington consensus*. Polity. Oxford.

Huntington, S.P., 1996, *The Clash of Civilizations and the Remaking of World Order*, Simon and Schuster, New York.

Hyden, G. 2004. Court, J. and Mease, K. 2004. *Making sense of governance: Empirical evidence from 16 Developing countries*. Boulder. London.

Irwin, T., 1985, *Aristotle Nicomachean Ethics translated with Introduction and notes Hackett*, Cambridge University Press.

Jackson, M.C., 2006, 'Knowledge management in the ERP Era', *Systems Research and Behavioural Science*, Vol. 23, No. 2.

Jones. B., 1990, Sleepers Wake! Technology and the Future of Work, 3rd ed., Oxford University Press, Melbourne.

Joy, B. 2000. Why the future doesn't need us Wired. Issue 8.04. http://www.wired.com/wired/archive/8.04/joy_pr.html accessed 30/04/2007

Rawls, J., 1999, The Law of Peoples with the Idea of Public Reason Revisited, Harvard University Press, London.

Kung, H, and Moltmann, J. 1992. Fundamentalism as an ecumenical challenge. SCM Press. London. Concilium .

Management Advisory Committee, 2004, Connecting Government: Whole of Government responses to Australia's Priority Challenges, APSC, Canberra.

McIntyre-Mills, J. 2000, *Global Citizenship and Social Movements: Creating Transcultural Webs of Meaning for the New Millennium*, Harwood academic publishers, Australia.

McIntyre-Mills, J., 2003, *Critical Systemic Praxis for Social and Environmental Justice: Participatory Policy Design and Governance for a Global Age*, Kluwer, London.

McIntyre, J. 2005 Working and re-working the conceptual and geographical boundaries of governance and international relations *Systemic Practice and Action Research* Vol. 18, No 2 157- 220.

McIntyre-Mills, J. *et al* 2006a, *Rescuing the Enlightenment from Itself: Critical and Systemic Implications for Democracy*, Springer. London, Boston, Vol. 1 of C. West Churchman Series.Preface : 11-15 and Prologue 17-44

McIntyre-Mills, J. *et al* 2006, *Systemic Governance and Accountability: working and re-working conceptual and spatial boundaries*, Springer. London, Boston, Vol. 3 of C. West Churchman Series, in press.

McIntyre–Mills, J., 2006b, 'Molar and Molecular Identity and Politics', in Van Gigch, J., with McIntyre-Mills, J., *Wisdom, knowledge and management*, Vol. 2, Springer, New York, Boston, London.

McIntyre-Mills, J. 2007.Challenging economic and religious fundamentalism: implications for the state, the market and the 'enemies within'. *International Journal of Applied Systemic Studies*. Forthcoming.

McLuhan, M. and Powers, B., 1989, *The Global Village: Transformations in World Life in the 21st Century*, Oxford University Press, Oxford.

Midgley, G. 2000. Systemic Intervention: philosophy, methodology, and practice. Contemporary Systems Thinking. New York. Kluwer.

Minogue, M. Polidano, C. and Hulme, D. 1998. *Beyond the New Public management: Changing Ideas and Practices in Governance*. Edward Elgar.Northampton.

National Economics/ALGA, 2003, *State of the Regions Report,* published by Australian Local Government Association.
Nussbaum, M 1995 *Women. Culture and Development: A study of human capabilities.* Oxford, Claredon.
Nussbaum, M. 2001 *Upheavals of thought: the intelligence of emotions.* Cambridge University Press.
Nussbaum, M., 2006, *Frontiers of justice, disability, nationality and species membership,* Harvard University Press, London.
O'Grady,P. 2005. *Meet the philosophers of ancient Greece.* Ashgate. Aldershot.
Pape, R.A., 2005, *Dying to win: the strategic logic of suicide terrorism,* Random House, New York.
Pierre, J. & Peters, B.G., 2000, *Governance, Politics and the State,* Macmillan, Hampshire.
Pierre, J., ed., 2000, *Debating Governance: Authority, Steering and Democracy,* Oxford University Press, Oxford.
Preston, N., Sampford, C. and Connors, C. 2002. *Encouraging ethics and challenging corruption.* The Federation Press. Sydney
Rawls, J. 1993 *Political Liberalism.* New York. Columbia University Press.
Rawls, J. 1999. *The Law of Peoples with The Idea of Public Reason Revisited.* Harvard University Press. London. 1999: see pages 61, 71).
Pilger, J., 2002, *The New Rulers of the World,* Verso, London.
Polanyi, M., 1962, *Personal Knowledge,* Routledge and Kegan Paul, London.
Reason, P. and Bradbury, H.2001 *Handbook of Action Research: Participative Inquiry and Practice.* London. Sage.
Reason, P., 2002, 'Justice, sustainability and participation. Inaugural lecture', *Concepts and Transformations,* 7(1):7-29.
Rhodes, RAW, 1997, *Understanding Governance. Policy networks, governance, reflexivity and accountability,* Open University Press, Maidenhead.
Sen, A., 2000, Development as Freedom, Knopf, New York.
Sharpe, L. 2005 *Creatures like us* Imprint Academic. Exeter.
Shore, C. 2006 Government without statehood? Anthropological perspectives on governance in the European Union. *European Law Journal. Vol 12, No 6: 709-724*
Singer, P., 2002, One World: *The Ethics of Globalisation,* The Text Publishers, Melbourne.
Somerville, M. 2000. *The ethical canary : science, society and the human spirit .* Pearson Penguin. Toronto.
Somerville, M. 2007 *The Ethical Imagination.* The Massey Lectures ,CBC Audio
Somerville,M. 2000. *The ethical canary: science, society and the human spirit.* Viking. Canada.
Stern, N, 2007. *The Economics of Climate Change: The Stern Review.* Cambridge University Press
Ulrich, W., 1983, *Critical Heuristics of Social Planning: A New Approach to Practical Philosophy,* Wiley, New York.
Ulrich, W., 2001, 'The quest for competence in systemic research and practice', *Systems Research and Behavioural Science,* 18:3-28
Van Gigch, J. in collaboration with McIntyre-Mills, J., 2006, 'Wisdom, Knowledge and Management', *C. West Churchman Legacy and Related Works,* Vol. 2, Kluwer, Springer.
Van Gigch, J., 2003, *Metadecisions: Rehabilitating Epistemology,* Kluwer Plenum, Springer
Vickers, G., 1983, *Human Systems are Different,* Harper and Row, London.

Von Foerster, H. 1995. *Cybernetics of cybernetics.* Second edition. Future Systems , Inc. Minneapolis

Wadsworth, Y., 2001, 'The Mirror, the magnifying glass, the compass and the map: facilitating participatory action research', in: *Handbook of Action Research*, P. Reason and H. Bradbury, Sage, London.

Wenger, E., 1998, *Communities of Practice: Learning, Meaning and Identity*, Cambridge University Press, Cambridge.

White, L., 2001, Effective governance: through complexity thinking and management science', *Systems Research and Behavioural Science*, 18(3):241-257.

White, L., 2002, 'Connection matters: exploring the implications of social capital and social networks for social policy', *Systems Research and Behavioural Science*, 19(2):255-270.

White, L., 2002, 'Connection matters: exploring the implications of social capital and social networks for social policy', *Systems Research and Behavioural Science*, 19(2):255-270.

Young,J. McIntyre, J. Drummond ,M. 2007 forthcoming "Overlapping identities in 'white Anglo' PRE WW2 (South) Australia: lessons for 21st century Australia. *People and Place*

Notes

1 Aristotle called this phronesis (or prudent decision making and action based on wisdom). West Churchman (1979, 1982) talked of using his design of inquiring system (based on questions to tap different kinds of knowledge) as a means to 'unfold' values and 'to sweep in' the social, cultural, political, economic and environmental factors within specific contexts. He did not explicitly focus on culture (see volume 1), but his design of inquiring systems lends itself to building in culture and gender sensitivity to develop a post colonial approach that helps to address the compartmentalised approach to addressing self-other and the environment. In the book " Rescuing the enlightenment from itself", McIntyre-Mills *et al* 2006 discuss the importance of considering that feedback loops , paradoxes and iterations as important for sustainable policy making.

2 My thanks to Professor Louis Kauffman for his comments on an earlier draft, any errors are mine alone.

3 This question was posed by Professor Adam Graycar in a workshop held at Flinders University in 2006. This section is based on commentary and extract from "Systemic Governance and Accountability", volume 3. In this volume I discuss the way in which people with lived experience (citizens and non citizens) are invited to tell their stories. 'If then' scenarios are modelled based on their stories. Data is collected on issues pertaining to wellbeing until saturation point on an issue is achieved. Then analysis is undertaken using Nvivo to produce a factor map. Voting is undertaken to determine which pathways are best and under what circumstances.

4 Levy, D. and Lotz, 2004, "The ethics of live sheep export trade", Centre for Applied Philosophy and public Ethics, University of Melbourne, 3 May, accessed 6/22/2004. http://www.animalsaustralia.org/default2.asp?idL1=1274&idL2=1668

5 "Multipolar: a balance of power arrangement; literally a billiard ball model;

Loose bipolar: two main opposing spheres with satellites of varying degrees of adherence to either side;

Tight bipolar: like 2, but with clear allegiances to one sphere;

Universal: a confederation; all groups controlled by one government;

Hierarchical; significant grouping that are functional rather than territorial; a federation;

Unit vet: each group can destroy all others, there is mutually assured destruction (MAD)."

6 Subsidiarity is based on the idea that those at the receiving end of a decision need to be party to the decision making process. People should be free to make decisions as they wish to the extent that they do not undermine the freedoms of others. Flood and Carson (op cit) review a number of works (Kaplan, Rosencrance, Modelski and Brecher, Weltman) that conclude that stability is functionally linked with a situation in which there are few variables with which to deal. Weltman (according to Flood and Carson, 1993: 144) concludes that systems ideas are merely functionalist. But as they point out (Flood and Carson, 1993: 145) the system of interest does not need to be states.

41. Increasing Cycle Commuting

Stephen McKernon
Supplejack Ltd, NZ

Cycling is increasingly promoted by transport planners worldwide to resolve urban transport problems. But use of cycling for transport (utility cycling) in developed countries varies considerably, and in New Zealand totals only a small percent of all kilometers traveled. About half of New Zealand's local authorities now have generic cycle travel strategies, which favour small infrastructure projects over more social approaches, such as educating motorists, promoting cycling, or enforcing road rules in relation to cycling. None have sought to understand utility cycling as a social system to ensure effective growth or longer term sustainability. This paper uses the social systems theory of Niklas Luhmann (1927 - 1998) to explore utility cycling as a social system, and to advance design of utility cycling as a solution. The result is practical social systems-based recommendations for managing and maintaining an increase in utility cycling.

Introduction

How to increase use of a marginal and dangerous mode?

Cycling is increasingly promoted in transport policy worldwide (Ogilvie, *et al.*, 2004) to resolve urban transport problems and to promote much more healthy, sustainable lifestyles. But use of cycling for transport (or 'utility cycling', which is mainly cycle commuting) in developed countries varies considerably, and in New Zealand totals about 1% of all vehicle kilometers traveled (Ministry of Transport, 2007a), or about 2.5% of commuters (Statistics NZ, 2007). The pattern since the 1970s is one of slow decline, so challenging planners to both reverse the trend and increase numbers from a very small base.

Further, accident data suggest the cyclist injury rate is some five times higher than that for car users (Ministry of Transport, 2007b). Aiming to increase utility cycling therefore poses the twin problems of reversing its decline and improving its safety.

About half of New Zealand's local authorities now have cycle strategies to encourage utility cycling (McKernon, 2007), and for example, Auckland authorities propose to double utility cycling numbers within the next decade (Auckland Regional Council, 2005). A feature of these strategies is the priority given to road infrastructure over social marketing, motorist education or skills training (Koorey, 2003). Auckland's record is indicative of the difficulties of achieving change: its first cycling strategy was published in 1980, and local cycle commuter numbers have decreased steadily since (Statistics NZ, 2007).

This paper discusses the task of increasing numbers of cycle commuters from a social systems perspective. It begins by introducing recent theoretical work on social systems, using this to explore cycling and cycle commuting. It then identifies two key system interventions, and finishes by outlining three communications strategies.

Why social systems?

New Zealand's orientation to safety and infrastructure-building is not unusual and reflects the general absence of social interventions worldwide (McKernon, 2007). It is only recently that cycling has been explored socially, such as through socio-technological (Rosen, 2002), semiotic (Cox, 2005) and historical (Herlihy, 2005) approaches.

Such approaches attempt to theorise cycling as complex relations between policy, commerce, communication and cyclists. But social science has not found such complexity easy to theorise, mainly because it has approached social phenomena through theories centered on individual action, hence the generic label *action theory* (Kampmann Walther, 2005). The counter-theory has been termed *communication theory*, though it might also be understood as *social systems theory* (Stichweh, 2000).

Action theory makes initial sense where a group's actions (such as cycle commuters) make it noteworthy, and where the aim is to increase the number of people acting this way. But the theory has difficulty explaining how an individual's actions are organized by and identified with a group. It holds that structures (such as institutions, values, norms and identities) organise and identify cycle commuters, but such structures cannot arise from action alone. At the least, action must be underpinned by meaning and communication to achieve structure. Critics therefore argue action theory is trafficking in metaphysical (non-action) concepts.

As a result the more sophisticated action theories posit systems-theoretical concepts such as 'structuration' (Giddens, 1979) and 'communicative action' (Habermas, 1987) to articulate the reflexivity of action, communication and structure. They retain individual action as their central operation, so treating communication as both action and medium. The problem then becomes theorizing communication-as-medium within action-based theory.

In contrast, systems-based theories argue for communication as the primary constitutive operation, and so for social phenomena as 'social' systems arising from, and in, self-referential communication. Action is then an effect of communication.

The most fully-worked of these theories is provided by Niklas Luhmann (1927-1998), and his theory is described and applied below. He is not well known outside Europe, and given his outspoken critiques of mainstream social science, is often regarded as controversial (Moeller, 2006). Applying his work to cycle commuting in New Zealand might be regarded as both eccentric and ambitious, yet it provides valuable insights for both the theory and practice of social change.

The analysis of cycling's social system that follows is based on cycle historians Herlihy (2004) and Kennett and Kennett (2005), who share a common interest in cycling's social dynamics.

How do social systems work?

Luhmann's theoretical work is abstract and complex. A brief summary can be provided here, and readers are referred to Moeller (2006) for a very readable account of Luhmann's fuller theory.

Luhmann (1994) defines communication as *information* (distinctions and meanings), its *utterance*, and its *understanding*. Framed this way, only communication is required to activate and maintain a social system, as communication generates further communication (Luhmann, 1995, Clam, 2000). Figure 1 below traces Luhmann's notion of a social system constituted in communication.

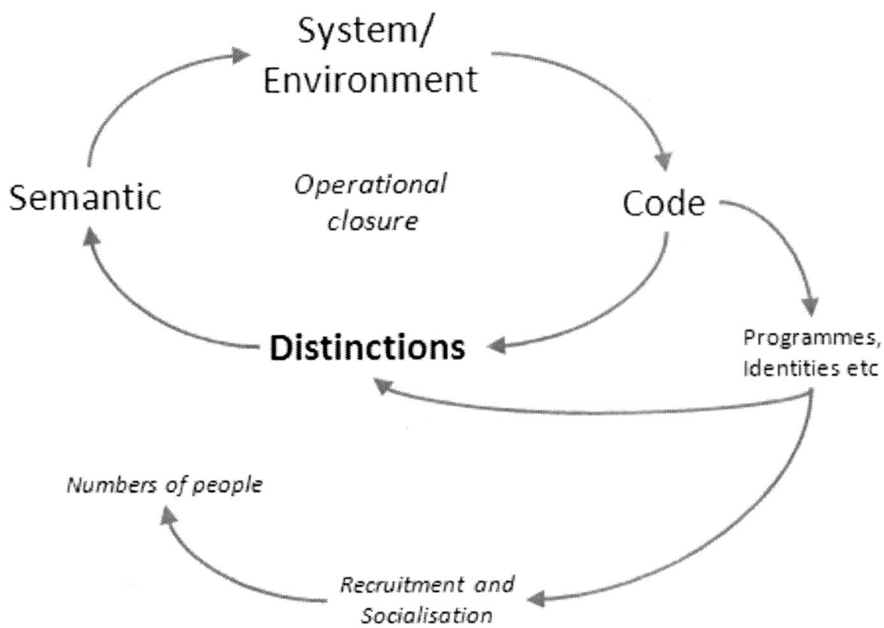

Figure 1 *Luhmann's Social Systems*

Social systems are activated through new *distinctions* arising in communication. As these are deployed over time they give rise to a *semantic* – a set of relatively stable meanings, statements and arguments. A social system emerges in the context of this semantic and is activated by a distinction between *system and environment*. Because the system arises in communication only, its environment can only do so too, and it therefore exists only as long as the system/ environment distinction is maintained, again in communication. That is, the system is not a difference between a 'real' system and a 'real' environment, but an emergent and evolving system in communication.

A social system's communications enrich its system/ environment distinction over time with new distinctions, so *codifying* this original distinction as the key to the system. The only communications then making sense within the system are those keyed to its code. A temporal effect of reflexive communication is the *operational closure* of the system. That is, codification also means it communicates only with itself and in its own terms – it is open to information from other systems but can use this only on its own terms.

Such closure allows it to enrich its distinctions, so also allowing it to evolve its internal complexity over time. That is, the system is adaptive and evolves, but not in the conventional sense. Rather, it evolves through re-configurations of its own complexity, and adaptation is evidenced through shifts in its semantic and internal structure.

Key adaptive structures are *programmes* and *identities*. A programme is a set of activities and interactions (often in relation to other systems), and an identity is its simplified social expression. These also contribute over time to the distinctions available within a system.

Luhmann argues that people are not part of social systems. Rather, people are recruited and socialized by social systems, and are only involved to the extent that a system's identities define them (Luhmann, 1994).

How does cycling communicate 'cycle commuting'?

Following Luhmann, cycling only communicates cycling. So for example, the cycle commuter on her practical cycle, wearing bright vest and backpack and negotiating roads and cars in peak hour traffic, is an effect of cycling's communications. In parallel, cycling communicates through transport's on-road communications (such as lanes, traffic lights and hand signals) but is not constituted by them. That is, the persons, actions and tangible contexts of cycling are effects of its communications as a social system, not its constitutive or causal elements. To fully appreciate how these communications work, it helps to understand how it arose as a social system.

Cycling arose during the energy and transport crisis of the Industrial Revolution. As cities grew, horses were less effective and increasingly vulnerable to food shortages, illnesses, and slaughter during wars. The horse was slowly replaced by engine-powered and human-powered innovation: the former lead to trains around the 1840s (and the motor car during the 1890s), and the latter to the bicycle from the 1860s.

Cycling distinguished itself as 'fast' in relation to the 'slow' modes it defined as its environment (walking, horse riding, and horse-drawn or steam-driven urban vehicles). An evolving semantic of speed gave rise to the modern Safety cycle in the 1880s, so achieving control, safety, durability and comfort at speed. Parallel innovations in cycle production and marketing fostered rapid frowth in cycling, and so contributed to improved roading, signage, maps, designated touring routes, hospitality partnerships, as well as touring and leisure events.

Because physical mobility also meant social mobility, cycling's fast/ slow code was re-interpreted as freedom/ constraint. This fast, cheap, mass-produced consumable expanded social boundaries and afforded sociopolitical freedoms previously unheard of. During an era of rapid urbanization and social unrest, cycling's freedoms aligned it with emancipatory and egalitarian movements.

Cycling's distinctions about its environment also evolved. For example, cycling's risks were initially from rider behavior and poor roading. As cycles and roads improved these risks declined and re-emerged from the 1930s as dangers arising from motorcars.

Note both cycling and motoring share a fast/ slow code, but differ considerably in their respective semantics. For example, the motorcar's semantic provides for high on-road speeds, high tolerance of danger, masculine identity, and endorsement of the status quo (Moser, 2003). The motorcar is also central to the growth of urbanization and has enabled urban sprawl.

Cycling's operational closure took place around the 1890s: it had matured to span all that cycling's social system affords today. Cycling's closure pre-dated motoring's by at least three decades, and actually contributed to the latter's development. From the time of its closure, cycling's three major evolutionary programmes have been leisure, activism and utility, as detailed below.

Cycling's leisure programme

The commoditization of leisure time from the mid 1800s (Gershuny, 2000) helped distinguish cycling as a leisure pursuit for the masses. Initially a pastime of wealthy males, by the early 1900s leisure cycling provided the middle and working classes with virtually free, healthy, enjoyable and highly social forms of relaxation.

Cycling's leisure programme grew more pronounced from the 1930s as cheap cars began to dominate urban transport, and re-shaped European markets from the 1960s onwards. This re-configuration drew on the commodification of the teenager and of healthy lifestyles, and leisure cycling's rapid growth was also made possible by the shift of global cycling production to Asia.

In New Zealand today there are approximately 1.274 million cyclists per year (Ministry of Transport, 2007), and virtually all are leisure cyclists. That is, roughly 1/3 of the population are leisure cyclists.

Figure 2 below traces changes in New Zealand's cycling programmes since cycling began. Leisure cycling is based on 85% of total cycles (manufactured and imported), and cycle commuting on available survey and anecdotal industry data (McKernon, 2007). Note the rapid increase in total cycling from the late 1970s.

A current marker of its local popularity is the increasing number of recreational and sporting events involving cycling, one of the oldest being the annual 160km ride around Lake Taupo.

Cycling's activism programme

Cycling's semantic of freedom/ constraint entangled it with emancipatory movements from its beginnings. Over time the act of cycling has variously symbolized protested against gender, class, and political constraints, as well as resistance to the dominance of the motorcar (Horton, 2006; Furness, 2005; Simpson, 2001; Rubenstein, 1999).

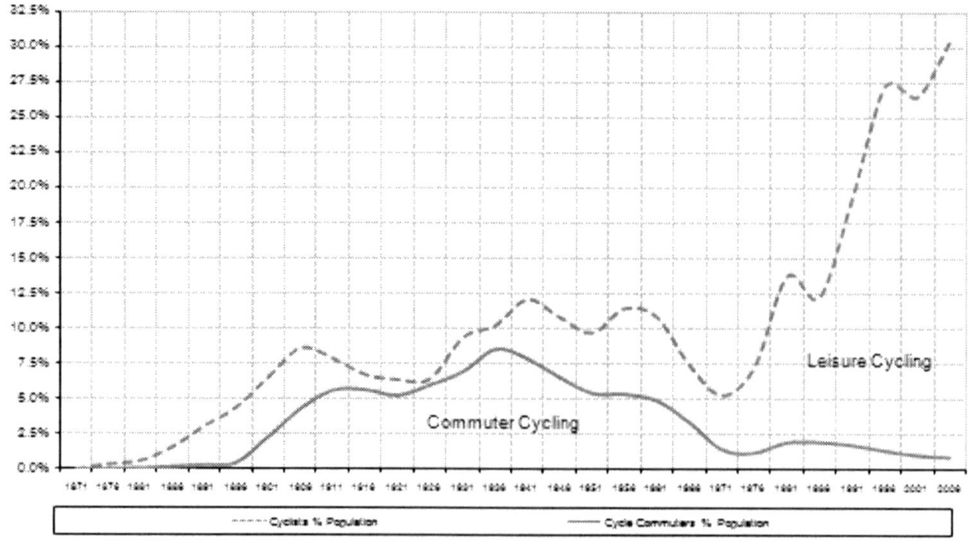

Figure 2 *Estimated Leisure and Utility Cycling in New Zealand*

For example, cycling was central to feminist suffragette and rational dress/ New Woman movements; socialist groups such as the German Worker's Cycle Federation, the American Socialist Wheelmen's Club and the British Clarion Cycling Club; and to radical urban design groups of the 1960s such as the Dutch Provos, who sought to ban cars and provide free bicycles. More recently it has figured in environmentalist movements, and so is locally endorsed by both Greenpeace and the Green Party.

In the New Zealand context, the Provo's radicalism informed McDonald's (1978) *Changing Gear*, which then became a manifesto for local advocacy groups, and one source for New Zealand's emerging cycle strategies (including Auckland's strategy of 1980).

Cycling's role within sustainable transport policy is ostensibly practical, but it connects cycling's utility and activism programmes. This opens policy to much more radical views of urban transport and urban life than immediately apparent.

Cycling's utility programme

Utility cycling can now be understood as a social programme in reserve. Peaking in the 1940s, it was eclipsed first by the motorcar from the 1930s, and then by leisure cycling from the 1960s.

In this sense utility cycling is doubly marginalized; transport communicates it as marginal, dangerous, and irritating, while leisure cycling views it as unpleasant and eccentric. Utility cycling's history and successes make it clear it is none of these, yet it is difficult to establish exactly what utility cycling communicates today. That is, the communications of both transport and leisure cycling mask the current identity of utility cycling.

To pursue this question, ten Auckland cycle commuters were interviewed using 1-hour qualitative interviews (Willig, 2001). The study (McKernon, 2007) showed cycle commuting communicates health and relaxation, high-self esteem, freedom, confidence, enjoyment, risk-tolerance, and 'making a difference'. The identity recruits people who are common sense, resilient, interested in self-improvement, and view cycle commuting as a low-key protest against the motorcar. These Auckland cycle commuters felt their most significant problem was the volume and speed of traffic.

This identity is clearly distinct from those afforded by both leisure cycling and motoring, yet is potentially appealing to both.

Understanding change: Cycle commuting's current system

The above account of cycle commuting suggests current cycle strategies are framed by paradox. They aim to address utility cycling's exclusion, yet isolate utility cycling from interventions in leisure cycling (a huge resource of cyclists), and from interventions in motorized transport (a key source of dangers). The causal loop diagram in Figure 3 below represents cycle commuting's current dynamics in simplified form, and from the perspective of cycle commuters.

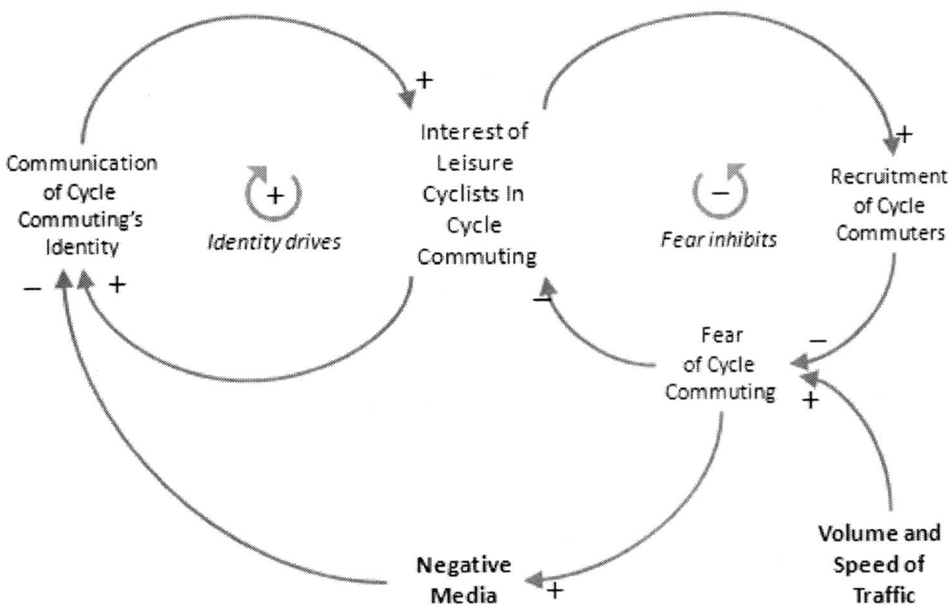

Figure 3 *Cycle Commuting as a Social System*

The diagram centres on leisure cyclists as cycle commuting's key resource. The constraining loop (right) shows how traffic drives fear of cycle commuting, so decreasing interest among leisure cyclists and contributing to negative media attributions.

The reinforcing loop (left) shows how interest in and communication of cycle commuting's specific identity reinforce each other, so contributing to increased recruitment of cycle commuters. One key effect of increased numbers of cycle commuters is a decrease in fears, which arises from a safety-in-numbers effect (Turner, *et al.*, 2006) that decreases accident rates, and would increase cycle commuting's acceptability (steps not shown).

In this account the two critical interventions are to reduce the speed of traffic and to communicate cycle commuting's identity accurately in mass media (in bold). The interventions would work in tandem to achieve rapid changes in cycle commuting.

This result challenges current ideas about what cycle commuting is and how its numbers should be increased. It also addresses the contradictions inherent in current cycle strategies. There are four points to note.

First, cycle commuting communicates powerfully. Utility cycling's code underpins those of both motorized transport and cycling, and its semantic now draws on cycling's activist programme. It offers a contemporary identity challenging motorized transport and linking with sustainable living. Communication of the identity is a key opportunity.

Second, cycle commuting is well-resourced. Utility cycling's identity appeals to cyclists, and to the large numbers of leisure cyclists in particular. This identity includes strands of self-improvement and activism – of 'making a difference' – that are contemporary and increasingly mainstream. Communicating with leisure cyclists specifically is a key opportunity.

Third, the full case for cycle commuting has yet to be made. It appears to offer significant gains in population health (from lowered obesity and related medical conditions), in economic performance (gains from decreases in work time lost and decreases in roading and parking expenditure), in ecological impacts, and in overall quality of life for cyclists and on-cyclists alike. But detailing such gains is clearly beyond the decision-making criteria afforded by the motorized transport sector.

Finally, traffic appears to the single largest barrier to change. Traffic reduction interventions are well-known in transport literature, and for example, are the part rationale for London's congestion zone. London's re-zoning doubled of cycle commuter numbers within a few years (Murray-Clarke, 2007).

Designing change: Communicating cycle commuting

While using media communications is also a well-known approach, the social systemic rationale is not. Three derived communications strategies are outlined below, important more for their rationale than for the specific media programmes they might invoke.

Talk about the identity, not the activity

Cycle commuting has a contemporary and energetic identity, with potentially strong appeal for leisure cyclists. Communicating this identity helps counter motorized transport's negative attributions about cycling, while amplifying its inherent appeal for leisure cyclists and its related benefits for individuals and the broader community.

Talk about all cycling, not just cycle commuting
Communicating the needs of all cyclists changes the frame of reference from 1% to 1/3 of the population. The case for cycle commuting is much stronger when total cyclist numbers and related benefits (such as health benefits) are understood. Talking about all cyclists draws motorists who cycle, the cycle industry and other sectors (such as health) into supporting cycle commuting.

Talk about traffic, not just cycle commuting infrastructure
Irrespective of traffic volumes or infrastructure provision, risks from motorized traffic remain a significant problem for cyclists. Communicating the need to behave with respect and comply with the Road Code is critical to change in both cycle commuting and motoring. Communicating the need to behave with respect and comply with the Road Code is critical to change in both cycle commuting and motoring. But cyclists' relative vulnerability means greater emphasis must fall on motorist attitudes and behaviors. Pro-cycling changes to Road Code and roading design, accident and insurance policies, driver education and traffic enforcement programmes may also effect change.

Summary: Two steps towards more cycle commuters

This paper argues for a social systems approach to social change. It uses Niklas Luhmann's social systems theory to develop an understanding of cycling and cycle commuting as social systems, and derives a systemic, communications-oriented approach to designing social change.

This involves the re-theorizing of cycling as communication, and in parallel, of change in cycle commuting. The result challenges transport's current communications about cycling and provides an approach to designing and managing change more effectively. The paper recommends two key interventions:

- Reducing motorized traffic;
- Communicating cycle commuting's identity accurately (to leisure cyclists in particular).

These interventions in tandem promise to increase cycle commuting significantly. An increase in numbers means improvements in both transport sustainability and flow-on effects in health, economic and other systems.

The social systems approach also notes the recent politicizing of cycle commuting through its links with cycle activism, and the politics of sustainable transport is likely to have a parallel effect. Where transport sees a marginal and irritating mode, cycle commuting envisions sustainability gains in transport as well as other systems. Communicating such a vision accurately may be very timely, both for increases in cycle commuting per se, and for mobilizing sustainability impacts elsewhere.

References

Auckland Regional Land Transport Strategy (2005). See www.arc.govt.nz/arc/index.cfm?20B5B7C1-BCD4-1A24-9518-FB9977DF621B, sourced March 2007.

Cox, P. (2005). "Conflicting agendas in selling cycling". *Proceedings of the Velo-City 2005 Conference*. Dublin.

Clam, J. (2000). "System's sole constituent, the operation: clarifying a central concept of Luhmannian theory". *Acta Sociologica,* ISSN (electronic): 1502-3869, 43: 63-79.

Furness, Z. (2005). " 'Put the fun between your legs!': the politics and counterculture of the bicycle". Unpublished thesis, Doctor of Philosophy, University of Pittsburgh.

Giddens, A. (1979). *Central Problems in Social Theory: Action, Structure and Contradiction in Social Analysis.* ISBN-10: 0520039750.

Gershuny, N. (2000). *Changing Times: Work and Leisure in Postindustrial Society.* ISBN-10: 019926189X.

Habermas, J. (1987). Trans. Lawrence, F. *The Philosophical Discourse of Modernity: Twelve Lectures.* ISBN-10: 0262581027.

Herlihy, D. (2004). *Bicycle: The History.* ISBN-10: 0300120478.

Horton, D. (2006). "Environmentalism and the bicycle". *Environmental Politics,* ISSN (printed): 0964-4016, 15 (1): 41-58.

Household Travel Survey 2003 – 2006. (2007a). Ministry of Transport. Wellington. See http://www.transport.govt.nz/ongoing-travel-survey-index/, sourced July 2007.

Injury Risks by Different Modes. (2007b). Ministry of Transport. See www.mot.govt.nz/risk-modes/, accessed March 2007.

Kampmann Walther, B. (2005). "Big theory – strong theory: the ontological ghost of post-ontological epistemology". *Cybernetics and Human Knowing,* ISSN (printed): 0907-0877, 11(3): 30-55.

Kennett, J., Kennett, S. (2005). *Ride: The Story of Cycling in New Zealand.* ASIN: B000EUH4DC.

Koorey, G. (2003). "Why a cycling strategy on its own will NOT increase cycling". Proceedings of the New Zealand cycling Conference 2003. See www.can.org.nz/activities/papers/koorey-2003-cycling-conf.ppt sourced July 2007.

Luhmann, N. (1994). " 'What is the case?' and 'what lies behind it?' The two sociologies and the theory of society". *Sociological Theory,* ISSN (electronic): 1467-9558, 126-137.

Luhmann, N. (1995). *Social Systems.* ISBN-10: 0804726256.

McDonald, P. (1978). *Changing Gear: Why and how to promote cycling in New Zealand.* Friends of the Earth, Wellington.

McKernon. S. (2007). *Design of change in cycle commuting.* Unpublished thesis, Master of Design Management, Unitec Institute of Technology, Auckland, New Zealand.

Moeller, H-G. (2006). *Luhmann Explained: From Souls to Systems.* ISBN-10: 0812695984.

Moser, K. (2003). "The dark side of 'automobilism', 1900-1930: Violence, war and the motor car". *Journal of Transport History,* ISSN (printed): 0022-5266, pp. 1-9.

Murray-Clarke, M. (2007). "Why the congestion zone has been extended". *BBC News.* 15th February 2007. See www.bbc.co.uk/london/content/articles/2007/02/15/congestion_malcolm_murrayclark_feature.shtml Accessed March 20007.

New Zealand Census 2006: Quickstats National Highlights Table 29. (2007). Statistics New Zealand. Wellington.

Ogilvie, D. Egan, M. Hamilton, V. & Petticrew, M. (2004). "Promoting walking and cycling as an alternative to using cars: systematic review". *BMJ,* ISSN (printed): 0959-8154, 763-775.

Rosen, P. (2002). *Framing Production: Technology, Culture, and Change in the British Bicycle Industry*. ISBN-10: 0262182254.

Rubenstein, D. (1977). "Cycling in the 1890s". *Victorian Studies*, ISSN (electronic): 1527-2052, Autumn: 47-71.

Simpson, C. (2001). "Respectable identities: New Zealand nineteenth-century New Women – on bicycles!" *The International Journal of the History of Sport*, ISSN (printed): 0952-3367, 18 (2): 54-77.

Sticheweh, R. (2000). "Systems theory as an alternative to action theory? The rise of 'communication' as a theoretical option". *Acta Sociologica*, ISSN (electronic): 1502-3869, 43: 5-13.

The New Zealand Official Year-Book 2005. Registrar-General's Office, New Zealand. ISSN: 0078-0170.

Turner, S., Roozenburg, A., Francis, T. (2006). "Predicting accident rates for cyclists and pedestrians". *Land Transport New Zealand Research Report 289*. Land Transport New Zealand. Wellington.

Willig, C. (2001). *Introducing Qualitative Research in Psychology: Adventures in Theory and Method*. ISBN-10: 0335205356.

THEME 9:
SYSTEM DYNAMICS

42. Local Solutions to Global Problems: An Integrated System Dynamics Model for Analyzing Policy Options for Tobacco Control in New Zealand

PLENARY PAPER

Robert Y. Cavana[1] and Martin Tobias[2]
[1]Victoria University of Wellington, Wellington, New Zealand
[2]Ministry of Health, Wellington, New Zealand.

Acknowledgements

The authors would like to thank the New Zealand Ministry of Health for permission to present this paper. However, the interpretations and opinions in this paper are the authors' own and do not necessarily reflect Ministry policy advice.

Tobacco use is a global problem and the health consequences are far reaching. The situation in New Zealand is similar to most other parts of the world. Holistic and systemic approaches are needed to help investigate policies to reduce the adverse health effects of tobacco use. This paper provides an overview of the system dynamics model that has been developed to assist the Ministry of Health to evaluate the dynamic consequences of tobacco control policies in New Zealand. The model consists of 6 sectors: population; smoking prevalences; tobacco consumption; second hand smoke; relative risks; and tobacco attributable deaths. The model is simulated for 20-30 years into the future. The simulation package used is 'iThink', and a user interface is presented for policy analysis. A couple of illustrative scenarios are provided, including: enhanced smoking cessation services and fiscal strategies involving less affordable cigarettes. The main output variables (performance measures) include current smoking prevalence, tobacco consumption, and tobacco attributable mortality. Finally areas for future model enhancement are identified.

Introduction

"The theme of this year's conference is systemic development: local solutions in a global environment. As the call to solve intractable problems in a globally-connected world increases, systems thinkers turn towards systemic problem solving. The challenge is to apply holistic, global systems concepts to local situations"

Source: ANZSYS 07 conference theme. http://anzsys07.unitec.ac.nz/

This paper addresses the conference theme, by examining the global health problems associated with tobacco smoking using a system dynamics model that has been developed to help the Ministry of Health (MOH) to evaluate the dynamic consequences of tobacco control policies in New Zealand (NZ).

Tobacco use can be thought of as a 'system' containing emergent properties, complexity, and nonlinear dynamics. Traditional epidemiological methods deal with complexity by breaking the issue down into parts simple enough to be controlled (randomised control trials) or observed (cohort or case control study). System dynamics (SD), by contrast, deals with complexity by abstracting the key elements and simulating their dynamic inter-relationships (using multiple simultaneous differential equations).

The focus of an SD model is thus on the behavior of the system *as a system*. Elements are retained only if necessary, and only relevant attributes incorporated.

"*Everything should be made as simple as possible – but not simpler*"
Albert Einstein

The specific objectives of the SD tobacco control model are:

1. To support evidence-informed tobacco control policy;
2. To provide a decision support tool when considering strategic policy options in tobacco control, and,
3. To assess the utility of system dynamics in formulating public health policy in the NZ context.

The Ministry of Health has a statutory responsibility to monitor use of, and harms caused by, tobacco products. Also such monitoring is required under the World Health Organization Framework Convention on Tobacco Control (WHO, 2005).

Previous system dynamics studies related to tobacco policy includes: the DYNAMO based system dynamics modelling work at MIT in the late 1970s and early 1980s on the impacts of smoking by Roberts *et al.* (1982); the Markovian system dynamics computer based simulation model developed in the USA by Tengs *et al.* (2001a,b; 2004a, b), Ahmad (2005) and Ahmad & Billimek (2005) for analyzing tobacco related policies; the computer simulation model called SimSmoke developed by Levy *et al.* (2006a, b) to assess the impacts of a broad array of public policies related to tobacco control; and the system dynamics pilot study by Cavana & Clifford (2006) at NZ Customs Service analysing the collection of tobacco excise duties and cigarette smoking in NZ.

The general approach used in this study follows the five phase integrated approach in Table 1, as outlined by Maani and Cavana (2000, 2007), following the general approach of the system dynamics methodology (e.g. see Forrester, 1961; Coyle, 1996; Sterman, 2000):

Phase	
1	Problem Structuring
2	Causal Loop Modelling
3	Dynamic Modelling
4	Scenario Planning and Modelling
5	Implementation and Organisational Learning

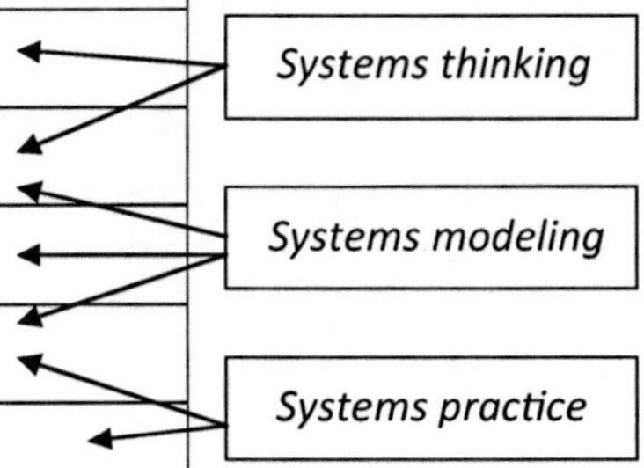

Source: Maani and Cavana (2000, Table 2.1, p16)

Table 1 *Integrated Systems Dynamics Methodology*

According to ISSS (2007):

"Systems thinking promotes holism as its primary intellectual strategy for handling complexity, whether the approach is hard or soft, carried out by academia or practitioners. Instead of analyzing complex systems by breaking them down into their parts, it advocates studying them as `wholes' using systems concepts..." [this relates to the problem structuring and casual loop modelling phases summarized in Table 1].

"Systems modeling aims at describing, analyzing and prescribing a real entity or phenomenon by constructing a variety of systems models. It includes mathematical models, conceptual models, computer models and simulation tools..." [this relates to the casual loop modelling, dynamic modelling and scenario planning/modelling phases summarized in Table 1].

"Finally, systems practice, or practical applications of systems thinking/ideas, is the greatest success of systems sciences in recent years. It has shown that systems sciences have the ability to translate theoretical notions into the practical domain through the use of systems methodologies, models and methods..." [this relates to the scenario planning/modelling and implementation/organizational learning phases summarized in Table 1].

This paper outlines progress to date of the tobacco policy modelling study. The next section provides the overview causal loop diagram that provided the conceptual framework for the development of the stock flow diagrams and simulation model outlined in the following section. The next part of this paper outlines a couple of scenarios with the tobacco policy model describing the experiments and the model performance measures for a range of tobacco control policies. Finally some limitations and areas for further work are outlined in the concluding section.

Causal Loop Modelling

The overall causal structure for the model is provided in Figure 1. This diagram shows the population aging chain and the various categories of smokers and non-smokers. The feedback effects of adult smokers and teen peer group smokers on initiation and on exposure to secondhand smoke can be clearly seen, and the effects of various tobacco control policies on initiation, net quitting (i.e., cessation minus relapse rates), and smoking intensity can also be observed in this diagram. Changes in tobacco control policy settings are represented in the model in two ways:

- Changes in smoking behavior, reflected in initiation and quit rates and smoking intensity.
- Changes in excess mortality risks (the relative risks of death for those exposed compared to those not exposed) for current smokers, ex-smokers, and never smokers exposed to secondhand smoke, by age and duration of exposure.

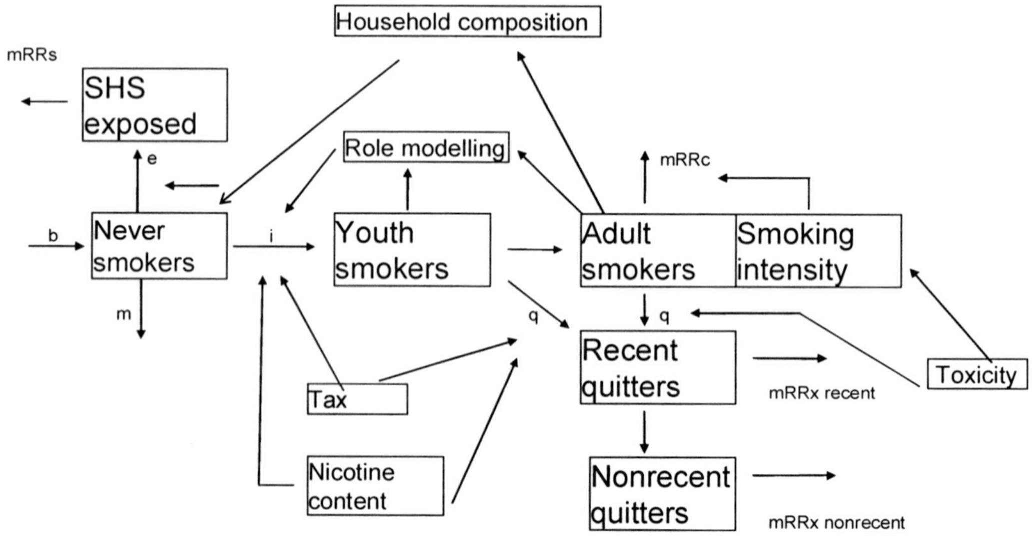

Key: i = smoking initiation rate; b = birth rate; e = exposure to second hand smoke; q = net quit rate; m = never smoker mortality rate; RR = relative risks of mortality; c = current smokers; s = second hand smoke; x = ex-smokers.

Figure 1 *Systems Diagram for the NZ Tobacco Policy Model*

This diagram provides the conceptual framework for the development of the 6 sector system dynamics simulation model, briefly outlined in the following section.

Dynamic Modelling

Overview of the Simulation Model

The system dynamics simulation model consists of 6 sectors (see Figure 2): population; smoking prevalences; tobacco consumption; second hand smoke; relative risks; and tobacco attributable deaths.

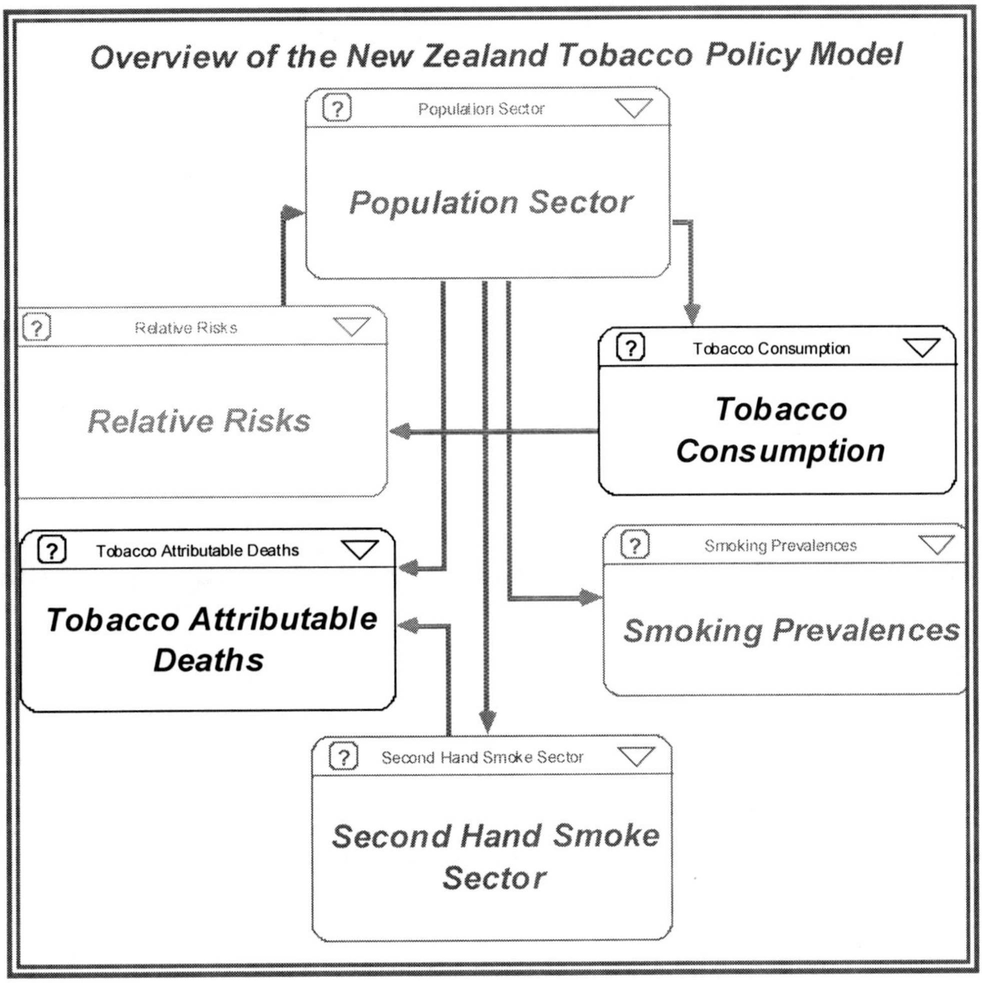

Figure 2 *Overview of the NZ Tobacco Policy Model*

The tobacco sector consists of population aging chains broken down into 10 year age groups representing stocks of 'never smokers', current smokers', 'recent ex-smokers', and 'non recent ex-smokers'. Flows are provided for births, aging between cohorts, initiation and net-quitting smoking, and mortality associated with smoking & ex-smoking. The prevalence sector calculates ratios for each of the stocks or combination of age related stocks in the population sector. The second hand smoke sector calculates the exposure and mortality associated with second hand (passive) smoking by age group in NZ. Finally the tobacco attributable deaths sector summarizes the mortality associated with smoking and second hand smoke by age cohort in NZ (smokers of course die from unrelated as well as smoking-related causes).

Only the simplified stock flow diagram for the population sector will be provided in this paper (see Figure 3). The variable names are classified as acronyms, *where for example*:

- 10G = age group from 10 to 19 years old
- NS = never smokers
- CS = current smokers
- XSR = recent ex-smokers
- XSNR = non recent ex-smokers
- Births = annual births
- D = annual deaths
- NSD 70G = annual deaths of never smokers in the 70 plus age group
- NS to 10G = annual aging into the age group starting at age 10 (flow - aging between the 1st two age cohorts)
- q = annual net-quit rate (ie rate of quitting smoking less restarting smoking)
- m = mortality rate
- ir = initiation rate
- RR CS30T69G = relative risk of mortality of current smokers in the 30 to 69 year old age group

The model is developed using the *iThink* v9.01 dynamic simulation software package (iSee systems, 2005). The sources for the data used to initialise the model are summarized in Table 2 below. The model can be simulated for 50 years, although the focus is on the medium term, 20-30 years into the future.

Calibrating and Testing the Model

The model was subjected to a number of verification and validation tests. Firstly we calibrated the model by checking that the base case reproduced current prevalence by age, consumption and tobacco attributable mortality (TAM) – this involved minor tweaking of initiation and quit rates. The 'validation' experiments included:

- Business as usual (BAU) scenario reproduces recent trends in prevalence
- Prevalence increases if never smoker mortality decreases or relative risk (RR) related to smoking decreases
- Prevalence, consumption and TAM behave appropriately if initiation and quit rates change
- Youth smoking prevalence changes appropriately if parental / peer feedbacks change
- Second hand or passive smoking (SHS)–attributable mortality changes appropriately if living arrangements change.

Prevalence (current, ex-smoking)	NZHS 02/03
Initiation rate (and responsiveness to parental and peer role modelling)	NZTUS 06
Net quit rates	NZTUS 06
Smoking intensity distribution	NZTUS 06
Never smoker mortality rates	$m_o = m / [p_c(RRc - 1) + p_x(RRx - 1) + 1]$
RR current smokers (by duration and intensity)	CPS II (duration = age −15)
RR ex-smokers (by duration)	CPS II
RR SHS exposure	NZCMS
Never smokers exposed to SHS	NZHS 02/03
Population estimates and projections (including mortality trend)	SNZ

Where:

NZHS 02/03 = 2002/03 New Zealand Health Survey
NZTUS 06 = 2006 New Zealand Tobacco Use Survey
CPS I I = American Cancer Society Cancer Prevention Study II
NZCMS = New Zealand Census Mortality Study
SNZ = Statistics New Zealand

Table 2 *Initializing the NZ Tobacco Policy Model*

Scenario Planning and Modelling

The user interface for the model (or management flight simulator) is provided in Figure 4. This shows the parameters that can be adjusted readily by the policy analysts or others experimenting with the model. Also, sensitivity analysis and scenario analysis can be carried out by undertaking 'what if' experiments with the user interface.

Two experiments are provided, to illustrate potential applications of the SD model:

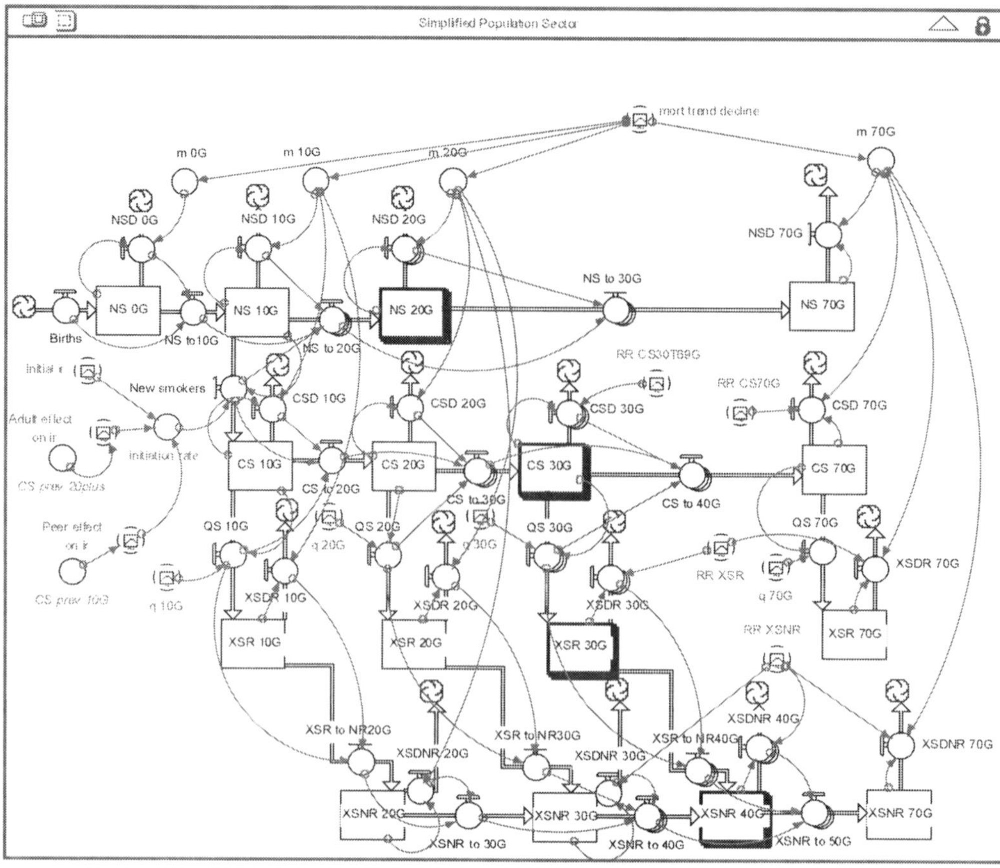

Figure 3 *Simplified Stock Flow Diagram for the Population Sector*

- Enhanced smoking cessation (increased investment in smoking cessation services and associated media campaigns);
- Fiscal strategies involving less affordable cigarettes (through raising the excise tax rate on tobacco products).

All intervention scenarios are compared with the status quo or 'business as usual' scenario.

Business as Usual (BAU) Scenario

The key model output for the business as usual (BAU) scenario (status quo or base case) is provided in Table 3.

The BAU scenario is required as the counterfactual against which all intervention scenarios must be compared.

Note that model predicts a very slow rate of decline in prevalence – 1.3 percentage points over 20 years or less than 0.1 percentage point per year. Per capita consumption falls from approximately 1000 CE/yr[1] today to about 900 CE/yr in 2031. Attributable mortality rate falls by less than 0.5% per year (from

1. 1 cigarette equivalent = 1 manufactured cigarette or 1 gram of 'roll your own' (RYO) tobacco.

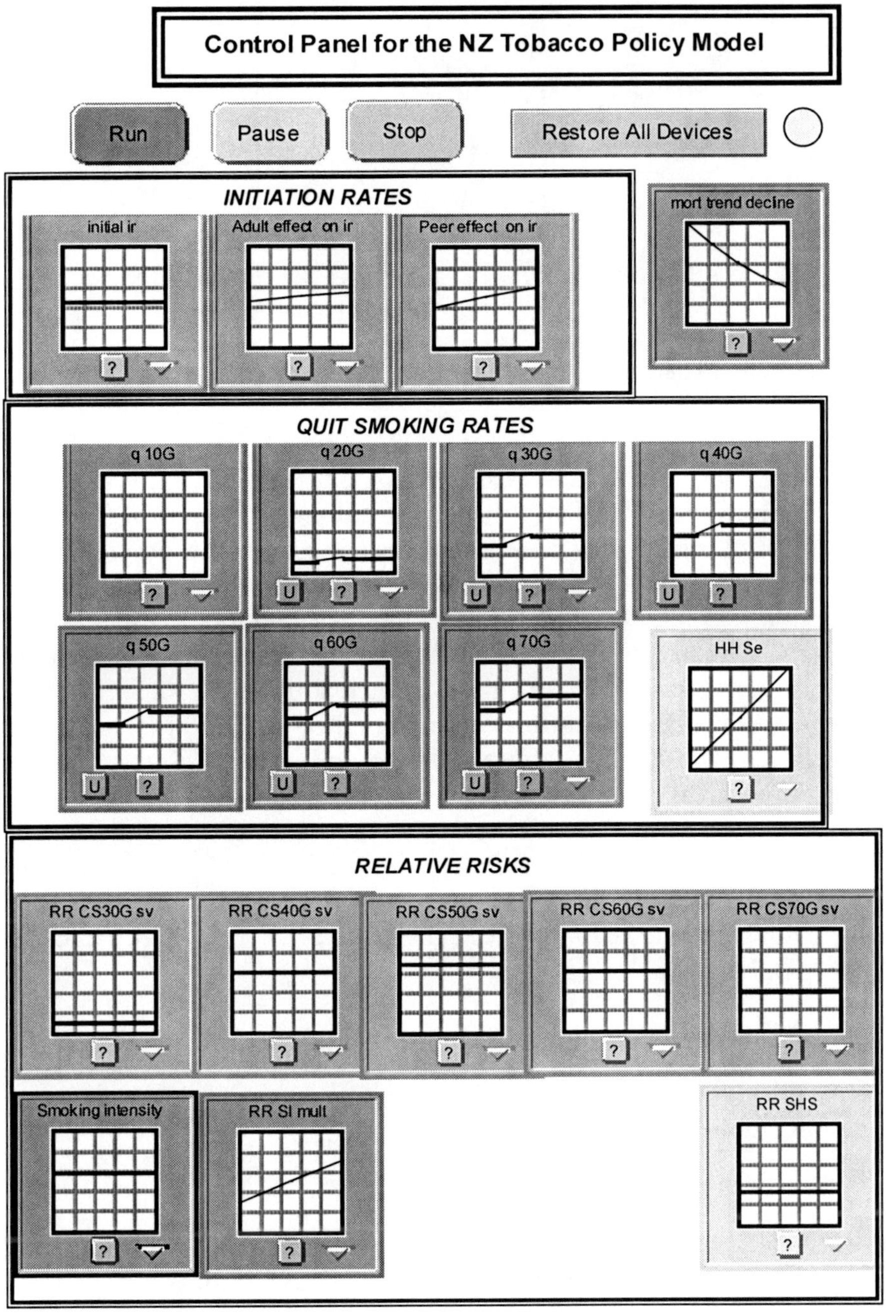

Figure 4 *User Interface for the NZ Tobacco Policy Model*

Year	Smoking prevalence		Tobacco consumption		Tobacco attributable mortality	
	Rate *(%)*	Count *(000/yr)*	per capita *(CE/yr)*	Total *(tonnes/yr)*	Rate *(per 100,000)*	Count *(people/yr)*
2001	23.3	744	1,023	3,259	114	4,254
2011	22.4	762	980	3,339	122	4,851
2021	21.6	770	947	3,375	119	4,891
2031	21.0	776	920	3,403	113	4,818

Table 3 *Major Performance Measures for the NZ Tobacco Policy Model – Business as Usual Scenario*

2011-2031) while the mortality count remains essentially stable (reflecting demographic trends).

Enhanced Cessation Scenarios

The first example we will briefly discuss is enhanced cessation (increased investment in smoking cessation services). Starting with the population of current smokers, each year a proportion M will make one or more quit attempts. Of these quit attempts, a proportion H will be assisted by nicotine replacement therapy (NRT) (illustrated in Figure 5). Unassisted attempts are associated with a short term success rate of 7% while assistance doubles the success rate. So the annual population cessation rate is determined by M and H (with the former parameter having the stronger effect). The net quit rate is about half the annual cessation rate because of later relapses.

Modelling parameters

Until recently we lacked robust national estimates for M and H, but such estimates have now become available from the 2006 NZTUS (NZ Tobacco Use Survey):

- 44% of adults currently make one or more quit attempts per year [M];
- 21% of these are currently NRT-assisted [H];
- Also, NRT doubles the successful quit rate, and;
- Relapses reduce long term net quit success rate by half.

Given these data, enhanced cessation scenarios can be designed and translated into the corresponding changes to the relevant model inputs.

Enhanced cessation scenarios

In this paper we will consider two enhanced cessation scenarios:

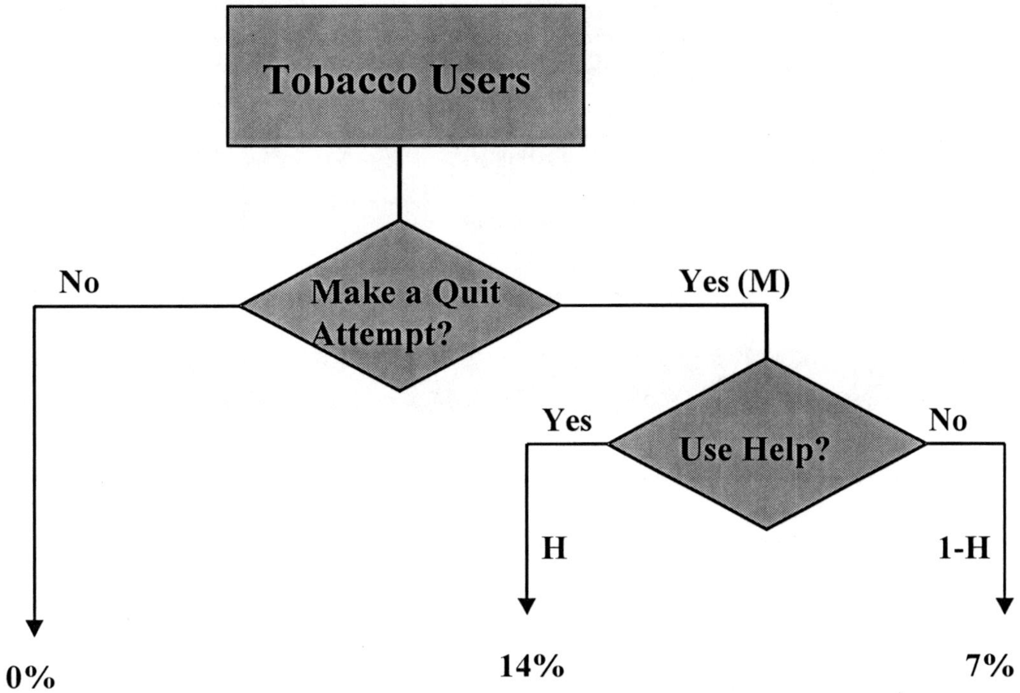

Figure 5 *Tobacco Cessation Decision Making Process*

- Scenario 1A:
  10% increase in M (44% to 48%)
  20% increase in H (21% to 25%)

- Scenario 1B:
  20% increase in M (44% to 53%)
  40% increase in H (21% to 29%)

The changes to the model are introduced progressively from 2006 to 2011, and sustained thereafter. Parameters for the model for the selected enhanced cessation scenarios (derived from the above data) are summarized in Table 4, and how these changes are incorporated into the model are summarized in Table 5:

The requisite changes are made to the flight management simulator (shown as Figure 4) and the model is simulated with the new parameter values. The main performance measures, including smoking prevalences (rate per 100 people over 10 years of age in NZ), per capita tobacco consumption (measured in cigarette equivalents per year), and the annual number of deaths in NZ attributed to tobacco smoking. The main output results for the enhanced cessation scenarios are provided in Table 6.

These results are compared with the 'business as usual scenario'. Clearly Scenario 1B, greater enhanced cessation, provides better results, with over 300 fewer people per year dying from tobacco related causes by 2031 (compared with the BAU scenario) and, on average, reduced per capita tobacco consumption of about 50 less cigarette equivalents per year (or about 2.5 standard packs

	Scenario 1A	Scenario 1B
si (smoking intensity)	unchanged	unchanged
ir (initiation rate)	unchanged	unchanged
q (net quit rate)	13% increase	26% increase

Table 4 *Enhanced Cessation Scenario 1 - Parameters*

		Base Case	Scenario 1A	Scenario 1B
si		12.0	12.0	12.0
ir		0.047	0.047	0.047
	10-19	0.003	0.003	0.003
	20-29	0.012	0.014	0.015
	30-39	0.016	0.018	0.020
q	40-49	0.020	0.023	0.025
	50-59	0.022	0.025	0.028
	60-69	0.024	0.027	0.030
	70+	0.027	0.031	0.034

Table 5 *Enhanced Cessation Scenario 1 - Model Input*

of cigarettes less per year per person). Nevertheless, this scenario only reduces the prevalence of tobacco smoking in the NZ population from 21.0 to 19.8 per-cent by 2031.

The dynamic behavior of the main variables for the enhanced cessation scenarios are summarized in Figure 6. The main performance measures include smoking prevalences, the number of current smokers and the annual mortality figures associated with tobacco smoking in New Zealand. Historical figures are shown for the period from 2001 to 2006, and the scenarios are provided for the period from 2006 to 2031.

Less Affordable Cigarette Scenarios

Two reduced affordability scenarios are considered, based on the recent history of price increases in NZ: 1991 (21%), 1998 (15%), 2000 (23%):

Year		Scenario 1A Smoking Prevalence (rate/100)	Scenario 1A Tobacco consumption (CE/capita)	Scenario 1A Tobacco attributable mortality (count)	Scenario 1B Smoking Prevalence (rate/100)	Scenario 1B Tobacco consumption (CE/capita)	Scenario 1B Tobacco attributable mortality (count)
2011	Base	22.4	980	4851	22.4	980	4851
	Expt	22.3	975	4822	22.2	972	4797
	Diff	0.1	5.0	29.0	0.2	8.0	54.0
	% diff	0.4%	0.5%	0.6%	0.9%	0.8%	1.1%
2021	Base	21.6	947	4891	21.6	947	4891
	Expt	21.2	926	4779	20.8	913	4686
	Diff	0.4	21.0	112.0	0.8	34.0	205.0
	% diff	1.9%	2.2%	2.3%	3.7%	3.6%	4.2%
2031	Base	21.0	920	4818	21.0	920	4818
	Expt	20.3	889	4631	19.8	869	4479
	Diff	0.7	31.0	187.0	1.2	51.0	339.0
	% diff	3.3%	3.4%	3.9%	5.7%	5.5%	7.0%

Table 6 *Key NZ Tobacco Policy Model Output - Enhanced Cessation Scenarios*

- Scenario 2A:
  10% reduction in affordability in 2006, sustained thereafter by annual CPI and income indexation;

- Scenario 2B:
  20% reduction in affordability as above.

Reduction in affordability (increase in costliness) equates to an increase in minutes of work required to earn 20 standard brand manufactured cigarettes or equivalent RYO tobacco at the ordinary average full-time wage (currently approximately 30 minutes). The price increase may include tax and trade components.

To translate the selected scenarios into model terms, data on the relevant elasticities (% change in smoking behavior for a 1% change in price) were derived from a meta-analysis of the literature (Chaloupka 2002) and other sources (Nicolas 2002, Forster & Jones 2000):

- Price elasticity of demand –0.4
- Conditional demand elasticity –0.2
- Prevalence elasticity –0.2
- Initiation elasticity –0.2
- Quitting elasticity +0.4

In each case, the change is modelled to take place abruptly in 2006 and is then maintained thereafter until 2031. Parameters for the model for the reduced affordability scenarios (derived from the above elasticity estimates) are summarized in Table 7 and how these changes are incorporated into the model are summarized in Table 8:

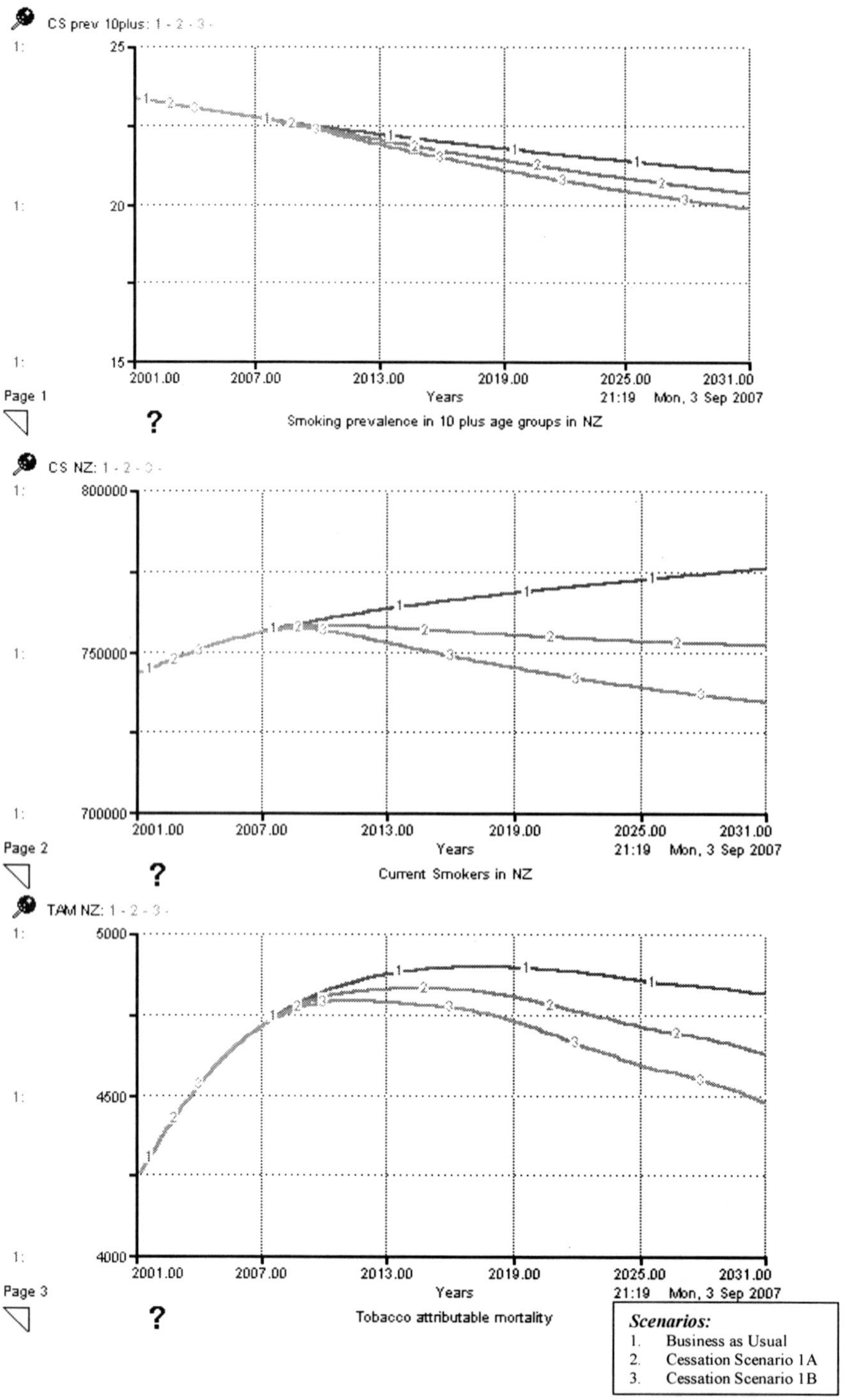

Figure 6 *NZ Tobacco Policy Model Output – Enhanced Cessation Scenarios*

	Scenario 2A	Scenario 2B
si (smoking intensity)	2% decrease	4% decrease
ir (initiation rate)	2% decrease	4% decrease
q (net quit rate)	4% increase	8% increase

Table 7 *Reduced Affordability Scenario 2 – Parameters*

		Base Case	Scenario 2A	Scenario 2B
si		12.0	11.7	11.5
ir		0.047	0.046	0.045
q	10-19	0.003	0.003	0.003
	20-29	0.012	0.012	0.013
	30-39	0.016	0.017	0.018
	40-49	0.020	0.021	0.022
	50-59	0.022	0.023	0.024
	60-69	0.024	0.025	0.026
	70+	0.027	0.028	0.029

Table 8 *Reduced Affordability Scenario 2 - Model Input*

The requisite changes are made to the flight management simulator (shown as Figure 4) and the model is simulated with the new parameter values. The main performance measures, including smoking prevalences (rate per 100 people over 10 years of age in NZ), per capita tobacco consumption (measured in cigarette equivalents per year), and the annual number of deaths in NZ attributed to tobacco smoking. The main output results for the reduced affordability scenarios (ie 10% and 20% reduction in affordability from 2006) are provided in Table 9 and Figure 7.

These results are compared with the 'business as usual scenario'. The impact on mortality of these scenarios – which involve only a single step change in affordability - is not as great as the enhanced cessation scenarios (1A & 1B) provided in Table 6 and Figure 6, although per capita tobacco consumption is significantly lower. Scenario 2B (20% reduced affordability), results in over 200 fewer people dying per year from tobacco related causes by 2031 (compared with the BAU scenario) and, on average, reduced per capita smoking of about 80 fewer cigarette equivalents per year (or about 4 standard packs of cigarettes less per year per person). However, this scenario only reduces the prevalence of tobacco smoking in the NZ population from 21.0 to 19.9 percent by 2031. Hence regular increases in costliness (possibly in combination with other strategies) may be needed to substantively reduce the prevalence of tobacco smoking in New Zealand.

The dynamic behavior of the main variables for the reduced affordability scenarios are summarized in Figure 7. The main performance measures include smoking prevalences, the number of current smokers and the annual mortality

Year		Scenario 2A			Scenario 2B		
		Smoking Prevalence *(rate/100)*	Tobacco consumption *(CE/capita)*	Tobacco attributable mortality *(count)*	Smoking Prevalence *(rate/100)*	Tobacco consumption *(CE/capita)*	Tobacco attributable mortality *(count)*
2011	Base	22.4	980	4851	22.4	980	4851
	Expt	22.2	932	4793	22.1	928	4747
	Diff	0.2	48.0	58.0	0.3	52.0	104.0
	% diff	0.9%	4.9%	1.2%	1.3%	5.3%	2.1%
2021	Base	21.6	947	4891	21.6	947	4891
	Expt	21.3	886	4807	20.9	877	4734
	Diff	0.3	61.0	84.0	0.7	70.0	157.0
	% diff	1.4%	6.4%	1.7%	3.2%	7.4%	3.2%
2031	Base	21.0	920	4818	21.0	920	4818
	Expt	20.5	849	4708	19.9	836	4606
	Diff	0.5	71.0	110.0	1.1	84.0	212.0
	% diff	2.4%	7.7%	2.3%	5.2%	9.1%	4.4%

Table 9 *Key NZ Tobacco Policy Model Output: Reduced Affordability Scenarios*

figures associated with tobacco smoking in New Zealand. Historical figures are shown for the period from 2001 to 2006, and the scenarios are provided for the period from 2006 to 2031.

Implementation and Organizational Learning

A number of different scenarios have been analyzed with the system dynamics model developed for tobacco policy control in New Zealand. These scenarios include enhanced cessation and reduced affordability strategies. Elsewhere, Cavana and Tobias (2007) have discussed other scenarios using an earlier version of this model.

From the results outlined, it can be seen that both enhanced smoking cessation services and sustained tobacco excise tax increases would be effective tobacco control strategies. However, these strategies on their own would appear to be only partial solutions to substantively reducing the prevalence of tobacco use in New Zealand.

In using these results, it should be understood that there are some limitations to the tobacco control model as it currently stands. These include:

- The model is age structured but not differentiated by gender, ethnicity or socio-economic group;
- Demographic trends (fertility, migration) are not fully captured, so population growth is under-estimated;
- Health effects are captured only by mortality, not morbidity;
- Some relevant dimensions of industry behavior and tobacco control are captured only crudely, if at all.

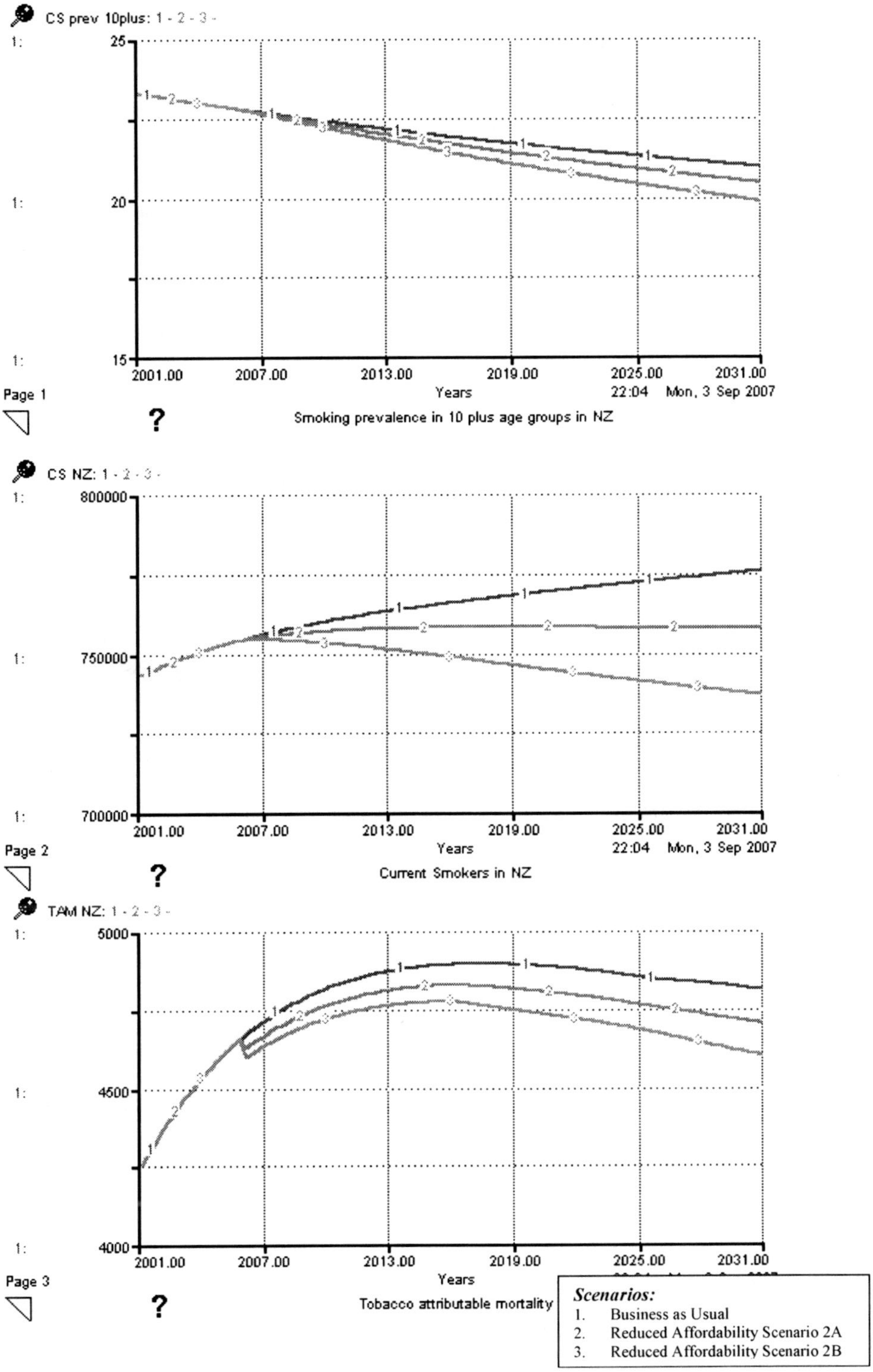

Figure 7 *NZ Tobacco Policy Model Output – Reduced Affordability Scenarios*

These limitations will be addressed by further development of the model. However, we maintain that integrated system dynamics provides a particularly appropriate methodological approach for examining the linkages between industry and tobacco control practice on the one hand, and tobacco use behaviors and health outcomes on the other.

References

Ahmad, S. and Billimek, J. (2005). Estimating the health impacts of tobacco harm reduction policies: a simulation modeling approach. *Risk Analysis*, **25**(4): 801-812.

Ahmad, S. (2005). Increasing excise taxes on cigarettes in California: a dynamic simulation of health and economic impacts. *Preventive Medicine*, **41**(1) 276-283.

American Cancer Society, Cancer Prevention Study II (various publications)

Cavana, R.Y. and Clifford, L.V. (2006). Demonstrating the utility of system dynamics for public policy analysis in New Zealand: the case of excise tax policy on tobacco. System Dynamics Review **22**(4): 321-348.

Cavana, R.Y. and Tobias, M. (2007). Using system dynamics to analyse policy options for tobacco control in New Zealand. Plenary paper. *Proceedings of the 25th International System Dynamics Conference*, July 07, Boston, USA.

Chaloupka, F.J., Wakefield, M. and Czart, C. (2001). Taxing tobacco: the impact of tobacco taxes on cigarette smoking and other tobacco use. In Rabin RL and Sugarman SD (editors) *Regulating Tobaco.* Oxford University Press.

Coyle, R.G. (1996). *System Dynamics Modelling: A Practical Approach.* Chapman & Hall: London.

Forrester, J.W. (1961). *Industrial Dynamics.* MIT Press: Cambridge, Mass.

Forster, M. and Jones, A. (2000). *The role of tobacco taxes in starting and quitting smoking: duration analysis of British data.* University of York Discussion Paper 176.

iSee Systems. (2005). *iThink Version 9.01 for Windows.* iSee Systems Inc.: Hanover NH.

ISSS (2007). *Theme "Integrated Systems Sciences: Systems Thinking, Modeling and Practice", the 51st annual meeting of the ISSS, to be held in Tokyo, Japan from August 5 to 10, 2007.* International Society for the Systems Sciences. Web site: http://projects.isss.org/Main/Tokyo2007. [accessed 31 May 2006].

Levy, D.T., Bauer, J.E. and Lee, H. (2006a). Simulation modelling and tobacco control: creating more robust public health policies. *American Journal of Public Health*, **96**(3): 61-65.

Levy, D.T., Bates, S., Lam, N.T. and Nikolayev, L. (2006b). The role of public policies in reducing smoking and deaths caused by smoking in Vietnam: results from the Vietnam tobacco policy simulation model. *Social Science & Medicine*, **62**: 1819-1830.

Maani, K.E. and Cavana, R.Y. (2007). *Systems Thinking, System Dynamics: Managing Change and Complexity.* 2nd ed. Pearson Education (NZ), Auckland.

Maani, K.E. and Cavana, R.Y. (2000). *Systems Thinking and Modelling: Understanding Change and Complexity.* Pearson Education (NZ), Auckland.

Ministry of Health (2005). New Zealand Census Mortality Study (data source)

Ministry of Health. (2004). New Zealand Health Survey 2002/03 (data source)

Nicolas, A.L. (2002). How important are tobacco prices in the propensity to start and quit smoking? *Health Econ,* **11**: 521-535.

Roberts, E., Homer, J., Kasabian, A. and Varrell, M. (1982). A Systems View of the Smoking Problem: Perspective and Limitations of the Role of Science in Decision-Making. *Int. J. Bio-Medical Computing,* **13**: 69-86.

SNZ. (2006). Demographic Trends 2005. Statistics New Zealand: Wellington, NZ.

[available from: http://www.stats.govt.nz/NR/rdonlyres/901D40E4-9607-4215-807F-9C22CDC98618/0/DemographicTrends20052.pdf]

Sterman, J.D. (2000). *Business Dynamics: Systems Thinking and Modeling for a Complex World.* Irwin McGraw-Hill: Boston.

Tengs, T.O., Ahmad, S., Moore, R. and Gage, E. (2004a). Federal policy mandating safer cigarettes: A hypothetical simulation of the anticipated population health gains or losses. *Journal of Policy Analysis and Management*, **23**(4): 857-872.

Tengs, T.O., Ahmad, S., Savage, J.M., Moore, R. and Gage, E. (2004b). The AMA proposal to mandate nicotine reduction in cigarettes: a simulation of the population health impacts. *Preventive Medicine*, **40**(2): 170-180.

Tengs, T.O., Osgood, N.D. and Chen, L.L. (2001a). The cost-effectiveness of intensive national school-based anti-tobacco education: results from the Tobacco Policy Model. *Preventive Medicine*, **33**(6): 558-570.

Tengs, T.O., Osgood, N.D, and Lin, T.H. (2001b). Public health impact of changes in smoking behavior: results from the Tobacco Policy Model. *Medical Care*, **39**(10): 1131-1141.

The Quit Group (2005). *The Quitline NRT Programme.* Research Report. He Pu¯rongo Rangahau. Prepared by The Quit Group, Na¯ Te Roopu¯ Me Mutu, September 2005. Available from:
http://www.quit.org.nz/file/research/publicationsAndPresentations/Evaluation_Quitline_RR_screenres.pdf)

WHO. (2005). *WHO Framework Convention on Tobacco Control.* World Health Organization: Geneva, Switzerland. [available from :
http://www.who.int/tobacco/framework/en/]

WHO. (2002). SACTob position statement on nicotine and its regulation in tobacco and non-tobacco products. Geneva: World Health Organization.

43. The Harnessing of Systems Methodologies to Enhance Understanding of the Systemic Structure of Industry Based Dilemmas

John Davies, Bronwyn Howell and **Victoria Mabin**
Victoria Management School, Victoria University of Wellington, NZ

This paper examines prima facie unrelated problem situations faced by those charged with enhancing service provision and market conditions in the health, telecommunications and mining sectors in Australasia. In particular, it examines the dilemmas faced by regulators seeking to improve price/quality relativities in the telecommunications sector, by politicians seeking to legislate the broadening of service provision in the primary healthcare sector and by competition authorities charged with determining access rights to the private transport infrastructure of mining companies. The paper demonstrates the mutually informing use of systems representational tools, as a means of building understanding of the systemic structure of such dilemmas, and as a means of providing an appropriate platform for decision making. In doing so, attention is drawn to how Senge's archetypes (1999) provide a basis for recognizing the communality of structures and to how the systems representations are able to contribute to the generation of meaning.

Introduction

This paper complements other work that has sought to demonstrate the benefits of building understanding of systemic structure through the use of systems representational tools, and then how systems representations are able to contribute to the generation of meaning (Lissack, 2004). In particular, the paper seeks to draw parallels between seemingly unrelated caselets - problem situations faced by those charged with enhancing service provision and market conditions in the health, telecommunications and mining sectors in Australia and New Zealand. We do so as a basis for examining the systemic structure of dilemmas faced by those charged with regulatory and legislative responsibilities for enhancing these roles.

The paper first outlines the three caselets, and then, in a subsequent section, attention is drawn to the commonality of systemic structure embedded in the systems representations, and how an understanding of that systemic structure may allow transfer of meaning and understanding from one problem domain to another, and from one time period to another. As such, it is hoped that not only will regulators, policy makers and decision makers be able to share contemporary experiences and understanding about existing dilemmas, but that lessons can be gained from problems and dilemmas that have been faced in the past, and assist with similar dilemmas in the future.

Caselets – Regulatory Dilemmas

The Primary Healthcare Sector in New Zealand – Maternity Care Services

Community-based general medical practitioners (GPs) have long been at the heart of NZ's state-funded primary healthcare services, with GPs maintaining a network of professional medical relationships with, for example, patients, hospitals, specialists and other social services. Prior to 1990, obstetrics-trained community-based GPs were also at the heart of primary healthcare maternity service provision, although patients without a GP could access hospital-based services; and those, giving birth in hospital could receive birth and post-natal care from midwives supervised by the GP. However, only GPs could take primary responsibility for the care of women through childbirth, and midwives were not allowed to provide maternity services unsupervised.

Yet, many considered that midwives' skills and services were an untapped resource, with maternity services suffering from the monopoly that had evolved around individual GPs and GP practices. Pressure to encourage better use of midwives, to make maternity services "more accessible to women by giving them childbirth choices" and to broaden the provision of services, led to the Nurses Amendment Act 1990. The Act gave midwives professional autonomy to operate as fully independent providers of pregnancy, childbirth and post-natal services without reference to, or supervision by GPs, and therefore reducing the *de facto* dominance of GPs.

These and other subsequent changes have provided midwives with access to a GP-facilitated and maintained network infrastructure of services and required relationships (HFA, 2000). As indicated by Howell (2006), midwives were able to 'bolt on' their human capital to the existing primary healthcare infrastructure developed by GPs. However, it has been suggested that whilst GPs would still be required to maintain the rest of their primary healthcare service infrastructure, returns on GP investment in obstetrics training would be compromised by the advent of midwives.

Howell (2006) has also suggested that if the regulated prices paid for use of such "infrastructure," and for the provision of required services, do not adequately compensate the incumbent, investment behavior will be such that investment may become "insufficient for maintaining the quality of ... infrastructure." The nature of changes in investment behavior is reflected in the falling number of doctors enrolling in postgraduate obstetrics and gynecology programmes (Chamberlain, 2006), in the paucity of GP-Obstetricians available to care for at-risk patients, and the accompanying inability or unwillingness of midwives to take responsibility for the care of such patients, formerly managed by GPs.

The Telecommunications Market in New Zealand – Unbundling and Telecom NZ

Ownership of telecommunications assets within NZ resides with the private sector. However, the NZ Government, as former owner, maintains a regulatory role within the sector, exercised through its Ministry of Economic Development (MED) and through its Telecommunications Commission. A continuing concern in the ever-expanding telecommunications sector has been the extent to which providers, led by Telecom NZ, are suppliers of a competitively priced range of quality internet, broadband and mobile services.

A contentious and interesting regulatory option relates to the regulated sharing or unbundling of Telecom infrastructure – the 'local loop unbundling' of copper wire cables - with current and would-be competitors, in the expectation that price/quality relativities would improve as competitors enter a market with features of deliberately lowered entry barriers. There is also the expectation that Telecom would take responsibility for managing the hardware / software interface between itself and its competitors, just as GPs would do for midwives.

In May 2006, the Minister announced that unbundling was deemed necessary to overcome perceived under-investment by Telecom, and to stimulate the introduction of a greater range of broadband products and services. Unbundling, he claimed, would lead to greater investment in the broadband markets by new entrants, expansion in the number of market participants competing with the incumbent provider, and therefore increased uptake of broadband connections (Minister of Communications, 2006).

However, the news promoted an adverse reaction on the Australian stock exchange – an immediate NZ$900 million drop in the company's market value, followed by a NZ$3billion drop over the subsequent six weeks. In addition, there was a view that the requirement to share its infrastructure will likely affect Telecom's incentives to invest in new infrastructure, and/or to maintain existing infrastructure that may also become subject to unbundling (Crandall, *et al.*, 2002; Shelanski, 2002).

The Mineral Extraction and Distribution Sector in Australia – Billiton BHP

BHP Billiton (BHP) is one of Australia's largest companies, reporting a A$6 billion profit in 2006 (Wright & Keenan, 2006). It is involved in iron-ore extraction, primarily for export to expanding markets in East Asia. It has major operations in the Pilbara region of north-west Australia, connected via its own rail network, along 426 and 210 kilometers of rail tracks, to its own seaport facilities at Port Hedland. BHP had already made a $A2 billion investment in its transport infrastructure of trains, track and rolling stock (BHP, 2006), and had announced plans in early 2007 to increase its iron-ore outputs to 155 million tonnes per annum via an A$2.3 billion expansion programme (Hoyle, 2007).

In the early part of the millennium, the newly formed Fortescue Mining Group (FMG) signed export agreements with Chinese steel companies that facilitated the A$1.92 billion funding of a new mine, a new 260km rail track and a new port site at Port Hedland (Phaceas, 2006). FMG also secured extraction rights to tenements at Mindy Mindy, but faced with the A$1 billion cost of duplicating a 200 km railway line to Port Hedland, FMG sought to gain access to BHP's rail network, so that its own haulage trains could roll onto the BHP network.

The National Competition Council (NCC), in June 2004, made a recommendation that such access be "declared", that the cost of duplication was not warranted, and would inhibit other investment in the project. BHP had argued that the railway was not a rail network, *per se*, but part of the company's integrated production system; and it would lose the flexibility to manage schedules, inhibiting export sales, if it had to accommodate another operator's trains (BHP, 2006a; Port Jackson Partners, 2006; IndustrySearch, 2005). On the other hand, FMG argued that their ability to contribute to the export market for iron-ore would not be economically viable if they had to build a rail network. The Federal Court ruled in favour of FMG, in December 2006, that BHP's two railway lines "were not part of the company's production process" (BHP, 2006) and that they were a "service" under the Trade Practices Act (ABC Rural, 2006).

The Markets

It is recognized that telecommunications markets differ fundamentally from the markets for many other goods and services because the capital required is typically very large, and is tied up predominantly in fixed assets that are specific to the production of telecommunications services. These assets are 'sunk', as their costs are neither avoidable nor recoverable (Wang & Yang, 2001). The same may be said about the capital requirements for those firms involved in the extraction and distribution of minerals like iron-ore, and about the human capital invested by GPs in obstetrics training. In each case, the markets are said to be characterized by significant economies of scale, leading to challenges for policy-makers and legislators in the design of the regulatory and market environments in which these firms operate (Laffont & Tirole, 2000).

Where there is a need for large economies of scale to exist, they are often accompanied by few firms choosing to invest, and by markets exhibiting limited competition. However, such limited competition, in some circumstances, may be necessary to provide sufficient incentives for investors to commit their capital to these large, or relatively large, sunk investments, especially where it is economically feasible for only one or two firms or providers to invest (natural monopoly or duopoly). This is especially important when investments are made in new technologies or, indeed, transport systems and infrastructure, with natural monopoly characteristics. In the case of obstetrics-trained GPs, the personal investment in medical training over a ten year period represents a significant sunk cost, comparable in order of magnitude, and possibly its effect as investment in telecommunications or rail infrastructure.

It has been claimed that a potential investor may be reluctant to commit to new infrastructure if another investor may also invest, or be allowed to use that infrastructure, placing the ability to receive an economic return on the original investment in jeopardy. Given that the natural monopoly nature of the businesses may preclude two firms competing with each other on different infrastructures, regulators began exploring the possibility of structurally separating parts of the business and providing a path for competitive provision of at least some parts of the business. Requiring incumbent providers to offer 'designated' bundles or elements of their integrated services to others, has have become known in the telecommunications sector as 'unbundling' (Crandall & Hazlett, 2000).

In the Australian mineral sector, BHP favours providing rail haulage services to competitors, but competitors favour leasing access to the physical rail network for their own trains and rolling stock. In the health sector, regulatory intervention requires GPs to facilitate access for other maternity carers to an almost intangible infrastructure of relationships and services. In each case, the nature of the infrastructure and the nature of the regulatory intervention is seemingly very different.

Building a Multi-methodological Approach

The following section seeks to represent and communicate the problem situation to provide an appropriate platform for understanding by legislative and regulatory decision makers. We do so by developing a multi-methodological approach that harnesses the use of two complementary systems representational tools.

The Initial Causal Loop Diagram

Our first tool is the causal loop diagram (CLD) of System Dynamics (SD). The CLD in Figure 1A displays how extending access in response to perceived shortcomings in the provision of maternity services, has impact beyond that which may have been expected. In particular, we see that whilst increasing the extent of independent nurse access to GP-provided healthcare infrastructure may have its desired and intended impact in the short term (see balancing loop B), it may also have unintended and unwanted effects on the willingness of GPs to invest in the healthcare infrastructure via qualifications and training that would be considered necessary to improve the provision and quality of maternity services.

Note that CLD convention requires entities to be described in neutral mode. The $+^{ve}$ S and $-^{ve}$ O annotations then allow relationships to be described in the context of starting or changing conditions. The $+^{ve}$ S annotation indicates that the *more* we do the action at the tail of the arrow, the *more* the effect at the head of the arrow. For example, the *more* we have X, the *more* Y is needed. By contrast, the $-^{ve}$ O annotation indicates that the *more* we do something, the *less* the effect. The double bar // across an arrow denotes a delay – the effect will occur over time or after a time.

As a consequence, improving access for independent nurses to the maternity services market may lead to reduction in the number of GPs available to provide requisite services (as indicated by the reinforcing loops R1), thus increasing concerns about the provision of maternity services. We thus note how our CLD structure can be identified as a version of Senge's *Fixes that Fail* (FTF) archetype – the *Quick Fix* making the problem worse in the longer term (Senge, 1994).

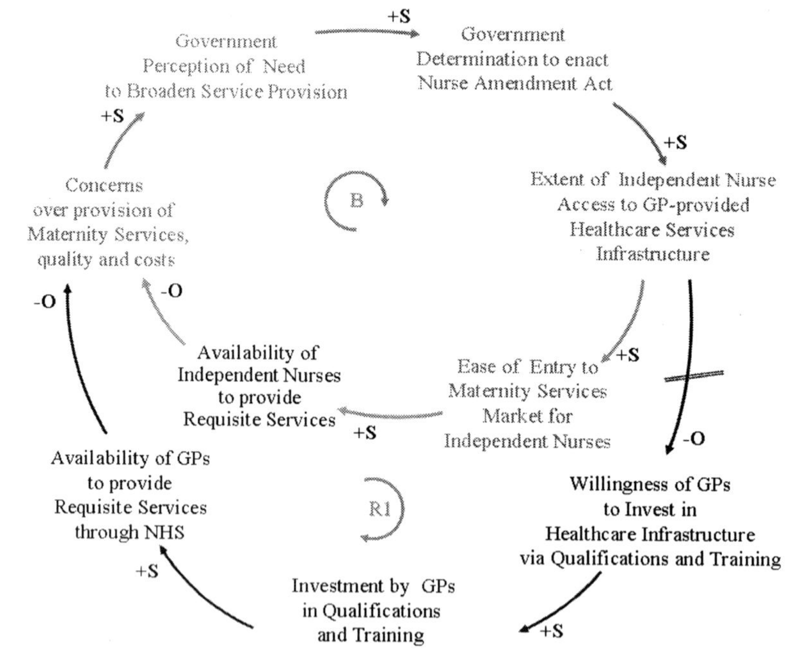

Figure 1A *An Illustrative CLD for the Primary Healthcare Case*

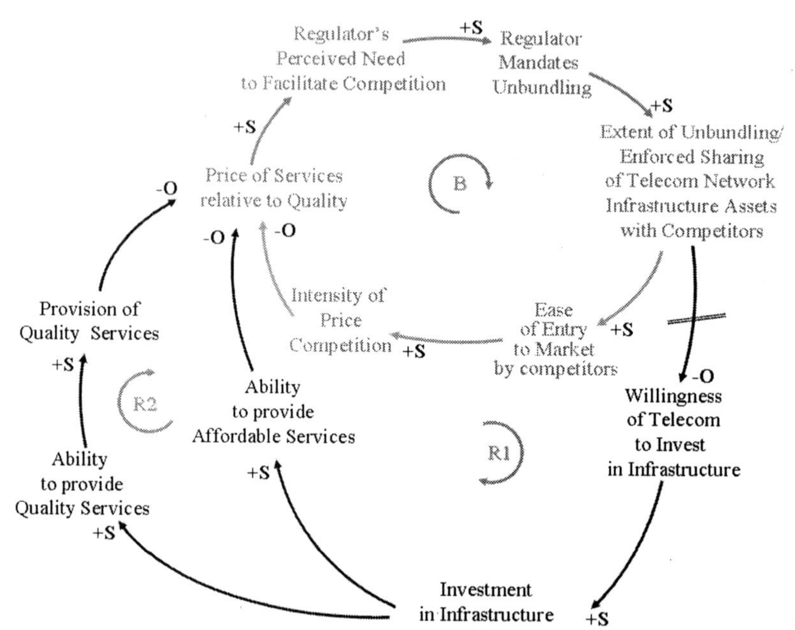

Figure 1B *An Illustrative CLD for the Telecom Unbundling Case*

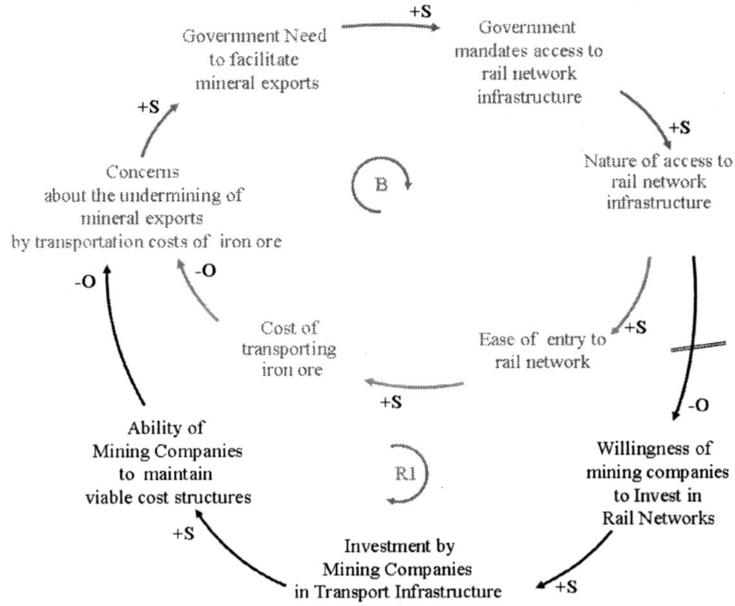

Figure 1C *An Illustrative CLD for the Australian Mineral Sector Case*

We also show as Figures 1B and 1C, the CLD representations of the Telecom Unbundling and the Australian Mineral sector situations, noting that they can also be identified as versions of the FTF archetype, sharing the common systemic structure. As such, we note that unbundling may lead to ease of access to market by competitors, increased competition, and improved price/quality relativities for services. Similarly, declaring open access to rail network services may lead to lower costs for transporting iron ore, and fewer concerns about export arrangements being compromised.

However, in both cases, ready access to telecom and rail network infrastructure may be seen as adversely impacting the willingness of Telecom and BHP to further invest in such infrastructure, thus leading over time, to deterioration in the price/quality relativity of telecom services, and the inability of incumbent rail providers to maintain viable cost structures and the consequent undermining of mineral exports.

In these representations, there is no attempt to reflect alternative choices, that is, to reflect any implicit dilemma faced by governments, or to reflect explicitly what may be the implicit system goal(s). As a consequence, we now show how TOC's conflict resolution process can help identify and structure a dilemma using the EC framework of Goldratt (Cox, *et al.*, 2003; Goldratt & Cox, 1992).

The Theory of Constraints - Evaporating Cloud (EC)/Conflict Resolution Diagram (CRD)

TOC as a methodology seeks to assist with the 'management of beneficial change' in general, and its EC tool, with the resolution of dilemmas, in particular. In Figure 2, we note how the dilemma has been framed as whether Government should legislate the sharing of GP-infrastructure, or mandate investment in training and qualifications. Using the EC framework allows one to draws explicit attention towards the choice dilemma, the overall system goal, and also the assumptions that underpin or give life to the dilemma. The reason for conflict can be explored by examining the assumptions that underlie the necessity-based logic relationships, depicted here by arrows connecting the boxes in the diagram.

In order to find a solution, we first need to provide a substantive rationale for the existence of the relationships, and to elicit any assumptions, perceptions or beliefs about why they are thought to hold. Some of these assumptions are shown in the thought bubbles of Figure 2.

This process not only helps to explain the dilemma, but also helps to enable the problem owners to generate one or more win-win solutions.

Figure 2A suggests that the dilemma can be interpreted as follows:

... that in order to ensure objective A the improved provision of maternity services, the Government must B facilitate a broadening of the provision of maternity services...
... and in order to B facilitate a broadening of the provision of maternity services, the Government must D enforce the sharing of GP-Obstetrician relationship infrastructure.

On the other hand, we also need that:

... that in order to ensure objective A the improved provision of maternity services, the Government must also C seek improvements in cost-effective quality provision ...
... and, in order to C seek improvements in cost-effective quality provision, the

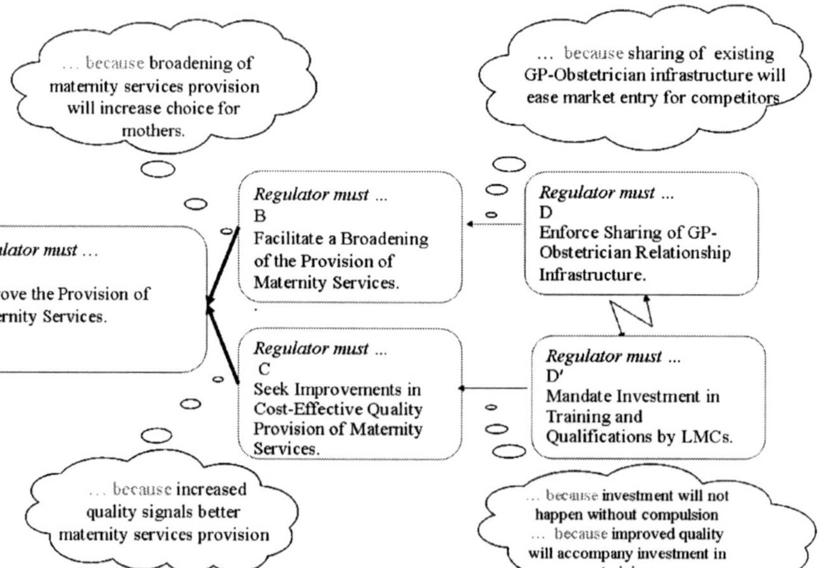

Figure 2 *TOC EC for the Primary Healthcare Case*

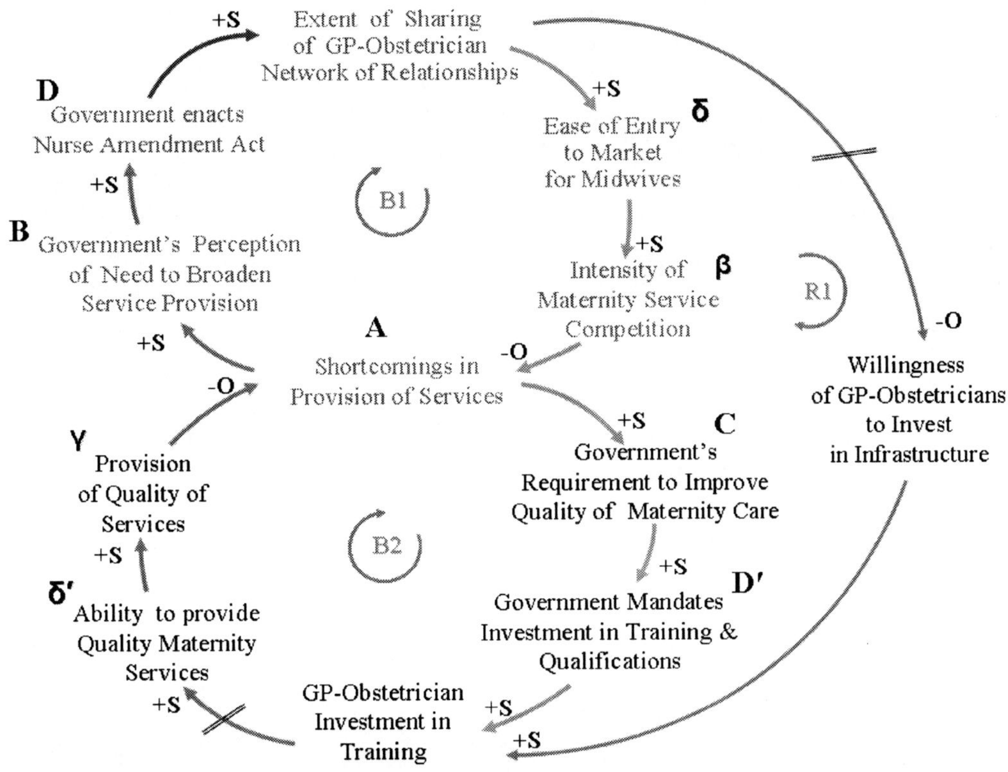

Figure 3 *A 2nd Illustrative CLD for the Primary Healthcare Case*

Government must D' mandate investment in training and qualifications by maternity carers.

Hence the conflict!

Extending the Causal Loop Diagram

Our second illustrative CLD for the primary healthcare case builds on the first, and takes account of the alternative views in conflict surfaced using the EC, in order to build a more comprehensive understanding of the dilemma facing the government as regulators and legislators.

Interpreting the loops in our second CLD suggests that the more the Government extends sharing of GP-Obstetricians' networks of relationships to midwives (Loop B1), the less will GPs invest in training and qualifications to practice obstetrics and provide maternity services, thus undermining the effectiveness of, say, Government initiatives to boost the quality of maternity care provision (B2). We note that these systemic effects or emergent properties are redolent of Senge's *Shifting the Burden* (STB) archetype, where the *Quick Fix* undermines our ability to execute an alternative *Fix*. From experience of multiple cases, we suggest that it is possible to transfer understanding from the CLDs back to the domain of TOC, especially where Senge's archetypes provide a basis for recognizing structures embedded within the chronic conflict situations already identified by practitioners using EC tools (Wolstenholme, 2004). However, we should surface and challenge assumptions about whose perceptions are being captured by the CLD, and why. Surfacing such assumptions can then raise other questions that may establish or undermine their validity, thus provoking alternative possibilities for solution (de Bono, 1994). Our illustrative analysis and interpretation thus illuminates how the EC and CLD approaches and representations can create a dialogue that can be seen to move the debate from arguing about which side or which argument is right, to finding a resolution, which is, in our cases, to provide quality maternity care services, to improve the viability of the mineral sector export market, or to improve the price/quality relativity of telecommunications services.

Discussion and Conclusions

This paper has examined a set of *prima facie* unrelated problem situations facing regulatory authorities in three distinctly different industry sectors – health, telecommunications and mining. In doing so, attempts have been made to capture the systemic essence of the problem situations using the representational tools of different systems methodologies.

We suggest that the use of such systems tools, for example, the CLDs of SD, in the manner undertaken here, facilitates clear analysis and communication of the understanding of problem situations, thereby supporting enhanced regulatory decision-making. The CLDs, in particular, demonstrate the communality of systemic structure that is embedded in the three cases. Further, we note that such recognition of systemic structure is further facilitated by the descriptive framework of system archetypes developed by Senge (1990). Our problem situations reflect the characteristics of Senge's *Fixes that Fail* and *Shifting the Burden* archetypes – that regulatory intervention may produce anticipated consequences in the short term, but also unforeseen and unwanted consequences in the longer term, reflecting the so called emergent properties of the system!

We note that our first CLD representations focused on examining the impact of a single action choice – legislated intervention to enforce sharing of an incumbent's infrastructure with its competitors, and that such analysis revealed a common systemic and emergent property that a *quick fix* intervention would, in the long term make the original problem worse. The use of the TOC systems representational tool known as the EC demanded explicit recognition of other possible actions and of the system's goal. These characteristics were then incorporated into an enhanced CLD for each problem situation.

The extended analysis, facilitated by harnessing complementary use of the systems representational tools, has suggested that enforced sharing of assets or infrastructure would likely have a long term unanticipated or unwanted effect on the investment behavior of an incumbent who is required to share those assets. As such the paper provides a demonstration of the mutually informing use of systems representational tools in understanding regulatory behavior and its impacts.

References

ABC Rural (2006). "Fortescue gains access to BHP Billiton rail lines," http://www.abc.net.au rural/news/2006/s1814769.htm

BHP (2006a). "BHP Billiton Welcomes Decision Not To Declare Mt Newman Rail Line," http://www.bhpbilliton.com/bb/investorsMedia/news/2006/bhpBillitonWelcomesDecisionNotToDeclareMtNewmanRailLine.jsp, Press Release Number 18/06, 23 May 2006

BHP (2006). "BHP Federal Court Decision Threatens Australian Exports," http://www.bhpbilliton.com/bb/investorsMedia/news/2006/bhp BHP Federal Court Decision Threatens Australian Exports.jsp, 18 Dec, Press Release Number 34/06.

Chamberlain, J. (2006). "Baby Don't Leave Me", *North and South*, Auckland NZ, February: 54.

Cox, J.F., Blackstone, J.J. and Schleier, S. (2003). *Managing Operations: A Focus on Excellence*, ISBN-10: 0884271722; ISBN-13: 978-0884271727.

Crandall, R.W., Sidak, J.G. and Singer, H.J. (2002). *The Empirical Case Against Asymmetric Regulation of Broadband Internet Access*, ISSN 1086-3818.

Crandall,R.W. and Hazlett, T.W. (2000). *Telecommunications Policy Reform in the United States and Canada*, Working Paper 00-09, ISBN: 0815702310.

de Bono, E., (1994). *de Bono's Thinking Course,* ISBN-10: 0816018952, ISBN-13: 978-0816018956.

Goldratt, E.M. and Cox, J. (1992). *The Goal* (2nd ed), ISBN:0884270610.

Health Funding Authority (2000), Maternity Services: A Reference Document, Health Funding Authority, Hamilton NZ, http://www.moh.govt.nz/moh.nsf/pagesmh/614., pp.94.

Howell, B. (2006). "Healthcare lessons for Telcos", *Competition and Regulation Times,* Issue 19, ISSN 1175-2912: 10-11.

Hoyle, J. (2007), "Editorial: Asian demand powers Australian heavy-haul," *International Railway Journal*, ISSN (printed): 0744-5326, http://www.railjournal.com/A/xfeature2.html, 07/06/28

IndustrySearch (2005). "BHP Billiton - sharing Pilbara rail will disrupt production", 23/11/05, http://www.industrysearch.com.au/news/printarticle.asp?id=18793

Laffont, J-J. and Tirole, J. (2000). *Competition in Telecommunications,* ISBN:0262621509.

Lissack, M. (2004). "Founding editor's note", *E:CO*, ISSN (printed): 1521-3250, Fall, 6(1-2): iv.

Phaceas, J. (2006), "New Yorkers lob $535m Fortescue's way" *Sydney Morning Herald,* July 19 2006, http://www.smh.com.au/news/business/new-yorkers-lob-535m-fortescues-way/2006/07/18/1153166382158.html#

Port Jackson Partners Ltd. (2006). *Economic Evaluation of the Impact of Lost Iron Ore Production and Share*, April, pp.39

Senge, P.M. et al. (1999). *The Dance of Change: The Challenges of Sustaining Momentum in Learning Organizations*, ISBN: 0385493223, ISBN-13: 9780385493222.

Senge, P.M. et al. (1994). *The Fifth Discipline Fieldbook: Strategies and Tools for Building a Learning Organization*, ISBN: 0385472560, ISBN-13: 9780385472562.

Senge, P.M. (2006). *The Fifth Discipline*, ISBN: 0385260946.

Shelanski, H.A. (2002). "Competition and Regulation in Broadband Services," in Crandall, R.W. & Alleman, J.H. (Eds). (2003). *Broadband: Should We Regulate High-Speed Internet Access?* AIE-Brookings Joint Center for Regulatory Studies, ISBN-10: 0815715927; ISBN-13: 978-0815715924.

Tibby, G. (2004). "Miners' rail fight just not cricket", *The Age*, Oct 1 2004, http://www.

theage.com.au/articles/2004/09/30/1096527864464.html?from=storylhs#

Wright, S. and Keenan, R. (2006). "BHP's rail line stays closed to rivals", *Sydney Morning Herald*, May 24, http://www.smh.com.au/news/business/bhps-rail-line-stays-closed-to-rivals/2006/05/23/1148150255375.html\

Wang, X.H. and Yang, W.Z. (2001). "Fixed and Sunk Costs Revisited", *Journal of Economic Education*, ISSN 0022-0485, Spring: 178-185.

Wolstenholme, E. (2004). "Using generic systems archetypes to support thinking and modelling. *System Dynamics Review*, ISSN (printed): ISSN 0883-7066, 20(4): 341-356.

44. Pandemic Influenza Mitigation Strategies and their Economic Impacts

Mary Ewers & Lori R. Dauelsberg
Los Alamos National Laboratory, USA

The current avian influenza in Asia, Africa, and Europe has sparked discussions of a new human pandemic influenza perhaps hitting the world. While the current influenza is not spread by human-to-human contact—a necessary characteristic for a human pandemic—there is a potential that it may become so. Since the pandemic does not currently exist, it is not known what characteristics—such as infectiousness and death rate—the disease will exhibit. The study conducted by the Critical Infrastructure Protection Decision Support System (CIPDSS) explores the possible mitigation strategies and their effect on the US economy. Results show that while many people may be infected, the economic costs for the US are relatively low especially in comparison to past economic perturbations.

Introduction

Influenza is very common in the world with 36,000 people dying annually in the US (www.cdc.gov) from seasonal outbreaks. More virulent strains have also occurred in the past and cause world-wide outbreaks. These outbreaks, called pandemics, can kill many millions of people around the world. More recent historic pandemics include the "Spanish Flu" of 1918 which killed at least 40 million people worldwide (Rosenwald, 2006), 500,000 in the United States, and the "Asian Flu" of 1957 caused around one to four million (CDC, 2006) deaths worldwide and the "Hong Kong Flu" in 1968 killed more than two million people. In addition to the deaths, another global pandemic on the scale of 1918 will have severe economic effects. The Congressional Budget Office estimates that a severe pandemic influenza will cause a 4.5% decline in the U.S. GDP (CBO, 2007).

All of these pandemics were originally an avian strain of flu circulating only in bird populations and not in humans—as is currently the case with H5N1 influenza virus in Asia, Africa and Europe. The 1918 "Spanish Flu" developed from a mutated strain of the virus H1N1. The 1957 influenza developed by reassortment from H2N2 and the 1968 "Hong Kong Flu" was caused by a strain of H3N2 which reassorted from H2N2.

Currently, the H5N1 avian virus is spread only in birds and is transmitted to humans mostly from direct contact with birds. Although there are some reports of human-to-human spread, the cases are isolated and mostly in families living in close quarters. The major concern with this virus is that the World Health Organization report the death rate among humans is currently 60%. Although it is most likely that the death rate will decrease if the virus mutates or reassorts to become a human pandemic, the death rate for this unknown disease may still be high. Most experts predict that the death rate will be anywhere from less than 2% up to 15% based on previous pandemics. For example, the death rate of the 1918 pandemic was approximately 2% (www.cdc.gov).

Government agencies and private industries worldwide are scrambling to prepare for a human pandemic caused by this virulent avian virus. Preparation involves not only the modeling the disease progression but also predicting the effects of mitigations available to the populations. CIPDSS is one of several programs that was tasked with this modeling effort.

In this paper we highlight the modeling efforts of Los Alamos and Sandia National Laboratories in identifying the economic impacts of a pandemic through the Critical Infrastructure Protection Decision Support System (CIPDSS) project. Several mitigation strategies are modeled using the CIPDSS tool to gauge resulting economic impacts. Mitigation strategies considered here include social distancing, targeted antivirals, and partially effective vaccines. The following sections will give an overview of the CIPDSS model, the epidemiological model, the economic impact model, as well as the resulting impacts from 7 mitigation strategies.

CIPDSS Overview

CIPDSS is a set of infrastructure models simulated almost entirely in system dynamics, coupled to a decision analytic tool designed to aid decision-makers with difficult choices between policies and mitigation strategies. CIPDSS is a joint modeling effort of Los Alamos, Sandia and Argonne National Laboratories sponsored by the Department of Homeland Security (DHS). The three labs are each the lead in one area although the work is completed collaboratively. Los Alamos National Laboratory has the lead for the metropolitan model (a model of the critical infrastructures from a generic metropolitan city), Sandia National Laboratories is the lead for the national model, and Argonne National Laboratory is the lead for the decision analytic tool.

The CIPDSS model consists of models of the major critical infrastructure as defined by DHS (Executive Office of the President, 2004). The individual infrastructure models are represented at each model scale (metropolitan and national) as is suitable: agriculture (national only), banking and finance, chemical and hazardous materials, defense industrial base (national only), emergency services (metropolitan only), energy, food (metropolitan only), information and telecommunications, postal and shipping, public health, transportation, water, and key assets. Because these listed infrastructures are not all inclusive of the US economy, other sectors are added in the models to help simulate the "real" workings of the infrastructures. For example, one additional model is the population—without people at work, all of these infrastructures grind to a halt. In addition, government and an economics "scorecard" model are included. For certain scenarios modeled, additional information—up to and including an entirely new model—is needed. An important example of this is the epidemiological model used in this study of pandemic influenza.

As mentioned above, the models are constructed using system dynamics and specifically in the commercial-off-the-shelf (COTS) system dynamics tool Vensim™. Each infrastructure, or sector, is modeled as a self-contained model with placeholder variables for the interdependencies with other sectors. A java tool written by project members, called Conductor, is used to integrate the necessary models for each simulation and create a single system dynamics model. The focus of these models is to represent the major stocks and flows of each infrastructure and the primary interdependencies with other sectors. For example, in the telecommunications model, phone calls are a major flow in the sector and are modeled including dropped calls, reattempts, and completed calls. In addition, interdependencies of the switching stations on telecommunications lines and the energy sector are included.

The model is designed to answer questions raised by decision-makers (mostly in city/county and national government) about what may occur in an event that may disrupt critical infrastructures. Some examples of events that have already been modeled by CIPDSS are: a telecommunications disruption, agricultural diseases, biological terrorism, a chemical release, hurricanes—including the spread of various diseases by contaminated flood waters—and pandemic influenza. The CIPDSS program has a goal of "order of magnitude" results and is therefore well-suited to comparisons of mitigation strategies—i.e. which mitigation strategy gives a significantly lower impact than others. As such, this pandemic flu study of seven different mitigation strategies is an ideal use of this model[1].

Epidemiological Infection/Disease Model

The infectious disease model is a modified Susceptible-Exposed-Infected-Recovered (SEIR) model (e.g., Hethcote, 2000). The stages are represented in a generic manner so that the model can be used for a large number of infectious agents by adjusting the input parameters appropriately. The model is written so that the user can enter either an R_0 value (the average number of people infected by a typically infectious individual) or a contact rate and infectivity rate with the R_0 value calculated as an output. For this study, R_0 was used as an input. Figure 1 shows displays the system dynamics diagram for a simple SEIR model with the resulting variable metrics highlighted in yellow.

Resulting variable metrics for the disease progression model are: Total Cumulative Deaths, Total Symptomatic, and Total Attack Rate. These metrics were used to validate our model against the results of other known disease progression models. The metrics then became inputs into labor and workforce models to determine the reduction in workforce.

The baseline scenario, representing a 1918-like influenza in the absence of interventions or mitigations, is described as follows.

- Clinical attack rate (i.e., the number of symptomatic cases divided by the age specific population):

1. For more information on the CIPDSS model and the Phase I Pandemic Influenza, please see the full paper for the study (Fair, 2005).

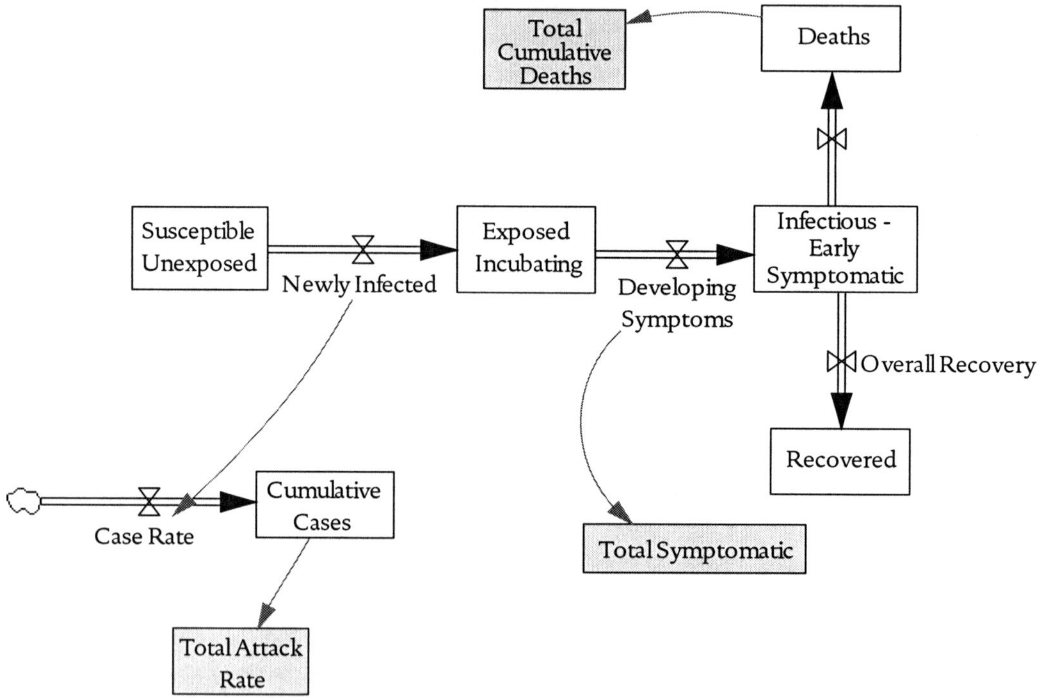

Figure 1 *SEIR Disease Progression Model*

  - Adult attack rate: 30% become symptomatic;
  - Student attack rate: 40% become symptomatic;
  - Fraction of infections that are symptomatic: 0.67;
- Mortality:
  - 2% of symptomatic cases, independent of age;
- Fraction of symptomatic people staying home from work, school (Halloran, 2002):
  - 50% of all adults;
  - 75% of all students;
  - 80% of all preschool children.

Additional scenarios (six total) included mitigations such as vaccines, self isolation, social distancing with masks, and quarantine. Most mitigations are input into the model before the "exposed incubating" stage of the model. The antivirals are administered after a person becomes symptomatic. Table 1 describes the details of the baseline scenario plus the 6 mitigation scenarios considered in this pandemic influenza study.

Economics Model

To estimate the magnitude of a possible pandemic influenza, a dollar value for economic impact is calculated within the CIPDSS models. For our study, eco-

Scenario	Description
Baseline	Adult attack rate: 30% Student attack rate: 40% Mortality rate: 2% of symptomatic cases Fraction of symptomatics staying home: • 50% Adults • 75% Students
Fear-Based Self Isolation ("Fear 40")	Baseline + 40% of total population self isolates (stays home) due to fear
NIH's Targeted Layered Containment (TLC)	Baseline + 60% of symptomatic cases stay home Antivirals given to symptomatic cases and their household contacts Symptomatic households are quarantined (30% compliance) Schools closed
NIH's TLC Lite	Same as TLC but with no school closure.
Antivirals	Baseline + Antivirals given to symptomatic cases and household contacts
Partially Effective Vaccine	Baseline + A partially effective vaccine is administered with 40% of vaccinated persons acquiring full immunity. The remaining 60% become infected but their illness is milder and they are less contagious.
Anticipated Intervention Strategy ("Nominal")	Baseline + Vaccine given to 5% of population 15% of total population self isolates due to fear 20% of schools are closed 15% social distancing with masks

Table 1 *Scenario Descriptions*

nomic impact includes only the lost productivity of those workers unable to work due to illness or family illness. We do not include cost specific economic impacts such as the cost of vaccinations and the cost of healthcare. In the CIPDSS model, the main figure for this estimate for the pandemic flu study is the lost gross domestic product (GDP).

GDP is a measure of productivity in the US. This model uses the GDP data from the 2004 estimate by the Bureau of Economic Analysis (BEA). The data from BEA is obtained by NAICS (North American Industrial Classification System) industry and then divided by the number of workers in each industry (also from BEA) to calculate the GDP that may be attributed to an individual worker. This number is then divided by 365 to get the average GDP contribution per worker per day.

Lost GDP is computed based on the Cobb-Douglas form of the production function: $Y=f(K,L)$. The change in GDP due to the pandemic influenza is given as $\Delta Y=Y_B-Y$ where (Y_B) represents the baseline GDP for the region and Y represents the GDP after the pandemic has taken place. . In the CIPDSS model of infrastructures such as electricity and telecom, capital (K) is measured as capacity available such as available electricity (e) and available communications via wire-lines (w). Labor (L) is measured by industry and by state. The change in labor is the driving force behind the economic impacts for this study. Lost value added (Lost GDP) is represented as:

$$\Delta Y=Y_B-e^a w^b L_g \tag{1}$$

The labor estimates in the model are derived in another "add-on" model for the population. This is directly influenced in this study by the disease model and the public health model. In this study, lost GDP is calculated from all workers who do not go to work (also called Unavailable Workers). This could be that they are sick, dead, self-isolated, or quarantined. We assume for this calculation that they do not work from home and therefore do not produce any output while in this status.

The GDP calculation is an estimate for the direct losses to the US economy over the time period studied. For this particular paper, the calculations were for the first year only. However, the following caveats apply: (1) although the events may cause structural changes to the economy, those changes are not evaluated in the economics model or in the rest of the CIPDSS infrastructure models (most of these changes will take more than a year to emerge); and (2) the ability to change business process and, for example, substitute inputs is limited during the scenario and generally is not modeled—this ability may decrease the actual GDP losses. In this study, though, capital losses do not occur and losses are derived only from reduced workforce.

The economic impacts estimated in this analysis stem from reductions in output due to reduced workforce participation attributable to the pandemic. One calculation not included in these results is the agricultural costs due to losses in stocks of poultry in the case of an avian form of the influenza. This study did not calculate potential losses in this or other areas, partially because although still high, the human costs of a pandemic influenza would far outweigh agricultural concerns. Figure 2 depicts the Cobb-Douglass production function methodology for determining losses to the US economy in a system dynamics diagram.

Mitigation Strategies

To simulate the seven scenarios that CIPDSS created (see Table 1 for detailed descriptions), several input variables for specific mitigations needed to be initialized at levels corresponding to the scenario run. Table 2 gives the initialized values for each of the input mitigation variables for each scenario. Some variables are the equivalent of an on/off switch (such as the use of masks) that activates a sub-model routine when switched "on". Other input variables have a specific value for initialization, such as "contact effectiveness."

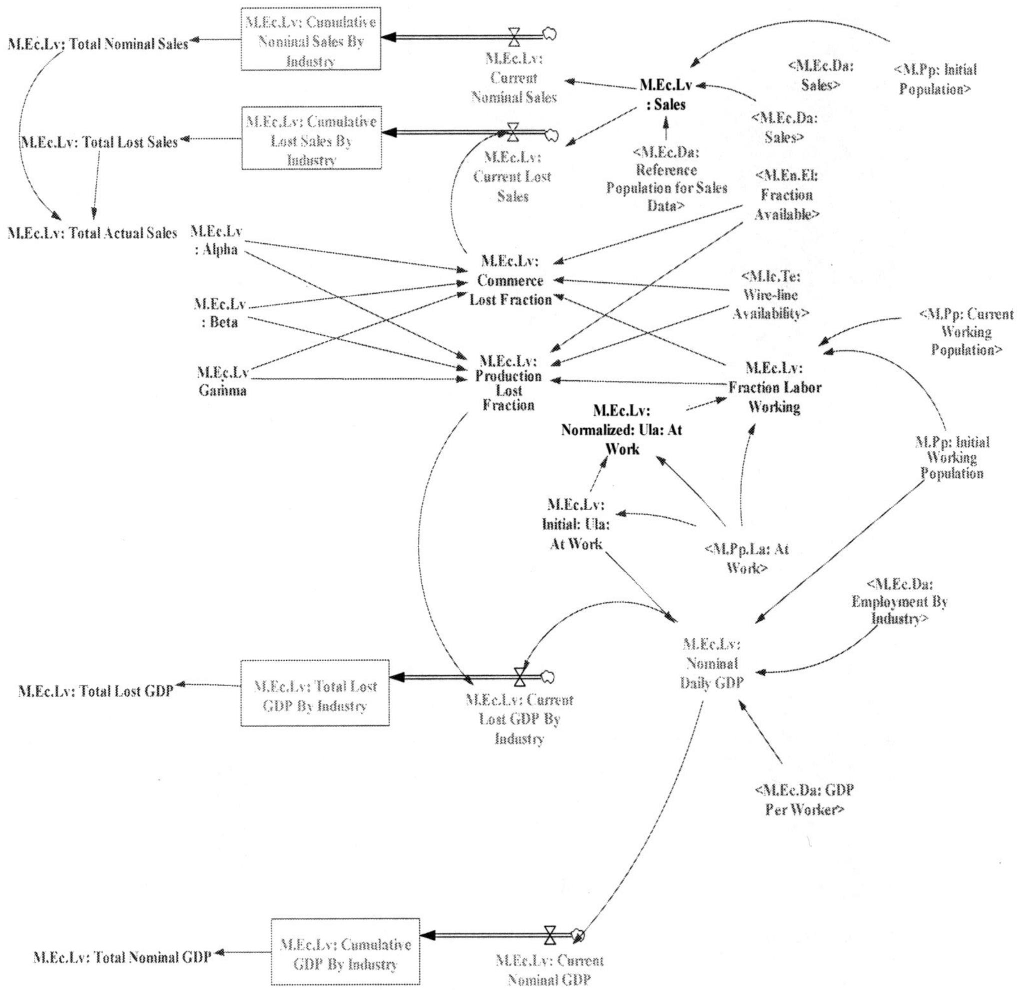

Figure 2 *Economics Model in Vensim™*

Results[2]

Lost GDP results from the CIPDSS model for all of the pandemic influenza simulations performed are shown in Figure 3. These values represent the loss in GDP over a period of 1 year. As mentioned previously, the main impact on the GDP is absenteeism in the workforce (either due to death, sickness, or self-isolation). Although the number of deaths in the base case is higher than in any other case, the cases with the largest initial economic impact are the Fear-Based Self-Isolation (Fear 40) and the Anticipated Intervention Scenario (Nominal). These cases have much larger impacts because of the extra workforce absenteeism (see Figure 4 for a graph of absenteeism).

A loss of $300 billion in 2002 dollars (the approximate value of loss in

2. Results are from the Phase I portion of the CIPDSS Pandemic Influenza study. The CIPDSS model has since been revised and updated for the Phase II portion and now includes 24 scenarios and a slightly modified disease progression model. Please contact the authors if you are interested in Phase II results which differ slightly from Phase I

Exogenous Model Parameters	Scenario 1 Baseline No mitigations	Scenario 2 40% population worried well and fear isolates	Scenario 3 TLC Antivirals given, targeted prophylaxis, social dist	Scenario 4 TLC lite	Scenario 5 Antivirals only, targeted prophylaxis	Scenario 6 Partially effective (50%) vaccination	Scenario 7 Nominal Intervention Strategy
Social Distancing (masks)	None	None	Yes	Yes	Yes	None	Yes
Self Isolation	None	Yes	Yes	Yes	Yes	None	Yes
Worried Well(parent to kid ratio)	On(.75)	On(4)	On(1)	On(.75)	On(.75)	None	On(1)
Vaccinations	None	None	Targeted	Targeted	Targeted	Mass	Mass
Avg contacts per case	20	20	10	1	2	20	20
Antivirals	None	None	Yes-unlimited	Yes-unlimited	Yes-limited	None	Yes-limited
Contact Effectiveness (fraction of contacts identified for prophylaxis)	.75	.75	.10	.078	.015	.75	.3
Targeted Prophylaxis	None	None	Yes	Yes	Yes	None	Yes
Death rate reduction from antivirals	n/a	n/a	100%	100%	100%	n/a	50%
Fraction antivirals applied to prophylaxis	n/a	n/a	94%	99%	90%	n/a	10%

Table 2 *Mitigation Strategies*

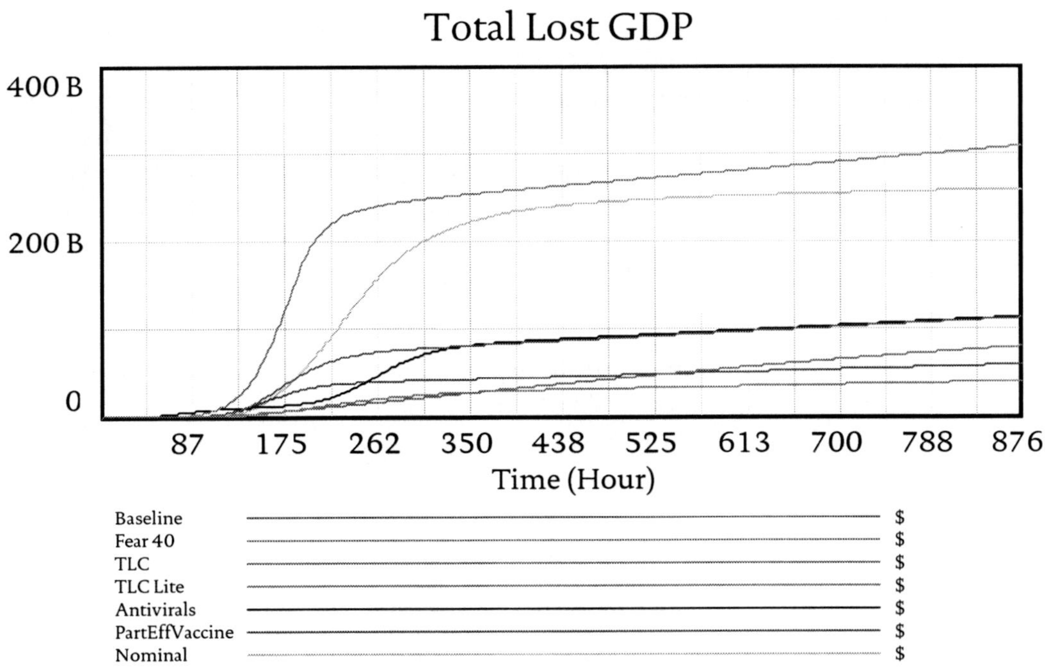

Figure 3 *Total Lost GDP for each scenario*

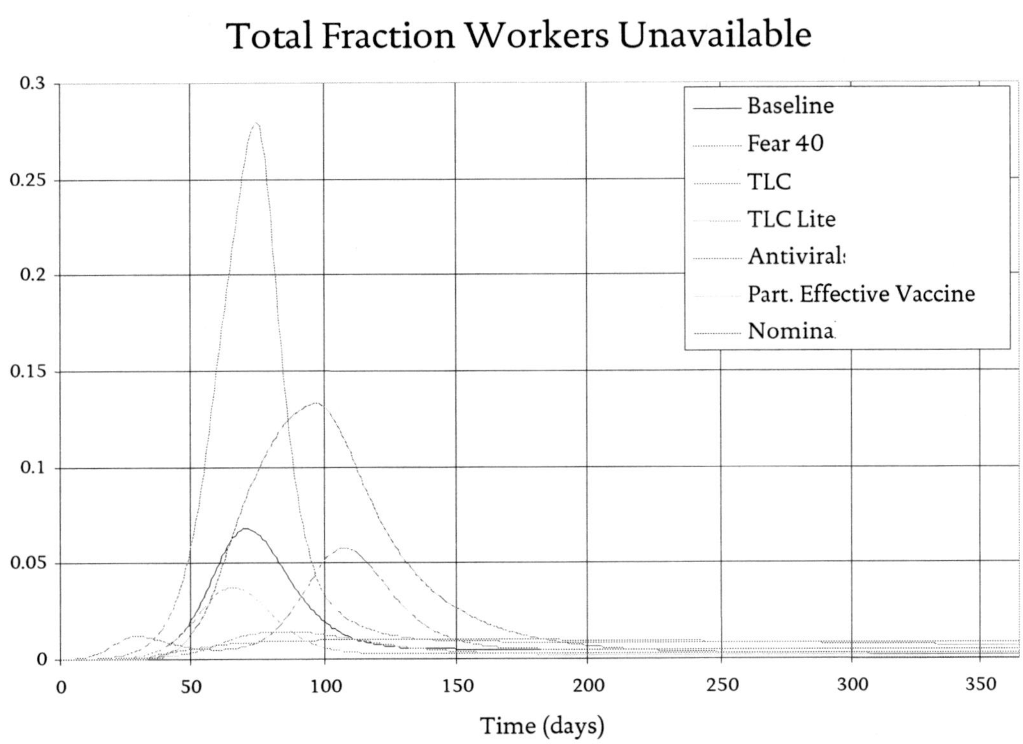

Figure 4 *Total fraction of workers unavailable for each scenario*

the Fear-Based Self-Isolation case) represents a 2.3% loss of GDP. In the base case, the losses are just over $100 billion. This result corresponds to a loss of <1% of the GDP. These base case results also correspond with several other pandemic influenza studies (Blitzer, 2006; Burns, 2006; Hanna, 2006).

Results of the other cases follow closely to absenteeism and death rates (see Table 3). That is, cases with very little to no self-isolation have much lower GDP losses than those with high rates. For example, the Partially Effective Vaccine case has a loss of approximately $60 billion (<1% of GDP) most of which is due to sickness and death (i.e. no self-isolation). Self-isolation was simulated in the Anticipated Intervention Strategy, though, and results from this are much higher at $260 billion (2% of GDP).

	Base Incident	Fear-Based Self-Isolation	TLC	TLC Lite	Antivirals	Partial Vaccine	Anticipated Intervention Strategy
Number Illnesses	74 M	61 M	1.2 M	28 M	69 M	39 M	2.6 M
Number Hospitalized	8.1 M	6.6 M	140,000	3.0 M	7.6 M	4.2 M	280,000
Number Deaths	1.5 M	1.2 M	25,000	550,000	1.4 M	780,000	52,000

Table 3 *Human Metrics for All Scenarios*

These economic results are comparable in general magnitude to the first-year results found by another DHS-sponsored project conducted by Los Alamos and Sandia National Laboratories, NISAC (National Infrastructure Simulation and Analysis Center), using a different economic modeling framework from Regional Economic Models, Inc. (REMI) (Treyz, 1992). Almost all of these cases lie within the ranges of GDP percent losses generated from the REMI modeling. Furthermore, both models provide the same rank ordering of all the scenarios based on year 1 lost GDP. The TLC Lite scenario has the lowest economic impacts in the first year according to both NISAC and CIPDSS estimates; this reduction over Baseline is due to (1) a reduction in the number of ill, which reduces workplace absenteeism; and (2) a reduction in death, which reduces the losses to U.S. economic capacity.

This analysis was conducted without considering the costs of formulation, implementation, or enforcement of the actions that implicitly comprise the scenarios. The cost is likely directly related to the number of public policy actions involved with the scenario. For example, the nominal integration scenario calls for school closures, quarantine, 150 day vaccine development, the sum of which is likely to be costly.

Conclusions

The estimated cost of a pandemic influenza in the United States may vary widely depending on the mitigation policy (or policies) that the government and the people themselves choose to implement. The range of direct economic impacts for one year is $60 billion to $300 billion in GDP (or less than 1% to 3.2% of 2006 GDP). According to the study performed by the CIPDSS and NISAC teams, the most effective strategy in terms of minimizing losses to the economy would be the Targeted Layered Containment Lite (TLC Lite) scenario followed by the Partially Effective Vaccine and TLC scenarios. One important note, though, is that these strategies minimize GDP losses, but do not necessarily minimize deaths.

In order to more fully evaluate the best strategy for the government to employ, a benefit-cost analysis or decision analysis should be performed. These analyses would not only include the economic impacts, but the number of deaths and the cost of the mitigation strategies themselves. This type of analysis was not performed during this particular study.

Another important note to this study is the fact that the disease parameters are currently unknown as the pandemic itself does not yet exist. Possible parameters were used, but may not be correct. In the future, the NISAC and CIPDSS plan to complete a sensitivity and uncertainty analysis (as well as a decision analysis) that will explore the unknown parameters of the disease and the epidemiological model that will better inform the results of this study.

References

Bush, B., L. Dauelsberg, S. DeLand, R. LeClaire, D. Powell, and M. Samsa. (2005). "Critical Infrastructure Protection Decision Support System (CIP/DSS) Project Overview," Report no. LA-UR-05-1870, Los Alamos National Laboratory, Los Alamos, NM. B

Bush, Brian W., Lori R. Dauelsberg, Michael H. Ebinger, Rene J. LeClaire, Dennis R. Powell, Steen Rasmussen, David R. Thompson, Cathy J. Wilson, Marc S. Witkowski, Andrew Ford, and Don Newsom. (2004). "Metropolitan Critical Infrastructure Model," (Version 8.1) LA-CC-04-088, Los Alamos National Laboratory, Los Alamos, NM.

Bush, Brian, Lori Dauelsberg, Sharon DeLand, Jeanne Fair, Rene LeClaire, Dennis Powell, and Michael Samsa. (2005). "Critical Infrastructure Protection Decision Support System: Evaluation of a Biological Scenario," report no. LA-UR-05-2799, Los Alamos National Laboratory, Los Alamos, NM.

Dauelsberg, Lori. (2006). "Economic Methodology in the CIPDSS Model for Avian Flu," report no. LA-UR-06-4170, Los Alamos National Laboratory, Los Alamos, NM.

Dauelsberg, Lori R. (2006). "The Potential Economic Impact of a Pandemic Flu in the United States," report no. LA-UR-06-4410, Los Alamos National Laboratory, Los Alamos, NM.

The Executive Office of the President, Office of Science and Technology Policy and The Department of Homeland Security, Science and Technology Directorate (2004). "The National Plan for Research and Development In Support of Critical Infrastructure Protection," available at http://www.dhs.gov/xlibrary/assets/ST_2004_NCIP_RD_PlanFINALApr05.pdf (accessed Aug. 31, 2007).

Fair, Jeanne, Rene LeClaire, Leslie Moore, Dennis Powell, and David Thompson. (2005). "Sensitivity Analysis of an Infectious Disease Model," report no. LA-UR-05-2799, Los Alamos National Laboratory, Los Alamos, NM.

Germann, Timothy C., Kai Kadau, Ira M. Longini, Jr., and Catherine A. Macken. (2006). "Mitigation strategies for pandemic influenza in the United States," *Proceedings of the National Academy of Sciences*, ISSN 0027-8424, 103(15), 11 April, 5935-5940.

Hethcote, H. W. (2000). "The Mathematics of Infectious Diseases," *SIAM Review*, ISSN 0036-1445, **42** (4), 599–653.

Powell, Dennis, Rene LeClaire, Jeanne Fair, Lori Dauelsberg, Laurie Wiggs, Perry Klare, Sharon Deland, Laurie Wiggs, and Michael Wilson. (2005). "Potential Impact of Avian Influenza Virus: Costs and Potential Consequences," report no. LA-UR-05-9050, Los Alamos National Laboratory, Los Alamos, NM.

Stroud, Phillip, et al. (2005). "Joint NISAC – CIP/DSS Analysis of Avian Influenza Virus Issues for the Catastrophic Assessment Task Force (CATF) Table-Top Exercise," report no. LA-UR-05-9254, Los Alamos National Laboratory, Los Alamos, NM.

Rosenwald, Michael. (2006). "The Flu Hunter," *Smithsonian*, ISSN 0886-2257, 36(10), 36-46.

Treyz, G. I., Rickman, D., and Shao, G. (1992). "The REMI Economic-Demographic Forecasting and Simulation Model," *International Regional Science Review,* ISSN 0160-0176 **14**:3, pp. 221–253.

U.S. Congress, Congressional Budget Office. (2007). "A Potential Influenza Pandemic: An Update on Possible Macroeconomic Effects and Policy Issues," http://www.cbo.gov/ftpdocs/72xx/doc7214/05-22-Avian%20Flu.pdf.

U.S. Department of Commerce, Bureau of Economic Analysis. (2006). http://www.bea.gov/ .

U.S. Department of Health & Human Services. (2006). "PandemicFlu.gov," http://www.pandemicflu.gov/.

U.S. Department of Health & Human Services, Centers for Disease Control and Prevention (CDC). (2006). "Influenza (Flu)," http://www.cdc.gov/flu/professionals/diagnosis/.

45. Reflections on SD Practice

PLENARY PAPER

Tim Haslett
Department of Management, Monash University, AUS

This paper is a series of reflections and lessons learned from 25 years of practice as a System Dynamics practitioner working in the business and government sectors. The overwhelming lesson is that the quality of the work is secondary to the manner in which projects are managed within organizations.

Introduction

This paper reflects on a body of work commissioned by commercial clients. While a number of academic papers have been published as a result, this work has essentially been pragmatic and driven by the fundamental consideration of the usability of the models that were developed. The process of making models usable is deeply embedded in the political and organizational processes of the client. This means that reflection on SD practice is about processes much broader than the process of model building itself.

The clients

The client group has been wide and diverse. The projects have included modelling the capabilities of the Joint Strike Fighter, the use of golf courses, restrictions to blood donor groups, the national superannuation system, the heroin trade, ambulance service demand, patient flows in hospitals, privatized garbage collection, the viability of WorkCover insurers, a call centre, oil and delivery transport systems, case management in the courts and an accident repair centre.

SD is inherently difficult to understand and the explanations more difficult

The theoretical foundations of System Dynamics are at once the greatest strength and the greatest weakness for our discipline. The strength is that, thanks to Jay Forrester, we have a very sure foundation upon which to proceed with our work. We are also fortunate that the body of literature, particularly that produced in the System Dynamics Review, has helped to define the methodology and the field of endeavour.

The downside of this however is that the body of theory that is needed to understand the discipline is relatively complex. For instance, the concept of feedback is commonly interpreted as meaning what people receive on their performance appraisals. Engineers understand feedback and control systems but many other do not. This is complicated by the fact that feedback comes in two forms, reinforcing or balancing. Because each has a quite different impact on the system in question, clients may begin to view the consultant with the degree of suspicion reserved for door-to-door vacuum salesmen and snake charmers. While the feedback concept is relatively easy to explain to an interested audience, the implications of its importance are not as easily understood.

The great power to be able to analyze systems in terms of positive and negative feedback subsystems rests in the fact that the results of the analysis are often counter-intuitive and provides insights that have not previously been possible. The difficulty is that the results of SD analysis can often be at odds with the thinking of managers and decision-makers whose mental processes are essentially linear. Linear thinking is characterized by an assumption that an intervention in a system will have a chain reaction effect uncomplicated by a feedback from unintended consequences.

Our failure to help a client understand these and other principles of SD modelling can have disastrous consequences. A recent presentation to a senior parliamentarian set out the preliminary stages of a large project. As the presentation progressed, signs of glazed eyes and a decreasing attention span became increasingly obvious. The explanation was clearly not getting through and as a consequence of this, one senior decision maker's confidence in the technique was seriously weakened. Within a fortnight, the project had been cancelled. Attributing causation, particularly when the causal structures are not well known, is always dangerous. However, it is likely that our failure to communicate clearly contributed to the cancellation of the project.

The problem of counter-intuitive outcomes

The more frustrating aspect of the failure to help the client to understand comes when the consequences of the lack understanding become obvious at the end of the project. Clients can be swept up by enthusiasm for a technique that has the potential to make the implications of policy decisions clear, but this is often supported by the hope that it will provide a justification for current policy. As the project progresses and the causal structures that come clearer, it becomes clear that counter-intuitive outcomes are not going to provide support for current policy. Often the project will be completed, only to be shelved.

A major motor services company that had developed an Accident Repair Centre (ARC) had encountered problems with bottlenecks developing within the system. The problem was multifaceted and involved work scheduling and spare parts availability. The spare parts problem led to cars being off-loaded from the production line to the extent that the whole system became grid locked. The client required a simulation model to see how the problem could be solved. The complexity of the model, shown in Figure 1, is an indication of the complexity of the system that had been developed. It was little wonder that it was unmanageable. The most noticeable complexity was the complicated sets of conditions that had to be met before cars could move from one station to another.

The as a result modelling can best be captured and the lives of the immortal poet Hillaire Belloc

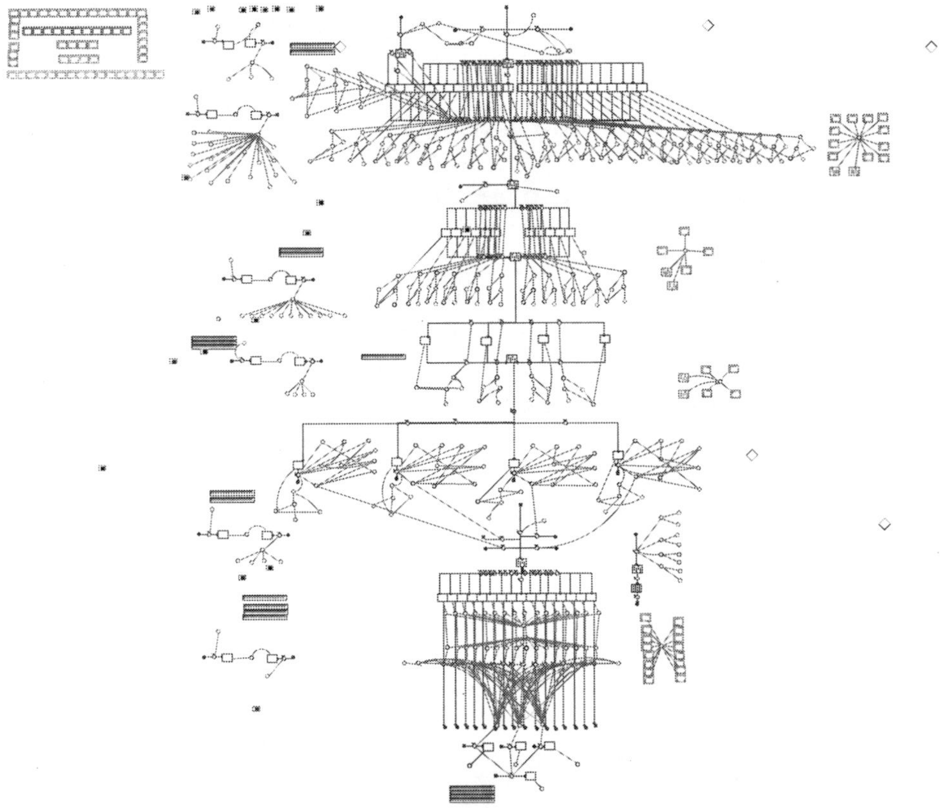

Figure 1 *The ARC model*

The Chief Defect of Henry King
Was chewing little bits of String.
At last he swallowed some which tied
Itself in ugly Knots inside.

Physicians of the Utmost Fame
Were called at once; but when they came
They answered, as they took their Fees,
"There is no Cure for this Disease.
Henry will very soon be dead."

The design of the ARC, which had cost millions of dollars and was to revolutionize car repair in Victoria, was so fundamentally flawed that it was never going to work properly. This was not what the client had expected. They had hoped that the problem would be solved, not proved to be insoluble. Within a short time, the client closed the ARC and began building a new one.

The tendency of SD modelling to produce counter-intuitive outcomes produces significant difficulties for some clients. Given that many organizations do not have an inbuilt capability for Systems Thinking and consequently an understanding of the impact of feedback, it is highly likely that some of the results of modelling exercises will run contrary to the accepted wisdom within the organization.

Some years ago, work with a provider of major emergency ambulance services wished to understand the drivers of demand for emergency ambulance services. The funding model was that ambulances were purchased when projected demand went above current capacity. The purchase of the new ambulance had the immediate effect that capacity went above current demand. The ambulance service was under pressure to use the increased capacity. This was often achieved by using expensive and well-equipped emergency ambulances for tasks such as ferrying patients between hospitals. The consequences of this were that the specialized vehicles took up some of the workload of less specialized vehicles that then had to look for some way to utilize their excess capacity. This meant a knock on effect down through the ambulance services with everybody looking for extra work. Anecdotal evidence existed of emergency ambulances being used to take patients to appointments at outpatients units. Very soon the demand for these services increased so that it was necessary to purchase new ambulances in a variety of categories where demand had been stimulated. Figure 2 shows how new ambulances then went out looking for work.

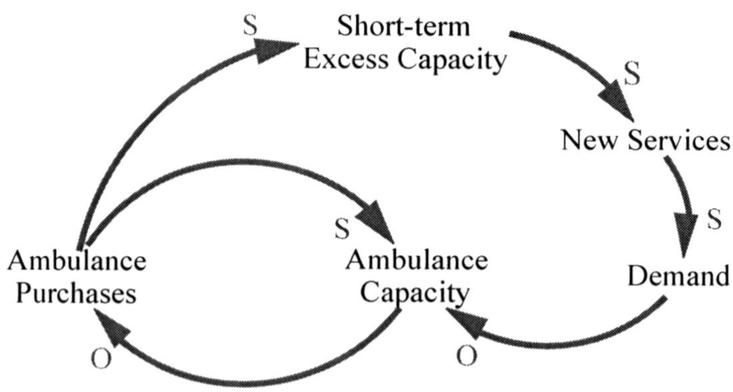

Figure 2 *Endogenous ambulance demand. An 'S' indicates that the causal variable has the Same effect on the dependent variable. As New Services go up then demand for those services also goes up. An 'O' indicates that the causal variable has the Opposite effect on the dependent variable. If Demand goes up then Ambulance Capacity goes down.*

The conclusion was that one of the key drivers of demand for ambulances was the purchase of ambulances and the provision of an increasing range of services. Demand was endogenously driven. This may not surprise the experienced modeler but it certainly came as a shock for the service and provided very little help in their budget submissions.

The first difficulty in this situation is that the model has produced a counter-intuitive outcome for the client. This outcome was based on the well-understood principle that systems generate their own behavior. The client must now face the difficult task of implementing major policy and behavioral changes to bring the system under control. It's very easy for the situations to fall into the "too hard basket".

Sometimes the opposite happens. A recent project involved the modelling of the impact of compulsory superannuation in Australia. The work that was conducted in the ATO Superannuation Branch was very successful for number of reasons. The first was the ability of the client group to accept the possibility of the counter-intuitive. One of the critical dynamics for the introduction of compulsory superannuation was that it takes 30 to 40 years before people are retiring with a maximum benefits. For significant periods of time, people would be leaving the workforce with relatively small amounts invested in superannuation. The question at issue was: "What will these people do in this situation?"

The consensus was that people would make additional payments into superannuation to increase their final benefit. However, it was agreed so there was no empirical evidence to support what seemed to be a fairly logical conclusion. The possibility of this assumption being wrong led to a significant investment in market research. The results of research justified the investment. Not only was it extremely unlikely that people would top up their superannuation, it was extremely likely they would take their superannuation as a lump sum and spend it on a caravan or trip around the world and then go on the pension. As one of the main thrusts of the superannuation policy was to make people less dependent upon government funded pensions, it looked likely that there would be a significant period of counter-intuitive outcomes in the superannuation sector. Current policy for superannuation in Australian now restricts the amount of money that retirees are able to take as a lump sum and effectively quarantines a proportion for an ongoing pension.

The problem of the short-term v. long term

By its very nature, SD modelling addresses problems that have a long-term and strategic focus for the organization. Many organizations have difficulty integrating long-term and strategic information into their decision-making. Many organizations are beset by the need to deal with short-term key performance indicators and the immediate effects of a turbulent environment. Some organizations find themselves constantly in "semi-crisis" mode. This is particularly true of organizations where resources are stretched to meet the demands of what appears to be an unpredictable environment. Health services appear to operate in this mode for good proportion of their time. A recent modelling assignment from a major hospital was commissioned as result of a number of the senior administrators completing SD programs at Monash. The discussions to develop a long-term modelling capability to predict and manage demand for hospital beds was frequently interrupted by quarter-hourly updates on the status of individual patients and a frequent absence of the manager to head off the latest crisis in bed allocation. Unfortunately, stamping out spot fires does not stop a major bushfire. While the immediate and practical reality is that the spot fires need to be fought, the difficulty is that the causes of the spot fires need to be managed. This dilemma is most acute in organizations that become "addicted to crisis". Managers become adept at dealing with the day-to-day crises of the organization. Often their efforts are nothing short of heroic and frequently life-saving. At a personal level, the hero manager has nothing to gain from improv-

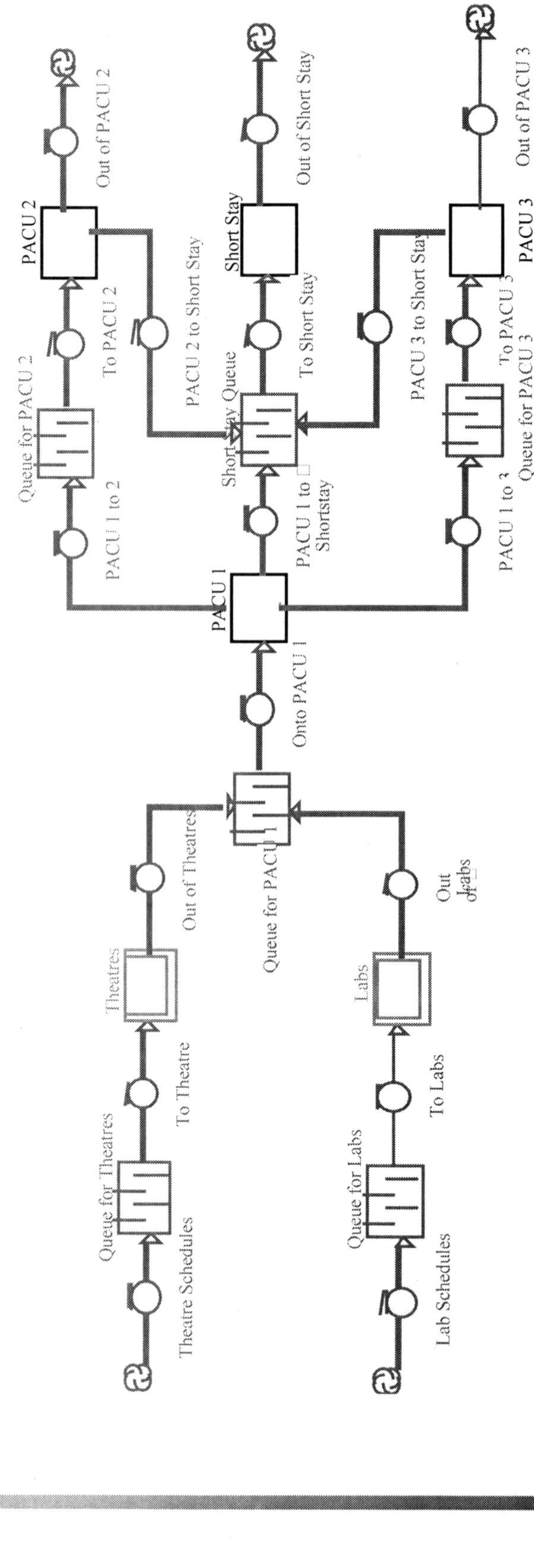

Figure 3 *Operating theatres and post-anaesthetic care units (PACU)*

ing the structures that provide opportunities for managerial heroism.

A senior medical administrator accounted with great pride how she had spent an entire Saturday searching one of our major cities for a compatible blood donor for a dying child. She finally located the child's aunt and brought her in to make a donation that saved the child's life. It is impossible to question the efficacy or importance of what was done in that situation. But when the administrator announced with pride that she was the only person who had the power and authority to do this, two questions inevitably arises: "But what if you weren't there? and "What systems do you have in place to deal with that?"

It is a truism that structures determine system behavior. It is equally true that the heroic efforts of individuals can overcome the influence of counter-productive structures in the short term. It is the heroism of individuals that often stands in the way of long-term strategic thinking. Structural change is time consuming, costly and risky. Often SD modelling indicates the need for significant structural change but when the immediate problems demand attention, managers rarely have time to make the necessary change.

A recent assignment in a major Victorian Hospital was able to deal with this problem in a different way. The hospital was building a short-stay facility and wished to know whether the plans that had been drawn up would meet the performance criteria set by the government. The critical dynamic in this case was that between the operating theatres, which generate patients, and the post-anaesthetic care units (PACU) where they recover. The new facility with its improved procedures was going to make significant improvements on patient throughput. While it is possible to bring about significant improvements in the processes surrounding the operating theatres, it is not possible to get patients to improve their post-anaesthetic recovery times. The issue was one of operating theatre capacity versus PACU capability shown in Figure 3.

Patients can only leave PACU when they are fully recovered and walking. Once PACU is full and there is no recovery space available, the operating theatres must stop. Failure to keep the operating theatres working efficiently has a highly detrimental effect on KPIs. This meant that PACU capacity was a key leverage point in the system.

The model simulations indicated that the PACU capacity in the original plans would not be sufficient to cope with all the services planned for the new facility. A decision was made to limit the procedures that would be carried out in the new facility and bring the output of the operating theatres within the PACU capacity.

This application of SD modelling was interesting for a number of reasons. It tested the assumptions of the design of a facility in a way that allowed in the managers to short-circuit potentially problematic situations before the facility was developed. It also combined architectural plans and SD modelling, certainly for the first time in the Victorian health system.

Internal sponsorship and the rich and famous

Someone who already has a working knowledge of SD often initiates SD modelling projects. In the Australian context, this has often been a student who has studied at Monash University. It is very important from the perspective of a consultant to have a very realistic view of the organizational status of the project initiator. Does their budgetary discretion encompass the cost of the project? If this is not the case, then there needs to be a series of presentations to approve the project. This broadens the roles of the stakeholders. The person who approves the budget now becomes the project sponsor within the organization and this role requires careful management on the part of a consultant. The same applies to the person who originally introduced to project the organization who is likely to become the internal project manager.

In every consulting assignment, someone must become rich and famous. It is important to have a very clear understanding of who those people will be. It is the project sponsor, the approver of budgets, who must become pre-eminently famous. The consultant becomes rich but never famous. To achieve their fame, the project sponsor must be in a position to demonstrate the progress, efficacy or importance of the project. They must be brought up to speed about the nature the SD modelling and provided with enough information to be able to speak formally and informally about the benefits of the project. In doing this they become famous. The consultant takes no role in representing the project in the organization. The emphasis on using the project sponsor and project manager to represent the project within the organization means that the emphasis is constantly on relating the progress and outcomes of the project to organizational objectives. It also enables the project manager and project sponsor to take ownership of the project.

The communication processes surrounding the project are as important as the project itself and structures need to be put in place to ensure that they work well. Stafford Beer's "Viable Systems Model", shown in Figure 4, provides an excellent template for structuring the project, and the communication processes that must support it.

The technical functionality of the project team is Beer's System 1. This is where the work of building causal diagrams and modelling is done. This group will clearly contain the project manager and if possible some members of the organization who have demonstrated enthusiasm for developing SD mapping and modelling skills. It is from this group that a replacement for the project manager must be found if the project manager moves to a new role. Developing requisite variety at all levels of the project serves as a protection against the loss of expertise as a result of staff movement.

The project manager will be effectively a one-person System 2 responsible for coordinating System 1. The project manager and the project sponsor will be members of System 3 which is responsible for maintaining the stability of the project, interpreting policy decisions from system five, allocating resources to System 1 and carrying out audits of progress. System 4 is the intelligence gathering function that will consist of the various stakeholders who have input to the modelling process. System 5 has a policy development role and will ulti-

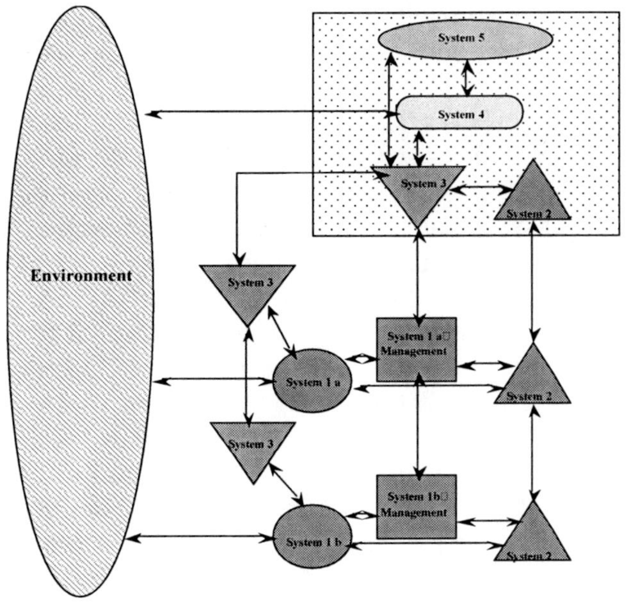

Figure 4 *Stafford Beer's Viable Systems Model*

mately be the user of the models.

Once the VSM has been established within the client organization, it is necessary to establish the membership of the five systems. The critical aspect of the membership of the systems is that membership should be multiple and overlapping. The project manager will need to be a member of System 5. Their expertise and knowledge of SD modelling will allow them to act as mentor to the modelling acolytes. They will also need to be a member of a least one other system, preferably System 3 with responsibility for resource allocation. The project sponsor should also be a member of System 3 and also of System 5 where policy is developed and the model will ultimately be used for scenario planning. Both the consultant and a project manager need to be members of System 4 where the major stakeholders who provide information for model, will meet. This multiple membership ensures that information about the status and progress of the project is held by a number people giving them the ability to influence all parts of the system. This structure has been used in two highly successful modelling exercises, those at the Australian Tax Office (ATO) and the Australian Red Cross Blood Service (ARCBS).

The Federal Treasurer, Peter Costello, in stating that superannuation reform was "on the agenda", initiated the ATO superannuation project as a result of a statement. The ATO was keen to become a major player in the superannuation policy debate and saw SD modelling as an alternative to the Federal Treasury's RIM model as a source of policy advice. This political imperative meant that the project sponsor was a Deputy Commissioner within the ATO. The focus of the Deputy Commissioner was on the macro-political elements of the Canberra bureaucracy rather than on any of the technical elements of SD modelling. The project manager was an enthusiastic convert to Systems Thinking in general and modelling in particular. He was also exceptionally politically astute and was able to position himself as a member of all systems within the VSM. The Deputy Commissioner and the project manager were both members of System 5.

System 4 was known as the High Level Modelling Team and consisted of stakeholders from ATO offices across Australia. In addition to this wide exposure that the project had through System 4, the ATO also ran a series of workshops on Systems Thinking and SD modelling techniques. It was from the participants in these workshops that the members of the System 1 modelling team were selected.

In addition to this significant level of organizational support, the modelling team also had a dedicated modelling room in the ATO offices. As the causal diagrams for the superannuation scheme were developed, they were displayed on the walls of the modelling room. ATO staff were free to come and look at the work and a number of presentations to external bodies were conducted in the modelling room. This enabled members of the modelling team to become moderately famous. The project leader became rather more famous and made presentations to other departments including one to the Assistant Treasurer. The project sponsor presented the work to a number of external industry bodies and later left the ATO to work for a major industry organization. Fame of course comes at a price. The project ended when Treasury offered all of System 5 and the project leader jobs in Treasury. All accepted. The move of these key players out of ATO Superannuation branch effectively removed any policy capability from the branch.

The counter-intuitive outcome of the ATO's desire to develop its policy capability in superannuation was that its success led all the key players to move on to policy roles within Treasury. The deputy commissioner had moved to work with a superannuation industry body. Everyone was famous and the consultant was slightly rich.

The pragmatics of SD modeling

As an academic and a teacher of SD, it is possible, and indeed necessary, to involve oneself in the more arcane aspects of SD modelling. However, the concerns of the academic community are rarely reflected in the concerns of the business and government sectors. Their concerns focus around outcomes, answers and action. The technical complexity of SD modelling opens it up to the accusation of being "academic", which is one of the more pejorative terms used in the business world. This "outcomes, answers and action" focus was shown in exercise modelling the patient flow in a subacute hospital facility. The project was stopped after the development of the causal diagrams and the early development of the simulation model. The project team believed that they now understood the problem sufficiently to be able to take effective action. The change program that arose from the modelling exercise reduced the patient stay time in the facility from 35 days to 17 with no change in level of patient care.

This experience neatly defines the role that our work plays in organizations. At best, we can be a catalyst for change by providing information for the decision-makers who must ultimately take responsibility for the change. We can provide little information about the way to initiate, implement or evaluate the change. The criteria for our work must be that we are able to provide information that allows responsible managers to make informed choices about the changes in their organization.

46. System Dynamics Modelling of National Design Infrastructure Development

Terence Love
Curtin University of Technology, AUS

Acknowledgements

I would like to acknowledge the three years of financial assistance for this project provided by the Office of Research and Development and the Faculty of Built Environment, Art and Design of Curtin University of Technology. In addition, I would like to thank the national design experts from governments, universities and businesses in the UK, Norway, Finland, and Australia that kindly contributed their time, expertise and knowledge to the research.

This paper describes system dynamic modelling of national design infrastructure following three-year research (approx. AU$200,000) developing a conceptual framework and gathering field data about five national design infrastructures: UK, Norway, Finland, Korea and Australia. The effects of design infrastructure are complex and located within multiple interrelated systems with high levels of complexity. Dynamic modelling is non trivial with a relatively large number of environmental variables different in each country and varying over time. The paper outlines the extended role of design in social, economic and cultural development, and discusses systemic aspects of national design infrastructure. It then describes preliminary modelling of: design knowledge, design education and the role of design in social and economic development, and identifies outcomes some of which are counter-intuitive. The research offers the basis for guiding the investment into the design infrastructure needed for innovation and the building of local and national knowledge-based economies.

Introduction

All developed and developing countries aim to improve their social and economic status. They do this through human instituted changes. Design activity is the foundation of all intentional human instituted change.

A commonly accepted definition of design as an activity was coined by Nobel Laureate Herbert Simon (1969). He defined design as to "[devise] courses of action aimed at changing existing situations into preferred ones". When used as a noun, typically 'design' is regarded as a specification for making something or doing something. This is a subtle but important point. The design is the *specification*, not the thing.

Much of the design activity that goes into changing human environments and, hopefully, improving societies' social and economic lot is relatively hidden regardless of our dependence on it. Any human, looking around themselves would find that the majority of their environment has been designed – even the most apparently nature-laden aspects. Most design work goes on behind the scenes, regardless of the illusion otherwise, that is implied by the tiny amount of objects in which the fact that they have been designed is a prominent part of their sales promotion. Mostly design activity is extensive, embedded systemically and out of the public view.

Take for example, the case of a simple set of IKEA wooden shelves. A practical and simple example first proposed on the PhD-Design discussion list on Jiscmail (Love, 2001). I am sat in my office looking at some IKEA timber bookshelves originally intended for use in garages and outhouses and visually acceptable for use in office settings The shelves consist of four different sorts of timber elements, one kind of coach bolt, some special twisted plated mushroom headed nails, a zinc plated cross brace, and four small zinc plated screws. The pack of shelves when supplied by IKEA is fastened together for transport by a glassfibre reinforced plastic strap whose ends are crimped with a zinc-plated steel sleeve. The shelving pack has a small black and white label with assembly instructions and several small barcode labels all attached using a pressure sensitive non-setting adhesive.

Many different sorts of designers were involved (see Table 1).

Now each of the machines/ buildings mentioned in the above table is also made of components that were designed and these designers and design fields should also be added as must the designers and design fields involved in transportation, logistics, business processes, information systems, computer systems, software, timber harvesting, environmental policy design, the design of the different training programs for the wide variety of individuals involved in the accounting etc, etc. Taken together, the design resources needed for specifying the activities, machines and other objects and processes needed for the creation and use of these IKEA shelves comprise the specific *design infrastructure* needed for the shelves to exist and provide social and economic benefits.

National Design Infrastructures

Viewed more broadly, *design infrastructure* is necessary for all change. At a national level, each country has an extensive design infrastructure, much of which is hidden and integrated into a wide variety of national and local systems. Elements of national design infrastructure include those listed in Table 2.

Design infrastructure provides the bridge between new knowledge generated by *research* and the actualization of designed products, systems, services, processes and organizations by governments, institutions and individuals. The role of design infrastructure in this process in relation to commercial products is shown in Figure 1.

In each country there is a different distribution of design infrastructure elements in relation to their quantity, quality and distribution. The elements of design infrastructure comprise a system shaped by the relationships between

designing the overall configuration	designing the coach bolts	designing the fancy nails
designing the cross cutting machine for the timber	designing the four head cutters for shaping the timber	designing the drilling machine for the holes for the bolts
designing the nailing machine and its jigs (a different designers job)	designing the steel smelting machines	designing the wiredrawing machines from which the nail blanks and the coach bolt blanks are cut
designing the labels	designing the plastic strap	designing the printing machinery
designing the nail making machine	designing the barcode system	design the policy standards for grading the wood
designing the cross brace (and the machines for making and plating it)	designing the die cutting machinery for cutting the labels	designing the software used to create the print instructions for labels
designing the hardware systems from computer to printer for the labels	designing the material content and properties of the steel	designing the plating machine for the fancy nails
designing the chainsaws to cut down the timber	designing the debarking machine for preparing the logs	designing the machines that make the glassfibre and the plastics for the strap
designing the paper making machinery		designing the saw mills for planking the logs (this includes a plethora of building designers/safety designers/ road designers etc/environmental designers/economic policy designers)

Table 1 *Different fields of design involved in making a simple wooden bookshelf*

design infrastructure elements and with other national systems and subsystems and the users.

A key question to ask is how well a country's design infrastructure system matches the country's development trajectory and its social, economic and technological developmental agendas.

Obviously, if a country's design infrastructure is primarily focused on designing new biotechnology, it suggests that there will be a certain innovation weakness if government focus is on economic development via shipbuilding. Similarly, if a country's design infrastructure is primarily dedicated towards craft and art, then it will not provide strong support for national aspirations to develop advanced computer system production. In fact, the situation is much more subtle for countries with a sharp awareness of the details of their design infrastructure systems. For example, Taiwan chooses to only manufacture certain *types* of computer chips and hardware – in line with their design infrastructure

design professionals	design centres
businesses undertaking design	government agencies to promote design
departments undertaking design within organisations	design-focused associations representing those undertaking design
national design policies	government agencies to develop design-focused policies
hardware and software tools available to support design	organisations commissioning and funding design research
organisations educating designers	organisations educating design researchers
design researchers	organisations undertaking design research
organisations commissioning design activity	organisations representing design research

Table 2 *Elements of national design infrastructure*

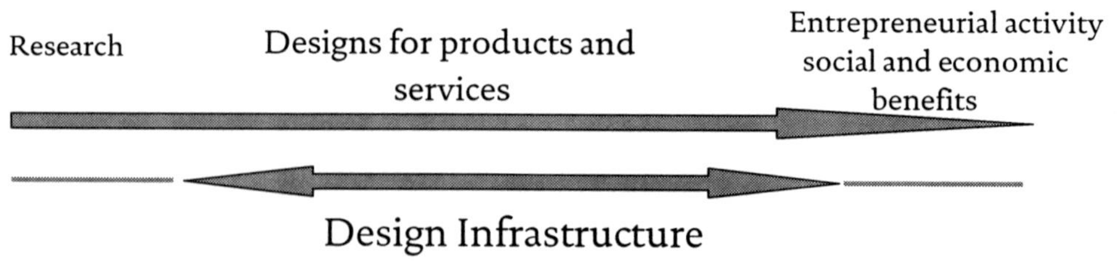

Figure 1 *Role of design infrastructure in relation to research and entrepreneurship.*

system and its planned evolution. Finland, a country that has committed its national development to expertise in design, has recently proposed a rejigging of its university elements of design infrastructure by combining the University of Art and Design with the Helsinki University of Economics and the University of Technology.

Systemically, at the largest scale, the behavior of design infrastructure systems can be envisaged as relatively simple: does the country have expertise to design particular things. Analytically, the problem comes in exploring how well a country has the capacity to support radical competitive innovation and the novelty and destabilizing social and economic changes that accompany the economic potential of disruptive designed outcomes.

Even at the largest scales of national design infrastructure systems, examples of the management cultural blindness cautioned against by Forrester and others (Forrester, 1975, 1998; Sterman, 2002) can occasionally be evident. An example is the case of Australia. Recent research by the author demonstrated an almost complete lack of awareness of the role of design infrastructure and design activity in innovation in Australian government, universities, research funding bodies and industry (Love, 2005, 2006). Instead, there had developed a bipolar view of innovation in which research gets magically transformed into commercial outcomes as in Figure 2.

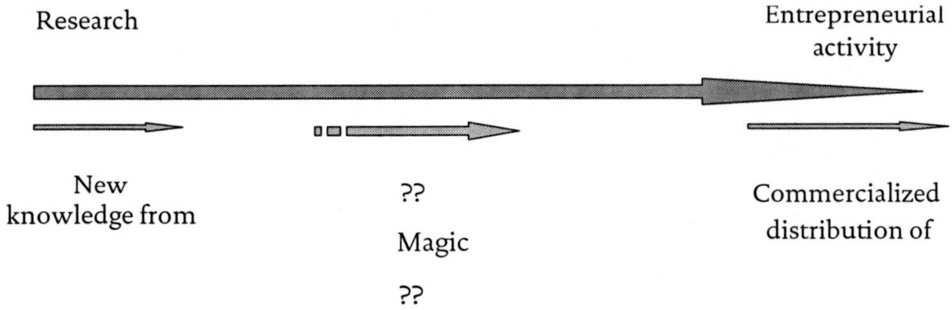

Figure 2 *'Hollow' model of innovation (e.g. Australian government policy and research funding circa 2005)*

This almost complete lack of awareness of the systemic role of design activity and in innovation and fulfilling national social and economic agendas did not mean that no design activity occurs. In fact, engineering design companies, particularly in the oil and gas and resources sectors are producing world-class designs for plant and equipment and there is increasing awareness of the work of some Australian art and craft designers. Systemically, in terms of Australia as a viable system (Beer, 1988, 1989), it means that management attention in levels, 2, 3, 4 and 5 fully commits its resources for innovative development on one hand to a limited subset of research for knowledge production that does not include design activity and its essential roles in innovation, and on the other hand to commercial activities that presume that the design work is done elsewhere. In essence, this is a system failure caused by management blindness.

The idea of development trajectory informs the why and wherefore of this problem. Australia's history is primarily as a colony of the UK on which it depended for value added or manufactured products, technical expertise and its professional services (for which again design has a primary role – e.g. lawyers design strategies for the courtroom, doctors primary role is in designing medical treatment programs). For most of this time, Britain discouraged the development of Australian design and innovation systems whilst at the same time committing heavily to the development of design infrastructure and research in UK innovation system. An example is the way that research into wool was divided between the UK and Australia where the UK undertook all the research into design-based development of value added outcomes, and Australian research was limited to finding ways of producing more wool (Boardman, 2001). In spite of this, Australian design activity has increased – without government and institutional support.

There is some evidence that the situation is changing in Australia as State governments have begun to realize the potential benefits of supporting design activity. Victoria for instance has now set up a small government department to oversee development of design-based industries. In general, however, the Australian culture remains one of hiding design infrastructure as in for example the 2007 Festival of Ideas in South Australia which ignores design activity except in terms of high profile aesthetically focused 'creative design', and instead substitutes the concept of 'magical discovery of fully formed ideas' . Similarly, but form a different tack, the Federal Australia-wide Festival of Innovation also ignores design activity and instead tries to cover the same ground with the magically discovered scientific 'inventions'. The role of design infrastructure as a production system for designs for new innovative and better products, systems, services, processes and organizations that is the common understanding in many other developed countries is ignored by both.

System Dynamics Model of National Design Infrastructure

Why is a systems dynamic model of national design infrastructure needed? There are four main reasons:

1. To provide a basis for government policymakers to explore which strategies of investment in design infrastructure/innovation are likely to have the best effects;
2. To address the high level of complexity in interactions between the large numbers of causal factors, intermediate processes and outcomes;
3. To provide dynamic modelling that includes and illustrates changes over time;
4. To identify counter-intuitive outcomes that are hidden to conventional research and lead to e.g. the errors of 'blindness' to aspects of design infrastructure found in Australia

For the dynamic modelling to be capable of refinement in scale and scope without needing to re-create the models and sub-models from scratch. System dynamics offers the means to develop sub models in a piecemeal fashion that can be integrated into a larger scale model.

This paper reports preliminary System Dynamic modelling of three aspects of design infrastructure: design knowledge, design education and design in business. The modelling is referenced against case studies of national design infrastructures in Australia, UK, Norway, Finland and South Korea involving desk-based review of design infrastructure and historic national development trajectory supported by semi-structured interviews with design experts from government, business and academia in each of the countries with the exception of South Korea. The primary focus of the research funding was to improve Australia's innovation processes. Preliminary desk research on Korea indicated that the significant differences in culture and development trajectories between South Korea and Australia meant that it would be difficult to successfully relate Korean developments to the Australian context.

The main focus at this time in developing System Dynamic models is to identify stocks and flows of key factors and positive and negative causal feedback loops.

Modelling Design-Related Knowledge

The quality of explicit design-related knowledge available is a key aspect of design infrastructure and is a major foundation for effective and efficient innovation and national development because it enables the use of rationalist/scientific approaches to developing and managing complex products, systems, services and organizations. Although it many 'intuitive/creative' designers from the craft traditions (graphic design, advertising, fashion etc) claim to eschew explicit, research-derived, design knowledge, there is increasing evidence of its use. Examples include readability heuristics of line length and font type, color forecasts and marketing information, usability studies.

Explicit design-related knowledge can both grow and become accessible, and become lost or inaccessible. For example, in a separate research project investigating design processes in the global outdoor clothing sector (findings to be published Oct 07), the author and colleagues discovered that the dynamics of design-related knowledge in that sector was dominated by persistent loss of knowledge due to the detail of the structure of design and manufacturing processes used in the sector. This understanding offers great potential competitive advantage.

Review of design infrastructure across the six countries showed a variety of factors shaped the dynamics of growth and loss of design-related knowledge. One way of representing this in systems terms is shown below in Figure 3.

The model is primarily symmetrical in that to the left there are a number of positive loops tending to increase design-related knowledge, and to the right there are positive loops tending to increase loss of design knowledge. Automated design has a dual role depending on whether explicit design knowledge is deliberately derived from it or not. One way increases design knowledge and the other leads to a potential loss of design-related knowledge. In policy-making terms, the system diagram suggests that gains can be made by amplifying the

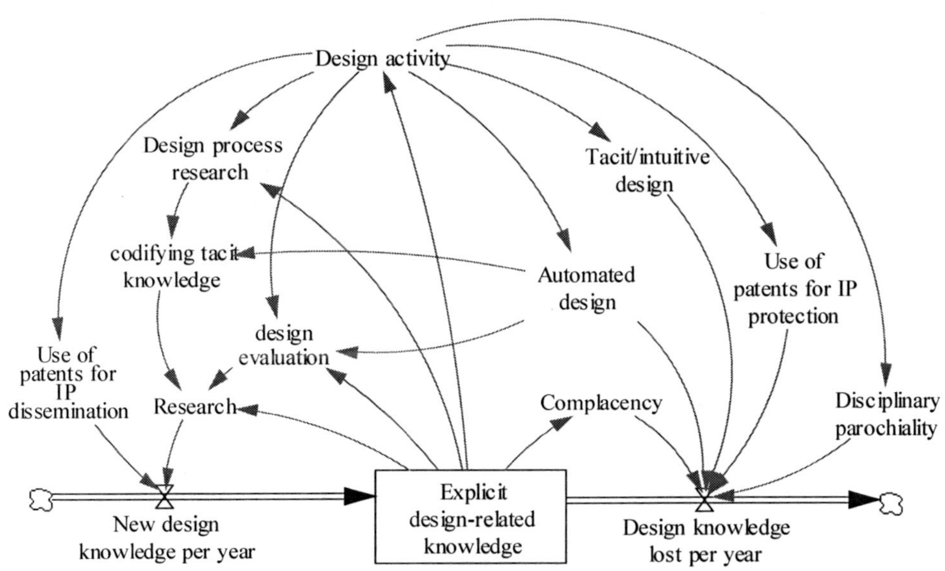

Figure 3 *Factors acting on development of explicit design-related knowledge*

effect of the factors to the left and attenuating the effects of the factors to the right.

Modelling Design Education

Design education has a single intention: of creating a pool of highly skilled designers. The research focused on investigating this aspect of the role of design education. It has become increasingly apparent, that another significant role of design education is to educate consumers and business managers to be more aware of the benefits of increased quality of design effort. In reality, most graduates of university-based design education become employed in ways that are not directly related to their design education, thus suggesting that a key role of design education is similar to that of classics education and finishing schools in earlier times.

There is currently a radical transformation of design professions. The three driving factors are: a transition from a traditional craft-based/art-based education to a more scientific university education as the basis for designers professional formation; increased dependence on tacit knowledge being made explicit and embodied in technological decision support for designers; and a vary high rate of change in the range and quality of design skills required by the market.

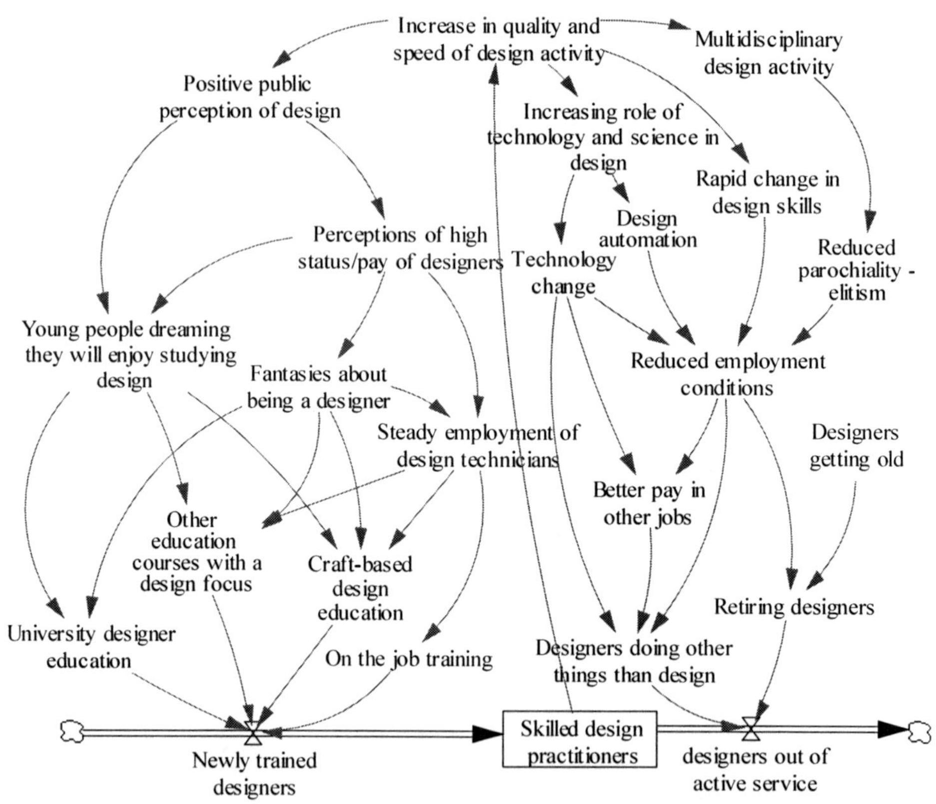

Figure 4 *Factors acting on design education and number of skilled design practitioners as perceived from the viewpoint of traditional established designers*

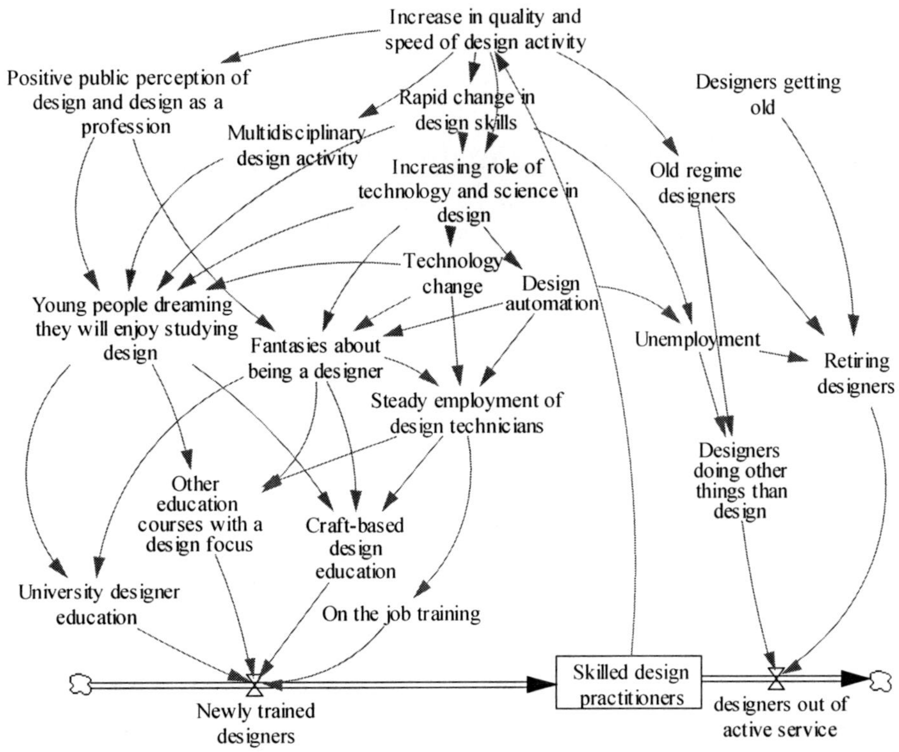

Figure 5 *Factors acting on design education and number of skilled design practitioners as perceived from the viewpoint of designers used to high levels of skill and technology change*

These overarching factors result in two very different pictures emerging from the design infrastructure research. Figure 4 below shows a systemic view as perhaps perceived from traditional design fields. In this, the impacts of technological and disciplinary change are primarily on the rate at which designers stop being employed as professional designers.

In contrast, Figure 5 below, shows a systemic view of the same factors as being perceived perhaps by a member of the newer sectors of design professionals who are used to high levels of change of design skills and disciplines; high technology use; and low interest in the benefits of traditional modes of skill evolution as the basis for improving design quality. In addition, for younger designers there appears to be, at the same time, respect for older designers and enthusiasm for older designers to leave the professional stage to make more room.

In essence, the difference between the two views is whether radical changes in design skills and technology skills are seen as positive or negative. The implications for design education, in design infrastructure terms, are complex. Current developed countries design infrastructures and design and innovation outputs are depending on a mix of design professionals from both positions. Both positions contribute to and support design output quality. In reality, at this point control of design activity appears to be held by those with more traditional design backgrounds and it is unclear whether a full transition to the new more technology based approach will offer the maximum benefits. At this stage, the main benefits of the above systems diagrams are to make explicit the factors impacting on the situation and the difference in perceptions between the two groups.

Modelling Design in Business

Design infrastructure has multiple roles in business. It impacts on the design of products, systems, services, organization structures, business strategies, business processes, and tools, personnel behaviors, marketing and sales activities as well as the external environment in which businesses operate. Figure 6 below shows a simple model of effects of design activity on asset levels that illustrates some of the multiple reinforcing loops by which assets accrue as a result of design activity, and assets are lost as products become obsolete, primarily as a result of new products and cultural change resulting form designed outputs.

The increase in assets at firm and national levels results in economic prosperity and cultural change that in turn affects the number of successful designs in a further set of positive feedback loops as shown below in Figure 7.

Significantly, economic and cultural change increases levels of critical awareness of designed solutions and also increases the strength and frequency of cycles of 'fashion' – in effect increasing the hunger for change via novel and better designed outcomes. This emerges as an increase in the rate at which designed outcomes become obsolete as represented in the right hand loops of Figure 7.

Taken together, the different feedback loops of Figure 7 illustrate the potential for several different scenarios in socio-economic development that is driven by design and innovation.

- Slow balanced scenario: Number of successful designs remains relatively stable and rates of design production and obsolescence are low. Often regarded as a 'sluggish' economy as it results in low asset increase;
- Fast balanced scenario: Number of successful designs remains relatively stable and rates of design production and obsolescence are high. This is often regarded as a high change 'booming' economy;
- Design hungry scenario: Rate of obsolescent (or potentially obsolescent) designs is high – usually due to poor performance rather than fashion. Number of successful designs is low. Rate of generation of successful new designs is low. Economy is sluggish. Offers high potential for change;
- Innovation driven scenario: Rate of new design production is high. Levels of successful designs are increasing. Designs become obsolescent as they are replaced by ones that provide socio-economic advantage;
- Effete society scenario: Rate of new design production is high. Levels of 'successful' designs are increasing. Designs become obsolescent as they are replaced by ones that are more fashionable. Society is driven by marketing/sales techniques and manipulation of desires. Design success is defined in terms of ability to create emotions of 'desire' rather than socio-economic benefit.

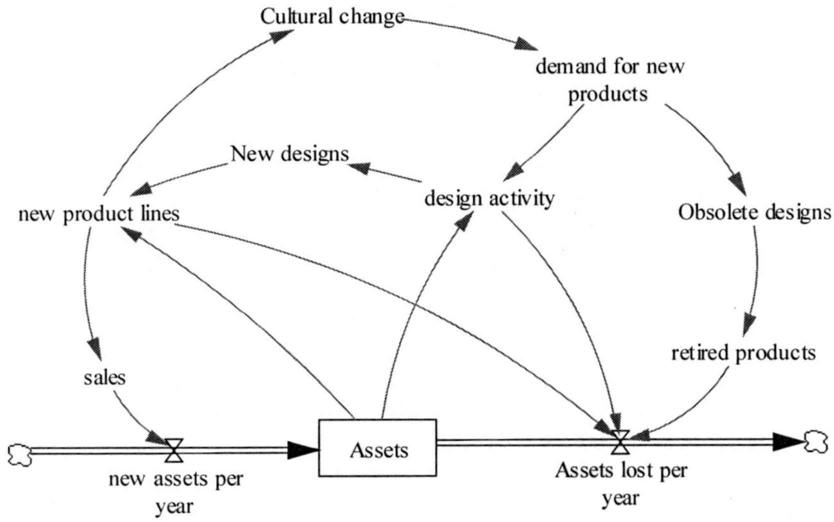

Figure 6 *Effects of design activity on asset levels*

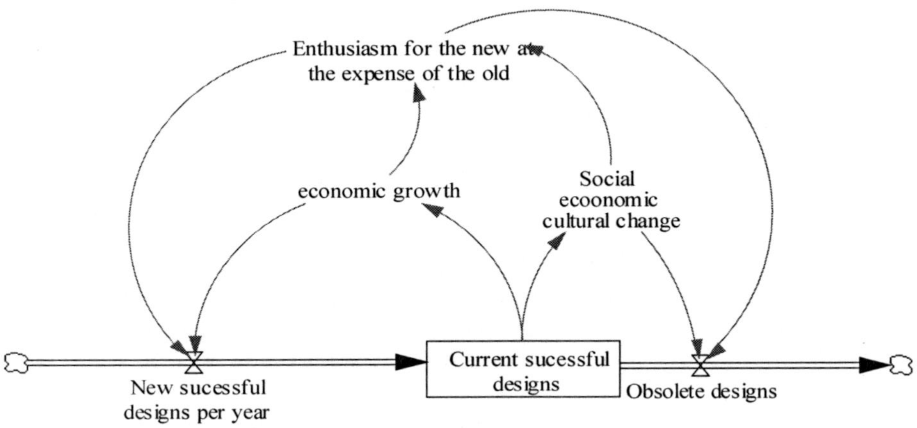

Figure 7 *Effects of economic growth and cultural change on numbers of successful designs*

Future Research

This paper describes one aspect of a larger project. It focuses on the preliminary modelling of: design knowledge, design education and the role of design in social and economic development, and identifies outcomes some of which are counter-intuitive. Other findings will be reported later. The aim is to develop a functional system dynamic model of national design infrastructures that incorporates delays and increased levels of modelling of interactions between subsystems. The next steps are to complete the range of system dynamics sub-system models that can be inferred from the data and literature reviews, and calibrate them. Future research as the analyses of existing data evolve will focus on identifying dominant feedback loops and key leverage points for interventions.

Summary

This paper has reported on preliminary outcomes from a three year research project investigating national design infrastructure systems in five countries.

The paper first introduces a larger view of design activity as a primary component of national social and economic systems than is usual, in which design has a more extensive role than is commonly perceived. An example was provided, a simple timber IKEA bookcase, in which the extent of the different roles of design activity was made more transparent.

This was followed by a description of the role of design infrastructures in national social, economic and cultural development and the importance of understanding the dynamics of design infrastructure development in terms of countries' histories and development trajectories. The importance of system dynamics as a potential tool for modelling the dynamics of design infrastructures was discussed.

Against this backdrop, the paper then provides preliminary systems models (using VenSim) based on selected findings of the design infrastructure research. These systems models illustrate some of complex behaviors found in the different dimensions of design infrastructure. This paper focuses particularly on three generic overarching issues: the dynamics of design knowledge, design education and the roles of design in business. Directions for future research are identified.

References

Beer, S. (1988). *Heart of Enterprise.* Chichester: John Wiley and Sons Ltd.

Beer, S. (1989). The Viable System Model: its provenance, development, methodology and pathology. In R. Espejo & R. Harnden (Eds.), *The Viable System Model: Interpretations and Applications of Stafford Beer's VSM*. Chichester, UK: John Wiley & Sons.

Boardman, K. (2001). Science and Innovation Centenary Article. from www.abs.gov.au

Forrester, J. W. (1975). Counterintuitive Behavior of Social Systems, 1970. In J. W. Forrester (Ed.), *Collected papers of Jay W. Forrester.* Cambridge Massachusetts: Wright-Allen Press Inc.

Forrester, J. W. (1998). *Designing the Future.* Seville: Universidad de Sevilla.

Love, T. (2001). Re: the political role of (graphic?) design doctorates (Identifying sub-fields of design). from http://www.jiscmail.ac.uk/cgi-bin/webadmin?A2=ind0108&L=phd-design&P=R10080&I=-1

Love, T. (2005). Design Infrastructure: Australian Developments. In *2005IDC New Design Paradigms Proceedings* (pp. N00000808ATLIP00000972.pdf [CDROM]). Douliou, Taiwan: National Yunlin University of Science and Technology, Taiwan.

Love, T. (2006). Design Centres as Elements of Design Infrastructure. *SEEDesign Bulletin (Design Wales)*(2), 3-5.

Simon, H. A. (1969). *The Sciences of the Artificial.* Cambridge Mass: MIT Press.

Sterman, J. D. (2002). All Models are Wrong: reflections on Becoming a Systems Scientist. *System Dynamics Review, 18*(4), 501-531.

47. Pitfalls in Managerial Decision Making: A Systemic Perspective

PLENARY PAPER

Kambiz Maani and **Anson Li**
Graduate School of Business, The University of Auckland, NZ

While numerous studies have dealt with the content of decision making, few have focused on the cognitive processes and the individual approach of the decision maker. Research, as well as decades of working with managers across diverse cultures, nationalities, and industries, has revealed consistent patterns of counter productive decision making in complex systems. In general, managers appear to have a tendency to "over intervene" in the systems they are responsible for, hence generating fluctuations and instability in their organizations. In this paper we describe and link the findings of two research projects which have dealt with these questions. The first project sought to identify patterns of cognitive processes that improve decision making outcomes, while the second investigates the factors that impact decision making in complex systems. We identify seven pitfalls that commonly betray managerial decisions and shed light on anti-systemic patterns of decision making that cause endemic poor performance.

Managerial Decisions

"For every complex question there is a simple answer, and it is wrong."

(Business Week 21 April 1980, p. 25)

In the past three decades, much research has explored the complexity of decision-making. This includes studies by Morecroft (1983, 1985), Senge (1990), and Sterman (1989, 2000) which have related this dilemma to systems thinking theories. According to Richmond (1994) systems thinking is "the art and science of making reliable inferences about behavior by developing an increasingly deep understanding of underlying structure". By understanding problem situations with a systems perspective, a more holistic understanding could be achieved in terms of the causal relationship between decisions, interventions, and their expected results.

Simon (1987) asserts that decisions made, even with the best intentions; do not always result in the favorable outcomes anticipated by the decision maker – "bounded rationality". Thus it is unrealistic to expect that interventions will yield the expected (and only the expected) results.

Other studies have also revealed counter intuitive behavior of complex systems, Meadows (1972, 1992), Morecroft (1983), Keating, *et al.*, (1999) and

Repenning, *et al.* (2001) to name a few. While these studies provide significant insights into the formulation and outcomes of decisions, the empirical work in the area of decision dynamics and interventions in complex systems remains elusive.

This paper identifies and addresses seven propositions (managerial decision pitfalls) listed below. To our knowledge there is no cohesive body of research that has dealt with these propositions.

1. Dramatic change leads to dramatic (positive) results;
2. The more change initiatives (interventions), the better the results;
3. Managers often ignore "soft" variables (e.g., morale, stress, burnout);
4. Managers are often oblivious to "systems delays";
5. Organizations and managers often judge performance by short-term results;
6. Organizations and managers tend to use too many performance measures;
7. Knowing the right actions is sufficient for success.

The paper seeks to identify patterns of decision-making which could assist in effective managerial decision making and formulation and implementation of intervention strategies in complex systems.

The Literature

At it roots systemic thinking is a cognitive processes which connects decision maker's mental models to understanding of complexity. Systems thinking has increasingly been accepted as a response to complexity as our default understanding in complex situations does not lead to adequate actions (Schaffernicht, 1999). Despite this most managers appear to have a great deal of difficulty thinking systemically. In this regard, Richmond (1994a, p. 213) observes that "We've grown up in a reality in which 'local' perspectives enabled us to do just fine; we have developed certain 'habits of thought' which make it difficult to learn in an interdependent reality."

Numerous studies illustrate non-systemic thinking by individuals confronted with complex problems (see for example Booth Sweeney & Sterman, 2000; Doyle, 1997; Buchner, 1995; Pennington, *et al.*, 1995; Brehmer, 1992; Funke, 1991; Sterman, 1989a, 1989b). Sterman (1989b: 336) describes participant behavior that "reflect an 'open-loop' conception of the origin of dynamics, as opposed to a mode of explanation in which change is seen as arising from the endogenous interactions of decision makers with their environment". Further, Cavaleri and Sterman (1997) found, in a case study of systemic intervention (Hanover Insurance), that subjects reported a much greater awareness of their thinking and changes in their behavior and went on to say that their management style became more "systemic" and that this helped in the design of new policies.

Despite the above studies, the link between systems thinking and effective decision making remains tenuous. According to Doyle (1997) "Many claims have been made concerning the ability of systems thinking interventions to change the nature and quality of thought about complex systems, [yet] important questions about the relationship between systems thinking and basic cognitive processes such as decision making, decision-making, and updating mental models remain unanswered."

According to Simon (1957), "bounded rationality is a property of decision making that reflects people's cognitive limitations. Individuals faced with complex choices are unable to make objectively rational decisions". Thus it is unrealistic to expect that interventions will yield the expected (and only the expected) results.

Morecroft (1983) study of human decision making concludes that "... there are severe limitations on the information processing and computing abilities of human decision makers. As a result, decision making can never achieve the ideal of perfect (objective) rationality." Morecroft (1985) further identifies six common practices that underlie the shortcomings of the human decision making process. They are:

1. Factored (fragmented) decision making;
2. Partial and certain information;
3. Rules of thumb or "quick fixes";
4. Goals and incentives;
5. Authority and culture (mental model);
6. Basic cognitive processes (delay, distortion, and bias).

To deal with the above shortcomings, many authors have suggested ways to improve the effectiveness of human decision-making. These include, among other tools, management and computer frameworks (Gilberto, 1995; Cayer, 2001), computer simulation models (Simon, 1987; Sterman, 1988), and use of systems thinking in decision-making (Senge, 1990; Maani, *et al.*, 2004).

Sterman's (1989) seminal article on "misperception of feedback" investigates the interpretation of information feedback by decision makers and the effects on the interventions derived. In this study "The decision making task is straightforward: subjects seek to minimize total costs by managing their inventories appropriately in the face of uncertain demand." In such a "simple" environment, however, things did not always go as planned for most participants, due to the rich simulated environment, which contains "multiple actors, feedbacks, non-linearity, and time delays." Similar to Morecroft's and Simon's notion of factored decision making, "the interaction of individual decisions with the structure of the simulated firm produces aggregate dynamics which diverge significantly and systematically from optimal behavior" (Sterman, 1989).

Keating, *et al.* (1999) carried out a study of the effectiveness of improvement programs. The motivation for the study arose from the fact that "most attempts by companies to use them have ended in failure" (Easton & Jarrell, 1998 in Keating, *et al.*, 1999) and that even "successful improvement programs have sometimes led to declining business performance, causing layoffs, low morale, and the collapse of commitment to continuous improvement." This dilemma was termed the "Improvement Paradox". The study sought to understand why improvement programs often fail. The findings suggest that "the inability to manage an improvement program as a dynamic process – one tightly coupled to other processes in the firm and to the firm's customers, suppliers, competitors and capital markets – is the main determinant of program failure. Failure to account for feedback from these tightly coupled activities leads to unanticipated, and often harmful, side effects that can cause the premature collapse and abandonment of otherwise successful improvement programs."

Collins (2001) and his research team studied 1,435 "good" companies' performance over a 40 years period, and identified a mere 11 organizations who had successfully transformed themselves from "good" to "great". The research team scrutinized the improvement/change strategies of these companies and identified unique styles of "change" that contributed to the success of the great companies. They tested several "*myths*" in relation to change management, none of which were "necessary" factors to transform from good to great.

- Change starts only when there's a crisis;
- Stock options, high salaries, and bonuses will grease the wheels of change;
- You can buy your way to growth;
- You can leapfrog the competition with technology;
- Change has to be wrenching, extreme, and painful.

Kanter (2003) studied several companies which had experienced successful "turn-around" through the interventions of their new leaders. These companies had experienced similar patterns of decline in their business, attributed to decisions made by various functions or divisions to apply quick fixes to various problems in order to achieve short-term goals under tight time frames. The findings suggest that short term fixes are common in troubled companies. These quick fixes usually make the situation worse in the longer term. For instance price cuts or discounting, although effective in increasing sales, would also reduce the funds available for marketing, which increases the organization's reliance on the promotional deals. Customers will also know that they can wait to get even better deals.

In summary, while the above studies shed light on complex decision making, they fall short of identifying the attributes or 'thought' skills that are effective for dealing with such problems. As a result, there are few practical guidance and established theories for managerial decision making in complex systems.

Does Systemic Thinking Improve Decision-making?

This research began with a simplistic (in retrospect) question that whether more systems thinking by a decision maker would lead to better task performance.

The findings suggest that this may not follow the simple notion that "the more systems thinking, the better the task performance". The results, however, suggest that although the overall amount of systems thinking does matter, the degree of higher-level systems thinking types performed (i.e., forest, closed-loop and operational) matters most. Further, the results show that participants who used all five systems thinking types and did this repeatedly throughout the simulation performed better (Maani & Maharaj, 2004).

This indicates that performance on a complex problem is an intricate and multi-dimensional process. The degree of high-level systems thinking and the consistent use of all levels of systems thinking throughout the decision-making exercise appear to have the greatest impact on task performance.

In previous studies of complex decision-making/problem-solving, characteristics that differentiate good and poor performers display strong parallels to aspects of the systems thinking studied. That is, individuals who display the characteristics of systems thinking, even if they are oblivious to the fact, perform better on complex decision-making tasks.

In those studies, the behavior of subjects who performed well reflects the attributes of systems thinking, while the behavior of those who performed poorly often mirrors the direct opposite of systems thinking, or 'linear thinking'. For instance, Dörner (1980: 91) observes "When solving such complex tasks, most people are not interested in finding out the existent trends and developmental tendencies at first, but are interested instead in the 'status quo'". This is a characteristic of static thinking, the polar opposite of dynamic thinking (Richmond, 1997b).

Further, this study adds support to the notion of "heuristic competence" construct. The construct is described as "a general competence for coping with complex systems" (Brehmer, 1992: 223). Participants who display 'heuristic competence' are described as those "who collect more information, who collect it more systematically, who construct adequate goals, who evaluate the effects of their decisions, and who generally behave in a systematic fashion ... Subjects who behave in a way that makes it more likely that they will acquire a good model of the task also learn to control the task better" (Dörner, *et al.* in Brehmer, 1992: 225). Thus, the heuristic competence behavior would lead to making fewer decisions, collecting more information before making decisions, and checking on results of decisions prior to making new ones.

Heuristic competence is highly analogous with the notions of systems thinking types and the *Conception- Planning- Action (CPA)* cycle that emerged in this study. The heuristic competence construct, however, is still loosely defined in the literature. The findings of this study propose a more clear description for the construct. Our findings suggest that systems thinking, when used in concert with the CPA cycle, manifest the characteristics of heuristic competence, as it involves understanding of the system structure, developing strategies, making decisions and carefully assessing the outcomes.

Several case studies suggests that most organizational decision processes do not follow the above cycle, partly because of time pressures as well as established norms and mental models (Kanter, 2003). In contrast, in organizations, decisions are often made at the "event" level without adequate attention to patterns of behavior and even less so to systemic structures underlying such patterns. This is a critical omission as our findings have suggested, understanding of systemic structures underlying organizational dynamics is a crucial prerequisite for the development of robust strategies. This highlights the need for group learning models such as microworlds and learning environments that utilize the elements of the CPA cycle in their conception and pedagogy.

Decision Making Pitfalls

The findings reported below are based on extensive laboratory experiments with 229 subjects using two simulation microworlds: The Service Quality Microworld (SQM) simulates a company operating at a *steady state*, whereas the Brand Management Microworld (BMW) is a start-up business (Maani & Li, 2004).

Magnitude and Frequency of Change

In general, the research results refute conventional wisdom and managerial truism underpinning Propositions 1 & 2 discussed earlier. For Proposition 1, the results indicate that frequent interventions correlate with inferior outcomes. For Proposition 2, the results are statistically significant, but are in opposite directions for the two microworlds. In the case of stable system (SQM), the results show that the greater the magnitude of change, the worse the result, while for the start-up system (BMW) greater magnitudes of interventions tended to improve performance.

The above finding is both surprising and illuminating and provides further insights. In order to explain this 'contradiction', we need to distinguish different natures of these microworlds. Viewing these dynamics in light of the Collins (2001) "Flywheel" analogy, the steady state model (SQM) is a "self-propelling" flywheel at the start, while the newly established organization is a flywheel at *stand still*, which requires a significant amount of effort to kick start. Thus, in the BMW case, initially, much greater effort/intervention is required to "fill" systems pipelines, i.e., heavily advertise, raise public awareness, and stock the stores in order to make sales happen. Once this happens, the system can be sustained with far less effort/interventions. However, as Collins observes, in order to start up the flywheel, effort should be applied "gradually [and] consistently", rather than using some "over hyped" changes that "lack accountability, fail to achieve credibility, and have no authenticity".

Even in a number of the BMW experiments dramatic change did result in great failures. In these cases, though large changes would have been appropriate, the subjects utilized 'wrong' levers (variables) for intervention – hence the choice of the decision variables also does matter. Further statistical analysis confirmed that the *mix* of decision variables does indeed make a difference in the outcomes of interventions.

In summary, the above results present counter-intuitive insights and lend support for the following observations.

1. High frequency of change could have negative impact on the outcomes of intervention strategies;
2. Dramatic ("over-hyped") change/interventions do not necessarily lead to positive results and, in fact, it could be counterproductive.

Awareness of "Soft" Variables

Analyzing participants' strategies and reflections before and after the game play, reveals remarkable patterns in relation to the awareness of "soft" variables in decision making in complex systems.

"Soft" variables are defined (Maani & Cavana, 2007) as the "subtle, 'invisible', and powerful factors" that influence the emotions and behavior of people and can be used as lead indicators of performance. Soft variables include morale, burnout, commitment, loyalty, confidence, and learning capacity, and can be regarded as the measures of the internal health and vitality of an organization.

In our experiments soft variables were not noted by the great majority of the participants in their strategies or post experiment reflections. In particular, only 50% of the subjects acknowledged the variable "time pressure". Twenty percent of the sample did acknowledge time pressure in their strategies, while the other 30% only mentioned it post experiment reflections.

Overall, in all the experiments, only a mere 3% *proactively* used time pressure as a critical performance indicator in their strategies. Another 2% of all participants reactively managed time pressure. (The subjects discovered the criticality of this variable during the simulation, usually as a result of their own poor performance during the game play, and therefore, tried to rectify the situation by easing off time pressure). 45% of the responses barely mentioned the existence of time pressure.

Acknowledgement of Systems Delays

Systems delays are embedded in complex systems. That is, changes in the target variables unfold over a period of time and not immediately noticeable. For instance, hiring, production goal, and quality changes could have an immediate impact upon the organization, however, their systemic and long term effects such as time pressure, burnout or turnover are only felt after considerable time delay.

The awareness of such delays by the participants were observed and coded from the strategies and reflections in their experiments (118 experiments from SQM and 105 experiments from BMW). The coding scheme and findings are presented in Table 1: As the table indicates, the awareness of systems delays is relatively consistent across the two different simulation models, SQM and BMW.

	SQM	BMW
Acknowledgement of delays	51%	44%
Acknowledgement of delays in strategy	43%	41%
Proactively acted with systems delays in mind	4%	4%
Reactively acted with systems delays in mind	5%	0%

Table 1 *Acknowledgement of Systems Delays*

At best, only about one-half of the participants showed awareness of systems delays. The majority of this group had anticipated this before the start of the simulation by noting possible delays that they could encounter in the course of their strategies. However, even though 51% of the subjects showed awareness of delays, only 4% of the entire sample indicated proactive decisions, taking into consideration the effect of time delay- for example, hiring more workers early on to allow time to gain experience, while keeping quality and production goals at lower levels to ease off the time pressure. In the experiments only 5% (SQM) of the subjects demonstrated learning from the game play. Those who did noticed the effect of systems delays after initial game plays and then reactively adjusted their future strategies with consideration of systems delays.

Number of Performance Measures

In our study, the variables that were mentioned by the participants in their strategies and/or reflections for tracking performance were considered as performance indicators/measures.

The results of the experiments were inconclusive as to the effect of the "number of" performance indicators or KPIs used to gauge performance. It is however plausible that the number of performance measures may have a material effect on performance but that it cannot be used as a dependable predictor for performance.

Order and Timing of Change

The importance of the sequence and timing of change was suggested by Keating, *et al.* (1999) in improvement projects where the authors had noted that in order to attain sustainable improvements, an advanced build up of capacity for improvement was necessary. Otherwise, performance would be jeopardized by increased pressure due to initial overwork associated with improvement initiative.

In this study, statistical tests indicate that in both models sequence and timing of interventions do matter. Particularly, initial capacity building decisions (e.g., increase in net hiring for SQM or advertising spending for BMW) were significantly superior to alternative decision sequences. The results concur with the findings of Keating, *et al.* (1999) in studies of the improvement paradox.

Discussion

The findings of this paper suggest the notion that systems thinking leads to better decision making and hence superior performance is rather simplistic. Our research indicates that the story is much more convoluted. While the degree of systems thinking does matter, the results suggest that certain *types* of systems thinking may be more relevant to superior performance. The 'type' of systems thinking, however, is not the only factor responsible for performance in complex problems. In our experiments, the subject's approach to the problem also appeared to be highly pertinent to task performance, as better performing subjects first attempted to gain understanding of the system structure, then developed and implemented strategies, and carefully assessed the outcomes of their decisions, in order to determine the validity of their understanding of system structure. Hence, better performing subjects consistently followed a cyclical thought pattern of conception, planning, and action (CPA). Using this cyclical pattern proved to be critical, as due to their intricate nature; understanding of complex problems appears to develop progressively.

Findings showed that systems thinking and particularly high-level systems thinking would affect performance indirectly, through intermediary step of task *understanding*. This would indicate that the amount of systems thinking would not necessarily correlate directly with task performance, but rather with understanding of task structure. However due to the opaque nature of complex problems, any understanding must be developed over time and thus it denotes a *gradual* and *cumulative* process. The subjects then utilized this understanding to develop strategies that improve performance. This purports that the use of systems thinking would correlate directly with better understanding of systems structure, rather than directly with task performance. The research revealed that differentiated systemic thinking would be more strongly linked to performance than systems thinking as a single construct.

Overall, the findings show that better performers displayed a distinctive pattern of thought that differed from that of the poor performers.

Conclusion

Cases studies as well as empirical and anecdotal evidence reveal endemic patterns of counter-intuitive managerial decision making with costly consequences for organizations. This research addresses the question why and how managerial interventions in complex systems often produce counter-intuitive results. In this regard seven pitfalls in managerial decision making were identified and empirically tested.

- Managers tend to over-intervene. This is manifested in the *frequency* and *magnitude* of their decisions. We contend that over-intervention behavior is caused and amplified by a lack of systemic thinking and misperception of dynamics of change. These behaviors are referred to variously as micro management, over-reaction, tampering, tinkering, etc.
- Managers and decision makers tend to ignore *soft* variables to the detriment of staff morale and organizational performance. Yet, soft indicators are pow-

erful lead indicators for individual and organizational performance.

- Managers are often oblivious to *systems delays*. Lack of awareness and attention to delay undermines performance and inhibits organizational stability.
- Organizations and managers tend to use too many and often inconsistent or *conflicting performance measures* (KPIs). Since the choice and number of KPIs impacts performance, excessive and inconsistent performance measures can cause low morale, poor results and unintended consequences.
- Managers generally focus on actions "getting things done". Our research indicates that *sequence and timing* of actions can be as consequential as the actions themselves.
- Managers (and organizations) often judge performance by *short-term results*. As performance often declines before it improves (worse before better), expectation of short-term results is unrealistic and misleading and can lead to counter productive outcomes.

Overall, the findings provide empirical evidence for anti-systemic patterns of managerial decision making that cause endemic poor performance in organizations. The results are aligned with findings of longitudinal and case studies, notably Keating, *et al.* (1999), Collins (2001) and Kanter (2003). The research paves the way for further empirical studies in this critical area.

References

Brehmer, B. (1992). "Dynamic Decision Making: Human Control of Complex Systems." Acta Psychologica **81**(3): 211-241.

Buchner, A. (1995). Basic Topics and Approaches to the Study of Complex Decision Making. Complex Decision Making. The European Perspective (pp. 27-63). P. A. Frensch and J. Funke. Hillsdale, New Jersey, Lawrence Erlbaum Associates, Inc.

Cavaleri, S. and J. D. Sterman (1997). "Towards evaluation of systems thinking interventions: a case study." System Dynamics Review 13(2): 171-186.

Cayer, C. (2001). Choosing appropriate business improvement tools. Annual Quality Congress Proceedings.

Collins, J. (2001a). Good to Great, Harper Business.

Collins, J. (2001b). "Level 5 Leadership: The Triumph of Humility and Fierce Resolve." Harvard Business Review January, 2001.

Dörner, D. (1980). "On the Problems People Have in Dealing with Complexity." Simulation and Games **11**: 87-106.

Doyle, J. (1997). "The Cognitive Psychology of Systems Thinking." System Dynamics Review **13**: 253-265.

Easton, G. S. and S. L. Jarrell (1998). "The effects of total quality management on corporate performance: An empirical investigation." The Journal of Business **71**(2): 253.

Funke, J. (1991). Solving Complex Problems: Exploration and Control of Complex Systems, Complex Decision making: Principles and Mechanisms R. J. Sternberg and P. A. Frensch. Hillsdale, New Jersey, Lawrence Erlbaum Associates, Inc.

Funke, J. (1988). "Using simulation to study complex problem solving: A review of studies in the FRG." Simulation and Games **19**: 277-303.

Gilberto, P. A. (1995). "The road to business process improvement - Can you get there from here?" Hospital Material Management Quarterly **17**(2): 12.

Kanter, R. M. (2003). "Leadership and the psychology of turnarounds." Harvard Business Review **81**(6): 58.

Keating, E. K., R. Oliva, et al. (1999). "Overcoming the Improvement Paradox." European Management Journal **17**(2): 120-134.

Maani, K. and R. Cavana (2007). Systems Thinking, System Dynamics - Managing Change and Complexity, Prentice Hall, Pearson Education, 2nd edition.

Maani, K. and A. Li (2004). Dynamics of Managerial Intervention in Complex Systems. Proceedings of the 22nd International Conference of System Dynamics Society, Oxford.

Maani, K. and V. Maharaj (2004). "Links between Systems Thinking and Complex Decision Making." System Dynamics Review **20**(1).

Service Quality Microworld (SQM) Manual (1994). Cambridge, MA, The Organizational Learning Centre.

Meadows, D. H., D. L. Meadows, et al. (1992). Beyond the Limits - Global Collapse or a Sustainable Future. England, Earth Scan.

Meadows, D. H. (1972). The Limits to Growth: a Report for the Club of Roam's Project on the Predicament of Mankind. London, Potomac Associates.

Morecroft, J. D. (1985). "Rationality in the Analysis of Behavioral Simulation Models." Management Science **31**(7): 900-916.

Pennington, N., A. Y. Lee, et al. (1995). "Cognitive Activities and Levels of Abstraction in Procedural and Object -Oriented Design." Human-Computer Interaction **10**: 171-226.

Repenning, N. P. and J. D. Sterman (2001). "Nobody ever gets credit for fixing problems that never happened." California Management Review **43**(4).

Richmond, B. (1998). "Operational Thinking." The Systems Thinker **9**(2): 6-7.

Richmond, B. (1997a). "The "Thinking" in Systems Thinking: How Can We Make it Easier to Master." The Systems Thinker **8**(2): 1-5.

Richmond, B. (1997b). "Dynamic Thinking: A Behavioral Context." The Systems Thinker **8**(6).

Schaffernicht, M. (1999). Managing Improvement Amongst Autonomous Actors with OMCA: The Case of the Chilean Educational Reform. Paper presented at the International Conference of the System Dynamics Society, Wellington, New Zealand.

Senge, P. M. (1990). The Fifth Discipline - The Art & Practice of The Learning Organization. Adelaide, Random House.

Simon, H. A. (1987). "Decision Making and problem Solving." INTERFACES **17**(5): 11-31.

Simon, H. A. (1979). "Rational Decision Making in Business Organizations." The American Economic Review **69**(4): 493.

Simon, H. A. (1957). Models of Man - Social and Rational. New York, John Wiley & Sons.

Sterman, J. D. (1989). "Modeling Managerial Behavior: Misperceptions of Feedback in a Dynamic Decision Making Experiment." Management Science **35**(3).

48. Elements of Client Confidence in System Dynamics Interventions: A Case-Based Ethnographic Study

Jason Yves Markham
Victoria University of Wellington, NZ

Acknowledgements

Associate Professor John Davies & Arun Elias, PhD (Masters thesis supervisors)

Despite ongoing debate (Pala, Vennix & Kleijnen, 1999) about the validity of system dynamics models, confidence in the broader model-building intervention has not been systematically explored from the client's perspective. The aim of this research was to develop a descriptive framework of client confidence, while studying ethnographically a system dynamics intervention for a military workforce planning problem. Framing methodology from Russo & Schoemaker (1989) was used to elicit the confidence criteria during client interviews, while constant comparative analysis methodology, as defined by Glaser & Strauss (1967), was used to construct the descriptive framework. The observed views of client confidence appeared to be extensive and diverse throughout the model-building intervention, and although client confidence proved to be an 'elusive' concept (Mitroff, 1969), framing methodology served as an effective filter for eliciting these elements.

Introduction

The technical perspective of the model builder, namely the 'validity' of model-building products, has dominated system dynamics research and model-building. The client's 'confidence' in the outcome of the model-based intervention, as the ultimate judge of its outcome (Coyle & Exelby, 2000), has been consequently neglected. Given that the model builder must 'build' (Forrester & Senge, 1980) and 'boost' (Coyle, 1996) the confidence of the client(s), there should be some methodology for determining the elements of client confidence. This research contributes to this need by demonstrating the use of framing methodology and content analysis as a multidisciplinary approach to the construction and interpretation of client confidence. This paper also makes a theoretical contribution of the confidence themes for this case study.

A comparison of existing frameworks of confidence themes is included in Table 1, matched to the 24 confidence themes developed during this study. These frameworks have been organized under four perspectives of confidence, along the epistemological spectrum from relativism to positivism. These four perspectives were drawn from three key philosophical papers of system dynamics and operations research literature: Naylor & Finger (1967), Barlas & Carpenter (1990) and Déry, Landry & Banville (1993).

Grappling with the Concept of Client Confidence

Confidence is subjective and relative to the client (Zhu, *et al.*, 1995), rather than having an absolute meaning, as suggested by the term validity (Forrester & Senge, 1980). It also became clear from this study that clients 'don't talk about validity', because the concept if unfamiliar and difficult to conceive. Selecting an appropriate research methodology to elicit these client views was therefore critical to the results of this study.

There is widespread doubt whether model builders typically conduct sufficient formal model tests (see for example Robinson, 1980; Wakeland & Hoarfrost, 2005) and only broad advice about how to use these tests or convey their results to clients. Van der Zouwen has demonstrated that it is 'very difficult' to assess the validity of models 'on the basis of their output only' (1997: 852). In the absence of 'objective quantitative methods ... for determining the validity of models from the viewpoint of the (client)' (Forrester, 1973: 35), it therefore becomes a matter of the client's judgement about the model-building intervention.

Framing methodology is useful in this situation because it provides a cognitive structure that sensitizes the observer to other perspectives (Davies & Mabin, 2001). Unlike model builders, who will tend to approach the issue of model validity with uniform, a priori notions (Meadows, 1980), clients will lack the a common or development mental framework for thinking about the qualities of an intervention. When De Bono (1971) investigated empirically the situation where non-experts were required to explain the behavior of a 'black box' technical phenomenon, he concluded that an individual's evaluation follows rules of 'everyday thinking'. The paradox of this pragmatism is that each client of a technical project will be right in their own view, but no one client will be completely right. Therefore, because all client views should be considered legitimate, framing was identified as a suitable methodology for obtaining the views of each client.

Research Methodology

The chronology and relationships between the research methodologies and techniques used in this case study are shown in Figure 1, demonstrating its multi-methodological character. The principal clients for the system dynamics intervention were identified using stakeholder analysis and interviewed prior to and immediately following the key stages of qualitative and quantitative model-building. Framing methodology was used to structure the interviews, which were then analyzed by a modified version of content analysis, known as 'constant comparative analysis' (Glaser & Strauss, 1967). This technique was used to construct a descriptive framework of the concept of client confidence, using as a foundation the four-part spectrum of perspectives of confidence identified from the literature of system dynamics (refer Table 1):

Perspectives of Confidence *(Refer note 1)*	Observed Client Confidence Themes *(Refer note 2)*	'Desirable characteristics' *Source: Randers (1980, p. xix)*	'Measures of validity' *Source: Lane (1995, p. 125)*	'Quality criteria' *Source: Coyle (1996, pp. 353-354)*
Relativity	Affect			
	Discourse		Meaningfulness & communicability	
	Satisfaction			
	Significance	Relevance	Relevance	
	Subjectivity		Cultural congruence	
	Trust		Trustworthiness	Credibility
Utility	Agency		System improvement	
	Benefit	Fertility	Fertility	Creativity
	Cost		Time & cost	Cost
	Model use			
	Suitability		Precision of insights	Suitability
	Solvency		Operational validity	Productivity
	Usability	Transparency	Ease of enrichment	Flexibility, simplicity & transparency
	Usefulness		Usefulness of intervention	Purpose
Empiricism	Accuracy	Formal correspondence with data & point predictive ability	Data validity	
	Analysis		Analytical quality	
	Experiment		Experimental validity	Sensitivity
	Fidelity	Descriptive realism & mode reproduction ability	Conceptual validity	Generality
Rationality	Caveat			
	Expertise		Guru status	
	Logic		Formulational validity	Basis
	Sophistication			Redundancy
	Soundness		Rigour & robustness	Promotion
	Understanding	Insight generating capacity	Insight generating	

Note 1. Adapted from Naylor & Finger, 1967; Barlas & Carpenter, 1990; and Déry et al., 1993.
Note 2. Observed during the study and developed into a framework using ground theory.
Note 3. Shading indicates new confidence themes.

Table 1 *Comparison of Frameworks for Confidence in System Dynamics Interventions*

relativity, utility, rationalism and *empiricism*. In the final phase of this study, the descriptive framework was used as a sensitizing framework to interpret and compare the views of each client at each key stage of the model-building project.

This enquiry occurred during a system dynamics model-building intervention intended to identify policy leverage points for a military workforce planning problem. The model-based intervention was conducted along similar lines to the methodology described in Maani & Cavana (2000) and the framing interviews were scheduled at three key stages during the model-based intervention, as shown in Figure 2. The iterative nature of system dynamics model-building is evident in Figure 2 from the occurrence of problem structuring and model testing activities during almost all stages of the project.

A semi-structured interview format was used in this study (after Cavana, Delahaye & Sekaran, 2001), based on the frame analysis questions shown in Figure 3. The clients were given a copy of the interview questions before the interview, to counter their lack of familiarity with the technique.

The idea of framing is commonly attributed to Erving Goffman's text *Frame Analysis* (1974, revised 1986), however those ideas have remained conceptually unclear (Gamsom, 1974) and 'vague' (Scheff, 2005). Russo & Schoemaker's book *Decision Traps* (1989) have cast framing into an explicit and unambiguous technique intended to serve as a tool for managers. The 10 frame analysis questions are intended by Russo & Schoemaker (1989) to help managers avoid their own *frame blindness* and lack of *frame control*. This study used the same set of frame analysis questions with slight modifications by Davies & Mabin (2001). These questions focus on the symbolic (*boundaries, yardsticks, reference points, metaphors, highlight* and *shadow*) and social (*why this frame, what others think* and *slogan*) elements of framing.

Ethnography means the study of a group from the 'inside', where the researcher comes to be regarded as 'one of them' (Rosenthal & Rosnow, 1991). This research context proved suitable for me because it was a continuation of my professional experience as a part-time system dynamics model builder in a military organization. This choice of research design was intended to improve the chances of success for this model-building intervention by ensuring it proceeded in an iterative fashion (Homer, 1996) and was conducive to my reflective involvement with the clients (Sterman, 2000).

A technique of content analysis known as constant comparative analysis was used to develop the confidence themes, following the steps described by Cavana, *et al.*, (2001: 171-175). Content analysis is an intensive, reflective coding methodology for developing grounded theory and was conducted in four phases, as shown in Table 2.

During the first reading of the interview transcripts, distinct confidence criteria (or 'sub-themes') were identified and grouped into preliminary themes (open coding). Then on the second reading for axial coding, the sub-themes were refined, expanded and reorganized. Selective coding, during the third reading of the data, was the main opportunity for simplification of the themes, concluding with the allocation of themes to the four meta-themes (or 'perspectives').

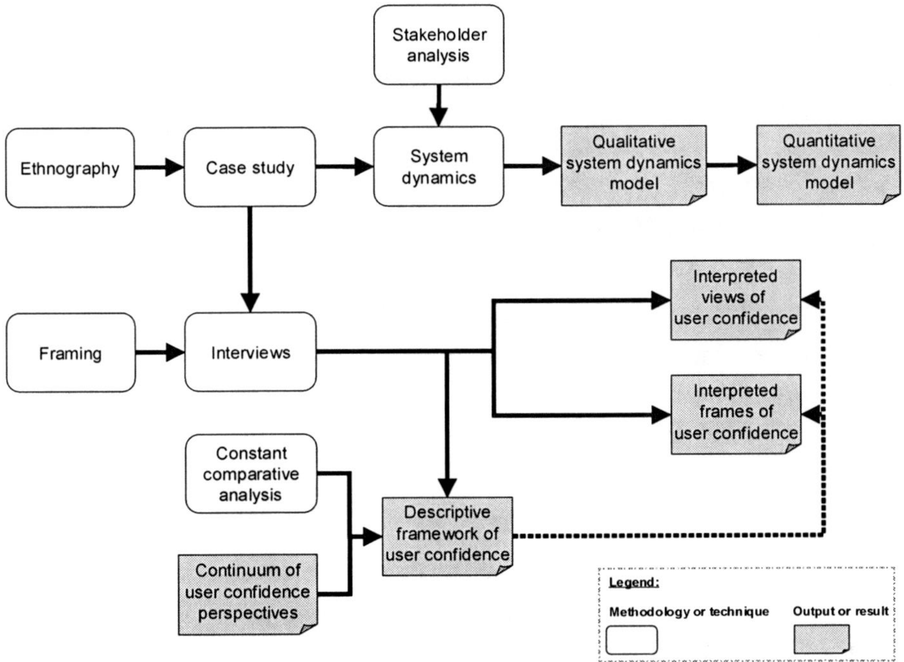

Figure 1 *Research Methodologies and Techniques*

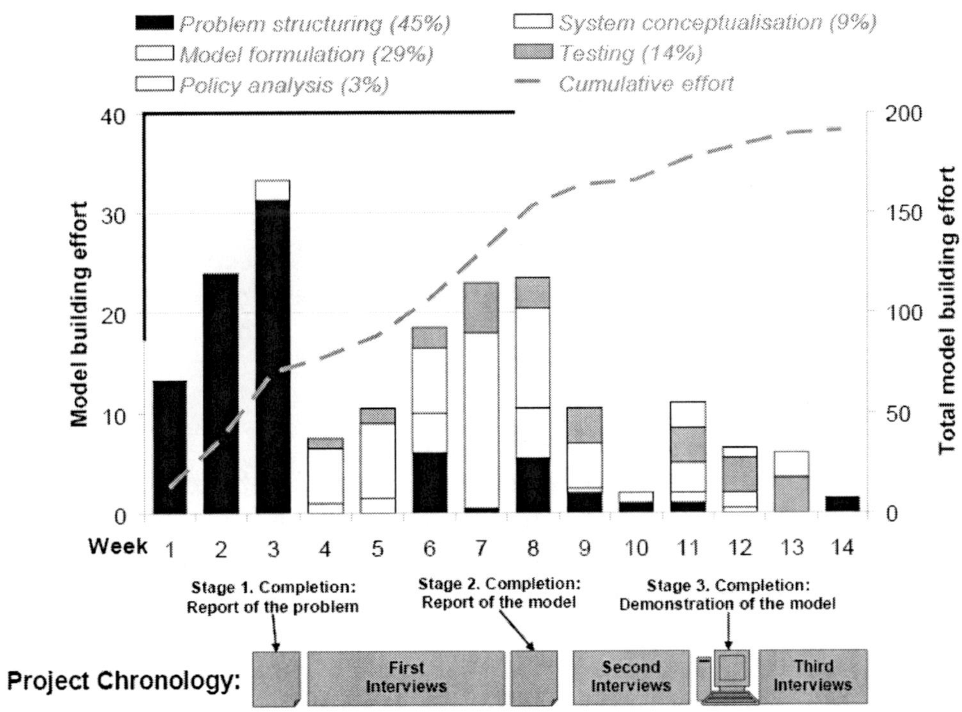

Figure 2 *Chronology of Model-Building and Framing Interviews*

FRAME ANALYSIS WORKSHEET

1. What issue or issues does your view of validity address? In other words, what are your validity criteria?
2. What boundaries do you put on the issue of validity? In other words, what other aspects of validity are left out of consideration?
3. What targets or reference points do you identify as success or failure, for the development and use of this workforce model?
4. What measures or scales do you use in conjunction with these targets?
5. Why do you think about the issue of the model's validity the way you do?
6. What does your view of validity emphasize or highlight?
7. What does your view of validity minimize or shadow?
8. Do other people in the Army or workforce planning think about the issue of validity differently from the way you do?
9. What metaphors—if any—do you use in thinking about the issue of validity?
10. Can you summarize your view of validity in a slogan?

Source: *Davies & Mabin (2001: 76); adapted from Russo and Schoemaker (1989: 43)*

Figure 3 *Frame Analysis Questions*

Stage of analysis	Analytical focus
Open coding	Development of 'themes'
Axial coding	Development of 'sub-themes'
Selective coding	Development of 'meta-themes'
Description of client views and frames	Integration and refinement of thematic levels

Table 2 *Stages of Content Analysis*

A fourth and final reading was undertaken to verify the confidence themes for each client and interpret the client frames, allowing for final adjustments and refinement of the descriptive framework. This process of constant comparative analysis became a living, ongoing activity that continues during this reporting stage of research and is likely to unfold further as further insights and meanings arise from reflection on the data and framework.

Results and Findings

Descriptive Framework of Client Confidence

The descriptive framework contained 120 distinct confidence criteria (i.e. 'sub-themes'). The confidence criteria were clustered into 24 'themes', each defined by a 'rule for inclusion' (Cavana, *et al.*, 2001). Those 24 themes were placed on the spectrum of perspectives of confidence (refer Table 1). This framework is clearly extensive because it includes all the explicit themes from existing frameworks (refer Table 1), while also identifying four new themes.

The 'mega-themes' of *proof* and *relevance* were included to highlight the perspectival extremes of the positivist-relativist spectrum. This idea resonates with the contrasting ideas of *representativeness* and *usefulness* proposed by Shannon (1975), has been extended by Lane (1995), and is also apparent in the title of Sterman's validation chapter: 'truth and beauty' (2000: 845). I attribute the notion of *proof* to Naylor & Finger (1967) for proposing a theory of validation by prediction based on *rationalism* and *empiricism.* This spectrum of confidence from *relevance* to *proof* demonstrates empirically the diverse range of elements within the notion of client confidence.

The themes of client confidence constructed in this study appear to fit isomorphically with Lane's (1995) more comprehensive framework. Although there are fewer thematic matches with the frameworks of Coyle (1996) and Randers (1980), the themes from this case study appear to be more extensive. This research generated four previously tacit themes of client confidence: *affect, model use, satisfaction* and *caveat.*

Tacit Themes of Client Confidence

The client confidence theme of *affect* was defined in this study as an 'emotional response towards the model, either positive or negative', demonstrated by the client comment: 'I am excited by this (model)'. The sub-themes for *affect* were *excitement, enthusiasm, encouraging* and *surprise.* Although Coyle, Exelby & Holt have also cited client enthusiasm as a confidence criterion (1999), authors have generally excluded the element of *affect* from the concept of client confidence.

The theme of *model use* was defined as 'employment of the model, including support or requests for further model-building effort', with its sub-themes being *implementation, operation, demand* and *support.* A common client statement for this theme was 'I am going to use it', similar to Forrester's idea that 'the validity and usefulness of dynamic models should be judged, not against an imaginary perfection, but in comparison with the mental and descriptive models which we would otherwise use' (1968: 3-3). By its frequent omission from the literature of confidence and validity, it appears the element of *model use* has been treated as external to the issue of client confidence.

Satisfaction was constructed as a theme of client confidence for data matching the description 'fulfillment of a desire'. One client expressed this idea in terms of the model results being 'within a bull's road of what I want'. *Satisfaction* is related to Lane's (1995) validity measure of *cultural congruence,* judging from the sub-themes of *acceptance, adequacy* and *intuitiveness.* Most of these ideas about client confidence have appeared in operations research literature, although not explicitly in any framework. For example: 'the model is "good enough" given the purpose' (Van der Zouwen, 1997: 850), '(the client's) satisfaction is a sufficient condition' (Roberts, 1978: 80), 'acceptable level of confidence' (Mihram, 1972: 25) and 'the model's accuracy is within its acceptable range' (Sargent, 2005: 130).

Caveat was defined as 'the bounds of client confidence in the model' with the sub-themes: *limitations, strengths & weaknesses, limited liability, unknown* and *control limit.* There was a significant volume of interview data for this theme covering a wide range of ideas. A few key examples of these ideas are:

Mega-themes	Meta-themes, or Perspectives	Themes
RELEVANCE	Relativity The art or aesthetics of model-building, i.e. personal confidence7	Affect Discourse Satisfaction Significance Subjectivity Trust
	Utility The ends or purpose of model-building, i.e. practical confidence	Agency Benefit Cost Model use Solvency Suitability Usability Usefulness
PROOF	Empiricism The science, validity or truth of model-building (a posteriori), i.e. scientific/ observed confidence	Accuracy Analysis Experiment Fidelity
	Rationality The verity or compliance with rules of model-building (a priori), i.e. reasoned confidence	Caveat Expertise Logic Sophistication Soundness Understanding

Table 3 *Summary of the Descriptive Framework of Client Confidence*

'garbage in ... garbage out', '(use the model) at your own risk', 'notwithstanding anomalies', 'I don't know what I don't know', 'we just cannot control or understand so many things', 'not even a sophisticated model could have taken it into account', and 'there could be things that happen that we just have absolutely no knowledge or control about'. Forrester recognized the element of *caveat* when he stated that 'the validity of industrial dynamics models is not separable from the effectiveness of industrial dynamics as a total viewpoint and discipline.' (1961, 115).

A notable common feature of these four themes is that they did not emerge from the data until the axial coding phase (refer to Table 2), appearing as ideas on their own merit after the simpler and more obvious themes had been clarified and refined. This result suggests that the concept of client confidence may be more extensive and complex than has been assumed. Framing methodology proved useful in this regard because it sensitized the model-builder, as an action researcher, to the quite complex themes of client confidence.

Observed Client Views of Confidence

The results of observed views and frames of all clients in this case study are included in the appendix, available on request. The three main columns represent the stages of interviewing; at an initial 'pre-model' stage, after the 'qualitative model' and finally after the 'quantitative model'. From this summary, I observed that each client's confidence themes, represented by 'x', tended to crystallize after they had seen the quantitative model. This result was expected because the clients had little or no prior experience with system dynamics. However, no clear pattern of thematic structure or development was apparent from longitudinal or cross-sectional comparisons of client views, suggesting that additional analytical methods might be needed to interpret these results.

The concept of client confidence also grew in complexity as it was explored. For some clients the idea of confidence became difficult to conceive, as illustrated by the statement: '...there are a lot of things that I think are important... I can't think this time, because the more I look at it the more things that are important... '. Most clients perceived confidence as a vague, ambiguous and confusing idea. For example: 'I am a little bit confused about validity as a concept.' These statements demonstrate, just as Mitroff (1969) discovered, that the concept of client confidence towards a computer-based management intervention can be 'elusive'.

Conclusions

A descriptive framework for the concept of client confidence in a system dynamics intervention was constructed from empirical data, with themes ranging across the positivist-relativist spectrum of perspectives. The framework from this study was extensive and diverse in nature.

The concept of client confidence was difficult to elicit and interpret, for the apparent reason that clients 'don't talk about validity'. This supports Mitroff's (1969) empirical finding that the concept of confidence in a computer model is 'elusive'. This case study also demonstrates the ability of framing methodology to deal with this conceptual elusiveness by acting as an 'interpretive filter' (Davies & Mabin, 2001).

Four previously tacit themes of client confidence were included in the framework of client confidence: *affect*, *model use*, *satisfaction*, and *caveat*. As the first three themes fall under the meta-theme of relevance, it highlights the need for model-builders to account for the relativist perspectives of their clients. Finally, this study has demonstrated the use of framing methodology as a 'sensitizing framework' (Davies & Mabin, 2001) to make explicit the elements underlying the elusive concept of client confidence.

It is hoped this research contribution will help to address the need for 'formal criteria for the establishment of confidence in, or the "validation" of, system dynamics models' (Coyle & Exelby, 2000: 27) that are aligned with client views of confidence. This paper may also serve to extend the debate about system dynamics validity beyond the traditional positivist paradigm common to model builders (Berends & Romme, 1999).

Implications for Research

This exploratory study could be extended by explanatory investigation of the concept of client confidence, by constructing a theoretical framework for the relationships between themes. This would involve tracing the explanatory connections between confidence themes, as described in Cavana, *et al.* (2001).

Further analysis might also look at the dependence of confidence themes on exogenous variables, to explore the potential for a typology of system dynamics clients.

Naturally, this case study has limited generalizability, being a study of the principal clients of a system dynamics intervention for a strategic military workforce planning problem in New Zealand.

References

Barlas, Y., and Carpenter, S. (1990). "Philosophical roots of model validation: Two paradigms," *System Dynamics Review,* ISSN 0883-7066, 6(2): pp. 148-166.

Berends, P., and Romme, G. (1999). "Simulation as a research tool in management studies," *European Management Journal,* ISSN 0263-2373, 17(6): pp. 576-583.

Cavana, R.Y., Delahaye, B.L., and Sekaran, U. (2001). *Applied Business Research: Qualitative and Quantitative Methods,* ISBN 0471341266.

Coyle, R.G. (1996). *System Dynamics Modelling: A Practical Approach,* ISBN 0412617102.

Coyle, R.G., and Exelby, D. (2000). "The validation of commercial system dynamics models," *System Dynamics Review,* ISSN 0883-7066, 16: pp. 27-41.

Coyle, R.G., Exelby, D., and Holt, J. (1999). System dynamics in defence analysis: Some case studies. *Journal of the Operational Research Society,* ISSN 0160-5682, 50(4): pp. 372-382.

Davies, J., and Mabin, V.J. (2001). "Knowledge management and the framing of information: A contribution to OR/MS practice and pedagogy," *Journal of the Operational Research Society,* ISSN 0160-5682, 52: pp. 856-872.

De Bono, E. (1971). *Practical Thinking,* ISBN 0140137831.

Déry, R., Landry, M., and Banville, C. (1993). Revisiting the issue of model validation in OR: An epistemological view. *European Journal of Operational Research,* ISSN 0377-2217, 66: pp. 168-183.

Forrester, J.W. (1961). *Industrial Dynamics,* ISBN 1883823366.

Forrester, J.W. (1968). *Principles of Systems,* ISBN 0262560178.

Forrester, J.W. (1973). "Confidence in models of social behavior with emphasis on system dynamics models." Unpublished paper no. D-1967. Cambridge, MA: MIT.

Forrester, J.W. and Senge, P. (1980). "Tests for building confidence in system dynamics models," *TIMS Studies in the Management Sciences,* 14: pp. 209-228

Glaser, B.G. and Strauss, A.L. (1967). *The Discovery of Grounded Theory,* ISBN 0202302601.

Goffman, E. 1974 (1986), *Frame Analysis: An Essay on the Organization of Experience,* ISBN 9780930350918.

Homer, J.B. (1997). "Structure, data and compelling conclusions: Notes from the field," (1997 Jay W. Forrester award lecture), *System Dynamics Review,* ISSN 0883-7066, 13(4): pp. 293-309.

Lane, D.C. (1995). The folding star: A comparative reframing and extension of validity concepts in system dynamics. *International System Dynamics Conference:* pp. 111-130.

Maani, K. and Cavana, R.Y. (2000). *Systems Thinking and Modelling: Understanding Change and Complexity,* ISBN 1-877258-00-8.

Meadows, D.H. (1980). "The unavoidable a priori". In J. Randers (Ed.) *Elements of the System Dynamics Method,* ISBN 1-883823-44-7: pp. 23-57.

Mihram, G.A. (1972). "Some practical aspects of the verification and validation of simulation models," *Operational Research Quarterly,* ISSN 1473-2858, 23(1): pp. 17-

29.

Mitroff, I.I. (1969). "Fundamental issues in the simulation of human behavior: A case in the strategy of behavioural science," *Management Sciences,* ISSN 1816-6075, 15(12): pp. B635-B650.

Naylor, T.H. and Finger, J.M. (1967). "Verification of computer simulation models," *Management Sciences*, ISSN 1816-6075, 14(2): pp. B-92-B101.

Pala, Ö., Vennix, J.A.M., and Kleijnen, P.C. (1999). "Validation in soft OR, hard OR and system dynamics: A critical comparison and contribution to the debate," *Proceedings of the 17th international conference of the system dynamics society*, Wellington, NZ.

Randers, J. (Ed.) (1980). *Elements of the System Dynamics Method,* ISBN 1-883823-44-7.

Roberts, E.B. (1978). "Strategies for effective implementation of complex corporate models", In E.B. Roberts (Ed.), *Managerial Applications of System Dynamics,* ISBN 0915299593: pp. 77-85.

Robinson, J.M. (1980). "Managerial sketches of the steps of modelling," In J. Randers (ed.) *Elements of the System Dynamics Method,* ISBN 1-883823-44-7: pp. 249-269.

Rosenthal, R., and Rosnow, R.L. (1991). *Essentials of Behavioural Research Methods and Data Analysis,* (2nd Ed.), ISBN 0073531960.

Russo, J.E. & Schoemaker, P.J.H. (1989). *Decision Traps,* ISBN 0385248350.

Sargent, R.G. (2005). "Verification and validation of simulation models," *Proceedings of the 37th conference on winter simulation,* Orlando, FL.

Shannon, R.E. (1975). *Systems Simulation: The Art and Science,* ISBN 0138818398.

Sterman, J.D. (2000). *Business Dynamics: Systems Thinking and Modeling for a Complex World,* ISBN 007238915X.

Van der Zouwen, J. (1997). "The validation of sociocybernetic models," *Kybernetes,* ISSN 0368-492X, 26(6/7): pp. 848-856.

Wakeland, W. and Hoarfrost, M. (2005). "The case for thoroughly testing complex system dynamics models," *Proceedings of the 22nd international conference of the system dynamics society*, Boston, MA.

Zhu, H. et al., (1995). "Road Maps Glossary," Unpublished memo D-4498, Cambridge, MA: MIT.

49. Is the Land Rehabilitation Project in Australia Using Coal-fired By-products Sustainable and Profitable? A Feasibility Analysis with System Dynamics

Kaoru Yamaguchi
Doshisha Business School, Kyoto, JAP

Yoshitaka Nitta & Takahisa Yokoyama
Central Research Institute of Electric Power Industry, JAP

Takayoshi Kato
Kyoto University, JAP

Acknowledgements

The research is jointly supported by the Omron Fund, Doshisha Business School and by the Central Research Institute of the Electric Power Industry, for which we are very thankful. The views presented in this paper are those of the authors, and do not necessarily reflect those of the institutions with which they are affiliated. Finally our special thanks are given to Kaye Spark for her editorial help.

The encroachment of sodicity, salinity and acidity on Australian land is of national concern. The land rehabilitation project, "COALA", aims to assess the feasibility of enhancing greenhouse gas reduction by sodic / acidic land reclamation in Australian using coal-fired power plant by-products. The technical feasibility of the project has been carried out using field trials for sodic soils and glasshouse pot trial for acidic soils. In this paper the sustainability and economic feasibility of the COALA Project are discussed using a system dynamics method. The major finding is that the COALA project is profitable under sustainable forest management.

Introduction

The encroachment of sodicity, salinity and acidity on Australian land is of national concern. A land rehabilitation project, COal industry by-product Applied to LAnd rehabilitation "COALA", was set up to study the feasibility of reducing greenhouse gas emissions by the forestation of sodic and acidic land in Australian reclaimed using coal-fired power plant by-products such as Flue Gas Desulphurization (FGD) gypsum or fly ash (coal-ash) derived fertilizers. The first part of this project, land reclamation carried out using field trials for sodic soils and glasshouse pot trial for acidic soils, has proven to be successful. This paper is concerned with the second part of the project, using a systems dynamics business model to evaluate the economic feasibility of enhancing greenhouse gas reduction from this type of land reclamation, as a sustainable business project in Australia jointly with Japan.

The Issue: By-products from Coal-fired Power Plant

There are 10 electric power companies (EPC) in Japan (Table 1), located in separate regions, and several whole sale electric companies such as Electric Power Development Company (JPOWER). The annual electricity generated by coal from these stations in 2004 (Table 1) constitutes 24% of the total electricity generated in Japan in that year. The coal-fired power generation depends on imported coals, mainly from Australia, China and Indonesia. For instance, in 2004, 63.3% of coals were imported from Australia and 18.7% and 11.6% were from China and Indonesia, respectively.

Electric Power Company (EPC)	Billion KWh/Year
Hokkaido EPC	14.49
Tohoku EPC	23.187
Tokyo EPC	5.832
Chubu EPC	29.206
Hokuriku EPC	15.644
Kansai EPC	0.409
Chugoku EPC	19.635
Shikoku EPC	7.377
Kyushu EPC	11.677
Okinawa EPC	4.468
Electric Power Development Co.	51.133

Table 1 *Annual coal-fired power generation by power companies in Japan (2004 data)*

The process of the generation of electricity results in the production of three major by-products, carbon dioxide (CO_2), FGD gypsum and fly ash. The structure of the pathways forming that process for the Hokkaido Electric Power Company (Figure 1) is typical of those for other power companies.

That structure is used as the basis of a sub-model for calculating the total domestic power generation from coal and its by-products by the above-mentioned electric power companies (excluding Okinawa EPC) in Japan as shown in Figure 2. The information arrows of inflows and outflows from the companies are not shown in the sub-model to reduce complexity.

In order to estimate the demand for electricity generated by coal in Japan over the period 2006 to 2060, a relatively conservative assumption is made

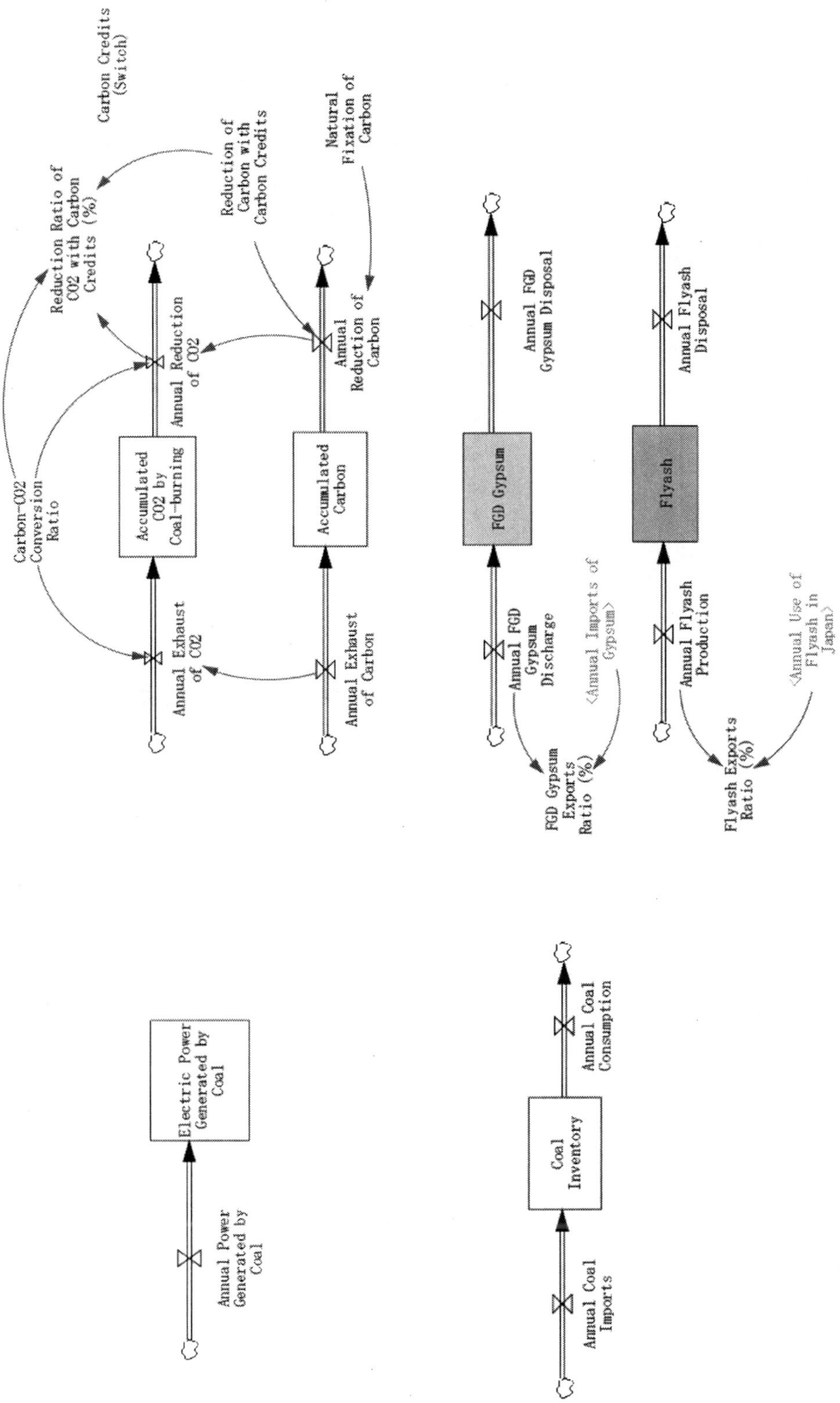

Figure 1 *Pathways of the power generation and by-products production of the Hokkaido Electric Power Company*

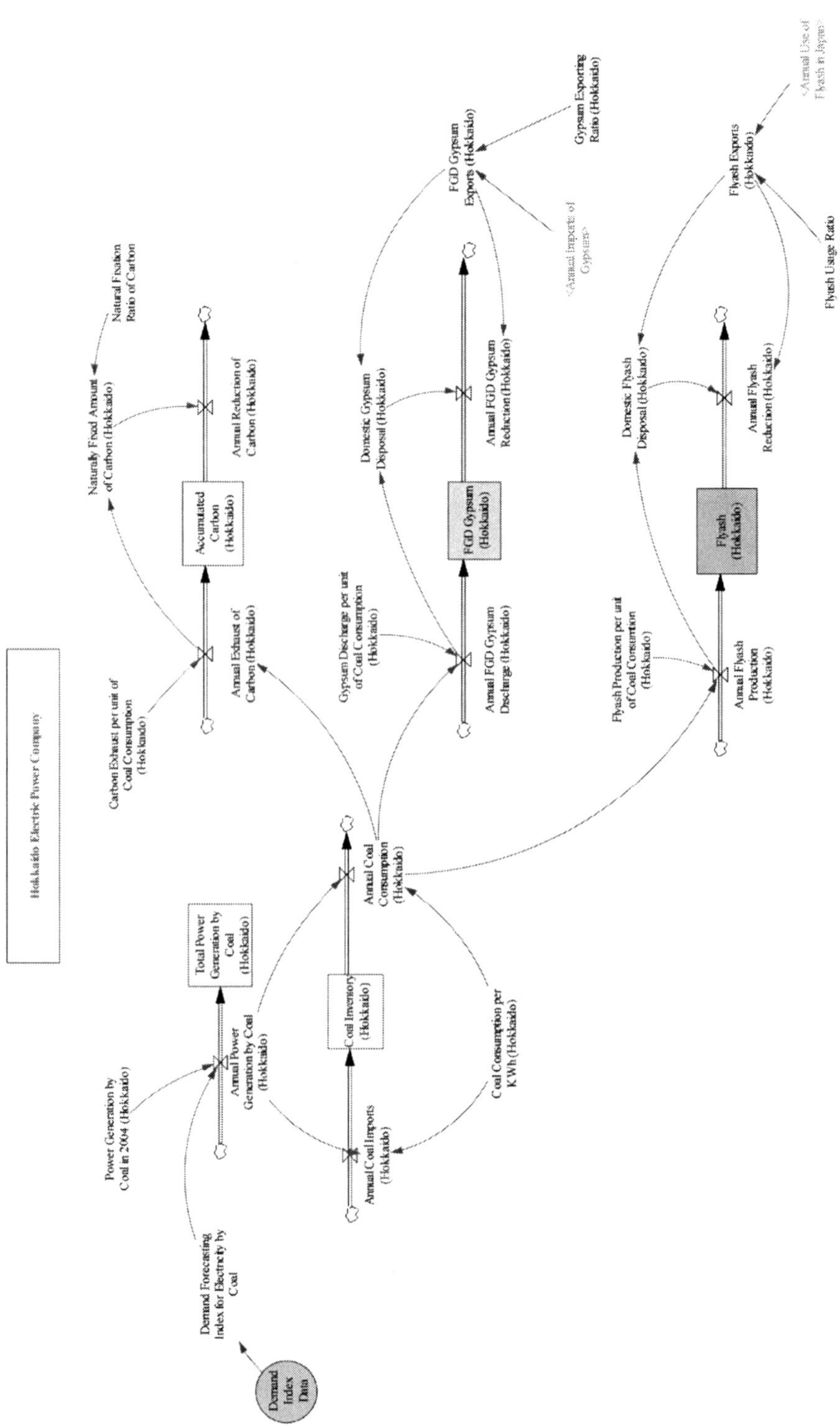

Figure 2 *The structure of the sub-model used to calculate the total coal-fired power generation and by-product production in Japan*

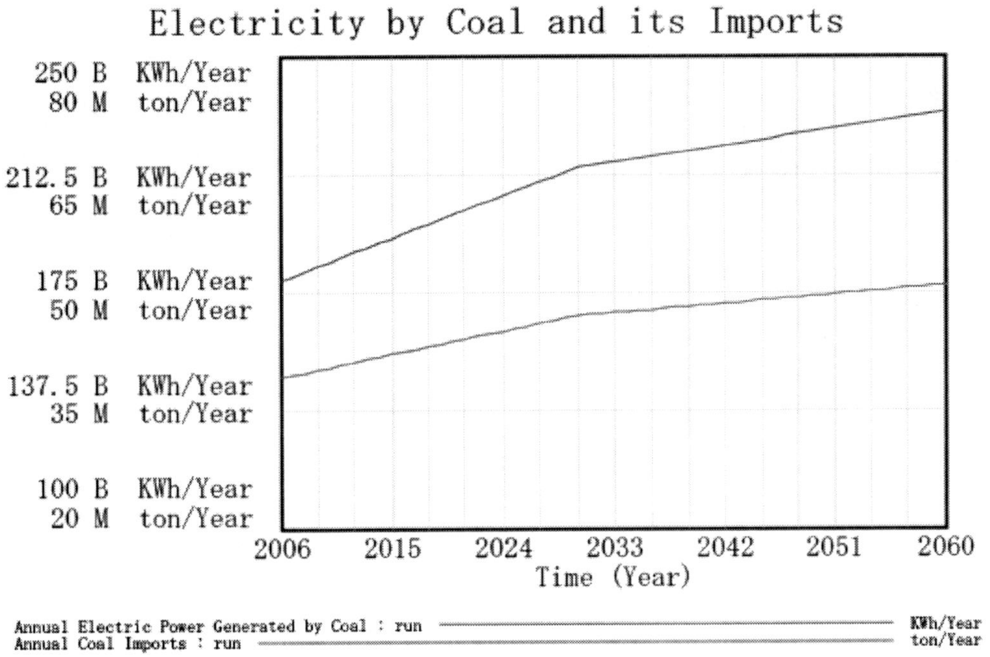

Figure 3 *The estimated future quantities of the Japanese annual coal imports and coal-fired power generation*

that the demand increases linearly by 20% to be 214.3 billion KWh in 2030 (or roughly 0.8% annually) and by a further 10% from 2030 to 2060 to be 232.16 billion Kwh in 2060 (about 0.33% annually from 2030-2060) (Figure 3). The estimated Japanese importation of coal, mainly from Australia, will be 46.93 million tons in 2030 and 50.84 million tons in 2060 (Figure 3).

The estimate of the additional accumulation of CO_2 from the levels present in 2006, due to the coal-fired emissions into the atmosphere less a small amount of natural fixation, would be 1.307 billion tons to 2030 and 3.154 billion tons to 2060 (Figure 4). In addition to the coal-fired CO_2 by-product, the corresponding amounts for the two other by-products generated annually would be 680,535 and 737,246 tons of FGD gypsum, and 4.693 and 5.084 million tons of fly ash, in 2030 and 2060 respectively (Figure 5).

In 2000, all of the FGD gypsum was reutilized, but approximately 20% of the fly ash (1.7 million tons) was disposed of as landfill. Hence, the disposal of coal-fired by-products, in particular fly ash, is an issue in Japan that needs to be solved whilst its energy remains dependent on imported coal.

COALA Project: A Win-Win Solution

Objectives

An estimated 580,000 hectares of land has already been badly affected by elevated levels of sodium and 5 more million hectares of land will be expected to be seriously affected within the next 20 years. Additionally, fifty million hectares (50% of agricultural land) has a surface pH ≤ 5.5 (Chartres, *et al.*, 1990), which is below the optimum pH for extremely acid-sensitive agricultural plants.

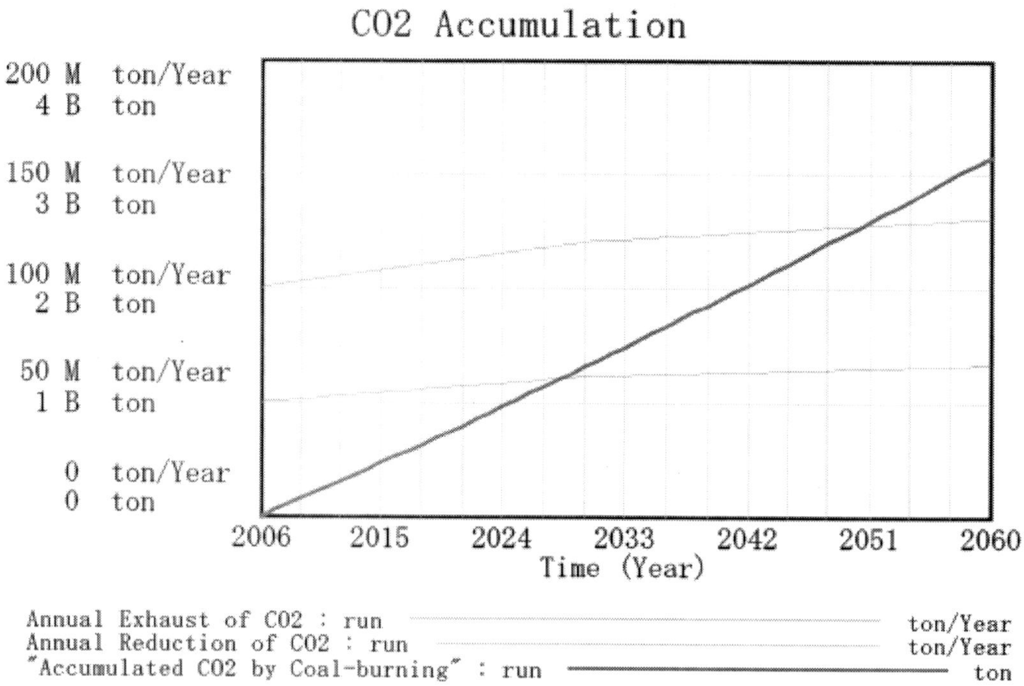

Figure 4 *The estimated additional accumulated carbon dioxide calculated as the difference between emissions ("exhaust") from coal burning and fixation ("reduction") by forest fixation.*

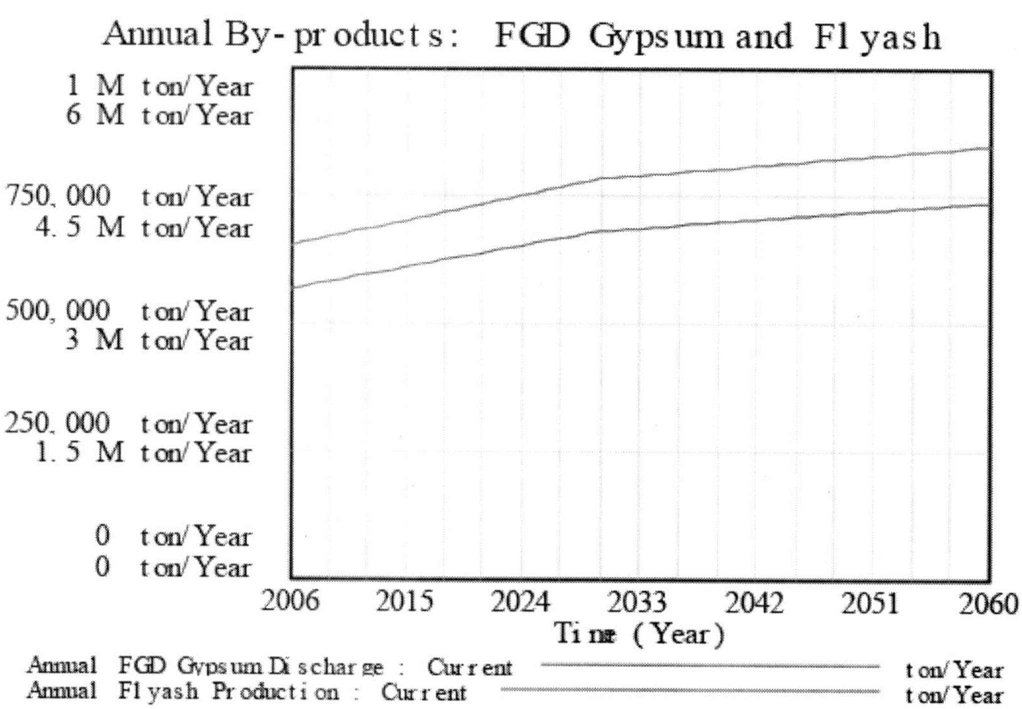

Figure 5 *The estimated production of coal-fired by-products FGD gypsum (0-1 M ton/year scale) and fly ash (0-6 M ton/year scale)*

In the COALA project, two of the by-products from coal-fired power generation have been assessed for their potential to amend sodic (Lu & Nitta, 2000) and acid soils (Spark & Swift, 2006). The implementation of this project has a potential benefit to Australia and Japan as trade partners. In Japan, the shift of fuel from coal to natural gas has been discussed as one of the options to reduce greenhouse gases, but it would require early retirement of existing coal-fired power stations, a very expensive option. Instead, if Japan could gain sufficient credits in carbon dioxide emission reduction, from the implementation of the concepts outlined in the COALA project to fully offset the emission differences between coal-fired and natural gas-fired power plants, there would be no greenhouse benefit in the switching of fuel. In addition Japan could gain extra time to attain a new balance of energy resources between coal, natural gas and nuclear power.

On the other hand, as Australia is a major supplier of some 60% of steam coal used in Japan, the implementation of this project could secure a major export market for Australia into the future. There would also be benefits to the agricultural and forestry sectors in Australia, obtained from the reclamation of marginal or unusable land. In addition, both countries would gain global environmental benefits from the increased carbon sink.

Soil Reclamation Experiments

The first stage of the COALA project consists of 2 sub-projects: the reclamation of sodic soils using FGD Gypsum, and the reclamation of acidic soils using fly ash derived fertilizers.

Sodic Soils sub-Project

This sub-project, detailed in Wearing, et al. (2003), was set up as an international collaboration between two Japanese companies, HEPCO (Hokuriku Electric Company) and CRIEPI (Central Research Institute of Electric Power Industry) and the University of Queensland (UQ) in Australia. The field trial was located on a sodic salt pan (Babcock block, Darbalara farm, UQ). Approximately 1,000 Australian native trees were planted in the trial, consisting of Casuarina glauca (Swamp Sheoak) planted in November 2000 and Eucalyptus moluccana (Gray box) and Eucalyptus camaldulensis x grandis (Saltgrow) planted in March 2001. The sodic soil was successfully reclaimed as demonstrated by the health and growth of the trees by 2004 (Figure 6).

This field trial demonstrated that FGD gypsum could be used to amend degraded saline-sodic soils in Australia enabling the use of the land for forestation (Lu & Nitta, 2000)

Acid Soils sub-Project

This sub-project, detailed in Spark and Swift (2006), concerned the potential of using fly ash derived fertilizers to reclaim acidic soils in a research collaboration between CRIEPI and UQ. All soils exhibited enhanced levels of nutrients and enhanced plant growth of the wheat and corn (Figure 7) with the podsol showing the greatest improvement, while the ferrosol showed the least improvement.

Figure 6 *Aerial photos of the field site used for the COALA sub-project using FGD gypsum on sodic soils at Darbalara farm, University of Queensland, Australia (left 2001, right March 2004)*

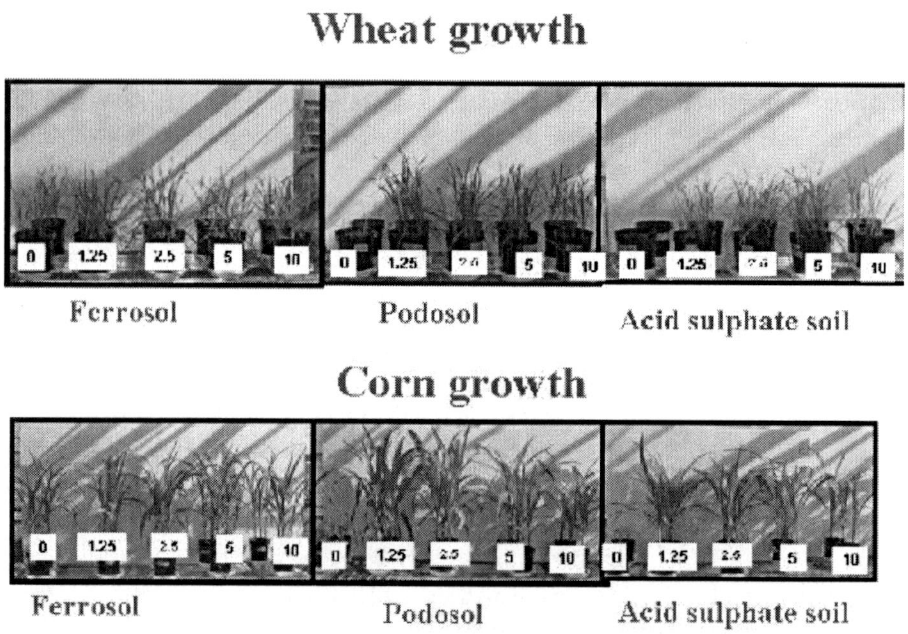

Figure 7 *The growth response of plants (8 weeks old) as a result of the incorporation of fly ash fertilizers into three types of acid soils at the rate of 0-10% w/w.*

Land Rehabilitation in Australia

The successful outcomes from both the sodic soil and acid soil sub-projects demonstrate that the FGD gypsum and fly ash fertilizers have the potential to reclaim poor quality land. Data based on the results of the two sub-projects has been used to build a system dynamics model of the COALA project to assess its economic feasibility when the COALA project is implemented. In the model the starting date is 2006, after which 1,000 hectare of sodic land is annually purchased at A$2,500 per hectare and reclaimed for the duration of 25 years. The application rate of 5 tons of FGD gypsum is used to reclaim one hectare of purchased sodic soils. Accordingly, 25,000 hectare of sodic lands in total will be reclaimed in 2030 for afforestation.

At the same starting date in 2006, 1,000 hectare of acidic land is annually purchased at A$ 2,500 per hectare and reclaimed for the duration of 25 years. One ton of fly ash is used to produce 1.1 tons of fly ash fertiliser in Japan, and 20 tons of fly ash fertilizer needs to be applied to reclaim one hectare of acid land. Accordingly, 25,000 hectare of sodic land in total will be reclaimed in total in 2030 for afforestation. Figure 8 illustrates the structure of land reclamation processes of both sodic and acid soils.

Sustainable Afforestation

Rotation of Forests

The afforestation data used to assess the model was 1,000 trees per hectare on the reclaimed land, classified into three groups according to their growth stages: seedlings (1-5 yrs), young trees (6-15 yrs) and matured trees (16-25 yrs). The reduction rate of trees (due to dying and pruning) was assumed to be 3, 2 and 0.5 % annually for the seedlings, young trees and mature trees, respectively.

Furthermore, trees that die or get pruned are to be replanted annually so that the total number of forest trees remains constant. Figure 9 illustrates the growth structure of afforestation on sodic land, with its rotation period of 25 years. Afforestation of acid land is similarly structured in the model. Figure 10 shows the annual figures for the number of seedlings, young trees and mature trees, and the number of mature trees logged.

Figure 11 illustrates the number of trees in stock at three stages of growth on the reclaimed sodic land of 25,000 hectare in terms of the numbers of seedlings, young trees and matured trees. That data illustrates that the total number of trees on the reclaimed sodic land will be stable at 25 million trees from the year 2031, and so a completely sustainable forest will be attained after 25 years of afforestation.

Carbon Credits

The above information can be used to calculate the number of tons of carbon absorbed annually from the forests on the reclaimed land. An additional assumption used in this calculation is that a seedling can absorb 0.0065 tons of carbon per year, while young and matured trees can absorb 0.0061 and 0.0054 tons of carbon, respectively. On the basis of this data, the total amount of carbon absorbed by the forest is about 300,000 tons per year after the year 2030 (Figure

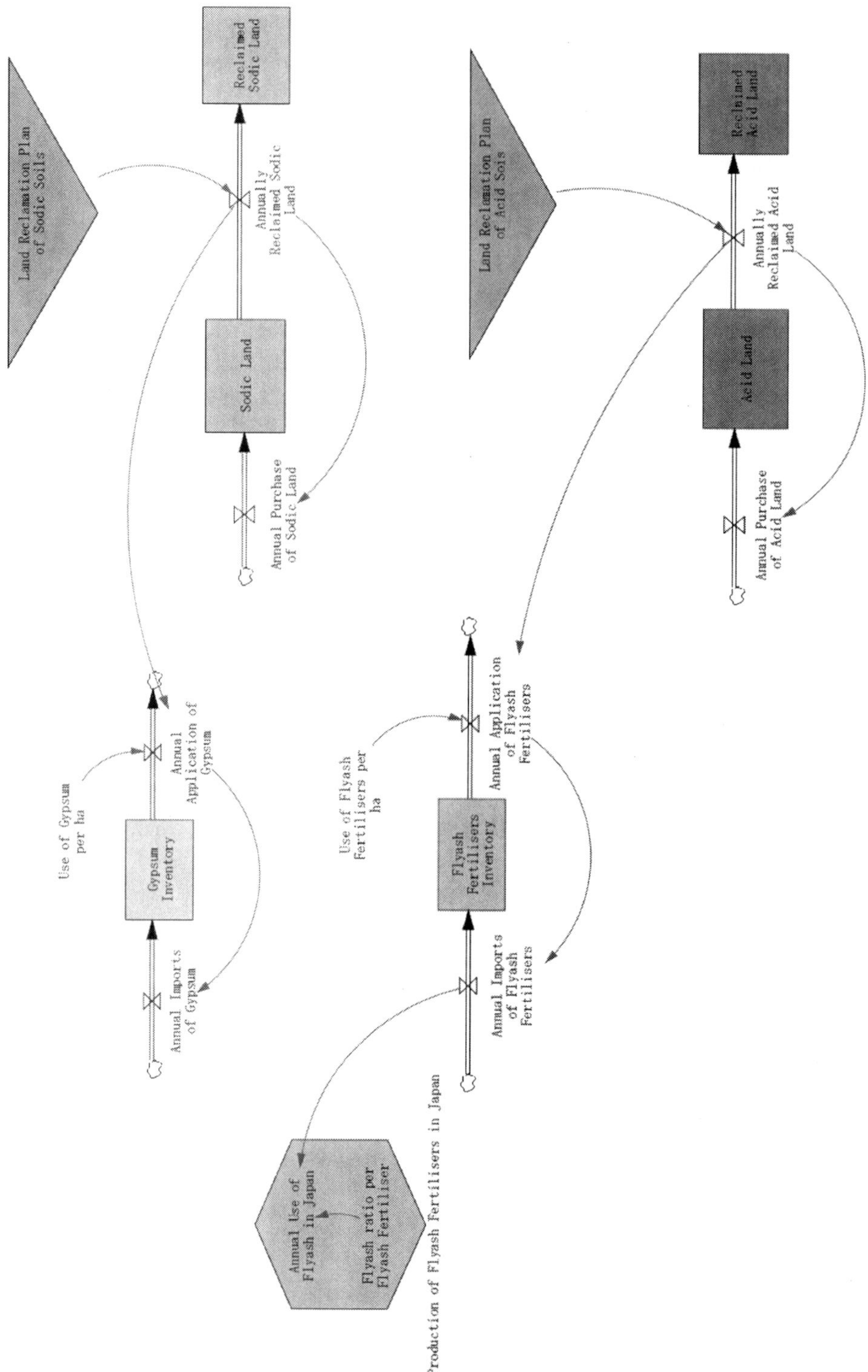

Figure 8 *Land Reclamation of Sodic and Acid Soils*

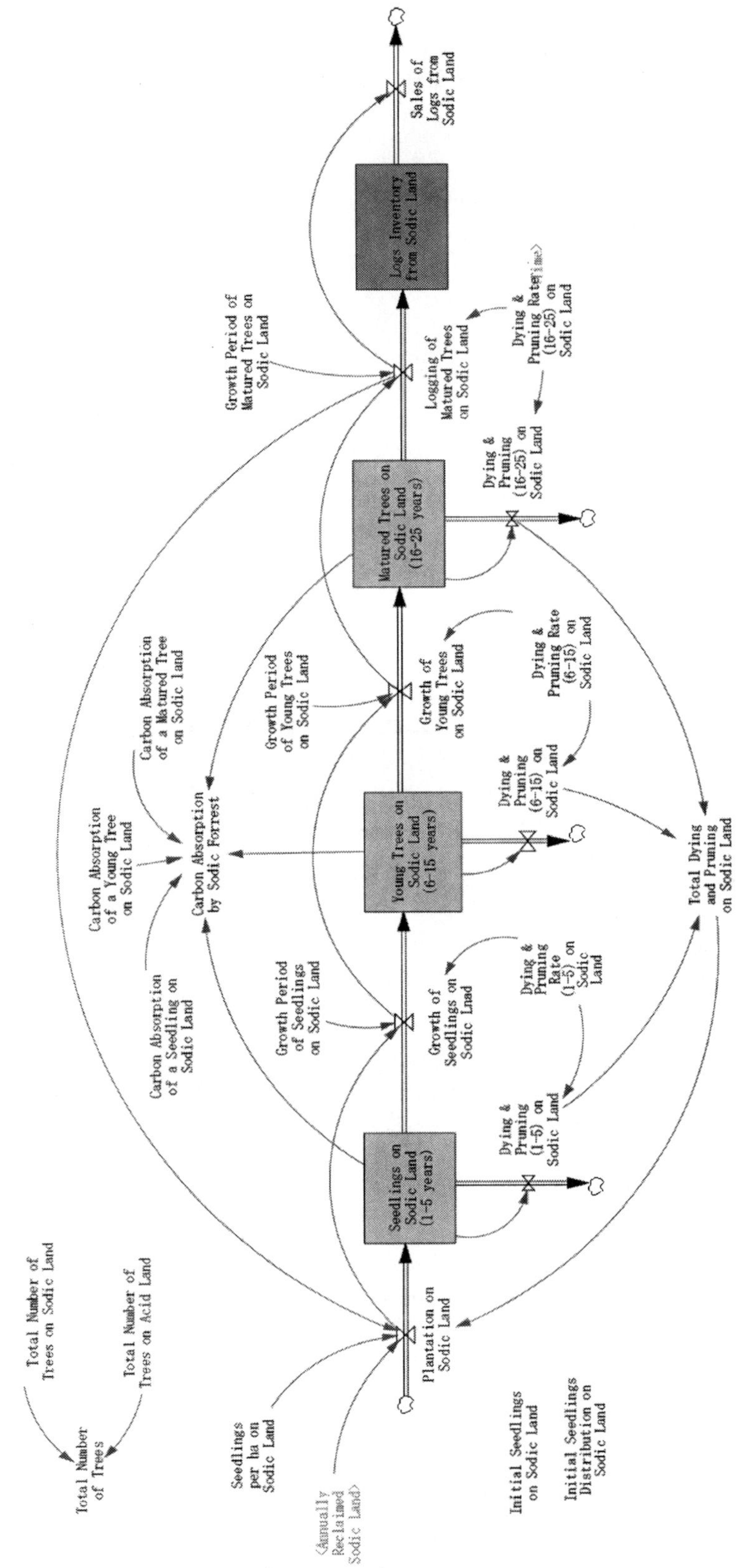

Figure 9 *Afforestation of Sodic Land*

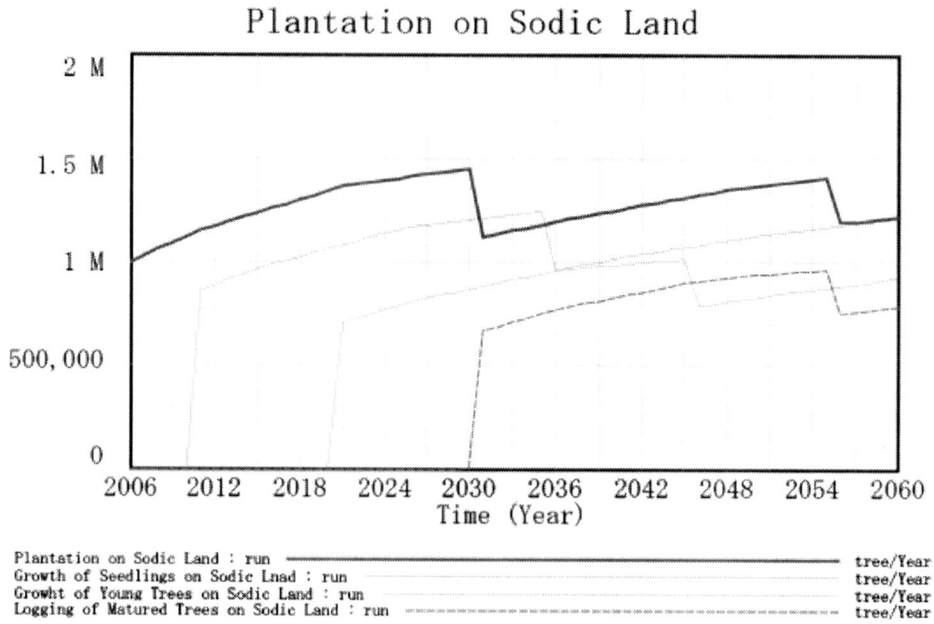

Figure 10 *The total number of trees for a plantation on sodic land: seedlings (blue line), young trees (red line) and mature trees (green line), and the annual number of mature trees logged (dotted purple line).*

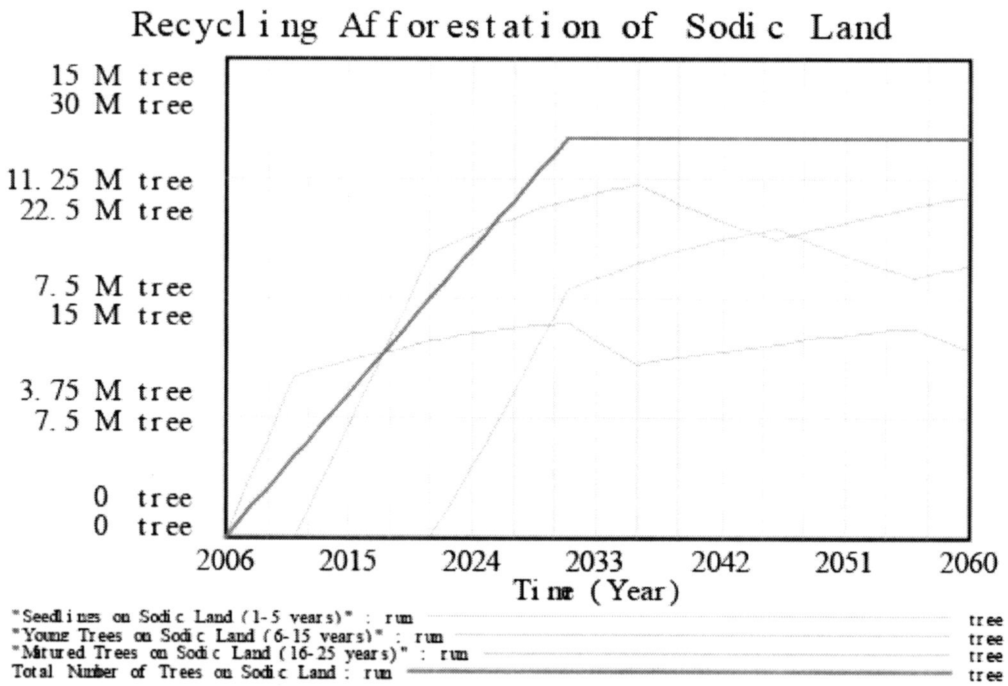

Figure 11 *The number of trees in stock on the reclaimed sodic land in terms of the three stages of growth (0-15 M trees scale) (seedlings (blue line), young (red line) and mature (green line) trees), and of the total number of trees (0-30 M trees scale) (grey line).*

12). This amount of carbon constitutes slightly less than 1 % of the Japanese annual carbon emissions resulting from coal-burning (Figure 12).

An Economic Feasibility Analysis

An economic feasibility analysis has been carried out to determine if the COALA project could be sustainable and profitable, if jointly implemented by Australia and Japan. The analytical method employed in this analysis is based on a principle of accounting system dynamics developed by Yamaguchi (2003).

Plantation Costs

The plantation unit costs of the project, as shown in Table 2, arise due to (1) the cost of producing fly ash fertilizers in Japan, (2) the transportation costs of FGD gypsum and fertilizers from Japan to Australia, (3) the land establishment and planting costs, (4) the plantation maintenance costs, and (5) the logging and shipping costs of trees.

The plantation costs are not recovered until the logged trees are sold. Therefore, until that sales revenue is realized these costs are treated as an afforestation investment and accumulated into forest assets in the balance sheet (Figure 13). When the logs are sold the plantation costs are subtracted from the forest assets as cost of goods sold.

Revenue

The sales revenue in the COALA project consists of three sources; the fly ash allowance, the sale of carbon credits and the sale of logs. In Japan an allowance of A$62 per ton can be expected to be paid for the disposal of fly ash by electric companies, which becomes project revenue. Although the price of carbon is hard to predict, it is assumed to be A$18 per ton. The price to be paid for the logs in 2030 and later is assumed to be A$60 per cubic meters. The volume of a tree is, on average, 3 cubic meters.

In addition to sales revenue, non-operational revenues which could be expected include the appreciation of reclaimed land due to the improvement of land quality, and the interest arising from cash holdings. Figure 14 illustrates the income statement of the project. Income taxes are not considered in the model, due to the lack of income tax data in Australia, but could be readily incorporated into a future revised model.

The relative amount of income from the sources of revenue is illustrated in Figure 15, with that arising from the fly ash allowance, sale of carbon credits and appreciation of reclaimed land being significantly less than that arising from the sales of logs and interest receipts. The amount of carbon absorbed by the growing trees, along with the revenue from carbon credits, increases continually until the number of trees in the forest is constant, in 2031. After that time the income from carbon credits will stabilize at A$5.3 million per year. In contrast, the sales revenue from logs increases sharply to A$240 million in 2031 and continues increasing to be A$346.7 million by 2055, significantly more than that gained for carbon credits.

Fertiliser and Transportation	
Fly ash fertiliser production (per ton)	A$25.00
Surface transportation (per ton)	A$100.00
Domestic transportation (per ton)	A$45.00
Establishment and Planting	
Fertilizing cost (her ha)	A$10.00
Seedling price (per tree)	A$1.00
Labor cost per seedling	A$2.485
Plantation Maintenance	
Maintenance (per ha)	A$1,000.00
Logging and shipping	
Logging (per tree)	A$36.00

Table 2 *Estimated plantation unit costs for the COALA project (investment)*

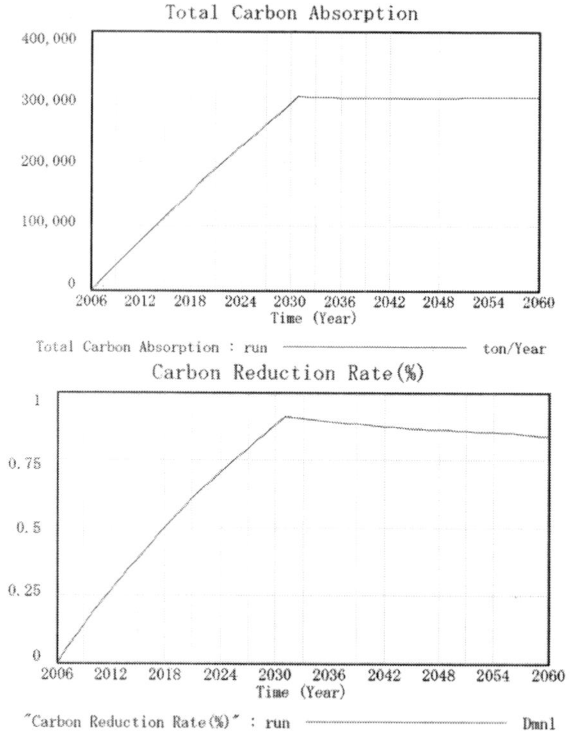

Figure 12 *The total carbon absorption (ton/year) by the forest in the COALA project (top) and the percentage decrease in Japanese emissions due to the carbon absorption by these trees (bottom).*

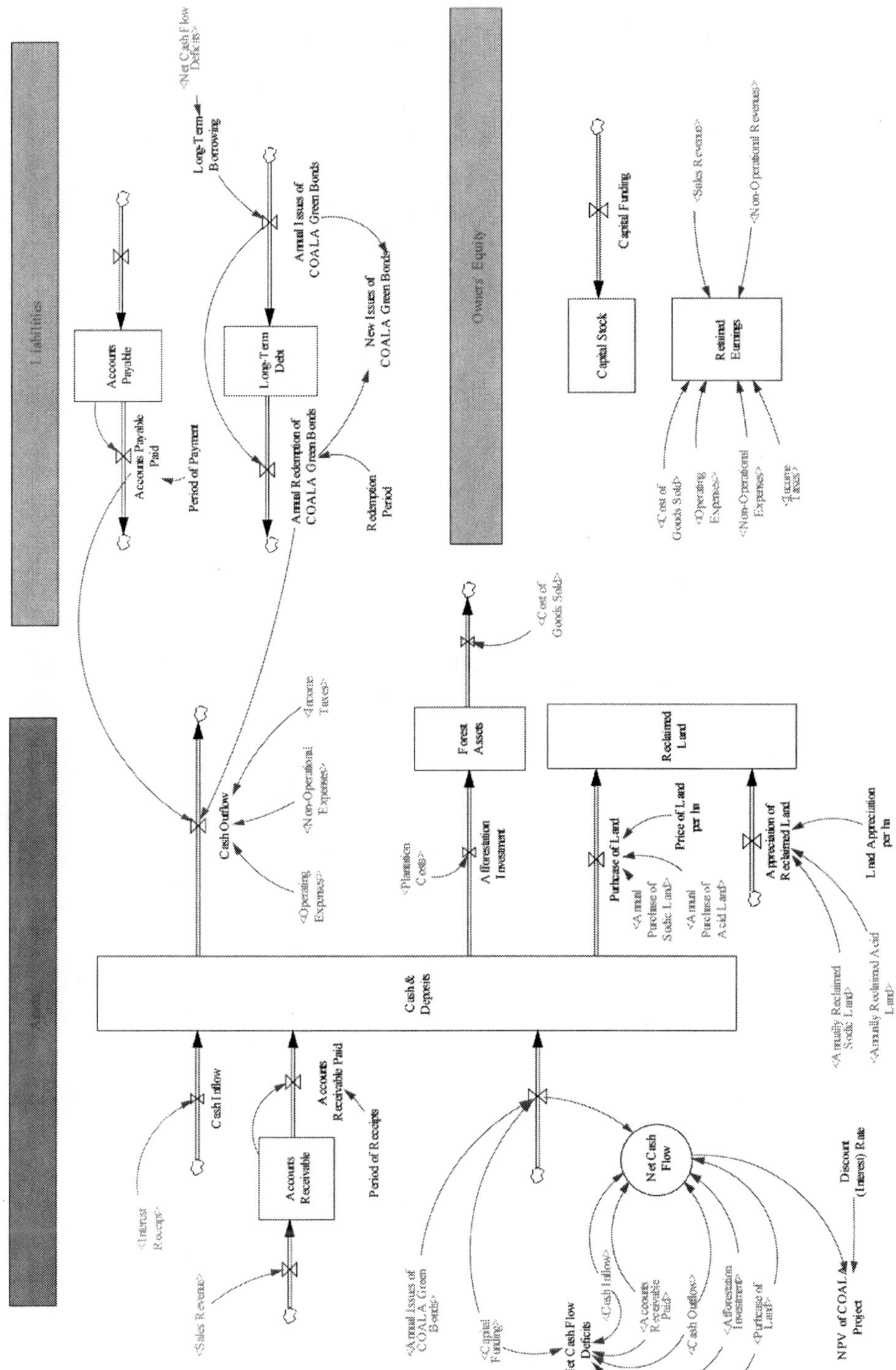

Figure 13 *The balance sheet for the COALA project.*

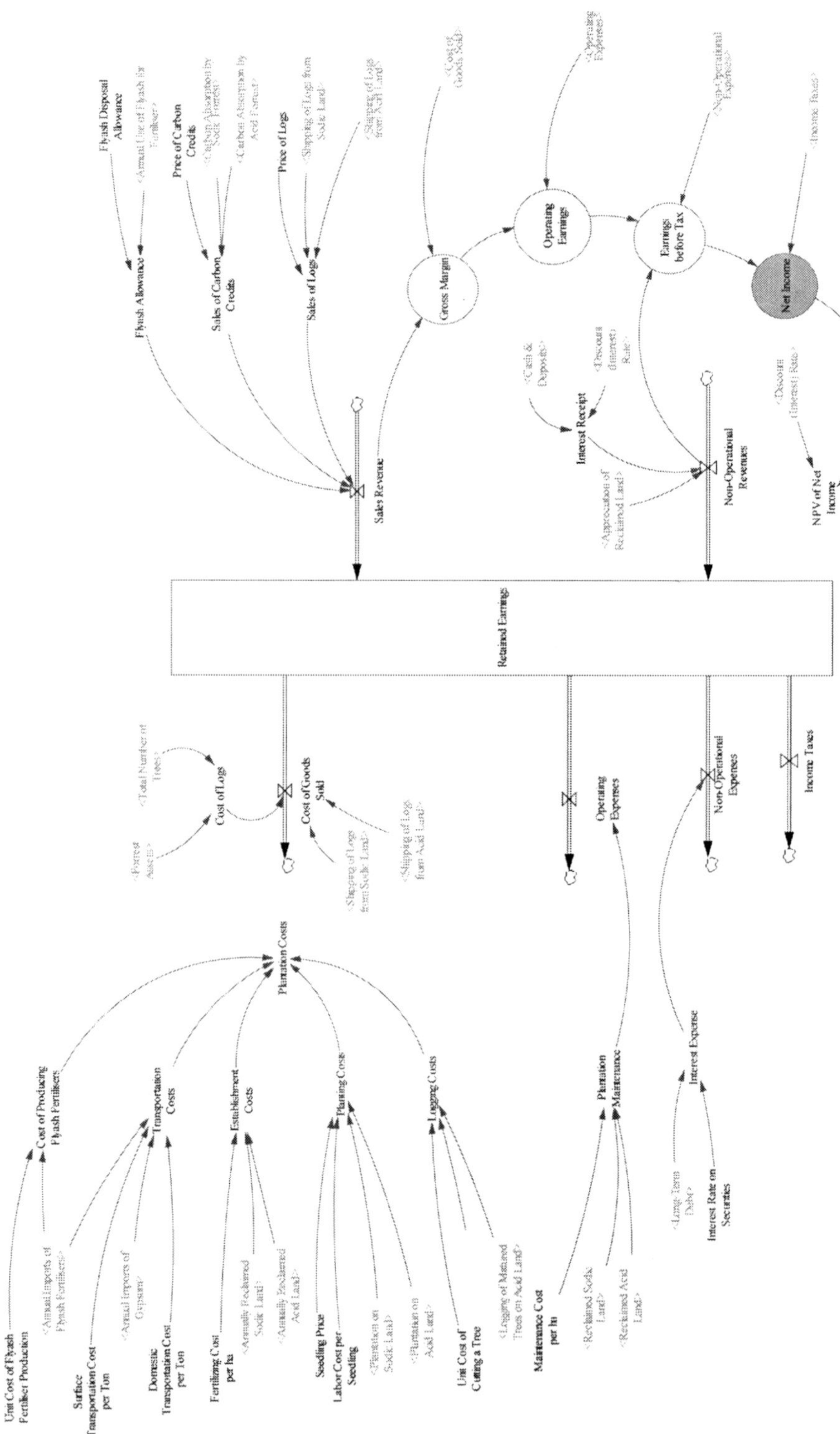

Figure 14 *The income statement for the COALA project.*

As illustrated in Figure 16, the sales revenue is not enough to cover the operating expenses of the plantation maintenance, and so that net income from the project is negative until 2030, even though cost of goods sold is not subtracted from the net income until logs are sold in 2030.

However, a more serious problem for the implementation of the project is the lack of cash flow (Figure 16) until 2031. As there are continual costs arising within the project, it is essential that a constant flow of cash is invested into the project until 2031 by which time the matured forest is sustainable.

COALA Green Bonds

To secure the investment in afforestation for 25 years it is proposed that the net cash deficits of the project are financed by issuing project bonds, called "COALA green bonds", which would have a redemption period of 10 years. These green bonds could be purchased by socially responsible investors or ecologically conscious investors. However, it would be preferred that the green bonds were also an attractive investment in the competitive financial markets.

To be competitive against corporate long-term bonds and government long-term securities in the Japanese financial markets the COALA green bonds would be offered at the interest rate of 3% as the current yield of Japanese government bonds (10 years) is 1.656%. Figure 17 illustrates how green bonds of 3% yield are planned to be issued and redeemed.

The bond issues will end in the year 2031 with the amount of A$226.47 million, followed by some adjustment issues between 2036 through 2041. The bond redemptions start in 2016 with the amount of A$16.11 million, and increases until 2041 at A$226.49 million, followed by some adjustment redemptions between 2046 through 2051. Total long-term debt of the project peaks at A$1.434 billion in 2032, but will be completely cleared by 2051.

The detail relating to the annual issues of the COALA green bonds are shown in Figure 18. The total assets of the project exceed liabilities in 2036, at which time the assets are at A$1.048 billion, but they continue to increase and eventually become significantly more than the liabilities (Figure 19).

The return of assets (ROA) (Figure 20) from the project peaks at 27.85 % in 2031 and remains more than 10% until 2047, after which it is around 5%, which is high relative to that of other industries. For instance, between 2000 and 2005, the ROAs of Toyota (the world largest and best performing automobile company) were calculated by the authors to range from 4.02% to 7.73%.

The results of a simulation based on a 5% of yield are shown in Figure 18 (annual issues of COALA green bonds) and Figure 20 (rates of returns of assets (ROA)). This higher and globally more competitive yield of 5%, returns of assets from the project still results in a profit in the COALA project in the long term. Hence, it is concluded that the green bonds of the project would be attractive in the competitive financial markets. However, the success of the project would be more assured if the green bonds were to be underwritten by the government as a part of their sustainable public policies. Sustainable business partially underwritten by the government would provide a new business model for creating sustainable futures, and the COALA project could initiate this practice.

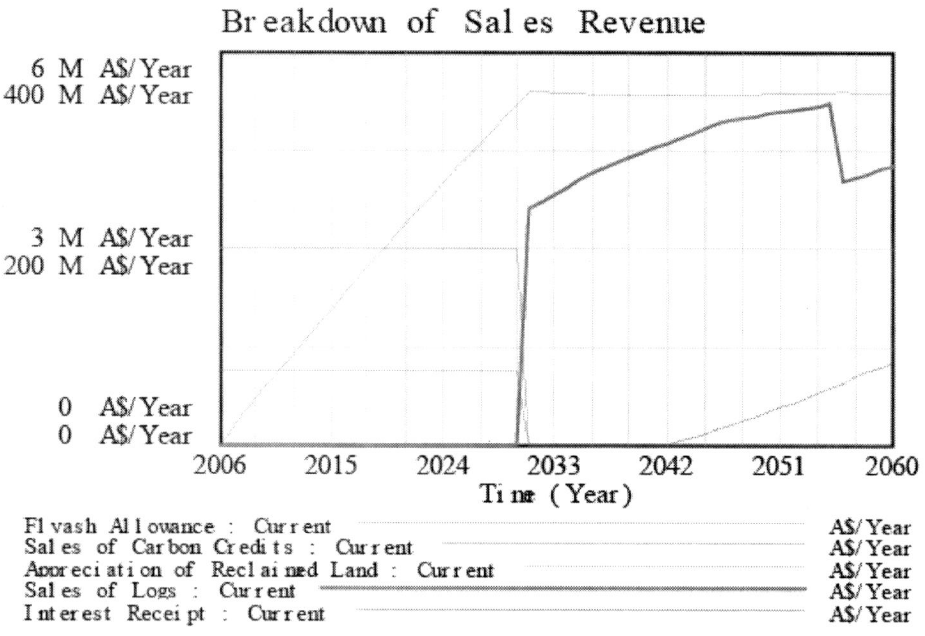

Figure 15 *Breakdown of Sales Revenue for the COAL project. The fly ash allowance (blue line), sales of carbon credits (red line) and appreciation of reclaimed land (green line) are associated with the 0-6 M A$/year scale and the sales of logs (thick gray line) and interest receipt (gray line) are associated with the 0-400 M A$/year scale.*

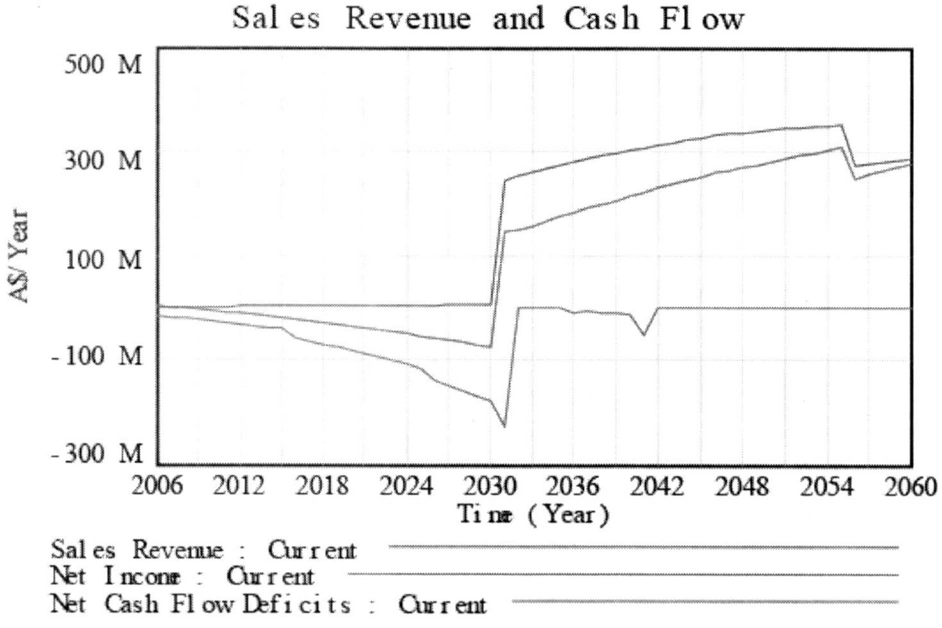

Figure 16 *The sales revenue (blue line), net income (red line) and cash flow (green line) for the COALA project.*

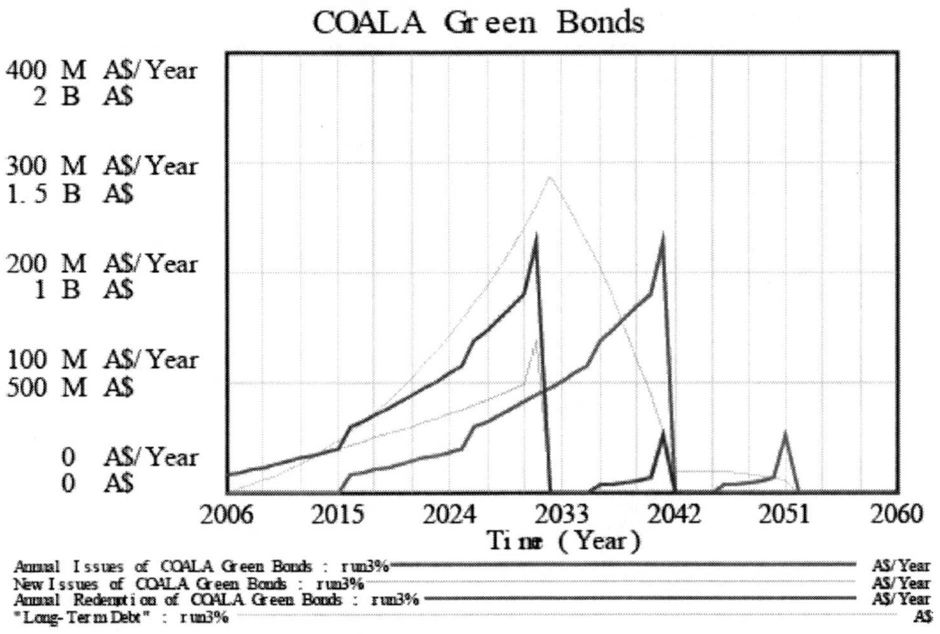

Figure 17 *The proposed schedule for annual issues (blue line) new issues (red line) and redemption (green line) of the COALA Green Bonds and the long term debt of the project (grey line).*

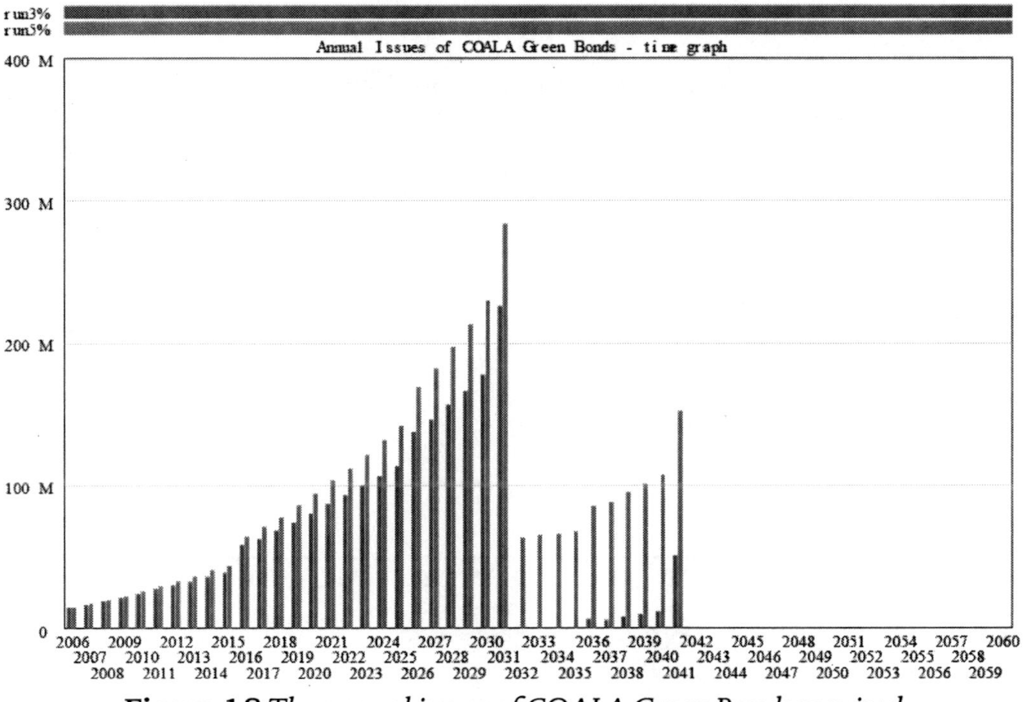

Figure 18 *The annual issues of COALA Green Bonds required for return yields of 3% (blue lines) and 5% (red lines).*

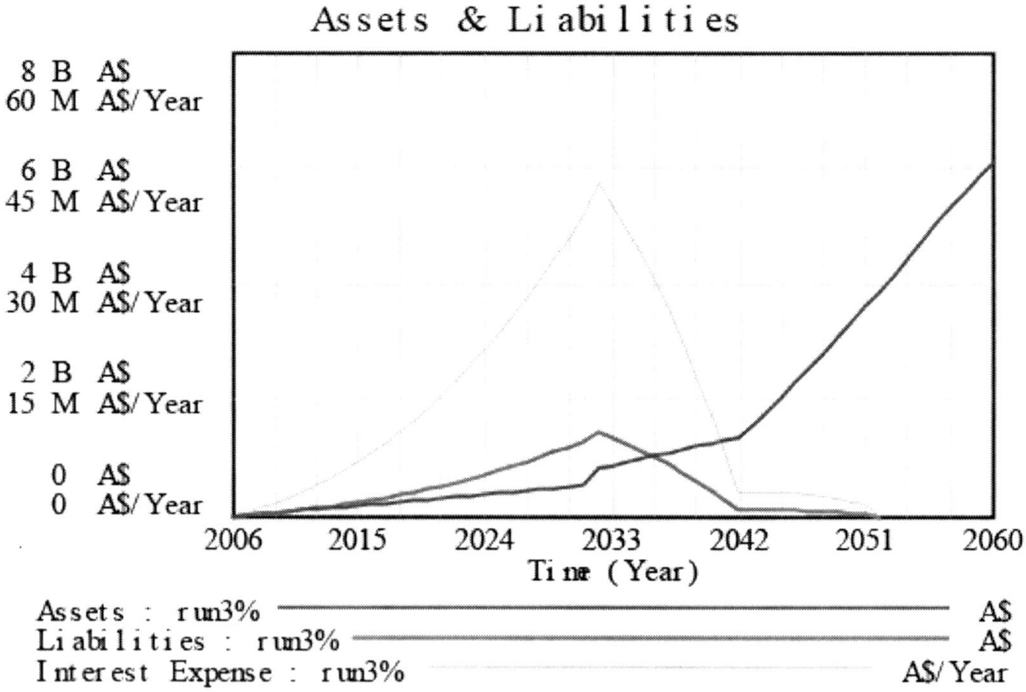

Figure 19 *The assets (red line) and liabilities (blue line) and interest costs (grey line) for the COALA project*

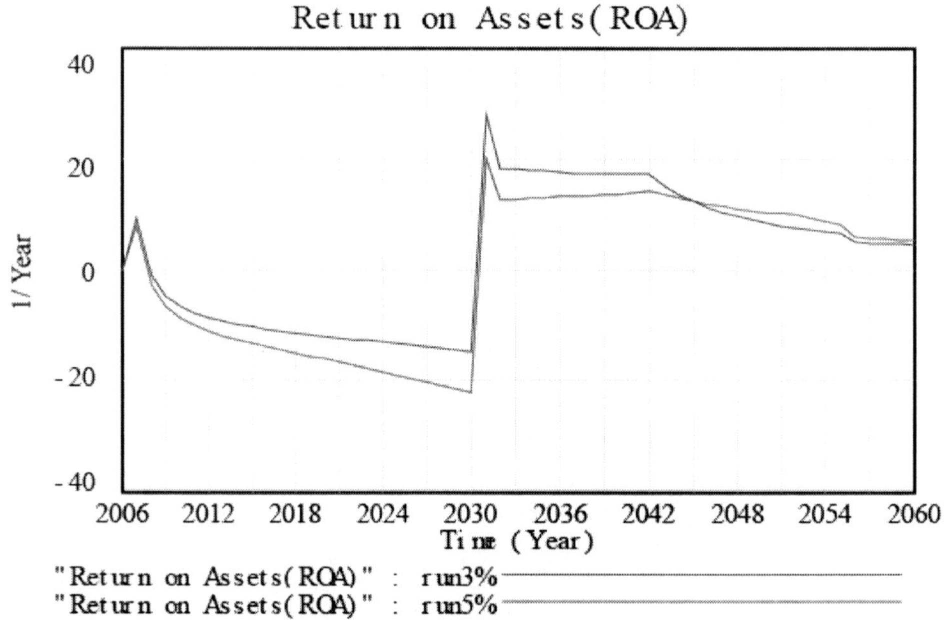

Figure 20 *The annual return on assets (ROA) for the COALA project for return yields of 3% (blue lines) and 5% (red lines).*

Green Management with Simulations

The feasibility analysis need not be confined to the information presented in this simulation. Interested investors could run their own simulations by selecting alternative assumptions on the parameters used in the model such as costs and prices before they make financial commitments to judge its economic feasibility and profitability to themselves.

An open and flexible style of repeated simulations is absolutely necessary for sustainable project management which usually takes a longer time than business-as-usual management. This new management style and strategy is recommended for green management and the system dynamics modeling method effectively meets this need. Model-based management is absolutely necessary for green management to attain public consensus as well as investors' support. It is concluded that this economic feasibility analysis demonstrates that the COALA project as a sustainable business is profitable in the long term. The authors are willing to provide their model to the concerned reader of the COALA project.

References

Chartres, C.J., Helyar, K.R., Fitzpatrick, R.W. and Williams, J. (2000), Land degradation as a result of European settlement of Australia and its influence on soil properties. In *Australia's renewable resources, sustainability and global change.* Gifford RM and Barson MM (eds). BRR Proceedings 14. Bureau of Rural Resources and CSIRO Division of Plant Industry, AGPS, Canberra. pp. 3-34.

Lu, G.Q. and Nitta, Y. (1999). Enhanced Greenhouse Gas Reduction by Application of Japanese FGD Gypsum for Alkali and Sodic Land Reclamation in Australia -a Pre-feasibility Study, COP, Germany

Wearing, C., Rudolph, V. and Lu, M. (2003). Coal Industry Byproduct Applied to Land rehabilitation (COALA) Project Report 1, Brisbane, Queensland, Australia, (12 May 2003)

Spark, K and Swift, R. (2006). Assessment of a Fly ash-Derived Fertiliser using Pot Trials. UniQuest Project No. 12952.02., Report prepared for Central Research Institute of the Electric Power Industry, Japan, by UniQuest Pty Ltd. Consulting and Research, The University of Queensland, Queensland 4072, Australia.

Yamaguchi, K. (2003). Principle of Accounting System Dynamics -- Modeling Corporate Financial Statements "Proceedings of the 21st International Conference of the System Dynamics Society", New York City, USA, July 20-24, 2003.

50. Working with "Living" System Dynamics Models: Emergent Methodological Contributions from Modeling for Critical Infrastructure Protection

Brian W. Bush, Dennis R. Powell
Los Alamos National Laboratory

Stephen H. Conrad, Sharon M. DeLand, Aldo A. Zagonel
Sandia National Laboratories[1]

Ignacio J. Martinez-Moyano, David R. Thompson
Argonne National Laboratory[2]

Acknowledgments

The Department of Homeland Security, Science & Technology Directorate, provided funding for this work.

Critical infrastructures are increasingly automated and interlinked, subject to possibly cascading vulnerabilities due to equipment failure, natural disasters, and terrorist attacks. The government seeks to ensure that disruptions are infrequent, brief, manageable, and cause the least harm possible. The system dynamics (SD) approach is particularly promising in understanding these complex systems, interactions, and issues. Problems in critical infrastructure protection are being investigated with a collection of SD models developed expressly for these concerns, including agriculture models. This paper discusses the technical and social modeling context that renders the development effort of these models uncommon. It involves a modular approach to modeling, a model reassembling technology, and a social process to manage the development of "living" models. These issues are discussed in light of a practical case of model testing and refinement.

1. Sandia is a multi-program laboratory operated by Sandia Corporation, a Lockheed Martin Company, for the United States Department of Energy's National Nuclear Security Administration under Contract DE-AC04-94AL85000.

2. This manuscript has been created in part by UChicago Argonne, LLC, Operator of Argonne National Laboratory ("Argonne"). Argonne, a U.S. Department of Energy Office of Science laboratory, is operated under Contract No. DE-AC02-06CH11357. The U.S. Government retains for itself, and others acting on its behalf, a paid-up non-exclusive, irrevocable worldwide license in said article to reproduce, prepare derivative works, distribute copies to the public, and perform publicly and display publicly, by or on behalf of the Government.

Introduction

This work is part of a larger effort to use system dynamics (SD) modeling to study critical infrastructures and their interdependencies in order to identify vulnerabilities and mitigate disruptions caused by equipment failure, human error, natural disasters, diseases, and terrorist attacks. The technical and social modeling context includes a modular approach to building and maintaining the models. Modules can be developed independently by different modelers at different sites. A technology specially developed for this work quickly assembles the modules, creating an executable composite model. Moreover, this ongoing, multi-modeler, multiproblem modular approach to working with "living" models calls for special considerations regarding the social processes for model development and application.

Critical infrastructure protection (CIP)

"Critical Infrastructure" encompasses systems and assets so vital that their incapacity or destruction would negatively impact national security, the economy, or public health and safety (USA PATRIOT, 2001). Critical infrastructures are considered potential terrorist targets due to the potential harm that can be done. Thus, the Homeland Security Act (HSA, 2002) formed the Department of Homeland Security (DHS) to evaluate vulnerabilities and ensure protection of high-risk elements of critical infrastructures, including agriculture.

A key research center involved in this effort is the National Infrastructure Simulation and Analysis Center (NISAC). NISAC is a repository for several large-scale, high-resolution simulation systems. Another related research effort is the Critical Infrastructure Protection Decision Support System (CIPDSS). CIPDSS has the charter to model all critical infrastructures, key asset categories, and infrastructure interdependencies. Additionally, CIPDSS was created to provide fast, order-of-magnitude assessments of potential impacts of disruptions (Bush, *et al.*, 2005).

Both NISAC and CIPDSS use System Dynamics as one of several modeling capabilities (see Ellison, *et al.*, 2007; Kelic, *et al.*, 2007). Additionally, CIPDSS has been used to analyze the introduction of infectious diseases (Powell, *et al.*, 2005), the loss of multiple telecommunications assets (LeClaire & O'Reilly, 2005), and the accidental release of toxic industrial chemicals (Samsa, *et al.*, 2007).

With respect to the agriculture infrastructure, HSPD-9 (2004) mandates sector vulnerability assessments to defend the agriculture and food systems against terrorist attacks, major disasters, and other emergencies. CIPDSS Project analyses include responses to disruptions of considerable magnitude in the beef and dairy economies (Conrad, 2004), and impacts of the introduction of windborne soybean rust in the United States following Hurricane Katrina (Soybean Rust Reports, 2005). But in assessing the sustainability of this research program, particularly in using the SD approach, it is important to consider the special nature of the modeling context involved in these efforts.

Technical and social modeling context

To our knowledge, modeling practice seldom resembles the CIP efforts just discussed. Examples that do include the Limits to Growth studies (Meadows, *et al.*, 1972), Pugh-Roberts Associates' experience in business strategy and project dynamics (e.g., Lyneis, 1980; Stephens, *et al.*, 2005), and Forrester's (1989) National Model. All draw upon "living" models, meaning models that can be reused, whether refined to revisit the same issues with more confidence, or adapted to address new questions. They tend to be large modeling projects involving multiple modelers that must be effectively coordinated, properly documented, systematically tested, and objectively evaluated for validity. Ideally, they would be supported by technology that facilitates and enables reuse, refinements, and linkages between models. They must use a social process for modeling that is conducive to creating an efficient multi-modeler development environment. The CIPDSS development effort additionally faced a geographically dispersed task force with some degree of turnover. Furthermore, submodels developed under CIPDSS focus on one infrastructure at a time, and scenario analyses involve multiple interacting infrastructures.

If modular modeling were supported, what form should the models and documentation take to facilitate understanding, refinements, and the reuse of existing models? If work in large projects under severe time constraints is required, how can model pieces readily be repeatedly assembled into a whole model, and then taken apart again? The experience, strengths, and weaknesses of modelers will vary. However, model building, testing, and documentation should be consistent and clear across model subsystems and over the lifespan of the modeling effort(s), requiring a large degree of coordination and some uniformity in practice.

Drawing upon their experience in software development, Thompson and Bush (2005) proposed the technological basis of modular program development for system dynamics modeling. The technology uses concepts such as scope definition, modularity, encapsulation, and modeling standards to create protocols that would support "living" models, promote reuse of formulations, and enable distributed development of models. The primary problem to be solved was that of variable identification and use in different models. To address this problem, we proposed and adopted a set of shared modeling conventions and standards that would support merging a set of files into a single file that could subsequently be simulated.

Here we discuss the tools and processes that we developed to enable solutions to the problems confronted in our CIP efforts. Our experience is organized around four main points:

1. A standards-based modular approach to modeling and documenting;
2. A model assembling technology for merging modules;
3. A formal process to test and evaluate the models and accumulate confidence;
4. A social process to support modular development.

The agriculture infrastructure

Background

We built an agriculture model to explore the propagating effects of large-scale disruptive events (Conrad, 2004). The initial version of the model contained three interconnected sectors — beef, dairy, and corn. These three commodities are tightly coupled; almost 60 percent of the corn production is used as animal feed. Together, they account for nearly 40 percent of the U.S. agricultural economy (see Figure 1).

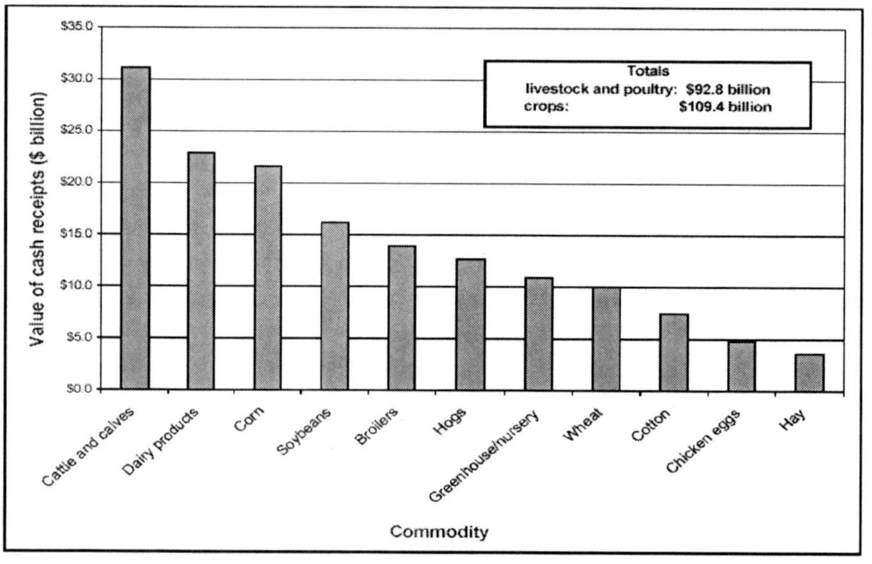

Source: *Agriculture Fact Book 1998*, U.S. Department of Agriculture, Office of Communications, November 1998, pp. 43-44.

Figure 1 *Values of the top 10 agricultural commodities in the U.S., 1996*

This work built upon Meadow's "hogs" model, addressing commodity production cycles. The basic feedback structure, including interactions between the three commodities is shown in Figure 2.

The prices of these commodities form the center of a pair of negative feedback loops that eliminate imbalances between demand and supply, promoting efficient allocation of resources. However, oscillations result from (1) producer delays in capacity acquisition and bounded decision making, and (2) very slow market demand and supply reactions to price. Corn is produced for animal feed, and the price of feed influences decisions regarding beef and dairy production rates, which in turn alter the corn consumption rate and influence corn prices.

This model was used in December 2003 to rapidly examine the consequences of the bovine spongiform encephalopathy (BSE) outbreak in Washington State, and to examine two policies aimed at addressing the effects of a foot-and-mouth disease (FMD) threat scenario. The simulations of short term decrease in demand for beef due to the BSE outbreak showed long-term reper-

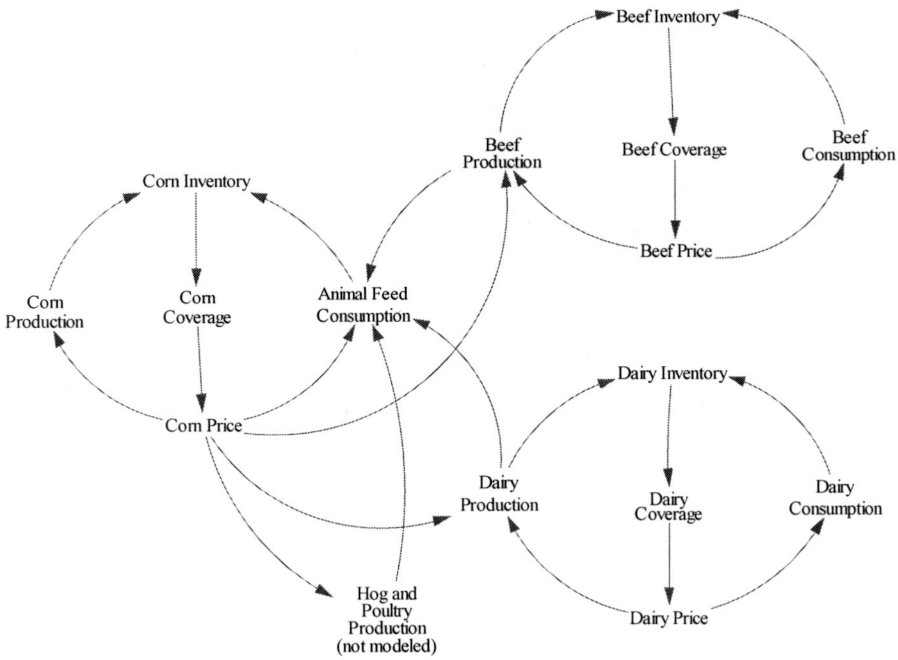

Figure 2 *Basic feedback structure of the three-commodity model*

cussions in the beef and corn markets. In the case of the less dangerous but more contagious FMD disease, the simulations showed that exempting cow-and-calf operations from the existing depopulation policy would help stabilize beef prices, beef sales, and beef cattle populations, without significantly increasing the risk of contagion (Conrad, 2004).[3]

Model testing and evaluation

The initial model was examined extensively. The tests performed were conducted by both external and internal reviewers (Rasmussen & Becker, 2004; Agriculture Model Report, 2004) and followed SD guidelines for confidence building and model refinement (Forrester & Senge, 1980; Sterman, 2000).

The original beef production module

The critical delays in capacity acquisition result primarily from the aging processes inherent in each of the commodities. For corn, this process involves planting, harvesting, storing, selling, and distributing. Also, corn is a seasonal crop, planted in the spring and harvested in the fall, with year-long dependencies upon boundedly rational decisions considering multiple factors such as expected demand, carrying inventory, subsidies and price, resulting in an aggregate desired harvest, which is then subject to weather conditions and crop diseases. Similarly, there are aging processes in the production of beef and milk associated with breeding and growing the cattle. Aging chains are used to cap-

3. Cow-and-calf operations tend to be relatively isolated and far less prone to contagion than other operations further along the aging chain, which are far more exposed to unfamiliar animals in transportation, trading farms, feedlots, and packing plants.

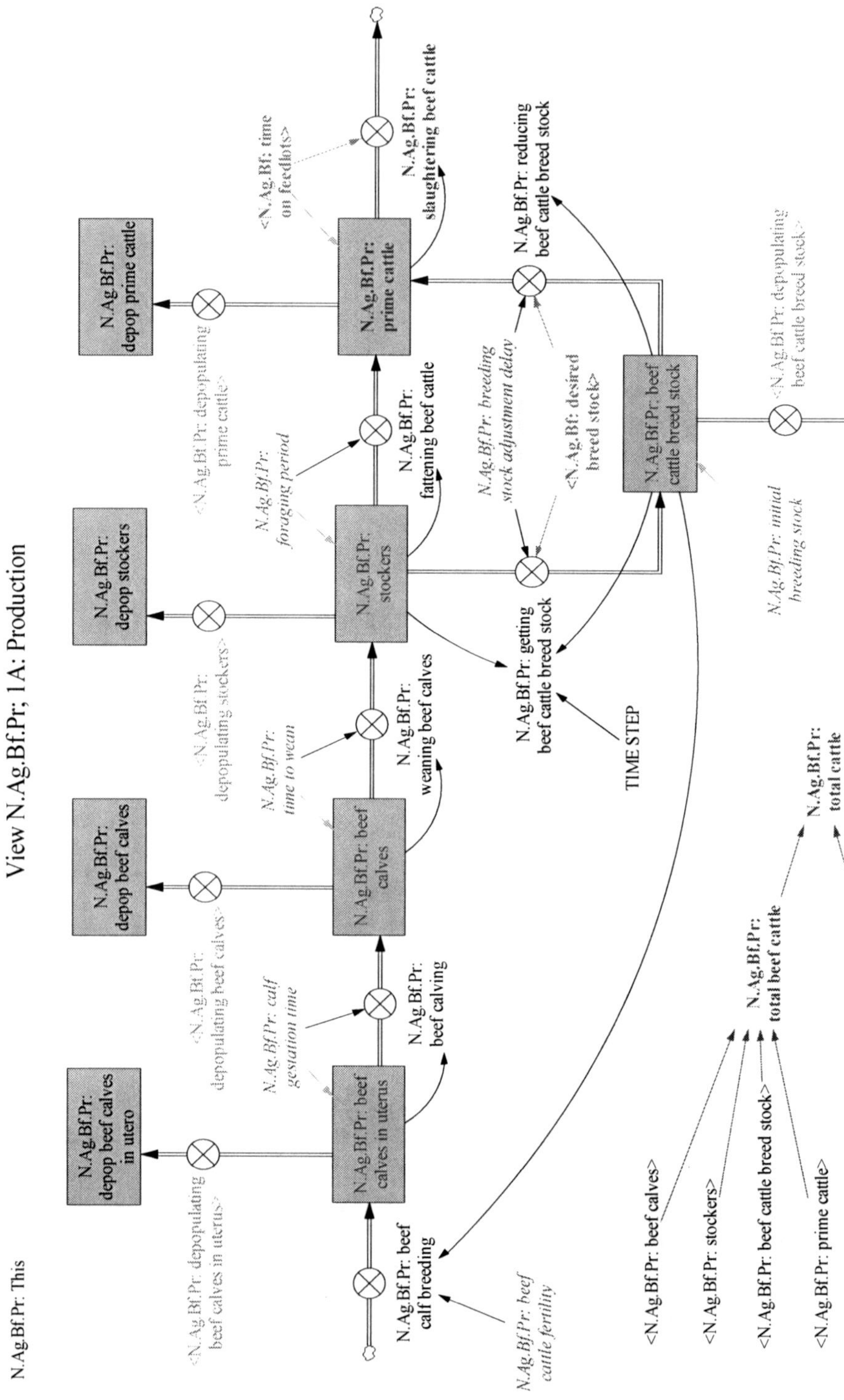

Figure 3 *The aging chain of the beef sector in the original beef production module*

ture the demographic structure of a population, its changes through time, and its response to disruptive events. The original beef production module used the aging chain represented in Figure 3 (see also supplemental file "N-Ag-Bf-Pr-Conrad.mdl").[4]

Related and ongoing applications

The production module for the beef commodity was revised with marginal additional effort and is captured in file "N-Ag-Bf-Pr.mdl." Both the original and the revised modules are operational and can be used interchangeably with the rest of the agriculture model (supplemental file "N-Ag without beef production. mdl").

Expanding and refining the original modules of this modeling effort can be used to explore a variety of agricultural disruptions such as a sudden change in demand for agricultural products, a food contamination incident, use of commodity crops for energy production, significant crop losses due to disease or drought, loss of exports (such as the United States experienced due to detection of BSE in Washington State), and widespread animal disease (such as bird flu), among many. Preliminary model analysis using a single-disruption scenario has shown promise in helping government agencies formulate improved policies for responding to major disruptive events in agriculture.

Emergent methodological contributions

What we have discussed in the previous section was the effort to test and refine only one sector of the agriculture infrastructure model. The current model has five sectors per commodity: production, inventory, market, willingness to supply, and willingness to demand. The beef aging chain is the stock-and-flow structure of the production sector. A full disclosure of the beef commodity unfolds into six components, one for each sector and one for the commodity as a whole. For three commodities, there are 19 components (six per commodity plus one for the interactions among them); for six there will be at least 37 components.

Agriculture is one of many critical infrastructures. The Congressional Research Service states that the meaning of critical infrastructures in the public policy context has been evolving and is still open to debate (CRS, 2004). Table 1 illustrates how this number has changed from six infrastructures in 1983 to more than 20 today.

Based upon present experience and a conservative assumption that the average infrastructure can be represented with ten sectors, it would take a minimum of 200+ sectors to capture all of the critical infrastructures. Moreover, for different purposes and problems, more than one sector representation may be needed for the same infrastructure component. Consequently, to be efficient, modeling teams must consider guidelines carefully to determine the breadth and depth requirements for SD infrastructure models (Becker, *et al.*, 2004).

4. The reader may ignore, for now, the variable prefixes and color coding used in the diagram. They serve to inform the model assembling process, as will be discussed later in the paper (see also Thompson & Bush, 2005; Powell, *et al.*, 2006).

Critical Infrastructure and Key Assets Over Time

Infrastructure	U.S. Government Reports and Executive Orders							
	CBO (1983)	NCPWI (1988)	E.O. 13010 (1996)	PDD-63 (1998)	E.O. 13228 (2001)	NSHS (2002)	NSPP (2003)	HSPD-7 (2003)
Transportation	X	X	X	X	X	X	X	X
Water supply /waste water treatment	X	X	X	X	X	X	X	X
Education	X							
Public health	X			X		X	X	X
Prisons	X							
Industrial capacity	X							
Waste services		X						
Telecommunications			X	X	X	X	X	X
Energy			X	X	X	X	X	X
Banking and finance			X	X		X	X	X
Emergency services			X	X		X	X	X
Government continuity			X	X		X	X	
Information systems				X	X	X	X	X
Nuclear facilities					X			
Special events					X			
Agriculture/food supply					X	X	X	X
Defense industrial base						X	X	X
Chemical industry						X	X	X
Postal / shipping services						X	X	X
Monuments and icons							X	X
Key industry / tech. sites							X	
Large gathering sites							X	

Table 1 *"Critical Infrastructures" Meaning (CRS, 2004)*

According to the National Infrastructure Protection Plan (NIPP, 2006), properly maintaining useful models, databases, simulations, and other tools will involve long-term support, coordination, and resource commitments. A modular approach to developing, documenting, and testing models seems a reasonable strategy for effective use of resources.

A modular approach to standardized modeling and documentation

Modular approaches to system design and development are well established in software and systems engineering. In system dynamics, from a technical perspective, a modular approach allows the modeler to formulate small, testable modules. Thoughtful delineation of module interfaces allows modules to be "extended" or interchanged to provide an appropriate level of abstraction for different analyses.

We have illustrated what a module would look like and how expansions and refinements can be used. We feel that two other elements are useful to complement this documentation. The first is a one-page summary that captures core information about a given module (illustrated in Appendix 1), which helps summarize the key elements of a module for a modeler working with the larger assembled model. The second is a subsystem diagram to show how this module relates to other modules or models (illustrated in Appendix 2), which is crucial for illuminating the interactions in the larger model.[5]

A model assembling technology for merging modules

In order to use either one of the two modules with other modules and/or models we need a model assembling technology. Ideally, SD modeling environments (e.g., Vensim™) would enable merging without cumbersome cutting and pasting. But since this is not the case, a "Conductor" tool was developed to achieve this result for the CIPDSS Project models. For the tool to work, the models must follow certain standards and conventions. The variables in the model must be linked to their specific modules; the tool performs and checks the links, relying on the standardized variable naming conventions (the prefixes preceding the variable names in the diagrams in Figure 3). The color conventions capture such things as variables that are exchanged between modules. For example, the red/bold "desired breeding stock" variable in Figure 3 is imported from the Willingness to Supply Module, whereas the blue/bold "slaughtering beef cattle" variable is exported to the Inventory Module. There have been several iterations in the development of the Conductor Tool. We demonstrated an earlier version at the 2006 SD Conference (Powell, *et al.*, 2006). A newer version captures and displays the exchange of variables between modules in tabular form, facilitating the construction of subsystem diagrams.

5. Automation technology has been used in supporting documentation of CIPDSS models where tables of variables, variable descriptions, and units were extracted from the model files using relatively simple scripts. Meta data elements required for more extensive automation are discussed in the current model standards document but are not yet implemented. We are currently working on automating the process of creating the one-page summaries directly from the models.

Tests for Assessment of Dynamic Models (Sterman, 2000, Chapter 21)		
√ Boundary adequacy √ Structure assessment √ Dimensional consistency √ Parameter assessment	√ Extreme conditions √ Integration error √ Behavior reproduction ▪ Behavior anomaly	▪ Family member ▪ Surprise behavior √ Sensitivity analysis ▪ System improvement

Table 2 *Tests performed to the Beef Production Module*

Decomposing large problems into interacting modules is a powerful software development paradigm; as applied to SD modeling, we believe it can make a significant contribution, particularly in the context of "living" models. The many benefits of a modular approach to modeling include improved maintainability of formulations and documentation, possibility of asynchronous model progress, and the use of shared protocols that tend to induce best practices and sustain model quality.

Modular testing and evaluation: Accumulating confidence

A related effort is underway to reorganize the tests to build confidence in SD models (Zagonel & Corbet, 2006). The idea is to produce a testing framework that specifies tests targeted to the variety of model purposes (e.g., understanding vs. forecasting) and serve as a guide to documenting model tests and refinements. Currently we document model testing using Sterman's (2000) classification. See Table 2 for an example.

Items unmarked have not been done at all pointing to opportunities or non applicability. More checked items do not imply acceptable levels of confidence in the module(s); however, these serve as a proxy for the accumulation of confidence in the module(s).

A social process to support modular development

An integral element of multimodule development is a social process in which modelers, project leaders, and other stakeholders must communicate on the standards "contract" as well as on module boundaries, testing, documentation, version control, etc. The Conductor tool requires a contract with the modelers in the form of a set of modeling standards that are complete and comprehensive to enable merging; however, the Conductor does not specify the standards — the modelers do. This was a challenging experience for the CIDPSS team. The technical staff at each participating site had to agree on a common set of standards. We began with a core set of standards adopted by all sites initially, then expanded and improved upon the core standards over a two-year period.[6]

6. A common objection was that namespace prefixes were cumbersome to use and interfered with the readability of the model. Several expressed the opinion that modules by their nature tended to "break up" the flow of feedback loops that traversed domains and interfered with the understandability of the whole system. More insidious were the feelings of some that modelers from another site desired to impose (unreasonable) stan-

Another aspect of social process in modular development is the identification of modules, module boundaries, and interfaces. The modularity expressed in the Agricultural model described in this paper is but one form of module partitioning. Other domains in the critical infrastructure models have different module partitions. We believe it would be beneficial to establish a common rationale for module creation, but that has tended to be more consistent at each site rather than among the sites. The general philosophy is to define a domain, such as Agriculture, and then describe the pertinent subdomains, e.g., beef, dairy, corn, soybeans, hogs, broilers, etc. Each subdomain is a module with possible connectivity to other modules. The domain is essentially defined by the performance of the subdomains, although it may include unique information and can be represented as a module that primarily links the subdomain models. Within a module the system is described as a SD model, but where information is required that must be found in another module, this identifies an interface variable for incoming information. This variable is defined to be exactly the variable name in the other module and given a default value, enabling the module to be run in standalone mode to test dynamic behavior. The Conductor, when merging the modules, will connect the local variable to the variable defined in the other module so that dynamic values are available to the module at runtime. The variables in the model that are meant to be used in other modules are specially designated as export variables and are denoted in the diagrams with a specific color. Conductor enforces the defined standards for import and export variables. This gives rise to the social process among the modelers to communicate their "public interface" for the module. A modeler working on a different module can still access non-import/export variables, but the practice is discouraged to promote encapsulation. Clearly, substantial discussion must occur among the model builders to create preliminary interface definitions and subsequently maintain interactions to assure that information needs of other modules are met.

In conclusion

The use of a modular approach to modeling and documentation, coupled with a model assembling technology for merging modules, can help manage the volume and quality of the models developed to investigate problems and threats in critical infrastructure protection. This technology addresses a call for a coordinated effort to build knowledge as analyses based upon SD models accumulate over time. The four novelties discussed in this paper are not trivial to implement and adopt, but they seem to be essential if a long-term consequential research agenda using SD modeling is to be fruitful in the area of critical infrastructure protection. These innovations address a challenging technical and social modeling context. With them, we hope to facilitate the use of existing resources and expedite the refinements and expansions of models

dards but were unwilling to consider or accept standards devised by developers from other sites. The social aspects of just establishing the standards contract requires time and careful reflective discussion and should not be underestimated. We feel that the airing of our modeling styles and differences was mutually beneficial, although at times somewhat painful.

as new problems arise for investigation. We intend to enable modeling work to progress in parallel, both at the subsystem and whole-model levels, aided by tools that bring together, as often as necessary, these two levels of development and analysis. Ideally, both model development and testing can progress and be documented using these innovations in ways that are conducive to an efficiency and quality-driven modeling effort.

References

Agriculture Model Report. December 2004. "Model testing and refinement of the CIPDSS Agriculture Model." Critical Infrastructure Protection Decision Support System Project. Sandia National Laboratories.

Becker N, Bettencourt L, Buehring W, Beyeler W, Brown T, Bush B, Conrad S, Dauelsberg L, DeLand S, Joslyn C, Kaplan P, LeClaire R, Loose V, North M, Powell D, Rasmussen S, Saeger K, Samsa M, Thompson DR, Whitfield R, Witkowski M. 2004. "Guidelines for Determining CIP/DSS Infrastructure Model Depth and Breadth Requirements." Report LA-UR-04-5324. Los Alamos National Laboratory.

Bush BW, Dauelsberg LR, LeClaire RJ, Powell DR, DeLand SM, Sansa ME. 2005. Critical Infrastructure Protection Decision Support System (CIPDSS) Project overview. *Proceedings of the 23rd International Conference of the System Dynamics Society*. Boston (July 17-21). http://www.systemdynamics.org/conferences/2005/proceed/papers/LECLA332.pdf

Conrad SH. 2004. The dynamics of agricultural commodities and their responses to disruptions of considerable magnitude. *Proceedings of the 22nd International Conference of the System Dynamics Society*. Oxford, England (July 23–27). http://www.systemdynamics.org/conferences/2004/SDS_2004/PAPERS/352CONRA.pdf http://www.systemdynamics.org/conferences/2004/SDS_2004/SUP_MAT/ - Supplemental file: 352.mdl

CRS. 2004. "Critical Infrastructure and Key Assets: Definition and identification." Congressional Research Service Report for Congress (RL32631). 16 pp. http://www.fas.org/sgp/crs/RL32631.pdf

Ellison J, Kelic A, Corbet TF. 2007. Is a natural gas strategic reserve for the U.S. necessary? A system dynamics approach. Submitted to the *25th International Conference of the System Dynamics Society*. Boston, USA (July 29–August 2). http://www.systemdynamics.org/conferences/soon.htm

Forrester JW. 1989. The system dynamics national model: macrobehavior from microstructure. In Milling PM, Zahn EOK (Eds.). *Computer-Based Management of Complex Systems: International System Dynamics Conference*. Berlin: Springer-Verlag.

Forrester JW, Senge PM. 1980. Tests for building confidence in system dynamics models. In Legasto Jr. AA, Forrester JW, Lyneis JM (Eds.). *System Dynamics. TIMS Studies in the Management Sciences* 14. New York: North-Holland: 209–228.

HSA. 2002. The Homeland Security Act, Public Law 107-296 (November 25) http://www.dhs.gov/xlibrary/assets/hr_5005_enr.pdf

HSPD-9. 2004. The White House Directive on Defense of United States Agriculture and Food (January 30) http://www.whitehouse.gov/news/releases/2004/02/20040203-2.html

Kelic A, Mathews E., Beyeler W. 2007. Telecommunications operations resiliency: labor shortages and the voice network. Submitted to the *25th International Conference of the System Dynamics Society*. Boston, USA (July 29–August 2). http://www.systemdynamics.org/conferences/soon.htm

LeClaire RJ, O'Reilly G. 2005. Leveraging a high fidelity switched network model to inform a SD model of the telecommunications infrastructure. *Proceedings of the 23rd International Conference of the System Dynamics Society*. Boston (July 17–21). http://www.systemdynamics.org/conferences/2005/proceed/papers/LECLA308.pdf

Lyneis JM. 1980. *Corporate Planning and Policy Design*. Cambridge, MA: Productivity Press.

Meadows DH, Meadows DL, Randers J, Behrens III WW. 1972. *The Limits to Growth: A Report for the Club of Rome's Project on the Predicament of Mankind*. New York: Universe Books.

NIPP. 2006. The National Infrastructure Protection Plan. http://www.dhs.gov/xlibrary/assets/NIPP_Plan.pdf

Powell DR, Fair J, LeClaire RJ, Moore LM, Thompson DR. 2005. Sensitivity analysis of an infectious disease model. *Proceedings of the 23rd International Conference of the System Dynamics Society*. Boston (July 17–21). http://www.systemdynamics.org/conferences/2005/proceed/papers/LECLA330.pdf

Powell DR, Thompson DR, Martínez-Moyano IJ. 2006. Workshop on the development of large system dynamics projects. *Proceedings of the 24th International Conference of the System Dynamics Society*. Nijmegen, The Netherlands (July 23–27). http://www.systemdynamics.org/conferences/2006/proceed/papers/POWEL256.pdf

Rasmussen S and N Becker. June 2004. "Initial stability and sensitivity studies of the CIPDSS agricultural sector models." Los Alamos National Laboratory.

Samsa ME, Powell DR, LeClaire R, Chang Y, Klare P, Martinez-Moyano IJ, Folga S, DeLand S. January 2007, "CIPDSS chemical threat capabilities case study: summary report." LA-UR-07-2382, Los Alamos National Laboratory.

Soybean Rust Reports. 2005. Critical Infrastructure Protection Decision Support System (CIPDSS) Project. Sandia National Laboratories.

Stephens CA, Graham AK, Lyneis JM. 2005. System dynamics modeling in the legal arena: meeting the challenges of expert witness admissibility. *System Dynamics Review* 21(2): 95–122.

Sterman JD. 2000. *Business Dynamics: System Thinking and Modeling for a Complex World*. Boston, MA: The McGraw-Hill Companies, Inc.

Thompson DR, Bush BW. 2005. Group development software for Vensim®." *Proceedings of the 23rd International Conference of the System Dynamics Society*. Boston (July 17–21). http://www.systemdynamics.org/conferences/2005/proceed/papers/LECLA437.pdf

USA PATRIOT. 2001. The Uniting and Strengthening America by Providing Appropriate Tools Required to Intercept and Obstruct Terrorism Act, Public Law 107-56 (October 26) http://frwebgate.access.gpo.gov/cgi-bin/getdoc.cgi?dbname=107_cong_public_laws&docid=f:publ056.107.pdf

Zagonel AA, Corbet TF. 2006. Levels of confidence in system dynamics modeling: a pragmatic approach to assessment of dynamic models. *Proceedings of the 24th International Conference of the System Dynamics Society*. Nijmegen, The Netherlands (July 23–27). http://www.systemdynamics.org/conferences/2006/proceed/papers/ZAGON374.pdf

Appendix 1
One-Page Module Summary

Name of module:	Brief description of module:
N.Ag.Bf.Pr **Production**	Aging chain of the beef cattle. The main input to this module is the desired breeding stock. The main output is the number of cows being slaughtered per time period. The amount of time on feedlots depends upon price gains due to weight gain, and feedlot costs per time period. The depopulating scenario depletes from the animal stocks

Imported variables: (**red & bold**)	Exported variables (**blue & bold**)
N.Ag.Bf: Desired Breeding Stock	**N.Ag.Bf.Pr: Slaughtering Beef Cattle**

Metrics (**bold & purple**)	Policy/scenario sliders (*yellow highlight*)
N.Ag.Bf.Pr: Depopulated Beef Cattle **N.Ag.Bf.Pr: Total Beef Cattle**	*N.Ag.B.Prf: Breeding Stock Adjustment Delay* *N.Ag.B.Prf: Time to adjust stock of female beef calves*

Data: (*grey & italic*)	Type:	Observations:
N.Ag.B.Pr: Average Beef Calving Interval *N.Ag.B.Pr: Beef Calving Percentage* *N.Ag.B.Pr: Time to Wean* *N.Ag.B.Pr: Foraging Period* *N.Ag.B.Pr: Breeding Stock Adjustment Delay* *N.Ag.B.Pr: Breeding Duration* *N.Ag.B.Pr: Initial Breeding Stock* *N.Ag.B.Pr: Beef Calf Mortality* *N.Ag.B.Pr: Beef Heifer Mortality* *N.Ag.B.Pr: Beef Cattle Mortality*	National-data	
N.Ag.B.Pr: Fraction of Male Births *N.Ag.B.Pr: Calf Gestation Time*	Constant	

Observations/questions/issues/problems/suggestions for refinements and changes:

Appendix 2
Module Subsystem Diagram

This example illustrates a simplified subsystem diagram highlighting the exchange of variables between the Beef Production Module, the Dairy Production Module, and the rest of the agriculture model.

Merged Model

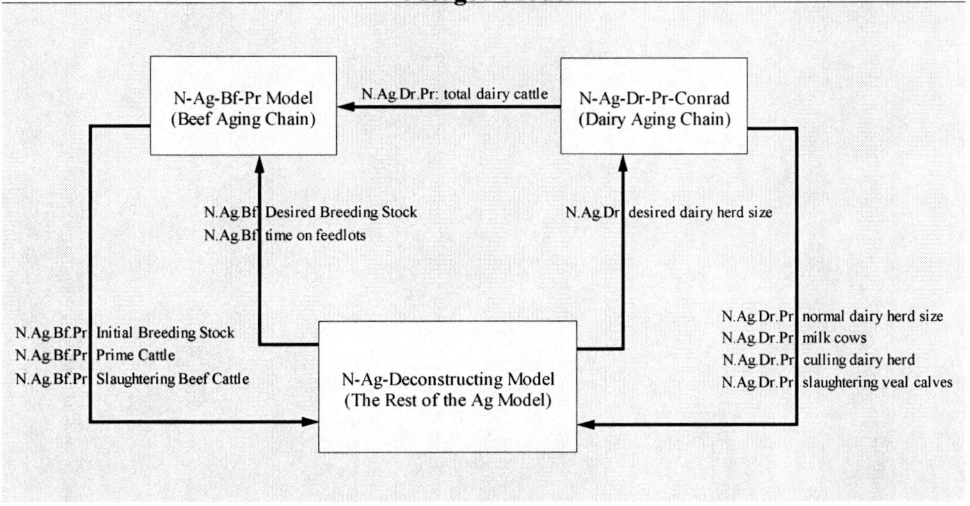

Theme 10: Systems Theory / Systems Thinking

51. Action Research: An Exploration of its Logic and Relationship to the Scientific Method

John Barton
John Barton Associates, AUS

John Stephens
Greyhound Racing Victoria, AUS

Tim Haslett
Monash University, AUS

This paper considers those interpretations of action research that can be traced to Kurt Lewin at the Research Center for Group Dynamics at the University of Michigan, and the work in social ecology by Emery and Trist at the Tavistock Institute. It locates the logical basis of these interpretations in the philosophy of pragmatism, particularly as it relates to Peirce's inferential logic and inquiry system. An outcome is the argument that both positivist science (which relates to closed systems thinking) and action research (which relates to open systems thinking) are both essential to any complete scientific approach.

Introduction

Reason and Bradbury (2001:3) observe that while many writers trace the origins of action research to "the social experiments of Kurt Lewin in the 1940s" and the "socio-technical experiments begun at the Tavistock Institute....there are others, which deserve acknowledgement". Consequently Reason and Bradbury correctly observe that:

"*...the term 'action research' has been used in so many different ways that the term has lost some of its original weight. Sometime it is used to describe positivist research in a 'field' context, or where there is a trade-off between the theoretical interests of the researchers and the practical interests of organization members; sometimes it is used to describe relatively uncritical organizational consulting based on information gathering and feedback... The action research family includes a whole range of approaches and practices, each grounded in different traditions, in different philosophical and psychological assumptions, pursuing different political commitments*" (Reason & Bradbury, 2001: xxiv).

In this paper we concentrate on those origins of action research attributable to Lewin and the Tavistock Institute.

There have been many attempts to establish the "scientific" credentials of action research. The usual approach is to first set down a set of basic tenets of scientific research and then compare action research to them. In most instances this version of scientific research is synonymous with one or more variations of positivist science. Blaikie (2004: 837) identifies three key versions- Comte's original version formulated in the first half of the 19th Century; logical positivism, formulated by the Vienna School in the 1920s; and a current "standard form" based on the tenet that phenomena must be explained as a specific case of a "covering law" and where explanation is based on observation resulting from objective research and the formation of refutable hypotheses.

Such an approach to comparison is doomed to fail because the test is constructed from the relatively narrow perspective of positivist science; narrow because positivist science does not entertain taking action in the broader world and in doing so attempts to exclude the importance of values in science and the possibility of changing contexts.

Two contemporary examples illustrate the shortcomings of positivist science when action is taken or at least contemplated. The first relates to newspaper reports (The Weekend Australian, August 18-19, 2007) concerning calls for a review of Australia's system for monitoring widely used medications. This follows the withdrawal of a drug for the treatment of arthritis that has been linked to liver failure. This has occurred despite the development and trialing of the drug under the most stringent "scientific" conditions.

The second example relates to the call by NASA's top climate scientist, James Hansen, to take action on climate change before all the facts are agreed. Hansen (2007: 32) writes:

"*...skepticism is at the heart of the scientific method and discovery. However, in a case such as ice-sheet instability and sea level rise, excessive caution also holds dangers*".

In each case we observe that when faced with the practicalities of action, positivist science is inadequate and we find ourselves either taking action, or at least contemplating it, on the basis of "inference to the best explanation" (Lipton, 1991). That is, a "best" hypothesis is formed and corresponding action taken in the context of monitoring, intervention to make adjustments, and eventual evaluation.

This process was described in logic by the American founder of pragmatist philosophy, Charles Sanders Peirce (1839-1914) and in this paper, it is argued that Peirce's triadic logic underpins action research and helps identify action research and positive research as complementary aspects of a more complete scientific method.

The importance of action research to systems thinking practice has become increasingly recognized (Checkland & Holwell, 1998; Flood, 2001) and Barton and Haslett (2006) have demonstrated how adopting the principles of action research can enhance particular systems methodologies, specifically, system dynamics.

Lewin's Action Research and Some Later Extensions

Blum (1955) provides one of the most useful accounts of Lewin's practice of action research at the Research Centre for Group Dynamics, University of Michigan, in the period 1945-1955. Blum (1955: 1) defines Lewin's action research as meaning "diagnosis of a social problem with a view of helping improve the situation. All action research has, therefore two stages:

1. A diagnostic stage in which the problem is being analyzed and hypotheses are being developed;
2. A therapeutic stage in which the hypotheses are tested by a consciously directed change experiment, preferably in a social "life" situation".

Blum argues that the inclusion of the second stage is the key differentiator from positivist science with fundamental consequences for the "overall research design, the methods and the techniques used".

Foremost amongst these implications is for the action researcher to develop a "mutual relationship" with stakeholders with possible consequences for objectivity and ethical behavior. In the therapeutic stage "people take part in an experiment which is consciously directed towards the implementation of certain values" (p.2). Consequently, Blum argues that "ideally action research should be undertaken by a team small enough to function as a group but which is sufficiently large to represent different (a) personality types (b) social values and (c) talents" (p. 3).

Blum identifies the main objection "which the action researcher has to meet squarely is that he confuses his role as a scientist with his role as a human, social, political and ultimately a religious being that he ceases to do objective research as he becomes entangled with the world of values" (p. 40). But he goes on to emphasise that positivist science is not immune from these issues: "values penetrate the whole conceptual framework since they affect such fundamental choices as between 'data' and 'variable'. They also determine the orientation of the whole structure of thought toward certain *problems* and hence the *meaning* of all theory" (p. 5).

The implication of Blum's account is that we need to adopt a more holistic approach to the scientific method and move away from a position that sees positivist science as "rigorous", where rigour is defined in somewhat circular terms within the bounds of positivist science, and action research is seen as not being rigorous.

Unfortunately, as Reason and Bradbury (2001) point out, there are many variants of action research, and not all involve the rigour involved in the processes developed by Lewin. In response to this situation Argyris *et al.* (1985) introduced the term "Action Science" - a *science* of human action in an attempt to bring action research back to its integrative roots as described by Lewin. In particular, Argyris *et al.* (1985) addressed the question of objectivity by recognizing three objectives as fundamental to Lewin's approach:

- Learning is the first and overarching objective;
- Any knowledge produced should be formulated into empirically disconfirmable propositions;
- Knowledge can be organized as theory.

In these terms they reinforce the distinctions made by Blum by arguing that attempting to use "standard scientific research" in the social sciences may be "self limiting":

"*We would be content to use the term "action research" if it was not for two factors. First, over the years action research has often been separated from theory building and testing. Leading social scientists distinguish action research from basic research by asserting that the intention of action research is to solve an important problem for a client and not necessarily to test features of a theory.... Second, many action researchers understandably conduct their empirical work by following the current ideas about standard scientific research. The dilemma is that some of the currently accepted ideas of rigorous research may be self-limiting*" (Argyris *et al.*, 1985: x).

Argyris *et al.*'s (1995) approach is an elaboration with a specific emphasis on implementation of Argyris and Schon's two theory-in-use models (I and II). Model 1 theory-in-use corresponds to a form of bounded rationality (Simon, 1964/1976) in which people impose their own meanings on action and become dogmatic about them. Consequently, it becomes difficult for them to openly reflect on their motivations and actions and they become defensive in conversation. Model 1 is also consistent with a closed-systems view of the world in which contexts and environments are locked out (Argyris, 1983: 120).

The capability of being able to effectively reflect on actions and motivations involves the adoption of Argyris and Schon's Model II. These two modes of learning have become popularized under the headings of single and double loop learning (Argyris & Schon, 1974, 1978, and 1996). (Argyris (1983) provides a succinct version of the action science perspective). Flood and Romm (1996) have added a third element of critical reflection that raises issues of power and systems of meaning and hence raises deep ethical considerations; triple loop learning. Checkland and Holwell (1997: 12) have further contributed to the development of Lewin's model by identifying from Argyris *et al.* (1985) four "crucial elements in a research approach which works within a specific social situation:

- A collaborative process between researchers and people in the situation;
- A process of critical inquiry;
- A focus on social practice, and;
- A deliberative process of reflective learning".

The important contribution that Checkland and Holwell make is the manner in which they articulate the difference between the traditional scientific method with its focus on the replication of results, and action research with its acknowledgement that, quoting from Keynes, social science is not dealing with phenomena that are "homogeneous through time". That is, in social science we are dealing with *open* systems.

Checkland and Holwell (1997) make this same point in their reference to the need for action researchers to increase their appreciation for a "declared epistemology and hence a recoverable research process" and make this explicit by defining action research as a process involving a framework (F) of ideas from which a methodology (M) is derived, and applied to an area of action (A). This FMA framework provides a useful approach to undertaking Argyris and Schon's "double loop learning".

The Tavistock Approach- Emery's ecological learning model.

In an attempt to overcome a range of (closed system) issues associated with socio-technical systems theory and practice, Emery and Trist led the development of the field of social ecology, (Trist *et al.*, 1993). The extant version of this is described by Merrelyn Emery as the "ecological learning model" (Emery, 1999).

Emery (1999: 54) points out that while approaches to learning such as those outlined above address questions such as "are we doing the right things right?" and is "rightness buttressed by power?" and espouse emancipatory practice, they do not adequately address the question of "learning from the environment". They are essentially assuming a closed system framework as distinct from the "ecological learning" approach that originates from contextualism and sits at the centre of the Emery Open System Model. This approach is best represented by Emery's open systems model (Emery, 1999, 2000), described in Figures 1 and 2.

There are two key aspects of this model that make it distinctive: it introduces a "causal texture" of relations in the system environment (L22); secondly, it emphasizes that the agents operating in the system can influence this environment (L12). This model is very much about the real time, coevolution of the system and its environment. The relationships L11, L12, L21, L22 capture the dynamics of this coevolution.

Throughout, participants use their perceptions and experience as the data on which they build their futures. In data collection, participants collectively contribute changes they have seen. There is no other source other than their perceptions and experience on which to judge the significance of their changes. The ground rule is that 'all perceptions are valid'. This has multiple effects, not the least of which is that people begin to restore their confidence in the value of their perceptions. It also has the effect of preventing those with more formal status from devaluing the perceptions of those with less status. (Emery, 1999: 69).

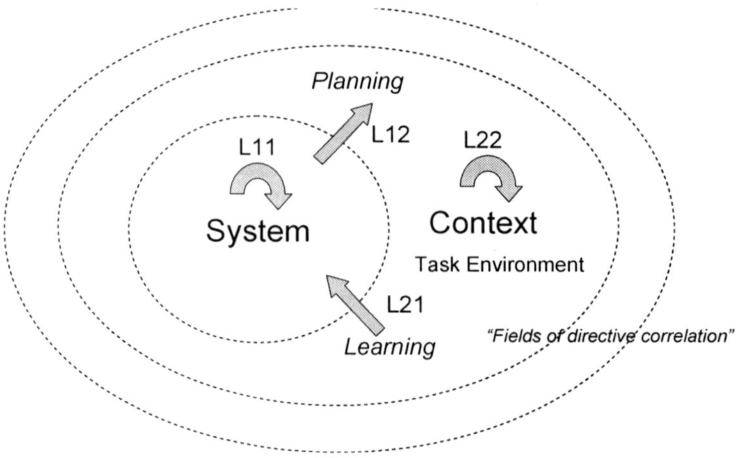

Figure 1 *Emery's Open Systems Model- A Static View (Emery, 1999)*

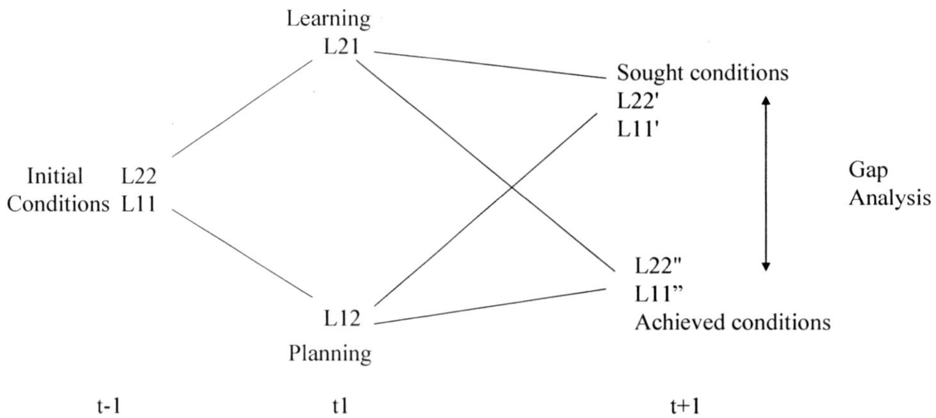

Figure 2 *Emery's Open Systems Model- A Dynamic View (Emery, 1999)*

This stage of ecological learning corresponds to the stage of inquiry associated with forming a hypothesis. The process of continuous ecological and experiential learning continues in the action phases provided the organization operates according to "Design Principle 2"; redundancy of functions (Emery, 1999: 105-136). This structure provides an organizational context within which ecological learning can operate.

Reframing the Scientific Method in terms of Open and Closed Systems.

The ecological approach to action research highlights the use of the open-closed systems dichotomy and provides the opportunity to associate positivist science with closed systems thinking, and action research with open systems (Blaikie, 2004: 838). Barton and Haslett (2007) provide details of this proposal. In this approach, the scientific process is interpreted an analysis-synthesis dialectic in which hypotheses are framed in systemic terms, the most primary constructs being open and closed systems.

In logic terms, irrespective of whether or not hypotheses are formed in open or closed systems terms, Peirce identified three modes of inference: abduction (the formation of hypotheses, deduction, and induction.

Peirce's Inferential Logic

In a significant departure from Kant's dichotomous treatment of deduction and induction, and their links to analysis and synthesis, Peirce returned to Greek dialectic involving three modes of inference: deduction, induction, and abduction (i.e., the logic of forming hypotheses).

In contrast to the more rigorous forms of inference (deduction and induction), abduction takes the form of making an observation about an outcome and proposing a cause for that outcome.

In his early period, Peirce used the terms "abduction" and retroduction" interchangeably but later he reserved the term abduction for the formation of hypotheses and retroduction as the process of testing and refining hypotheses and their final selection (Rescher, 1978).

Peirce argued that abduction was the only form of inference that extends knowledge- deduction simply develops logical results from hypotheses, and induction uses data to quantify and test arguments. Abduction is now recognized as an essential part of the scientific method (Houser, 2005) and has a particular significance for management decision-making (Powell, 2002) and the field of artificial intelligence (Josephson & Josephson, 1994). Haack summarizes the importance of abduction:

"The method of science requires abduction. Scientific inquiry is creative; it requires imagination to come up with abductive hypotheses. But there are 'trillions and trillions of hypotheses' that might be made, of which only one is true; we succeed as well as we do, Peirce suggests, because evolution has given human beings an instinct for guessing which 'though it goes wrong oftener than right, yet the relative frequency with which it is right is ... the most wonderful thing in our constitution'" (Haack, 2006: 25).

Peirce uses these three modes of inference to define a "logic of inquiry". Abduction, deduction, and induction provide a cycle of inference in which experience is used to develop a small set of hypotheses from what may arguably be an infinite set of possibilities; deduction can be used to reformulate hypotheses into forms suitable for testing using inductive inference. This gives rise to Peirce's experimentalism as the pragmatic basis for inquiry and the background to Dewey's instrumentalism. This process supports the analysis-synthesis dialectic described by Barton and Haslett (2007) and forms the logical basis to both action research and positivist science.

As noted above, Peirce's form of inquiry forms the basis of Dewey's experiential learning model (Dewey, 1910) and its extant versions including, for example, Kolb (1984), Shewhart (1939) and Deming (1950), and Argyris *et al.*'s (1985) "Action Science".

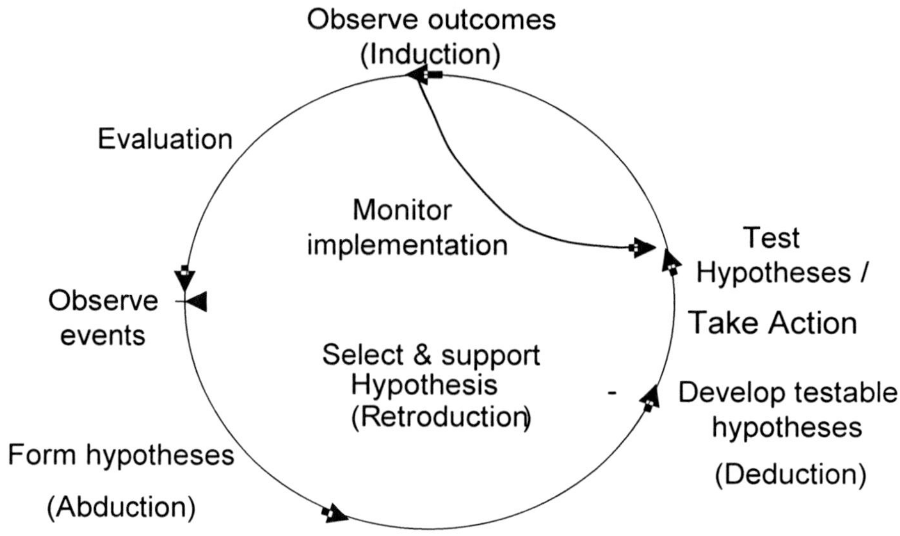

Figure 3 *Peirce's Inquiry Process*

Reason & Bradbury	**Peirce**
Improve the human condition	Resolution of doubt
Practical outcome	Pragmatic maxim
New forms of understanding through reflection & experience	Three modes of inference
Participative processes	Community of inquiry

Table 1 *Comparison of Reason & Bradbury's View of AR with Peirce.*

Despite the emphasis on rigour, Peirce was aware that this process was subject to error (fallibilism) and that all inferences were conditional. On this basis, we can differentiate between the logics of laboratory sciences and social science methods. In a laboratory science, and within reasonable limits, the conditionals (such as room temperature) can be identified, measured, and controlled. In systems terms, a "closed" system is created. In the social sciences, this is rarely possible: we are dealing with "open systems" in which not all conditionals are knowable, let alone controllable. In this sense, laboratory science is a "special case" of social science! To minimise the problems of fallibilism, and to facilitate the multiple perspectives advocated by Lewin, team processes are essential to the inquiry process and correspond to what Peirce termed "communities of inquiry".

It may not be surprising to note that, although dealing at a high level of aggregation, there is a correspondence between the key characteristics of action research described by Reason and Bradbury, and the modes of scientific inquiry proposed by Peirce; see Table.1.

Does Action Research Constitute "Rigorous" Science?

We now want to complete this path of increasing rigour by integrating the threads of this received thinking in action research into the model of science described by Barton and Haslett (2007). Dewey's experiential learning cycles and its popularization in more recent times through the work of Kolb (1984) and others, and its adoption in quality management via Shewhart and Deming (1982: 88) helps us establish this link. They are articulations of the analytic-synthetic dialectic and this, together with Peirce's triadic logic of inquiry, provides a rigorous basis to action research.

However, when we pose the question about action research and rigour, we are framing it in terms of the received position of positivist science. When posed in these terms, it is not surprising that, as Susman and Evered (1978) conclude, action research in its various guises, does not constitute "rigorous" science. Checkland's response is that action research attempts to replicate *processes*, and we might suggest that the learning structures described by Argyris, Emery, Checkland and Holwell, Kolb and others represent particular cases of a "covering law" defined by Peirce's system of inquiry.

As Susman and Evered point out, and as has been mentioned previously, there are many deficiencies in positivist science. Social science and management in particular, is about action in open systems. Whether we are talking about positivist science, or action research, action is taken on the basis of a hypothesis that is always going to be conditional on circumstances relating to the system of knowledge of which the hypothesis is part. As discussed above, in the closed systems world of positivist science, we make the presumption that these conditionals are both known and controllable. In open systems, neither assumption is true. So we act on the basis of our best explanation- a decision which is value driven.

The critical quest that we face with positivist science is that it only confirms hypotheses under strict conditions. What happens when we act on these hypotheses in the context of an open system? In the example cited earlier, what happens when a drug that has been extensively trialled under laboratory conditions is released into the open community? Do the hypotheses established by

Property	**Positivist Science**	**Action Research**
Systems frame	Closed	Open
Repeatability	Experimental result	Process
Conditionals on hypotheses	Known and controllable	Unknown and not controllable
Objectivity	Apparent independence of researcher but dependent on the norms of peers	Triple loop learning evaluation; dependent on values of the community of inquiry
Dominant mode of inference	Deduction	Abduction
Action based	No	Yes

Table 2. A Comparison of Action Research and Positivist Research

positivist research still hold? We never know, until we try! That is, we are acting on the basis of our hypothesis to the best explanation and have transitioned from a positivist research domain to an action research domain. In this sense the positivist research has simply been part of what Peirce process of "retroduction". On the basis of the above, Table 2 provides a comparison between positivist research and action research.

Conclusions

In summary, we have argued that action research and positivist science play complementary roles in the broader scope of the scientific method in which hypotheses are proposed, tested, and acted upon and that the logic underlying this process can be explained by reference to framing hypotheses in open and closed system contexts.

From the perspective of action research, Lewin's process has been made increasingly rigorous through a number of refinements and innovations. The problem of objectivity is addressed by Argyris and Schon's concept of single and double loop learning, which involves open reflection of processes. This process has itself been extended in two ways: by Flood and Romm's triple loop learning, and by Checkland and Howell's use of the FMA structure and its usefulness in guiding the double loop learning phase. However, as Fred and Merrelyn Emery argue, these approaches fail to sufficiently emphasise the importance of the environment. Instead, Fred and Merrelyn Emery provide an action learning approach rooted in theories of perception and "ecological learning" which help define the dynamics implicit in Lewin's model. In turn, the ecological approach is grounded in Pepper's (1942) world view of contextualism and with its basis in Peirce's triadic logic of inquiry.

Scientific research and action research are not competing approaches to science, but complementary, albeit as Blum points out, where the design of the scientific method ideally needs to be influenced by the social objectives of the research.

The need for practical outcomes, place action research within a social context where interaction between the environment of the "experiment" and the experiment itself interact and in which values place a critical role. Inevitably, this includes interactions between researcher and subjects, and context and draws on four fundamental premises that are associated with pragmatist philosophy:

1. Peirce's tenet that all human concepts are defined by their consequences;
2. James' tenet that truth is embodied in practical outcomes;
3. Dewey's logic of controlled inquiry, in which rational thought is interspersed with action;
4. Mead's tenet that human action is conceptualized socially and human conceptualization is also a social reflection.

References

Argyris, C. (1983). Action Science and Intervention. *Journal of Applied Behavioral Science, 19*, 115-140.

Argyris, C., & Schön, D. A. (1996). *Organizational Learning II*. Reading Mass.: Addison Wesley.

Argyris, C., Putman, R., & McLain Smith, D. (1985). *Action Science*. San Francisco: Jossey-Bass.

Barton, J and Haslett, T (2002). Fresh Insights into System Dynamics Methodology-Developing an abductive inference perspective. Proceedings, 24th International Conference of the System Dynamics Society, Nijmegen, The Netherlands July 23 -27

Barton, J., & Haslett, T. (2007). Analysis, Synthesis, Systems Thinking and the ScientificMethod: Rediscovering the Importance of Open Systems. *Systems Research and Behavioral Science, 14*, 143-155.

Blaikie, N. (2004) Positivism. Entry in The SAGE Encyclopedia of Social Science Research methods, Vol. 2. Lewis-Beck, Bryman, & Liao (Ed). Thousand Oaks: SAGE

Blum, F., H. (1955). Action Research- A Scientific Approach? *Philosophy of Science, 22*(1), 1-7.

Checkland, P. (2000). Soft Systems Methodology: A Thirty Year Retrospective. *Systems Research and Behavioral Sciences, 17*, S11-S58.

Checkland, Peter & Holwell, Sue. (1998) Action Research: Its nature and validity. *Systemic Practice & Action Research*, Vol 11, No 1, 1998.

Deming, W. E. (1982). *Out of Crisis*. Cambridge: CUP.

Dewey, J. (1938). *Logic: The Theory of Inquiry*. NY: Holt, Rinehart and Winston.

Emery, M. (1999). *Searching*. Amsterdam: John Benjamins Publishing Co.

Emery, M. (2000). The Current Version of Emery's Open Systems Theory. *Systemic Practice & Action Research, 13*(5), 623 - 644.

Flood, R.L. Action Research and Systems Thinking in Reason, P. and H. Bradbury (2001). *Handbook of Action Research. Participative Inquiry and Practice*. London: UK, Sage Publications.

Flood, R. L., & Romm, N. R. A. (1996). *Diversity Management- Triple Loop Learning*. Chichester: Wiley.

Haack, S. (Ed.). (2006). *Pragmatism, Old & New: Selected Writings*. Amherst: Prometheus.

Hansen, J. (2007). Climate Catastrophe. *New Scientist*. 28 July. Pp 30-34.

Houser, N. (2005). Peirce in the 21st Century. *Transactions of the Charles S. Peirce Society, 41*(4), 729-739.

Josephsen, John R. and Josephsen Susan G. (1994). *Abductive Inference*. New York: Cambridge University Press.

Kolb, D. A. (1984). *Experiential Learning: Experience as The Source of Learning and Development*. Englewood Cliffs, New Jersey: Prentice-Hall.

Lipton, P. (2004). Inference to the Best Explanation (2nd. Ed.) London: Routledge.

Pepper, S. C. (1942). *World Hypotheses*. Berkeley: University of California Press.

Powell, T., C. (2002). The Philosophy of Strategy. *Strategic Management Joumal, 23*, 873-880.

Reason, P. and H. Bradbury (2001). *Handbook of Action Research. Participative Inquiry and Practice*. London: UK, Sage Publications.

Rescher, N. (1978). *Peirce's Philosophy of Science*. Notre Dame: University of Notre Dame Press.

Shewhart, W.A. (1939) *Statistical Method from the Viewpoint of Quality Control*. Grad

School of the Dept of Agriculture, Washington. (Dover, 1986).

Simon, H. A. (1964). *Administrative Behavior: A Study of Decision-Making Processes in Administrative Organizations.* (3rd Ed). New York: The Free Press.

Trist, E., Emery, F., & Murray, H. (Eds.) (1993). The Social Engagement of Social Sciences Vol. III. The Socio-Ecological Perspective. Philadelphia: Uni. of Pennsylvania Press.

Susman, G. I., & Evered, R. D. (1978). An Assessment of the Scientific Merits of Action Research. *Administrative Science Quarterly, 23*, 582 - 603.

52. Emerging Themes in Sustainability and the Need for Applied Systems Solutions

Simon Chun Kwan Chui
The University of Auckland, NZ

The world since the industrial revolution has seen improvements to human welfare on a massive scale, but also environmental problems on a massive scale. A summary of the emerging sustainability fields of environmental economics, industrial ecology, sustainable urbanism and lean management reveals a call for a sophisticated whole-system perspective in tackling these problems, emphasizing decentralised and streamlined relationships between system elements. Taken as a whole, these initiatives indicate a cross-discipline paradigm-shift towards the application of systems theory as practical solutions to the shortcomings of industrialism, and suggest directions where future developments in systems theory and thinking will be most useful.

Introduction

Two of the most pressing problems in the contemporary world are resource depletion and environmental degradation, both results of the massive and pervasive industrialization of human activity. While industrialism has provided tremendous improvements to human welfare over the past two and a half centuries, it also inherently neglects to factor in environmental constraints until substantial damage is done. This paper briefly summarizes four fields that have emerged to address the shortcomings of industrialism, namely environmental economics, industrial ecology, sustainable urbanism, and lean management. This reveals some commonalities that suggest that a pervasive culture of sustainability, in contrast to the existing culture of consumerism, may be reached through the widespread application of systems theory to all facets of human endeavour. This paper identifies some specific issues where the application of systems theory will greatly benefit the continued development of the four fields.

The global industrial system

Industrialization is a series of mutually supporting technological innovations developed some 250 years ago that changed human activity from predominantly agrarian to predominantly industrial (Grübler, 1994). Practically synonymous with human activity, industry mobilizes hundreds of billions of metric tons of raw materials every year (Hawken, *et al.* 1999: 50-53), extracting and transporting raw materials across the globe to sprawling factories and industrial zones to be transformed into the myriad consumer goods that are distributed to the cities and homes of the world's consumer population (Graedel, *et al.* 1995:

8). In our industrial world, socio-economic success flows from technology applied to material production to maximise labour productivity (Kam, 2001: 35-68; Swamidass, 2000: 4).

Mass production and the division of labour

From the beginning of the industrial revolution over 200 years ago, the hierarchical subdivision of labour was identified as the basis of successful industrialism, utilizing specialization to enable improved worker skill and focus, and, most importantly, the utilisation of specialist tools and machines (Smith, 1979: 110-115; Womack, *et al.* 1991: 12-13). Since 1750, human industrial output has grown by a about factor of 100, the outcome of the increasing utilisation of sophisticated mechanical tools to multiply labour productivity (Grübler, 1994: 41). By all measures, overall human welfare has been improved by industrialization: people live longer; infant mortality is reduced; food supply per capita is greater and more stable; people work fewer hours while output has increased; education levels have improved; and people are more likely enjoy the benefits of living in a democratic and pluralistic society (Goklany, 2003: 195-198).

Resource depletion and environmental degradation

Despite the benefits of industrialism, there have also been substantial costs. Industrialism, by definition, is a process that transforms natural resources into human-made artefacts (Bourg, 2003: 59), and the success of industrialism came hand in hand with the large scale depletion of natural resources and damage to the environment (Hawken, *et al.* 1999: 2). Of the hundreds of billions of metric tons of raw materials mobilized every year, some 90 percent are immediately discarded as they are not the resources that are actually desired, but only material that is disrupted by the processes of extraction (Graedel, *et al.* 1995: 19). Less than 2 percent of the material is actively recycled at the end of their use (Hawken, *et al.* 1999: 50-53), and only 1 percent remains in use within the system six months after its extraction (Dale, 2006: 4). In other words, the industrial system is one where materials flow rapidly from un-extracted resource to discarded waste, in processes that involve substantial environmental disruption.

Four responses to environmental limits

In the past, the response to localized resource depletion has simply been to find more resources or to find substitutes (Bourg 2003: 58, Graedel, *et al.* 1995: 66), while the response to local environmental degradation has been to capture and control effluents and to remediate any damage done (Bringezu, 2003: 21; Graedel, *et al.*, 1995: 47). As both industrial activity and environmental constraints become increasingly global in scope, these responses become inadequate. The four developing fields summarized below take a different approach: they seek to address some fundamental shortcomings in traditional industrialism.

Environmental economics

Economics is the codification and quantification of human needs and wants, and the activities we conduct in order to satisfy them (Graedel, *et al.*, 1995: 63-64). A primary shortcoming of current economic systems is the presence of "externalities": activities that have real costs and benefits, but which are not entirely factored into prices, and therefore not fully accounted for in decision-making mechanisms (Graedel, *et al.*, 1995: 86). The aim of environmental economics is to adjust market incentive/disincentive mechanisms so that as many externalities as possible are internalized, and that these enter decision-making processes early enough to significantly influence outcomes. Possible initiatives include waste taxes and recycling subsidies that reflect the true costs and benefits of these activities to society (Graedel, *et al.*, 1995: 82; Griefahn, 1994: 424-425; Hawken, *et al.*, 1999: 41-42, 159-167), and the realignment of prices so that they focus on services provided, rather than on products sold, thereby removing the market's emphasis on material throughput (Graedel, *et al.*, 1995: 305; Hawken, *et al.*, 1999: 10-11; Kazazian, 2003: 85-86; Stahel, 2003: 266). By adjusting the rules of the system, environmental economics hopes to address a dysfunction that pervades all aspects of the system at every scale.

Industrial ecology

Industrial ecology looks to natural ecological systems as a model for redesigning human industrial systems (Bringezu, 2003: 20; Hawken, *et al.*, 1999: 10). In contrast to the resource depleting model of human industrialism, material flows in natural ecosystems are overwhelmingly cyclic: the outputs of any one organism become inputs for other organisms, and the volume of material cycling within the system are much greater than the volume entering or leaving it. If human industry can successfully mimic this cyclic paradigm, then the problems of resource depletion and environmental degradation can be largely eliminated (Bringezu, 2003: 22; Dale, 2006: 3; Graedel, 1994: 23-26; Graedel, *et al.*, 1995: 93-94). The primary challenges of industrial ecology are the re-conceptualization of "wastes" as "resources", the development of process technologies that retain the embedded utility of residues from industrial processes (Graedel, *et al.*, 1995: 113, 183-186), and the development of markets for the exchange and redeployment of these residual resources (Braungart, 1994: 335-336; Graedel, *et al.*, 1995: 83; Kincaid, 2003: 97-99; Yap 2006: 101). From the perspective of industrial ecology, the industrial system is incomplete in its current configuration, so existing resource distribution mechanisms need to be extended and augmented to include residual products.

Sustainable urbanism

After Second World War, urbanism in the West has been characterized by substantial amounts of sprawl: low-density development that, while attractive and in demand in the market, require high infrastructure costs, consumes large amounts of land, and necessitates expensive private automobile use (Burchell, *et al.*, 1998: 1-26; Grant, 2006: 50-53). This unsustainable, consumerist approach to urbanism been met by initiatives like New Urbanism and Smart Growth that, among other things, advocate for geographical limits on urban development to preserve agricultural lands and natural habitats (Yaro, 1999: 23-25), better integration and coordination of civic governance to prevent conflicting priorities in civic management (Orfield, 1999: 65-69), and the creation of concentrated and mixed use neighbourhood centres to improve urban vitality (Barnett, 1999: 73-77; Norquist, 1999: 97-99; Plater-Zyberk, 1999: 79-82). Most significantly, sustainable urbanism recognizes that complex and highly interconnected urban influences require holistic solutions, and that attempting to address specific urban problems in a piecemeal manner will only aggravate system dysfunction.

Lean management

Under conventional management hierarchies, the increasing complexity of the subdivision of labour results in highly inflexible and unresponsive production systems. In aversion to costly stoppages, non-critical defects and mistakes are simply allowed to continue and be passed down the line to be remedied later. Processes are seldom changed or improved due to the high costs, resulting in unnecessary waste (Womack, *et al.,* 1991: 12-14, 24-26). Lean production overcomes these shortcomings through pervasive modularization, dividing the production line into discreet process stages that are linked together with streamlined communication and inventory management mechanisms. Each stage of the work is then associated with a work cell, a small and semi-autonomous team of multi-skilled workers. Responsiveness is improved by allowing routine decision-making to be done at a lower management level, and flexibility is increased as cells can be added to or removed from the system without disruption to the larger system. This reduces, with the aim of eliminating, the unnecessary and non-value-adding consumption of resources (Black, 2000: 177-178; Feld, 2001: 3-6; McCreery & Bloom, 2000: 97-101; Womack, *et al.,* 1991: 49-68).

Common strategies for systemic sustainability

On the surface, the four fields vary widely in scope and in focus. However, there are significant commonalities in the different approaches to addressing the shortcomings of contemporary industrialism. These commonalities, summarized below, indicate that the solution will involve the widespread practical application of systems theory. Although the concerns are conceptually separated into three major themes here, it should be noted that they are mutually supportive, and unlikely to be useful if each is considered and implemented in isolation.

Whole-system perspective

The most frequently expressed concern is the need for a whole-system perspective in process design and implementation (Fischer-Kowalski, 2003: 44-45; Hawken, *et al.,* 1999: 64; Hodge, 2006: 159; Kazazian, 2003: 85; Stahel, 2003: 267-268). While the division of labour creates highly proficient specializations, it does not guarantee that they will come together into a complete system. This is evident in a market system that neglects and inadvertently promotes resource depletion and environmental damage on a massive scale, in industrial systems that neglect the residues they produce (Graedel, *et al.,* 1995: 8), and in a piecemeal approach to urban design that neglects the interdependency of social, economic, and infrastructural issues. In all cases, the benefits of specialization need to be complemented by a whole-system perspective that creates an understanding of the relationship between each specialist and the whole system, allowing the active building of useful connections between entities in order to capture potential synergies and prevent dysfunctional system behavior (Côté & Wallner, 2006: 130; Dale, 2006: 10; Gibson & Peck, 2006: 137-138; Stahel, 2003: 273). Obviously it would be counterproductive if increased connections between entities simply resulted in excessive complexity and information overload. Therefore, the challenge is to devise mechanisms to transfer and internalize only the useful types and amounts of information, and to devise mechanisms that can quickly detect and highlight the presence of externalities so that they can be acted upon.

Modular networks

A second major theme is the use of modularity as a means to achieve systemic flexibility and upgradability where modules can be added, subtracted, or modified with minimal system disruption (Duray, 2000: 280-281; Stahel, 2003: 272). The need is for modular systems where each module has the sufficient mix of resources to perform its function while remaining small enough to be agile and responsive (Graedel, *et al.,* 1995: 328-332; Stahel, 2003: 273-274). System-wide coordination is achieved through unobtrusive yet pervasive and powerful incentive/disincentive mechanisms that can translate overarching goals into specific actions to be performed in each module of management (Andrews, 1994: 406-410, 412-415; Gibson & Peck, 2006: 141-144; Graedel, *et al.,* 1995: 80-82, 293-295; Griefahn, 1994: 424-425; Hawken, *et al.,* 1999: 41-42, 90-93, 159-167; Panayotou & Zinnes, 1994: 389-391; Stahel, 2003: 271; Yap 2006: 105-107). This modularity retains the advantages of the specialization and the division of labour while employing more flexible and streamlined connections between process segments that facilitate effective transfer of materials and knowledge, avoiding specialization isolation. Minor disruptions are autonomously handled within modules, and are prevented from spilling out beyond individual modules to affect the larger system. The deployment and management of modules may be substantially automated by the careful design of rules and guidelines that determine optimum module size and composition in relation to the system, and the design of the mechanisms of exchanges between modules such that they network into a successful system.

Pervasive knowledge

Any system that is as complex and dynamic as cities or large industrial systems will exhibit unpredictable behavior and non-linear interactions between elements (Bourg & Erkman, 2003: 14; Gibson & Peck, 2006: 139-140; Hawken, *et al.,* 1999: 113-121; Hodge, 2006: 159). In such a complex system, detailed centralised planning is impractical as it necessitates the collection and analysis of vast amounts continuously changing data in an attempt to monitor dynamic and multi-faceted situations (Lister, 2006: 18-21). An alternative strategy is to incorporate into each system element effective feedback and feed-forward mechanisms that are designed to allow them to automatically optimize themselves in shifting conditions, which, in turn, allows the system to find its own "plan" (Hawken, *et al.*, 1999: 127-131). Such a system would require a sophisticated and pervasive knowledge infrastructure to continuously collect accurate and useful information when and where it is generated, to be distributed to wherever feedback action is required (Hill, 2006: 44-46). The point of pervasive knowledge is to avoid flooding a centralised decision-making mechanism with excessive data and to direct information effectively to wherever it will be useful, with minimum or no input necessary from a centralised decision-making mechanism. An essential aspect of pervasive knowledge is the translation of raw data from any one system element into information that will be useful and applicable to other system elements, or, in other words, the development of an effective knowledge infrastructure. The "pervasive" aspect of pervasive knowledge highlights the need for knowledge to be collected and be made applicable at all levels and in all situation; the knowledge infrastructure itself, like all the system elements that it serves, should have mechanisms that constantly collects and processes feedback information to ensure that it is functioning effectively.

Conclusion

Sustainability, in addressing the problems of resource depletion and environmental degradation in human industrialism, has identified the problem as an inability to sufficiently understand the complex interrelationships between all aspects of natural and human activity, and an inability to effectively coordinate the complexity of increasing specialization. It is not surprising that the four fields summarized in this paper, in dealing with the problem of sustainability, all begin to look to concepts from systems theory for solutions to dealing with complexity across issues that vary so widely in scope and in focus. The significance is that these four fields do not simply propose to "patch up" industrialism's negative symptoms with localized fixes; these are paradigm-shifting proposals that aim to re-engineer the entire industrial system by reassessing its basic strategies and underlying assumptions. If these initiatives, and others like them, eventually come to affect every aspect and scale of human activity, just as industrialism has done in the past centuries, then it may be that the practical application of systems theory will also become as routine and commonplace as the tools of industrialism are today. Tools that will need to be developed will likely include: automated mechanisms for the collection, processing, and distribution of useful information at local and global scales; techniques for quickly detecting and highlighting the existence of externalities; a framework for assembling multi-skilled, self-managed teams as a module of a larger system, and; protocols and infrastructure for the streamlined transfer of information, materials and incentives between system elements.

References

Andrews, C. (1994). "Policies to Encourage Clean Technology," in R. H. Socolow, C. Andrews, F. Berkhout and V. Thomas (ed.), *Industrial ecology and global change*, ISBN 0521471974, pp. 405-422.

Barnett, J. (1999). "Ten; The neighborhood, the district, and the corridor are the essential elements of development and redevelopment in the metropolis. The form identifiable areas that encourage citizens to take responsibility for their maintenance and evolution," in M. Leccese, K. McCormick and Congress for the New Urbanism (ed.), *The charter of the new urbanism*, ISBN 0071355537, pp. 73-77.

Black, J. T. (2000). "Lean Manufacturing Implementation," in P. M. Swamidass (ed.), *Innovations in competitive manufacturing*, ISBN 0792378962, pp. 177-186.

Bourg, D. (2003). "Industrial Ecology; Philosophical and Political Meanings," in D. Bourg and S. Erkman (ed.), *Perspectives on industrial ecology*, ISBN 1874719462, pp. 58-61.

Bourg, D. and Erkman, S. (ed.). (2003). *Perspectives on industrial ecology*, ISBN 1874719462.

Braungart, M. (1994). "Product Life-Cycle Management to Replace Waste Management," in R. H. Socolow, C. Andrews, F. Berkhout and V. Thomas (ed.), *Industrial ecology and global change*, ISBN 0521471974, pp. 335-337.

Bringezu, S. (2003). "Industrial Ecology and Material Flow Analysis; Basic Concepts, Policy Relevance and Some Case Studies," in D. Bourg and S. Erkman (ed.), *Perspectives on industrial ecology*, ISBN 1874719462, pp. 20-34.

Burchell, R. W., United States. Federal Transit Administration., National Research Council (U.S.). Transportation Research Board, Transit Development Corporation. and Transit Cooperative Research Program. (1998). *The Costs of sprawl-- revisited*, ISBN 030906306X.

Côté, R. P. and Wallner, H. P. (2006). "From Clusters and Networks to Islands of Sustainability," in R. P. Côté, J. Tansey and A. Dale (ed.), *Linking industry and ecology : a question of design*, ISBN 9780774812139, pp. 114-133.

Dale, A. (2006). "Linking Industry and Ecology in Canada: A Question of Design," in R. P. Côté, J. Tansey and A. Dale (ed.), Linking industry and ecology : a question of design, ISBN 9780774812139, pp. 3-11.

Duray, R. (2000). "Mass Customization," in P. M. Swamidass (ed.), *Innovations in competitive manufacturing*, ISBN 0792378962, pp. 275-282.

Feld, W. M. (2001). *Lean manufacturing : tools, techniques, and how to use them*, ISBN 157444297X.

Fischer-Kowalski, M. (2003). "On the History of Industrial Metabolism," in D. Bourg and S. Erkman (ed.), *Perspectives on industrial ecology*, ISBN 1874719462, pp. 35-45.

Gibson, R. B. and Peck, S. W. (2006). "From Advanced Eco-Efficiency to Systemic Sustainability: What Leading Companies are Doing and What Assistance and Pressure They Need from Governments and Other Players," in R. P. Côté, J. Tansey and A. Dale (ed.), *Linking industry and ecology : a question of design*, ISBN 0774812133, pp. 134-150.

Goklany, I. M. (2003). "The Future of the Industrial System," in D. Bourg and S. Erkman (ed.), *Perspectives on industrial ecology*, ISBN 1874719462, pp. 194-222.

Graedel, T. E. (1994). "Industrial Ecology: Definition and Implementation," in R. H. Socolow, C. Andrews, F. Berkhout and V. Thomas (ed.), *Industrial ecology and global change*, ISBN 0521471974, pp. 23-41.

Graedel, T. E., Allenby, B. R. and American Telephone and Telrgraph Company. (1995). *Industrial ecology*, ISBN 9780131252387.

Grant, J. (2006). "Industry in the City: From Industrial Ghettos to Eco-Parks," in R. P. Côté, J. Tansey and A. Dale (ed.), *Linking industry and ecology : a question of design*, ISBN 9780774812139, pp. 50-66.

Griefahn, M. (1994). "Initiatives in Lower Saxony to Link Ecology to Economy," in R. H. Socolow, C. Andrews, F. Berkhout and V. Thomas (ed.), *Industrial ecology and global change*, ISBN 0521471974, pp. 423-428.

Grübler, A. (1994). "Industrialization as a Historical Phenomenon," in R. H. Socolow, C. Andrews, F. Berkhout and V. Thomas (ed.), *Industrial ecology and global change*, ISBN 0521471974, pp. 43-68.

Hawken, P., Lovins, A. B. and Lovins, L. H. (1999). *Natural capitalism : creating the next industrial revolution*, ISBN 0316353167.

Hill, S. B. (2006). "Redesign as Deep Industrial Ecology: Lessons from Ecological Agriculture and Social Ecology," in R. P. Côté, J. Tansey and A. Dale (ed.), *Linking industry and ecology : a question of design*, ISBN 9780774812139, pp. 29-49.

Hodge, R. A. (2006). "Mining, Minerals, and Sustainability," in R. P. Côté, J. Tansey and A. Dale (ed.), *Linking industry and ecology : a question of design*, ISBN 9780774812139, pp. 151-175.

Kam, W. P. (2001). "From Leveraging Multinational Corporations to Fostering Technopreneurship: The Changing Role of S&T Policy in Singapore," in L. Low and D. M. Johnston (ed.), *Singapore Inc. public policy options in the third millennium*, ISBN 9812101594, pp. 35-84.

Kazazian, T. (2003). "The Ecodesign Process," in D. Bourg and S. Erkman (ed.), *Perspectives on industrial ecology*, ISBN 1874719462, pp. 82-90.

Kincaid, J. (2003). "Metropolitan Industrial Ecosystem Development," in D. Bourg and S. Erkman (ed.), *Perspectives on industrial ecology*, ISBN 1874719462, pp. 95-100.

Lister, N.-M. (2006). "Industrial Ecology as Ecological Design: Opportunities for Re(dis) covery," in R. P. Côté, J. Tansey and A. Dale (ed.), *Linking industry and ecology : a question of design*, ISBN 9780774812139, pp. 15-28..

McCreery, J. K. and Bloom, M. C. (2000). "Teams: Design and Implementation," in P. M. Swamidass (ed.), *Innovations in competitive manufacturing*, ISBN 0792378962, pp. 95-106.

Norquist, J. O. (1999). "Fourteen; Transit corridors, when properly planned and coordinated, can help organize metropolitan structure and revitalize urban centers. In contrast, highway corridors should not displace investment from existing centers," in M. Leccese, K. McCormick and Congress for the New Urbanism (ed.), *The charter of the new urbanism*, ISBN 0071355537, pp. 97-99.

Orfield, M. (1999). "Nine; Revenues and resources can be shared more cooperatively among the municipalities and centers within regions to avoid destructive competition for tax base and to promote rational coordination of transportation, recreation, public services, housing, and community institutions," in M. Leccese, K. McCormick and Congress for the New Urbanism (ed.), *The charter of the new urbanism*, ISBN 0071355537, pp. 65-69.

Panayotou, T. and Zinnes, C. (1994). "Free-Lunch Economics for Industrial Ecologists," in R. H. Socolow, C. Andrews, F. Berkhout and V. Thomas (ed.), *Industrial ecology and global change*, ISBN 0521471974, pp. 383-397.

Plater-Zyberk, E. (1999). "Eleven; Neighborhoods should be compact, pedestrian-friendly, and mixed-use. Districts generally emphasize a special single use, and should follow the principles of neighborhood design when possible. Corridors are regional connectors of neighborhoods and districts; they range from boulevards and rail lines to rivers and parkways," in M. Leccese, K. McCormick and Congress for the New Urbanism (ed.), *The charter of the new urbanism*, ISBN 0071355537, pp. 79-82.

Smith, A. (1979). *The wealth of nations : books I-III*, ISBN 0140432086.

Stahel, W. R. (2003). "The Functional Society; the Service Economy," in D. Bourg and S. Erkman (ed.), *Perspectives on industrial ecology*, ISBN 1874719462, pp. 264-282.

Swamidass, P. M. (2000). "Innovations in competitive manufacturing: From JIT to e-business," in P. M. Swamidass (ed.), *Innovations in competitive manufacturing*, ISBN 0792378962, pp. 3-14.

Womack, J. P., Jones, D. T. and Roos, D. (1991). *The machine that changed the world*, ISBN 0060974176.

Yap, N. T. (2006). "Cleaner Production and Eco-Efficiency: Charting a Course for Sustainability," in R. P. Côté, J. Tansey and A. Dale (ed.), *Linking industry and ecology : a question of design*, ISBN 9780774812139, pp. 97-113.

Yaro, R. D. (1999). "Two; Metropolitan regions are finite places with geographic boundaries derived from topography, coastlines, farmlands, regional parks, and river basins. The metropolis is made of multiple centers that are cities, towns, and villages, each with its own identifiable center and edges" in M. Leccese, K. McCormick and Congress for the New Urbanism (ed.), *The charter of the new urbanism*, ISBN 0071355537, pp. 23-25.

53. Semantic-Pragmatic Driven Complexification: A Proposal for an Extension of the Phenomeno-Semantic Model Complexity

Darek M. Eriksson
Luleå University of Technology, SWE

In a recent contribution we proposed a notion of the Phenomeno-Semantic Complexity as a complement to the mainstream notion, that typically understands complexity as the interaction of adaptive agents governed by local rules yet giving rise to novel unpredictable global behavior. The phenomeno-semantic notion, on the other hand, focuses on the process of semantic and syntactical transformations of message when communicated between sense-making actors, and unintentionally giving rise to a new meaning, potentially leading to unpredicted and contra-intuitive behavior, hence to complexity. This communication-oriented understanding of complexification implies alternative strategies for both the practical management of complexity in human affairs and for its research to seek understanding of its underlying constitutions and mechanisms. A suggested further area of such inquiry was the multi-faceted relation between the syntactic, the semantic, and the pragmatic aspects of communication. While relation between the syntactic and the semantic aspects alone was addressed during the mentioned introduction, this text focuses on the introduction of their relation with the pragmatic component as the driver of complexification. This extension completes the loop between the three semiotic constituents: the sign, the signification, and the signifier, giving rise to a more complete notion of complexity, the Model of Semiotic Complexification. This model is regarded as complementary to the mentioned more conventional notion of complexity based on the interaction of adaptive agents. Some implications for the complexity research are presented as well as practical implications for the management of complexity in human affairs and organizations.

Introduction

In a recent contribution (Eriksson, 2007), we presented intermediate findings from an ongoing research into the management of complexity in human affairs, in the form of the *Model of Phenomeno-Semantic Complexification*. This text presents a further extension of that model. While the mentioned previous presentation articulated the *syntactical* and *semantic* components of communication as sources of complexification, the account given here articulates the *pragmatic* component as a source of complexification of human affairs. Together they give rise to a *Semiotic Model of Complexification*, which holds that complexity in human affairs emerges from the communication process between sense-making actors, where unintended transformation occurs in one or several of the three semiotic components; hence three distinct types of complexity-drivers: the syntactical transformation, the semantic transformation, and the pragmatic transformation.

This semiotic notion of complexification may be juxtaposed with the more conventional notion of complexity, the ontological-syntactical, typically understood as system constituted by interacting adaptive agents, governed by local rules, giving rise to unpredictable global behavior. The here advanced *semiotic notion* of complexity and the conventional *ontological-syntactical notion* are regarded as complementary.

The here proposed Semiotic Model of Complexification also constitutes a source for the generation of guidelines for how-to-deal with complexity in human affairs, particularly in terms of communication between people.

This text continuous with a brief recall of the previously introduced Phenomeno-semantic notion to complexification, thereafter the here introduced pragmatic component is allocated into that notion. In the section thereafter the full Semiotic Model of complexification is articulated and briefly juxtaposed with the more conventional notion of complexity. A summary and suggestions for next steps close this text.

An explicit notion of *complexity* is central to the proposals given herein, and will unfold as their presentation is progressed; therefore, tentatively assumed, complexity is here regarded as the perception or conception of unpredictable and/or contra-intuitive yet intelligible behavior in a phenomenon under consideration.

The Model of Phenomeno-Semantic Complexification

We cannot assume here that an informed reader is familiar with the recently proposed *Phenomeno-Semanic* notion of complexity (Eriksson, 2007). On the other hand that notion is essential for the understanding of the here introduced *pragmatic-source* of complexification, which motivates a summarized recall of the Phenomeno-Semantic model.

In a broad sense, the phenomeno-semantic notion of complexification, as well as the one proposal herein, are inspired and derived from a French School of Systemics and its founding Projective Constructivist Epistemology (see Le Moigne, 1990; Eriksson, 1997).We start this recall with a brief account of Ogden's *Triangle of Meaning*, and its three interacting semiotic components; thereafter the recall proceeds with Neass-insired interpretation of the interrelations between the three components. Next is the Shannon-Weaver's *Model of Communication*, which incorporates Ogden's Triangle of Meaning in terms of two communicating and sense-making agents. This gives a framework for the articulation of the two sources, or drives, of complexification in human affairs: the *syntactical-transformation* and the *semantic-transformation*, during communication between two sense-making agents. In the following section, this framework is used to further extend this model by articulating the *pragmatic-component* as a source of complexification.

The inaccessibility to meaning

Ogden model of meaning proposes a concept of meaning constituted by a three-component structure. One is the very idea or mental concept held by a sense-making actor, a man, in his or her mind. Second is the thing, object or referent that is supposed to be conceived by the mental concept mentioned. Thirdly is the symbol, term, or signal, that is supposed to represent the mental concept and thereby the reference-object, see Figure 1 for an illustration of this structure.

The very interrelation between the three mentioned components is here interpreted with A. Naess' (1953) notion of *empirical semantics*, in contrast to *formal semantics* or logics. This implies that there is no absolute and exclusive one-to-one relation between the referred object and the mental concept, nor is there any such a relation between the mental concept and the symbol that is supposed to represent it, and hence the object. For example, the sentence "*Putin is ill*" and the sentence "*Putin is bad*" may both mean that [Putin is not healthy]. Yet, the sentence "*Putin is bad*", may also mean that [Putin is a poor politician]. Further, Naess states that there is no one-to-one direct and exclusive relationship between our mental concepts, ideas or meanings, on the one hand, and the actual situation, or objects or facts in the world, on the other. For example, the expression "*morning star*" typically means [the strongest shining star in the morning, in the east], while in fact it is the {the second planet from the sun, in the Milky Way}. A second expression "*evening star*" typically means [the strongest shining star in the evening, in the west], while it is in fact the {the second planet from the sun, in the Milky Way}. To make the example even more compelling, a third expression "*Venus*" typically means [the second planet from the sun, in the Milky Way] and in fact is the {the second planet from the sun, in the Milky Way}.

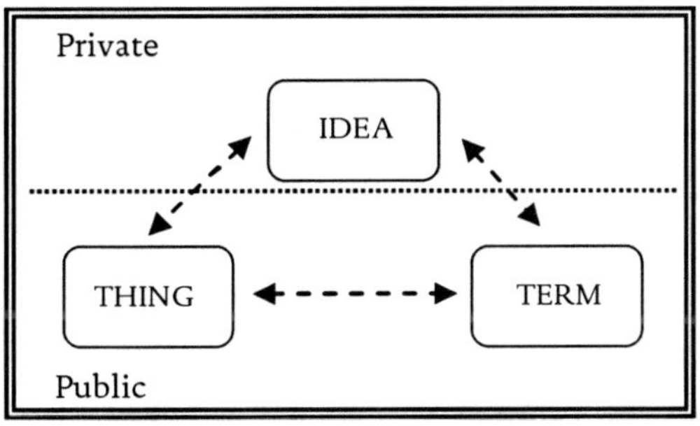

Figure 1 *Illustrates the so-called Ogden's triangle of meaning, consisting of three related components: (i) the meaning, or mental concept, or Idea; (ii) object, or referent, or Thing, which is the mental concept is about; (iii) the symbol, Term, or signal, representing the mental concept. The Idea is private for the individual as only he or she may access it directly while the Thing and the Term are public, as they may be accessed by other individuals.*

The lack of direct and exclusive relation between the three components of the meaning-triangle gives rise to difficulties in communication and hence understanding between people and human affairs. An example is the vagueness of terms, such as in the expression "*being bald*"; a more careful investigation gives rise to the question: how much – or little – hair does a person need to be described as "bald"?

The in-directness of Communication

Next step is the realization that when two sense-making actors interact in order to communicate, it means that two meaning-triangles interact. Hence, individual A holds a mental concept A that represents object A, and that is represented with symbol A, which is communicated, or transferred, to Individual B, where its interpretation gives rise to Mental Concept B, which he or she refers to Object B. The intention of such a communication is that the Individual B's Mental Concept B is to be equivalent with the Mental Concept A of Individual A, where both are supposed to refer to the same object, hence Object A to be the same as Object B. – Figure 2 illustrates these relationships. The above mentioned room for ambiguous relations between the three components, within a triangle of meaning, is further extended when two triangles of meaning are interacting. The source of this ambiguity, or miscommunication, is more formally and specifically articulated when employing Shannon and Weaver (1949) model of communication.

In *Shannon-Weaver's Model of Communication*, the sender, here 'Man 1', has an 'Idea 1', which he encodes resulting in 'Term 1', a symbol or signal. This is then physically communicated to the receiver, here 'Man 2', who decodes the symbols received, resulting in 'Idea 2'. Typically, the intention of the sender, here 'Man 1', is that the receiver, here 'Man 2', shall have the same idea, hence 'Idea 1' = 'Idea 2'. Figure 3 illustrates this concept.

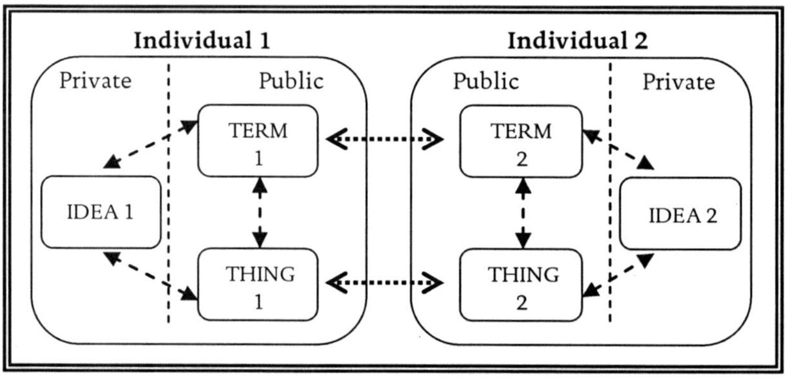

Figure 2 *Illustrates the relation between two Triangles of Meaning attempting to communicate. The two individuals communicate about the Thing with the help of the Term; where the latter two are public while the individuals' ideas are private.*

The Transformation of the Signal

The usefulness of Shannon's Model of Communication is that it facilitates the identification of two types of sources of noise, or transformation of the message, in the process of communication. These are (i) the *Semantic Transformation* and the (ii) *Syntactic Transformation*. This is illustrated in Figure 3.

Syntactic Transformation emerges when the actual syntax, symbol or signal, here 'Term 1', is physically transferred from the sender to the receiver. In electronic communication this often occurs as a result of various interferences with other electronic signals. In human mouth-to-mouth communication, this may occur due to interference with other sound waves, for example, when a construction machine generates sounds outside an open window to a room where two people are talking. For instance, while the sender, 'Man 1', says to the receiver, 'Man 2': "*I am not ill*", the sound interference may make the 'Man 2' hear "*I am ill*".

Secondly, the *Semantic Transformation* may emerge in two places in the communication model presented. Firstly, when an idea of a sender, here 'Idea 1' of 'Man 1', is encoded, i.e., formalized, into symbols, here 'Term A', and in the process of encoding or formalization, some of the meaning is missed. We can denote that here as *formalization-noise*, or encoding-noise. An intuitive example of this is a textbook on how to ski or swim; anyone who skis or swims knows that even though such a book may be instructive in many aspects, it is not enough to merely read the textbook to acquire sufficient knowledge and skills to be able to ski or swim.

The second instance of Semantic Transformation is when a receiver decodes a received symbol, hence *interpretation-noise*, or decoding-noise. Here 'Man 2' receives the 'Term 1' that is supposed to give rise to 'Idea 1'. In the process of assigning meaning to a symbol some meaning may be lost, or alternative meaning may be assigned.

A further distinction was introduced in the introduced model of phenomeno-semantic complexification, namely between *1st order* and *2nd order* of semantic complexification. Breifly, given a system in focus, the 1st order of semantic complexification refers to the transformation of the semantic component when a subject-system (i.e., the observing, inquiring, investigating) communicates about the object-system (i.e., system in focus that is investigated, observed, inquired), while the 2nd order of semantic complexification refers to transformation of the semantic component when the mentioned object-system communicates.

To summarize, we have now advanced a model of transformation of both the syntax and the semantics of a message. Hence, if a message communicated between two sense-making individuals, for example two employees in an organization, is utilized to stimulate the design and execution of actions, thus behavior, the unintended transformation of such a message may be understood as a foundation or a driver of the emergence of unpredicted behavior in psychological and social phenomena, hence giving rise to *complexity*! The given account summarizes the previously introduced model of phenomeno-semantic complexification, articulating the syntactical and the semantic drivers of complexification. In the following section, an additional driver of complexification is introduced, namely the *pragmatic component*.

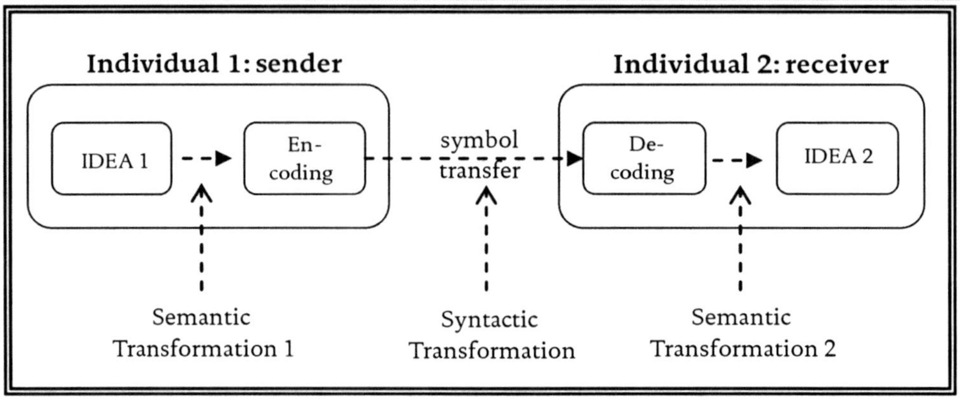

Figure 3 *Illustrates the semantic and syntactic transformation respectively, within Shannon & Weaver Model of Communication. In this, a sender, Individual 1, has an Idea 1 that is formalized into a symbol, by means of encoding and then physically transferring it to the receiver, here Individual 2. The latter interprets the received symbol by decoding it, which gives rise to an Idea 2. The purpose of this communication is to secure that Idea 1 of the sender is the same as the Idea 2 of the receiver. This goal is challenged by two types of transformation: the semantic transformation that occurs during encoding and decoding, and the syntactic transformation that occurs during the physical transfer of the symbol.*

The Pragmatic Source of Complexification

While the above recalled phenomeno-semantic complexity articulated the syntactical and the semantic drivers of complexification, that model may be further extended with an additional source of complexification: the *pragmatic component*.

Recalling that a sense-making agent, a human actor A, transfers a message to another sense-making agent, a human actor B, this very transfer exposes for the opportunity for syntactical and/or semantic transformation. However, *independently* of whether such transformation occurs or not, the receiver in the communication process, actor B may conduct some action(s) as a consequence of, or triggered by, the message received from actor A. This very phase from the reception of a message to the conduct of a consequent action may be a source of complexification in itself. For example, while a sender, actor A, may send a message to the receiver, the actor B, directing the latter to do an action, for instance to drive a car from point 1 to point 2, the action actually executed may be different from the type of action directed, hence the receiver may drive the car from point 1 to point 2, yet on the wrong side of the road, left instead of right, giving rise to unpredicted behavior, hence complexity. Figure 4 illustrates the position of the pragmatic driver on the receivers end, hence receiver-driven pragmatic complexification.

However, the pragmatic driver may also occur on the sender's side. This is so as an Event E, perceived by the Actor A, may trigger or give rise to Idea A1, yet the same Event E may also give rise to Idea A2, for Actor B. Depending on whether Idea A1 or A2 emerged from Event E, different messages may be communicated to Actor B, giving rise to different consequent actions, hence unpredicted behavior, or complexification.

The pragmatic complexification, both the *sender-driven* and the *receiver-driven*, may typically depend on the human actors' body of pre-understanding, his or her intentions and interests, and similar, hence factors that are utilized for the process of interpretation of perceived actions and for the directing of intended actions. A key contributing factor is that communication process, i.e., message transfer, is often limited, as it is seldom possible to be totally explicit about all aspect of received-action and consequent-action. In the mentioned example of the driving of a car, from point 1 to point 2, it may be possible to prevent the Actor B from driving the car on the unintended side of the road, by explicitly communicating this. An alternative strategy is to assure that the receiver pre-understands which side to drive the car on. Another example from our research is the sales operations of companies, where a sales representative communicates with a potential customer. The representative's task is typically to interpret the various customer-activities as sales-signals. Investigations have shown that similar customer-activities are interpreted differently by different representatives, which leads both to different sales strategies customized for a given customer and to different sales actions. On the sender end, we have experienced when a set of sales representatives, given seemingly the same product-information regarding the product to be detailed, interpret it rather differently and also conducts different sales activities toward a customer regarding the same product, which lead to unpredicted customer-behavior on the market.

This conception of the pragmatically driven complexification also opens two strategic avenues for dealing with it. One is the attention to the formulation of the content of the message, second is the selection of the actual actors to act as senders and receivers of the message. Hence, a carefully formulated message may know what kind of information is needed for the receiver in order to eliminate the emergence of pragmatically driven complexification. Likewise, carefully selected actors, with the desired pre-understanding and interests, may also eliminate the opportunity for such complexification. Interestingly, based in practical experiences, the operations within highly regulated industries, such as the pharmaceutical, the nuclear power, or the air traffic, all seem to have realized these two strategies, by means of detailed documentations and by means of regulation for actors' professional knowledge. Yet, this strategy has not always been fully successful as is evident by the various accidents when nuclear power stations blow up, pharmaceutical drugs are withdrawn from markets, and air traffic accidents occur.

The Emerged Model of Semiotic Complexification

The Model of Semiotic Complexification

The introduction of the pragmatic-driver of complexification, both by the sender and by the receiver, provide us with a more complete understanding of the emergence of complexity in psychological and social systems, or in human affairs. We propose to label this new notion the Model of Semiotic Complexification, as each of the three semiotic components – semantics, syntax,

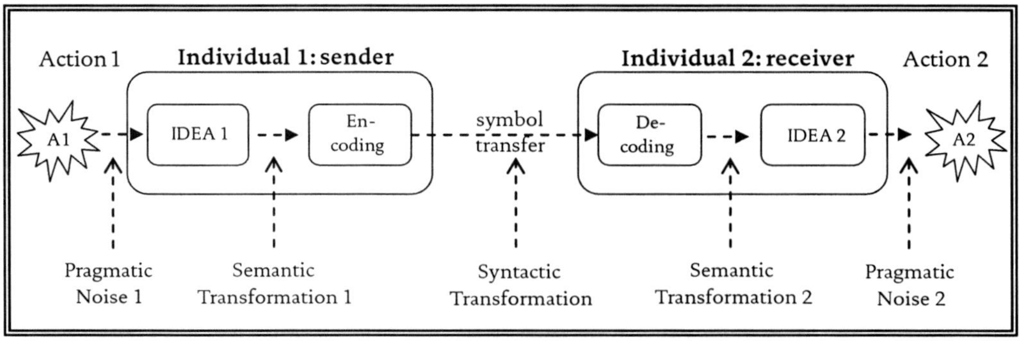

Figure 4 *Illustrates the here proposed Model of Semiotic Complexification, based upon the Shannon & Weaver Model of Communication. In this, a sender, Individual 1, is experiencing or perceiving Action 1, that gives rice to Idea 1, which is formalized into a symbol, by means of encoding and then physically transferring it to the receiver, here Individual 2. The latter interprets the received symbol by decoding it, which gives rise to an Idea 2, which triggers Action 2. This chain of actions, interpretation, encodings, transferring, decodings and acting creates opportunity for three types of complexification of the psycho-social systems: the pragmatic, the semantic, and the syntactic. Regarded from left hand, the first ambiguity emerges when one and the same Action 1 may give rise to different Ideas at the perceiving agent, here Individual 1, hence also unintended ideas, which is here understood as Pragmatic Noise 1, or perceiver-driven complexification. Secondly is the Semantic Transformation 1, where one and the same Idea 1 may be encoded, or represented by means of different semantics (signal or symbol). Thirdly is the transfer of the selected semantics to the receiver, where its unintended transformation may occur, giving rise here to the Semantic Transformation. Next is the decoding of the received symbol or signal into a mental concept, here Idea 2, this decoding may give rise to Semantic Transformation 2. Finally, the same Idea 2 may trigger various Actions 2, including some unintended, hence Pragmatic Noise 2. Together, there are two types of Pragmatic Noise, two types of Semantic Transformation, and one type of Syntactic Transformation. All may give rise to unintended, complex or unpredictable behavior in human affairs.*

pragmatics – are included, and each on its own accounts for the emergence of complexity. Hence, human affairs may manifest complex behavior – unpredictable, contra intuitive – where this complexity may emerge by means of semantic complexification – i.e., the transformation of the meaning in the transition process, weather in the formulation or the interpretation phase – or by means of syntactical transformation – i.e., the transformation of the signal or symbol in the transition phase – and by means of the pragmatic complexification – i.e. sender's alternative interpretation of a received-action and receiver's alternative consequent-action.

The Conventional Naturalist Model of Complexity

The Model of Semiotic Complexification may then be juxtaposed to the more conventional notion of complex system that is typically understood as a Complex Adaptive System (CAS); (Holland, 1994, 1995, 1998) – which we also understand as the Naturalist Model of Complexity.

The behavior of a CAS is regarded as dynamic, out-of-equilibrium, and thus highly non-linear. Such systems manifest the emergence of laws and patterns of order through cooperative effects of the sub-units, agents of a complex system, i.e., local coordination. CAS employ feedback mechanisms, parallel processing and simple local rules directing adaptive agents, which in turn can give rise to collective or global behavior of great complexity and variety, where deduction of the emergent behavior is very difficult. CAS is typically characterized by internal in-homogeneity of the system (i.e. it consists of a number of different classes of autonomous agents), adaptation of agents in the system, non-linear interaction between parts of the system, and the net-like causal structure of the system (high connectivity); (see Holland, 1995, 1998; Casti, 1997). They are therefore modelled as a set of agents, with local rules for behavior providing local coordination giving rise to an emerged global behavior and self-organization.

An example of CAS is an ant colony that organizes itself without a leader i.e., without any central and top-down directed coordination. Each ant appears to go about its own business, following a few simple rules determining its interaction with its environment or its fellow ants. An incredibly complex and organized society emerges from this interaction, displaying adaptation to changing circumstances.

The contemporary notions of complexity as outlined above may be understood in terms of some of their key characteristics. First *naturalism*, where the empirical observations made as a basis for induction of theoretical propositions, are most frequently based in physical, chemical, and biological phenomena. The peculiar characteristics of mental systems, both psychological and socio-psychological, such as sense-making or power-structures are not accounted for. Secondly, *syntactic-orientation* where understanding of complex behavior of studied phenomena emerges from numerical simulation models using a set of rules guiding the interaction of the constituting components. This is shown by syntactic manipulation, i.e., representation, rather than focusing on the pragmatic and semantic aspects of the phenomena studied. Thirdly, *objectification*, where studies of complexity focus mainly on the observed-system and do not seriously account the observing-system - in this endeavour, such studies typically assume a kind of ontological representation, i.e., direct correspondence between the model and the modelled phenomena. These three characteristics allow us to label the contemporary notions of complexity as '*Onto-Syntactic*'.

The Two Notions of Complexity are Complementary

Tentatively speaking, the here presented Model of Semiotic Complexification and the more conventional notion of complex systems, the model of the Complex Adaptive System, may be regarded as complementary to each other.

Considered together they may extend the research areas and approaches into complexity, and also enrich the set of managerial tools available for dealing with complexity.

The two models have different empirical sources, in terms of the observation and induction of proposals. While the semiotic approach has its source in psychological and social phenomenon, where interacting sense-making agents are the key phenomenon, the adaptive system approach has its typical source in physical, chemical and biological phenomena. Taken together, the two approaches cover the typical layers of systems, from physical, via chemical, biological, mental, to social. This is important at least for one key reason: it supports the avoidance of reductionism (yet, does not guard), here understood as an attempt to understand a phenomenon of a given complexity, e.g., mental, in terms of a phenomenon of a lower complexity, e.g., chemical. By derivation, the question in this context is then whether the Complex Adaptive System approach is capable to make enough of justice to the complexity of mental and social phenomena? One support for the inability is that contemporary social sciences focuses extensively on the communicative aspects of sense-making actors, for instance Habermas' (1984, 1987) communicative rationality and Searl's (1969) speech act theories, among others. While the Complex Adaptive System disregards from this communicative aspect in its notion of complexity.

Turning from differences into similarities, between the two approaches to complexity, we may notice that both account for the interactions of intelligent agents, the semiotic of sense-making agents only while the CAS approach seemingly of all type of agents. Also, both approaches account for the emergence of complex behavior, generally understood as contra-intuitive, unpredictable yet intelligible. Given the similarities and differences suggested here, the CAS approach may be regarded as more general encompassing all type of systems, from physical to social, while the semiotic approach may be regarded as more specific, accounting only for psychological and social systems.

Some Direction for the Complexity Research and Management

The highlighted differences, similarities and complementary understanding of the two approaches to complexity also have implications of the formulation of research strategies into complexity as well as practical management of complexity. One clear difference is the role of Information and Communication Technology (ICT). In the CAS approach, the key role of ICT is for the execution of relevant models of CAS, hence for the study of complexity. On the other hand, in the semiotic approach the role of ICT is within the complex system as such, the execution of its actual operations. In this, ICT may potentially enable, for example, the reduction of the unwanted emergence of semiotic and semantic driven complexification. As a consequence, the CAS approach requires formulation of novel formal languages for the representation of CAS while the semiotic approach may require novel languages and protocols for communication between sense-making agents. Even though in different manner, in both approaches representation, languages, and ICT seem to be central for the management of complexity.

Turning attention to the practical management of complexity in human affairs, the semiotic approach to complexity seems particularly fruitful to contemporary organizations and society that increasingly relies on knowledge workers and citizens. In this, the role of financial and natural resources seem to be reduced in favor of the knowledge and human capital. Whether in public or industrial organizations, among many others, knowledge, meaning, language, communication, seem all to be central for a successful conduct of their operations. Therefore, the recommendations from the semiotic notion of complexification put attention to the means of explicit conceptualizations of central concepts utilized in key operations, the languages and protocols employed for such communications, including documentation standards. Also, an explicit contextualization of such meanings is central, in terms of the cultural, political, and operational structures governing particular utilization of key concepts as well as execution of related actions. Finally, a deliberate design and utilization of appropriate symbolism for the support of representation, for communication processes, and for the execution of operations in human affairs, deserves managerial attention.

Summary and Further Research

Our civilization seems to face increasing challenges from experiences in human affairs that manifest unpredicted and contra-intuitive behavior, yet in some manner intelligible, whether this may be failures in managing patients at hospitals, managing safety operations at nuclear stations, or more generally failing in achieving productive and effective operations in human endeavor. Seemingly as a reaction, a fairly recent domain of inquiry has emerged, still in its infantry, called typically as *Complexity Sciences.* A well accepted approach to the comprehension of complexity is the so-called Complex Adaptive System approach. This understands complexity as the interaction of adaptive agents governed by local rules, yet giving rise to novel unpredictable global behavior. While this approach has its merits it also manifests some limitation, especially with regard to the comprehension of complexity generated by psychological and social systems. To remedy this, an alternative and complementary approach has been proposed, the so-called phenomeno-semantic notion of complexity. The latter suggests that complex behavior in psychological and social phenomena emerges in the communication process between two sense-making agents, more specifically when unintended syntactical and semantic transformation of the message occurs. In this text, we have proposed an addendum to this notion of complexity, namely the pragmatic component. This accounts for two types of pragmatic drivers of complexification and both for the multi-faced relation between an action or event in human affairs and the mental concept related to it. The sender-driven pragmatic complexification occurs when a particular event gives rise to an unwanted conception in the mid of its perceiver while the receiver-driven pragmatic complexification occurs when an unwanted event is animated by the receiver given a specific mental concept to trigger that event.

It is proposed here that both approaches to the comprehension and management of complexity – the Complex Adaptive System notion and the Semiotic notion – are complementary to each other, both in terms of needed research agendas and also their role in the toolbox in dealing with complexity in human affairs. In both cases representation, languages, communication protocols, and Information and Communication Technology play a central role, yet in different manner.

References

Casti, J. (1997). *Would-be Worlds: how simulation is changing the frontiers of science.* John
Wiley & Sons, New York. ISBN: 0-471-12308-0

Eriksson, D.M. (1997). A principal exposition of Jean-Louis Le Moigne's Systemic Theory.
Cybernetics & Human Knowing. Vol. 4, No. 2-3, pp. 35-77. ISSN 0907-0877

Eriksson, D.M. (2007). Phenomeno-Semantic Complexity: A proposal for an alternative notion of complexity as a foundation for the management of complexity in human affairs. *Emergence: Complexity & Organization,* Vol. 9, No. 1-2, 2007. ISSN 1521-3250

Holland, J. (1994). Echoing emergence: objectives, rough definitions, and speculations for ECHO-class models. In: *Complexity – Metaphors, Models, and Reality*; Vol. XIX of Studies in the Science of Complexity; Crownan, G. Pines, D. Meltzer, D. Eds., Santa Fe Institute, pp. 310-334. ISBN: 0-201-62606-3

Habermas, J. (1984). *The theory of communicative action – reason and the rationalisation of society* (Vol. I). Beacon Press, Boston, MA.

Habermas, J. (1987). *The theory of communicative action – Volume Two: life world and systems: A critique of functionalist reason.* Beacon Press, Boston, MA.

Holland, J. (1995). *Hidden Order.* Addison-Wesley, Reading. ISBN 0-201-40793-0

Holland, J. (1998). *Emergence.* Oxford University Press, Oxford. ISBN 0-201-14943-5

Le Moigne, J.L.(1990). *La modélisation des systèmes complexes,* Dunod, Paris. ISBN: 2-10-004382-X

Naess, A. (1953). *Interpretation and preciseness: a contribution to the theory of communication.* Det norske videnskaps-akademi i Oslo. No ISBN.

Searle, J.R. (1969). *Speech Acts, an Essay in the Philosophy of Language.* Cambridge University Press, London, U.K. ISBN: 0-521-07184-4

Shannon, Claude E. & Warren, Weaver (1949): *A Mathematical Model of Communication.* Urbana, IL: University of Illinois Press. No ISBN.

54. An Evaluation of R. L. Ackoff's Interactive Planning: A Case of Systemic Development of an Organizational Unit

Darek M. Eriksson
Luleå University of Technology, SWE

Russel L. Ackoff, regarded as a leading authority within management and systems thinking, designed the Interactive Planning (IP) methodology. It is a conceptual tool to guide systematic and systemic organizational development. One of its unique features is that the organizational development should be ideal-oriented yet informed by experimental experience. IP has been appreciated within management science in general and within the systems thinking community in particular, and more than 300 applications of IP have been mentioned. However, the question "what is the empirical usefulness of IP?" cannot be easily answered, as there exist no independent, systematic, empirically grounded, and critical evaluations of IP's usefulness – the study presented here does offer such a unique evaluation. In this case, IP was employed to support the comprehensive development of a Medical Department at a pharmaceutical company. This IP application was evaluated using a set of predefined evaluation criteria derived from the IP as such and from its critique. The results show that IP is indeed a powerful methodology for guiding organizational development. While IP does have several positive merits, a set of limitations were identified and serve as a basis for deriving recommendations for the practitioners using IP and also areas that merit further development by its researchers.

Introduction

This text presents a case study based, evaluation of Interactive Planning (IP) methodology. Russell Ackoff, regarded as a leading management and systems thinking authority, has developed IP as a methodology for the support of organizational development. Among many such methodologies, IP has some unique features, including its focus on an ideal-driven design of organizations as well as their experimentally-based development.

Even though more than 300 IP applications have been mentioned in the literature (e.g. Ackoff, 1981; Jackson, 2000: 246) these applications do not provide an informed answer to the question: *what is the empirical usefulness of IP?* The study presented here attempts answering this question, by the conduct of a real life application of IP that is systematic, empirically grounded, and informed by the critique of IP. This case study applied IP to the development of a Medical Department at a pharmaceutical company. Among others, the results show that

IP is indeed a feasible and powerful methodology for the guidance of organizational development. The results also show that there are challenges that may emerge in the course of IP application, which the future practitioners as well as researcher may find of relevance. These challenges also confirm the current the critique of IP and expand further.

The cases study was conducted in an action research manner (Checkland & Holwell, 1998), however given the space limitations the research methodology is not explicated here, yet the reader may it implicitly derive from the descriptions given here. Next section presents the organization that was subjected to the transformation. Then comes the summary of the results obtained in the study, hence the very evaluation of the IP application. The text ends with Conclusions.

The Transformed Organization

The organization subjected to the deliberate transformation, as guided by Ackoff's Interactive Planning, is described in this section, in terms of its structure, processes, and motivation for the intervention.

Structural Overview of the NorPhar

The transformed organization was a Medical Department within the Nordic Branch of a major international pharmaceutical company (hereafter Pharmaco). This Nordic Branch (hereafter NorPhar) was responsible for marketing and sales of pharmaceutical products in the Nordic Countries.

Organizational Structure: NorPhar had approximately 250 employees distributed over a number of organizational units. The organizational structure included four Market Organizations, one for each country, (Denmark, Finland, Norway, Sweden) while operations in Iceland were outsourced. The NorPhar organization included a number of shared-services units such as: Medical Department, Regulatory Department, Human Resources Department, Public Affairs Department, Business Development Department, and Financial Department which also included the Information Systems Unit and Logistics Unit. NorPhar was managed by the Nordic Management Team, constituted by the Directors from each Department and Market Organization, and led by the Managing Director who, in turn, reported to the European President. See Figure 1 for an overview of the organizational structure of NorPhar. Each Market Organization was led by a Country Manager and included a number of Business Units, each led by a Business Unit Manager, and made up of one or more Market Assistants and Product Managers, and one or more Field Sales Managers, where the latter managed a number of Product Specialists, also referred to as sales representatives. See Figure 2 for an overview of the Market Organizations.

Operations of the Medical Department

The Medical Department was structured into five medical units: the Safety Unit, the Medical Information Unit, the Medical Advisory Unit, the Clinical Trial Unit, and the Health Economic Unit.

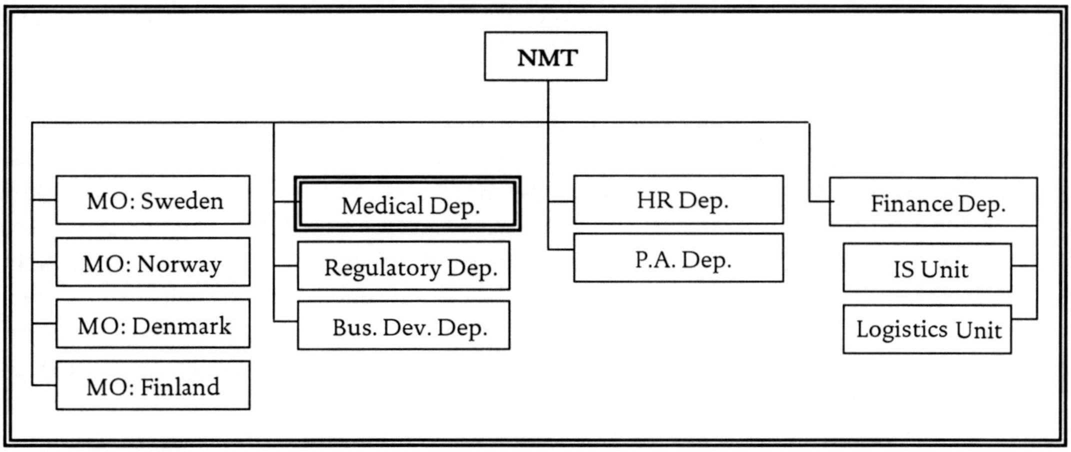

Figure 1 *Illustrates an overview of the organizational structure of the NorPhar.*

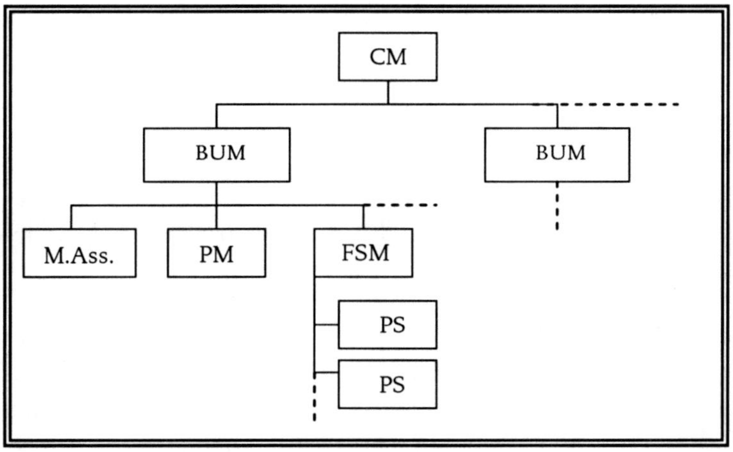

Figure 2 *Illustrates a structural overview of the four Market Organizations. Each is managed by a Country Manager (CM), who typically has several Business Unit Managers (BUM), managing the Business Unit. A Business Unit has typically one or two Market Assistants (M.Ass.), one or twoProduct Managers (PM), one or several Field Sales Managers (FSM), where the latter manage several Product Specialists (PM).*

The *Safety Unit* was made up of Safety Officers with sole responsibility for management and execution of the so-called Adverse-Event-Reporting process. The *Medical Information Unit* had Medical Information Officers (MIO) who handled the Medical Information & Advisory toward internal and external inquires. The Medical Advisors within the *Medical Advisory Unit* were involved in both the Clinical-Trial process and the Medical Information & Advisory process. Medical Advisors were also responsibility for the medical validity of the marketing material. The *Health Economic Unit* was responsible for Generation-of-Relevant-Health-Economic-Data-and-Arguments when pricing negotiations were conducted between the NorPhar and the local pricing authorities, i.e., customers. Finally, the Medical Director was responsible for Management-

Control, i.e., the planning, budgeting, directing monitoring and controlling, of the Medical Department's operations.

The Rationale of the Initiative

The dynamics of the business environment together with the offensive business growth objectives inclined NorPhar to choose a *customer-oriented business strategy*, aiming at increasing the customer-base of current products. This gave rise to a new need to establish a type of medical operations never previously realized in the business environment. A key challenge of this development need was how to develop or transform this organizational entity, as there was no best practice available on the market to be studied and copied into the NorPhar. Therefore, the company and its Medical Department literally needed to invent their future operations. This development was objectified in terms of establishing medical operations that (a) manifest flawless coordination with the marketing and sales units, (b) manifest a high level of customer-orientation in its operations, and (c) manifest a high level quality of all the operations conducted at the Medical Department.

The Evaluated Interactive Planning

The following section presents the Interactive Planning methodology in terms of *IP-postulates*; these summarize and operationalize the IP-methodology, the key sources utilized were Ackoff (1968, 1970a, 1970b, 1974, 1981, 1999a, 1999b; Ackoff, *et al.*, 2006).

Further, a set of published IP application cases was identified (i.e., Ackoff 1968, 1970a, 1970B, 1974, 1981, 1999a, 1999b; Ackoff & Emshoff, 1975a; 1975b; Ackoff, *et al.*, 1976; Ackoff, *et al.*, 2006; Ozbekhan, 1977; Ciccantelli & Magidson, 1993; Jackson 2000; Leemann, 2002). However, none of these represents an independently conducted evaluation, based on empirically based and critically oriented case.

Interactive Planning

Interactive Planning (IP) is a procedure that prescribes how to develop and management social systems, i.e., organizations, whether business or other. Ackoff (1981:246) expresses the intention of IP in the following terms: *"The objective of interactive planning is an effective pursuit of an idealized state. The state is formulated as a design of that system with which the current system's stakeholders would replace it if they were free to do so. Such a system should be technologically feasible and operationally viable, and it should provide the system with an ability to learn and adapt quickly and effectively."*

IP as such is summarized below in terms of thirteen *Postulates of Interactive Planning*; these were used as a guide for the actual use of IP in this case and also served as criteria for its evaluation. Two additional IP-Postulates are presented further on, providing the evaluation with a total of sixteen IP-Postulates.

IP-Postulate 1: Organizational Self-Development
The overall purpose of IP is to establish a successful, self-developing organization.

IP-Postulate 2: Ideal-Seeking Procedure
IP provides conceptual support for the design and realization of an ideal-seeking organizational sub-set (procedures and resources), that is capable of effective ideal-seeking.

IP-Postulate 3: Learn & Adapt
IP provides conceptual support for the establishment of an organization which is able to learn and to adapt.

IP-Postulate 4: Participation
All stakeholders of the organization subjected to development should participate in the process of plan formulation for that organization.

IP-Postulate 5: Continuity
Formulation of plans for the organization subjected to development should be conducted continuously, i.e. in a never-ending process.

IP-Postulate 6: Holism
Formulation of plans for an organizational unit should include representatives from the unit subjected to development, from all units at the same horizontal level and from units one level above and one level below in the vertical structure.

IP-Postulate 7: Current & Uninterrupted Future
Formulation of developmental plans should generate a detailed description of (i) the current operations in their environment, including (ii) identified obstructions, and (iii) a future state of the operations when no deliberate developmental intervention is realized.

IP-Postulate 8: Ideal Organization
Formulation of developmental plans should generate a detailed description of an ideal and desired organization, as conceived by its stakeholders at the given time.

IP-Postulate 9: Management System
Formulation of developmental plans should generate a detailed description of a customized Management System that is capable of identifying the current situation, comparing it with the ideal situation, and conducting informed decision-making regarding necessary corrective measures and re-formulation of the defined ideal striven after.

IP-Postulate 10: Organizational Structure
The ideal organization of the operations should be structured in three dimensions in relation to (i) the *consumers* of the outputs, to (ii) the *outputs*, and to (iii) the *inputs*.

IP-Postulate 11: Activity Plan
Formulation of developmental plans should generate a detailed description of a plan of means that accounts for all the key activities needing to be conducted to bring operations from their current situation toward their desired ideal situation.

IP-Postulate 12: Resource Plan
Formulation of developmental plans should generate a detailed description of a resource plan that accounts for all the resources needed to execute the activities defined in the Activity Plan.

IP-Postulate 13: Controlled Implementation
Implementation of the formulated plans should comprise the realization of planned activities followed by monitoring and control of realized activities versus the planned ideal; when the difference between the actually-realized and the planned-to-be-realized has been identified, corrective activities should be formulated and executed.

Key Criticism of Interactive Planning

Since Ackoff's introduction, Interactive Planning has attracted some criticism, mainly from a Marxist-oriented sociological point of view. Jackson (2000: 244-246) summarizes this critique in two key issues. One is that IP is not capable of addressing *prevailing social power-structures* inherent in a situation; such power structures influence the execution of the IP-process and hence its result. In this matter, a particular concern is the inequality of the political power of all stakeholders, the so-called '*irresolvable conflicts*'. It is said that such situations make it impossible to agree upon a consensus-based ideal of a social system.

Secondly, and related to the above, is the fact that not all stakeholders will always be *allowed* to participate in the execution of an IP-process, which is a key feature of the latter, both for its validity and its ethical concerns. Ackoff responded to this criticism (1975, 1982; Jackson, 2000: 246) yet not very convincingly. This criticism was utilized in the evaluation of the this IP application. More specifically, it was operationalized in terms of two following additional evaluation criteria:

IP Postulate 14: IP cannot resolve power structures
The procedures of IP do not provide any means for identification and resolution of potential social power structures inherent in the addressed managerial situation.

IP Postulate 15: IP cannot include all stakeholders

The procedures of IP do not provide any means for the identification of all relevant stakeholders of the addressed managerial situation and their inclusion in the execution of the IP-process.

Evaluation of Interactive Planning Application

This part reports the results obtained form the IP-application, in relation to the defined IP-postulates.

Evaluation of the Interactive Planning Process

This section presents the results of the evaluation of the IP process as such, i.e. the *procedural intra-case analysis*; Table 1 presents a summary of the outcome. The text below gives a summary of the IP assessment in terms of each evaluation criteria.

1. *Organizational Self-Development* was judged *positively* as the establishment of organizational procedures and sub-organization did already work in accordance with the IP-process resulting in actual and continuous self-development.
2. *Ideal-Seeking Procedure* was judged *positively* as the established procedures for self-development of the Medical Department organization did formulate visionary and ideal notions of operations. The key issue identified in this process was how to *validate the content* generated by the ideal-seeking procedure, i.e., the very ideal formulated. IP's answer to this is that a *consensus* among the involved stakeholders provides validity status for a proposal. However, the issue identified was: what if all stakeholders hold a consensus about an ideal, yet the agreed ideal lacks feasibility in the actual operations, for example, as the stakeholders' understanding of the competitive market place at hand is not adequate? IP does not give any substantial answer to this.
3. *Learn and Adapt* was judged *positively* in so far as a learning-procedure was established, due to the Management System commented below, which continuously monitored performance and detected any divergence from the plans, which became subject to modifications and changes. However, the observation was made that such learning and adaptation was limited to predefined goals and ideals, and thus did not promote learning and adaptation in regard to issues outside such a definition. This may be hazardous if the content of such a definition lacks relevance for the prevailing conditions, whether they are external or internal.
4. *Participation* of the stakeholders was judged *negatively,* and a key problem in the employment of IP and hence the development of the Medical Department. IP prescribes that all stakeholders should be involved in the formulation of the ideal to be striven after. If a stakeholder is understood to be someone or something –e.g. a person or an institution– that holds an interest, in the organization in the broad sense, the immediate question is then what is really meant by a stake or an interest, and where should the boundary be

set? The whole developmental effort suffered from a lack of participation of the stakeholders, both the absence of several internal stakeholders and various external stakeholders. The reason for this was twofold; for the internal stakeholders it was a mix of a lack of interest and prioritization and the fact that they were not invited to the process, while even the external stakeholders were not invited. This lack of invitation was motivated by the position that the department had to get its operations stable before opening it up externally.

5. *Continuity* was judged *positively* as the execution of the IP-process included regular work, typically on a weekly basis, on organizational development. In addition, the formulated ideals including desired operations as well as the means and resource plans were reviewed regularly and modified where the need was identified.
6. *Holism* includes the principles of coordination and of integration, i.e., that the departments or units hierarchically immediately above and below the studied department ought to participate in the IP-process of the Medical Department. This overlaps the participation postulate as discussed above, as it specifies the type of stakeholders needing to participate. As mentioned above, no other units or departments within the company were represented in the IP-process executed therefore a *negative* outcome for this IP-postulate was logged.
7. *Current and Uninterrupted Future* was judged *positively* after extensive modelling of the department's current situation as well as of its obstacles, problems and scenarios for the future assuming that no intervention was conducted – all as suggested by IP.
8. *Ideal-Organization* was also judged *positively*. The participants were asked to conceive and propose ideal situations, with the only limitations suggested by IP. In several senses this ideal-focused approach to design was regarded as positive by the participants, in that they experienced that suddenly someone was seriously asking for their personal opinions with regard to their profession – something they did not experience often.

Even though the ideal-focused approach was experienced as positive with regard to its procedure, or way of working with the design, it was not perceived as positive with regard to the decision as to content of the ideal design. This was particularly manifested in the Clinical Trial unit, where two different roles of employees attempted to find a consensus of the ideal way of conducting clinical trials. The Clinical Managers considered that they should be responsible for the whole clinical trial process while Medical Advisors should be used as advisors in the initial phase of the design of a trial and later in the final phase when conclusions were derived. The Medical Advisors, on the other hand, had the view that they should be responsible for the whole trial, and that Clinical Managers should be used for the operational work of setting-up a study and for gathering of data. Even though various attempts were made to find a consensus, and the final decision became a policy document stipulating the second solution, this conflict with regard to the content of the future ideal significantly contributed to the employees leaving the department for other jobs, which also created operational disturbances in the department – in other words, the conflict was not solved while maintaining the system constituents!

9. *Management System* was judged *positively*, as an explicit procedure was established for managing the whole IP-process, with dedicated roles and staff members and their activities.
10. *Organizational Structure* was judged *negatively*, as it was never established strictly in accordance with the IP-directive. This stipulates that the customer-related units, the output units, and the input units be separated from each other. The Medical Department was structured mainly according to its outputs, e.g. Adverse Event reports and Clinical Trials, for two main reasons. One was that the Department was regarded as too small, in terms of number of its employees, i.e., approx. 20, to justify the stipulated three-dimensional organization as a meaningful and cost-effective operational structure. Secondly, the department was part of a Nordic company, which in turn was part of a Global company with general global policies regarding organizational structure; these global policies did not promote the structuring approach stipulated by IP.
11. *Activity Plan and...*
12. *Resource Plan* were both judged *positively* and shown to be a powerful input to the implementation phase. Once the desired situation and the current situation had been explicitly and consistently described, it became an analytical task to derive the activities and resources needed to move the organization from its current state to its future one.
13. *Controlled Implementation* was judged *positively*, however an aspect was experienced in relation to the controlled implementation work, the fact that an ideal design easily promotes formulation of new types of solutions that have typically not been realized before, within or outside the organization. This means that the proposed solutions are highly hypothetical and lack empirical experience. Implementation of such solutions can easily be dangerous – i.e., give rise to the emergence of unanticipated and unwanted consequences – and is resource-consuming, as it is not always feasible to re-use previous solutions. To cope with the management of the above-mentioned danger, Ackoff (1981: 237) proposes experimentation: *"...if an organization's ability to improve its performance continuously is to be developed, the implementation of plans should be undertaken experimentally. Experimentation is controlled experience; it enables us to learn much more rapidly and effectively than we can from ordinary experience and trial and error."* However, the experience is that such experience is also highly resource consuming. At the end, the implementation of ideals can easily become a matter of a cost-benefit analysis.
14. *Lack of Conflict Resolution* facilitation capability by IP was judged *negatively*. As mentioned above, the emerged conflict between the two roles, Medical Advisors and Clinical Managers, in the design of the ideal clinical trial pro-

cess, could not be resolved while maintaining these individuals within the Department, hence the system; it led instead to the employee deflection. No conceptual support was found in the IP-literature with regard to handling such conflicts. The only IP-suggestion identified was to focus on ideals even further away in time: *"In general, people disagree less about ideals that about short-range goals and means for obtaining them"* (Ackoff, 1981:118). However, the ideal-oriented focus of the design was assumed for the very start of the design-process yet the conflict emerged.

15. *Lack of Stakeholder Participation* was also judged *negatively*. As mentioned in the discussion, IP's directive to include all stakeholders is intuitively reasonable yet was conceptually unclear and operationally not feasible in this case. Conceptually regarded, there is a need to support the definition of what or who is a stakeholder and why. Practically regarded, the number of stakeholders may easily become unmanageably large, challenging both the resources needed to include all and also the lead-time needed to execute the IP-process.

Summary and Conclusions

This text presents an evaluation of the practical usefulness of Interactive Planning methodology, based in a case study that applied IP to the development of a Medical Department in a pharmaceutical company. The results are regarded as unique, as there seem not to be any previous report of an independently conducted, empirically based and critically oriented evaluation of IP. The results obtained suggest that IP is indeed a feasible and powerful methodology for the support of the development of an organization. The results also showed a set of challenges that may emerge during the process of IP application, including the challenge to *secure participation of stakeholders* and the challenge to *manage deliberately prevailing power-structures* in social settings - both experienced challenges confirm current critique of IP. Additional results include the observation that IP *implicitly promotes a decentralised organizational leadership and culture* and seem to assume that it is always preferable, and the observation that IP's stipulation for *an ideal-driven organizational development potentially opens organizations for a greater risk and higher costs* during the development process – something that is not always desirable.

The here presented challenges, observations, and experiences may all inform both researchers and practitioners of organizational development. The primer by suggesting areas that merit further empirical and conceptual development, the latter by suggesting areas that need careful attention when actually developing an organization by means of Interactive Planning.

References

Ackoff, R.L.(1968). Toward an Idealized University. *Management Science*,15,B-121-131. ISSN: 0025-1909

Ackoff, R.L.(1970a). *A concept of corporate planning*. Wiley, NewYork.ISBN:0-471-00290-9

Ackoff, R.L.(1970b). A black ghetto's research on a university, *Op.Res*,18:761-771.

#	Label	Outcome	Comment
1	Organizational Self-Development	Yes	Yes, until the deflection of employees.
2	Ideal-Seeking Procedure	Yes	What should be the content of the ideal, how to be sure about its validity?
3	Learn & Adapt	Yes	Learning & adaptation is limited to the detractions from the ideal defined.
4	Participation	No	Difficult to get all stakeholders involved.
5	Continuity	No	Disturbed, as majority of the employees of the department left it.
6	Holism	No	Yes, with other units horizontally, not with the top management, i.e., not vertically
7	Current & Uninterrupted Future	Yes	Powerful didactic tool, and also operational prerequisite for derivation of valid activity and resource plans
8	Ideal Organization	Yes	How to determine the validity of the content of a proposed ideal?
9	Management System	Yes	Powerful and needed for implementation control, decision making criteria needed.
10	Organisational Structure	No	Too small organisation, and global policy driven
11	Activity Plan	Yes	Careful prioritisation needed.
12	Resource Plan	Yes	Careful prioritisation needed.
13	Controlled Implementation	Yes	Resource demanding.
14	IP cannot resolve power-structures	No	Unable to resolve.
15	IP cannot include all stakeholders	No	Situations emerge easily where the number of stakeholders is unmanageable; also the power-structures may hinder stakeholder participation.

Table 2 *Presents the fourteen evaluation criteria employed in the evaluation of Interactive Planning. The left-hand rows present the labels of the criteria, the Outcome row represents whether the criteria was fulfilled or not in the present case, while the Comment row presents any observations made that may have relevance for the future use of IP.*

ISSN: 0030-364X

Ackoff, R.L.(1974). *Redesigning the Future*. Wiley, New York.ISBN:87-17-03277-6

Ackoff, R.L.(1981). *Creating the Corporate Future*. Wiley, NewYork. ISBN:0-471-09009-3

Ackoff, R.L.(1982). On the hard headedness and soft heartedness of M. C. Jackson. *J.Appl.Sys. Anal*, 9: 31, ISSN: 0960-085X

Ackoff, R.L.(1999a). *Ackoff's Best: his classic writings on management.* Wiley, NewYork.ISBN:0-471-31634-2

Ackoff, R.L.(1999b). *Re-creating the corporation: A Design of organizations for the 21st Century*, Oxford Univ.Press, NY. ISBN: 0-19-512387-5

Ackoff, R.L.(1976).*Designing a National Scientific and Technological Communications Systems: The SCATT Report.* Co-authored with: Cowen, T., Davis, P., Elton, M.,
Emery, J.C., Meditz, M. Sachs, W. University of Pennsylvania Press, Philadelphia.

Ackoff, R.L., Emshoff, J.R.,(1975a).Advertising research at Anheuser-Busch, Inc. (1963-1968). *Sloan Manage. Rev*,16 (Winter),1-15.ISSN:0019-848X

Ackoff, R.L.,Emshoff,J.R.,(1975b). Advertising research at Anheuser-Busch, Inc. (1968-1974).*Sloan Manage.Rev*,16 (Spring),1-16.ISSN:0019-848X

Ackoff, R.L.,Magidson,J.,Addison,H.J.(2006).*Idealized Design. Creating an Organization's Future.* Wharton School Pub.NJ.ISBN:0131963635

Checkland, P.B..,Holwell,S.(1998).Action Research: Its Nature and Validity. *Systemic Practice and Action Research*.Vol.11,No.1,pp.9-21.ISSN:1094-429X

Ciccantelli, S., Magidson, J,(1993).Consumer idealized design: involving consumers in the product development process. *J.Prod. Innov. Manag.* 10(4), 341-347. ISSN:0737-6782

Jackson, M.C. (2000). *Systems approaches to management.* Kluwer, N.Y. ISBN: 0306474654

Leemann, J.E..(2002).Applying Interactive Planning at DuPont: The Case of Transformation a Safety, Health, and Environmental Function to Deliver Business Value. *Systemic Practice and Action Research*,Vol.15,No.2,85-109.ISSN:0737-6782.

55. Retaining Organizational Knowledge: Learning Histories Revisited

Kevin Laws
Faculty of Education and Social Work, The University of Sydney, AUS

Robert McLeod
University of New South Wales Foundation Studies Programme, AUS;
Northern Beaches English College, AUS

Considerable attention has been given to the acquisition, dissemination and utilisation of knowledge within an organization. During the 1990s researchers undertook studies of major business organizations to discover answers to questions such as: What types of learning efforts work? Why do they work, and why do they not? They devised the concept of creating a learning history as a means of answering these questions. However these histories took considerable time to produce, involved considerable costs and involved large numbers of employees. During the past decade the authors of this paper have investigated ways in which the concept of a learning history (LH) may be used at levels below that of a whole organization to address issues of immediate concern to departments and teams. This paper reports on a number of projects which were undertaken in this regard.

Introduction

In today's world a new managerial mindset is demanded to successfully confront the substantial challenges and the unprecedented and continuous changes that are occurring. An important aspect of this new mindset is the acceptance that we live in the era of the 'knowledge society'. Knowledge acquisition, dissemination, utilisation and retrieval have become essential strategies in organizations and this has placed a significant emphasis on the importance of continuous learning at the individual, team, departmental and organizational levels.

Previously, the authors have discussed the suitability and effectiveness of a number of organizational learning methodologies (see for example Laws & McLeod, 1996, 1997, 1998, 2004). This paper will focus on organizational learning and the use of learning histories (LHs) as a means of facilitating organizational change and as a means of retaining knowledge within an organization for use in the future.

Organizational Learning

All organizations can be thought of as learning systems with both formal and informal processes and structures that facilitate learning. The nature of learning and the way in which it occurs is determined by the organization's culture and sub-cultures. Over the past twenty years there have been many who have tried to create 'learning organizations' through the use of different strategies, such as computer simulations, systems analysis, systems dynamics, management science and operations research.

Van Aken, Berends and van der Bij (2007: 118) focused on problem solving in organizations and suggested that learning for the future can be enhanced when organizations reflect on both the successes and the failures of the past. However, they warned that learning from experience is not automatic and requires reflection, and that reflection is greatly enhanced if there is an external point of reference. For Girard and Lambert (2007) the written story proved to be a motivator for organizational change and an effective way to share knowledge. Kok (2007) used qualitative methods to help reveal a new framework for the measurement and management of 'Intellectual Capital'. O'Sullivan and Azeem (2007) analyzed the nature of different collaborative group structures, while Papoutsakis (2007) described 'Knowledge Sharing Networks' that facilitated the complicated task of organizational learning.

Cutcher-Gershenfeld and Ford (2005: 151-154) emphasized the importance of 'bold vision (i.e., the linking of data, knowledge, and action) and of 'harsh realities' in the dynamic business world. They acknowledged that learning took place at a number of different levels (organizational, group and local), and that organizations were involved in different forms of learning that included: incremental learning, experimental learning, continuous learning, synergistic learning, entrenched learning and revolutionary learning. According to them organizations with viable learning environments created a framework for sustained transformational change, especially when members of the organization were able to adjust their mindsets to learn from 'disconnects' as well as successes (Cutcher-Gershenfeld & Ford 2007: 178-182).

Traditionally, approaches to organizational management emphasized the analysis of individual problems and focused mainly upon incremental change, but this was no longer sufficient as organizations continued to experience complex changes and uncertainty. It was becoming increasingly more difficult to see the consequences of decisions and to learn from experience (Kofman & Senge, 1993). Systems thinking, in combination with other organizational change strategies, provided organizations with a tool to help them address continuous change (Gardner & Demello, 1993). The importance of systems thinking and effectively changing the 'mind sets' of all participants was a hallmark of the work of Senge (1990).

Wheatley (1999) and Garmston and Wellman (1995: 6-12) considered the 'new science' offered insights into alternative approaches to organizational improvement by acknowledging that organizations are nonlinear systems that change radically with the folding and refolding of feedback into themselves. Such rapid changes lead to new concepts that include 'networks', 'nonlinearity', 'chaos', and 'complexity'. The systems that change themselves and interact with their context as they change are sometimes called 'self-renewing systems' or 'living systems'. Caine and Caine (1997: 62) prefer to call them 'complex adaptive systems' with their chief characteristic being 'self-organization'.

Capra (1996: 83) claimed that 'self-organization' has emerged as the central concept in the systems view of life and defined it as the ability to organize patterns and structures without any externally imposed plans or direction. Self-organization was thus one of the most potent messages of the new science. It was fundamentally different from the traditional view of the organization, which depended on: top-down control; the specification of rules of behavior and communication; the use of constant supervision; oversight, and predictable outcomes. The new paradigm of 'self-organization' requires 'bottom up and top-down thinking'.

Learning Histories

When one looks closely at how 'learning organizations' have evolved it is clear that what is required is a highly sophisticated set of strategies or methodologies that acknowledge the process of change. Over the past decade the authors of this paper have been identifying and evaluating a set of methodologies that have been effective in facilitating organizational learning for improvement. LHs remain at the forefront of this research and this paper will report on some of the recent findings.

LHs draw upon techniques from ethnography, oral history, action research, and learning and process consultation in the promotion of reflection and inquiry within an organization. Action research adds focused inquiry skills and effective methods for developing people's capacities to reflect upon and assess the results of their efforts. The analysis of data from interviews, observation, and written documents follows from traditional qualitative data analysis processes. An emphasis of the analysis process is to develop grounded theory based upon what people said happened and the issues which faced them as they deal with the changing work environment (Roth, 1996).

A LH is the story of a project or a change initiative. It is designed to portray the project as participants experience it, and to invite participants to draw their own conclusions. A LH describes what happens in a learning and change process, in the voice of participants. It documents 'hard' facts and events, and focuses on what people thought about events, how they perceived their own actions and how the perceptions of others differ from their own. Effective cultural change in an organization is a complex phenomenon that requires skillful transformational leadership (Legotlo & Mathibe, 2007) engaging the whole organization in decision making. LHs provide an opportunity for the whole community to be involved in such processes.

A LH includes not just reports of action and results, but also the underlying assumptions and reactions of a variety of people. The final report might take many forms, but its story is always larger than any single person's experience. The power of the learning history depends on its ability to convey multiple perspectives on problematic events. Every participant, reading the learning history, should feel that their own point of view has been treated fairly, and that they understand how other people came to their personal perspectives (Roth, 1995). In constructing a LH the participants also evaluate the program or change and determine how the processes adopted might be modified and improved in the future.

As originally developed by Roth the LH process involved a fixed number of steps to be followed: for example interviewing, observing, analyzing, writing, editing, circulating drafts, following up and conducting dissemination workshops. The intention of the history was to broaden and deepen learning throughout the organization by providing a forum for reflecting on learning and substantiating results. The LH process can be beneficial not only for the original participants, but also for researchers who advised them, and ultimately for anyone who is interested in an organization's learning processes (Roth, 1996).

Initially, it was argued that an external learning historian was an essential part of the process of constructing a LH (Roth, 1996). The learning historian worked with people in the organization to help them reflect and assess their own efforts, and then utilized the data from reflection and assessment as the basis for documents which were more broadly disseminated. Multiple perspectives were sought - those of the people in the organization involved in the efforts, other people in that organization, and the action researchers themselves. The learning historian team creates 'jointly told tales' that describe work issues and learning experiences from multiple and often contending perspectives.

Roth and others at MIT worked with major international corporations to develop the methodology. The histories developed were frequently very long (up to more than one hundred pages), took considerable time to compile (over twelve months to research and write) and involved the whole or a major part of the organization.

In recent times Parent and Beliveau (2007) suggested that the LH methodology is typically used within an action research environment and designed to allow recognition of what has been learned in the past to guide stakeholders in the dialogical generation of a new future. They illustrated the effectiveness of using LHs to facilitate a large scale knowledge transfer among three workplaces. Clearly such a large scale attempt to link three organizations using LHs was very ambitious. Parent and Beliveau (2007: 79) suggest there were a number of lessons to be learned including: obtaining clear and early involvement from all participants; the 'softer' aspects of the LH serve as opportunities to capture participant perspectives and stimulate conversations on what happened, why it happened and how future action can be improved; the closer to real time the history is developed and shared the more opportunities it provides for the group to change and improve performance and the time and effort put into the LH is far outweighed by the value of the knowledge generated.

A New Approach to Learning Histories

We consider that LHs are an appropriate tool to use at a much lesser scale than the whole organization level. Our approach to LHs was to train key people inside an organization to act as a learning historian. We adopted this approach because most of our work involved not-for-profit or small organizations that were without the resources of the very large corporations that were involved in the LH approach developed at MIT. We also considered that it would be possible to develop multiple LHs, each focused on a particular issue in a department or team, and to retain these as a record of organizational learning and as models for future projects and learning. We considered multiple histories would provide multiple perspectives on how successful change could occur, and how unsuccessful practices could be identified and shared with those who came into the organization at a later stage.

In recording the LH we advocated the use the two column format as did Roth (1995). In the right-hand column comments were recorded by a particular individual about the selected theme, and it is here that participants tell their part of the story. Their comments were then passed onto the next participant. This process continued until all participants had contributed. In the left-hand column, critical observations and key questions were recorded by the learning historian. Text running across the width of the full page provided the context and background for each part of the story and led into the narrative in the two-column format (Roth, 1995).

In our own research at a private school we attempted to facilitate the use of multiple LHs within single subject departments and on a very small scale. One leader used LHs to develop administration policy for the Year 12 Exhibition. Another leader developed a LH document outlining the need for a new Drama space. Another used LHs to develop policy areas in her Faculty so that the Faculty handbook could be completed and reported that:

"*At a faculty meeting we discussed and listed the policies we felt needed attention. It was a long list. To sit and discuss each one and formulate it through discussion would have been very time consuming. We decided that two policies (student welfare/discipline and differentiation) did require this sort of discussion to write an effective policy ...but for the others we decided to use LHs.*"

She further commented that this was achieved by:

1. A member of staff took responsibility for 1-3 policy areas;
2. The member of staff prepared a LH document and circulated it for comment. This had been very efficient, taking only 2-3 days for each document to circulate to 8 members of staff;
3. On receiving it back, the initiator of the document acting as the learning historian made some adjustments and recirculated it. This continued until the document was publishable;
4. Staff were made aware that their comments would be read by other mem-

bers of the faculty, so to make any unpublishable comments to the author;

5. The final policy was then transferred onto a disk so that they could be published in the faculty handbook, which was ready for publication later in the year.

The History faculty at the same school used three LHs to modify the year 9 History programme. When the opportunity to use LHs to improve the Year 9 History programme was mooted, it was welcomed by all staff members. The LHs promoted valuable written 'discussion' and the faculty leader was delighted with the staff reactions to the LHs and was confident that they would become part of the normal procedures utilized by the faculty. The faculty leader stated that 'staff was happy to be able to work on the LHs in their own time and the fact that faculty meetings were shorter and more efficient was pleasing to all concerned'. The leader also claimed that the LHs had been a very useful methodology and had allowed for the development of a top class Year 9 programme with all participants being able to add valuable input.

Other faculties used the methodology as well and this provided a new opportunity to develop cultural change throughout the whole school. The use of LHs created a new opportunity for all staff to be fully involved in the change processes that were being undertaken. LHs were seen as a positive way to implement change at all levels in the school and were considered appropriate irrespective of the scale of the issue at hand. Matters that ranged from inter/intra faculty policy decisions to whole school policy decisions were considered appropriate. The high expectations of staff involvement in decision making was made possible by using LHs. Staff sanctioned their opinions and ideas to be revealed on the LHs and this embellished rich debate on key issues by all members of staff. The LHs therefore allowed the school to move forward in developing a more collaborative and effective policy process that was owned by those that were going to be most affected by such policies.

In another setting LHs were studied as part of a course offered as a Master of Education degree. This course focused on participants developing a deep understanding of what is meant by organizational learning and some of the methodologies, including LHs, that may be implemented to facilitate organizational learning. Each participant was required to read a range of literature on these methodologies and to implement projects in their work places to evaluate the methodologies.

The overall opinion of participants was that LHs are a very effective methodology to assist organizations to become learning organizations. They stated that LHs complemented the methodology of dialogue and allowed all members of the organization to contribute to a very systemic and inclusive sharing of ideas. One participant commented 'the suggestion of having group meetings where the results of the LH are discussed in an open forum seems to have the best appeal to me'. By using a LH opinions from staff and the wider community were heard and respected and even the most marginal views were exposed.

One participant wrote "a LH allowed an organization and its members to learn by sharing experience.... It was a way of capturing, assessing, and diffusing pilot projects within the organization." Another made the observation that LHs:

"enhance whole school development. We can have input from teachers, parents, administration staff etc. In a school environment you would hope that learning is taking place in all facets, not only through student comprehension, but learning by the teachers.... I truly believe in this tool and that only good can come from it being applied. It may seem like a lengthy process but I feel the outcome is one to be desired."

Another participant claimed that LHs are an:

"essential documentation in any organization, as it provides information on two different scales. It helps an organization evaluate what worked well and therefore what they should repeat in the future. Additionally, it helps an organization to identify any mistakes that were made or problems that occurred so they can be avoided in the future."

The importance of the scale of the LH was reviewed in relation to the storage of knowledge created when one participant commented 'larger organizations may use computer databases whilst small organizations may keep written logs'.

Not all comments were positive, but reflected the practicalities of work. One participant suggested that the processes involved were 'too long and complicated'. Another participant was concerned that 'the recording and analysis of LHs looks to be the biggest drawback. ... Who would have the time to record and analyze each event within the organization?' Another stated that there is an 'opportunity for miscommunication due to the amount of the stages involved, although it is recognized that the participants are given the opportunity to revise and amend the document'. The question of whether organizations were sufficiently aware to take advantage of LHs was raised by a participant who commented 'LHs would not be positively received in some (organizations). Some organizations aren't ready for this kind of reflection, unfortunately'.

The flexibility in the use of LHs was reinforced when one participant commented that 'in the school setting LHs can be used by individual departments, the executive, and individual classroom teachers.... The process will encourage reflection among all staff'. Another stated 'the information (obtained) could also be used between schools. Thus the learning history can be both internal and external. Schools can learn a lot from each other when they share information'.

The fact that all staff can be engaged in a LH was considered a very positive quality when one participant stated 'everyone involved is allowed to speak, not only the senior manager.... this makes the process very democratic'. Another participant stated 'members are encouraged to tell their personal view, no matter how critical it might be. They expect to be taken seriously. This is one of the qualities: the emotional connection with members' needs'.

Concluding Comment

Clearly learning histories are a valuable tool for change agents to consider for use in any organization. Our research has shown that LHs can be applied to departments and teams within organizations, and can be applied to any project from small to large scale. LHs do not have to be controlled by outsiders, and can quickly become part of the culture of any organization as staff gain the confidence in their use. LHs are a useful tool for recording the development and learning that takes place within an organization. The compilation of LHs provides a valuable insight into the successes as well as the shortcomings of efforts to achieve organizational change. They can be used to make it unnecessary to 'reinvent the wheel' as personnel in organizations change.

References

Caine, R.N. & Caine, G. (1997). *Education on the edge of possibility*, ISBN 0871202824

Capra, F. (1996*) The Web of Life*. ISBN 0385476760.

Cutcher-Gershenfel, J. & Ford, J. K. (2005). *Valuable Disconnects in Organizational Learning Systems. Integrating Bold Visions and Harsh Realities*, ISBN 0195089065

Gardner, B.H. & Demello, S. (1993) Systems thinking in action. *Healthcare Forum*, ISSN 0899-9287: 25-28.

Garmston,R. & Wellman,B (1995). Adaptive schools in quantum universe. *Educational Leadership*, ISSN 0013-1784: 6.

Girard,J.P.& Lambert,S. (2007). Writing Stories that Guide Organizations into the Future.

Electronic Journal of Knowledge Management. ISSN 1479-4411: 161-173

Kofman,F. & Senge,P.M. (1993). Communities of commitmenet: The heart of learning organizations. *Organizational Dynamics*. ISSN 0090-2616: 5-22.

Kok, A. (2007). Intellectual Capital Management as Part of Knowledge Management Initiatives at Institutions of Higher Learning. *Electronic Journal of Knowledge Management*. ISSN 1479-4411:181-193.

Laws, K. & McLeod, R. J. (1996). Assisting educational institutions to become better learning organizations: some preliminary findings. Paper presented at the Second Australia and New Zealand Systems Conference Learning through Systems Thinking. Monash University, Melbourne.

Laws, K. & McLeod, R. J. (1997). Assisting schools to become better Learning Organizations: some suggested methodologies. *Third Australia and New Zealand Systems Conference*, ISBN 0909816328.

Laws, K. & McLeod, R. J. (1998). Schools, organizational learning and the use of 'learning histories': Some research results. Paper presented at the 4th Annual Australia and New Zealand Systems Conference,University of Western Sydney.

Laws, K. & McLeod, R. J. (2004). Case study and grounded theory: Sharing some alternative qualitative research methodologies with systems professionals. Paper presented at the Twentith Second Systems Dynamics Conference. Oxford University.

Legotlo, M.W. and Mathibe I.R (2007). "The leadership of the school community as sharing power and decision making in the school. http://www.weleadinlearning.org

O'Sullivan, K.J. & Azeem, S.A. (2007). An Analysis of Collaborative Group Structure Technological Facilitation from a Knowledge Management Perspective. *Electronic Journal of Knowledge Management*. ISSN 1479-4411: 223-231

Papoutsakis, H. (2007). "Sharing Knowledge in the Organization: A Retrospective Analysis and an Empirical Study," Technological Facilitation from a Knowledge Management Perspective. *Electronic Journal of Knowledge Management.* ISSN 1479-4411: 231-245

Parent, R. & Beliveau, J. (2007). "Organizational Knowledge Transfer: Turning Research into Action through a Learning History," *Electronic Journal of Knowledge Management.* ISSN 1479-4411: 73-79

Roth, G. L. (1995). "Learning about Organizational Learning- Creating a Learning History." http://www.solonline.org/res/wp/18001.html

Roth, G. L. (1996). "Learning Histories: Using Documentation to Assess and Facilitate Organizational Learning" http://www.solonline.org/res/wp/18004.html

Senge, P. M. (1990.) *The Fifth Discipline: The Art and Practice of the Learning Organization.* ISBN 00912827264

Van Aken, J.E., Berends, H. & Van Der Bij, H. (2007). *Problem Solving in Organizations,* ISBN 139780521869768

Wheatley, M. (1999). *Leadership and the New Science.* ISBN 1576751198.

56. Examining the Implementation of Automated Performance Management Systems: A Critical Realist Perspective

J. Myles, P. Dobson and **P. Jackson**
Edith Cowan University, Perth Western Australia, AUS

Although there have been a number of calls for an increased use of critical realism in Information Systems Research this approach has been little used to date. This paper seeks to address the dearth of practical examples of research in the area by proposing that critical realism be adopted as the underlying research philosophy for an enterprise systems evaluation. The paper addresses some of the implications of adopting such an approach for the evaluation and implementation of Automated Performance Measurement Systems (APMS).

Introduction

Many recent articles from within the Information Systems arena present an old-fashioned view of realism. For example, Iivari, Hirschheim and Klein (1998) see classical realism as seeing "data as describing objective facts, information systems as consisting of technological structures ("hardware"), human beings as subject to causal laws (determinism), and organizations as relatively stable structures" (p. 172). Wilson (1999) sees the realist perspective as relying on "the availability of a set of formal constraints which have the characteristics of abstractness, generality, invariance across contexts".

Fitzgerald and Howcroft (1998) present a realist ontology as one of the foundational elements of positivism in discussing the polarity between hard and soft approaches in IS. Realism is placed alongside positivist, objectivist, etc epistemologies and quantitative, confirmatory, deductive, laboratory focussed and nomothetic methodologies. Such a traditional view of realism is perhaps justified within the IS arena as it reflects the historical focus of its use, however, there now needs to be a greater recognition of the newer forms of realism – forms of realism that specifically address all of the positivist leanings emphasized by Fitzgerald and Howcroft (1998). A particular example of this newer form of realism is critical realism. This modern realist approach is primarily founded on the writings of the social sciences philosopher Bhaskar (1979, 1989) and is peculiarly European in its origins.

Critical realism is becoming influential in a range of other disciplines, but the application of critical realism within the IS field has been limited to date. Mingers (2002) examines the implications of a critical realist approach particularly in its support for pluralist research. Dobson (2001) argues for a closer integration of philosophical matters within IS research and suggests a critical realist approach has particular potential for IS research. Carlsson (2003) examines IS evaluation from a critical realist perspective. This paper seeks to address the dearth of practical examples of critical realist use in IS by proposing the review of APMS implementation from such a perspective.

Initial Observations

The Sarbanes-Oxley Act was introduced in 2002 to address recent high profile accounting scandals in the US. The Act requires that senior executives must advise stockholders immediately of any issues that are likely to affect company performance. This liability is personal and thus makes senior executives personally liable for the effectiveness and immediacy of their internal measurement systems and reporting. Current business intelligence and business activity monitoring tools will necessarily play an important role in such so-called Corporate Performance Management (CPM) tools (Gartner, 2005).

The development of effective performance reporting and management tools is one necessary consequence of the Sarbanes-Oxley act. The requirement for executives to have unfettered access to organizational data also suggests that such tools require minimal or no human intervention in the analysis and collection of the data. This automated component in CPM systems will lead to the growth of a new class of monitoring system distinct from traditional Business Intelligence (BI) and Business Activity Monitoring (BAM) tools – these so-called Automated Performance Management Systems can be argued to ultimately rest on a lack of trust in traditional reporting tools and management structures. This paper describes the implementation of two such performance measurement systems and proposes the adoption of critical realism as a basic philosophy to examine the important issues involved in their implementation.

Realist Review as a Foundational Platform

The lack of practical examples of critical realist use is perhaps not difficult to understand given the philosophy provides little real guidance as to methodological development. Contemporary realist examination requires precision and contextualized detail, this contextualization being a necessary consequence of an underlying ontologically bold philosophy (Outhwaite, 1987). Along with most realist approaches, critical realism encompasses an external realism in its distinction between the world and our experience of it. This assumption necessarily implies that any knowledge gained of an external world must typically be provisional, fallible, incomplete and extendable. As Stones (1996) suggests realist methodologies and writings need to reflect a continual commitment to caution, scepticism and reflexivity.

In contrast to traditional realist approaches critical realism also suggests a so-called depth realism and argues for a stratified ontology. This concept suggests that reality is made up of three ontologically distinct realms – first, the empirical, that is experience; second, the actual, that is events (i.e., the actual objects of experience); and third, the transcendental, non-actual or deep, that is structures, mechanisms and associated powers. Critical realism argues that "the world is composed not only of events and our experience or impression of them, but also of (irreducible) structures and mechanisms, powers and tendencies, etc. that, although not directly observable, nevertheless underlie actual events that we experience and govern or produce them" (Lawson, 1997: 8). The deep structures and mechanisms that make up the world are the primary focus of such an ontological realism. The realist seeks a deep knowledge and understanding of a social situation. It argues against single concentration on observed events and requires an understanding of the deeper structures and mechanisms that often belie the surface event level observation.

Bhaskar (1979) presents fundamental difficulties with the way that prediction and falsification have been used in the open systems evident within the social arena. For the critical realist a major issue with social investigation is the inability to create closure - the aim of "experiment" in the natural sciences. Bhaskar argues that this inability implies that theory cannot be used in a predictive manner and can *only* play an explanatory role in social investigations.

Implications for APMS Examination

The realist focus on context and setting

Pawson *et al.* (2005) describes realist review as "a relatively new strategy for synthesizing research which has an explanatory rather than a judgemental focus. It seeks to unpack the mechanisms of how complex programmes (or why they fail) in particular contexts and settings" (p. 21) Such methods are becoming more prevalent in the analysis of the effectiveness of social programs. It is the contention of this paper that a similar approach can be effective in examining the heavily social and contextual nature of complex APMS implementation. Critical realist evaluation moves from the basic evaluative question - *what* works - to what is it about this implementation that works for whom in what circumstances. As Sayer (2000) suggests the target for realist research is not the determination of an "objective" or generalizable truth but the achievement of the best we can do at the time i.e., "practically adequate" explanations. This practical focus within critical realism sees knowledge as existing in a "historically specific, symbolically mediated and expressed, practice-dependent form" (Lawson, 1997) that is potentially transformable as subsequent deeper knowledge is gained. The realist denies easy generalizability and requires a heavy focus on context.

Automated performance management systems reflect a growing emphasis on agile reporting and integrated systems. APMS have been variously described as Corporate Performance Management Systems, Business Activity Monitoring Systems, and Business Intelligence Systems, yet such descriptions are perhaps not descriptive enough.

Kueng *et al.* (2001) described Performance Measurement Systems as having five components, These were people, procedures, data, software and hardware. Descriptions of these components are detailed in Table 1, below. Kueng *et al.* also state that the various systems that deliver performance-relevant data are integrated and that manual intervention (for extraction, verification, conversion, loading of data) is not required, i.e., data collection is completely automated.

People	Procedures	Data	Software	Hardware
Owner of PMS	Procedures and rules for definition of performance indicators	Performance-relevant Data (as-is values)	Software for extraction, transformation and loading of data	Personal Computer or other visual display unit Server
People accountable for the units measured	Rules for data management	To-be values of performance indicators	Database Mgmt software / Data Warehouse software	Communication infrastructure
People who set-up and maintain the PMS	Rules for data communication	Performance results (calculated data)	Data analysis software	Storage system
Data suppliers	Rules for use of performance results	Meta-data: description of performance indicators	Presentation and communication software	
Internal and external users of the PMS				
Internal and external stakeholders				

Table 1 *Components of a Performance Measurement System (Kueng, Meier et al. 2001)*

Table 1 illustrates the technical, operational, social and political complexities that exist within APMS's. With this complexity comes the need to develop frameworks for relating functional or local performance to overall business level performance as well as examining the interaction between a performance measurement system and its internal and external environment (Lockamy & Spencer, 1998). Limited published material exists on the successes or failures of APMS software implementations (Bititci, Cavalieri, *et al.*, 2005; Bourne, 2005; Nudurupati & Bititci, 2005) but there are indications that performance management systems appear to have a high percentage of failures (Bourne, Neely *et al.*, 2002). McCunn (1998, cited in Bourne, 2005) quotes figures that 70% of performance measurement initiatives fail.

The two APMS systems examined in this study were founded on large-scale data warehousing applications that were developed as a basis for proposed Automated Business (or Corporate) Performance Measurement Systems. The projects were based on SAP's Business Warehouse product and both data warehouses sourced their data from SAP's R3 Enterprise Resource Planning (ERP) systems but also included a myriad of other non-SAP production systems. One organization was a mid to large Government Business Enterprise and the other was a large global commodity company.

The data warehousing systems had the common objective of producing automatic performance measurement management reporting via a mixture of Microsoft Excel spreadsheets and Web based reports. The information was presented in a form where no manipulation was required and in most cases any such change was not in fact possible because of the existing security/authorisation layer that protected the reporting document.

One system languished as implementation and process change management failed to get traction and the system did not become embedded as a meaningful tool. It is now used in an ad hoc fashion and is seen by some as just an expensive toy.

The other system was nearly complete (90%) and was partially operational (approx. 70% of the business processes covered) with over 60% of managers and information analysts using the tool throughout the business. Production benefits were occurring and the system had already paid for itself within the first 12 months. All of a sudden the project was stopped, seemingly for no apparent reason. The project was under budget (85%) and was scheduled to deliver on time. It wasn't finished and with some of the data not collected holes exist in high level management reports and hence manual intervention is still required. Senior Managers remain frustrated at management reporting delays and are sceptical on the metrics being reported.

Discussions with the I/S Managers for both of the organizations did not indicate any reason for failure, in fact both were very supportive as they struggled to understand how to complete implementation of these systems and integrate them in to their respective businesses.

Realist emphasis on explanation and ex-post evaluation

The realist focus on explanation rather than prediction necessarily encourages an emphasis on ex-post evaluation. The realist would suggest that ex-ante or predictive evaluation is difficult given the highly complex nature of the implementation environment. Ex-post evaluations after the event are more in keeping with the underlying realist focus on explanation rather than prediction.

The emphasis on explanation also must impact the associated research question. Critical realism focuses on retroductive propositional type questioning where the research question may be "Under what conditions might APMS implementation prove successful?" rather than "What are the critical success factors for an APMS implementation?". A critical success factors approach suggests a greater predictive possibility and tends to deny the heavy contextuality of a realist study.

The original Delone and McLean model (1992) of IS success in Figure 1 is realist in focus as it emphasizes causal factors – however the critical real-

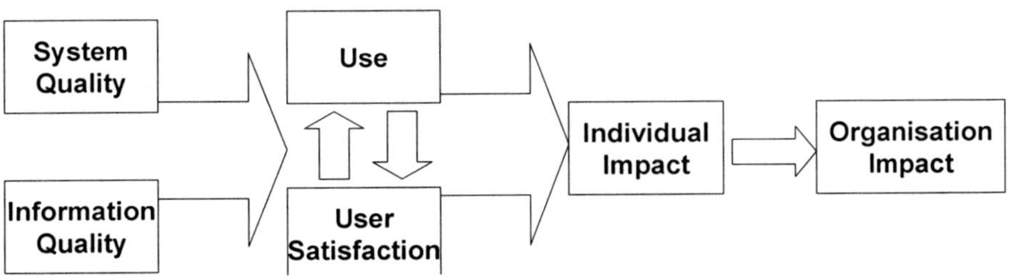

Figure 1 *Delone and Mclean Model of IS Success (1992)*

ist would have difficulty agreeing with the simplistic notion that organizational impacts are solely pre-determined by individual factors. The realist argues for a deeper multi-level analysis that recognizes that individual agency (micro) level impacts are only one of the components - such an analysis ignores the duality of structure in that agency actions are both constrained and enabled by pre-existing structures. Any research study founded on critical realism needs to reflect this duality of structure and agency. Archer (1995) and Hedström and Swedberg provide guidance on how to accommodate this duality in a research context.

An emphasis on the social nature of IT implementation

The defining characteristic of APMS is that it is *automated* and involves the communication of key performance indicators. As such the implementation and operation of such a system can be highly political. Performance measurement can be defined as the process of quantifying the efficiency and effectiveness of action and a performance measurement system as the set of metrics used to quantify both the efficiency and effectiveness of actions (Bourne, Neely, *et al.*, 2003). The development of any performance management system must adhere to the following definite stages:

- Define the performance to be measured;
- Determine and agree on appropriate performance metrics;
- Implement systems to monitor performance against these metrics;
- Implement systems to communicate these metrics to concerned stakeholders.

Each stage in the development of a performance management system can be expected to be potentially highly political and affect the acceptance of the final management system.

The final communication of performance figures is inherently social. As Pawson, *et al.* (2005) suggest this collection of performance figures is usually followed by public disclosure of under performing sectors. Such a public disclosure ideally leads to “sanction instigation” whereby the broader organizational community act to “boycott, censure, reproach or control the under performing party”. The final phase is termed “miscreant response” in which “failing parties are shamed, chastised, made contrite and so improve performance in order to be reintegrated”. As Pawson argues these social processes are all fallible and can all lead to unintended outcomes. The initial performance metric may be inappropriate or measuring the wrong problem, the dissemination may be inappropriate, public reactions may take the form of apathy or panic rather than reproach thus leading to attempts to “resist, reject, ignore or actively discredit the official labelling”. The potential for active resistance seems more likely given the automated nature of an APMS system. Automated communication may be seen to imply a lack of trust in intervening management structures and could lead to active resistance.

The "critical" view of APMS

Organizational goals are set by management, high level requirements are set by management, as are timelines, resources and objectives (Abdel, *et al.*, 1999). The design solution of APMS, its overarching principles and objectives, depend upon the ideologies, requirements and principles of these decision makers. These principles are based upon a normative threat (the Sarbanes-Oxley legislation) as well as the drive to maximise productivity through control and early intervention. The ideology of industrialization, that increasing labor productivity is the foundation of increasing wealth and the improvement of social and economic conditions, also makes rational resistance difficult. The solution of APMS is therefore conservative, preserving the power *status quo* and serving the needs of those who need to control, measure and manipulate. Here we can observe a structure of legitimated management and regulation interacting with the agency of individual and idiosyncratic leadership. Critical realism allows that these structures have a causative function, derived from the ontological commitment of protagonists. These causal events may have elements which can be generalized, but their universality need to be understood in the context of agency and individualism.

New divisions of labour and requirements for cooperation, a transcendence of current work processes, will break down existing divisions of labour and require extensive cooperation. Particularly in organizations with command and control management paradigms and Fordist conceptions of the structure of work, boundary spanning and the unimpeded flow of information will be perceived as threat to those whose authority is based upon the existence of boundaries and fiefdoms. The adjustment and threat to power structures defined through knowledge is a high risk area for projects whose focus and objective is to codify knowledge and ways of doing things and make them freely available. The case of APMS is particularly interesting because it is managers whose knowledge is being codified and commoditized and whose ability to intervene and massage production figures is being withdrawn. It is managers whose fiefs are becoming subject to a super-Panopticon, accessed by the CEO himself, who may ring up at 8:00 a.m. and complain about the previous day's poor production quality. The stance of critical realism can sensitize researchers not only to the collision of conflicting structures, but also to the motivations of the protagonists who inhabit those structures and have careers to build or mortgages to pay.

People in organizations are usually aware of the importance of their knowledge to their position, status and remuneration and any reduction may well be met with lack of full cooperation. The implementation of APMS moves this to the next level. Martin (1988) states that "the major resource distribution by technological change is knowledge: groups with knowledge of the old system may lose control of knowledge under the new system".

Scarbrough and Corbett (1992) assert that the higher the levels of autonomy and job specialization, the greater the power of the job holder. If this is correct, then if these two parameters are reduced by technological change, it is more than likely that the change will be resisted at some stage of the technology change project: either in design, implementation or use. This resistance is a denial of the legitimacy of the technological solution – and may have nothing to do with whether the solution is "the best for the company" or even represents a best possible reorganization of work processes. Critical realism recognizes the role of individual agency in the withdrawal of support and legitimation for the normative and regulative structures implied by the "organization as machine" metaphor in which APMS finds its validation.

Conclusion

The preceding section aims to provide guidelines for progressing the examination of APMS implementation. Critical realism is proposed as an under-laborer for the research - the term under-laboring taken from Locke (1894: 14) as "clearing the ground a little...removing some of the rubbish that lies in the way of knowledge". This initial paper suggests some of the issues that need to be addressed in examination of APMS implementation. The above discussion demonstrates the multi-dimensional complexity of APMS projects and highlights the salient feature of the technology as being the total and immediate exposure of production performance to senior management. This exposure, accompanied by the vulnerability to direct intervention, reveals the prominence of social issues such as power, control and surveillance as potential factors in the success of APMS projects. The social philosophical stance of critical realism offers a foundation upon which to make sense of the actions and beliefs of APMS project stakeholders.

It is the contention of this paper that an instrumental approach confined to assessing technology acceptance, system quality or user perceptions would be inadequate to uncover the diverse range of potential impacting factors.

References

Archer, M. (1995). *Realist Social Theory: The Morphogenetic Approach*, ISBN 0521484421, Cambridge University Press, Cambridge.

Bhaskar, R. (1979) *The possibility of natur*alism, ISBN 0415198747, Harvester Wheatsheaf, Hemel Hempstead.

Bhaskar, R. (1989). *Reclaiming Reality: A Critical Introduction to Contemporary Philosophy*. ISBN 041545493X, London: Verso.

Bititci, U. S., S. Cavalieri, et al. (2005). "Editorial: Implementation of performance measurement systems: private and public sectors." *Production Planning &* Control, ISSN 0953-7287, 16(2): 99-100.

Bourne, M. (2005). "Researching performance measurement system implementation: the dynamics of success and failure." *Production Planning & Control,* ISSN 0953-7287, 16(2): 101-113.

Bourne, M., A. Neely, et al. (2002). "The success and failure of performance measurement initiatives: Perceptions of participating managers." *International Journal of Operations & Production Management,* ISSN 0144-3577, 22(11): 1288-1310.

Bourne, M., A. Neely, et al. (2003). "Implementing performance measurement systems: a literature review'." *International Journal of Business Performance Management,* ISSN 1368-4892, 5(1): 1-24.

Carlsson, S. (2003). Advancing Information Systems Evaluation (Research): A Critical Realist Approach, *Electronic Journal of Information Systems Evaluation,* ISSN 15666379, Volume 6 Issue 2 (2003) 11-20.

Collier, A. (1994). *Critical realism: an introduction to the philosophy of Roy Bhaskar.* ISBN 0860916022, London: Verso.

DeLone, W. H. and E. R. McLean (1992). "Information Systems Success: The Quest for the Dependent Variable." *Information Systems Research* , ISSN 1047-7047, 3(1): 60-95.

Dobson, P. (2001). The Philosophy of Critical Realism - An Opportunity for Information Systems Research, *Information Systems Frontiers*, ISSN 1387-3326, July 2001.

Fitzgerald, B. and Howcroft, D. (1998). Towards dissolution of the IS research debate: from polarization to polarity, *Journal of Information Technology*, ISSN 1846-3908, vol. 13, pp. 313-326.

Hedström, P., and Swedberg, R. (1998). "Social Mechanisms: An introductory essay," in: *Social Mechanisms: An Analytical Approach to Social Theory,* P. Hedström and R. Swedberg (eds.), ISBN 0521596874, Cambridge University Press, New York, pp. 1-31.

Iivari, J, Hirschheim, R. Klein, H.K. (1998). A paradigmatic analysis contrasting information systems development approaches and methodologies, *Information Systems Research,* ISSN 1047-7047, Vol: 9, Iss: 2, pp: 164-193.

Kanter, R. M. (1996). When a Thousand Flowers Bloom: Structural, Collective, and Social Conditions for Innovation in Organizations, in P. S. Myers, (ed.) *Knowledge Management and Organizational Design*, ISBN 0750697490, Butterworth-Heinemann, Newton, MA.

Kueng, P., A. Meier, et al. (2001). "Performance Measurement Systems must be Engineered." *Communications of the Association of Information Systems* , ISSN 1529-3181, 7(3).

Layder, D. (1993), *New Strategies in Social Research: An Introduction and Guide*, ISBN 0745608817, Polity Press, Cambridge.

Lockamy, A. I. and M. S. Spencer (1998). "Performance measurement in a theory of constraints environment." *International Journal of Production Research* , ISSN 1366-588X, 36(8): 2045± 2060.

Martin, R. (1988). Technological Change and Manual Work. In D. Gallie (Ed.), *Employment in Britain* (pp. 102-127). ISBN 0631160213, Oxford: Basil Blackwell.

McCunn, P. (1998). "The balanced scorecard...the eleventh commandment." *Management Accounting* , ISSN 0025-1682, 76(11): 34.

Mingers, J. (2002). Real-izing Information Systems: Critical Realism As An Underpinning Philosophy For Information Systems, *Proceedings Twenty-Third International Conference on Information Systems*, p. 295-303.

Nudurupati, S. S. and U. S. Bititci (2005). "Implementation and impact of IT-supported performance measurement systems." *Production Planning & Control,* ISSN 0953-7287, 16(2): 152-162.

Outhwaite, W., (1987). Realism and Social Science, in M. S. Archer, R, Bhaskar, A. Collier, T. Lawson. A. Norrie (Eds), *Critical realism: Essential Readings.* ISBN 0415196329, Routledge, UK, p 282-293

Pawson, R., T. Greenhalgh, et al. (2005). "Realist review – a new method of systematic review designed for complex policy interventions." *Journal of Health Services Research & Policy,* ISSN 1355-8196, 10(1): 21–34.

Pratt, A., (1995). Putting Critical Realism to Work: The Practical Implications for Geographical Research, *Progress in Human Geography,* ISSN 0309-1325, (19:1), 1995, pp. 61-74.

Sayer, A. (2000). *Realism and Social Science.* ISBN 0761961240, London, Sage Publications Ltd.

Scarbrough, H. & Corbett, J. M. (1992). *Technology And Organization: Power, Meaning And Design*, ISBN 0415059410, Routledge, London.

Smith, M. L. (2005). *Overcoming theory-practice inconsistencies: Critical realism and information systems research.* Unpublished manuscript, Department of Information Systems, London School of Economics and Political Science, Working Paper 134.

Stones, R. (1996), *Sociological Reasoning: Towards A Past-Modern Sociology*, ISBN 0312160771, MacMillan.

Wilson, F. (1999). Flogging a dead horse: The implications of epistemological relativism within information systems methodological practice, *European Journal of Information Systems*, ISSN 0960-085X, Vol: 8, Iss: 3, pp: 161-169.

57. Insider Action Research: Beyond Participation in Action Research

Rod Sarah
Melbourne, AUS

Tim Haslett
Dept of Management, Monash University, AUS

In action research studies, participation is a core defining principle wherein the local members are engaged in learning about and the improvement of the larger system of which they are a part. In this paper, we report on the researchers experiences conducting insider action research in a business organization. There are recoverable insights from this research that extends the concept of local participation and researcher membership roles in the practice of action research studies in business organizations.

Introduction

Change projects are regarded by those they affect as very important during the period of the program – they have attention and focus, excitement and enthusiasm and are supported by significant resource allocations. However, change projects don't exist in a vacuum – they can be conceived as a 'system' of activities directed toward some purpose that occur in an 'environment', and are therefore are subject to changes in this extended environment. Systems theorists have been long aware of the concept of 'systems-in-environments' and open systems theory (von Bertalanffy, 1950; Emery, 1981) which is as a core principle behind achieving the fundamental cultural change required for a desirable future upon (Emery, 1999).

Sustaining large-scale change is a significant challenge and therefore how to avoid a situation when the initial focus and interest fades away after an initial period of enthusiasm is an ongoing concern. This challenge (Olsen & Haslett, 2002; Sarah, *et al.*, 2002; Sarah & Haslett, 2005; Sarah, 2006) where the difficulties in sustaining change projects using action research has been outlined previously.

Based as part of an ongoing study based out of Monash University, this paper specifically focuses on one aspect of sustaining one category of action research – doing research in your own organization. This paper focuses on the role of insider action researchers (Coghlan & Brannick, 2001, 2005) and how this unique positioning situation contributes to the durability of the research project. The proposition behind this paper is that durable change projects are a feature of successful change, and successful projects have the potential to be mutually reinforcing. It is this mutual reinforcement dynamic whereby local 'system' solutions to problems can influence the system environment. As such, the focus of this paper is to explore how the positioning of the action researcher adds to successful local solutions that have the potential for replication in other places.

The Context

The case study that forms the basis of this paper is an organizational transformation of a student services organization at Monash University. This paper reports on one element of a model for linking a Masters Degree in Management as an employer-sponsored 'capability building program.' In this study, the primary author was employed at the beginning of the change program in an ongoing capacity as an action researcher engaged to write the history of the change program. Specifically, the paper discusses the positionality of the insider action researcher as a vital element for leveraging local change for whole system transformation. However, we begin with a brief overview of action research and the insider action researcher role before exploring the contribution to the literature from this case study.

Action Research

The origins of action research are at best problematic and writers suggest it is difficult to provide a coherent history of action research in the literature (Reason & Bradbury, 2001). What is not in dispute is that action research as evolved significantly since its coined beginnings in the 1940's (Collier, 1945; Lewin, 1946) and while Lewin may not have been the first to use of advocate action research, however he was the first to develop a theory of action research as a 'research methodology' in the social sciences field. Lewin saw knowledge as something created from 'problem solving' in real-life situations (Lewin, 1946, 1948) where the early action research studies, and those that it inspired, had an insistence on 'participation' as an important element of their development.

Some 60 years later, participation remains a central core feature of this major field of research that involves a cyclical process comprising a variety of activities and phases that integrate research and action in living systems (Coghlan & Brannick, 2001; Reason & Bradbury, 2001). *'A primary purpose of action research is to produce practical knowledge...a wider purpose (of action research) is to contribute through this practical knowledge to the increased well being...of human persons and communities...'* (Reason & Bradbury, 2001: 3). Clearly action research is a systems approach where members of the system work to improve their system.

Insider Action Research

Traditionally, action researchers were seen as outside change agents where the research was initiated by an outsider and a central issue was how to involve insiders in the research. This relationship between insiders and outsiders and the 'positionality' of the researcher is a part of the aforementioned evolving practice that is action research. Today, with the advent of professional managers who have acquired research skills enrolled in postgraduate programs, action research is often done by organizational insiders who see it as a way to deepen their own reflection of practice toward problem-solving and professional development. One increasingly popular category of action research in business organizations is being performed by the insider-researcher.

Yet, doing field research inside organizations is not new. Adler and Adler (1987) describe three ideal-type membership roles in field research that reflect the degree of involvement in the study group:

- Peripheral membership;
- Active membership, and;
- Complete membership.

Their typology is categorized by membership affiliation where the differentiation point is the research role. Their topology is represented as a continuum. At the high end of the continuum – the complete member – are those researchers who become so committed to the group that they abandon their ties to the scientific/research community and fail to return from the field. At the time of their study, the 'on-going' insider was an exception to contemporary field research practice. Adler and Adler do however acknowledge a special case in their study – the opportunistic researcher (based on Riemer, 1977, quoted in Adler & Adler, 1987), where the researcher studies settings where they are already members. In contemporary literature, insider action researchers where are complete members, and ongoing employees of the host organization (Coghlan & Brannick, 2005).

This is what Monash embraced as the practitioner-scholar model - a model whereby professional practice is informed by scholarly inquiry. As a practitioner scholar, insider action researchers begin as practicing managers however the researcher and practitioner roles may become one and the same.

Insider-Outsider Continuum

Coghlan and Brannick (2005) discuss several important aspects of doing action research in your own organization. These three aspects are positioned as differentiating insider action researchers from outsider action researchers and represent different dynamics for the Action Researcher. We briefly summarize the literature on these three aspects highlighting important and unique insights not specifically covered in the literatures.

Pre-understanding: The notion of pre-understanding of the setting is thought to be a unique advantage for the inside action researcher where their prior immersion in the setting provides valuable insights and knowledge about cultures and informal structures of the host (Coghlan & Brannick, 2005: 61). In this sense they are an 'insider-inside' the host organization. However, prior immersion is thought to create a challenge in terms of the capacity to observe the unfolding of the cycles of action, learning and reflection.

The researcher who joins the organization as a temporary member not only has the political and cultural challenge of negotiating access to the organization and data, but to understanding the culture and history of the research setting. In this sense, they are an 'outsider-inside' the host organization. The challenge then is a lack of pre-understanding.

In this case study however, the researcher's role can be thought to lie between these two dimensions. The researcher was a new employee, contracted for permanent on-going employment. Therefore the researcher would be categorized as an insider. But as a new employee, without prior exposure to the culture and history of the setting, the researcher was still an outsider. In this sense, they were an 'outside-insider' in the host organization.

This third position is therefore somewhat unique – in that being inside the organization you have physical access but being a recent arrival, the pre-understanding level is the same as the outsider-inside. However, due to the absence of a closeness to the issues and organization, otherwise unrecognized assumptions and norms are more easily identifiable (Coghlan & Brannick, 2005: 63).

Access: The literature on insider action research makes a distinction between primary and secondary access. Primary access is the ability to get into the organization and be allowed to undertake research (Coghlan & Brannick, 2005: 67). As an organizational member, an inside action researcher has primary access. In regard to 'secondary access', this refers to access to specific parts of the organization and information that are relevant to the research (op cit, p. 67).

Much of the literature refers to 'physical' membership. However, this is only one dimension of membership. Another element of membership relates to psychological and social membership of the organization and the dynamics surrounding this.

An insider action researcher does not have a detached interest in the research setting or topic and therefore is denied some of the detachment of the outsider. It is then a risk for the insider that they are likely to encounter elements of the research that are frustrating if not distasteful and that may lead to degrees of alienation because of being deeply connected to the research and the research setting. As an organizational member, there is genuine commitment to the organization as host and to the group as co-researchers and collaborators.

Role Duality: The literature reports a challenge of adding a research role to a pre-existing organizational role. My role, as a new role and as a new member, was a practitioner-scholar who was both doing an organizational project and a PhD research project as two co-joined cycles of project work. I was simultaneously producing results and generating knowledge for the organization community and results and knowledge for the academic community. This dynamic is similar to concept of a core project and a thesis project (Perry & Zuber-Skerritt, 1992; Zuber-Skerritt & Perry, 2002). The 'complete member' inside action researcher role also brings to the researcher legitimacy with their fellow organizational members. The legitimacy is in respect of internal acceptance as an ongoing member and status as employee that creates an initial connection. In comparison, an outsider has to negotiate the organizational boundary established between employees and non-employees, the organization.

	Research Description	Pre-understanding	Access	Role
Outsider-Inside (Traditional Field Researcher)	Traditional external coming inside to conduct research	None	Political challenge	External role dominates where the researcher will withdraw from the study and return to a prior membership organisation
Insider-Inside (Inside Action Researcher)	Insider Action Researcher who is already a permanent on-going employee	Yes due to historical lived experiences in the organisation.	Access assumed due to employment engagement	Role clarity (but proposed as an IAR that his will develop into practitioner-scholar)
Outside-Insider (sub-category of Inside Action Researcher)	The new inside action researcher who seeks to have an ongoing employment/ career relationship with the host organisation	None	Access assumed due to employment engagement	Role clarity (but proposed as an IAR that his will develop into practitioner-scholar)

Table 1 *Insider-Outsider Continuum*

The above can be summarized in the following table with a new sub-category of insider action researcher – the outsider inside. :

As the inside action researcher moves beyond participation, we can also summarize the dynamics of engagement in the following mutually reinforcing causal feedback description (see Figure 1 below):

The researcher, as an engaged member of the host organization, increasingly does 'member work' that is core to the host organization. This leads to the researcher taking on the obligations and commitments of the member of the organization, further reinforcing their engagement as a member. This feedback loop is show as R1 in Figure 1.

As an engaged member, undertaking member work, you also gain access to 'secret information', and possession of this information is known only to members. This is a privilege and increases the obligations and commitments of and to the host organization, and further reinforces the membership status of the researcher. This feedback loop is shown as R2 in Figure 1.

Recommended Practice

We have demonstrated that the positionality of the researcher in undertaking an action research study in their own organization is increasingly important. Inside action researchers, as practicing managers, or as practitioner-scholars have three duties where we need to seek active membership roles to sustain our local practice.

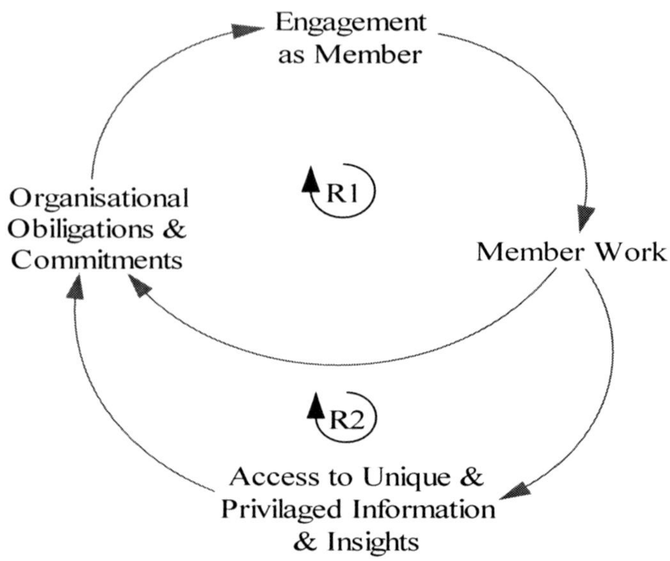

Figure 1 *Dynamics of Insider Action Research Engagement*

We need to build a role for our research in our organizations as a core element of legitimizing the new work of practice scholarship. Our own experiences, emotions and therefore our interpretations and constructions are equally important in the knowledge creation process. As the researcher, it is we who eventually decide what is reported and what is not. Indeed, Checkland and Holwell (1998) implore us to declare in advance our framework of ideas in any research setting. To do otherwise is mere story telling and findings at best are anecdotal (p. 14).

We need to create learning communities inside the organization where we can communicate our work. This is the true essence of cogeneration of knowledge and action. The creation of learning organizations provides an infrastructure for inside action researchers and practitioner scholars to generate knowledge from the local solution to the wider global community. It is an integration of first, second and third-person action inquiry (Reason & Torbert, 2001; Torbert, 2001) that compliments Reason and Marshall's popular notion of three audiences for research – for me, for us and for them (1987). This is how the local solutions can shape and influence the larger system.

Insider-Action Researchers on the Outside

The literatures focus on pre-understanding, access and role duality for the insider action researcher. What about the insider action researcher who suddenly finds themselves on the 'outside' before their core thesis project research is completed? In concluding this paper, we will briefly report on what happens when rather than withdrawing from the field of study, the field of study was withdrawn from the researcher. I explore my recent experience of employment separation from the host organization (and the organizations subsequent winding up) and my adaptation of to a new role of the insider action researcher on the outside.

In this part of the paper, as it was personal to the primary author, it is written in the first person from their perspective.

1. Separation: While the engagement dynamics were unique to this setting, the disengagement was not what I had expected. Having identified myself as an insider researcher, I saw this as an enduring role. This had been reinforced by the research sponsor and CEO and we had already begun scoping the post-doctoral study. Thus, with no ongoing membership, the role identity with the group and/or host ceased. After over 30 years of full-time work, I could talk the talk of a full-time PhD student finalizing his research thesis, but the walking the talk by just writing the writing was much more challenging.
2. Community: In their introduction to the Handbook of Action Research, Reason and Bradbury (2001) acknowledge the intimate relationship between knowledge and power and in action research studies. Knowledge creation is a political process, just as undertaking any research activity in any organization is a political act (Punch, 1994). Doing research in your own organization is particularly political. It also has an ethical dimension. I have a strong commitment to, and self-identification with, the workgroup that for 5 years were my colleagues and co-researchers. Upon separation, I experienced a challenge in portraying the research 'appropriately'. I didn't want to feel that my final thesis report would be biased because of my personal trauma of separation or to feel I was misrepresenting my colleagues and our study in anyway.
3. Writing the research: As an inside action researcher on the outside, the challenge of extracting something to say out of 5 years of data seems herculean as much as it was incomprehensible. Where and how do you start? For six months, I started and restarted, pick-up, put down, read, re-read, copied, took more notes, took notes of the notes and summaries of the summaries, until finally it clicked. The story is the story – it is what happened as I interpreted it through my experiences. The blindingly obvious became obvious - insider action research is a subjectivist methodology in that it employs subjective means to study subjective phenomenon. The insider on the outside was a six month distraction.

Conclusion

Conducting insider action research is more than participation – it is beyond participation. It is a highly personal approach that requires emotions and intimacy, traits that aren't always acknowledged in the world of business. And while insider action research literature is written from a single 'researcher' perspective, it is collaborative and depends on mutual support and respect from your professional and academic colleagues. When these requirements are met, insider action research is transformative.

Insider action research changes the researcher and the organization of which they are a part – therefore *caveat emptor*, let the 'insider researcher' beware:

- That being inside is more than physical access – it is an emotional standpoint;
- That research is not just an add-on to another role but can change the practicing manager role to a practitioner-scholar;
- The practitioner-scholar who produces knowledge for the community is part of the dynamic of leveraging local solutions in a wider organizational (if not societal) environment;
- That in any longer term action research change program expect the unexpected, anticipate the unanticipated, and embrace both since it is from these novel and surprising events that deep insights and transformational knowledge and learning can emerge.

Yet counter-intuitively, it is this emotional dimension of insider action research that provides the drive and energy to sustain local level action research based knowledge creation and learnings that when successful, beget further success. Insider action research can be one of the elements of creating the positive reinforcing feedback that is essential if local solutions are to have any impact in the larger system of which they are a part.

References

Adler, P. A. and P. Adler (1987). Membership roles in Field Research. ISBN: 0-8039-2578-6

Checkland, P. and S. Holwell (1998). "Action Research: Its Nature and Validity." Systemic Practice and Action Research: ISSN: 1094429X 11(1): pp9-21.

Coghlan, D. and T. Brannick (2001). Doing Action Research in Your Own Organization. ISBN: 0-7619-6887-3.

Coghlan, D. and T. Brannick (2005). Doing Action Research in Your Own Organization (Second Edition). ISBN: 1-4129 0247 9.

Collier, J. (1945). "United States Indian Administration as a laboratory of ethnic relations." Social Research: 12: pp275-286.

Emery, F. E. (1981). Systems Thinking, Vol 1. ISBN: 0-1408-0396-3.

Emery, M. (1999). Searching: The theory and practice of making cultural change. ISBN: 90-272-1774-2.

Lewin, K. (1946). "Action research and minority problems." Journal of Social Issues: ISSN: 0022-4537. 2: pp 34-46.

Lewin, K. (1948). Resolving Social Conflicts. ISBN: 0-285-64719-9.

Olsen, J. E. and T. Haslett (2002). "Strategic Management in Action." Systemic Practice and Action Research. ISSN: 1094429X. 15(6): pp449-464.

Perry, C. and O. Zuber-Skerritt (1992). "Action Research in Graduate Management Research Programs." Higher Education ISSN: 0022-1546. 23(2): 195-208.

Punch, M. (1994). Politics and ethics in qualitative research. In *Handbook of Qualitative Research.* N. K. Denzin and Y. S. Lincoln. ISBN: 0-7619-1512-5. pp83-97.

Reason, P. and H. Bradbury, Eds. (2001). Handbook of Action Research: Participative Inquiry and Practice. ISBN: 0-7619-6645-5.

Reason, P. and J. Marshall (1987). Research as personal process. In *Appreciating Adults Learning.* D. Boud and V. Griffin. ISBN: 1-8509-1275-0: pp112-126.

Reason, P. and W. R. Torbert (2001). "The action turn: Toward a transformational social science." Concepts and Transformation. ISSN: 1884-8639. 6(1): pp1-37.

Riemer, J. W. (1977). "Varieties of opportunistic research." Urban Life. ISSN: 1552-5414. 5(4): pp467-477.

Sarah, R. (2006). "Using Action Research to provide the necessary 'stability' to manage the instability of organizational change." ALAR Journal. ISSN: 1326-964X. 10(2)

Sarah, R. and T. Haslett (2005). Using stability to manage the instability of organizational change. ANZSYS 2005, Christchurch, NZ.

Sarah, R., T. Haslett, et al. (2002). "Business Action Research in Practice - A Strategic Conversation about Conducting Action Research in Business Organizations." Systemic Practice and Action Research. ISSN: 1094429X. 15(6): 535-546.

Torbert, W. R. (2001). The Practice of Action Inquiry. In *Handbook of Action Research: Participative Inquiry and Practice.* P. Reason and H. Bradbury. ISBN: 0-7619-6645-5: pp251-260.

von Bertalanffy, L. (1950). The Theory of Open Systems in Physics and Biology. In *Systems Thinking: Selected Readings.* F. E. Emery. ISBN: 0-14-080396-3. pp70-85.

Zuber-Skerritt, O. and C. Perry (2002). "Action research within organizations and university thesis writing." The Learning Organization. ISSN: 0969-6474. 9(3/4): pp171-179.

58. Does Health Care for Systemic Development?

James Sheffield
Department of Information Systems and Operations Management,
University of Auckland, NZ

The paper critically evaluates systems approaches to knowledge management to identify if health cares for (i.e., values) systemic development. Research in knowledge management and health informatics is reviewed to see if multiple systems perspectives exist, and if and how concepts from multiple systems perspectives are integrated, or 'swept in' to a complex whole. The first finding is that knowledge management strategies in health do 'sweep in' insights from three systems perspectives: personal learning (knowledge creation); communities of practise (knowledge normalization); and the exercise of technical expertise and technology (knowledge application). The second finding is that health knowledge management has an architecture that does promote systemic development. An empirical case example of systemic intervention by an executive team is discussed in terms of micro evolution in social ecology.

Introduction

"Knowledge management, as a field of study, has suffered from issues of definition since before the term caught the attention of practicing managers and IS professionals. Put simply, it is unclear what it is that everyone is trying so hard to manage." (Kay & Goldspink, 2005)

A new discipline requires definitional papers that focus on basic theory by defining terms and establishing relationships between concepts (Croasdell, *et al.*, 2003). The literature on knowledge management in organizations now contains a variety of conceptual papers, including those associated with systems thinking and systemic development (Marshall & Brady, 2001; Panagiotidis & Edwards, 2001; Rubenstein-Montano, *et al.*, 2001; Jackson, 2005). Contrary to the above quote, knowledge research in influential journals has always had well-articulated theoretical perspectives, research paradigms, and research methods. However knowledge management research tends to focus on business organizations and prioritizes utility over human agency and power relations (Guo & Sheffield, in press). It is unclear to what extent research under the rubric of knowledge management promotes systemic development.

Three perspectives on foundational theory may be discerned in the business-oriented knowledge management literature. The *first* perspective proposes that organizations have different types of knowledge, and that identifying and examining these will lead to more effective means for generating, sharing and managing knowledge in organizations. This perspective treats knowledge as a representational object to be studied from a "hard systems" (positivist) viewpoint. A *second* perspective on organizational knowledge proposes that knowledge is inseparable from knowing how to get things done in complex organizational work. This perspective proposes that organizations enact a collective capability in organizing. It examines 'practice', i.e., the "situated and ongoing accomplishment that emerges from people's everyday actions" (Orlikowski, 2002: 269). This perspective treats knowledge as a social phenomenon to be studied from a "soft systems" (interpretive) viewpoint. A *third* perspective on organizational knowledge proposes that knowing how to get things done in organizations cannot be separated from politics, i.e., how power is attached to knowledge and vice versa. This perspective treats knowledge as a double-edged weapon to be studied from a "critical systems" (critical pluralist) viewpoint. In systemic development the three paradigms are considered as not mutually exclusive or incommensurable (Kuhn, 1970), but as points of triangulation on knowledge. The assumption is that knowledge is multifaceted, and an individual's initial assumptions may well be naive. A corollary is that power should not be employed to hide systemic problems. Inquiry should emerge from discourse (Schultze & Leidner, 2002) that "sweeps into" practice (Churchman, 1971) an awareness of theoretical perspectives, research paradigms, and research methods (Klein & Hirschheim, 2001), and vice versa. We therefore define systemic development as inquiry into theory and practice that constitutes, and is constituted by, a complex pluralistic whole.

Knowledge management in a particular domain, such as health *may,* or *may not,* be approached pluralistically via a blending of the three systems perspectives (hard, soft and critical) and related research paradigms. In combination, positivism and interpretivism - the paradigms most frequently employed in practice - capture much of the fluidity and interconnectedness important to a systemic approach. Yet neither provides a standard against which to critique the selective application of facts, or aberrant norms, or conflict about work practices. Only the critical paradigm prioritizes approaches that are sensitive to dissensus, conflict and power relations. Systemic research in health knowledge management is defined as a blending of all three paradigms to improve patient care.

But *does* health care for systemic development? This paper reviews knowledge management research in health to see *if* multiple systems perspectives exist, and *if* and *how* concepts from multiple systems perspectives are integrated, or 'swept into' a complex whole. The paper closes with a discussion of an empirical case example of systemic intervention by an executive team.

Multiple but separate systems perspectives

"On the table there are several documents: a rehabilitation plan, paper-based patient records and personal notebooks for each of the professionals. The atmosphere in the room is marked by intense concentration" (Ellingsen, 2003: 45)

"An enormous challenge, however, is how to construct representations that are meaningful to all health professionals who work with a patient" (*ibid.*: 49).

There is evidence that multiple systems perspectives are applied, albeit separately, in health knowledge management. For example, Hansen *et al.* (1999) is an influential early study that may be read as suggesting that a whole organization can adopt a single systems perspective, and thereby avoid the complexity of systemic development. Hansen *et al.* (1999) ascribes quite separate knowledge management strategies to two healthcare organizations, Access Health and the Memorial Sloan-Kettering Cancer Centre in New York City. Access Health, a call-in medical centre, seeks to manage costs by ensuring that patient consultations are supported by the efficient application of pre-existing knowledge and standard pre-defined processes. Extensive classification codes and data gathered from previous cases are employed by each physician to expedite reduction of ambiguity about symptoms and choice of an appropriate treatment. Access Health views knowledge as clear or *explicit* and adopts a 'codification' strategy based on rules and the re-use of pre-existing knowledge. This *a priori* information is prepared by technical specialists outside the clinical practice and delivered via computer technology. No information is provided on how the computer data is updated in the light of practice. The assumption at Access Health is that knowledge about *all* symptoms and treatments is standardized or independent of the local context, and will retain its usefulness and meaning as it is captured from many individual physicians and re-used by many others (*knowledge application*).

In contrast, Memorial Sloan-Kettering Cancer Centre in New York City typically deals with cases that are difficult to understand. Extensive consultations based on the needs of each case are regularly held among specialists to reach a consensus position on the interpretation of a patient's symptoms, and the implications for their treatment. Memorial Sloan-Kettering views knowledge as emergent from a local community of practice, or *tacit*, and adopts a 'personalization' strategy based on the creative channelling of individual capabilities via the norms guiding each semi-autonomous community of practice. Because technical expertise is located inside the clinic it is updated as an integral part of the individual and organizational learning that occurs naturally in clinical practice. The assumption at Memorial Sloan-Kettering is that *all* cases are unique, and that innovation stems from the sharing of intuition and know-how by individual physicians in a particular context (*knowledge normalization*).

Yet tacit and explicit strategies for managing knowledge do not directly address issues of personal learning and self-knowledge. Such knowledge is required in situations where individuals must exercise prospective and retrospective sense making to surface evidence on how to proceed. The active sharing of personal insights by individual agents is a precondition for the possibility of knowledge normalization. Negotiation across heterogeneous roles (health worker, operations management, financial, governance) is required to resolve conflict among multiple views (Harrop, *et al.*, 2006). Authors such as Ellingsen and Monteiro (2003) provide considerable evidence that an individual's own value commitments and their commitments to the values and norms associated with their role and/or professional group (viz., patient, health practitioner specialty, academic researcher, or a mixture of these, and other roles) are important in personal and organizational learning (*knowledge creation*).

In summary, the authors cited above provide examples of health knowledge management research that proceeds from separate systems perspectives (Table 1). These approaches must be developed synchronously to illuminate the challenges identified by Ellingsen (2003).

Systems perspective	**Research paradigm**	**Knowledge management perspective**	**Sample research**
Critical systems	Critical pluralist	Knowledge creation	Harrop *et al.* (2006); Ellingsen and Monteiro (2003)
Soft systems	Interpretive	Knowledge normalization	Hansen *et al.* (1999)
Hard systems	Positivist	Knowledge application	Hansen *et al.* (1999)

Table 1 *Multiple perspectives in health knowledge management*

Are multiple systems perspectives integrated?

"*Before Hanna even enters the scanning room, a contradiction arises. Ultrasound examinations are a routine element of Western maternity care. They are designed to reduce anxiety, and often succeed in doing so, yet at the same time they provoke it*" (Büscher & Jensen, 2007: 25).

"*She steps forward and points at the indication of the blood pressure on the monitor screen and tells Michael, 'I think this is pain'*" (Svensson, 2007: 18).

In practice, reliance on a single strategy is not without its difficulties. Knowledge application via the use of standardized ("global") electronic patient record systems in heterogeneous areas has proven difficult for "local" users (Ellingsen &Monteiro, 2003). Knowledge normalization based on the collection and dissemination of evidence has failed to banish heterogeneity (Jaded, *et al.*, 2000). As suggested by the above quotes, knowledge created in the patient-health worker encounter may be unique to that context, retaining an emergent character difficult to understand from other systems perspectives. This difficulty may lead to operational systems that neglect the user perspective (Harrop, *et al.*, 2006).

A duty of care informs the knowledge created in the patient-health worker encounter in a particular context, such as in a rehabilitation clinic (Ellingsen, 2003), maternity care (Büscher & Jensen, 2007), or an operating theatre (Svensson, 2007). In such contexts knowledge emerges directly from individuals, their social resources, and emergent patterns of conduct, communication and collaboration. Information and other technologies are not separate objects bound to rules but capabilities embedded in the flow of work (Hindmarsh, *et al.*, 2007).

Martin, *et al.* (2007) provides an overview of the ongoing work required to integrate disparate technical systems, semi-autonomous workplace procedures, and specific creative work practices within wider organizational requirements (Table 2).

Perspective	Integration work required
Knowledge creation	Integration of hard and soft systems perspectives with specific aspects of front-line patient-health worker encounters in a particular context
Knowledge normalization	Coordination of semi-autonomous workplace procedures in different but interdependent specialty units that form elements of generic process flows
Knowledge application	Technical integration of disparate systems used in different but interdependent specialty units such as accident and emergency, pathology and imaging

Table 2 *Integrating multiple perspectives in health knowledge management*

The architecture of (health) knowledge management can be represented diagrammatically as three intersecting domains each with a distinctive mode of existence, access and validation. These domains are distinguished by social actors whose cognitions (intentions) and enactments (outcomes) are defined by their relationships to each domain (Sheffield, 2007a) (Figure 1).

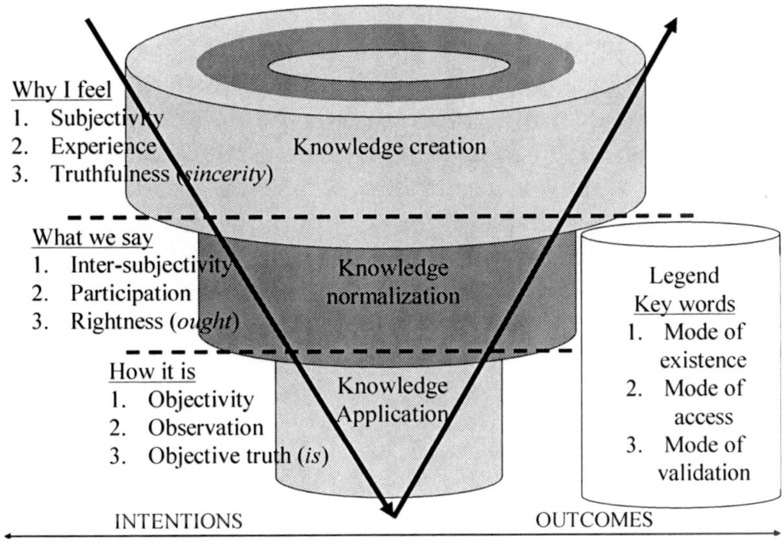

Figure 1 *Architecture of knowledge management*

In summary, many authors in heath knowledge management adopt a pluralistic approach so as to "sweep in" concepts from multiple systems perspectives that constitute a complex whole. They seek to integrate the three perspectives developed above: application of standardized pre-existing codified knowledge and technology (knowledge application); effective channelling of individual capabilities via the norms guiding a local community of practice (knowledge normalization); and value-based personal and organizational learning (knowledge creation). As suggested by the quotes from Büscher and Jensen (2007) and Svensson (2007), such a pluralistic approach lies at the very heart of patient care.

So how does health care for knowledge management?

"Self-reflection on, and expression of, personal values is required in any examination of how knowledge is, and ought to be, linked to power, and power to knowledge."

Interdependencies arise as distinctions recognized by individuals whose interlocked behaviors enable and constrain a collective (social) ecology (Weick, 1979). Each social actor experiences a unique patterning of personal values, social norms and technical facts. Re-organizing mutual expectations requires local actions to reflect holistic or global assumptions about patient care that must emerge from actors' own behavior. Weick describes this sense making process as a "consensually validated grammar for reducing equivocality" about "structures of mutual expectation, attached to roles which define what each [organizational member] shall expect from others and from himself" (*ibid.*: 3). Weick presents a model of systemic development based on natural selection in which consensual validation occurs as a result of a four step process - ecological change, enactment, selection and retention (*ibid.*: 134) (Figure 2). Systemic development that integrates knowledge creation and knowledge normalization occurs naturally as a result of the self-organizing character of personal and interpersonal learning in a particular context. A systemic intervention by a management group may be required to coordinate semi-autonomous workplace procedures in different but interdependent specialty units that form elements of generic process flows. The appropriate use of power is central to such an intervention. Self-reflection on, and expression of, personal values is required in any examination of how knowledge is, and ought to be, linked to power, and power to knowledge. A systemic intervention facilitated by the author and supported by electronic meeting technology (Sheffield & Gallupe, 1994, 1995) is briefly reviewed.

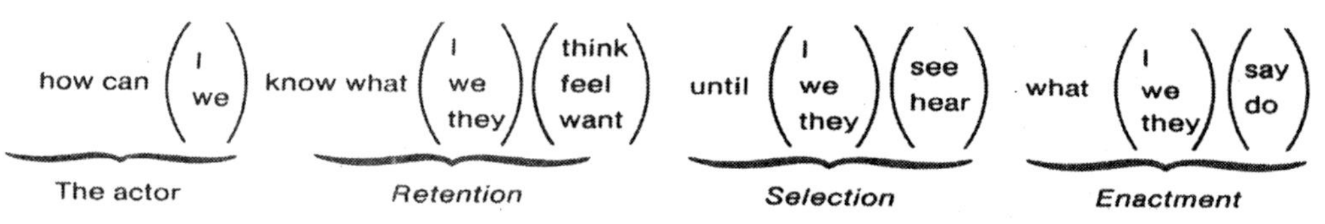

Figure 2 *A four step model of systemic development (Weick 1979, p. 134)*

The executive team in a New Zealand district health board hospital wishes to review expectations and workplace procedures in different but interdependent specialty units. While the general nature of process flows, and the roles of those responsible are understood, these are somewhat fluid and cannot be rigidly determined ahead of time. Six of the ten members of the executive team are directly responsible for medical areas of the hospital and the coordination of departments in their area. The other four include the hospital director and directors of non-medical areas. The hospital is at the time experiencing capacity problems in emergency care, problems that may be exacerbated by the lack of a permanent EC director. Because emergency care relies heavily on consultants from other specialty areas, these problems have a ripple effect that creates downstream problems. Like members of a football team, health specialists move the action downfield, passing the work to one another. In football passing depends on how sender and receiver are positioned at the time and success is not automatic. In a hospital making a pass requires specialist medical skill and a keen prospective and retrospective sense of 'the way we do things around here". What counts as a good pass is subject to cultural misunderstanding. Departments that are heterogeneous yet marked by strong interdependencies tend on occasion to "drop the ball". This is a sensitive issue for patients, frontline healthworkers, their department heads, area directors and the hospital director. The executive team sees the problem as systemic.

The hospital director invites all ten members of his executive team to a half day meeting. The purpose is to reach consensus on ways to improve interdependencies within and between departments. The date of the meeting changes several times to accommodate schedule conflicts. In the event not all that were expected to attend do so. The hospital director opens the meeting by thanking those present and briefly giving a personalized account of some challenges he has been facing since the team last met. Each participant responds in kind so that the resourceful presence (pre-sense) of each is enacted as a group resource. Some of the stories recounted, such as the discovery of the disappearance of a significant quantity of methadone from the drug rehabilitation department, have potentially serious implications and need urgent attention. The sharing of personal experiences among area directors serves as a 'check in' procedure that establishes the degree to which each was able to be present and to attend to the issues at hand. While the interpersonal bonds among those who represent (re-present) different cultures appear strong, it is clear that attendees are already very busy on other matters.

Each participant uses a personal computer to prepare his or her own statement of meeting objectives. They employ electronic meeting technology to concatenate all statements of objectives, and to display them on each participant's screen. On seeing their own work product displayed along with those of others, each participant is able to verbally identify elements of best practice, and is keen to have another go at typing. Over the next few more rounds participants make considerable progress in "seeing what they say and knowing what they think" (Figure 2). The joint statement of the problem is collectively enacted as "How can each of those of us responsible for a medical area facilitate coordination among their own departments, and in directly related areas." Participants in previous electronically supported meetings have expressed their belief that the synchronous use of keyboards reduces blockages, competition for airtime, and promotes fairness and efficiency. The 'posting' of work products from unidentified sources to a common and neutral area appears to promote equality of participation, collaboration and problem solving. In this meeting participants faithfully appropriated the technology for their own purposes. The facilitator did not detect any lack of trust or other barriers to exploring issues that were sensitive and could reflect poorly on participants.

The way the participants choose to move from problem statement to policy consensus is of theoretical interest. Key concepts in an emergent grammar are bracketed (literally) for further study. The process used to develop a consensus statement of meeting objectives is used recursively to refine each element in the policy. Collectively the elements identify a web of interdependencies and the way that these are to be surfaced and evaluated. The result is a document ready for publication that effectively moves the organizing process down one level. The policy asks each area director to facilitate a similar process within and among their various departments. Recurring problems ("pressure points") are to be identified, own expectations for service levels clarified, and negotiated with those in the departments concerned, to coordinate activities linked to form generic process flows. A summary of achievements, documenting service levels and any unresolved issues, is to be presented by each area director to the hospital director by a certain date. The meeting generates personal commitment to speech acts that, when "frozen" into text, constitute a representation (re-present-ation), stable across space and time, useful in the ongoing recursive organizing of a systemic intervention. Participants in the systemic intervention (including the author, whose mother died in the hospital) experience systemic development as micro evolution (natural selection) in social ecology (Figure 3).

As participants in systemic intervention

we experienced choosing a term from each of the braces:
"How can {I, he, she, you, they, we} (The actor)
know what {I, he, she, you, they, we} {think, feel, want} (Retention)
Until {I, he, she, you, they, we} {see, hear} (Selection)
What {I, he, she, you, they, we} {say, do} (Enactment)"

Weick, K. (1979). The Social Psychology of Organizing (p. 134)

in an iterative, reflective, recursive, social yet often silent process that constitutes
"A consensually validated grammar for reducing equivocality by means of sensible interlocked behaviours"

Ibid. (p. 3)

Figure 3 *Systemic intervention as micro evolution in social ecology*

Results and discussion

In total, the paper is an illustration of how patient care depends on efforts to resolve tensions among systems perspectives that privilege technical expertise, or community norms, or personal values. The empirical example of systemic intervention by an executive team illustrates how health cares for systemic development. This intervention appears successful in large measure because the culture of the executive team is sensitive to conflicting agendas and resource constraints. The willingness of members of the executive team to negotiate mutual expectations with each other promises to expand in a virtuous circle to 'sweep in' other health workers, including those from heterogenous work groups who have in the past occasionally "dropped the ball". The author's own experience suggests that many managers refuse to recognise their own complicity in systemic problems because such recognition costs additional effort and diminishes their position power. That this executive team cares for systemic development can be seen in the way they take care to "walk the talk" and "eat their own cooking".

The findings may be useful to researchers and practitioners in systemic development for three reasons. Firstly, the objective or factual basis for the study constitutes a resource supportive of technical excellence. Secondly, the social or normative basis of the article is supportive of resourceful practical action towards, and emergent interpersonal consensus about, issues that are recursively intertwined. Thirdly, the personal or value-driven aspects of the theory may resonate with the self-reflection of individuals who experience conflict between technical and practical approaches, and conflict between how knowledge *is,* and *should be,* linked to power. More generally, the paper contributes to the literature that seeks to understand systemic complexity via awareness of one's epistemic commitments and those of others. Another research study (Sheffield 2007b) presented at this conference examines the knowledge management literature for pluralistic approaches useful in systemic development.

References

Büscher, M. and Jensen, G. (2007). "Sound sight: Seeing with ultrasound," *Health Informatics Journal*, ISSN:1460-4582, 13(1):23-36.

Churchman, C.W. (1971). *The design of inquiring systems: Basic concepts of systems and organizations*,ISBN:0465016081.

Croasdell, D., Jennex, M., Yu, Z., Christianson, T., Chakradeo, M. and Makdum, W. (2003). "A Meta-Analysis of Methodologies for Research in Knowledge Management, Organizational Learning and Organizational Memory: Five Years at HICSS", in Proceedings of the 36th Hawaii International Conference on System Sciences.

Ellingsen, G. (2003). "Coordinating work in hospitals through a global tool: Implications for the implementation of electronic patient records in hospitals," *Scandinavian Journal of Information Systems*, ISSN:0905-0167, 15:39-54.

Ellingsen, G. and Monteiro, E. (2003). "A patchwork planet: Integration and cooperation in hospitals," *Computer Supported Cooperative Work*, ISSN:0925-9724, 12(1):71-95.

Guo, Z. and Sheffield, J. (in press). "A Paradigmatic and Methodological Examination of Knowledge Management Research: 2000-2004," *Decision Support Systems*, ISSN:0167-9236.

Hansen, M., Nohria, N., Tierney, T. (1999). "What's your strategy for knowledge management?," *Harvard Business Review*, ISSN:0017-8012, March-April:104-116.

Harrop, N., Wood-Harper, T. and Gillies, A. (2006). "Neglected user perspectives in the design of an online hospital bed-state system: implications for the National Programme for IT in the NHS," *Health Informatics Journal*, ISSN:1460-4582, 12(4):293-303.

Hindmarsh, J., Jenkins, K.N. and Rapley, T. (2007). "Special issue introduction to healthcare technologies in practice," *Health Informatics Journal*, ISSN:1460-4582, 13(1):5-8.

Jackson, M. (2005). "Reflections on Knowledge Management From a Critical Systems Perspective," *Knowledge Management Research and Practice*, ISSN:1477-8238 3:187-196.

Kay, R. and Goldspink, C. (2005). "Organizational Knowledge and Autopoiesis: Implications for Knowledge Management," in Proceedings of the 11th ANZSYS/Managing the Complex V Conference, Christchurch, New Zealand.

Klein, H. and Hirschheim, R. (2001). "Choosing Between Competing Design Ideals in Information Systems Development," *Information Systems Frontiers*, ISSN:1387-3326, 3(1): 75-90.

Kuhn, T. (1970). *The Structure of Scientific Revolutions*, ISBN:9780226458083.

Marshall, N., and Brady, T. (2001). "Knowledge Management and the Politics of Knowledge: Illustrations from Complex Products and Systems," *European Journal of Information Systems*, ISSN:0960-085X, 10(2):99-112.

Martin, D., Mariana, J. and Rouncefield, M. (2007). "Managing integration work in an electronic patient record (EPR) project," *Health Informatics Journal*, ISSN:1460-4582, 13(1):47-56.

Orlikowski, W. (2002). "Knowing in Practice: Enacting a Collective Capability in Distributed Organizing," *Organization Science*, ISSN:1047-7039, 13(3):249-273.

Panagiotidis, P. and Edwards, J. (2001). "Organizational Learning-A Critical Systems Thinking Discipline," *European Journal of Information Systems*, ISSN:0960-085X, 10:135-146.

Rubenstein-Montano, B., Liebowitz, B., Buchwalter, J., McCaw, J., Newman, D. and Rebeck, B. (2001). "A Systems Thinking Framework for Knowledge Management," *Decision Support Systems*, ISSN:0167-9236, 31(1):5-16.

Schultze, U. and Leidner, D. (2002). "Studying Knowledge Management in Information Systems Research: Discourse and Theoretical Assumptions," *MIS Quarterly*, ISSN:0276-7783, 26(3): 213-242.

Sheffield J. (2007a). "Habermasian Analysis of Comprehensive Urban Planning," in Proceedings of the 40th Annual Hawaii International Conference on System Sciences.

Sheffield, J. (2007b). "Pluralisms in knowledge management," In Proceedings of Australia New Zealand Systems Conference 2007, 2nd-5th December, Auckland, New Zealand.

Sheffield, J. and Gallupe, R.B. (1995). "Using Group Support Systems to Improve the New Zealand Economy Part II: Followup Results," *Journal of Management Information Systems*, ISSN:0742-1222,11(3):135-153.

Sheffield, J. and Gallupe, R.B. (1994). "Using Electronic Meeting Technology to Support Economic Policy Development in New Zealand: Short Term Results," *Journal of Management Information Systems*, ISSN:0742-1222, 10(3):97-116.

Svensson, M.S. (2007). "Monitoring practice and alarm technology in anaesthesiology," *Health Informatics Journal*, ISSN:1460-4582, 13(1):9-22.

Weick, K. (1979). *The social psychology of organizing*. ISBN:0075548089.

59. Pluralisms in Knowledge Management

James Sheffield
Department of Information Systems and Operations Management, University of Auckland, NZ

Acknowledgement

The author wishes to thank Edward Lau who authored an initial draft of this research.

Knowledge management constitutes a fertile yet problematic area of systemic development. The literature is dominated by a hard systems (positivist) approach that prioritizes observation and global generalizations over local action to improve practice in a particular context. It is not clear that pluralistic approaches to knowledge management exist, and are used in practice. This research surveys knowledge management theory to surface underlying systems perspectives, and to identify pluralisms that support systemic development. A brief example of practical application is provided. Primarily the study is theoretical, and builds theory of importance to knowledge management and systemic development. Further guidelines for practice are presented in another research study presented at this conference that examines systemic development in health knowledge management.

Introduction

"*Our objective with this analysis is to raise IS (information systems) researchers' awareness of the potential and the implications of the different discourses in the study of knowledge and knowledge management*" (Schultze & Leidner, 2002: 213).

Knowledge management is a broad and relatively new field central to understanding the modern service-based, knowledge-intensive economy. Researchers come to knowledge management from different disciplinary backgrounds, to work on a broad range of topics, using a variety of images (Morgan, 2006), analogies, and research approaches. A popular working definition of the field is provided by Davenport and Prusak (1998):

"*Knowledge is a fluid mix of framed experience, values, contextual information, and expert insights that provides a framework for evaluating and incorporating new experiences and information. It originates and is applied in the minds of knowers. In organizations, it often becomes embedded not only in documents or repositories but also in organizational routines, processes, practices, and norms.*" (*ibid.*: 5)

Three perspectives maybe discerned here. Firstly, knowledge that originates in a particular local context through the framed experiences and values of knowers is the emergent ("tacit") knowledge (Polanyi, 1967) prized in systemic development. Secondly, expertise and documented knowledge is the emerged ("explicit") knowledge (Zack, 1999) that constitutes the knowledge representations or boundary objects available to members of both local and global communities. Thirdly, it is the aggregate of the action originated by knowers that, over space and time, appears as organizational routines, processes, practices and norms. Another paper in this conference under the rubric of knowledge management identifies three systems perspectives (hard, soft, and critical); three research paradigms (positivist, interpretive, and critical pluralist); and three knowledge management domains (knowledge application, knowledge normalization, and knowledge creation) (Sheffield, 2007a). The three knowledge management domains constitute a typology of knowledge management practice. These are seen as emphasizing the factual, interpersonal, and personal aspects of knowledge phenomena, respectively. Figure 1 illustrates how these perspectives may used to deconstruct the Davenport and Prusak (1998) definition.

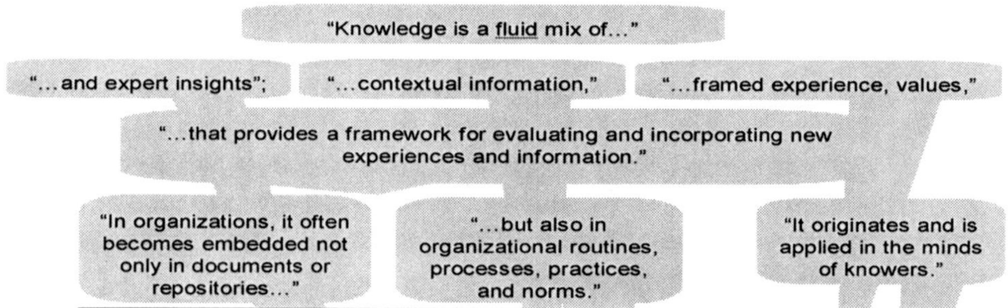

Systems perspective	Hard	Soft	Critical
Research Paradigm	Positivist	Interpretivist	Pluralist
Knowledge Perspective	Knowledge application	Knowledge normalization	Knowledge creation

Figure 1 *Pluralism in knowledge management*

It is not clear if the holism and pluralism of the Davenport and Prusak definition carries over to research and practice. The literature is dominated by a hard systems (positivist) approach that prioritizes observation and global generalizations over local action to improve practice in a particular context (Guo and Sheffield, in press). The current study aims to surface systems perspectives underlying knowledge management theory, and to identify any frameworks that embrace the pluralism that lies at the heart of systemic development.

Frameworks in knowledge management

The knowledge management literature is searched for frameworks influential in developing a common vocabulary among members of knowledge management research communities. Promising frameworks are those that score against three criteria: *foundational theory* (that is, frameworks that develop and/or review concepts and relationships, taxonomies and perspectives of theoretical importance and/or broad application to knowledge management researchers); *impact* (frameworks frequently cited by knowledge management authors); *inquiry* (frameworks that develop or review the philosophical assumptions underlying knowledge management research and/or research paradigms). The search process delivered more than 50 frameworks that scored well against a single criterion, including the following:

- Foundational theory: Baskerville and Dulipovici, 2006; Croasdell, *et al.*, 2003; Grover and Davenport, 2001; Holsapple and Joshi, 2004; Lehaney, *et al.*, 2004; Peachy and Hall, 2005; Rubenstein-Montano, *et al.*, 2001; Shin, *et al.*, 2001; Stenmark, 2002;
- High impact books: Wenger, 1999 (5000 citations); Nonaka, 1994 (3000 citations); Nonaka and Takeuchi, 1995 (3000 citations); Davenport and Prusak, 1998 (2000 citations);
- High impact articles: Hansen *et al*, 1999 (1000 citations); Nonaka and Konno, 1998 (900 citations); Blackler, 1995 (700 citations); Alavi and Leidner, 2001 (500 citations); Orlikowski, 2002 (300 citations); Earl, 2001 (200 citations);
- Inquiry: Guo and Sheffield, 2006; Jackson, 2005; Marshall and Brady, 2001; Orlikowski, 2002; Panagiotidis and Edwards, 2001; Schultze and Leidner, 2002, Sorensen and Kakihara, 2002.

Eight frameworks are chosen that, collectively, perform well against all three criteria. These are briefly described below. An initial indication is given of the dominant system perspective.

Hierarchy: from data to information to knowledge (Stenmark, 2002). The theme that objective data is the ultimate source of both socially useful knowledge and personal knowledge, is seen as focusing on knowledge as context-independent facts (Hard systems).

Flow: the knowledge management value-chain (Shin, 2001). This framework treats knowledge as an organizational resource to which value is added as it moves downstream through the local activities in the value chain. This is a workflow metaphor that focuses on achieving success in a technical sense through instrumental action that attempts to control the way in which knowledge works in an organization (Hard systems).

Exchange: the knowledge market (Grover and Davenport, 2001). The exchange and flow frameworks are both oriented to promoting organizational success through efficient knowledge transfer. However, unlike the knowledge management value-chain the exchange framework attempts to describe individuals' rational motivations for sharing knowledge with each other. This framework assumes that the very act of sharing knowledge will lead to benefits and so the imperative for the organization is to find means of increasing the efficiency of the market (Hard systems).

Transformation: Knowledge conversion (Nonaka, 1994). SECI (socialization, externalization, combination, internalization) focuses on the social processes at work in the transformation of explicit to implicit knowledge, and vice versa. Insomuch as the SECI model does not dwell on the technical systems required for the (non-transformative) storage and dissemination of explicit knowledge, nor on the preconditions required to address power relations, it does not fully investigate the role of objective facts and personal values (Soft systems).

Systems thinking: Emergence (Rubenstein-Montano, et al., 2001). Systems thinking is not well represented in knowledge management research. The single article encountered (Rubenstein-Montano *et al.*, 2001) interprets knowledge management themes in terms of systems concepts such as people, learning and technology. While a holistic approach is recommended there is no explicit or implicit recognition of any particular underlying knowledge perspective. (Pluralistic)

Critical systems (Jackson 2005); scientific discourses (Schultz & Leidner, 2002); the Habermasian inquiring system (Guo & Sheffield, 2006). These pluralistic frameworks are investigated below.

Perspectives and frameworks in knowledge management

Table 1 provides a simple graphical representation that links the eight frameworks to systems perspectives, research paradigms, and knowledge management domains, and classifies them as pluralistic or non-pluralistic.

Pluralisms in knowledge management

This section explores the three frameworks that support pluralism via well-defined systems perspectives. All three constitute pluralisms useful in analyzing "the potential and the implications of the different discourses" (Schultze & Leidner, 2002: 213).

Critical systems: Conflict and power

Jackson (2005) broadens the dialogue between knowledge management and systems thinking to include a variety of theories and methods, and employs the latter to critique knowledge management frameworks. A particular focus is how knowledge management deals with the conditions enabling knowledge creation (Tackeuchi & Nonaka, 2004). Knowledge creation is seen as a dialectical process in which the deeply held beliefs and (value) commitments of individuals "is dynamically created out of contradictions in a dialectical process" whereby "individuals confront their own most cherished assumptions and a synthesis of different perspectives emerges" (Jackson, 2005: 190). A social systems approach that champions human agency and employs an interpretivist approach

Perspectives			
Systems perspective	**Hard systems**	**Soft systems**	**Critical systems**
Research paradigm	Positivist, focusing on objective facts	Interpretive, focusing on social norms	Critical pluralist, focusing on personal values
Knowledge management domain	Knowledge application	Knowledge normalization	Knowledge creation
Non-pluralistic knowledge management frameworks			
Hierarchy: Data, information, knowledge (Stenmark, 2002)	XXX		
Flow. Value chain (Shin, 2001)	XXX		
Exchange. Market (Grover and Davenport, 2001)	XXX		
Transformation: SECI (Nonaka, 1994)	X	XXX	X
Pluralistic knowledge management frameworks			
Systems thinking (Rubenstein-Montano *et al.*, 2001)	XXX	XX	X
Critical systems (Jackson 2005)	XXX	XXX	XXX
Scientific discourses (Schultz and Leidner, 2002)	XXX	XXX	XXX
Habermasian inquiring system (Guo and Sheffield, 2006)	XXX	XXX	XXX

Table 1 *Perspectives and frameworks in knowledge management*

to inquiry is considered a necessary but insufficient move away from more static and mechanistic approaches that focus on objective facts. Knowledge management still needs to confront the conflict, and relations to power, that are inherent in knowledge creation (Marshall & Brady, 2001; Müller-Merbach, 2004; Panagiotidis & Edwards, 2001; Pozzebon & Pinsonneault, 2006). Insomuch as the dialectical process at the heart of organizational learning requires conflict, and involves the exercise of power, "a critical systems approach, embracing ethical concerns, is essential" (Jackson, 2005: 191).

Scientific discourses

According to Schultze and Leidner (2002), "In information systems, most research on knowledge management assumes that knowledge has positive implications for organizations. However, knowledge is a double-edged sword: while too little might result in expensive mistakes, too much might result in unwanted accountability. The purpose of this paper is to highlight the lack of attention paid to the unintended consequences of managing organizational knowledge and thereby to broaden the scope of IS-based knowledge management research" (*ibid.*: 213). Schultze and Leidner (2002) adopt a framework developed by Deetz (1996) for classifying scientific discourses. Although Deetz's framework is intended to provide a taxonomy of research for organization science, it can also be used to "make sense of knowledge management research as well as knowledge management itself" (Schultze & Leidner, 2002: 215) (Figure 2).

The framework consists of two dimensions: the "origin of concepts and problems" dimension and the "relation to dominant social discourse" dimension. The first dimension is concerned with how research concepts and problems are developed. At the local/emergent end of the continuum concepts are *developed from* a specific situation whereas at the elite/a priori end existing concepts are *applied to* a specific situation. The second dimension is concerned with the stance of the researcher in relation to the status quo. The consensus end of this continuum seeks to maintain order and equilibrium and regards this as the natural state of social systems. In contrast, the dissensus end is at odds with the dominant social structure and "considers struggle, conflict, and tension as the natural state" (*ibid.*: 216).

These two dimensions create four quadrants, each of which is oriented towards a particular scientific discourse: normative, interpretive, critical, and dialogic. The normative discourse is characterized by "codification, the normalization of experience, and the search for law-like relationships" (*ibid.*: 17). 'Normalization' in the context of scientific discourse emphasizes objective facts. The interpretive discourse assumes reality is socially constructed and seeks consensus on organizational activities from participants' "own frame of reference" (Collis & Hussey, 2003: 53). 'Normalization' in the context of communities of practice (Wenger, 1999) revolves around social norms, and hence the interpretive scientific discourse. The objective of critical discourse is to make apparent forms of domination and conflict which implicitly lead to power imbalances between organization members. Finally, the dialogic discourse recognizes that reality is socially constructed yet the multiple narratives and perspectives are disjointed and incoherent. The dialogic discourse differs from the critical discourse "in that it considers power and domination as situational and not owned by anything or anyone" (Schultze & Leidner, 2002: 217). Only the dialogic and critical discourses emphasize power relations, and the explicit need for personal commitments and values.

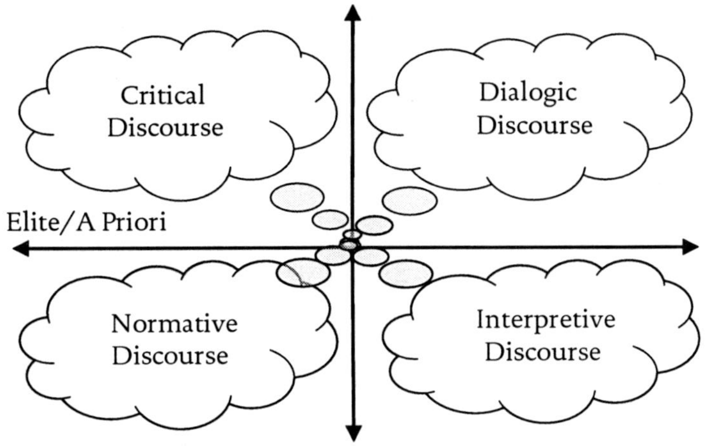

Figure 2 *Deetz's scientific discourses*
Source: Schultze and Leidner, 2002: 216

Habermasian inquiring system

Guo and Sheffield (2006) develop a framework that synthesizes concepts from Churchman's inquiring systems and Habermas (1985, 1987, 1989) that, the authors suggest, provide a "universally pragmatic framework useful in managing the complexity, and conceptualizing the richness, of knowledge phenomena" (*ibid.*: 1). The framework is organized as a three-level integrating structure based on Habermas's three knowledge interests (technical, practical, and emancipatory) and the rationality associated with each. The other three design elements (Churchman's roles, knowledge dynamics, research paradigms) are then positioned according to these three encompassing levels, the sum of which "represents a complex learning system, where there are bidirectional loops between each pair of the three levels of rationality" (*ibid.*: 4) (Figure 3).

The relevance of the framework to knowledge management is established through knowledge dynamics associated with the intersecting domains of knowledge creation, knowledge normalization, knowledge application. A knowledge initiative in one domain 'always already' assumes a horizon of possibilities made possible through the existence of the other two domains. Fundamentally, *knowledge creation* is enacted by individual stakeholders (clients, in terms of Churchman's roles) through their own unique cognitive processes, including those associated with power relations, social justice and ethics (Sheffield & Guo, 2007), and serves Habermas's emancipatory knowledge interest.

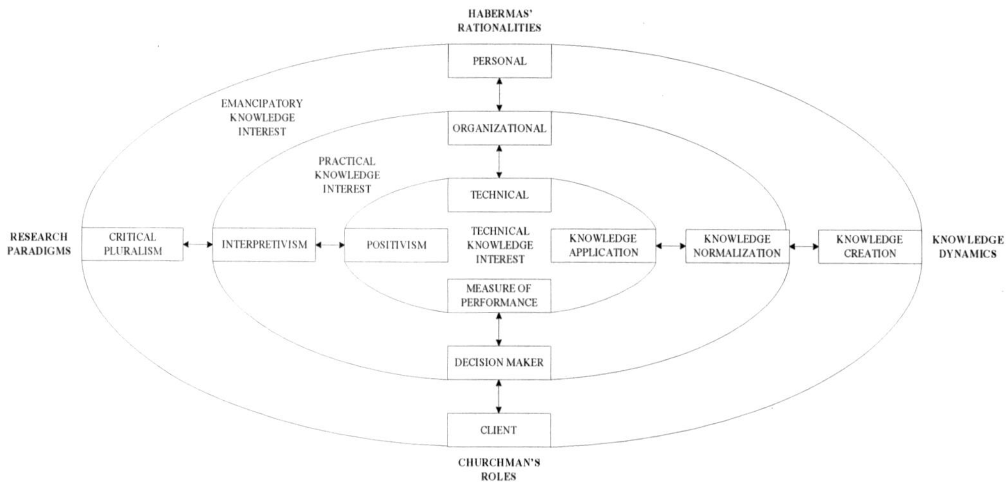

Figure 3 *The Habermasian inquiring system for knowledge management*
Source: Guo and Sheffield, 2006: 7

Critical pluralism is seen as an appropriate paradigm for studying the diverse beliefs, values, aspirations, etc. of various stakeholders (Mingers, 2001). The idea of *knowledge normalization* is similar to Nonaka's knowledge spiral, in which knowledge is developed, refined, and amplified from the individual to organizational level. Knowledge normalization serves Habermas's practical knowledge interest and Churchman's organizational decision maker role - clients' personal knowledge is *normalized* (socialized) according to the collective values of the decision maker in order to become organizational knowledge. The interpretive paradigm is seen as appropriate for research investigating inter-subjective meaning and mutual accommodations central to the normalization process (Orlikowski, 2002). Finally, *knowledge application* refers to how knowledge - created at the personal level, and normalized at the organizational level - is ultimately utilized in day-to-day operations to achieve organizational results (competitive advantage, organizational capability). By performing against measures such as these, knowledge application 'realizes' organizational knowledge, thus serving Habermas's technical knowledge interest. The positivist paradigm is seen as appropriate in evaluating technical excellence validated by objective truth.

Pluralisms in practice

Awareness of 'different discourses' appears important in comprehensive urban planning (Sheffield, 2007b) and health knowledge management (Sheffield, 2007a). Aidemark (2005) proposes that implementing a hospital intranet involves a "delicate trade-off between social and cognitive perspectives" and that "these two aspects must be handled in an interconnected and balanced way". Ellingsen and Monteiro (2003) argue that today's hospitals must combine codification and personalization strategies in an environment of technological, organizational, institutional, and political complexity. In this environment, individual's own value commitments and their commitments to the values and norms associated with their role and/or professional group (viz, patient, health practitioner specialty, academic researcher, or a mixture of these, and other roles) are important in personal and organizational learning.

Ellingsen (2003) provides a case study in the contradictions that lie at the very heart of coordinating work in hospitals. Three vignettes are provided about the case of a single patient who attends a department of rehabilitation over a period of one to two years. Care of the brain-damaged patient relies for success on the professional expertise and coordination of seven types of professionals (physician, nurse, occupational therapist, physiotherapist, speech therapist, psychologist, and social worker). But who will say what these highly educated people know? And how will the knowledge distributed among them be recorded? According to the chief physician "we need a common framework (such as a global tool for surveying patient functionality) or an ideology; for instance, there is a connection between body impairment and how to manage things in everyday life...This means that everything is interconnected and accordingly must be regarded as a whole." (*ibid.*: 50) A global tool is introduced in the form of a structured format for an electronic record. The ideology which governs the local use of the tool reflects hierarchical structures along boundaries of disciplinary specialization as well as informal accommodations. The formal documentation of patient care necessitates negotiation about major changes to work practices. The use of the tool becomes the occasion for promoting the professionalism of some specialties and the downgrading of others. Additional accommodations and accountability are required. "It implies hard work...The participants had to accept that some of their professional assessments were evaluated in a more critical perspective." (*ibid.*: 51) Accountability, norms governing interdisciplinary coordination, and power relations constitute three different discourses, each of which has a logic that contradicts the others. A normative critique of patient care requires sensitivity to the way each discourse facilitates, and constrains, the others.

Conclusion

The interdisciplinary nature and variety of areas of application speaks to the relevance, if not the rigour, of knowledge management research and practice. Researchers come to knowledge management and systemic development from different disciplinary backgrounds and work in different domains. The knowledge management literature as a whole is dominated by a single systems perspective (hard systems), a single research paradigm (positivism, focusing on objective facts), and a single knowledge management domain (knowledge application). This singular (non-pluralistic) approach produces theories about knowledge that has already emerged. Yet the popular definition of knowledge examined in the introduction, and the literature surveyed, includes two other perspectives – soft systems and critical systems – that focus on the organizational and individual aspects of emergence, respectively. Four pluralistic knowledge management frameworks are identified. Three of these - critical systems, scientific discourses, and the Habermasian inquiring system – describe knowledge as emergent from all three systems perspectives. All three recognise that dissensus or conflict is the precondition to knowledge creation, and that power relations, value commitments, and ethics are central to knowledge management. The contribution of the paper is to build concepts and relationships among three pluralistic frameworks of importance to both knowledge management and systemic development. More generally, the paper contributes to the literature that seeks to understand systemic complexity via awareness of one's epistemic commitments and those of others. The contribution is therefore theory building. Another research study presented at this conference examines systemic development in health knowledge management and provides an empirical example of a systemic intervention by an executive team.

References

Aidemark, J. (2005). "Implementing intranet for social and cognitive knowledge processes," *International Journal of Healthcare Technology and Management,* ISSN: 1477-8238, 6: 357-367.

Alavi, M. and Leidner, D. (2001). "Knowledge management and knowledge management systems: Conceptual foundations and research issues," *MIS Quarterly,* ISSN: 0276-7783, 25(1): 107-136.

Baskerville, R. and Dulipovici, A. (2006). "The theoretical foundations of knowledge management," *Knowledge Management Research and Practice,* ISSN: 1477-8238, 4(2): 83-105.

Blackler, F. (1995). "Knowledge, knowledge work and organizations: an overview and interpretation," *Organization Studies,* ISSN: 0170-8406, 16(6): 1021-1046.

Collis, J. and Hussey, R. (2003). *Business research.* ISBN 0333983254.

Croasdell, D.T., Jennex, M., Yu, Z., Christianson, T., Chakradeo, M. and Makdum, W. (2003). "A meta-analysis of methodologies for research in knowledge management, organizational learning and organizational memory: five years at HICSS," In *Proceedings of the 36th Annual Hawaii International Conference on System Sciences.*

Davenport, T. H., and Prusak, L. (1998). *Working knowledge: How organizations manage what they know.* ISBN 0875846556.

Deetz, S. (1996). "Describing differences in approaches to organization science: rethinking Burrell and Morgan and their legacy," *Organization Science,* ISSN 1047-7039, 7(2): 191-207.

Earl, M. (2001). "Knowledge management strategies: toward a taxonomy," *Journal of Management Information Systems,* ISSN:0742-1222, 18(1): 215-233.

Ellingsen, G. (2003). "Coordinating work in hospitals through a global tool: implications for the implementation of electronic patient records in hospitals," *Scandinavian Journal of Information Systems,* ISSN: 0905-0167, 15: 39-54.

Ellingsen, G. and Monteiro, E. (2003). "A patchwork planet: integration and cooperation in hospitals," *Computer Supported Cooperative Work,* ISSN: 0925-9724, 12(1): 71-95.

Grover, V. and Davenport, T. (2001). "General perspectives on knowledge management: fostering a research agenda," *Journal of Management Information Systems,* ISSN: 0742-1222, 18(1): 5-21.

Guo, Z. and Sheffield, J. (in press). "A paradigmatic and methodological examination of knowledge management research: 2000-2004," *Decision Support Systems,* ISSN: 0167-9236.

Guo, Z. and Sheffield, J. (2006). "Habermasian inquiring systems: toward a general framework for knowledge management research," In *Proceedings of the 39th Annual Hawaii International Conference on System Sciences.*

Habermas, J. (1985). *The theory of communicative action Volume 1: reason and the rationalization of society,* ISBN: 0807015075. Reprint edition.

Habermas, J. (1987). *Knowledge and human interests.* ISBN: 0745604595.

Habermas, J. (1989). *The theory of communicative action Volume 2: lifeword and system,* ISBN: 080701401X. Reprint edition.

Hansen, M., Nohria, N., Tierney, T. (1999). "What's your strategy for knowledge management?," *Harvard Business Review,* ISSN: 0017-8012, March-April: 104-116.

Holsapple, C. and Joshi, K. (2004). "A formal knowledge management ontology: conduct, activities, resources, and influences," *Journal of the American Society For Information Science and Technology,* ISSN: 1532-2882, 55(7): 593-612.

Jackson, M. (2005). "Reflections on knowledge management from a critical systems perspective," *Knowledge Management Research and Practice,* ISSN: 1477-8238, 3(4): 187-196.

Lehaney, B., Clark, S., Coakes, E. and Jack, G. (2004). *Beyond knowledge management,* ISBN: 9781591402237.

Marshall, N. and Brady, T. (2001). "Knowledge management and the politics of knowledge: illustrations from complex products and systems,". *European Journal of Information Systems,* ISSN: 0960-085X, 10(2): 99-112.

Mingers J. (2001). "Combining IS research methods: towards a pluralist methodology," *Information Systems Research,* ISSN: 1047-7047, 12(3): 240-259.

Morgan, G. (2006). *Images of Organization,* ISBN: 9781412939799.

Müller-Merbach, H. (2004). "Creative conflict," *Knowledge Management Research and Practice,* ISSN: 1477-8238, 2(2): 129-130.

Nonaka, I. (1994) "A dynamic theory of organizational knowledge creation," *Organization Science,* ISSN: 1047-7039, 5(1): 14-37.

Nonaka, I. and Konno, N. (1998). "The concept of 'Ba': building a foundation for knowledge creation," *California Management Review,* ISSN: 0008-1256, 40(3): 40-54.

Nonaka, I. and Takeuchi, H. (1995). *The knowledge-creating company: how Japanese companies create the dynamics of innovation,* ISBN, 0195092694.

Orlikowski, W. (2002). "Knowing in practice: enacting a collective capability in distributed organizing," *Organization Science,* ISSN: 1047-7039, 13(3): 249-273.

Panagiotidis, P. and Edwards, J. S. (2001). "Organizational learning - a critical systems thinking discipline," *European Journal of Information Systems,* ISSN: 0960-085X, 10(3): 135-146.

Peachy, T. and Hall, D. (2005). "Knowledge management and the leading IS journals: an analysis of trends and gaps in published research," In *Proceedings of the 38th Annual Hawaii International Conference on System Sciences.*

Polanyi, M. (1967). *The tacit dimension.* ISBN: 0844659991.

Pozzebon, M. and Pinsonneault, A. (2006). *A study of power and knowledge in the implementation of configurable information technologies.* HEC Montreal, ISSN 0832-7203.

Rubenstein-Montano, B., Liebowitz, J., Buchwalter, J., Mccaw, D., Newman, B. and Rebeck, K. (2001). "A systems thinking framework for knowledge management," *Decision Support Systems,* ISSN: 0167-9236, 31(1): 5-16.

Schultze, U. and Leidner, D. E. (2002). „Studying knowledge management in information systems research: discourses and theoretical assumptions," *MIS Quarterly,* ISSN: 0276-7783, 26(3): 213-242.

Sheffield, J. (2007a). "Does health care for knowledge management?" In Proceedings of Australia New Zealand Systems Conference 2007, 2nd - 5th December, Auckland, New Zealand.

Sheffield J. (2007b). "Habermasian analysis of comprehensive urban planning," in Proceedings of the 40th Annual Hawaii International Conference on System Sciences.

Sheffield, J and Guo, Z. (2007). "Ethical inquiry in knowledge management," *International Journal of Applied Systemic Studies,* ISSN: 1751-0589, 1(1): 68-81.

Shin, M., Holden, T. and Schmidt, R. A. (2001). "From knowledge theory to management practice: towards an integrated approach," *Information Processing and Management,* ISSN: 0306-4573, 37(2): 335-355.

Sorensen, C. and Kakihara, M. (2002). "Knowledge discourses and interaction technology," In *Proceedings of the 35th Annual Hawaii International Conference on System Sciences.*

Stenmark, D. (2002). "Information vs. knowledge: the role of intranets in knowledge management," In *Proceedings of the 35th Annual Hawaii International Conference on System Sciences.*

Tackeuchi, H. and Nonaka, I. (2004). Editors, *Hitosubashi on knowledge management.* ISBN: 0470820748.

Wenger, E. (1999). *Communities of Practice: learning, meaning, and identity*, ISBN: 0521663636.

Zack, M. H. (1999). "Managing codified knowledge," *Sloan Management Review,* ISSN: 1532-9194, 40(4): 45-58.

60. Action Research: Its History and Relationship to the Scientific Method

John Stephens
Greyhound Racing Victoria, AUS

John Barton
John Barton Associates, AUS

Tim Haslett
Department of Management, Monash University, AUS

This paper presents a Western philosophical view on the development of belief systems and theory-based methods over time and their relationship to the development of Action Research (AR). It is the first of two papers that seek to demonstrate the close relationship between traditional scientific methods and Action Research.

A philosophical basis for Action Research (AR): The Greeks

There is no simple answer to the question "What is AR?" (Checkland & Holwell, 1998a; Reason & Bradbury, 2001). This paper therefore presents a Western philosophical view on the development of belief systems and theory-based methods over time and their relationship to the scientific method and the development of Action Research (AR).

In Ancient Greece the "rise of mental coherence" (Singer, 1959) involved inquiry, debate and discovery of concepts of reality. But while his predecessors had asked "what is it made of", Pythagoras (569 - c.500 BC) asked "what is its pattern" (Bateson, 1964) implying that the essential components of matter were numbers and particularly geometry. In other words from a broad "inductive" perspective, some concepts of reality which started with observations, ended up with theories. Hence from about this time some of the first theories about the conceptualization of reality followed (Singer, 1959; Spangenburg & Moser, 2004) and a religious philosophy was perhaps first challenged by mathematically based inquiry processes and the concept of a Mathematical Universe (Checkland, 1993).

For Heraclites (c. 500 BC) inquiry and conceptual thinking involved a "becoming" reality where all things involved unending struggles and strife in a continual state of flux. The only thing of permanence was the principle of change itself (Singer, 1959). However opposing Heraclites, Parmenides (c. 515 - 450 BC) presented a "being" concept of reality interpreting it not experientially, but by using an early form of dialectic inquiry to think logically. Attacking observational science, Parmenides asserted the primacy of logic claiming that the senses were deceptive and that observation was inferior to logical argument. Also from a dialectic perspective, Socrates' (469 - 399 BC) largely abandoned inductive inferences (Ellinor & Gerard, 1998) to favour broadly "deductive" inference where concepts of reality started with theories and from them, sets of action principles were synthesized. Importantly Socratic "truth by discussion" perhaps first allowed for a mixture of inductive and deductive inferences. From this question and answer technique, early "abductive" inferences thus allowed for a "scientific method" via the formation of hypotheses and promotion of contextual action. Aristotle (384 - 322 BC) further contributed to the foundation of the scientific method by basing his knowing on testing, inquiry and experience.

In summary the Greeks had "argued for the sole purpose of arriving at the truth and, with argument as their chief weapon; argument used deliberately, consciously, and carefully, developed into a technical method" (Checkland, 1993). This foreshadows Pepper's (1942) root metaphor of *Formism* and we therefore associate rudimentary observational science, never-ending change and different forms of inferential logic as embryonic contributors to Western philosophical thinking, the scientific method and the very early development of AR.

The philosophical basis for Action Research: The Scientific Age

Leading to the scientific age, Ackoff (1993) paints a bleak picture of the Middle Ages, Singer (1959) agrees referring to this time as "the failure of knowledge". However, during this time, the Arabs preservation and translation of Greek texts ensured that the systemic development of knowledge might be progressive and cumulative. Later we stress the cumulative importance of reflective thinking in contemporary AR but as the scientific era dawned deductive logic increased its legitimacy as a method for securing truth.

The "revival of learning" of the *renaissance* (Singer, 1959) saw what Walsh (1992) encapsulates as man's focus shifted from *a fulfillment beyond this world, to a state of perfection within it.* Observation and measurement became co-contributors to the 'neo-sciences', the intermediary phases that preceded what were later to become methods of the scientific methodology. Checkland (2000: 36) provides a succinct account of method and methodology and we take his view that a methodology is at a meta-level with respect to a method. Methodology is therefore a body of methods used in a particular activity.

With the application of observation and logic to the neo-sciences came great discoveries and a greater attention to their methods of creation. Soon "incredible" discoveries in the new field of *science* began to threaten the conformist theological doctrine. Hence Francis Bacon (1561 - 1626) emphasized the importance of data but Harvey (1578 - 1657) went further showing how to record accurate data from observations. His seminal theory of blood circulation demonstrates the importance of three aspects of scientific enquiry: speculative reason in the formation of hypotheses, accurate quantitative analysis and a blend of induction and deduction.

Now observation followed by mathematics, the dialectic and logic aggregated into a holistic scientific technique. Consequentially, the iterative interplay of inductive and deductive inference consciously and carefully brought maturity to the emerging scientific technique. In addition, the processes of reflective assessment and iteration were established as its tools of refinement. In setting prediction as a standard for scientific theory, man moved away from divine determinism. We acknowledge the immense power of the dialectic as a method for establishing concepts of reality through discussion. As Einstein (1879 - 1955) put it "science without religion is lame, religion without science is blind". Hence classical Socratic thought evaluated the scientific and theological doctrines. Thus Butterfield (1958: 17) suggested that "how things worked" became the catch cry of the next worldview the *scientific revolution.*

In the *scientific revolution* we had a time labeled as *the* most extraordinarily productive in the entire history of pure science (Debus, 1992). There we had an emerging technique where tools of measurement represented a triumph of observation (experience) over logic. We believe this brought an important and interesting ongoing dynamic in the form of the induction-deduction process, which in addition to an early form of abductive logic, inference in which explanatory hypotheses are formed and evaluated provided the basis for the reflective iteration within the double loop learning processes that characterise contemporary methods of Action Research (Bateson, 1964; Argyris, 1982; Nonaka, 1994; Nonaka & Takeuchi, 1995; Checkland, 2000). But perhaps more importantly, we also link reflective iteration with the refinement of a whole of AR methodology. This view is evident in Checkland's (2000: 19) description of his Soft Systems Methodology (SSM);

"*...the methodology is presented as a sequence of stages with iteration back to previous stages, the sequences being: analysis; root definition of relevant systems; conceptualization; comparison and definition of changes; selection of change to implement; design of change and implementation; appraisal.*"

We contend that the dialectic of analysis/induction and synthesis/deduction created a cyclic process for a universal scientific paradigm. The steps of that paradigm: observation, hypothesis, experimentation and generalization became indoctrinated into all particular methods of science. Newton's thinking often began with intuition, the great abductive process, later supported by experiment, deductive inference and mathematical confirmation. Supporting this view, Stuewer (1970) says that 'Newton invents theories, he proposes a radically empiricist methodology, and he claims that he has obtained the former with the help of the latter'. Philosophically, the scientific paradigm suggested that belief secured from the pillars of physics, chemistry and biology could be explained by relatively simple sets of mathematical laws. However, problems in physiology, psychology and some of the newer sciences on the whole struggled with attempts to integrate Newtonian mechanics into their methodologies. Hence the appropriateness of subjecting the metaphysical and social scientific worlds with strains of measurement appropriate to the physical sciences came to the fore.

The subsequent development of "softer" perspectives of reality can be linked to the times of the German Idealist Immanuel Kant (1724-1804). Kant suggested that empiricism and rationalism went hand in hand creating a resolution of paradox. But from Kant's reflection on failed attempts to explain various aspects of human nature came his concept of *a priori* knowledge where, though common principles have to be accepted as existing independently from our sense perceptions, they cannot be proved. Kant also declared that the methods of the physical sciences were founded on *a priori* concepts "as well as" sensory experiences. He went on to say that the securing of knowledge in the physical world really occurred by using subjective perspectives of rational systems such as mathematics. He therefore contested the appropriateness of the scientific methodology as a means for dealing with reality in the metaphysical and social scientific worlds. Kant's thinking is an important precursor to Piaget, C.S.Peirce and Pavlov. We highlight the significance of Peirce's logic, semiotics and four main methods of fixing belief (tenacity, authority, a priori and science) in linkages we make in a later paper (Barton, *et al.*, 2007) through James, Singer, Simon, Churchman, Forrester and Ackoff to culminate in Beer's (1972, 1979, 1985) Viable Systems Diagnosis (VSD). Applebaum (1992: 169) says that Peirce (1839-1914) rectified an empirical imbalance by suggesting not only the justification of analysis or "scientific" knowledge, but by positing the issue of knowledge growth through the circular reflection and a blend of empiricist views and *a priori* concepts of logic to improve knowledge. This "pragmatic" view of epistemology thence gained popularity in areas other than the physical sciences, as an acceptable way of securing reality.

At the turn of the 19th century empiricism and induction contributed to rigor in the observational and formation of hypothesis steps on one hand, while on the other, the deductive or rational approaches advanced rigor in the experimentation and generalization steps. The importance of this is shown by Kemeny quoted in Quade and Miser (1985) who describe the scientific methodology by way of Einstein (1879 - 1955):

"*As Einstein has repeatedly emphasized, First of all the scientist is an observer. Next he tries to describe in complete generality what he saw, and what he expects to see in the future. Next he makes predictions on the basis of his theories, which he checks against the facts again. The most characteristic feature of the method is its cyclic nature. It starts with facts, ends in facts, and the facts ending one cycle are the beginning of the next cycle. A scientist holds his theories tentatively, always prepared to abandon them if the facts do not bear out his predictions. If a series of observations, designed to verify certain predictions, force us to abandon our theory, then we look for a new and improved theory.*"

This definitive expression of the scientific methodology also depicts a *four stage, continuous and iterative learning cycle* which is consistent with many AR learning frameworks. For example Dewey (1943), Deming (1982), and Flood (1999) base their action-learning frameworks on the "cyclic" method described by Einstein. However as Walsh (1992:142) explains, the study of man and society is different from the study of planets and electrons because human reality becomes largely known *through participation in it.* We clearly acknowledge the disparities between systems science and systemic intervention research practices, and the necessity of taking into account multiple standpoints on perceptions of reality. Using the root metaphors of Pepper's (1942) *World Hypotheses,* we have thus associated the time of the Greeks with *Formism* and Newtonian science with the *Mechanism.* We now associate the third of Pepper's root metaphors *Organicism* with the *Modern era* worldview to look at the formalization of Systems Thinking and the development of the Organizational Behavior (OB) and AR intellectual streams.

Formism and *Mechanism* have not disappeared during the *modern era.* Whereas the mechanistic view had claimed that analysis and reductionism could explain all objects and events, Vitalists were among those biologically minded who queried the capacity of *Mechanism* and/or *Formism* to sufficiently explain behavior in complex entities where intrinsic properties could not be derived merely from an understanding of their parts. In describing *equifinality* as a mechanism whereby a system has a specified goal, or final state which it may reach in different ways from different working conditions - the goal is equifinal, we agree with Beer's (1959: 168-9) inference that Von Bertalanffy's (1950) proof that closed systems cannot behave equifinally effectively rebutted Vitalism.

In the *modern era,* von Bertalanffy's (1968) General Systems Theory (GST) and the biological metaphor underpinned methods that explored complex systems including then embryonic organizations and laid the claims of the Vitalists to rest. Our views on organizations and thinking in the *modern era* are however strongly influenced by Systems Thinking with its foundations in the both biological and mechanistic metaphors. The concept of inherent feedback systems was fundamental to knowledge about the functionality of organizational systems. Systems Thinking is now strongly endorsed (Simon, 1979; Senge & Sterman, 1992; Park, 1999) as a valid approach for securing of knowledge about functionality in organizational systems. Our belief is that the enhanced systemicity of the 1990's introduced new ways of thinking to people concerned about understanding through Kant's *a priori* knowledge.

Our line of thinking suggests that some discontentment with mechanistic thinking led to the formalisation of Systems Thinking around the middle of the 20th century. From that time, OB has progressed to become a justifiable way of securing knowledge about management practices in complex organizational systems. However some disappointment with some of the OB methods, basically generated through the analysis-synthesis dialectic then germinated a different but not unrelated interest in knowledge created *in and of* organizations, rather than that created by the application of static prescriptions *onto* them. Hence AR, a different stream of thinking, was founded.

Restating that there is no simple answer to the question 'What is AR?' (Checkland & Holwell, 1998a; Reason & Bradbury, 2001), it is broadly agreed that AR was founded by Kurt Lewin (1946; 1947; 1951). We think of Lewin's founding work in Sarton's (1952) terms as a particular "cut" in social history where an interconnection of Systems Thinking, OB and AR gave substance to a paradigm shift about how research might be conducted in and about organizations.

As Midgley (2003: xviii) puts it "by drawing upon the full variety of systems ideas, we should be able to produce a more rounded understanding of people, organizations, societies and the world we live in, than could emerge from any of the traditional (*deterministic*) scientific disciplines" [*our emphasis*]. Here, Midgley (2007) means that the traditional scientific approaches are useful but limited unless integrated into a more systemic perspective. Scientific methods can become part of a systems thinker's toolkit, but whether those purposes are appropriate needs to be assessed systemically. This view emphasizes a potential shift in thinking as research is conducted *in and by* rather than *on* organizations.

We have now presented a Western philosophical view on the development of belief systems and theory-based methods in the light of recognized worldviews. That view is grounded on our core belief that knowledge may be developed through an analysis-synthesis dialectic. In promoting Systems Thinking, OB and AR as meaningful "new" ways of producing knowledge, our view is that Pepper's *Organicism* root metaphor has been influential in the development of knowledge. It is also our belief that Pepper's fourth root metaphor, *Contextualism* grows in importance, particularly for emerging worldviews such as *Post-modernism.*

Barton and Haslett (2007) argue that the scientific method and the development of knowledge can be described in terms of the analysis-synthesis dialectic and that this process can be used to describe both the "grand" developments in science and "micro" developments at the organizational and personal levels. When supported by the system of inferential logic described the 19th Century pragmatist philosopher, Charles Sanders Peirce (Peirce, 1878), this process also

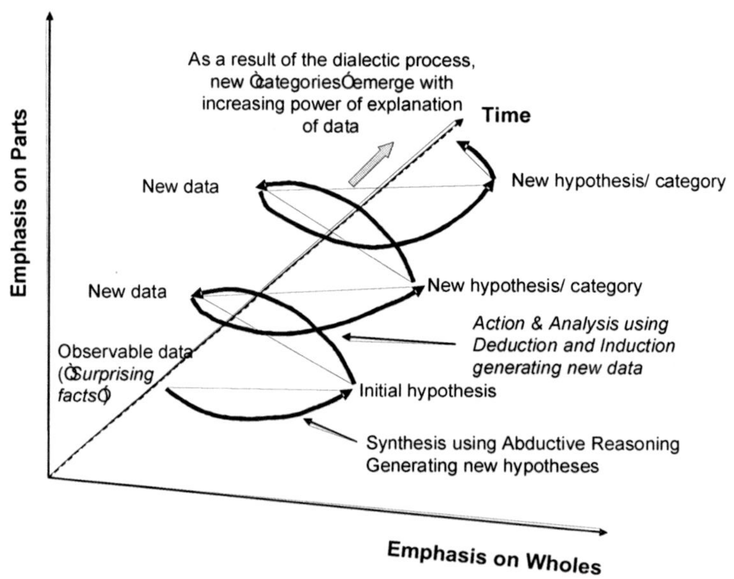

Figure 1 *The Scientific Method as Analysis and Synthesis Dialectic*

provides a rigorous framework for defining both AR and Positivist Research and demonstrates that they are complementary processes.

The process is described in Figure 1. It starts with the observation of a number of events for which there is no obvious and immediate explanation and for which there is a desire to gain a coherent explanation. In Ackoff's terms these situations are described as "messes" (Checkland, 1981). Peirce describes these as "surprising facts".

A new synthesis of these "facts" occurs which provides a primary "thesis". Analysis, experimentation, and/or action taken on the basis this thesis leads to differences between the explanatory powers of the thesis and observation.

This leads to the development of an "antithesis" and so the dialectic is established. The resolution of this dialectic results in a new synthesis or hypothesis, which becomes the thesis for the next cycle of dialectic. The concept of the cycle of dialectic is central to scientific method in the same way that the process of cyclic reflection is important to Action Research. The essential distinction is between an open and closed system of enquiry. Traditionally scientific enquiry takes place in a closed system where the influence of the environment is minimized whereas in Action Research the influence of the environment is part of the experiment.

Senge (1990) identified "five disciplines" that define a set of capabilities for any organization aspiring to become a "learning organization". Importantly, in each case these factors form part of a coherent, systemic framework, which can be used to explain what initially appears as an ill-defined and largely intuitive set of observations and ideas. In each case, a number of "surprising facts" are synthesized into a systemic framework in the sense that they describe an integrative framework based on an organizing principle- the systems principle (Emery etc). Over time, these frameworks will be tested and compared with other possible frameworks leading to the emergence of new frameworks and theories. For example, Senge's learning framework can be compared and tested against Nonaka's (1991, 1994) knowledge creation construct based on a tacit knowledge-explicit knowledge dialectic (Takeuchi, 2004). What is significant is that each of these frames is "systemic".

Einstein identifies a similar process in physics (Figure 2) as the jump from the observed facts to the set of "Axioms of Fundamental Principle"- Speculative leap based on hunch, conjecture, inspiration, and guesswork.... We are dealing, after all, with the private process of theory construction or innovation, the phase not open to inspection by others and indeed perhaps little understood by the originator himself. But the leap to the top of the schema symbolizes precisely the precious moment of great energy, the response to the motivation of "wonder" and the "passion of comprehension" (Holton, 1998a: 31).

In summary, each cycle of dialectic described in Figure 1 can be described as a learning process starting with "surprising facts" which lead to the formation of a systemic framing of the ideas; that is, an the explanatory hypothesis. Barton and Haslett (2007) argue that this is describes the role of the systems concept in science- the framing of explanatory hypotheses.

There is a close similarity between this description of the scientific process with that identified by Peirce as being analogous to Cuvier's evolutionary

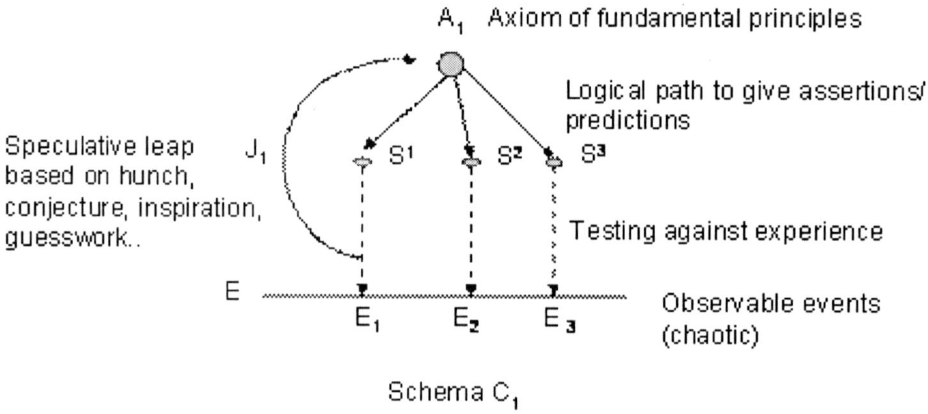

Figure 2 *Einstein's Model for Constructing a Scientific Theory (Holton, 1998)*

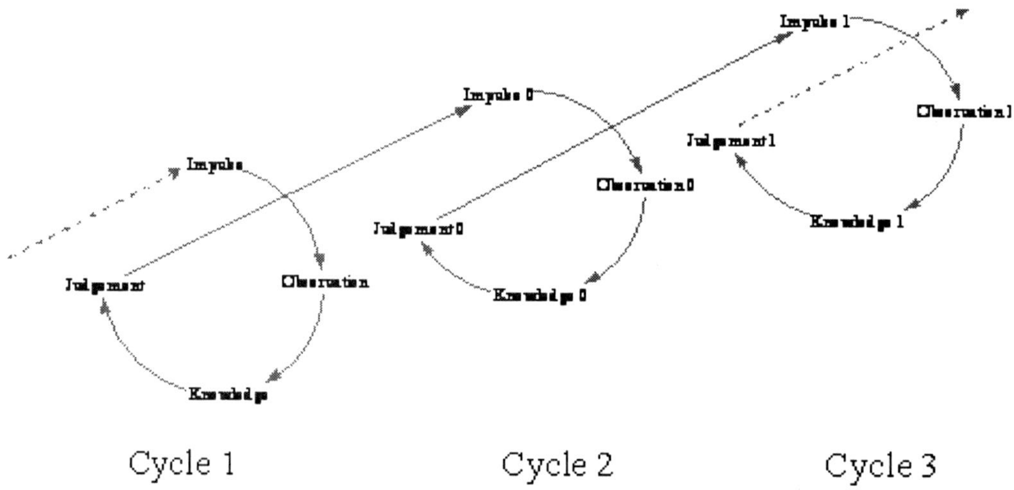

Figure 3 *Dewey's Experiential Learning Cycle (Kolb, 1984)*

process. This process emphasizes that science advances in leaps, compared to the more stable evolutionary processes identified with Darwin and Lamarck (Sharpe, 1970; Tuomi, 1992). (It is this type of "speculative leap that sets abduction apart from induction- see below).

To relate this dialectic version of the scientific method to Action Research, it is necessary to relate it to experiential learning theory. In particular, the process described in Figure 1 can be related to Dewey's "Spiral of Learning" (Figure 3).

But to make this connection explicit, it is necessary to articulate the role of inferential logic in this process, and abductive inference in particular. Dewey's experiential logic is drawn from Peirce's notion of the continuity of inquiry supported by his description of inferential logic (Dewey, 1938).

Conclusions

The development of knowledge comes through an analysis-synthesis dialectic. While scientific enquiry takes place in a closed system where the influence of the environment is minimized, Action Research recognizes and integrates the influence of the environment into the enquiry process. This places Action Research in an open, rather than a closed, systems context. It is thus able to integrate learning into the scientific and organizational process.

References

Ackoff, R. L. (1993). From Mechanistic to Social Systemic Thinking (video). Cambridge MA: USA, Pegasus Communications.

Argyris, C. (1982). "The Executive Mind and Double Loop Learning." Organizational Dynamics **11**(2): 5-22.

Applebaum, W. (1992). Epistemological and Political Implications of the Scientific Revolution. Science, Pseudo-Science, and Utopianism in early Modern Thought. S. A. McKnight. London: UK, University of Missouri Press.

Barton, J., T. Haslett, et al. (2007). Action Research: Its logic and relationship to the scientific method. ANZSYS. Auckland: NZ.

Bateson, G. (1964). Steps to an Ecology of Mind. New York: UK Ballantine Books.

Beer, S. (1972). Brain of the Firm. Allen Lane: UK, The Penguin Press.

Beer, S. (1979). The Heart of the Enterprise. London: UK, John Wiley and Sons.

Beer, S. (1985). Diagnosing the System for Organizations. London: UK, John Wiley and Sons.

Butterfield, H. (1958). Origins of Modern Science: 1300 - 1800. London: UK, G.Bell and Sons.

Checkland, P. B. (1993). Systems Thinking, Systems Practice. Chichester: England, John Wiley and Sons.

Checkland, P. B. (2000). "Soft Systems Methodology: A Thirty Year Retrospective[a]." Systems Research and Behavioral Science **17**: S11-58.

Checkland, P. B. and S. Holwell (1998a). "Action research: Its nature and validity." Systems Practice and Action Research (SPAR) **11**(1): 9-21.

Debus, A. G. (1992). Science and History. The Birth of a New Field. Science, Pseudo-Science, and Utopianism in early Modern Thought. S. A. McKnight. London: UK, University of Missouri Press.

Deming, W. E. (1982). Out of Crisis. Cambridge MA, Mass. Inst. Of Technology.

Dewey, J. (1938). Logic: The Theory of Inquiry. New York: USA, Holt, Rinehart and Winston.

Dewey, J. (1943). The Child of the curriculum and the School and Society. Chicago: USA, University of Chicago Press.

Ellinor, E. and G. Gerard (1998). Dialogue: Creating and Sustaining Collaborative Partnerships at Work. Canada, John Wiley and Sons.

Flood, R. L. (1999). Rethinking the Fifth Discipline: Learning within the unknowable. London, Routledge.

Holton, G (1998) Einstein and the cultural roots of modern science Daedalus. Vol. 127, Iss. 1; pg. 1 - 44

Kolb, D. A. (1984). Experiential Learning. Englewood Cliffs NJ. , Prentice–Hall.

Lewin, K. (1946). "Action Research and minority problems." Journal of Social Issues. **2**(4): 34-46.

Lewin, K. (1947). "Frontiers in group dynamics: Channels of group life; Social planning and action research." Human Relations. **1**(2): 143-153.

Lewin, K. (1951). Field Theory in Social Science: Selected Theoretical Papers. New York: USA, McGraw-Hill.

Midgley, G. (2003). Systems Thinking. Vol I-IV. London: UK, Sage Publications.

Midgley, G. (2007). Traditional Scientific Disciplines and Systems Thinking. Melbourne: Australia: e mail communication.

Nonaka, I. (1994). "A Dynamic Theory of Organizational Knowledge Creation." Organizational Science. **5**(1): 14-37.

Nonaka, I. and H. Takeuchi (1995). The Knowledge Creating Company: How the Japanese Companies create the dynamics of Innovation. New York: USA, Oxford University Press.

Park, P. (1999). "People, knowledge, and change in participatory research " Management learning **30**(2): 141-157.

Pepper, S. C. (1942). World Hypotheses. Berkeley, CA: USA, University of California Press.

Quade, E. S. and H. J. Miser (1985). Handbook of Systems Analysis: Overview of Uses, Procedures, Applications and Practice. Systems Thinking. G. Midgley. London: UK, Sage Publications. **2:** 241-270.

Reason, P. B. and H. Bradbury (2001). Handbook of Action Research. Participative Inquiry and Practice. London: UK, Sage Publications.

Sarton, G. (1952). A Guide to the History of Science. New York: USA, The Ronald Press Company.

Senge, P. M. and J. D. Sterman (1992). "Systems Thinking and Organizational Learning: Acting Locally and Thinking Globally in the Organizations of the Future." European Journal of Operational Research **59**(1): 137-150.

Simon, H. A. (1979). "Rational Decision Making in Business Organizations " American Economic Review **69**: 493-513.

Singer, C. J. (1959). Short History of Scientific Ideas to 1900. London: UK, Oxford University Press.

Singer, E. A. (1959). Experience and Reflection. Philadelphia: USA, University of Philadelphia Press.

Spangenburg, R. and D. K. Moser (2004). The Birth of Science: Ancient Times to 1699. New York: USA, Facts on File.

Stuewer, R. H. (1970). Historical and Philosophical Perspectives of Science. New York: USA, University of Minnesota, Gordon Breach.

Sharpe, R. (1970). Induction. Abduction, and the Evolution of Science. Transactions of the Charles S. Peirce Society, VI(1), 17-33.

Takeuchi, H. (2004). Knowledge Creation within a Dialectic Organization. In H. Takeuchi & I. Nonaka (Eds.), Hitosubashi on Knowledge Management. Singapore: John Wiley & Sons (Asia).

Tuomi, J. (1992). Evolutionary Synthesis: A Search for the Strategy. Philosophy of Science, 59, 429-438.

von Bertalanffy, L. (1968). General Systems Theory: Foundations, Developments, Applications. New York G.Braziller.

Walsh, D. (1992). A Mythology of Reason. Science, Pseudo-Science, and Utopianism in early Modern Thought. S. A. McKnight. London: UK, University of Missouri Press.

61. The Great Ashby

John Stephens
Greyhound Racing Victoria, AUS

Tim Haslett
Monash University, AUS

For practitioner/scholars Action Research (AR) involves multiple reflective cycles. Each cycle has three steps that are iterative, recursive and cumulative. One step involves the definition and explanation of theories broadly dominated by inductive inference. A second step involves a broad emphasis on deductive inference whereby theories are arranged into coherent action principles. A third step involves hypotheses developed broadly through abductive inference and contextual action. An emergent AR intervention is described which relies heavily on cybernetics, Beer's Viable Systems Diagnosis and Ashby's Law of Requisite Variety. The paper makes two conclusions. The first is that Ashby's Law is an 'in-built' and undeniable feedback mechanism in AR. The second is that by exerting itself irrespective of the theories and AR practices involved Ashby is at the heart of AR. Through interplay of induction and deduction Ashby's Law is a root cause of abduction in AR.

Introduction

This paper takes the view that for practitioner/scholars, managers who employ problem solving methods while working and learning within their workplace at the same time (Stephens, 2007), Action Research (AR) involves multiple reflective learning perspectives that move toward the creation of 'a distinctive way of thinking rather than a specific concrete subject' (Bateson, 2000/1964). In that regard, reflective thinking often involves phases such as planning, doing, checking and acting. Deming (1982), Dewey (1943), and Senge (1990) cite not dissimilar models and others including Kolb (1984), Revans (1982), Weinstein (1995) and Flood (1999) consider knowledge creation via various action-learning perspectives.

But in looking for distinctive ways of thinking we believe that early on in 'messy' situations (Ackoff, 1978; Mitroff & Linstone, 1993) practitioner/scholars are provided with enabling conditions for AR interventions, initially through the raising of anxiety levels. Here, despite having no critical or immediate impact, unsettling patterns of events arouse concerns. In this context, novice practitioner/scholars are often attracted to various problem solving methods (Flood & Jackson, 1995). For example, Haslett, *et al.*(2002) have found that Checkland's (1985) FMA action-research template underpins a simple and popular method for use in AR interventions. However while the early engagement of various problem solving methods may infer building requisite (necessary) variety into AR processes, our experience is that at this time, specific awareness of Ashby's (1956: 207) Law of Requisite Variety (LRV) 'only variety can destroy variety' is highly improbable. We expand on Ashby's LRV later but here it is sufficient to say that the LRV exerts itself *regardless* of the methods and operational templates introduced into AR interventions (Beer 1979).

Here we are going to consider the employment of Checkland's template in a specific AR intervention to illustrate our argument that distinctive ways of thinking may emerge from messy situations, because of Ashby's Law. Checkland's (1985) FMA action-research template underpins one problem solving method that is strongly supported by many of our practitioner/scholar colleagues (Haslett, 2005). While other methods have similar interrelated and iterative parts Checkland's template involves a framework of ideas 'F', a methodology 'M' and an area of application 'A'. Thereby a chosen 'M' has the potential to promote change in each and all of 'F', 'M' and 'A', with a primary objective to ameliorate 'A'. In this light, we concur with Checkland and Howell's (1998a) view that AR needs to be conducted in such a way that the whole AR process is subsequently recoverable by anyone interested in critically scrutinizing the research. In regards messy situations, we believe that at the start, distinctive ways of thinking proceed with a relative *tabula rasa* background of the chosen method, reflective learning perspectives and theories of management. And while Checkland (2000: S42) says AR requires 'declaring explicitly, at the start of the research the intellectual frameworks and the process of using them which will be used to define what counts as knowledge' it is our view that for initial AR cycles 'finding a way forward' generates knowledge during the processes that determine the parts (in this case, 'F', 'M' and 'A'). In the case at hand, that led to cybernetics, Beer's Viable Systems Diagnosis and Ashby's Law of Requisite Variety. The paper goes on to discuss the way in which three methods of inference (induction, deduction and abduction) may be tied back to a chosen problem solving method, the development of knowledge and the need to make AR processes recoverable.

Finding a way forward

Our experience (Stephens and Haslett 2002 a; 2005 a; 2005 b) is that finding a way forward in AR interventions involves inductive, deductive and abductive inferences that (a) occur before and during the process of determining 'F', 'M' and 'A', and (b) are associated with definite stages within the process.

We define Inductive Inference *(II)* as; Statement [X] is true because it has observable supporting data. Statement [Y] must be true because it results from [X]. Hence it can be concluded that [X] causes [Y]. For example, in a particular messy situation (Stephens 2007), the observable data supported the inductive contention 'the company follows cyclical boom and bust financial periods' - is a true statement [X]. 'The company's finances are about to turn' - [Y] must then be true because this statement results from [X]. Conclusion or theory; bust will follow the current boom causing financial disaster. Actually, the pending financial disaster was aligned with theory about changing environmental factors. So for the purposes of this discussion, we take the broad view that inductive inference may be aligned with theory and the formation of hypotheses via the determination and explanation of observable data involving messy situation. In other words, very broadly, we start with some observations and we end up with a theory (about the mess). This provides the basis for deciding on 'M' (methodology) and the specific 'A' (Area for action) for a first AR cycle.

Progression of this messy situation will next involve Deductive Inference *(DI)*. Deductive inference is acknowledged as a popular and rigorous form of argument and we define deduction as; [X] is true because its theory is well established. If [X] is true, [Y] is true. Therefore [Y] must be true. For example, based on the mathematical theory of sine curves 'bust follows boom' [X] pattern and given current boom-times, then bust will follow. This argument may be followed by 'that depends on what we do' and the consideration of action principles that may prevent the bust. So again for the purposes of this discussion, we take the broad view that deductive inference derived from the earlier inductive phase, may refocus that set of ideas or principles into a new set of action principles about the 'mess'. In other words, very broadly we start with theory and from it we synthesise a set of action principles (about the mess).

Finally, abductive inference *(AI)* is what Churchman describes as Singer's process of 'sweeping in' (Barton & Haslett, 2007: 151). The 'sweeping in' process develops multiple perspectives of the 'mess' and attempts their synthesis. While Barton and Haslett suggest abduction is the least rigorous form of inference, they also say it is the only form of inference that can generate new knowledge. We define abduction as: [Y] an outcome is true. Our understanding is that [X] causes [Y]; hence we assume [X] is true. In our example, the boom is a current outcome [Y]. Our understanding is that 'cyclical boom and bust' has been demonstrated. We therefore assume that without contextual action, pending 'bust' - is true. But we have taken contextual action based on the successive development of inductive and deductive inferences. Thus as a final component of this process, we take the broad view that abductive inference implies the formation of hypotheses that promote contextual action. This hypothesis is tested in the next cycle of action where information on the success (or otherwise) of the hypothesis is collected. In other words, we broadly look at multiple perspectives of dealing with the 'mess' (theory and action principles) and we set about doing things to 'right the mess' (contextual action). This is where the 'sweeping in' process of abductive inference allows for the results of contextual actions to deal with the boom bust cycle to be integrated into the boom bust hypothesis. It is at this point in the AR process where the 'F' (Frameworks) of the FMA are revised, that the potential for the development of recoverable hypotheses exists.

Our hypothesis is that the processes of inductive, deductive and abductive inferences are central to the conduct of AR and the development of recoverable knowledge. We are indicating that from our experience, finding a way forward involves these types of inferences and that the subsequent consideration of theory, a coherent set of action principles and contextual action are integral to the determination of 'F', 'M' and 'A'. To illustrate this point we cite some salient points from our AR intervention cycles.

Cycle One

With the value of hindsight, this first AR intervention might now be described as crude and elementary. In that regard we do however briefly highlight the sort of messy situation we are talking about, the preparatory nature of this first cycle, the likelihood of 'failure' and the need to get smarter when working in AR. From this overall AR intervention, we now believe that getting smarter in managing the variety exposed in AR projects means designing attenuators and amplifications (Beer, 1985) in terms of inductive, deductive and abductive inferences.

Framework of Ideas (F)	Methodology (M)	Area of Application (A)
THEORY: Cause and effect thinking: If I do this (present the data) then that (positive action) will follow	Action Research using Checkland's template: Determination of F, M and A	Business stagnation in respect to responding to concerning 'boom and bust' data
ACTION PRINCIPLES: Presentation of: Computer simulation Discussion papers Internal search External search Left-field search Proposal for election	**CONTEXTUAL ACTION**: Reflective analysis of: Rationality and decision making of Board and CEO	**RESULT**: abject failure Progression to cycle two

Table 1 *Features from the cycle one intervention*

In that light, one of the long-term objectives of the project was to change the ways in which new board members were elected. The principle had been for many years 'once you are in you are in forever'. There was a perceived need to begin electing people to the board based on the skills they brought rather than their longevity.

The results of this first AR intervention were not immediately encouraging. The initial inductive inference, 'people can be taught to do things better' had been incomplete at best and deeply flawed at worst. The data from this first cycle was that there had been little behavioral change and little or no progress towards some key organizational goals. During the reflective process, it was decided that 'nothing never happens' and that this cycle needed to be viewed as creating the prepared mind. One critical piece of data was that there appeared to be little inclination within the organization to change decision-making processes and strategies. A different approach was needed. It was decided that instead of adopting a 'this is where we want you to be with your decision-making' approach, a 'let's take you from where you are with your decision making' approach would be used. This approach also involved treating the participants' current decision-making processes as strengths to be built on, rather than changed.

Cycle Two

In briefly considering cycle two from an AR learning perspective we highlight (a) the development of theory and (b) the introduction of action principles and their consequences for contextual action - in simple or Ashbian terms, we got smarter. We were now able to deduce that some approaches (Checkland's 'M') had not worked. We also deduced that the 'A' (area of action) needed to be changed from a directive approach to a self-development approach.

Framework of Ideas (F)	Methodology (M)	Area of Application (A)
THEORY: Systems Thinking, Motivation, Models of Learning , SSM, Learning Styles	Action Research	Business stagnation in respect to 'getting smarter'
ACTION PRINCIPLES: Presentation of: Theory-based Diagnostic methodologies Consideration of Journal documents Proposal for election	**CONTEXTUAL ACTION**: Reflective analysis of: The role of the Action Researcher Individual and Group cognition, defence mechanisms, single and double loop learning	**RESULT**: Success at the election A distinctive way of thinking Theory based methods 'help' Action principles 'help' Reflection is important A template is handy This is tough stuff Getting smarter is important

Table 2 *Features from the cycle two intervention*

The second cycle was far more successful in terms of outcomes in the form of election results but also in the form of the Boards participation in the process and an increased willingness to participate in change.

In the light of cycles one and two, three very important markers had emerged to signify the broadening of our thinking. We recognized that a new learning framework had evolved. The framework revealed; our somewhat idiosyncratic continuous reading/reflective approach to AR, the need for greater attention to inductive, deductive and abductive inferences and the consequential impact of theory, a coherent set of action principles and contextual action as integral parts of our thinking. That smarter approach now encompassed an ardent cognitive focus, the employment of a designated template to focus the direction of the AR intervention and a realization that AR was indeed a difficult task. Nonetheless a fundamental view on the nature of AR *(Diagram Three)*, 'a distinctive way of thinking rather than a specific concrete subject' had emerged.

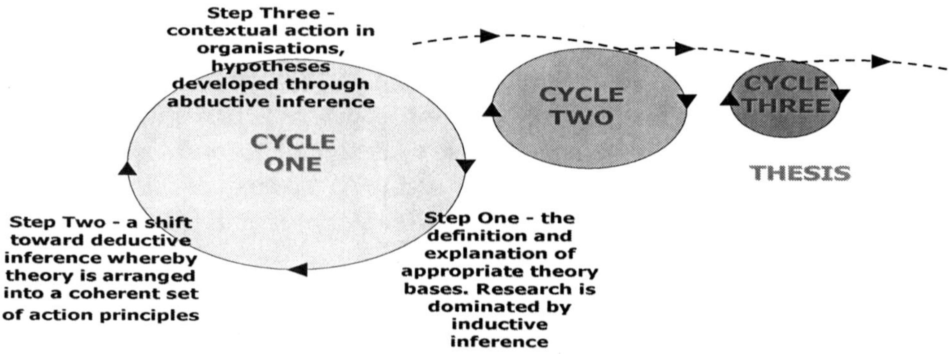

Figure 1 *Our view on the nature of Action Research*

Our view on the nature of AR is that cycles of AR each have three iterative, recursive and cumulative steps. We have labelled them as steps one, two and three but believe that their relative influence is incommensurable. Here step one involves the definition and explanation of research theory broadly dominated by analysis and inductive inference. A second step involves a broad emphasis on synthesis and deductive inference whereby the theory is arranged into coherent action principles. A third step then involves hypotheses developed broadly through abductive inference and contextual action. Hence this cumulative synthesis of 'what is true' may push the practitioner/scholar towards the construction of a primary 'thesis' whereby further development via experimentation and/or contextual action may further progress the distinctive way of thinking.

Cycle Three

Reflection via inductive, deductive and adductive inference during cycle two had led to our awareness that we needed to become smarter in managing the variety exposed in the AR intervention. This meant strengthening the Frameworks within the FMA template. There had been a strong emphasis on the development of 'M' and 'A' in cycles one and two but the theoretical frameworks needed to be further developed for continuing progress to be made in the improvement of the AR process. The work in cycles one and two had been based implicitly on the theory of building requisite (necessary) variety into the decision processes of the Board without us having a detailed understanding of Ashby's (1956) views on cybernetics and specifically his Law of Requisite Variety (LRV). The fundamental hypothesis was 'that the success of theory-based management methods is reliant on their application within emergent action-learning frameworks'. The emphasis thus now needed to be on 'raising the bar' in relation to managing the variety exposed in the AR intervention via the development of knowledge about appropriate theory bases. This would again occur through designing attenuators and amplifications in terms of inductive, deductive and abductive inference. Fundamentally this involved Ashby's Law of Requisite Variety (LRV).

Ashby's (1956: 207) LRV states that 'only variety can destroy variety'. The importance of requisite variety as a learning principle should not be trivially understated as the LRV exerts itself *regardless* of the operational formats that

Issue	Inductive Inference Define and explain theory about	Deductive Inference Arrange the theory into a coherent set of action principles involving
Juggling the best you can	Management	Management science Cybernetic Theory (VSD)
Keeping operations under control	Homeostasis or organisational equilibrium	General Systems Theory
'Internal' environments have to cope with unpredictable 'external' environments	Environmental complexity (variety) - Open and closed org. systems	Open Systems Theory Socio – Technical Theory
Sub-systems need to be able to talk to each with common understanding	Recursion	Set Theory
How a manager might become smart enough to 'turn up' or 'turn down' operational variety	Variety dial	Ashby's - Requisite Variety Conant- Ashby - Residual Variety

Table 3 *Features from the cycle three intervention*

may be followed. Further, Beer (1979: 89 our emphasis) profoundly states that [Ashby's Law] stands in 'the same relation to management as the law of gravity stands to Newtonian physics'. As such we believe it is absolutely central to a coherent account of complexity control in AR interventions and for that matter, organizations.

This principle was now made explicit in a theory of the development of organizational capability that would be progressed as part of the ongoing AR project. Hence to this point, in finding a way forward we had created a distinctive way of thinking rather than a specific concrete subject in our AR. Our distinctive thinking involved the identification of messy situations, engagement of problem solving methods, identification of inductive, deductive and abductive inference to manage the variety exposed and fundamentally, the importance of Ashby's in-built and undeniable feedback mechanism to AR.

The Development of a Requisite Variety Model of Management

To finish up, we now briefly describe how this distinctive way of thinking led to the development of a requisite variety model of management which is based on Stafford Beer's (1972, 1979, 1985) original drawings. Thus the paper ties the three methods of inference (induction, deduction and abduction) back to the chosen problem solving method (Checkland's FMA), the subsequent development of knowledge and the need to make AR processes recoverable.

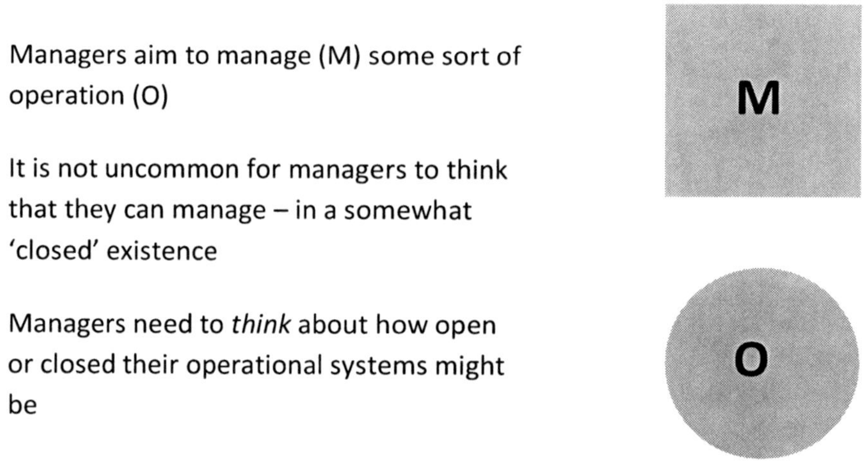

Figure 2 *Managers aim to Manage (M) some sort of Operation (O)*

As managers move from a relatively closed system view of the relationship between Management and the organization to an open systems view (Emery & Trist, 1965; Emery, 2000), the question that will arise is 'How do I, as a manager, interact with the organization?' and then 'How does the organization interact with me?' This is recognition of the need to 'absorb the (lack of) variety' (Beer, 1974: 30 our emphasis) of managers, by improving their skills and capabilities in both domains and also by recognizing that management is a symbiotic relationship. In learning about open systems, the relationship between the Manger and the organization expands to recognise that the relationship with the 'external' environment needs to be included in the model.

The newer model therefore assumes that the interrelationships between the three elements of the model operate in an open system, in theory, if not in practice.

That only variety can destroy variety or 'you need to become smarter than the system you are managing' (Barton, 2002) is shown in the inter-relations of the system. Both the manager and the organization need the variety to manage each other. Both manager and organization need the variety to manage the 'external' environment.

The final diagram shows the specific development of this model for Greyhound Racing Victoria. It includes our concept of a 'Variety Dial' (Stephens & Haslett, 2003, 2005a) which is turned up or down to attenuate or amplify the signals between the elements in the model.

Conclusion

This paper is the first stage of a discussion of the manner in which inferential reasoning has formed the basis for the development of a major AR project. It also begins the discussion of the development of the applica-

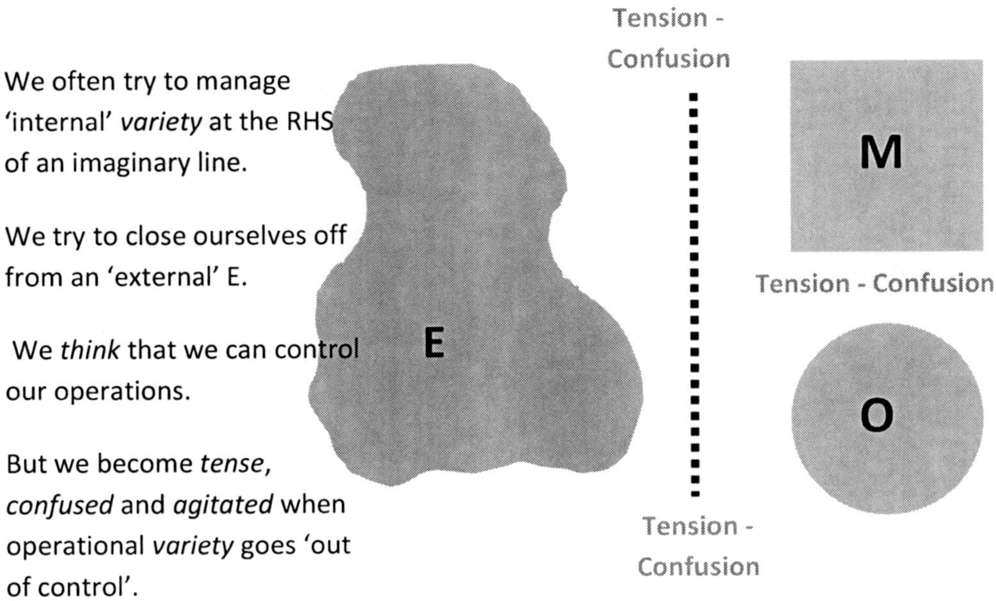

Figure 3 *Tension, confusion and environmental disturbances*

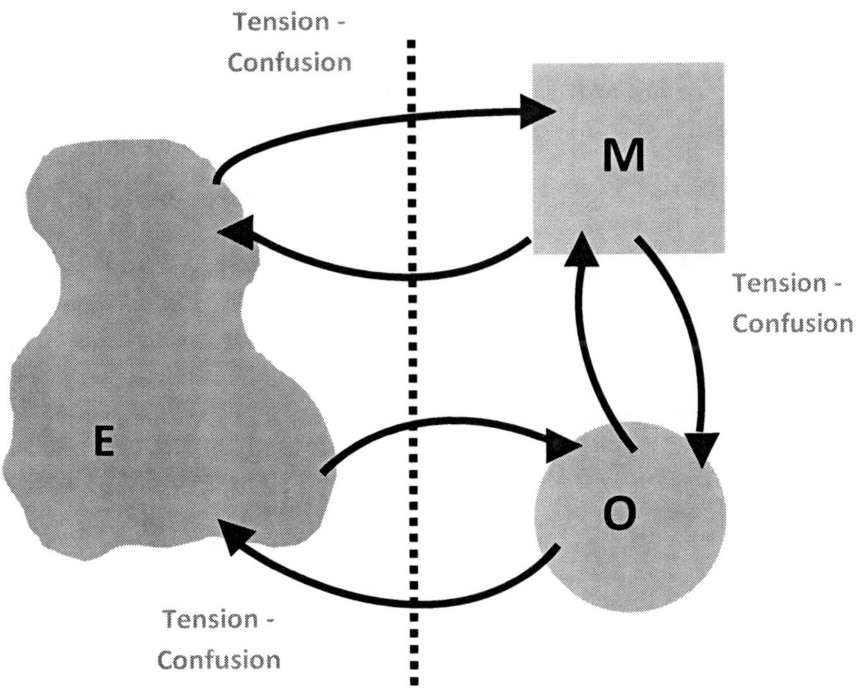

A question becomes - how might a manager might become smart enough to 'turn up' or 'turn down' tension and confusion emanating from operational variety?

Figure 4 *The interconnectiveness of tension, confusion and environmental disturbances*

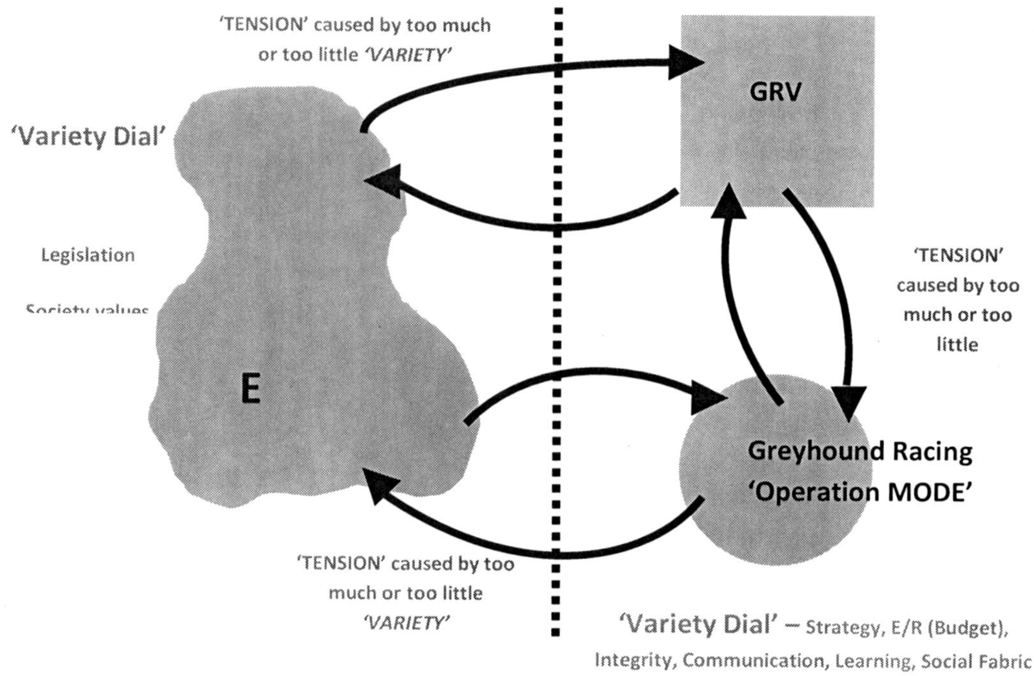

We impose conditions from *strategic planning* and *budget* to take *variety* out of our operations. The environment provides us with intelligence that influences our behaviours

Figure 5 *A Cybernetic model for homeostatic management*

tion of Ashby's (1956) LRV in project. We make two conclusions here. The first is that Ashby's LRV is the 'in-built' and undeniable feedback mechanism that is pivotal to all AR cycles. The second is that by exerting itself, irrespective of the theories or the AR practices involved, Ashby is at the heart of cyclical learning schemes. Because it causes the interplay of induction and deduction, Ashby's Law is a root cause of abduction in AR. A subsequent paper will demonstrate the application of the organizational structures that follow as a consequence of this and demonstrate how it is applied to the strategic planning process. As such the Great Ashby 'stands in the same relation to management as the law of gravity stands to Newtonian physics' (Beer, 1979: 89).

References

Ackoff, R. L. (1978). The Art of Problem Solving. New York: USA, Wiley.

Ashby, W. R. (1956). An Introduction to Cybernetics. London: UK, Chapman and Hall

Barton, J. (2002). Monash University, Melbourne: Australia.: Informal verbal discussions: Management in practice.

Barton, J. and T. Haslett (2007). "Analysis, Synthesis, Systems Thinking and the Scientific Method: Rediscovering the Importance of Open Systems." Systems Research and Behavioral Science 24: 143-155.

Bateson, G. (2000/1964). Introduction. Steps to an Ecology of Mind. M. C. Bateson. Chicago: USA, University of Chicago Press.

Beer, S. (1974). Designing Freedom. London: UK, John Wiley and Sons.

Beer, S. (1979). The Heart of the Enterprise. London: UK, John Wiley and Sons.
Beer, S. (1985). Diagnosing the System for Organizations. London: UK, John Wiley and Sons.
Checkland, P. B. (1985). "Achieving Desirable and Feasible Change: An Application of SSM." Journal of Operational Research Society. 36(9): 821-831.
Checkland, P. B. (2000). "Soft Systems Methodology: A Thirty Year Retrospective[a]." Systems Research and Behavioral Science 17: S11-58.
Checkland, P. B. and S. Holwell (1998a). "Action research: Its nature and validity." Systems Practice and Action Research (SPAR) 11(1): 9-21.
Demming, W. E. (1982). Out of Crisis. Cambridge MA, Mass. Inst. Of Technolog
Dewey, J. (1943). The Child of the curriculum and the School and Society. Chicago: USA, University of Chicago Press.
Emery, F. E. and E. L. Trist (1965). "The Causal Texture of Organizational Environments." Human Relations. 18: 21-32.
Emery, M. (2000). "The Current Version of Emery's Open Systems Theory." Systemic Practice and Action Research. 13(5): 623-644.
Flood, R. L. (1999). Rethinking the Fifth Discipline: Learning within the unknowable. London; UK, Routledge.
Flood, R. L. and M. Jackson (1995). Creative Problem Solving: Total Systems Intervention. Chichester: UK, John Wiley and Sons.
Haslett, T., Barton, J., Molineux, J., Olsen, J., Sarah, R., Stephens, J., Tepe, S., Walker, B. (2005). "Creating actionable knowledge: Reflections of an Action Research Cohort." International Journal of Knowledge, Culture and Change Management. **4**: 1241-1252
Haslett, T., J. R. Stephens, et al. (2002). Collaborative Learning in PhD Programs: A model from the Department of Management. Sixth International Research Conference on Quality, Innovation and Knowledge Management, Kuala Lumpur, Monash University.
Kolb, D. A. (1984). Experiential Learning. Englewood Cliffs, NJ: USA, Prentice-Hall.
Mitroff, I. I. and H. A. Linstone (1993). The Unbounded Mind: Breaking the Chains of Traditional Business Thinking. New York: USA, Oxford University Press.
Revans, R. W. (1982). The Origins and Growth of Action Learning. London: UK, Chartwell Bratt.
Senge, P. (1990). The Fifth Discipline: The Art and Practice of the Learning Organization. Melbourne: Australia, Random House.
Stephens, J. R. (2007). An Action Research Study of Theory-based Management Methods and Emergent Action-learning Frameworks. Business and Economics (Management). Melbourne, Monash University. PhD: 469.
Stephens, J. R. and T. Haslett (2002 a). Viable Systems Diagnosis: An Adaptive Agent?
International Research Conference on Quality, Innovation and Knowledge Management., Kuala Lumpur Monash University.
Stephens, J. R. and T. Haslett (2003). Demystifying Beer - do you want fries with that?. Australia and New Zealand Systems Society (ANZSYS) - Systems in Management., Melbourne: Australia, Monash University.
Stephens, J. R. and T. Haslett (2005 a). "From Cybernetics and VSD to Management and Action." Systemic Practice and Action Research. 18(4): 395-407.
Stephens, J. R. and T. Haslett (2005 b). "Peirce and Beer." Systemic Practice and Action Research. 18(5): 519-530.
Weinstein, K. (1995). Action Learning: A Journey in Discovery and Development. London: UK, Harper-Collins.

62. As it was Intended: About the Standard Use of System's Methods and Methodologies

Jorge Vélez-Castiblanco
Victoria Management School, Victoria University of Wellington, NZ

The standard use of systems methods and methodologies has been defined in terms of intentions. However the concept of intention in itself is neither developed nor questioned. To advance a discussion of the concept, some debates in philosophy of action are introduced. Subsequently the concepts of methods and methodology are put forward. Finally it is argued that it is problematic to define standard uses of those in terms of intention. From this perspective they do not seem possible at all. Therefore it is suggested that intentions are not a way to standardize but a way to a better reflective practice.

Introduction

Systems thinking use a wide range of methods and methodologies for problem solving (Jackson, 2000). Methods and methodologies represent the main way in which practitioners describe and encode the knowledge gained in interventions (Keys, 2002). It is not strange then, that a lot of effort has been devoted to standardize how these tools can be use by practitioners (Keys, 1997).

Now what has been understood as the standard use in systems thinking has been defined based on the concept of intention. However, the concept of intention itself is neither developed nor questioned. It seems that the concept has been taken for granted in systems thinking literature. The purpose of this paper is to more critically examine the notion of intention and outline some of its implications for systems thinking.

This paper starts by introducing some debates in relation to intention from the point of view of philosophy of action. Subsequently the concepts of methods and methodology are explained in relation to intention. Finally the notion of standard uses is discussed using thought experiments involving intention.

Intention

In philosophy the word intentionality has two different meanings (Malle, *et al.*, 2001). In the first sense intentionality is "the aboutness or directedness of mind (or states of mind) to things, objects, states of affairs, events" (Siewert, 2007). In other words certain states of the mind such as belief, hope, and desire are directed or can be directed towards something (e.g. you can desire a new car. The state of mind (desire) is directed to something (a new car)). This sense of intentionality has been explored in management science mainly through phenomenology and the work of authors such as Fuenmayor (1991a, 1991b) and Georgiou (2003, 2007).

The second meaning that falls in the field of philosophy of action is not explored in Systems Thinking. This meaning refers to the property of actions that make them purposeful, (Malle, *et al.*, 2001). Wittgenstein (2001: §621) expresses this through the question: "What is left over if I subtract the fact that my arm goes up from the fact that I raise my arm?". In this way Wittgenstein is making a distinction between something that merely happens and something that happens when we put our mind into it. Actions are interesting because of the intentions that we put there gave them meaning (Juarrero, 1999; Mele, 1997).

The notion of intention is used daily in many ways. They can be used to control and guide our actions. They are important in making sense of other people's actions, for instance a mere description of movements does not make much sense unless we attach them to an intention. Additionally as a consequence of our use of intentions to make sense of behaviors, they are fundamental to help in the coordination of social dynamics (Baldwin & Baird, 2001).

Currently there is a significant body of work in areas such as philosophy, psychology, cognitive science, law, child development, primatology, language and artificial intelligence (Malle, *et al.*, 2001; Zelazo, *et al.*, 1999).

Here the purpose is not to make a detailed explanation of the field. The purpose is to make a brief exploration of the topic from a conceptual-philosophical point of view, just enough to discuss some implications for systems thinking. In this line the paper falls in what Ormerod (2006: 892) calls "mining philosophy for the purpose of informing OR[Operational Research]". The spirit here is to use philosophy with the aim of clarifying concepts (Benett & Hacker, 2003), in this case the concept of intention.

My approach is to explain the concept in terms of layers. Some core ideas will be explained and on top of them in an iterative way more ideas will be added. Basically every addition will represent additional debates.

In the kernel of ideas it seems there is strong agreement. Intentionality have a cognitive component and a motivational component expressed as beliefs (cognitive) and desire (motivational) (Davis, 1997; Mele, 1997). Part of the problem is how to interlink both components in order to get intention. Davis (1997: 147) proposes that "S intends that p iff[if and only if] S believes that p because he desires that p and believes his desire will motivate him to act in such a way that p".

However, Bratman (1987) argues that this is enough. For Bratman we need the notion of intentions to predict and explain others people actions. Additionally we also need them to coordinate our projects and actions with others. To achieve all this Bratman ties the notion of intention to planning. Plans are used as inputs for further consideration and reasoning about our actions. Plan demands internal consistency, a coherence between my actions and believes. Consequently they help to justify our actions and play a central role in initiating and sustaining intentional actions (Mele, 1997).

Bratman also makes the important distinction of intention as a two faced phenomenon. "We do things intentionally, and we intend to do things" (Bratman, 1987: 111). Doing things intentionally is about the present. Intending to do things is about the future. Much of the present discussions about these two concepts refer to what is exactly the nature of their relationship.

There are two views about this relationship (Mele, 2003). In one, if a subject S intentionally does A, it is because S intended A. This is called the simple view. The other view is that in some cases S intentionally does A, but he never intended A, but nevertheless S intended something. This is called the simple phenomenon view. Both positions in some way imply that intentional action is more complex than intending to do something because the latter is a component of the former. The discussion here centres in the nature of the intention in an intentional action.

Now, in order to characterize intentional actions, additionally to the concept of intention, Mele & Moser (1997) suggest to add evidence, awareness and skill. However the work of Knobe (2003) challenges the notion of skill and proposes moral features as part of the characterization. To the skill-moral debate, Adams & Steadman (2004) reply that the pragmatics effects of language are being forgotten in the analysis.

This concludes a brief review of some of the debates regarding intention. I remind you that this is only a brief outline of the debates and is not a substantive review of the theory. For instance I presented just one definition of intention (Davis) because compared to others in the field is simple and short. More complex definitions involving more elements are beyond of the scope an intention of this paper. Many of the debates are still unresolved and the arguments in favour of one or another view are complex and lengthy. Obviously how they will be resolved and how the relationships between different elements come to be will impact on how the concept of intention will be used in other disciplines.

However a lesson that we can still take with us is that the concepts of intention and intentional action cannot be taken for granted. They reflect complex relationships between desires, belief, plans, evidence, skill, language and moral features.

Method and methodology

Many meanings are attached to the words 'method' and 'methodology', and sometimes the meanings overlap and interchange. For example, on methodology Lehaney & Vinten (1994) identify the following uses in Management Science: scientific methodologies, ways in which techniques are chosen, ways in which problems are chosen, method or techniques, modelling process and chronological planning of events.

Instead of dealing with all the diverse meanings above I will focus on following the etymological roots explored by Kotarbiński (1966) and in turn utilized by Checkland(1981). These are perhaps the most influential meaning in Systems Thinking.

The roots of the term methodology can be traced to Greek language, not as methodology but as a derivative of method (Kotarbiński, 1966). The concept of method has suffered many transformations. It started as "the path of a person who follows or pursues another person". Later it came to mean a path to something, and the way to do something. In a more modern interpretation it is "expert behavior in the field of analyzing, bringing out ideas, formulating one's thoughts" (Kotarbiński, 1966: 439)

Kotarbiński (1966: 446), proposes method as "a mode of action used with the consciousness of a repetition of its application in similar cases". The definition is concerned with the stages that are seen as important for the description of the mode of action. Actions can be described in innumerable ways. In a method "All the respects which play a role in determining the method used in a given action are determined univocally by the intention of the agent" (Kotarbiński, 1966: 449).

Now, methodology interpretations are in some way different derivations from the concept of method. Checkland (1981) working on MS/ST methodologies suggests following what Kotarbiński calls a praxiological (action oriented) approach to methodology. A methodology is then a "set of principles of method" (Checkland, 1981: 161). Consequently a methodology:

"*would cover such recommendations as the proper order of actions, the principle that earlier actions should be the best possible preparations for later actions, distinctions as between synthesis (when a whole is being built of elements) and analysis (when elements are being extracted from the whole)*" (Kotarbiński, 1966: 439)

Methodology is concerned with principles and they "are used to underlie, justify and inform the things which are actually done in response to a particular human problem situation" (Checkland, 2000: 36). Intentions in this regard have a similar role to methodologies. However while intentions are rooted in particular actors, methodology's principles look to be used by actors in many different situations.

It is important to clarify that for Kotarbiński, methodology is a discipline in its own right, and consequently there is only one methodology. However Checkland's interpretation carries the possibility of many possible sets of principles, therefore there can be many possible methodologies.

Another important clarification is the difference between method and methodology. The concept of method conveys the idea of following a course of action in a systematic way. Methodologies are not prefigured courses of action, they propose frameworks of ideas that can be used to decide how to prepare for action and consequently can be used to decide what and how methods can be applied.

However most contemporary methodologies around propose specific methodological stages that resemble the idea of modes of action in a method. In this light it is useful to keep in mind Kay & Halpin's (1999) argument about methodology. They suggest that we cannot find out about methodologies in books, we can only find out about methods. They suggest that if the ideas proposed by a methodology are not used to reflect but they are just followed as they are stated, they are really being used as method. In order to have methodology it is necessary to have the reflective involvement of the practitioner. From the point of view of intention perhaps we can only have methodologies when they are carried out as intentional actions.

Additionally to the methodological stages there is another strong connection between method and methodology. When a methodology is used to reflect how to act in a situation, over time some "modes of action" - using here Kotarbiński language – will arise. If these modes of action become systematized and applied to similar cases we have a method (Checkland, 2000). As a consequence of this process methods became intrinsically attached and associated to the methodologies, in fact perhaps this is the origin of the methodological stages.

Standard Uses

The interest in defining what is a standard method or methodology seems to derive from Flood and Romm's (1995: 377) work. They suggested that it was possible to use methods to "meet purposes not provided by their founding theoretical underpinnings". They call this use *oblique*. In consequence a distinction was made. It is possible to use methods in oblique use, and by contrast is also possible to use them in the "direct", "straight", "pure", "standard way". Midgley (1997: 317) uses the term 'pure' to mean "in the form its creator intended". Standard use is defined as "the way that they were originally intended" (Mingers, 2006: 236).

Standard use of methodologies is a special case. The literature in general does not refer to them. Accordingly to the definition of methodology in terms of principles, it will not be possible to define their use as standard. However it is possible to see how recognized methodologies such as Interactive Planning and Soft Systems Methodology are treated as methods and in this way their standard use is implicit (Flood & Romm, 1995; Mingers, 2003, 2006). This situation has been already pointed out by Jackson (2003).

One possible source of confusion is the methodological stages. They as it was already mentioned are a kind of mode of action or method. So in certain way it can be said that the analysis to methods can be applied to methodologies up to certain extend. Consequently it can be considered that the argumentation here applies to methods and to the methodological stages imbedded in methodologies.

As we saw the concept of intentions in philosophy has different elements that can be used to analyze standard uses. Not all aspects will be developed here. The argumentation here relies in metal experiments about how the trajectory of actions can be affected when following a method or methodological stages.

How standard?

Intentions are ways to make sense of actions. In describing a complex set of actions, what is going to identify what method was followed is how the actor decides to group and describe them. Instead of focusing on every little nuance, methods rely on intentions to pinpoint salient aspects that serve as reference to a set of actions (Kotarbiński, 1966).

With the aim of visualizing the arguments let us consider two elements: Possible actions and steps given by a method. Here a plane metaphorically will represent all the possible actions in a situation. Some dots on the plane will represent specific actions corresponding to the salient aspects of action accordingly to a method (Figure 1).

Based on this, it is now possible to represent a specific intervention as a line or trajectory crossing the plane. If the course of action is being driven by a method we can represent this by the trajectory crossing the points representing the actions prescribed in the method (Figure 2).

Kotarbiński says that there are innumerable ways to describe what has been done. This means that is possible to choose different points as references for the method. It also implies the other way around. Namely, that there are infinite ways to apply a method (Figure 3).

All these possibilities use a continuous line, but it also possible to think that the line can behave as a discontinuous function and "jump" to the specific steps in the method without changing the general trajectory of the actions (Figure 4).

Here despite that a hypothetical practitioner complies with the stages in the method, it seems very safe to say that the trajectory followed was not intending to follow the method. Perhaps the situation here is more about disguising the process as if was carried out using a particular method. It resembles a process of saving face.

While standards can be defined in terms of compliance to some stages, this is insufficient to avoid situations such as highly deviant trajectories in Figure 3 or the saving face trajectory in Figure 4. Surely in the last Figure the method was not followed as it was intended.

If complying with some stages cannot secure a standard use, what could happen if we turn to more developed concepts of intention? In the light of the previous section the situation can only go worse. Trajectories affected by belief, desires or skills would be more difficult to defines in terms of a standard.

However, there is another alternative. We can consider intentionality not as a source of standardization, but as a source of self knowledge and self understanding. This has been suggested in the action philosophy literature (Setiya, 2003). If we can be more aware of the impact of our intentions, we can have additional avenues for a reflective practice, and perhaps we will not be able to follow a method or methodology as it was intended but as we intended.

Final Reflections

The argument of this paper is that the concept intention cannot be taken for granted. It argues that if standard uses of methods and methodologies are defined in terms of intention, standard uses are at the best unlikely.

There are two paths here. One it will be possible to define standard uses in terms of something else. The second, it is to study how methods and methodologies are affected by practitioners' intentions. This second option has certain appealing. It can help to increase practitioners awareness of the process and at the same time expand the possibilities of use of methods and methodologies.

Figure 1 *Method as points of reference in a plane of actions*

Figure 2 *The application of a method as a trajectory of actions*

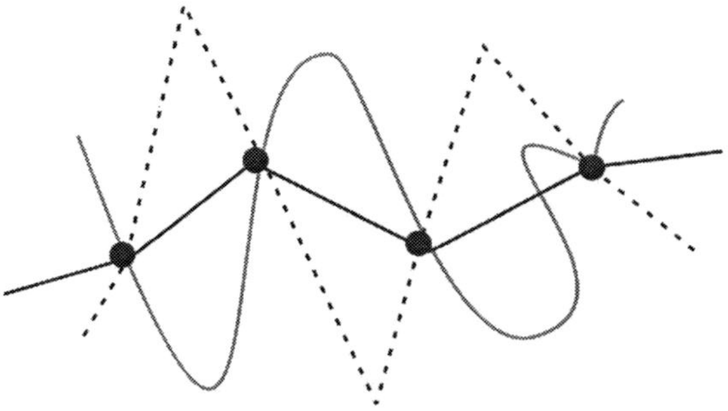

Figure 3 *Multiple trajectories following the same method*

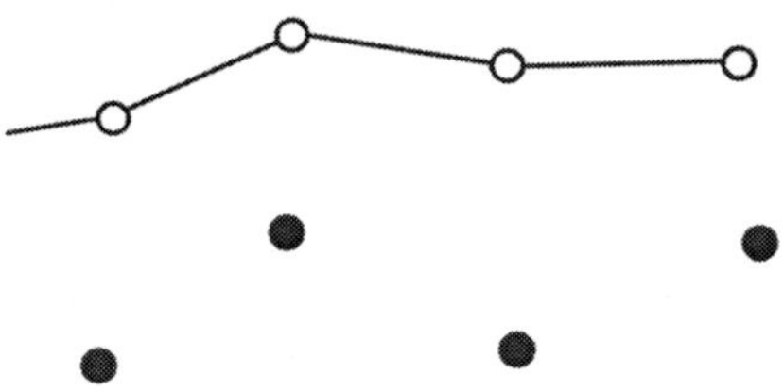

Figure 4 *Following a method in a discontinuous trajectory*

This path also suggests that ethics is fundamental.

If our intentions do not affect the modes of actions and our reflections about how to guide those modes of action, then we are not responsible and accountable for the use of methods and methodologies. In this case we can proceed just to blame or praise our methods and methodologies. However as this paper argues this is not the case, so how methods and methodologies are used will make us responsible and accountable for their use.

References

Adams, F., & Steadman, A. (2004). "Intentional action and moral considerations: still pragmatic". *Analysis, 64*(3), ISSN: 0003-2638, pp. 268-276.

Baldwin, D. A., & Baird, J. A. (2001). "Discerning intentions in dynamic human action". *TRENDS in Cognitive Sciences,* 5(4), ISSN: 1364-6613, pp. 171-178.

Benett, M. R., & Hacker, P. M. S. (2003). *Philosophical Foundations of Neuroscience,* ISBN: 1-4051-0838-X.

Bratman, M. E. (1987). *Intention, Plans, and Practical Reason,* ISBN: 0-674-45818-4.

Checkland, P. (1981). *Systems Thinking, Systems Practice,* ISBN: 0-471-27911-0.

Checkland, P. (2000). "Soft Systems Methodology: A Thirty Year Retrospective". *Systems Research and Behavioral Science, 17*ISSN: 1099-1743, pp. 11-58.

Davis, W. A. (1997). "A Causal Theory of Intending". In A. R. Mele (Ed.), *The Philosophy of Action*, ISBN: 0-19-875174-5, pp. 131-148.

Flood, R. L., & Romm, N. (1995). "Enhancing the process of choice in TSI, and improving chances of tackling coercion". *Systems Practice, 8*(4), ISSN: 0894-9859, pp. 377-408.

Fuenmayor, R. (1991a). "The self-referential structure of an everyday-living situation: A phenomenological ontology for interpretative systemology". *Systems Practice, 4*ISSN: 0894-9859, pp. 449-472.

Fuenmayor, R. (1991b). "Truth and openness: An epistemology for interpretative systemology". *Systems Practice, 4*ISSN: 0894-9859, pp. 473-490.

Georgiou, I. (2003). "The idea of emergent property". *The Journal of the Operational Research Society, 54*(3), ISSN: 01605682, pp. 239.

Georgiou, I. (2007). *Thinking Through Systems Thinking*, ISBN: 0415405203.

Jackson, M. C. (2000). *Systems Approaches to Management*, ISBN: 0-306-46506-X.

Jackson, M. C. (2003). "The power of multi-methodology: some thoughts for John Mingers". *The Journal of the Operational Research Society, 54*(12), ISSN: 01605682, pp. 1300.

Juarrero, A. (1999). *Dynamics in Action: Intentional Behavior as a Complex System*, ISBN: JUADH 0-262-10081-9.

Kay, R., & Halpin, D. (1999). "Redefining the role of the practitioner in critical systems methodologies". *Systems Research and Behavioral Science, 16*(3), ISSN: 1099-1743, pp. 273.

Keys, P. (1997). "Approaches to understanding the process of OR: Review, critique and extension". *Omega, 25*(1), ISSN, pp. 1-13.

Keys, P. (2002). "Process of MS/OR". In H. G. Daellenbach & R. L. Flood (Eds.), *The Informed Student Guide to Management Science*, ISBN: 1-86152-542-7, pp. 211-212.

Knobe, J. (2003). "Intentional action in folk psychology: an experimental investigation". *Philosophical Psychology, 16*(2), ISSN: 0951-5089, pp. 309-324.

Kotarbiński, T. (1966). *Gnosiology: The Scientific Approach to the Theory of Knowledge* (O. Wojtasiewicz, Trans.), Oxford, Pergamon

Lehaney, B. A., & Vinten, G. (1994). "'Methodology': An analysis of its meaning and use". *Work Study, 43*(3), ISSN: 00438022, pp. 5.

Malle, B. F., Moses, L. J., & Baldwin, D. A. (Eds.). (2001). *Intentions and Intentionality: Foundations of Social Cognition*. Cambridge, Massachusetts: MIT Press, ISBN: 0-262-63267-5.

Mele, A. R. (1997). "Introduction". In A. R. Mele (Ed.), *The Philosophy of Action*, ISBN: 0-19-875174-5, pp. 1-26.

Mele, A. R. (2003). "Intentional action: controversies, data, and core hypotheses". *Philosophical Psychology, 16*(2), ISSN: 0951-5089, pp. 325-340.

Mele, A. R., & Moser, P. K. (1997). "Intentional Action". In A. R. Mele (Ed.), *The Philosophy of Action*, ISBN: 0-19-875174-5, pp. 223-255.

Midgley, G. (1997). "Developing the Methodology of TSI: From the Oblique Use of Methods to Creative Design". *Systems Practice, 10*(3), ISSN: 0894-9859, pp. 305-319.

Mingers, J. (2003). "A classification of the philosophical assumptions of management science methods". *The Journal of the Operational Research Society, 54*(6), ISSN: 01605682, pp. 559.

Mingers, J. (2006). *Realising Systems Thinking: Knowledge and Action in Management*

Science, ISBN: 0-387-28188-6.

Ormerod, R. J. (2006). "The history and ideas of pragmatism". *The Journal of the Operational Research Society, 57*(8), ISSN: 01605682, pp. 892.

Setiya, K. (2003). "Explaining Action". *The Philosophical Review, 112*(3), ISSN, pp. 339-393.

Siewert, C. (2007). Consciousness and Intentionality. *The Stanford Encyclopedia of Philosophy* Spring 2007. Retrieved June 29, 2007, from http://plato.stanford.edu/archives/spr2007/entries/consciousness-intentionality/

Wittgenstein, L. (2001). *Philosophical Investigations* (G. E. M. Ascombe, Trans. 3rd ed.), ISBN: 0-631-23127-7.

Zelazo, P. D., Astington, J. W., & Olson, D. R. (Eds.). (1999). *Developing Theories of Intention*. Mahwah, NJ: Lawrence Erlbaum Associates, ISBN: 0-8058-3142-8.

Appendix A:
MISCELLANEOUS ABSTRACTS

System Structuring in Procedural Level with the Application of DCSYM Methodology and DCSYM Case Tool v1.0

Nikiras A. Assimakopoulos
Department of Informatics, University of Piraeus, Piraeus, Greece

Maria M. Konstantopoulou
Department of Public Management, Panteio University, Athens, Greece

DCSYM (Design and Control Systemic Methodology) complexity compensation abilities is based on the unique notion of layers. The system analyst, problem solver and designer creates sequential layers that encapsulate different aspects of the system or problem. The layers can then be matched together to create the whole picture or decoupled for fine tuning. DCSYM's basic category layers are the subsystem, individual, communication and control layers. Furthermore each layer has a mathematical output as a matrix that can be used as an input in mathematical packages for further analysis and simulation.

We have designed and constantly evolving a software system (DCSYM Case Tools) that vastly expands DCSYM's capabilities. The system analyst can use dedicated design tools for the creation of DCSYM's structure communication and control layers. He may manipulate his charts easily and output them in XML format for sharing and for future reference. He can also apply the software in team sessions of system or company agents that want to intervene existing structures or strategically plan future structures. The software introduces the notion of recursion in dealing with systems since it can handle nested structures easily (recurring XML structures).

In this paper we will briefly present DCSYM's main theoretical aspects and functionality in procedural sections. We will demonstrate the use of DCSYM Layers and underlying mathematical matrices. We will also demonstrate the use of our software in its current form and a pre release of the new layer, the semantic layer, which we are going to incorporate in software assisted DCSYM to enhance readability and comprehension of DCSYM structured graphs. Finally, we shall give some research inclinations for the use of DCSYM in our research concerning the design of the appropriate infrastructure for initiating self organising and evolving Virtual Enterprises including legal coverage.

System Structuring in Strategic Organizational Level with the Application of DCSYM Methodology

Nikiras A. Assimakopoulos and **Ioannis C. Theocharopoulos**
Department of Informatics, University of Piraeus, Piraeus, Greece

DCSYM (Design and Control Systemic Methodology) originates from a cybernetic approach and is designed to create powerful representations of the subsystems of a system together with the positionings of the individuals, their roles and their communications network in strategic organisational level. It is also capable of depicting hierarchy and flow of control between the subsystems and individuals. Aiming at in-depth analysis and problem solving, DCSYM can handle a considerable amount of complexity due mainly to the coexistence of a consistent schematic and mathematical representation based on a strict, yet simple set of structuring rules. We have applied DCSYM in a wide range of structures in the business sector (banks, companies), in the Public Management sector, the social sector (health, education), IT sector and knowledge creation sector (DCSYM Ontologies). Finally, we shall present an application in a Greek Public Hospital of Athens.

Systems Thinking, Quality and Higher Education: Insights and Challenges

Don Houston
Massey University, NZ

Solving the quality problem in higher education has been on various agendas since at least the mid-1980s. Attempts to address the problem have seen the imposition and largely uncritical acceptance of accountability mechanisms and improvement methodologies such as TQM imported from industry as universal solutions. These approaches have provided little obvious benefit. This paper reflects on my experience as an insider researcher attempting to use critical systems ideas and practices to promote authentic improvement in a university academic department.

Critical review of the quality management literature demonstrates clearly that TQM is a poor fit with higher education. The discussion points to the importance of purpose, language, values and boundary judgements and images of organizations in the determining the transferability of concepts and methods for 'quality' between organizational types.

The integrative purpose of learning – through research, teaching and service –proposed by Bowden & Marton (1998) is presented as the point of departure from which local quality improvement should be developed. For staff and students, the quality problem mainly relates to better promoting learning. Analysis and reflection on the problem and context drawing on systems methodologies shaped interventions for improvement in learning. This experience provides insights about what might be achieved and about the systemic challenges to systemic intervention for improvement.

What Will Come After the Investment, Innovation and Affluence Phases of Social Development?

Matjaž Mulej, Vojko Potočan, Zdenka Ženko, Damjan Prosenak and Anita Hrast

Porter and Kramer (2006) model the evolution of competitiveness based on natural resources (phase 1), investment (phase 2), innovation (phase 3), and affluence (phase 4). Economic laws about satisfying needs with scarce resources predict that growing affluence will kill the ambition to create in order to have. Yet social responsibility requires humankind not to stop evolving upon reaching the fourth phase. New measures of value and economic success are needed to explain the ambition to create and be beneficial beyond the ambition to have. Psychologists and sociologists offer such measures under the common denominator of 'happiness'. When the goal is happiness innovativeness is seen not only as a technological or profit-oriented phenomenon, but an attribute that uses and develops human creativity, capacity for cooperation, and professionalism. These concepts reach beyond the material content into the spiritual one, because it helps life make sense.

Printed in the United States
142344LV00005B/11/P